Jefferson & Madison
on Separation of Church and State

WRITINGS ON RELIGION AND SECULARISM

Jefferson & Madison
on Separation of Church and State

WRITINGS ON RELIGION AND SECULARISM

EDITED BY LENNI BRENNER

Fort Lee, New Jersey

Published by Barricade Books Inc.
185 Bridge Plaza North
Suite 308-A
Fort Lee, NJ 07024

www.barricadebooks.com

Library of Congress Cataloging-in-Publication Data
Jefferson, Thomas, 1743-1826.
    Jefferson & Madison on separation of church and state / edited by Lenni Brenner.
        p. cm.
    Includes bibliographical references and index.
    ISBN 1-56980-273-4 (pbk.)
    1. Jefferson, Thomas, 1743-1826--Views on church and state. 2. Jefferson, Thomas,
1743-1826--Correspondence. 3. Madison, James, 1751-1836--Views on church and state.
4. Madison, James, 1751-1836--Correspondence. 5. Church and state--United States--
History--18th century. 6. Church and state--United States--History--19th century. 7.
Religion and politics--United States--History--18th century. 8. Religion and politics--
United States--History--19th century. 9. Presidents--United States--Correspondence. I.
Madison, James, 1751-1836. II. Brenner, Lenni, 1937- III. Title.

E332.2.J475 2004
973.4'6'092--dc22
                                                                                    2004047785

First Printing
Manufactured in Canada

CONTENTS

To locate a specific document, please refer to the Documents and Letters List.

EDITOR'S NOTE TO READERS

This book aims to bring the full range of Thomas Jefferson and James Madison's writings on religion to the broad public. There are previous collections of Jefferson's writings. Ditto for Madison. But editions of one individual's writings don't give a systematic picture of what the other was writing at the same time. And few focus on religion. Putting their writings together, chronologically, gives us a more three-dimensional picture of their religious politics. This is especially rewarding for particular periods rich in historic writings. In 1784-89, Jefferson was U.S. Minister to France, with its revolutionaries meeting in his home, while Madison passed Virginia's Statute for Religious Freedom and then the Constitution and Bill of Rights. Their retirements after their Presidencies, Jefferson 1809-1826, Madison 1817-1836, produced some of their most profound commentaries on religion.

The book arises out of 2004's intense debates over the meaning of Jefferson's celebrated 1802 letter to the Danbury Baptist Association:

"I contemplate with sovereign reverence that act of the whole American people which declared that their legislature should 'make no law respecting an establishment of religion, or prohibiting the free exercise thereof,' thus building a wall of separation between Church and State."

His quote is from the First Amendment of America's Bill of Rights, Madison's contribution to humanity.

A proud veteran of the struggle for Black American civil rights, I have equally strong views on religion and secularism. So as not to allow them to get between these two splendid writers and their readers, my analysis of their stature is reserved for a final "Scholar's Afterword."

For now you get editorial explanation of the problems regarding digesting our twosome into readable shape so that you can understand them.

I'm with the editorial majority of historians in retaining their spelling. 'Recieved Wisdom' would be the perfect literary title for their works. That's how they spelled received. But there is method to our madness. Retaining their archaisms graphically reminds us that, for all their centrality in the present and future intellectual world, they are 18th and 19th century figures. They were profound within profound limitations. We must be aware of them, without losing appreciation of what they achieved.

Jefferson was a super linguist. He knew Anglo-Saxon and used its "thorn," a letter symbol for th, as in this, that and the other in private notes. English lost the thorn, so editors substitute a y, as in ys, yt and y oyer.

Their punctuation was dramatically, sometimes painfully, different from ours. Jefferson rarely used Capitals to start sentences in his copies of his writings. Reading him becomes an ordeal. So modern editors cap sentence starts, except in prep notes, and the problem goes away.

They put periods where we put commas, and after every abbreviation. This is tolerable to our eyes in short texts. Usage at length is too much stop and go, unsettling for moderns. Their fine writing becomes a scholarly chore. So their old fashioned punctuation is retained in short pieces, but a handful of documents are modernized for readers' convenience.

Both constantly cap words, mid-sentence, in ways foreign to contemporary English, however these are retained. They are not as distracting as staccato punctuation.

Sentences are ellipsed internally by [...]. Ellipses between 2 or more sentences are [....].

Previous editorial sleuths solved problems via unreadable letters and words in the originals, by putting them into brackets for scholarly exactness. But here smooth reading turns pedantic po[wer] into power.

Some original documents come with additions and deletions by the authors. Additions are [bracketed]. My introductory notes, translations and explanations are [bracketed]. Deletions are placed in <acute brackets>.

Jefferson frequently used very long sentences, extended via semicolons. Page-long paragraphs are common. Again, for your convenience, I've modernized a few sentences, i.e., made 2 shorter sentences out of a Jefferson giant, and broken up elephantine paragraphs.

There are many excerpts here. Some have gone through many editions, and have been modernized to some degree. And sometimes they used two forms of the same thing in a document. Sometimes its & co., other times &c, etc. Don't trouble yourself over such trivia. They weren't pedants, & wouldn't care.

Past such technicalities, the reward is that Jefferson & Madison are two of the clearest writers who've ever lived. With most documents you don't need to know about other topics taken up in them to understand what they say about religion. Hence many have no editorial introductions. Introductions are reserved for those requiring readers being factually prepped so that they can make sense of the author's dated references.

———

Separate chronologies for the two authors follow the text. These provide further clues to assist readers in grasping the contexts of their opuses.

They were fluent in Greek, Latin, and French. Material in those languages is translated. Some previous editors provided translations of such passages. With others I received valuable assistance from Umit Singh Dhuga concerning Greek, Latin, and French, and Carl Lesnor concerning French. But demotic medieval Latin and French legal and theological terms are the Dakota badlands of translations. Certainty doesn't exist there. I presumed to occasionally play sheriff to their educated conjectures, and therefore assume responsibility for all translations.

A collection of excerpts is automatically guilty of including too much and too little. But my goal always was to give you no more and no less than the religious parts of these texts, in a manner understandable to the reader. Naturally everyone is encouraged to seek out the complete originals. However such a digest is required where Jefferson wrote 19,000 letters, and our pair wrote 1,200 to each other.

Some writings found in scholarly tomes on Jefferson & Madison are not included here. Madison's student jottings on William Berkitt's "Expository Notes" deal with religion. Unfortunately all editors agree that his lists of biblical passages tell us nothing about what he thought was significant in them. Similarly, Jefferson maintained a youthful "Common-place Book," quotes and paraphrases from authors he was impressed with. While it is important to know of these mentors, it doesn't genuinely qualify as a work by Jefferson.

In February 1804, the reelected President of the United States took a razor to the New Testament and cut and pasted passages into what he called *The Philosophy of Jesus of Nazareth extracted from the account of his life and doctrines as given by Matthew, Mark, Luke and John. being an abridgment of the New Testament for the use of Indians unembarrassed with matters of fact or faith beyond the levels of their comprehensions.* The title is his joke. He publicly compared his clerical Federalist enemies to Indians who didn't want to come to terms with oncoming American civilization. Unfortunately the collection, in Jefferson's papers when he died, was subsequently lost.

In 1983, Dickinson Adams and Princeton University Press's *Papers of Thomas Jefferson* series reconstructed the lost work. It is based on cut up Bibles actually used to produce the collection. While the reconstruction is approximately 90 percent correct, the rest is speculation about what Jefferson might have ultimately included, and doesn't belong in a digest of his definitive works. Instead, Adams' *Jefferson's Extracts from the Gospels* is highly recommended as follow-through reading after examining Jefferson's similar but more exacting 1819 compilation, *The Life and Morals of Jesus,* AKA *Jefferson's Bible,* included here.

Also omitted are passing references. Our writers frequently list freedom of religion among American rights. But beyond the notation, the quote doesn't touch on religion. Including such snippet references would be pointless pedantry. Thus, what you get, via dabs of editing, is Jefferson, author of America's Declaration of Independence, and Madison, who presented the Bill of Rights to its first Congress, in full throat on religion and secularism. Enjoy them, profit from their wisdom. Then, only after you read them for yourself, after their revolutionary youth, their Presidential years, retirement and death, will you get my chat about them in their time, and their relevance for America and the world's future. See you then in the Scholar's Afterword.

Lenni Brenner
September 2004

Part 1

THE REVOLUTIONARIES AS STUDENTS

1762 – 1774

Youths produce adults. But the youths of these two sons of Episcopalian slaveholders were somewhat different. Jefferson, 1743-1826, robust at 6'3", went to William & Mary in Virginia, where he studied law under distinguished names. Later in life, Jefferson told of his youthful disbelief in the doctrine of the trinity. From that developed his life-long loathing for what he called priestcraft, expressed throughout this book in criticism of all the major religious denominations in America. Yet the great anti-cleric maintained friendships with many ministers.

Madison, 1751-1836, went to what is now Princeton University in New Jersey. Both studied Greek and Latin, but Madison also studied Hebrew, while Jefferson took French and Italian. Madison, no more than 5'6", developed a nervous disorder on his return to Virginia in 1772, feared he would die early and thought much about the afterlife. When he recovered, he went from preoccupation with death to a sharp focus on freedom of religion. He gives us much on the positions of the Virginia sects in the struggle for religious freedom, but he doesn't deal with their theologies.

The two met in 1776, and became friends for life. For weal and for woe, they went on to invent the official ideology of the United States of America, the Declaration of Independence and the Bill of Rights of the first republic of modern times.

THOMAS JEFFERSON TO JOHN PAGE
December 25, 1762

Editor's note: Page was Jefferson's closest friend at the College of William & Mary.

This very day, to others the day of greatest mirth and jollity, sees me overwhelmed with more and greater misfortunes than have befallen a descendant of Adam for these thousand years past, I am sure; and perhaps, after excepting Job, since the creation of the world. I think his misfortunes were somewhat greater than mine: for although we may be pretty nearly on a level in other respects, yet, I thank my God, I have the advantage of brother Job in this, that Satan has not as yet put forth his hand to load me with bodily afflictions. You must know, dear Page, that I am now in a house surrounded with enemies, who take counsel together against my soul; and when I lay me down to rest, they say among themselves, come let us destroy him. I am sure if there is such a thing as a Devil in this world, he must have been here last night and have had some hand in contriving what happened to me. Do you think the cursed rats (at his instigation, I suppose) did not eat up my pocket-book, which was in my pocket, within a foot of my head? And not contented with plenty for the present, they carried away my Jemmy worked silk garters, and half a dozen new minuets I had just got, to serve, I suppose, as provision for the winter. But of this I should not have accused the Devil, (because, you know rats will be rats, and hunger, without the addition of his instigations, might have urged them to do this), if something worse, and from a different quarter, had not happened. You know it rained last night, or if you do not know it, I am sure I do. When I went to bed, I laid my watch in the usual place, and going to take her up after I arose this morning, I found her in the same place, it's true but! *Quantum mutatus ab illo!* [How changed from what it was!] all afloat in water, let in at a leak in the roof of the house, and as silent and still as the rats that had eat my pocket-book. Now, you know, if chance had had anything to do in this matter, there were a thousand other spots where it might have chanced to leak as well as at this one, which was perpendicularly over my watch. But I'll tell you; it's my opinion that the Devil came and bored the hole over it on purpose. Well, as I was saying, my poor watch had lost her speech. I should not have cared much for this, but something worse attended it; the subtle particles of the water with which the case was filled, had, by their penetration, so overcome the cohesion of the particles of the paper, of which my dear picture and watch-paper were composed, that, in attempting to take them out to dry them, good God! *Mens horret referre!* [The mind shutters to recall it.] My cursed fingers gave them such a rent, as I fear I never shall get over. This, cried I, was the last stroke Satan had in reserve for me: he knew I cared not for anything else he could do to me, and was determined to try this last most fatal expedient. *Multis fortunae vulneribus percussus, huic uni me imparem sensi, et penitus succubui!* [Pierced through by the many wounds of fate, I felt myself unequal to this one and succumbed utterly.] I would have cried bitterly, but

I thought it beneath the dignity of a man, and a man too who had read των οντων, τα μεν εστιν εφ᾽ ἡμιν τα δ᾽οὐ εφ᾽ ἡμιν [on the one hand the things which pertain to us, and on the other hand things which do not pertain to us.]

However, whatever misfortunes may attend the picture or lover, my hearty prayers shall be, that all the health and happiness which Heaven can send may be the portion of the original, and that so much goodness may ever meet with what may be most agreeable in this world, as I am sure it must be in the next. And now, although the picture be defaced, there is so lively an image of her imprinted in my mind, that I shall think of her too often, I fear, for my peace of mind; and too often, I am sure, to get through old Coke this winter; for God knows I have not seen him since I packed him up in my trunk in Williamsburg.

Well, Page, I do wish the Devil had old Coke, for I am sure I never was so tired of an old dull scoundrel in my life. What! Are there so few inquietudes tacked to this momentary life of ours, that we must need be loading ourselves with a thousand more? Or, as brother Job says, (who, by the bye, I think began to whine a little under his afflictions) 'Are not my days few? Cease then, that I may take comfort a little before I go whence I shall not return, even to the land of darkness, and the shadow of death.' But the old fellows say we must read to gain knowledge, and gain knowledge to make us happy and admired. Mere jargon! Is there any such thing as happiness in this world? No. And as for admiration, I am sure the man who powders most, perfumes most, embroiders most, and talks most nonsense, is most admired. Though to be candid, there are some who have too much good sense to esteem such monkey-like animals as these, in whose formation, as the saying is, the tailors and barbers go halves with God Almighty; and since these are the only persons whose esteem is worth a wish, I do not know but that, upon the whole, the advice of these old fellows may be worth following.

You cannot conceive the satisfaction it would give me to have a letter from you. Write me very circumstantially everything which happened at the wedding. Was she there? Because, if she was, I ought to have been at the Devil for not being there too....

If there is any news stirring in town or country, such as deaths, courtships, or marriages, in the circle of my acquaintance, let me know it. Remember me affectionately to all the young ladies of my acquaintance, particularly the Miss Burwells, and Miss Potters, and tell them that though that heavy earthly part of me, my body, be absent, the better half of me, my soul, is ever with them, and that my best wishes shall ever attend them....

THOMAS JEFFERSON TO JOHN PAGE
January 20, 1763

I have not attempted to read anything since a few days after Jack Walker went down, and God knows when I shall be able to do it. I have some thoughts of going to Petersburg if the actors go there in May.

THOMAS JEFFERSON TO JOHN PAGE
July 15, 1763

The most fortunate of us, in our journey through life, frequently meets with calamities and misfortunes which may greatly afflict us; and, to fortify our minds against the attacks of these calamities and misfortunes, should be one of the principal studies and endeavors of our lives. The only method of doing this is to assume a perfect resignation to the Divine will, to consider whatever does happen, must happen; and that, by our uneasiness, we cannot prevent the blow before it does fall, but we may add to its force after it has fallen. These considerations, and others such as these, may enable us in some measure to surmount the difficulties thrown in our way; to bear up with a tolerable degree of patience under this burthen of life; and to proceed with a pious and unshaken resignation, till we arrive at our journey's end, when we may deliver up our trust into the hands of him who gave it, and recieve such reward as to him shall seem proportioned to our merit. Such, dear Page, will be the language of the man who considers his situation in this life, and such should be the language of every man who would wish to render that situation as easy as the nature of it will admit. Few things will disturb him at all: nothing will disturb him much.

THOMAS JEFFERSON TO WILLIAM FLEMING
[ca. October 1763]

From a crowd of disagreeable [companions] among whom I have spent three or four of the most tedious hours of my life. I retire into Gunn's bedchamber to converse in black and white with an absent friend. I heartily wish you were here that I might converse with a Christian once more before I die: for die I must this night unless I should be releived by the arrival of some sociable fellow.

THOMAS JEFFERSON TO JOHN PAGE
October 7, 1763

In the most melancholy fit that ever any poor soul was, I sit down to write to you.... I had dressed up in my own mind, such thoughts as occurred to me, in as moving language as I knew how, and expected to have performed in a tolerably creditable manner. But, good God! When I had an opportunity of venting them, a few broken sentences, uttered in great disorder, and interrupted with pauses of uncommon length, were the too visible marks of my strange confusion!

THOMAS JEFFERSON TO JOHN PAGE
[Devilsburg] January 19, 1764

Editor's note: Williamsburg was "Devilsburg" to our young Tom,
courting a young woman.

The contents of your letter have not a little alarmed me: and really upon seriously weighing them with what has formerly passed between αδνιλεβ [mock Greek] and myself I am somewhat at a loss what to conclude. Your *'semper saltat, semper ridet, semper loquitur, semper solicitat'* [Always dancing, always laughing, always chatting, always friendly] & c. appear a little suspicious, but good god! it is impossible!

THOMAS JEFFERSON TO JOHN PAGE
[Devilsburg] January 23, 1764

My letter of Jan. 19, may have been opened, and the person who did it may have been further incited by curiosity, to ask you if you had recieved such a letter as they saw mentioned therein; but God send, and I hope this is not the case.

THOMAS JEFFERSON TO WILLIAM FLEMING
March 20, 1764

You say you are determined to be married as soon as possible: and advise me to do the same. No, thank ye; I will consider it first. Many and great are the comforts of a single state, and neither of the reasons you urge can have any influence with an inhabitant and a young inhabitant too of Wmsburgh. For St. Paul only says that it is better to be married than to burn. Now I presume that if that apostle had known that providence would at an after day be so kind to any particular set of people as to furnish them with other means of extinguishing their fire than those of matrimony, he would have earnestly recommended them to their practice.

THOMAS JEFFERSON, RESOLUTIONS FOR AN ANSWER TO GOVERNOR
BOTETOURT'S SPEECH
May 8, 1769

Editor's note: This is Jefferson's first state paper, as a member of the Virginia House of Burgesses.

Expressing our firm Attachment to his Majesty's sacred Person and Government.... Assuring his Excellency, that we shall, with Candour, proceed to the important Business on which we are met in General Assembly; and that, if in the Course of our Deliberations, any Matters shall arise, which may in any way affect the Interests Great Britain, these shall ever be discussed on this ruling Principal, that her Interests, and Ours, are inseparably the same: And, finally, offering our Prayers, that Providence, and the Royal Pleasure, may long continue his Lordship the happy Ruler of a free and an happy People.

THOMAS JEFFERSON TO BERNARD MOORE
[Ca. 1769]

Editor's note: Jefferson sent a study plan to Moore. This is missing, but he modified it and sent it to another correspondent in 1814. The part relating to religion is given here.

Till VIII o'clock in the morning employ yourself in Physical studies, Ethics, Religion, natural and sectarian, and Natural law, reading the following books....

Ethics & Natl Religion. Locke's Essay. Locke's conduct of the mind in the search after truth. Stewart's Philosophy of the human mind. Enfield's history of Philosophy. Condorcet, Progrès de l'esprit Humain. Cicero de officiis. Tuscalana. de Senectute. Sommium Scipionis. Senecae Philosophica. Hutchinson's Introduction to Moral Philosophy. Ld. Kaim's Natural Religion. Traite elementaire de Morale et Bonheur. La Sagesse de Charron.

Religion. Sectarian Bible. New Testament. Commentaries on them by Middleton in his works, and by Priestley in his Corruptions of Christianity, & Early opinions of Christ. Volney's Ruins. The sermons of Sterne, Masillon & Bourdaloue.

THOMAS JEFFERSON TO THOMAS ADAMS
July 11, 1770

I take the liberty of interceding for your friendly aid to Mr. James Ogilvie a gentleman of my acquaintance now in London. Purposing last fall to go to Britain for orders he made the usual application to the commissary for his recommendatory letter to the bishop. This man, partly from an evil disposition to defeat the wishes of some gentlemen, no favorites of his, who bore a warm friendship to Mr. Ogilvie, and partly from that elation of mind which usually attends preferment without merit and which has no other object in view but to hang out to the world it's own importance, peremptorily refused his recommendation. The cause of refusal which he assigned unfortunately gave the lie to his own conduct of a few weeks before. He thought Ogilvie not qualified for the sacred function because he did not possess a critical knowlege of the Greek; tho' but a very few weeks before he had thought his sadler properly qualified who was not only a stranger to the characters, but perhaps even to the present existence of that language. He did however condescend to promise Ogilvie that he would not oppose his ordination with the bishop; a promise which seems to have been made with no other than the wanton purpose of sporting with truth: For tho' Ogilvie sailed within a few days after receiving this promise the commissary's letter found means to be before him, and to lodge with the bishop a caveat against his ordination. Here then the matter rests, till his friends can take proper measures for counteracting the designs of this worthy representative of episcopal faith; and as he is obliged to remain in London in the mean time and probably went unprovided for so long a stay, I would ask the favor of you, and I shall deem it a very great one, to procure him credit with your mercantile friends in London for any monies of which he may be in need, for the repaiment of which I enter myself security.

THOMAS JEFFERSON TO PEYTON RANDOLPH
July 23, 1770

I am to beg the favor of your friendly interposition in the following case, which I hope you will think sufficient to excuse the freedom of the application. Sometime last fall Mr. Jas. Ogilvie proposing to go to Britain for orders he made the usual application to the commissary for his recommendatory letter to the bishop. The commissary finding him somewhat deficient in his Greek, expressed some doubts whether he could recommend him. Ogilive to remove them did without thought to be sure make use of a very unfortunate argument; mentioning to the commissary the case of Stevenson who without understanding a word of greek had been lately recommended.

The commissary took flame at the hint and peremptorily refused his recommendation. In several subsequent visits Ogilvie attempted to soften him and did at length prevail so far as to obtain a promise that he would not oppose his ordination with the bishop. With this assurance, and with an actual nomination to a parish in his pocket he took his departure.

But whether the commissary's frame is such as that he does not feel the obligations of an engagement, or whether he really thought he had done wrong in entering into it I cannot say, but before Ogilvie reached London he had lodged a letter with the bishop in which were these words 'Mr. Ogilive applied to me last spring for a recommendation to your Lordship for holy orders. For reasons which then existed I refused him. He has now applied to me a second time, as these reasons are not removed I have denied him again, but he goes home in opposition.'

Nothing could have been more artfully couched to do him a prejudice. The bishop observed to Colo. Mercer, who had espoused Ogilvie's interest with some warmth, that had Mr. Horrocks mentioned his objections, it would have left him to judge whether they were such as he might have overlooked; but that a charge so general laid his whole character open to censure in such a manner as to put it out of his power to vindicate it. This young gentleman seems to have been guided thro' life by the hand of misfortune itself. Some hard fatality which presides over all his measures has rendered abortive every scheme which either his prudence or the anxiety of his friends have ever proposed for his advancement.

His present undertaking was peculiarly unfortunate. Before he went to London he paid a visit to his father a presbyterian minister in Aberdeen, who received him with all the joy with which an absence of many years would inspire a parent. Yet, so wonderful is the dominion of bigotry over her votaries that on the first information of his purpose to receive episcopal ordination he shut him from his doors and abjured every parental duty.

Thus rejected by that hand from which he had expected some assistance necessary even for the short residence on that side the water which he had then in contemplation, he hastened to London, and there received the last stroke which fortune had reserved for him. The distresses of his situation operating on a mind uncommonly sensitive to the pains as well as to the pleasures of life, may be conceived even by those to whom fortune has been kinder. There he still remains then, and there he must remain (for it is his last stake) till the commissary can be prevailed on either to withdraw his opposition or to explain the grounds of it, or till we can take such other measures as may counteract its malignity.

The former is the easier and shorter relief to Ogilvie's distress, and it may not be impossible but that the commissary may by this time be disposed to assist him.

For this purpose I have ventured to ask your interposition with him on behalf of this gentleman in whose cause I have warm feelings. This liberty I have taken with you not on any assumed rights of friendship or acquaintance, but merely on the principles of common humanity to which his situation seems to recommend him, and in the hope that you will think with the good man in the play *'homo sum: humani nil a me alienum puto.'* [Terence - "I am a man: nothing human is alien to me."]

I have no interest at our episcopal palace, and indeed any application if known to come from me would rather be of disservice. I flatter myself your interposition there would have certain effect, and assure you it would lay me under lasting obligations. I suppose the most certain assistance would be a letter from the commissary to the bishop. But one thing I must conjure you to do; to see the letter yourself, that you may judge whether it be really friendly or not. I confess to you Mr. Speaker that I put not the least confidence in the most solemn promises of this reverend gentleman. And unless yourself can be assured of the sincerity of his endeavors I had rather proceed at once in such measures as may answer our purpose tho' 'in opposition.'

After your application I have one further favor to ask of you, that if it is unsuccessful you will give me notice by a line lodged in the post office, if successful (as I doubt not but it will be) you would be so kind as to inclose his letter under cover to Ogilvie, and direct to him at Mrs. Ballard's Hungerford street in the Strand London; as this would be a more speedy communication of relief to him then sending the letter viâ Albemarle. I have no proffers to make you in return for all this trouble; fortune seems to have reserved your obligations for herself. You have nothing to ask, I nothing to give. I can only assure you then that I sincerely rejoice in the independance of your situation; I mean an independance on all but your own merit, than which I am sure you cannot have a more permanent dependance. I am Sir with much truth Your very humble servt.

THOMAS JEFFERSON TO JAMES OGILVIE
February 20, 1771

About the same time I wrote from Wmsburgh to a gentleman of the vestry in Orange to secure for you a vacancy which had happened in that parish by the death of Martin. I have had no answer, but the parish is still vacant which gives me hopes it is kept for you. Mr. Maury incumbent in Fredericksville parish (of which I was when you were here) has a tempting offer from another quarter. I know not whether he will accept of it. If he should we shall do for you all that can be done in your absence. But for God's sake let not that be a moment longer than is of absolute necessity.

THOMAS JEFFERSON TO ROBERT SKIPWORTH
August 3, 1771

Editor's note: Prices of the books, and the number of volumes, listed below are omitted.

I sat down with a design of executing your request to form a catalogue of books.... In Law I mention a few systematical books, as a knowlege of the minutiae of that science is not necessary for a private gentleman. In Religion, History, Natural philosophy, I followed the same plan in general....

RELIGION.
Locke's conduct of the mind in search of truth
Xenophon's memoirs of Socrates. by Feilding
Epictetus. by Mrs. Carter
Antoninus. by Collins
Seneca. by L'Estrange
Cicero's Offices. by Guthrie
Cicero's Tusculan questions
Ld. Bolingbroke's Philosophical works
Hume's essays
Ld. Kaim's Natural religion
Philosophical survey of Nature
Oeconomy of human life
Sterne's sermons
Sherlock on death
Sherlock on a future state

HISTORY. ANTIENT.
Bible
Rollin's Antient history

JAMES MADISON TO WILLIAM BRADFORD
November 9, 1772

You moralize so prettily that if I were to judge from some parts of your letter of October 13 I should take you for an old Philosopher that had experienced the emptiness of Earthly Happiness. And I am very glad that you have so early seen through the romantic paintings with which the World is sometimes set off by the sprightly imaginations of the Ingenious. You have happily supplied by reading and observation the want of experiment and therefore I hope you are sufficiently guarded against the allurements and vanities that beset us on our first entrance on the Theatre of Life. Yet however nice and cautious we may be in detecting the follies of mankind and framing our Oeconomy according to the precepts of Wisdom and Religion, I fancy there will commonly remain with us some latent expectation of obtaining more than ordinary Happiness and prosperity till we feel the convincing argument of actual disappointment. Tho I will not determine whether we shall be much the worse for it if we do not allow it to intercept our views towards a future State, because strong desires and great Hopes instigate us to arduous enterprizes, fortitude, and perseverance. Nevertheless a watchful eye must be kept on ourselves lest while we are building ideal monuments of Renown and Bliss here, we neglect to have our names enrolled in the Annals of Heaven. These thoughts come into my mind because I am writing to you and thinking of you. As to myself I am too dull and infirm now to look out for any extraordinary things in this world, for I think my sensations for many months past have intimated to me not to expect a long or healthy life, yet it may be better with me after some time, tho I hardly dare expect it, and therefore have little spirit and alacrity to set about any thing that is difficult in acquiring and useless in possessing after one has exchanged Time for Eternity. But you have Health, Youth, Fire, and Genius to bear you along through the high tract of public Life, and so may be more interested and delighted in improving on hints that respect the temporal though momentous concerns of man.

I think you made a judicious choice of History and the Science of Morals for your winter's study. They seem to be of the most universal benefit to men of sense and taste in every post and must certainly be of great use to youth in settling the principles and refining the Judgment as well as in enlarging Knowledge & correcting the imagination. I doubt not but you design to season them with a little divinity now and then, which like the philosopher's stone, in hands of a good man will turn them and every lawful acquirement into the nature of itself, and make them more precious than fine gold.

JAMES MADISON TO WILLIAM BRADFORD
September 25, 1773

Since you first hinted to me your suspense as to the settled business of your life, I have partook of your anxiety & though it has been often in my thoughts I feel a backwardness to offer my opinion in so critical a matter and the more so for the weight you are pleased to give it. I have too much esteem and affection for you and am too conscious of my want of capacity and experience to direct in so important an Affair. I must therefore premise that it is my earnest request that you would act the candid open friend as well as in rejecting as in asking advice; for I consult nothing but your real interest, and am sensible of my insufficiency to be a counsellor much more a preceptor. You forbid any recommendation of Divinity by suggesting that you have insuperable objections therefore I can only condole with the Church on the loss of a fine Genius and persuasive Orator. I cannot however suppress thus much of my advice on that head that you would always keep the Ministry obliquely in View whatever your profession be. This will lead you to cultivate an acquaintance occasionally with the most sublime of all Sciences and will qualify you for a change of public character if you should hereafter desire it. I have sometimes thought there could be no stronger testimony in favor of Religion or against temporal Enjoyments even the most rational and manly than for men who occupy the most honorable and gainful departments and are rising in reputation and wealth, publicly to declare their unsatisfactoriness by becoming fervent Advocates in the cause of Christ, & I wish you may give in your Evidence in this way. Such instances have seldom occurred, therefore they would be more striking and would be instead of a "Cloud of Witnesses."

JAMES MADISON TO WILLIAM BRADFORD
December 1, 1773

I should be well pleased with a scetch of the plan you have fixed upon for your studies, the books & the order you intend to read them in; and when you have obtained
sufficient insight into the Constitution of your Country and can make it an amusement to yourself send me a draught of its Origin & fundamental principals of
Legislation; particularly the extent of your religious Toleration. Here allow me to
propose the following Queries. Is an Ecclesiastical Establishment absolutely necessary to support civil society in a supream Government? & how far is it hurtful to a
dependent state? I do not ask for an immediate answer but mention them as worth
attending to in the course of your reading and consulting experienced Lawyers &
Politicians upon. When you have satisfied yourself in these points I should listen
with pleasure to the Result of your reserches.

You recommend sending for the Reviews as the best way to know the present
State of Literature and Choicest Books published. This I have done and shall continue to do: but I find them loose in their principals and encouragers of free enquiry
even such as destroys the most essential Truths, Enemies to serious religion &
extreamly partial in their Citations, seeking them rather to Justify their censures and
Commendations than to give the reader a just specimen of the Authors genius. I can
rely with greater confidence on your judgment after you have read the Authors or
have known their Character from your judicious friends. I am meditating a Journey
to Philada which I hope to accomplish early in the spring if no unforeseen hin-
drances stop me. I shall bring a brother with me to put to school somewhere there,
perhaps at Mr. Smith's. I need not say how far the desire of seeing you and others is
a powerful Inducement and that my imagination daily anticipates the pleasure of
this tour. Who were the authors of the Sermons you sent me? What is the exchange
with you now & what is it likely to be in the spring? Write speedily & and forgive
my troublesome questions.

JAMES MADISON TO WILLIAM BRADFORD
January 24, 1774

*Editor's note: Six Baptists were jailed in 1773-4 in Culpeper County for preaching without
a license. Madison refers to a Presbyterian Synod.*

Political Contests are necessary sometimes as well as military to afford exercise and
practice and to instruct in the Art of defending Liberty and property. I verily believe
the frequent Assaults that have been made on America, Boston especially, will in the
end prove of real advantage. If the Church of England had been the established and
general religion in all the Northern Colonies as it has been among us here and uninterrupted tranquility had prevailed throughout the Continent, it is clear to me that
slavery and Subjection might and would have been gradually insinuated among us.
Union of Religious Sentiments begets a surprizing confidence and Ecclesiastical

Establishments tend to great ignorance and Corruption all of which facilitate the Execution of mischievous Projects. But away with Politiks!....

I want again to breathe your free Air. I expect it will mend my Constitution & confirm my principles. I have indeed as good an Atmosphere at home as the Climate will allow: but have nothing to brag of as to the State and Liberty of my Country. Poverty and Luxury prevail among all sorts: Pride ignorance and Knavery among the Priesthood and Vice and Wickedness among the Laity. This is bad enough. But It is not the worst I have to tell you. That diabolical Hell conceived principle of persecution rages among some and to their eternal Infamy the Clergy can furnish their Quota of Imps for such business. This vexes me the most of any thing whatever. There are at this [time] in the adjacent County not less than 5 or 6 well meaning men in close Gaol for publishing their religious Sentiments which in the main are very orthodox. I have neither patience to hear talk or think of any thing relative to this matter, for I have squabbled and scolded abused and ridiculed so long about it, to so little purpose that I am without common patience. So I leave you to pity me and pray for Liberty of Conscience to revive among us.

I expect to hear from you once more before I see you if time will admit: and want to know when the Synod meets & where.

JAMES MADISON TO WILLIAM BRADFORD
April 1, 1774

Editor's note: The Calpipnis Letters were 20 letters by an Anglican minister.

Our Assembly is to meet the first of May when It is expected something will be done in behalf of the Dissenters: Petitions I hear are already forming among the Persecuted Baptists and I fancy it is in the thoughts of the Presbyterians also to intercede for greater liberty in matters of Religion. For my part I can not help being very doubtful of their succeeding in the Attempt. The Affair was on the Carpet during the last Session; but such incredible and extravagant stories were told in the House of the monstrous effects of the Enthusiasm prevalent among the Sectaries and so greedily swallowed by their Enemies that I believe they lost footing by it and the bad name they still have with those who pretend too much contempt to examine into their principles and Conduct and are too much devoted to the ecclesiastical establishment to hear of the Toleration of Dissentients, I am apprehensive, will be again made a pretext for rejecting their requests. The Sentiments of our people of Fortune & fashion on this subject are vastly different from what you have been used to. That liberal catholic and equitable way of thinking as to the rights of Conscience, which is one of the Characteristics of a free people and so strongly marks the People of your province is but little known among the Zealous adherents to our Hierarchy. We have it is true some persons in the Legislature of generous Principles both in Religion & Politicks but number, not merit, you know, is necessary to carry points there. Besides, the Clergy are a numerous and powerful body, have great influence at home by reason of their connection with & dependence on the Bishops and

Crown and will naturally employ all their art & Interest to depress their rising Adversaries; for such they must consider dissenters who rob them of the good will of the people and may in time endanger their livings & security.

You are happy in dwelling in a Land where those inestimable privileges are fully enjoyed and public has long felt the good effects of their religious as well as Civil Liberty. Foreigners have been encouraged to settle amg. you. Industry and Virtue have been promoted by mutual emulation and mutual Inspection, Commerce and the Arts have flourished and I can not help attributing those continual exertions of Genius which appear among you to the inspiration of Liberty and that love of Fame and Knowledge which always accompany it. Religious bondage shackles and debilitates the mind and unfits it for every noble enterprize every expanded prospect. How far this is the Case with Virginia will more clearly appear when the ensuing Trial is made.

I am making all haste in preparing for my journey ... it will answer so exactly with the meeting of the Synod.... Luckey on his Return to Virginia will bring me whatever publications you think worth sending and among others Calpipnis Letters.

Part 2

THE MAKING OF REVOLUTIONARIES

1774 – 1776

H ere we see Jefferson first operating politically within the pious confines of colonial protest within British imperialism, then the proclaimer of the independent republic against that empire. Virginia becomes politically free, but the old world's local representative, the Episcopalians, still are the established church. To his dying day, Jefferson felt that his campaign for disestablishment ranked second among his accomplishments only to the Declaration of Independence.

Madison goes from revolutionary thoughts of tarring and feathering a pro-British "Tory" clergyman, to formulating some of the basic early documents in the history of the struggle for American freedom of religion.

THOMAS JEFFERSON, RESOLUTION OF THE HOUSE OF BURGESSES DESIGNATING A DAY OF FASTING AND PRAYER
May 24, 1774

Editor's note: Jefferson describes the designing of this resolution in his Autobiography, *which see.*

This House being deeply impressed with Apprehension of the great Dangers to be derived to British America, from the hostile Invasion of the city of Boston, in our Sister Colony of Massachusetts Bay, whose Commerce and Harbour are on the 1st Day of June next to be stopped by an armed Force, deem it highly necessary that the said first Day of June be set apart by the Members of this House as a Day of Fasting, Humiliation, and Prayer, devoutly to implore the divine Interposition for averting the heavy Calamity, which threatens Destruction to our civil Rights, and the Evils of civil War; to give us one Heart and one Mind firmly to oppose, by all just and proper Means, every Injury to American Rights, and that the Minds of His Majesty and his Parliament may be inspired from above with Wisdom, Moderation, and Justice, to remove from the loyal People of America all Cause of Danger from a continued Pursuit of Measures pregnant with their Ruin.

Ordered, therefore, that the Members of this House do attend in their Places at the Hour of ten in the Forenoon, on said 1st Day of June next, in Order to proceed with the Speaker and the Mace to the Church in this City for the Purposes aforesaid; and that the Reverend Mr. Price be appointed to read Prayers, and the Reverend Mr. Gwatkin to preach a Sermon suitable to the Occasion.

THOMAS JEFFERSON AND JOHN WALKER,
TO THE INHABITANTS OF THE PARISH OF ST. ANNE
[Before July 23, 1774]

Editor's note: Walker was a fellow house member from Albemarle, in St. Anne's parish. Jefferson was a parish vestryman. See Jefferson's Autobiography *for discussion of this.*

To the Inhabitants of the parish of Saint Anne.

The members of the late house of Burgesses having taken into their consideration the dangers impending over British America from the hostile invasion of a sister colony, thought proper that it should be recommended to the several parishes in this colony that they set apart some convenient day for fasting, humiliation and prayer devoutly to implore the divine interposition in behalf of an injured and oppressed people; and that the minds of his majesty, his ministers, and parliament, might be inspired with wisdom from above, to avert from us the dangers which threaten our civil rights, and all the evils of civil war. We do therefore recommend to the inhabitants of the parish of Saint Anne that Saturday the 23rd instant be by them set apart for the purpose aforesaid, on which day will be prayers and a sermon suited to the occasion by the reverend Mr. Clay at the new church on Hardware river, which place is thought the centrical to the parishioners in General.

John Walker

Thomas Jefferson

RESOLUTIONS AND ASSOCIATION OF THE VIRGINIA CONVENTION OF 1774
August 1-6, 1774

Editor's note: Jefferson was a member of this convention.

We his Majesty's dutiful and loyal Subjects, the delegates of the Freeholders of VIRGINIA.... have, unanimously, and with one Voice, entered into the following Resolutions and Association, which we do oblige ourselves, by those sacred Ties of Honour and Love to our Country, strictly to observe: And farther declare, before God and the World, that we will religiously adhere to and keep the same inviolate in every Particular, until Redress of all such American Grievances as may be defined and settled at the General Congress of Delegates for the different Colonies shall be fully obtained, or until this Association shall be abrogated or altered by a general Meeting of the Deputies of this Colony, to be convened as is herein after directed.

JAMES MADISON TO WILLIAM BRADFORD
November 26, 1774

The proceedings of the Congress are universally approved of in this Province & I am persuaded will be faithfully adheared to. A spirit of Liberty & Patriotism animates all degrees and denominations of men. Many publickly declare themselves ready to join the Bostonians as soon as violence is offered them or resistance thought expedient. In many counties independent companies are forming and voluntaraly subjecting themselves to military discipline that they may be expert & prepared against a time of Need. I hope it will be a general thing thro'ought this province. Such firm and provident steps will either intimidate our enemies or enable us to defy them. By an epistle from the yearly meeting of the Quakers in your City to their bretheren & friends in our Colonies I observe they are determined to be passive on this Critical occasion from a regard to their religious principles mixed I presume with the Leaven of civil policy.

JAMES MADISON TO WILLIAM BRADFORD
January 20, 1775

There will by the Spring, I expect, be some thousands of well trained High Spirited men ready to meet danger whenever it appears, who are influenced by no mercenary Principles, bearing their own expences and having the prospect of no recompence but the honour and safety of their Country. I suppose the Inhabitants of your Province are more reserved in their behavior if not more easy in their Apprehensions, from the prevalence of Quaker principles and politics. The Quakers

---

are the only people with us who refuse to accede to the Continental Association.... When I say refuse to accede to the Association my meaning is that they refuse to Sign it, that being the method used among us to distinguish friends from foes and to oblige the Common people to a more strict observance of it: I have never heard whether the like method has been adopted in the other governments.

JAMES MADISON TO WILLIAM BRADFORD
March 10, 1775

Editor's note: The material in brackets was inserted by a previous editor for clarity.

I lately saw in one of our Gazettes a pamphlet in answer to the friendly address [a tract by an Anglican clergyman] &c: by what you informed me I conjecture it to have been written by Genl. [Charles] Lee. It has much Spirit and Vivacity & contains some very sensible remarks. Some of our old bigots did not altogether approve the Strictures on the Clergy & King Charles: but it was generally, nay with this exception, universally, applauded. I wish most heartily we had [James] Rivington [a Tory journalist] & his ministerial Gazetteers for 24 hours in this place. Execrable as their designs are, they would meet with adequate punishment. How different is the Spirit of Virginia from that of N York? A fellow was lately tarred and feathered for treating one of our county committees with disrespect; in N Y they insult the whole Colony and Continent with impunity!

THOMAS JEFFERSON AND JOHN DICKINSON, DECLARATION OF THE CAUSES AND NECESSITY FOR TAKING UP ARMS
[June 26 to July 6, 1775]

Editor's note: The thirteen colonies had united in a confederation and de facto the struggle for independence had begun. Material in brackets are deletions and other changes by Jefferson.

Thomas Jefferson, Composition Draft:
The large strides of late taken by the legislature of Great Britain towards establishing over the colonies their absolute rule.... it behoves those who are called to this great decision to be assured that their cause is approved before supreme reason so is it of great avail that it's justice be made known to the world whose [prayers cannot be wanting intercessions] affections will ever [be favorable to a people] take part with those encountring oppression. Our forefathers, inhabitants of the island of Gr. Britn. having long endeavored to bear up against the evils of misrule, left their native land to seek on these shores a residence for civil & religious freedom....

We do then, most solemnly [in the presence of] before God & the world declare that, regardless of every consequences, at the risk of every distress [that] the arms we have been compelled to assume will wage with perseverance, exerting to the utmost energies all those powers which our creator hath given us to preserve that Liberty which he committed to us in sacred deposit & to protect from every hostile hand our lives & our properties.

Thomas Jefferson, Fair Copy for the Committee:

A Declaration by the representatives of the United colonies of America now sitting in General Congress setting forth the causes & necessity of their taking up arms.

The large strides of late taken by the legislature of Great Britain towards establishing over these colonies their absolute rule ... it behoves those, who are called to this great decision, to be assured that their cause is approved before supreme reason, so it is of great avail that it's justice be made known to the world, whose affections will ever take part with those encountering oppression. Our forefathers, inhabitants of the island of Great Britain left their native land to seek on these shores a residence for civil & religious freedom, at the expence of their blood.... we call for & confide in the good offices of our fellow subjects beyond the Atlantic, of their friendly disposition we do not yet cease to hope; aware, as they must be, that they have nothing more to expect from the same common enemy than the humble favor be being last devoured, and we devoutly implore the assistance of Almighty god to conduct us happily thro' this great conflict to dispose his majesty, his ministers, & parliament to reconciliation with us on reasonable terms & to deliver us from the evils of a civil war.

THE DECLARATION AS ADOPTED BY CONGRESS
July 6, 1775

Editor's note: There is considerable scholarly debate as to their individual contributions to the final document by the Congress of the thirteen colonies.

If it was possible for Men, who exercise their Reason to believe, that the Divine Author of our Existence intended a part of the human Race to hold an absolute Property in, and an unbounded Power over others, marked out by his infinite Goodness and Wisdom, as the Objects of a legal Domination never rightfully resistible, however severe and oppressive, the Inhabitants of these Colonies might at least require from the Parliament of Great-Britain some Evidence, that this dreadful Authority over them has been granted to that Body. But a Reverence for our great Creator, Principles of Humanity, and the Dictates of Common Sense, must convince all those who reflect upon the subject, that Government was instituted to promote the Welfare of Mankind, and ought to be administered for the Attainment of that End.... Our forefathers, Inhabitants of the Island of Great-Britain, left their Native Land, to seek on these Shores a Residence for civil and religious Freedom. At the Expence of their Blood, at the Hazard of their Fortunes, without the least Charge to the Country from which they removed, by unceasing Labour and an unconquerable Spirit, the effected Settlements in the distant and inhospitable Wilds of America....

We gratefully acknowledge, as signal Instances of the Divine Favour towards us, that his Providence would not permit us to be called into this severe Controversy, until we were grown up to our present strength, had been previously exercised in warlike Operation, and possessed of the means of defending ourselves. With hearts fortified with these animating Reflections, we must solemnly, before God and the

World, declare, that, exerting the utmost Energy of those Powers, which our benef-icent Creator hath graciously bestowed upon us, the Arms we have been compelled by our Enemies to assume, we will, in defiance of every Hazard, with unabating Firmness and Perseverence, employ for the preservation of our Liberties; being with one Mind resolved to die Freemen rather than live Slaves....

With an humble Confidence in the Mercies of the supreme and impartial Judge and Ruler of the Universe, we most devoutly implore his Divine Goodness to pro-tect us happily through this great Conflict, to dispose our Adversaries to reconcilia-tion on reasonable Terms, and thereby to relieve the Empire from the Calamities of civil war.

JAMES MADISON TO WILLIAM BRADFORD
July 28, 1775

Editor's note: Material in brackets is added for clarity.

A letter to Mr. Smith is in company with this.... I have requested him to bring me two pamphlets, "An apology for the Church of England as by Law Established" &c by Josiah Tucker - and An Essay on Toleration with a particular view to the late Application of the Dissenting Ministers to Parliament &c by Phil. Furneaux. If he should not be in Town after he recieves this & you could procure them and send them with Priestly before he sets off for Virginia you would lay me under another Obligation.

A Scotch Parson in an adjoining County refused to observe the fast or preach on that day [of 'public humiliation, fasting and prayer,' called by the Continental Congress]. When called on he pleaded Conscience, alledging that it was his duty to pay no regard to any such appointments made by unconstitutional authority. The Committee it seems have their Consciences too: they have ordered his Church doors to be shut and his salary to be stopped, and have sent to the convention for their advice. If the Convention should connive at their proceedings I question, should his insolence not abate if he does not get ducked in a coat of Tar & surplice of feathers and then he may go in his new Canonicals and act under the lawful Authority of Gen. Gage if he pleased. We have one of the same Kidney in the parish I live in. He was sometime ago published in the Gazette for his insolence and had like to have met with sore treatment: but finding his protection to be not so much in the law as the favor of the people he is grown very supple & obsequious.

THOMAS JEFFERSON TO FRANCIS EPPES
October 10, 1775

In the spring 10,000 men more are to come over. They are to be procured by taking away two thirds of the Garrison at Gibralter (who are to be replaced by some Hessians) by 2000 Highlanders and 5000 Roman Catholics whom they propose to raise in Ireland. Instead of the Roman Catholics however some of our accounts say foreigners are to be sent.

THOMAS JEFFERSON TO JOHN RANDOLPH
November 29, 1775

Beleive me Dear Sir there is not in the British empire a man who more cordially loves a Union with Gr. Britain than I do. But by the god that made me I will cease to exist before I yeild to a connection on such terms as the British parliament propose and in this I think I speak the sentiments of America.

JAMES MADISON, AMENDMENTS TO THE VIRGINIA DECLARATION OF RIGHTS
[May 29 to June 12, 1776]

Editor's note: Madison was a member of the committee of Virginia's Revolutionary Convention assigned "to prepare a declaration of rights." George Mason was the author of the declaration, but Madison had problems with Mason's usage of "toleration," and presented an amendment also disestablishing the Church of England. When it became clear that he lacked votes for disestablishment, he presented another amendment to the Committee's proposal.

Below, Mason's statement is followed by Madison's amendment. Then the Committee's draft is followed by Madison's second amendment. Finally, the article passed by the Convention is given. We shall see, later, that Madison and Jefferson did ultimately disestablish the church.

George Mason's Article:

That as Religion, or the Duty which we owe to our divine and omnipotent Creator, and the Manner of discharging it, can be governed only by Reason and Conviction, not by Force or Violence; and therefore that all Men should enjoy the fullest Toleration in the Exercise of Religion, according to the Dictates of Conscience, unpunished and unrestrained by the Magistrate, unless, under Colour of Religion, any Man disturb the Peace, the Happiness, or Safety of Society, or of Individuals. And that it is the mutual Duty of all, to practice Christian Forbearance, Love and Charity towards Each other.

Madison's Amendment to Mason's Article:

That Religion or the duty we owe to our Creator, and the manner of discharging it, being under the direction of reason and conviction only, not of violence or compulsion, all men are equally entitled to the full and free exercise of it accordg to the dictates of Conscience; and therefore that no man or class of men ought, on account of religion to be invested with peculiar emoluments or privileges; nor subjected to any penalties or disabilities unless under &c.

The Committee's Proposal:

That religion, or the duty which we owe to our CREATOR, and the manner of discharging it, can be directed only by reason and conviction, not by force or violence; and therefore, that all men should enjoy the fullest toleration in the exercise of religion, according to the dictates of conscience, unpunished and unrestrained by the magistrate unless, under colour of religion, any man disturb the peace, the happiness, or safety of society. And that it is the mutual duty of all to practice Christian forbearance, love and charity, towards each other.

Madison's Amendment to the Committee's Article:
That religion, or the duty which we owe to our CREATOR, and the manner of discharging it, can be directed only by reason and conviction, not by force or violence; and therefore, that all men are equally entitled to enjoy the free exercise of religion, according to the dictates of conscience, unpunished and unrestrained by the magistrate, Unless the preservation of equal liberty and the existence of the State are manifestly endangered; And that it is the mutual duty of all to practice Christian forbearance, love, and charity towards each other.

The Article as Passed by the Committee:
That religion, or the duty which we owe to our CREATOR, and the manner of discharging it, can be directed only by reason and conviction, not by force or violence; and therefore, all men are equally entitled to the free exercise of religion, according to the dictates of conscience; and that it is the mutual duty of all to practice Christian forbearance, love, and charity towards each other.

THE VIRGINIA CONSTITUTION
THOMAS JEFFERSON, FIRST DRAFT
[Before June 13, 1776]

Editor's note: The bracket below is Jefferson's.

Whereas George Guelph, King of Great Britain & Ireland and Elector of Hanover, heretofore entrusted with the exercise of the kingly office in this government, hath endeavored to pervert the same into a detestable & insupportable tyranny.... the sd. George Guelph has forfeited the kingly office, and has rendered it necessary.... to reestablish such antient principles as are friendly to the rights of the people....

All persons shall have full & free liberty of religious opinion, nor shall any be compelled to frequent or maintain any religious service or institution [but seditious behavior to be punble by civil magistrate accdg to the laws already made or hereafter to be made.].... the qualifications of all officers, Execve, judicial, military & eccles: oath of fidelity & no bribery.

THOMAS JEFFERSON, SECOND DRAFT
[Before June 13, 1776]

Editor's note: The words in < > were dropped.

All person shall have full & free liberty of religious opinion: nor shall any be compelled to frequent or maintain any religious institution. <but this shall not be held to justify any seditious preaching or conversation against the authority of the civil government.>

The Qualifications of all officers Civil, military & Ecclesiastical shall be an oath of fidelity to the state and the having given no bribe to obtain their office.

THOMAS JEFFERSON, THIRD DRAFT
[Before June 13, 1776]

Editor's note: The bracket is in the manuscript.

All persons shall have full and free liberty of religious opinion; nor shall any be compelled to frequent or maintain any religious institution....

No person shall be capable of acting in any office, Civil, Military [or Ecclesiastical] who shall have given any bribe to obtain such office, or who shall not previously take an oath of fidelity to the state.

THE VIRGINIA CONSTITUTION AS ADOPTED
June 29, 1776

In case of death, incapacity, or resignation, the Governour, with the advice of the privy Council, shall appoint Persons to succeed in Office, to be approved or displaced by both Houses. These Officers shall have fixed and adequate Salaries, and together with all others holding lucrative Offices, and all Ministers of the Gospel of every Denomination be incapable of being elected Members of either House of Assembly, or the Privy Council.

THOMAS JEFFERSON, NOTES ON PROCEEDINGS IN THE CONTINENTAL CONGRESS
June 7 to July 4, 1776

Editor's note: Jefferson's Notes were written sometime before 1783 and inserted into his Autobiography in 1821. What is presented here is a piece from his Notes, which discusses changes by others in the Declaration, and then excerpts from the document itself.

Where Jefferson says "The parts struck out by Congress shall be distinguished by a black line drawn under them; & those inserted by them shall be placed in the margin or in a concurrent column," here deletions from his draft are inside acute brackets, < >. Inserts by others are placed in regular brackets within the text.

Be aware that his original "inalienable rights" came to be printed "unalienable rights."

July 2.

Congress proceeded the same day to consider the declaration of Independance, which had been reported & laid on the table the Friday preceding, and on Monday referred to a commee. of the whole. The pusillanimous idea that we had friends in England worth keeping terms with, still haunted the minds of many. For this reason those passages which conveyed censures on the people of England were struck out, lest they should give them offence. The clause too, reprobating the enslaving the inhabitants of Africa, was struck out in complaisance to South Carolina & Georgia, who had never attempted to restrain importation of slaves, and who on the contrary still wished to continue it. Our Northern brethren also I believe felt a little tender under those censures; for tho' their people have very few slaves themselves yet they had been pretty considerable carriers of them to others.... As the sentiments of men are known not only by what they recieve, but what they reject also, I will state the form of the declaration as originally reported. The parts struck out by Congress shall be distinguished by a black line drawn under them; & those inserted by them shall be placed in the margin or in a concurrent column.

A DECLARATION BY THE REPRESENTATIVES OF UNITED STATES OF AMERICA, IN GENERAL CONGRESS ASSEMBLED

When in the course of human events, it becomes necessary for one people to dissolve the political bands which have connected them with another, and to assume among the powers of the earth the separate & equal station to which the laws of nature and of nature's God entitle them, a decent respect to the opinions of mankind requires that they should declare the causes which impel them to the separation.

We hold these truths to be self evident: that all men are created equal; that they are endowed by their Creator with [certain] <inherent and> inalienable rights; that among these are life, liberty, and the pursuit of happiness....

The history of the present king of Great Britain is a history of [repeated] <unremitting> injuries and usurpations....

<He has waged cruel war against human nature itself, violating it's most sacred rights of life and liberty in the persons of a distant people who never offended him, captivating and carrying them into slavery in another hemisphere, or to incur miserable death in their transportation hither. This piratical warfare, the opprobrium of INFIDEL powers, is the warfare of the CHRISTIAN king of Great Britain. Determined to keep open a market where MEN should be bought and sold, he has prostituted his negative for suppressing every legislative attempt to prohibit or to restrain this execrable commerce. And that this assemblage of horrors might want no fact of distinguished die, he is now exciting those very people to rise in arms among us, and to purchase that liberty of which he has deprived them, by murdering the people on whom he also obtruded them: thus paying off former crimes committed against the LIBERTIES of one people, with crimes which he urges them to commit against the LIVES of another>....

We, therefore, the representatives of the United states of America in General Congress assembled, [appealing to the supreme judge of the world for the rectitude of our intentions], do in the name, and by the authority of the good people of these [colonies, solemnly publish and declare that these United colonies are and of right ought] to be free and independant states.... And for the support of this declaration, [with a firm reliance on the protection of divine providence,] we mutually pledge to each other our lives, our fortunes and our sacred honor.

Part 3

THE STRUGGLE FOR THE DISESTABLISHMENT OF RELIGION IN VIRGINIA

1776 – 1785

The Declaration established the American nation, but Jefferson's primary field of activity remained Virginia and in 1779 he is elected Governor. His goal is to remake the state, removing all vestiges of British feudalism, including the established Church of England. This period ended with a British raid on Virginia on December 29, 1780, with Jefferson forced to flee from his plantation at Monticello on June 4, 1781. With the British withdrawal, he reverted to his civilian life as ex-Governor during the revolution.

After his wife's death in 1782, his focus becomes increasingly national, he becomes a delegate to the national congress, meeting in Annapolis and Princeton, and is then appointed Minister plenipotentiary to negotiate treaties in Europe. He traveled extensively to the north of Virginia to gather information on the country he was to represent, before leaving for Paris in 1785.

With Jefferson engaged on the national level, the struggle for religious freedom in Virginia was lead by Madison, and his 1785 Memorial and Remonstrance Against Religious Assessments is the major document in that campaign, and the basis of his subsequent thinking with regard to government and religion on the national level.

THOMAS JEFFERSON TO JOHN PAGE
July 30, 1776

Editor's note: This refers to a proposed seal for Virginia.

I like the device of the first side of the seal much. The second I think is too much crouded, nor is the design so striking. But for god's sake, what is the *'Deus nobis haec otia fecit.'* [God has made this leisure for us] It puzzles everybody here; if my country really enjoys that otium, it is singular, as every other colony seems to be hard struggling. I think it was agreed on before Dunmore's flight from Gwyn's island so that it can hardly be referred to the temporary holiday that has given you. This device is too aenigmatical, since if it puzzles now, it will be absolutely insoluble fifty years hence.

THOMAS JEFFERSON, REPORT ON A SEAL FOR THE UNITED STATES
August 20, 1776

Editor's note: This was one of Jefferson's proposals. John Adams also wrote that "Mr. Jefferson proposed the children of Israel in the wilderness, led by a cloud by day and a pillar of fire by night; and on the other side, Hengist and Horsa, the Saxon chiefs from whom we claim the honor of being descended, and whose political principles and form of government we have assumed."

The suggestion for the motto has been attributed to Jefferson, Ben Franklin, and Pierre Du Simitière of Philadelphia, who drew the designs. Most scholars think that Franklin was the author.

Jefferson's proposal.
Pharaoh sitting in an open chariot, a crown on his head and a sword in his hand passing thro' the divided waters of the Red sea in pursuit of the Israelites: rays from a pillar of fire in the cloud, expressive of the divine presence, and command, reaching to Moses who stands on the shore and, extending his hand over the sea, causes it to overwhelm Pharaoh. Motto. Rebellion to tyrants is obedience to god.

THOMAS JEFFERSON, NOTES ON LOCKE AND SHAFTESBURY
[Between October 11 and November 19, 1776]

Editor's note: "Arians," below, refers to the supporters of Arius, who preached that God existed first and then created his son. "Athans" stands for Athanasians, followers of St. Athanasius, author of the Roman Catholic creed on the trinity.

Here and elsewhere, Jefferson uses the letter y as a substitute for the thorn, an Anglo-Saxon symbol for th, as in ye = the.

The square brackets below that do not refer to an illegible point in the manuscript, are by Jefferson. Material between acute brackets < > are deleted words.

Why persecute for diffce. in religs. opinion?

---

1. for love to the person.
2. because of tendency of these opns. to dis [...]

When I see them persecute their nearest connection & acquaintances for gross vices, I shall beleive it may proceed from love. Till they do this, I appeal to their own conscences. If they will examine, why they do nt. find some other principle. Because of tendency. Why not then level persecution at the crimes you fear will be introduced? Burn or hang the adulterer, cheat &c. or exclude them from offices.

Strange should be so zealous against things which tend to produce immorality & yet so indulgent to the immorality when produced. These moral vices all men acknolege to be diametrically against Xty. & obstructive of salvation of souls, but the fantastical points for which we generally persecute are often very questionable, as we may be assured by the very different conclusions of people.

Our Saviour chose not to propagate his religion by temporal punmts or civil incapacitations, if he had it was in his almighty power. But he chose extend it by it's influence on reason, thereby shewing to others how [they] should proceed.

Commonwealth is 'a society of men constituted for preser[ving] their civil <rights> interests.'

Interests are 'life, health, indolency of body, liberty, property.'

The magistrate's jurisdn extends only to civil rights and from these considns:

The magistrate has no power but wt ye people gave hm.

The people hv not givn hm <power> the care of souls bec y cd nt,

y cd nt because no man hs right to abandon ye care of his salvation to another.

No man has power to let another prescribe his faith. Faith is not faith witht believing. No man can conform his faith to the dictates of another.

The life & essence of religion consists in the internal persuasion or belief of the mind. External forms [of wor]ship, when against our belief, are hypocrisy [and im]piety. Rom. 14:23 'he that doubteth is damned, if he eat, because he eateth not of faith: for whatsoever is not of faith is sin.'

If it be said the magistrate may make use of a[guements] and so draw the heterodox to truth: I [answer] every man has a commission to admonish, exhort, convince another of error.

[A church] is a 'voluntary society of men, joining themselves together of their own accord, in order to the publick worshipping of god in such a manner as they judge acceptable to him & effectual to the salvation of their souls.' It is voluntary because no man is by nature bound to any church. The hopes of salvation is the cause of his entering into it. If he find any thing wrong in it, he should be as free to go out as he was to come in.

What is the power of that church &c.? As it is a society <of voluntary> it must have some laws for it's regulation, time & place of meeting, admitting & excluding members &c. must be regulated.

But as it was a spontaneous joining of members, it follows that it's laws extend to it's own members only, not to those of any other voluntary society: for then by the same rule some other voluntary society might usurp power over them.

Christ has said 'wheresoever 2 or 3 are gatherd togeth in his name he will be in the midst of them.' This is his definition of a society. He does not make it essential that a bishop or presbyter govern them. Without them it suffices for the salvation of souls.

From the dissentions among sects themselves arises necessarily right of chusing & necessity of deliberating to which we will conform.

But if we chuse for ourselves, we must allow others to chuse also, & so reciprocally. This establishes religious liberty.

Why require those things in order to ecclesiastical communion which Christ does not require in order to life eternal? How can that be the church of Christ which excludes such person from it's communion as he will one day recieve into the kingdom of heaven.

The arms of a religious society or church are exhortations admonitions & advice, & ultimately expulsions or excommunication. This last is the utmost limit of power.

How far does the duty of toleration extend?

1. No church is bound by the duty of toleration to retain within her bosom obstinate offenders against her laws.

2. We have no right to prejudice another in his civil enjoinments because he is of another church. If any man err from the right way, it is his own misfortune, no injury to thee, nor therefore art thou to punish him in the things of this life because thou supposest he will be miserable in that which is to come. On the contrary accdg to the spirit of the gospel, charity, bounty, liberality is due to him.

Each church being free, no one can have jurisdiction over another; no not even when the civil magistrate joins it. It neither acquires the right of the sword by the magistrate's coming to it, nor does it lose the rights of instruction or excommunication by his going from it, it cannot by the accession of any new member acquire jurisdiction over those who do no accede. He brings only himself, having no power to bring others.

Suppose for instance two churches. One of Arminians another of <Lutherans> Calvinists in Constantinople. Has either any right over the other? Will it be said the orthodox one has? Every church is to itself orthodox, to others erroneous or heretical.

No man complains of his neighbor for ill management of his affairs, for an error in sowing his land, or marrying his daughter, for consuming his substance in taverns, pulling down, build &c. In all these he has his liberty: but if he do not frequent the church, or there conform to ceremonies, there is an immediate uproar.

The care of every man's soul belongs to himself. But what if he neglect the care of it? Well what if he neglect the care of his health or estate, which more nearly relate to the state. Will the magistrate make a law that he shall not be poor or sick? Laws provide against injury from others; but not from ourselves. God himself will not save men against their wills.

If I be marching on with my utmost vigour in that way which according to the sacred geography leads to Jerusalem streight, why am I beaten & ill used by others because my hair is not of the right cut; because I have not been kept right, bec I eat flesh on the road, bec I avoid certain by-ways which seem to lead into briars, bec among several paths I take that which seems shortest & cleanest, bec I avoid travellers less grave & keep company with others who are more sour & austere, or be I follow a guide crowned with a mitre & cloathed in white. Yet these are the frivolous things which keep Xns at war.

If the magistrate command me to [bring my commodity to a publick store house] I bring it because he can indemnify me if he erred & I therefore lose it; but what indemnification can he give me for the kdom of heaven?

I cannot give up my guidance to the magistrate; because he knows no more of the way to heaven than I do & is less concerned to direct me right than I am to go right. If the Jews had followed their kings, amongst so many what number would have led them to idolatry? Consider the vicissitudes among the emperors, Arians, Athans or among our princes, H.8, E.6, Mary, Elizabeth.

Compulsion in religion is distinguished peculiarly from compulsion is every other thing. I may grow rich by art I am compelled to follow, I may recover health by medicines I am compelled to take agt my own judgmt, but I cannot be saved by a worship I disbelieve & abhor.

Whatever is lawful in the Commonwealth, or permitted to the subject in the ordinary way, cannot be forbidden to him for religious uses; & whatsoever is prejudicial to the commonwealth in their ordinary uses & therefore prohibited by the laws, ought not to be permitted to churches in their sacred rites. For instance, it is unlawful in the ordinary course of things or in a private house to murder a child. It should not be permitted any sect then to sacrifice children: it is ordinarily lawful (or temporarily lawful) to kill calves or lambs. They may therefor be religiously sacrificed. But if the good of the state required a temporary suspension of killing lambs (as during a seige); sacrifices of them may then be rightfully suspended also. This the true extent of toleration.

Truth will do well enough if left to shift for herself. She seldom has received much aid from the power of great men to whom she is rarely known & seldom welcome. She has no need of force to procure entrance into the minds of men. Error indeed has often prevailed by the assistance of power or force.

Truth is the proper & sufficient antagonist to error.

If any thing pass in a religious meeting seditiously & contrary the public peace, let it be punished in the same manner & no otherwise than as if it had happened in a fair or market. These meetings ought not to be sanctuaries for faction & flagitiousness.

Locke denies toleration to those who entertain opns contrary to those moral rules necessary for the preservation of society; as for instance, that faith is not to be kept with those of another persuasion, that kings excommunicated forfeit their crowns, that dominion is founded in grace, or that obedience is due to some foreign prince, or who will not own & teach the duty of tolerating all men in matters of religion, or who deny the existence of a god. [It was a great thing to go so far (as he himself sais of the parl, who framed the act of tolern.) But where he stopped short, we may go on.*]

He sais 'neither Pagan nor Mahamedan nor Jew ought to be excluded from the civil rights of the Commonwealth because of his religion.' Shall we suffer a Pagan to deal with us and not suffer him to pray to his god?

Why have Xns been distinguished above all people who have ever lived for persecutions? Is it because it is the genius of their religion? No, it's genius is the reverse. It is the refusing toleration to those of a different opn which has produced all the bustles & wars on account of religion. It was the misfortune of mankind that during the darker centuries the Xn priests following their ambition & avarice & combining with the magistrates to divide the spoils of the people, could establish the notion that schismatics might be ousted of their possessions & destroyed. This notion we have not yet cleared ourselves from. In this case no wonder the oppressed should rebel, & they will continue to rebel & raise disturbances until their civil rights are fully restored to them & all partial distinctions, exclusions & incapacitations removed.

1. Shaftesbury. charact.

As the antients tolerated visionaries & enthusiasts of all kinds so they permitted a free scope to philosophy as a balance. As the Pythagoreans & later Platonicks joined with the superstition of the times the Epicureans & Academicks were allowed all the use of wit & raillery against it. Thus matters were balanced; reason had [full] play & science flourished. These contrarieties produced harmony. Superstition & enthusiasm thus let alone never raged to bloodshed persecution &c. But now a new sort of policy which considers the future lives & happiness of men rather than the present, has taught to distress one another, & raised an antipathy which no temporal interest could ever do, now uniformity of opn, a hopeful project! is looked on as the only remedy agt. this evil & is made the very object of govmt itself. If magistracy should vouchsafe to interpose thus in other sciences we should [have] as bad logic, mathematics & philosophy as we have divinity in countries where the law settles orthodoxy.

[Suppose the state should take into head that there should be an uniformity of countenance. Men would be obliged to put an artificial bump or swelling here, a patch there &c. But this would be merely hypocritical.] [Or if the alternative was given of wearing a mask, 99/100ths must immediately mask. Would this add to the beauty of nature? Why otherwise in opinions.] [In the middle ages of Xty, opposition to the state opns was hushed. The consequence was, Xty became loaded with

---

*Footnote by Jefferson:

Will not his own excellent rule be sufficient here too, to punish these as civil offences, e. gr. to assert that a foreign prince has power within this commonwealth is a misdemeanor. The other opns may be despised. Perhaps the single thing which may be required others before toleration to them would be an oath that they would allow toleration to others.

---

all the Romish follies. Nothing but free argument, raillery even ridicule will preserve the purity of religion.]

2. Cor. 1. 24. The apostles declare they had no dominion over the faith.

Locke's system of Christianity is this.
Adam was created happy & immortal: but his happiness was to have been Earthly, and earthly immortality. By sin he lost this, so that he became subject to total death (like that of brutes) & to the crosses & unhappinesses of this life. At the intercession however of the son of god this sentence was in part remitted. A life conformable to the law was to restore them again to immortality. And moreover to those who believed their faith was to be counted for righteousness, not that faith without works was to save them; St. James c.2. sais expressly the contrary; & all make the fundamental pillars of Xty to be faith & repentance, so that a reformation of life (included under repentance) was essential, & defects in this would be made up by their faith; i.e. their faith should be counted for righteousness. As to that part of mankind who never had the gospel preached to them, they are 1. Jews. 2. Pagans, or Gentiles. The Jews had the law of works revealed to them. By this therefore they were to be saved: & a lively faith in god's promises to send the Messiah would supply small defects. 2. the Gentiles. St. Paul sais Rom. 2:13. 'the Gentiles have the law written in their hearts' i.e. the law of nature: to which adding a faith in God, & his attributes that on their repentance he would pardon them, they also would be justified. This then explains the text 'there is no other name under heaven by which a man may be saved.' i.e. the defects in good works shall not be supplied by a faith in Mahomet, Foe, or any other except Christ.

The fundamentals of Xty as found in the gospels are 1. Faith. 2. Repentance, that faith is every[where] explained to be a belief that Jesus was the Messiah who had been promised. Repentance was to be proved sincere by good works. The advantages accruing to mankind from our Savior's mission are these: 1. The knolege of one god only. 2. A clear knolege of their duty, or system of morality, delivered on such authority as to give it sanction. 3. The outward forms of religious worship wanted to be purged of that farcical pomp & nonsense with which they were loaded. 4. An inducement to a pious life, by revealing clearly a future existence in bliss, & that it was to be the reward of the virtuous.

The Epistles were written to persons already Christians. A person might be a Xn then before they were written. Consequently the fundamentals of Xty were to be found in the preaching of our savior, which is related in the gospels. These fundamentals are to be found in the epistles dropped here & there & promiscuously mixed with other truths. But these other truths are not to be made fundamentals. They serve for edification indeed & explaining to us matters in worship & morality. But being written occasionally it will readily be seen that their explanations are adapted to the notions & customs of the people they were written to. But yet every sentence in them (tho the writers were inspired) must not be taken up & made a fundamental, without assent to which a man is not to be admitted a member X's church here, or to his kingdom hereafter. The Apostles creed was by them taken to contain all things necessary to salvation & consequently to a communion.

THOMAS JEFFERSON, ROUGH DRAFT OF RESOLUTIONS FOR DISESTABLISHING THE CHURCH OF ENGLAND AND FOR REPEALING LAWS INTERFERING WITH FREEDOM OF WORSHIP
[Between October 11 and November 19, 1776]

Editor's note: Only fragments of the preamble have been found.

Fragment 1:
for restoring to the <inhabitants> Citizens of this Comm'w. the right of maintaining their religious opinions, & of worshipping god in their own way; for releasing them from all legal obligations to frequent churches or other places of worship, & for exempting them from contributions for the support of any <church> religious society independant of their good will, & for discontinuing the establishment of the church of England by law & <thereby> taking away the privilege & pre-eminence of one religious sect over another, and thereby <establish [....] & equal rights among all>.

Fragment 2:
<for discontinuing the establishment of the English church by law, taking away all privilege & pre-eminence of one religious sect over another; & totally and eternally restraining the civil magistrate from all pretentions of interposing his authority or exercise in matters of religion>.

Resolved & C.
That the statutes 1.E.6.c.1, 5&6.E.6.c.1, 1El.c.2, 23.El.c.1.28, El.c.6, 35.El.c.1, 1.Jac.1.c.4, 3.Jac.1.c.1, 3.Jac.1.c.4, 3.Jac.1.c.21, and the act of ass 1705.c.6. & so much of all older acts or statues as render criminal the maintaining any opinions in matters of religion or the exercising any mode of worship whatever or as prescribe punishments for the same ought to be repealed.

Resolved that it is the opn of this Commee that so much of sd. petitions as prays that the establishment of the Church of England by law in this Commonwealth may be discontinued, and that no pre-eminence may be allowed to any one Religious sect over another, is reasonable; & therefore that the several laws establishing the sd. Church of England, giving peculiar privileges to <the> it's ministers <thereof> & levying for the support thereof <the same> contributions on the people independent of their good will ought to be repealed; saving to such incumbents as are now actually seised of Glebe lands, their rights to such Glebe lands during their lives, & to such parishes as have received private donations for <use of> support of the sd. Church <of England> the perpetual benefit of such donations.

THOMAS JEFFERSON, MISCELLANEOUS NOTES ON RELIGION
[Between October 11 and December 9, 1776]

Editor's note: The first brackets are in the manuscript. The other brackets contain illegible words obtained from the Act discussed. The material between astericks is from different fragments in Jefferson's papers.

1662.c.3. Pervis. An act against persons that refuse to have their children baptized.

1663.c.1. Pervis. An act prohibiting the unlawful assembling of quakers.

[1692.c.5. An act encoraging the erecting of a post office in this country.] This was to confirm the establishmt of that office made in England.

1659. Mar. 13

An act for the suppressing the Quakers. I doubt whether the laws of this session are in H. B. office. The substance is to lay penalty of £100 Sterl. on any captain of ship who shall bring in a Quaker to be levied by an order from the Gov. & council on the justices of the county.

That all Quakers already questioned or which shall hereafter arrive shall be apprehended & imprisoned without bail or mainprize till they abjure this country, or give security to depart the colony immediately & not to return.

If they return, to be proceeded against & pursued as contemners of the laws & magistracy:

If they return a second time to be proceeded against as felons.

No person to entertain any of the Quakers questioned by the Gov. & council or who shall hereafter be questd.

No person to permit any assembly of Quakers in or near his house in penalty of £100 Sterling.

No person, at their peril, to dispose or publish their books with their tenets & opinions.

Justices & other officers at their peril to take notice of this act to see it fully effected and executed.

****

Impropriety of time - invasion
nevr complnd befre
Hierarchy & Monarchy Congenl.

Threatg.

Practice Tolern nt Leg.

Stat. of Tolern. Adopted

Propriety of an Estabmt.
Obj. Most states have establmt.
Ans. yn every Relign hs bn establd.
Ds ys Prove Infallibility

Examp Holland
Pennsylva &c.
[....]

Public Regulns. necessary
1. Open doors

2. Tendcy of opns.
Regenern
Future state
Ys wd subjct Religs opn.
Ys supportd Monksh ignorce.
Trust to Ministers
Wch. is smallst Inconvce.

3. Ordinatn
Leave it to each sect
Yr own interest lead to it
Quakers

4. Fixed Contributn.
Laborer worthy of hire

[....]
While contins worthy - shd b indepdt
Wll be afrd to censure
Ans. The reverse is true
Obj. Rich Philadelphns refuse

Inequality of Parishes
Contribn wll not suppt.
Contribn mst go to difft. sect or be lost
Decln Rts. Freedm of conscce
Force to support Error
Quakers
Foreigns. discoraged
Law deft cts. - Value Xn Examp.
Ruin church

[....]
Ye Stat: Justified by hist times.
Ans. Shd hve bn repealed.
All Stat: After 4. [....] Whimsicl.
Ys is determin of law
Obj. Act of parl. repeald. Mst be in force here.
Yn in repeal Magn Charta. Stat. of Wills
Ys gives up Americn qu.
Genl ct so thought it
Ans. Y dd nt.

Obj. Act. ass. is agt swearg. Drunkss. - Wll be licence to practice [....]
None but Chst men obligd to go to Chch.
Obj. Wt [...] Sentiments
Obj.

★★★★

Do not [...] inculcate principles of morality.
Why then give peculir privileges to any.
Romn. Cathol. in Congress - grt. confidce.
Canada
Frdly interchange of Citizens wth all ye colonies.
[....]
Shadford the petner. is appd by Rankins for Virga.
Westly has written in favr of ministry
has been advertzd in Maryld gazette as having written agt Junius's lres.
E. of Dartmouth, principl secretary, a methodist
Shadfd has signed witht authority.

Methodsts in Albem. signd petns.
Co. L. 11. 260. Hob. 79.
1 Bl. c.8.Co. 106.
Spelman. Admir. flotsam.
Jacob. beaconage.
2. Shower 232. Comb. 474.

THOMAS JEFFERSON, NOTES ON HERESY
[Between October 11 and December 9, 1776]

Editor's note: The following two fragments are of the same period, divided by asterisks. The brackets are in the manuscripts.

A heretic is an impugner of fundamentals. What are fundamentals? The protestants will say those doctrines which are clearly & precisely delivered in the holy scriptures. Dr. Waterland would say the Trinity. But how far this character [of being clearly delivered?] will suit the doctrine of the Trinity I leave others to determine. It is no where expressly declared by any of the earliest fathers, & was never affirmed or taught by the church before the council of Nice. [Chillingw. Pref. § 18.33.] Irenaeus says 'who are the clean? Those who go on firmly, believing in the father & in the son.' The fundamental doctrine or the firmness of the Xn. faith in this early age then was to beleive in the father & son. - Constantine wrote to Arius & Alexr. treating the question 'as vain foolish & impertinent as a dispute of words without sense which none could explane nor any comprehend &c.' This lre is commended by Eusebius [Vit. Constant. 1b.2.c.64 &c.] and Socrates [Hist. Eccles. 1.1.c.7] as excellent admirable & full of wisdom. 2. Middleton 115 remarks on the story of St. John & [....]

Le saint concil [de Nicée anno 330] ayant defini que le fils de dieu est de meme sustance que no pere & qu'il est eternel comme lui, composa une Simbole [the Nicene creed] où il explique la divinete du pere & du fils, et qu'il finit par ces paroles 'dont le regne n'aura point de fin.' car la doctrine qui regarde le saint esprit ne fut ajoutée que dans le second concile tenu contre les erreurs de Macedonius, ou ces questions furent agitées. Zonare par Coussin. abb. 330. [The holy council (of Nicea anno 330) having defined that the son of god is of the same substance as our father and that, like him, he is eternal, formulated a Symbol (the Nicene creed) where the divinity of the father and of the son is affirmed and which ends with the words, 'whose reign shall never end,' for the doctrine regarding the holy spirit was only added by the second council, where these questions were brought up to refute the errors of Macedonius.] The second council meant by Zonares was that of Constantinople ann. 381. D. hist. Prim. Xty. pref. XXXVIII. 2d. app. to pref. 49. The Council of Antioch [ann   ] expressly affirmed of our savior ουκ εςτιν ομοουςιος that he was not Consubstantial to the father. The Council of Nice affirmed the direct contrary. D. hist. Prim. Xty. Pref. CXXV.

****

Sabellians. Xn. heretics. That the Father is the one only god; that the Word is no more than an expression of ye godhead & had not existed from all eternity, that Jes. Christ was god no otherwise than by his superiority above all creatures who were put in subjection to him by the father, that he was not a Mediator, but sent to be a pattern of conduct to men, that the punishmts of hell are nt eternl.

Arminians. They think with the Romish church (agt. the Calvinists) that there is an universal grace given to all men, & that man is always free & at liberty to receive or reject grace. That god creates men free, that his justice would not permit him to punish men for crimes they are predestinated to commit. They admit the prescience of god, but distinguish between fore-knowing & predestination on his authority.

Arians. Xn. heretics. They avow there was a time when the Son was not, that he was created in time, mutable in nature, & like the Angels liable to sin. They deny the three persons in the trinity to be of the same essence. Erasmus & Grotius were Arians.

Apollinarians. Xn. heretics. They affirm there was but one nature in Christ, that his body as well as soul was impassive & immortal, & that his birth, death & resurrection was only in appearance.

Macedonians. Xn. heretics. They teach that the Holy ghost was a meer creature but superior in excellence to the Angels.

See Broughton. verbo [word] 'Hertics' an enumeration of 48 sects of Christians pronounced Heretics.

THOMAS JEFFERSON, NOTES ON EPISCOPACY
[Between October 11 and December 9, 1776]

Gr. Επιςκοπος Lat. Episcopus. Ital. Vescovo.
Fr. Evesque. Saxon Biscop. Bishop. (overseer)
The epistles of Paul to Timothy & Titus are relied on (together with tradition) for
    the Apostolic institution of bishops.
As to tradition, if we are protestants we reject all tradition, & rely on the scripture
    alone, for that is the essence & common principle of all the protestant churches.

As to Scripture.
1. Tim.3.2, 'a bishop must be blameless &c. Επιςκοπς.'
v. 8, 'likewise must the deacons be grave &c. Διακονος' (ministros)
c.5v.6, he calls Timothy a 'minister' 'Διακονος'
c.4.v.14. 'Neglect not the gift that is in thee, which was given thee by prophecy with
the laying on the hands of the presbytery. πρεςβυτεροι'
c.5, 'rebuke not an elder πρεςβυτερω'

5.17, 'let the elders that rule well &c. πρεςβυτεροι'
5.19, 'against an elder (πρεςβυτερου recieve nt an accusan.'
5.22, 'lay hands suddenly on no man χειρας επιτιθει'
6.11. he calls Timothy 'man of god ανθρωπε του θεου'
2.Tim.1.6. 'Stir up the gift of god which is in thee by the putting on of my hands
επιθεςεως των χειρων μου.' But ante c.4 v.14, he said it was by the hands of the
presbytery. This imposition of hands then was some ceremony or custom frequently repeated, & certainly is as good a proof that Timothy was ordained by the elders
(& consequently that they might ordain) as that it was by Paul.

1.11. Paul calls himself 'a preacher' 'an apostle' 'a teacher.' 'κηρυξ και αποϛτολος και διδαϛκαλος' Here he designates himself by several synonims as he had before done Timothy. Does this prove that every synonim authorizes a different order of ecclesiastics.

4.5, 'do the work of an Evangelist, make full proof of thy ministry εργον ποιηϛον ευαγγελιϛτου, την διακονιαν ϛου πληποφορηϛον.' Timothy then is called 'επιϛκοπος, διακονος, ευαγγελιϛτος, ανθρωπος θεου.'

4.11, He tells Tim. to bring Mark with him for 'he is profitable to me for the ministry διακονια.'

Epist. to Titus 1.1. He calls himself 'a servant of god δουλος θεου.' 1.5. 'For this cause left I thee in Crete that thou shouldst set in order the things that are wanting, and ordain (καταϛτησης) elders in every city, as I had appointed thee, If any be blameless the husband of one wife, having faithful children, not accused of riot or unruly, for a bishop must be blameless as the steward of god &c.' Here then it appears that as the elders appointed the bishops, so the bishops appointed the elders, i.e. they are synonims. Again when telling Titus to appoint elders in every city he tells him what kind of men they must be, for said he a bishop must be &c. so that in the same sentence he calls elders bishops.

3.10: 'a man that is an heretic after the first & second admonition, reject.' 'αιρετικον.'

Jas. 5.14, 'is any sick among you? Let him call for the elders (πρεϛβυτερους) of the church, & let them pray over him, anointing him with oil in the name of the lord.'

Another plea for Episcopal government in Religion in England is its similarity to the political governmt by a king. No bishop no king. This then with us is a plea for governmt by a presbytery which resembles republican governmt.

The clergy have ever seen this. The bishops were alwais mere tools of the crown.

The Presbyterian spirit is known to be so congenial with friendly liberty, that the patriots after the restoration finding that the humor of people was running too strongly to exalt the prerogative of the crown, promoted the dissenting interest as a check and balance, & thus was produced the Toleration act.

St. Peter gave the title of Clergy to all god's people till pope Higinus and ye succeeding prelates took it from them & appropriated it to priests only. 1. Milt. 230.

Origen, being yet a layman, expounded the scriptures publickly & was therein defended by Alexander of Jerusalem & Theoctistus of Caesarea, producing in his behalf divers examples that the privilege of teaching was antiently permitted to laymen. The first Nicene council called on the assistance of many learned lay brethren, ib. 230.

Bishops were elected by the hands of the whole ch. Ignatius (the most antt. of the extant fathers) writing to the Philadelphians sais 'that it belongs to them as to the church of god to chuse a bishop.' Cambden in his description of Scotld. sais 'that over all the world bps had no certain diocese till pope Dionysius about the year 268 did cut them out, & that the bps of Scotld exd their function what place soever they came, indifferently till temp. Malcolm 3. 1070'

Cyprian epist. 68, sais 'the people chefly hath power either of chusing worthy or refusing unworthy bps.' The council of Nice writing to the African churches exhorts them to chuse orthodox bps in the place of the dead. 1. Milt. 254.

Nicephorus Phocas the Greek emperor ann. 1000 first enacted that no bp shd be chosen without his will. Ignatius in his epistle to those of Tra[...] confesseth that the presbyters are his fellow-sellers & fellow benchers, and Cyprian in the 6.41.52, epist, calls the presbyters, 'his Compresbyters,' yet he was a bp. - A modern bp, to be moulded into a primitive one must be elected by the people, undiocest, unrevenued, unlorded, 1.Milt. 255.

THOMAS JEFFERSON, BILL FOR THE NATURALIZATION OF FOREIGNERS
October 14, 1776

Editor's note: The Bill is in Edmund Pendleton's handwriting, with the last paragraph by Jefferson. There are significant alterations by Jefferson, the most important being those that would extend citizenship to Jews. The material after the asterisks is entirely by Jefferson, on the back of the Bill. Words in acute brackets were deleted, presumably by Jefferson.

For the encouragement of <Foreign Protestants> foreigners to settle in this Countrey

Be it enacted by the Senate and House of Delegates of Virginia now met in General Assembly

That all <Foreign Protestants> (foreigners) (now settled) persons born in other countries and now residing in this <Colony and not naturalized> Commonwealth, and all who may hereafter migrate into the same, who shall go before any Court of Record with the same, and give Satisfactory proof by their own Oath or Affirmation or Otherwise, that they have resided or intend to reside in this countrey for the space of years at the least; and who shall take an Oath of Fidelity to the Common Wealth and subscribe to be Obedient to the Laws thereof, shall be considered as Free Citizens of the same and shall be entitled to all the Rights, privileges and immunities, civil and religious, of this Commonwealth, as if born therein. And the Clerk of the Court shall enter such an Oath and Subscription of Record, and give the Person a Certificate thereof, for all which he shall receive the fee of and no more.

And be it further Enacted that <all Foreign Protestants who> where any foreigners have acquired Lands in the Countrey, and have conveyed the same to others by deed or will, or transmitted them to their children or other Relations; The title of every person now in Actual Possession of such Lands under such conveyance, or transmission, is hereby confirmed in as full and ample manner as if the same had conveied by natural born <Subjects> citizens of this Commonwealth.

And be it further enacted that there shall be paid by the Treasurer of this <Colony> Commonwealth out any public money in his hands the sum of 20 dollars to every foreigner who shall come to settle in this Commonwealth for the purpose of defraying his passage hither over sea, and that there shall be also be granted to him fifty acres of unappropriated lands, wherever he shall chuse the same to be held in <free and absolute> fee simple.

****

Physical advantages
    Consumption
    Labor
    Procreation
    [....]

Moral
    Honesty - veracity
    Religion - Is theirs less moral
    Will the amendmt take ym. better
    all who have not full rights are secret
        enem[ies]

Obj. No nation allows them to realize
    Jews advantageous

Ys wll narrow ground of formg. act
    Ass.

THOMAS JEFFERSON, OUTLINE OF ARGUMENT IN SUPPORT OF HIS RESOLUTIONS
[Before November 30, 1776]

Editor's note: Again, Jefferson uses the letter y as a substitute for the Anglo-Saxon symbol known as a thorn, i.e., th, as in ys, yt & y oyer, this that and the other.

Befre. ent. on Propr. Redress - see wt. is Injury - ye sta. Religs. Lib.

Apostacy. act. 1705.c.6.

    1st. offce. disabled. to hold office
    2nd. disabled to sue, incapb. of gift or legacy
    3rd. three years imprismt. however conscients. ye Conversion

Heresy. <1.EL.c.1.> Heretico combura [burn for heresy].
  State hs. adoptd. Athanasn. creed.
  Arians therefore Heretics
  eithr. Civl. or Eccles. judge in burn 1.H.P.c.405
    2. Arians burnt in El. & Jac.
Socinians.

Recusancy.
  Sacramt.1.E.6.c.1.
    to deprave it, imprismt. & fine ad libitum [according to will]
    Quakers

Commn. Prayr. 1.El.c.2.
  (a) derogate frm. it — or attend any other Commd. to
    prison tll. Conform if not. Confrm. in 3 Months, abjure,
  act of ass. addnal. 5/except on dissentrs.
  wch. is deragn
  Athanasn. creed.
  Commination
  XXXlX Articles
    11th. Faith - Works.
    13. Works sinfl. befre. grace & Inspirn.
    17. Predestination.
    18. No name cn. save bt. Christ.
  Obj. Insultg. & Revilg. offensve. to good men
  ans. so evy. oth transgrn. divne. commd. is yt. sfft. to
    justify coercn.
  Revilr. wll. be contemd. - Ministers if Punish, people
    wll. Pity.
  cool reasg. refutn. compsn. bst. arms fr. Revilrs. to tke.
    refge. in Fi & Imprmt. seems hd. n. bettr. suppt.

Tenets & Formulars. plannd. by Clergy, yo. stabld. by
    civl. hist. Synods, convocns, councils -
      intrig. Cabls. animos. anathem.
      smll. Majorts. -
      cross in baptm. carrd. by 1. in Convocn. E1.
    Obj. shll. w. lve. mn. propagte. wt. opn. please?
  ans. Truth cnt. sufr. by fre. Enquiry - only w. propag.
      Free enquiry enemy only to Error
    if m. forbd. free Argum' - Mahomsm
      prevnt. Reformn.
  (b) No attendg. Chch. whre. Com. Prayr.
    23. El. c.1, 28. El.c.6, 35.El.c1, 3.Jac.1.c.4.

41

20£ a month - or 2/3 of lands:

10£ a month for keepg. a person wh. ds. nt. or Imprismt & Abjurn.

(d) Attending Conventicles

same punmts.

Free govnt, forgets own princ. whn. becmes. intolrt.

4. Popery.

5. Profaneness. 3.Jac.1.c.21.

jestingly speakg. name of God, Christ, Ghost, Trinty. £10.

for every offence.

6. Contribn.

is it just?

yse. peop. p. dble. Contribns.

ys. is Persecn in degree

is it Geners. in Clerg. hire whre. nevr. labord.

Gent. wll. b. surprizd. at detl. yse persecutg. stat.

mos. men imagne. persecn. unknn. t. our ls.

legl. sta. Relign. little undstd.

ye. persecn. gos. nt. t. death bt. in 1. case - Fi. Impr.

happly. ye. Spirt. of times in favr. of rts. of Conscce.

if just sch. rts. possed. in Xtnt. wch. lenity of ti. allows

just shd. be fxd by law.

at ys. ti. of reformn. no laws incompble left unrepd.

Lt. gent. wh hapn. of Relign. of sta. mke. ca. of oth. yr. own

wt. wd. b. yr. Sensns. if n. Secty. civl. rts. bt. Modern.

of ti.

wd. b. uneasy till fxd. on legal basis.

Rts. of Conscce mch. mo. tendr.

Obj. yse. acts only interrorm [as a warning].

Ans. acts in terrm. nt. justfble. -m. presme. wll. b. xd.

leave evy. one at mercy of Bigot.

evy. one shd. kn. undr. wt. law lives

shd. nt. b. oblgd. recr. to Spirt. of ti. fr. protctn.

ys. is nt. Secure govmt. - bt. at mercy of events

Spirt. ti. m. altr. - single Zealt. m. undtke. refrm.

bad complmt. to law. yt. peop. discrn. iniqty. & nt. xte. it

former attempts at tolern. how have succeeded

Presbyterian wd. open just wide enough for hms.

others wd. open it to infidelity, bt. keep out fanaticism

True mode only for all to concur, & throw open to all.

---

ye. prest. chch. too strong for any 1 sect, bt. too weak agt. all.

Hs. State Right to adopt an Opn. in mattr. Relign.
    whn. mn. ent. Socty. Surrendr. litt. as posble.
    Civl. rts. all yt. r. nec. to Civl. govmt.
    Religs. rts. nt. nec. surrd.
    Indivd. cnt. surrdr. - answble. to God
       If is unalienable right,[...] is Religs.
    God reqres. evy. act acdg. to Belief
    yt. Belf. foundd., on Evdce. offd. to his mind.
       as yngs. appr. to hims. nt. to anoth.

Obj. oth. mens Undstgs. better
Ans. hs. own Undstg., wh. mo. or less. judics. only faclty. god

True line betw. Opn. or tendcy. of opn. - & Overt act.
    humn. 1. nothg. t. d. wth. Opn. or tendcy. - only Overt acts.
    if magistr. restrn. prins. bec. of tendcy. & h. judge yn.
       Relign. no longer free
    Coercn. exercd. by fallible men.

Obj. Belief of Future State necess.
Ans. Jewish theocrcy.
    God dd. nt. revl. in Bible.
    Sadducees.

Obj. Religion will decline if not supported
Ans. Gates of Hell shall not prevail...

Is a Relign. of State <Use> Expedt.
    Purpose mst. be Uniformty.
(a) Is Uniformty. desirble?
    if evr. cd. b. obtd. wd. be b. suffoctg. free enqry.
       all imprvmts. in relign. or Philos. hve. bn. frm. settg.
       up privte. jdmt. agt. Public - ventrg. dept. Uniformty.

    Monksh. imposns. - ignorce. - darknss. suppd. on
       ruins Enqry.
    Glorious Reformn. effect of shakg. off Pub. opn.
    Mahomsm. supportd. by stiflg. free enqry.
    Philos. reformd by freeenq.
       Galileo. Newton

Unifmty. no. mo. nec. in Relign. yn. Philos.

   no consqce. if Newtonn. or Cartesn.

   Overt acts all yt. nec.

Diffce. in Religs. opn. supplies place Censor Morum [Moral Censor]

Teachrs. evy. sect inculcte. sa. mor. princ. wh. yn gve.

   peculr. priv. to any?

(b) Is Unifmty. Attainable?

   by Inquisn.

   by lessr. Punmts. - Burng heretic - Fine. Impr. Abjurn.

Constrt. m. prodce. Hippocr. - nt. prevt. sentimt.

Coercn. mst. b. xrcd. by fallib. men - abusd.

  Experce. hs. provd. Unattnb.

Millns. burnt - tortd. - find. - mprisd. yet men differ.

In Romn. Cath. countr. most infidelty.

If Relign. of sta. mst b. stabld. Is ours right?

   Zealots wll. ans. yes.

   1/10,000 of men of our Relign.

Obj. all states have establmt.

Ans. then all religions have been established

<Ans> hve Govng. pwrs. of earth shewn Infallibility. by this?

     nevr. pretendd. to it till Xty.

     Exam. effects since yt.

   hs. God stampd. us wth. mark

     r. w. whiter - handsmr. - athletc. - wisr.

   if n. sch. Ear-mark whence ys. Confidence?

   ans. Reason.

     true evy. mn's Reasn. judge fr. hms. Prebn. fr.

    Presbn. - Episcn. for Episcn.

  bt. wh. m. reasn. step int. jdmt. seat of yours?

Advantags. to Relign.to put all on footg.

   Strengthn. Church.

     oblige it's ministers to be Industrs. Exemplary

     Northern clergy

     wh. depdce. or Indepdce. mst. likely to mke. industrs.

      Lawyers - Physicns.

     Xty. florshd. 300. y. witht. establmt.

      soon as establd. declined.frm. Purity

     betrays wnt. confdce. in doctrnes. of chch. to suspct. yt.

---

reasn. or intrinsck. xcllce. insfft. wtht. seculr. prop.
Gates of hell shall never prevail

Attach People
    20,000 beyd. & adjg. Blue ridge.
    55,000 in all.
    ceding wll. attach.

Obj. Fixed. Contribn.
    inequalty. of Parishes
    no. of dissentrs. difft. in difft. parishs.
    Contribn. wll. nt. supprt. Preachrs. in some Chch. min. in
      other
    Contribn. of sme. yn. wll be lost or givn. agt. Conscce.
    Decln. of rts. is freedm. of Religion
      force mn. to contribte. wn. n. teachr. of sect to recve. is t.
        force to supprt. heresy
    Quakrs. give no Contribns.
    Discorge. fornrs.
    N. Engld.

THOMAS JEFFERSON, DRAFT OF A BILL EXEMPTING DISSENTERS FROM CONTRIBUTING TO THE SUPPORT OF THE CHURCH
November 30, 1776

Editor's note: The Princeton University edition of The Papers of Thomas Jefferson, *Vol. 1, tells us that "it is plausible to conclude that the Bill as here presented had been agreed upon before TJ left the legislature on 29 Nov." Indeed it is an elaboration of Jefferson's Rough Draft, and is considered as his doing.*

Whereas it is represented by many of the Inhabitants of this Country who dissent from the Church of England as by Law established that they consider the Assessments and Contributions which they have been hitherto obliged to make towards the support and Maintenance of the said Church and its Ministry as grievous and oppressive, and an Infringement of their religious Freedom. For Remedy whereof and that equal Liberty as well religious as civil may be universally extended to all the good People of this Common Wealth, Be it Enacted by the General Assembly of the Common Wealth of Virginia and it is hereby Enacted by the Authority of the same that all Dissenters of whatever Denomination from the said Church shall from and after the passing this Act be totally free and exempt from all Levies Taxes and Impositions whatever towards supporting and maintaining the said Church as it now is or may hereafter be established and its Ministers. Provided nevertheless and it is hereby farther Enacted by the Authority aforesaid that the Vestries of the several Parishes where the same hath not been already done shall and may and they are hereby authorized and required at such times as they shall appoint to levy and assess on all Tithables within their respective Parishes as well Dissenters as others all such Salaries and Arrears of Salaries as are or may be due to the Ministers or Incumbents of their Parishes for past Services; moreover to make such Assessments on all Tithables as will enable the said Vestries to comply with their legal parochial Engagements already entered into and lastly to continue such future Provision for the poor in their respective Parishes as they have hitherto by Law been accustomed to make. And be it farther Enacted by the Authority aforesaid that there shall in all time coming be saved and reserved to the Use of the Church by Law established the several Tracts of Glebe Land already purchased; the Churches and Chapels already built for the use of the Parishes; all Books Plate & ornaments belonging or appropriated to the use of the said Church and all arrears of Money or Tobacco arising from former Assessments or otherwise and that there shall more-over be saved and reserved to the use of such Parishes as may have received private Donations for the better support of the said Church and its Ministers the perpetual Benefit and enjoyment of all such Donations.

And whereas great Varieties of Opinions have arisen touching the Propriety of a general Assessment or whether every religious society should be left to voluntary Contributions for the support and maintenance of the several Ministers and Teachers of the Gospel who are of different Persuasions and Denominations, and this Difference of Sentiments cannot now be well accommodated, so that it is thought most prudent to defer this matter to the Discussion and final Determination of a future assembly when the Opinions of the Country in General may be better known. To the End therefore that so important a Subject may in no Sort be prejudged, Be it Enacted by the Authority aforesaid that nothing in this Act contained shall be construed to affect or influence the said Question of a general Assessment or voluntary Contribution in any respect whatever.

Provided always that in the mean time the Members of the Established Church shall not in any Parish be subject to the payment of a greater tax for the support of the said Church & its Minister than they would have been, had the Dissenters not been exempted from paying their accustomed proportion, any Law to the contrary notwithstanding.

And whereas it is represented that in some Counties Lists of Tithables have been omitted to be taken, For remedy whereof be it further enacted, that the Courts of the several Counties, where it may be necessary, shall have Power & they are hereby required so soon as may be convenient to appoint some of their own Members to take the Lists of Tithables throughout their respective Counties.

THOMAS JEFFERSON, BILL FOR PROPORTIONING CRIMES AND PUNISHMENTS 1778

Editor's note: Jefferson drafted this Bill in 1778. It wasn't voted on until 1785, when it was presented to the Virginia legislature by Madison. It lost by a single vote. It finally passed in 1796.

Jefferson reduced penalties for crimes, death, flogging, etc., law by law. Yet here, if we judge Jefferson and Madison as if they were alive today, they are still barbarian. But that is simply looking through the wrong end of the historical telescope. In the 18th century they were radical, first as republicans under the British crown, later, in this case, as penal reformers, denounced by American bigots upholding unmitigated "biblical" ferocity of punishments in colonial laws they encountered.

Privilege or benefit of clergy, referred to below, started in Britain, exempting clergy from temporal jurisdiction, with church courts substituted. Then an exemption from minor temporal charges and extreme punishments, death, flogging, etc. Eventually lay church functionaries were covered, then peers of the realm. Extending privileges to some laity was a manner of reforming brutal punishment within a feudal framework, without granting full equality to all commoners.

Section l: And forasmuch as the experience of all ages and countries hath shewn, that cruel and sanguinary laws defeat their own purpose, by engaging the benevolence of mankind to withhold prosecutions, to smother testimony, or to listen to it with bias; and by producing in many instances a total dispensation and impunity under the names of pardon and privilege of clergy; when, if the punishment were only proportioned to the injury, men would feel it their inclination, as well as their duty, to see the laws observed; and the power of dispensation, so dangerous and mischievous, which produces crimes by holding up a hope of impunity, might totally be abolished....

Section ll: Be it enacted by the General Assembly, that no crime shall be henceforth punished by the deprivation of life or limb, except those herein after ordained to be so punished....

Section XII: Suicide is by law punishable by forfeiture of chattels. This bill exempts it from forfeiture. The suicide injures the State less than he who leaves it with his effects. If the latter then be not punished, the former should not. As to the example, we need not fear its influence. Men are too much attached to life, to exhibit frequent instances of depriving themselves of it. At any rate, the quasi-punishment of confiscation will not prevent it. For if one be found who can calmly determine to renounce life, who is so weary of his existence here, as rather to make experiment of what is beyond the grave, can we suppose him, in such a state of mind, susceptible of influence from the losses to his family from confiscation? That men in general, too, disapprove of this severity, is apparent from the constant practice of juries finding the suicide in a state of insanity; because they have no other way of saving the forfeiture. Let it then be done away....

Section XIII: Whenever sentence of death shall have been pronounced against any person for treason or murder, execution thereof shall be done on the next day but one, after such sentence, unless it be Sunday, and then on the Monday following....

Section XXIX: All attempts to delude the people, or to abuse their understanding by exercise of the pretended arts of witchcraft, conjuration, enchantment, or sorcery, or by pretended prophecies, shall be punished by ducking and whipping, at the discretion of a jury, not exceeding fifteen stripes....

Section XXXII: Pardon and privilege of clergy, shall henceforth be abolished, that none may be induced to injure through hope of impunity.

THOMAS JEFFERSON TO DAVID RITTENHOUSE
July 19, 1778

Editor's note: Rittenhouse (1732-1796) was a celebrated astronomer.

Without having ascended mount Sina for inspiration, I can pronounce that the precept, in the decalogue of the vulgar, that they shall not make to themselves 'the likeness of any thing that is in the heavens above' is reversed for you, and that you will fulfill the highest purposes of your creation by employing yourself in the perpetual breach of that inhibition.

THOMAS JEFFERSON, DRAFT OF THE VIRGINIA STATUTE FOR RELIGIOUS FREEDOM
[1777 - 1779]

Editor's note: Jefferson drafted this bill in 1777. It was introduced into the Virginia Assembly in June 1779. It was debated but not adopted, largely due to the opposition of Patrick Henry. Madison reintroduced it again in October 1785 and it passed in January 1786.

In his Autobiography, Jefferson remarked that "[When] the bill for establishing religious freedom ... was finally passed.... a singular proposition proved that its protection of opinion was meant to be universal. Where the preamble declares that coercion is a departure from the plan of the holy author of our religion, an amendment was proposed, by inserting the word 'Jesus Christ,' so that it should read 'a departure from the plan of Jesus Christ, the holy author of our religion.' The insertion was rejected by a great majority, in proof that they meant to comprehend within the mantle of its protection the Jew and the Gentile, the Christian and Mahometan, the Hindoo and infidel of every denomination."

In his design for his tombstone epitaph, Jefferson listed "the Statute of Virginia for religious freedom" as his second greatest achievement, "most to be remembered," after the Declaration. As Madison pushed it thru, while Jefferson was in France as Minister Plenipotentiary, it was Madison's first major personal accomplishment as well.

The Statute is given below with phrases from the original draft cut in final passage, printed within brackets and the two additions within < >.

SECTION I. [Well aware that the opinions and belief of men depend not on their own will, but follow involuntarily the evidence proposed to their minds; that] <Whereas> Almighty God hath created the mind free, [and manifested his supreme will that free it shall remain by making it altogether insusceptible of restraint;] that all attempts to influence it by temporal punishments, or burthens, or by civil incapacitations, tend only to beget habits of hypocrisy and meanness, and are a departure from the plan of the holy author of our religion, who being Lord both of body and mind, yet chose not to propagate it by coercions on either, as was in his Almighty power to do, [but to extend it by its influence on reason alone;] that the impious presumption of legislators and rulers, civil as well as ecclesiastical, who, being themselves but fallible and uninspired men, have assumed dominion over the faith of others, setting up their own opinions and modes of thinking as the only true and infallible, and as such endeavoring to impose them on others, hath established and maintained false religions over the greatest part of the world and through all time: That to compel a man to furnish contributions of money for the propagation of opinions which he disbelieves [and abhors], is sinful and tyrannical; that even the forcing him to support this or that teacher of his own religious persuasion, is depriving him of the comfortable liberty of giving his contributions to the particular pastor whose morals he would make his pattern, and whose powers he feels most persuasive to righteousness; and is withdrawing from the ministry those temporary rewards, which proceeding from an approbation of their personal conduct, are an additional incitement to earnest and unremitting labours for the instruction of mankind; that our civil rights have no dependance on our religious opinions, any more than our opinions in physics or geometry; that therefore the proscribing any citizen as unworthy the public confidence by laying upon him an incapacity of being called to offices of trust and emolument, unless he profess or renounce this or that religious opinion, is depriving him injuriously of those privileges and advantages to which, in common with his fellow citizens, he has a natural right; that it tends also to corrupt the principles of that [very] religion it is meant to encourage, by bribing, with a monopoly of worldly honours and emoluments, those who will externally profess and conform to it; that though indeed these are criminal who do not withstand such temptation, yet neither are those innocent who lay the bait in their way; [that the opinions of men are not the object of civil government, nor under its jurisdiction;] that to suffer the civil magistrate to intrude his powers into the field of opinion, and to restrain the profession or propagation of principles on supposition of their ill tendency is a dangerous falacy, which at once destroys all religious liberty, because he being of course judge of that tendency will make his opinions the rule of judgment, and approve or condemn the sentiments of others only as they shall square with or differ from his own; that it is time enough for the rightful purposes of civil government for its officers to interfere when principles break out into overt acts against peace and good order; and finally, that truth is great and will prevail if left to herself; that she is the proper and sufficient antagonist to error, and has nothing to fear conflict unless by human interposition disarmed of her natural weapons, free argument and debate; errors ceasing to be dangerous when it is permitted freely to contradict them.

SECTION II. [We the General Assembly of Virginia do enact] <Be it therefore enacted by the General Assembly,> That no man shall be compelled to frequent or support any religious worship, place, or ministry whatsoever, nor shall be enforced, restrained, molested, or burthened in his body or goods, nor shall otherwise suffer, on account of his religious opinions or belief; but that all men shall be free to profess, and by argument to maintain, their opinions in matters of religion, and that the same shall in no wise diminish, enlarge, or affect their civil capacities.

SECTION III. And though we well know that this Assembly, elected by the people for the ordinary purposes of legislation only, have no power to restrain the acts of succeeding Assemblies, constituted with powers equal to our own, and that therefore to declare this act irrevocable would be of no effect in law; yet we are free to declare, and do declare, that the rights hereby asserted are of the natural rights of mankind, and that if any act shall be hereafter passed to repeal the present or to narrow its operation, such act will be an infringement of natural right.

THOMAS JEFFERSON TO BROTHER JOHN BAPTIST DE COIGNE
June 1781

Editor's note: Jefferson was Governor of Virginia when he made this address to de Coigne, a chief among the Wabash and Illinois Indians. At that time Kentucky was still part of Virginia and he was concerned that the Indians there remain friendly to the Americans against the British.

I hope it will please the Great Being above to continue you long in life, in health and in friendship to us; and that your son will afterwards succeed you in wisdom, in good disposition, and in power over your people.... I have joined with you sincerely in smoking the pipe of peace; it is a good old custom handed down by your ancestors, and as such I respect and join in it with reverence. I hope we shall long continue to smoke in friendship together.

THOMAS JEFFERSON, NOTES ON THE STATE OF VIRGINIA
[1781 - 1782]

Query VI - A Notice of the mines and other subterraneous riches, its trees, plants, fruits, etc.

Thus nature seems to have drawn a belt of separation between these two tremendous animals, whose breadth, indeed, is not precisely known, though at present we may suppose it about 6 1/2 degrees of latitude; to have assigned to the elephant the region south of these confines, and those north to the mammoth, founding the constitution of the one in her extreme of heat, and that of the other in the extreme of cold. When the Creator has therefore separated their nature as far as the extent of the scale of animal life allowed to this planet would permit, it seems perverse to declare it the same, from a partial resemblance of their tusks and bones. But to whatever animal we ascribe these remains, it is certain such a one has existed in America, and that it has been the largest of all terrestrial beings....

Query XII - A notice of the counties, cities, townships, and villages?

The state, by another division, is formed into parishes, many of which are commensurate with the counties; but sometimes a county comprehends more than one parish, and sometimes a parish more than one county. This division had relation to the religion of the State, a portion of the Anglican church, with a fixed salary, having been heretofore established in each parish. The care of the poor was another object of the parochial division....

Query XlII - The constitution of the state, and its several charters?

Queen Elizabeth by her letters-patent, bearing date March 25, 1584, licenced Sir Walter Raleigh to search for remote heathen lands, not inhabited by Christian people, and granted to him, in fee simple, all the soil within 200 leagues of the places where his people should, within 6 years, make their dwellings or abidings; reserving only, to herself and her successors, their allegiance and one-fifth part of all the gold and silver ore they should obtain....

When this colony, therefore, which still maintained its opposition to Cromwell and the parliament, was induced in 1651 to lay down their arms, they previously secured their most essential rights, by a solemn convention, which having never seen print, I will here insert literally from the records....

"11ly. That the use of the booke of common prayer shall be permitted for one yeare ensueinge with referrence to the consent of the major part of the parishes, provided that those things which relate to kingshipp or that government be not used publiquely, and the continuance of ministers in their places, they misdemeaning themselves, and the payment of their accustomed dues and agreements made with them respectively shall be left as they now stand dureing this ensueing yeare"....

Query XlV - The administration of justice and description of the laws?

Marriages must be solemnized either on special licence, granted by the first magistrate of the county, on proof of the consent of the parent or guardian of either party under age, or after solemn publication, on three several Sundays, at some place of religious worship, in the parishes where the parties reside. The act of solemnization may be by the minister of any society of Christians, who shall have been previously licenced for this purpose by the court of the county. Quakers and Menonists however are exempted from all these conditions, and marriage among them is to be solemnized by the society itself....

Among the blacks is misery enough, God knows, but no poetry. Love is the peculiar cestrum of the poet. Their love is ardent, but it kindles the senses only, not the imagination. Religion indeed has produced a Phyllis Whately; but it could not produce a poet. The compositions published under her name are below the dignity of criticism. The heroes of the Dunciad are to her, as Hercules to the author of that poem. Ignatius Sancho has approached nearer to merit in composition, yet his letters do more honour to the heart than the head. They breathe the purest effusions of friendship and general philanthrophy, and shew how great a degree of the latter may be compounded with strong religious zeal. He is often happy in the turn of his compliments, and his style is easy and familiar, except when he affects a Shandean fabrication of words. But his imagination is wild and extravagant, escapes incessantly from every restraint of reason and taste, and, in the course of its vagaries, leaves a tract of thought as incoherent and eccentric, as the course of a meteor through the sky....

The man, in whose favor no laws of property exist, probably feels himself less bound to respect those made in favour of others. When arguing for ourselves, we lay it down as a fundamental, that laws, to be just, must give a reciprocation of right: that, without this, they are merely arbitrary rules of conduct, founded in force, and not in conscience: and it is a problem which I give to the master to solve, whether the religious precepts against the violation of property were not framed for him as well as his slave? And whether the slave may not as justifiably take a little from one, who has taken all from him, as he may slay one who would slay him? That a change in the relations in which a man is placed should change his ideas of moral right and wrong, is neither new, nor peculiar to the colour of the blacks....

The opinion, that they are inferior in the faculties of reason and imagination, must be hazarded with great diffidence.... let me add too, as a circumstance of great tenderness, where our conclusion would degrade a whole race of men from the rank in the scale of beings which their Creator may perhaps have given them. To our reproach it must be said, that though for a century and a half we have had under our eyes the races of black and of red men, they have never yet been viewed by us as subjects of natural history. I advance it therefore as a suspicion only, that the blacks, whether originally a distinct race, or made distinct by time and circumstances, are inferior to the whites in the endowments both of body and mind....

Pardon and privilege of clergy are proposed to be abolished; but if the verdict be against the defendant, the court in their discretion, may allow a new trial....

Another object of the revisal is, to diffuse knowledge more generally through the mass of the people.... The first stage of this education being the schools of the hundreds, wherein the great mass of the people will receive their instruction, the principal foundations of future order will be laid here. Instead therefore of putting the Bible and Testament into the hands of the children, at an age when their judgements are not sufficiently matured for religious inquiries, their memories may here be stored with the most useful facts from Grecian, Roman, European and American history. The first elements of morality too may be instilled into their minds, such as, when further developed as their judgements advance in strength, may teach them how to work out their own greatest happiness, by shewing them that it does not depend on the condition of life in which chance has placed them, but is always the result of a good conscience, good health, occupation, and freedom in all just pursuits....

Query XV - The colleges, and public establishments, the roads, buildings, & c.?
The College of William and Mary is the only public seminary of learning in this state.... By its charter.... a professorship of the Greek and Latin languages, a professorship of mathematics, one of moral philosophy, and two of divinity, were established. To these were annexed, for a sixth professorship, a considerable donation by

Mr. Boyle of England, for the instruction of the Indians, and their conversion to Christianity. This was called the professorship of Brafferton.... After the present revolution, the visitors ... undertook to change the objects of the professorships. They excluded the two schools for divinity....

The purposes of the Brafferton institution would be better answered by maintaining a perpetual mission among the Indian tribes, the object of which, besides instructing them in the principles of Christianity, as the founder requires, should be to collect their traditions, laws, customs, languages, and other circumstances which might lead to a discovery of their relation with one another, or descent from other nations. When these objects are accomplished with one tribe, the missionary might pass on to another....

The only public buildings worthy [of] mention are the Capitol, the Palace, the College, and the Hospital for Lunatics, all of them in Williamsburg.... There are no other public buildings but churches and court-houses in which no attempts are made at elegance....

Query XVII - The different religions received into that state?
The first settlers in this country were emigrants from England, of the English church, just at a point of time when it was flushed with complete victory over the religious of all other persuasions. Possessed, as they became, of the powers of making, administering, and executing the laws, they showed equal intolerance in this country with their Presbyterian brethren, who had emigrated to the northern government. The poor Quakers were flying from persecution in England. They cast their eyes on these new countries as asylums of civil and religious freedom; but they found them free only for the reigning sect. Several acts of the Virginia assembly of 1659, 1662, and 1693, had made it penal in parents to refuse to have their children baptized; had prohibited the unlawful assembling of Quakers; had made it penal for any master of a vessel to bring a Quaker into the state; had ordered those already here, and such as should come thereafter, to be imprisoned till they should abjure the country; provided a milder punishment for their first and second return, but death for their third; had inhibited all persons from suffering their meetings in or near their houses, entertaining them individually, or disposing of books which supported their tenets. If no capital execution took place here, as did in New-England, it was not owing to the moderation of the church, or spirit of the legislature, as may be inferred from the law itself; but to historical circumstances which have not been handed down to us. The Anglicans retained full possession of the country about a century. Other opinions began then to creep in, and the great care of the government to support their own church, having begotten an equal degree of indolence in its clergy, two-thirds of the people had become dissenters at the commencement of the present revolution. The laws indeed were still oppressive on them, but the spirit of the one party had subsided into moderation, and of the other had risen to a degree of determination which commanded respect.

The present state of our laws on the subject of religion is this. The convention of May 1776, in their declaration of rights, declared it to be a truth, and a natural right, that the exercise of religion should be free; but when they proceeded to form on that declaration the ordinance of government, instead of taking up every principle declared in the bill of rights, and guarding it by legislative sanction, they passed over that which asserted our religious rights, leaving them as they found them. The same convention, however, when they met as a member of the general assembly in October 1776, repealed all acts of parliament which had rendered criminal the maintaining any opinions in matters of religion, the forbearing to repair to church, and the exercising any mode of worship; and suspended the laws giving salaries to the clergy, which suspension was made perpetual in October 1779. Statutory oppressions in religion being thus wiped away, we remain at present under those only imposed by the common law, or by our own acts of assembly. At the common law, heresy was a capital offence, punishable by burning. Its definition was left to the ecclesiastical judges, before whom the conviction was, till the statute of the 1 El. c. 1. circumscribed it, by declaring, that nothing should be deemed heresy, but what had been so determined by authority of the canonical scriptures, or by one of the four first general councils, or by some other council having for the grounds of their declaration the express and plain words of the scriptures. Heresy, thus circumscribed, being an offence at the common law, our act of assembly of October 1777, c. 17. gives cognizance of it to the general court, by declaring, that the jurisdiction of that court shall be general in all matters at the common law. The execution is by the writ De haeretico comburendo [Of burning heretics]. By our own act of assembly of 1705, c. 30, if a person brought up in the Christian religion denies the being of a God, or the Trinity, or asserts there are more Gods than one, or denies the Christian religion to be true, or the scriptures to be of divine authority, he is punishable on the first offence by incapacity to hold any office or employment ecclesiastical, civil, or military; on the second by disability to sue, to take any gift or legacy, to be guardian, executor, or administrator, and by three years imprisonment, without bail. A father's right to the custody of his own children being founded in law on his right of guardianship, this being taken away, they may of course be severed from him, and put, by the authority of a court, into more orthodox hands. This is a summary view of that religious slavery, under which a people have been willing to remain, who have lavished their lives and fortunes for the establishment of their civil freedom.

The error seems not sufficiently eradicated, that the operations of the mind, as well as the acts of the body, are subject to the coercion of the laws. But our rulers can have authority over such natural rights only as we have submitted to them. The rights of conscience we never submitted, we could not submit. We are answerable for them to our God. The legitimate powers of government extend to such acts only as are injurious to others. But it does me no injury for my neighbour to say there are twenty gods, or no god. It neither picks my pocket nor breaks my leg. If it be said, his testimony in a court of justice cannot be relied on, reject it then, and be the stigma on him. Constraint may make him worse by making him a hypocrite, but it will never make him a truer man. It may fix him obstinately in his errors, but will not cure them. Reason and free enquiry are the only effectual agents against error. Give a loose to them, they will support the true religion, by bringing every false one to their tribunal, to the test of their investigation. They are the natural enemies of error, and of error only. Had not the Roman government permitted free enquiry, Christianity could never have been introduced. Had not free enquiry been indulged, at the era of the reformation, the corruptions of Christianity could not have been purged away. If it be restrained now, the present corruptions will be protected, and new ones encouraged. Was the government to prescribe to us our medicine and diet, our bodies would be in such keeping as our souls are now. Thus in France the emetic was once forbidden as a medicine, and the potatoe as an article of food. Government is just as infallible too when it fixes systems in physics. Galileo was sent to the inquisition for affirming that the earth was a sphere: the government had declared it to be as flat as a trencher, and Galileo was obliged to abjure his error. This error however at length prevailed, the earth became a globe, and Descartes declared it was whirled round its axis by a vortex. The government in which he lived was wise enough to see that this was no question of civil jurisdiction, or we should all have been involved by authority in vortices. In fact, the vortices have been exploded, and the Newtonian principle of gravitation is now more firmly established, on the basis of reason, than it would be were the government to step in, and to make it an article of necessary faith.

Reason and experiment have been indulged, and error has fled before them. It is error alone which needs the support of government. Truth can stand by itself. Subject opinion to coercion: whom will you make your inquisitors? Fallible men; men governed by bad passions, by private as well as public reasons. And why subject it to coercion? To produce uniformity. But is uniformity of opinion desirable? No more than of face and stature. Introduce the bed of Procrustes then, and as there is danger that the large men may beat the small, make us all of a size, by lopping the former and stretching the latter. Difference of opinion is advantageous in religion. The several sects perform the office of a Censor morum [moral censor] over each other. Is uniformity attainable? Millions of innocent men, women, and children, since the introduction of Christianity, have been burnt, tortured, fined, imprisoned; yet we have not advanced one inch towards uniformity.

What has been the effect of coercion? To make one half the world fools, and the other half hypocrites. To support roguery and error all over the earth. Let us reflect that it is inhabited by a thousand millions of people. That these profess probably a thousand different systems of religion. That ours is but one of that thousand. That if there be but one right, and ours that one, we should wish to see the 999 wandering sects gathered into the fold of truth. But against such a majority we cannot effect this by force.

Reason and persuasion are the only practicable instruments. To make way for these, free enquiry must be indulged; and how can we wish others to indulge it while we refuse it ourselves. But every state, says an inquisitor, has established some religion. No two, say I, have established the same. Is this a proof of the infallibility of establishments? Our sister states of Pennsylvania and New York, however, have long subsisted without any establishment at all. The experiment was new and doubtful when they made it. It has answered beyond conception. They flourish infinitely. Religion is well supported; of various kinds, indeed, but all good enough; all sufficient to preserve peace and order: or if a sect arises, whose tenets would subvert morals, good sense has fair play, and reasons and laughs it out of doors, without suffering the state to be troubled with it. They do not hang more malefactors than we do. They are not more disturbed with religious dissensions. On the contrary, their harmony is unparalleled, and can be ascribed to nothing but their unbounded tolerance, because there is no other circumstance in which they differ from every nation on earth. They have made the happy discovery, that the way to silence religious disputes, is to take no notice of them. Let us too give this experiment fair play, and get rid, while we may, of those tyrannical laws. It is true, we are as yet secured against them by the spirit of the times. I doubt whether the people of this country would suffer an execution for heresy, or a three years imprisonment for not comprehending the mysteries of the Trinity. But is the spirit of the people an infallible, a permanent reliance? Is it government? Is this the kind of protection we receive in return for the rights we give up? Besides, the spirit of the times may alter, will alter. Our rulers will become corrupt, our people careless. A single zealot may commence persecutor, and better men be his victims. It can never be too often repeated, that the time for fixing every essential right on a legal basis is while our rulers are honest, and ourselves united. From the conclusion of this war we shall be going down hill. It will not then be necessary to resort every moment to the people for support. They will be forgotten, therefore, and their rights disregarded. They will forget themselves, but in the sole faculty of making money, and will never think of uniting to effect a due respect for their rights. The shackles, therefore, which shall not be knocked off at the conclusion of this war, will remain on us long, will be made heavier and heavier, till our rights shall revive or expire in a convulsion.

Query XVIII - The particular customs and manners that may happen to be received in that state?
It is difficult to determine on the standard by which the manners of a nation may be tried, whether catholic or particular. There must doubtless be an unhappy influence on the manners of our people produced by the existence of slavery among us.... And can the liberties of a nation be thought secure when we have removed their only firm basis, a conviction in the minds of the people that these liberties are of the gift of God? That they are not to be violated but with his wrath? Indeed I tremble for my country when I reflect that God is just: that his justice cannot sleep for ever; that considering numbers, nature and natural means only, a revolution of the wheel of fortune, and exchange of situation, is among possible events: that it may become probable, by supernatural interference! The Almighty has no attribute which can take side with us in such a contest. — But it is impossible to be temperate and to pursue this subject through the various considerations of policy, of morals, of history natural and civil. We must be contented to hope they will force their way into every one's mind. I think a change already perceptible, since the origin of the pres-

ent revolution. The spirit of the master is abating, that of the slave rising from the dust, his condition mollifying, the way I hope preparing, under the auspices of heaven, for a total emancipation, and that this is disposed, in the order of events, to be with the consent of the masters, rather than by their extirpation....

Query XlX - The Present State of manufactures, commerce, interior and exterior trade?

Those who labor in the earth are the chosen people of God, if ever He had a chosen people, whose breasts He has made His peculiar deposit for substantial and genuine virtue. It is the focus in which he keeps alive that sacred fire, which otherwise might escape from the face of the earth. Corruption of morals in the mass of cultivators is a phenomenon of which no age nor nation has furnished an example.

Query XXll - The public income and expences?

The clergy receive only voluntary contributions: suppose them on an average 1/8 of a dollar a tythe on 200,000 tythes.... 25,000.... And if we strike out the 25,000 dollars for the services of the clergy, which neither makes part of that administration, more than what is paid to physicians or lawyers, and being voluntary, is either much or nothing as every one pleases, it leaves 225,000 dollars, equal to 48,208 guineas, the real cost of the apparatus of government with us.

JAMES MADISON TO EDMUND PENDLETON
July 23, 1782

Editor's note: On May 4, 1782, Ireland's Catholics were allowed to set up their own schools and own real estate.

Ireland is reaping a large share of the harvest produced by our labours. Besides a free trade & a free legislation, the shackles are taken off the poor Catholicks in the articles of their religious worship & the tenure of real property.

JAMES MADISON TO EDMUND RANDOLPH
July 23, 1782

Editor's note: Charles lll of Spain had limited the powers of the inquisition in his empire. And, in March 1782, the Pope made an unsuccessful trip to Austria to try to get the Emperor to rescind his reform, granting some civil rights to Protestants and Greek Orthodox in his realm.

Ireland is likely to be indulged in every thing. In addition to a free trade & and a free Legislation, they have obtained the assent of the Ld. Lieutt. to an act of Parliament for emancipating the Catholics from the shackles on their religious rights, & on their tenures of real property. Your philanthropy will be gratified by my adding as other proofs of the progress of light & freedom, the abolition of the inquisitorial jurisdiction in Sicily, the only part of the Neapolitan dominions where it was in force, and the inefficacy of the Pope's visit to Vienna in checking the liberal innovations of the Emperor in his ecclesiastical polity.

JAMES MADISON TO EDMUND RANDOLPH
August 27, 1782

Editor's note: In retirement, Madison wrote in the name initialed:

I cannot in any way make you more sensible of the importance of your kind attention to pecuniary remittances for me than by informing you that I have for some time past been a pensioner on the favor of H. S. [Haym Solomon] a Jew Broker. Will not the Agent of Mr. Morris give a draught payable to me for notes payable to the bearer?

Editor's note: Madison thought highly of Solomon (who spelled it Salomon). Everyone in Philadelphia, including Salomon, referred to him as a "Jew Broker." On September 30th he wrote Randolph that:

"The kindness of our little friend in Front Street near the Coffee House is a fund which will preserve me from extremities, but I never resort to it without great mortification, as he obstinately rejects all recompense. The price of money is so usurious that he thinks it ought to be extorted from none but those who aim at profitable speculations. To a necessitous Delegate he gratuitously spares a supply out of his private stock."

Editor's note: In retirement, January 20, 1827, Madison answered Salomon's son's inquiry regarding their relationship:

"Among other members of Congs. from Virginia whose resources public & private had been cut off, I had occasion once, perhaps twice myself to resort to his pecuniary aid on a small scale for current wants. We regarded him as upright, intelligent and friendly in his transactions with us."

THOMAS JEFFERSON TO ELIZABETH WAYLES EPPES
October 3, 1782

Editor's note: This was Jefferson's first personal letter after his wife's death.

The girls being unable to assure you themselves of their welfare the duty devolves on me and I undertake it the more willingly as it will lay you under the necessity of sometimes letting us hear from you.... This miserable kind of existence is really too burthensome to be borne, and were it not for the infidelity of deserting the sacred charge left me, I could not wish it's continuance a moment. For what could be wished? All my plans of comfort and happiness reversed by a single event and nothing answering in prospect before me but a gloom unbrightened with one cheerful expectation. The care and instruction of our children indeed affords some temporary abstractions from wretchedness and nourishes a soothing reflection that if there be beyond the grave any concern for the things of this world there is one angel at least who views these attentions with pleasure and wishes the continuance of them while she must pity the miseries to which they confine me.

JAMES MADISON, REPORT ON TREATY AND CONVENTION WITH THE NETHERLANDS
January 23, 1783

Editor's note: The Article 4 referred to below guaranteed "entire and perfect liberty of conscience" to "subjects and inhabitants of each party," on consideration that they submit "as to the public demonstration of it, to the laws of the country."

The Committee consisting of Mr. Madison Mr. Hamilton & Mr. Elseworth to whom were referred the letter of the 8th. of Ocr. 1782 from the Minister Plenipo: at the Hague with copies of a Treaty of Amity & Commerce, and of a convention concerning vessels recaptured, Report, That on a comparison of the former with the instructions given to the said Minister Plenipo: on that subject, they find that no variations have taken place which effect the substance of the plan proposed by Congress. Those which the Committee have thought most worthy of being remarked to Congress are

1st. the clause in Art. 4. which imposes some degree of restraint on the exercise of religious worship.

JAMES MADISON, ADDRESS TO THE STATES
April 26, 1783

The plan thus communicated and explained by Congress must now receive its fate from their Constituents.... Let it be remembered finally that it has ever been the pride and boast of America, that the rights for which she contended were the rights of human nature. By the blessing of the Author of these rights on the means exerted for their defence, they have prevailed against all opposition and form the basis of thirteen independant States. No instance has heretofore occurred, nor can any instance be expected hereafter to occur, in which the unadulterated forms of Republican Government can pretend to so fair an opportunity of justifying themselves by their fruits. In this view the Citizens of the U.S. are responsible for the greatest trust ever confided to a Political Society. If justice, good faith, honor, gratitude & all the other Qualities which enoble the character of a nation, and fulfil the ends of Government, be the fruits of our establishments, the cause of liberty will acquire a dignity and lustre, which it has never yet enjoyed: and an example will be set which can not but have the most favorable influence on the rights of mankind. If on the other side, our Governments should be unfortunately blotted with her reverse of these cardinal and essential Virtues, the great cause which we have engaged to vindicate, will be dishonored & betrayed: the last & fairest experiment in favor of the rights of human nature will be turned against them; and their patrons & friends exposed to be insulted & silenced by the votaries of Tyranny and Usurpation.

THOMAS JEFFERSON, DRAFT OF A CONSTITUTION FOR VIRGINIA
[May-June 1783]

The General assembly shall not have the power to infringe this constitution; to abridge the civil rights of any person on account of his religious belief; to restrain him from professing and supporting that belief, or to compel him to contributions, other than those he shall himself have stipulated, for the support of that or any other.

THOMAS JEFFERSON TO MARTHA JEFFERSON
December 11, 1783

I hope you will have good sense enough to disregard those foolish predictions that the world is to be at an end soon. The almighty has never made known to any body at what time he created it, nor will he tell any body when he means to put an end to it, if ever he means to do it. As to preparations for that event, the best way is for you to be always prepared for it. The only way to be so is never to do nor say a bad thing. If ever you are about to say any thing amiss or to do any thing wrong, consider before hand. You will feel something within you which will tell you it is wrong and ought not to be said or done: this is your conscience, and be sure to obey it. Our maker has given us all, this faithful internal Monitor, and if you always obey it, you will always be prepared for the end of the world: or for a much more certain event which is death. This must happen to all: it puts an end to the world as to us, and the way to be ready for it is never to do a wrong act.

THOMAS JEFFERSON TO ELIZA TRIST
December 11, 1783

I take the liberty of adding my wishes for your health and happiness, and assurances that I feel myself much interested in those events which may affect either. I hope the day is near when Mr. Trist's return will make amends for the crosses and disappointments you complain of, and render the current of life as smooth and placid as you can wish. In the mean time you are supported by a certainty that you are again to meet. If you wish to know the value of this circumstances, ask if of the many wretched from whom that consolation is cut off. They will tell you it is from heaven you are looking down on them. It is not easy to reconcile ourselves to the many useless miseries to which Providence seems to expose us. But his justice affords a prospect that we shall all be made even some day.

JAMES MADISON TO THOMAS JEFFERSON
July 3, 1784

Several Petitions came forward in behalf of a Genl. Assessmt. which was reported by the Come. of Religion to be reasonable. The friends of the measure did not chuse to try their strength in the House. The Episcopal Clergy introduced a notable project for re-establishing their independance of the laity. The foundation of it was that the whole body should be legally incorporated, invested with the present property of the Church, made capable of acquiring indefinitely — empowered to make canons & by laws not contrary to the law of the land, and incumbents when once chosen by Vestries to be immovable otherwise then by sentence of the Convocation. Extraordinary as such a project was, it was preserved from a dishonorable death by the talents of Mr. Henry. It lies over for another Session.

JAMES MADISON TO RICHARD HENRY LEE
November 14, 1784

You will infer therefore that little business of moment has yet been done. Excepting a few Resolutions.... Our time has been cheifly taken up with the scheme of a Genl. Assessment. The one proposed & supported, comprehends Christians alone and obliges other sects to contribute to its maintenance. It was opposed not only on the general principle that no Religious Estabts. was within the purview of Civil authority, but on the [...] ground on which it was placed; and the infraction [...] the last article of the Decl: of Rights. On the question 47 were for the proposition, 32 against it. The majority was produced by a Coalition between the Episcopal & Presbyterian Sects. A memorial presented since the vote by the Clergy of the latter shews that a Schism will take place. They do not deny but rather betray a desire that an Assessment may be estabt. but protest agst. any which does not embrace all Religions, and will not coincide with the Decl: of Rights. It is probable that the Foundation of the scheme will finally be enlarged, & that an experiment at least of its practicability will be made.

JAMES MADISON TO JAMES MONROE
November 27, 1784

The Bill for a Religious Assesst. has not been yet brought in. Mr. Henry the father of the Scheme is gone up to his Seat for his family & will no more sit in the H. of Delegates, a circumstance very inauspicious to his offspring.

JAMES MADISON TO JAMES MONROE
December 4, 1784

The bill for the Religious Asst. was reported yesterday and will be taken up in a Come. of the Whole next week. Its friends are much disheartened at the loss of Mr. Henry. Its fate is I think very uncertain.

JAMES MADISON, NOTES ON DEBATE OVER RELIGIOUS ASSESSMENT
December 23-24, 1784

Editor's note: Matter in brackets added for clarity.

Outline A.
Debate on Bill for Relig. Estabt. proposed by Mr Henry

1. limited
2. in particular
3. What is Xnty? Courts of law to Judge
4. What edition, Hebrew, Septuagint, or vulgate? What copy — what translation?
5. What books canonical, what apochryphal? The papists holding to be the former what protestants the latter, the Lutherans the latter what other protestants & papists the former
6. In What light are they to be viewed, as dictated every letter by inspiration, or the essential parts only? Or the matter in general not the words?
7. What sense the true one, for if some doctrines be essential to Xnty, those who reject these, whatever name they take are no Xn Society?
8. Is it Trinitarianism, arianism, Socinianism? Is it salvation by faith or works also — by free grace, or free will — &c&c&c -
9. What clue is to guide Judge thro' this labyrinth? When the question comes before them whether any particular Society is a Xn society?
10. Ends in what is orthodoxy, what heresy?

Outline B.
I.   Rel: no within purview of Civil Authority
     tendency to Estabg. Xnty
1.   to project of Uniformity
2.   to penal laws for supportg. it.

Progress of Gen: Assest. proves this tendency
differences between estabg. & tolerating errour

II. True question not - Is Rel: necesy.?
     are Religs. Estabts. necessy. for Religion? no.
1.   propensity of man to Religion
2.   Experience shews Relig: corrupted by Estabt.
3.   downfall of States, mentioned by Mr. H[enry], happened where here was Estabts.
4.   Experience gives no model of Gel. Asst?
5.   Case of Pa. explained — not solitary. NJ.
     See Const: of it. R.I. N.Y. D.
     factions greater in S.C.
6.   Case of primitive Xnty
     of Reformation
     of Dissenters formerly

III. Decl: Rig[hts].
7.   Progress of Religious Liberty

IV. Policy.
1.   promote emigrations from State
2.   prevent into it as asylum

V. Necessity of Estabts. inferred from State of Conty.

true causes of disease
1. War common to other States &
2. bad laws produces same complts. in N.E.
3. pretext from taxes
4. State of Administration of Justice.
5. transition from old to new plan.
6. policy & hopes of friends to G. Asst.

true remedies not Estabt. but being out war
1. laws cherish virtue
2. Administ: justice
3. personal example - Association for R.
4. By present vote cut off hope of G. Asst.
5. Education of youth

Probable defects of Bill
dishonor Xnty

4. panegyric on it on our side
4. Decl: Rights

Thomas Jefferson to James Madison
December 8, 1784

The proposition for a Convention has had the result I expected. If one could be obtained I do not know whether it would do more harm than good. While Mr. Henry lives another bad constitution would be formed, & saddled for ever on us. What we have to do I think is devoutly to pray for his death, in the mean time to keep alive the idea that the present is but an ordinance & to prepare the minds of the young men. I am glad the Episcopalians have again shewn their teeth & fangs. The dissenters had almost forgotten them.

James Madison to Richard Henry Lee
December 11, 1784

The bill for a general assessment has not yet undergone a discussion; the same is the case of the militia bill.

JAMES MADISON TO JAMES MADISON SR.
January 6, 1785

The Genl. Assesst. has been put off till next Session & is to be published in the mean time. Mr. Porter has a number of printed copies for our County. The inclosed Act for incorporating the Episcopal Church is the result of much altercation on the subject. In its original form it was wholly inadmissible. In its present form into which it has been trimmed, I assented to it with reluctance at the time, and with dissatisfaction on a review of it. There has been some error in the case too, for it was unquestionably voted in the House that two laymen should be deputed from each Parish to the Convention spoken of. I had taken it for granted also that the Clergy were hereafter to be elected by the Vestries, and was much surprised on examining the Act since it was printed to find that the mode in which vacant parishes are to be filled, is left to be provided for by the Convention. I consider the passage of the Act however as having been so far useful as to have parried for the present the Genl. Assesst. which would have otherwise have certainly been saddled upon us: & If it be unpopular among the laity it will soon be repealed, and will be a standing lesson to them of the danger of referring religious matters to the legislature.

JAMES MADISON TO THOMAS JEFFERSON
January 9, 1785

I reached this place the 14th day after that fixed for the meeting of the Assembly.... According to my promise I subjoin a brief review of its most material proceedings....

An act for incorporating the Protestant Episcopal Church

This act declares the ministers & vestries who are to be trienially chosen, in each period a body corporate, enables them to hold property not exceeding the value of £800 per annum, and gives sanction to a Convention which is to be composed of the Clergy and a lay deputy from each parish, and is to regulate the affairs of the Church. It was understood by the House of Delegates that the Convention was to consist of two laymen for each clergyman, and an amendment was received for that express purpose. It so happened that the insertion of the amendment did not produce that effect, and the mistake was never discovered till the bill had passed and was in print. Another circumstance still more singular is that the act is constructed as to deprive the Vestries of the uncontrouled right of electing Clergymen, unless it be referred to them by the canons of the Convention, and this usurpation actually escaped the eye both of the friends and adversaries of the measure, both parties taking the contrary for granted throughout the whole progress of it. The former as well as the latter appear now to be dissatisfied with what has been done, and will probably concur in a revision if not a repeal of the law. Independently of those oversights the law is in various points exceptionable. But the necessity of some sort of incorporation for the purpose of holding & managing the property of the Church could not well be denied, nor a more harmless modification of it now obtained. A negative of the bill too would have doubled the eagerness and the pretexts for a much greater evil, a General Assessment, which there is good ground to believe was parried by this partial gratification of its warmest votaries. A Resolution for a legal provision for the "teachers of Christian Religion" had early in the Session been proposed by Mr. Henry, and in spite of all the opposition that could be mustered, carried by 47 agst. 32 votes. Many petitions from below the blue ridge had prayed for such a law; and though several from the presbyterian laity beyond it were in a contrary Stile, the Clergy of that Sect favoured it. The other Sects seemed to be passive. The Resolution lay some weeks before a bill was brought in, and the bill some weeks before it was called for, after the passage of the incorporating act it was taken up, and on the third reading, ordered by a small majority to be printed for consideration. The bill in its present dress proposes a tax of blank per Ct. on all taxable property for support of Teachers of the Christian Religion. Each person when he pays his tax is to name the society to which he dedicates it, and in case of refusal to do so, the tax is to be applied to the maintenance of a school in the County. As the bill stood for some time, the application in such cases was to be made by the Legislature to pious uses. In a committee of the whole it was determined by a majority of 7 or 8 that the word "christian" should be exchanged for the word "Religious." On the report to the House the pathetic zeal of the late governor Harrison gained a like majority for reinstating discrimination. Should the bill ever pass into a law in its present form it may & will be easily eluded. It is chiefly obnoxious on account of its dishonorable principle and dangerous tendency.

JAMES MADISON TO MARQUIS DE LAFAYETTE
March 20, 1785

Nature seems on all sides to be reasserting those rights which have so long been trampled on by tyranny & bigotry. Philosophy & Commerce are the auxiliaries to whom she is indebted for her triumphs. Will it be presumptuous to say that those nations will shew most wisdom as well as acquire most glory, who, instead of forcing her current into artificial channels, endeavour to ascertain its tendency & to anticipate its effects.

JAMES MADISON TO JAMES MONROE
APRIL 12, 1785

The only proceeding of the late Session of Assembly which makes a noise thro' the Country is that which relates to a Genl. Assessmt. The Episcopal people are generally for it, tho' I think the zeal of some of them has cooled. The laity of the other Sects are equally unanimous on the other side. So are all the Clergy except the Presbyterian who seem as ready to set up an establishmt. which is to take them in as they were to pull down that which shut them out. I do not know a more shameful contrast than might be formed between their Memorials on the latter & former occasion.

JAMES MADISON TO THOMAS JEFFERSON
April 27, 1785

The Bill for a Genl. Assesst. has produced some fermentation below the Mountains & a violent one beyond them. The contest at the next Session on this question will be a warm & precarious one.... The elections as far as they have come to my knowledge are likely to produce a great proportion of new members.

JAMES MADISON TO JAMES MONROE
April 28, 1785

Our Elections as far as I hear are likely to produce a great proportion of new members. In some Counties they are influenced by the Bill for a Genl. Assesst. In Culpeper Mr. Pendleton a worthy man & acceptable in his general character to the people was laid aside in consequence of his vote for the Bill, in favour of an Adversary to it.

JAMES MADISON TO JAMES MONROE
May 29, 1785

It gives me much pleasure to observe by 2 printed reports sent me by Col. Grayson that in the latter Congs. had expunged a clause contained in the first for setting apart a district of land in each Township, for supporting the Religion of the Majority of inhabitants. How a regulation, so unjust in itself, so foreign to the Authority of Congs. so hurtful to the sale of the public land, and smelling so strongly of an anti-quated Bigotry, could have received the countenance of a Commtee is truly a matter of astonishment. In one view it might have been no disadvantage to this State in case the Genl. Assesst. should take place, as it would have given a repellent quality to the new Country, in the estimation of those whom our own encroachments on Religious Liberty would be calculated to banish it. But the adversaries to the Assesst. begin to think the prospect here flattering to their wishes. The printed Bill has excited great discussion and is likely to prove the sense of the Community to be in favor of the liberty now enjoyed. I have heard of several Counties where the late representatives have been laid aside for voting for the Bill, and not of a single one where the reverse has happened. The Presbyterian Clergy too who were in general friends to the scheme, are already in another tone, either compelled by the laity of that sect, or alarmed at the probability of further interferences of the Legislature, if they once begin to dictate in matters of Religion.

Part 4

JEFFERSON INSPIRES THE FRENCH REVOLUTION. MADISON FATHERS AMERICA'S CONSTITUTION AND BILL OF RIGHTS

1785 – 1790

Jefferson was the United States' Minister plenipotentiary to the King of France, America's ally in the struggle against Britain. He kept Madison and others well informed on the situation in that country and Europe. He came to love France, which he toured, as well as northern Italy, the German Rhineland and Holland.

As the author of the Declaration, his presence was an inspiration to the reform elements within the society, around the Marquis de Lafayette, who fought in the American revolution. In his last period in Paris, they met in his home. It can be said that, while maintaining the best of relationships with the court, Jefferson, by his presence, performed the secularist version of the laying on of hands. His revolution was the direct inspiration for the French revolution of 1789 and the subsequent European epoch of revolution.

In his absence, Madison became the central national organizing force in America. From his own day until now, historians are unanimous in seeing him as "the father of the Constitution." In effect, he was the manager of the 1787 Constitutional Convention. Although originally opposed to attaching a Bill of Rights to the Constitution, he was converted to the need for it, by Jefferson and others, and he presented it to the first House of Representatives in 1789. The two efforts certainly made him, then and forever more, one of humanity's most important historical figures.

JAMES MADISON, MEMORIAL AND REMONSTRANCE
AGAINST RELIGIOUS ASSESSMENTS
June 20, 1785

Editor's note: The Memorial was in response to a general assessment bill in the 1784 Virginia Assembly. The major change between 1776 and 1784-5 in the politics of Virginia's religious controversy was that the supporters of religious establishment moved from supporting maintaining the Church of England, alone, to omnibus support for all "teachers of the Christian religion." The quote in point 1 is from Article 16 of the 1776 Virginia Declaration of Rights.

See James Madison to George Mason, July 14, 1826, below, a letter to a descendant of Col. George Mason, for additional material on the circumstances of the Memorial and Remonstrance.

To the Honorable the General Assembly of the Commonwealth of Virginia
A Memorial and Remonstrance

We the subscribers, citizens of the said Commonwealth, having taken into serious consideration, a Bill printed by order of the last Session of General Assembly, entitled "A Bill establishing a provision for Teachers of the Christian Religion," and conceiving that the same if finally armed with the sanctions of a law, will be a dangerous abuse of power, are bound as faithful members of a free State to remonstrate against it, and to declare the reasons by which we are determined. We remonstrate against the said Bill,

1. Because we hold it for a fundamental and undeniable truth, "that religion or the duty which we owe to our Creator and the manner of discharging it, can be directed only by reason and conviction, not by force or violence." The Religion then of every man must be left to the conviction and conscience of every man; and it is the right of every man to exercise it as these may dictate. This right is in its nature an unalienable right. It is unalienable, because the opinions of men, depending only on the evidence contemplated by their own minds cannot follow the dictates of other men: It is unalienable also, because what is here a right towards men, is a duty towards the Creator. It is the duty of every man to render to the Creator such homage and such only as he believes to be acceptable to him. This duty is precedent, both in order of time and in degree of obligation, to the claims of Civil Society. Before any man can be considered as a member of Civil Society, he must be considered as a subject of the Governor of the Universe: And if a member of Civil Society, do it with a saving of his allegiance to the Universal Sovereign.

We maintain therefore that in matters of Religion, no man's right is abridged by the institution of Civil Society and that Religion is wholly exempt from its cognizance. True it is, that no other rule exists, by which any question which may divide a Society, can be ultimately determined, but the will of the majority; but it is also true that the majority may trespass on the rights of the minority.

2. Because Religion be exempt from the authority of the Society at large, still less can it be subject to that of the Legislative Body. The latter are but the creatures and vicegerents of the former. Their jurisdiction is both derivative and limited: it is limited with regard to the coordinate departments, more necessarily is it limited with regard to the constituents. The preservation of a free Government requires not merely, that the metes and bounds which separate each department of power be invariably maintained; but more especially that neither of them be suffered to overleap the great Barrier which defends the rights of the people. The Rulers who are guilty of such an encroachment, exceed the commission from which they derive their authority, and are Tyrants. The People who submit to it are governed by laws made neither by themselves nor by an authority derived from them, and are slaves.

3. Because it is proper to take alarm at the first experiment on our liberties. We hold this prudent jealousy to be the first duty of Citizens, and one of the noblest characteristics of the late Revolution. The free men of America did not wait till usurped power had strengthened itself by exercise, and entangled the question in precedents. They saw all the consequences in the principle, and they avoided the consequences by denying the principle. We revere this lesson too much soon to forget it. Who does not see that the same authority which can establish Christianity, in exclusion of all other Religions, may establish with the same ease any particular sect of Christians, in exclusion of all other Sects? that the same authority which can force a citizen to contribute three pence only of his property for the support of any one establishment, may force him to conform to any other establishment in all cases whatsoever?

4. Because the Bill violates the equality which ought to be the basis of every law, and which is more indispensable, in proportion as the validity or expediency of any law is more liable to be impeached. If "all men are by nature equally free and independent," all men are to be considered as entering into Society on equal conditions; as relinquishing no more, and therefore retaining no less, one than another, of their natural rights. Above all are they to be considered as retaining an "equal title to the free exercise of Religion according to the dictates of Conscience." Whilst we assert for ourselves a freedom to embrace, to profess and to observe the Religion which we believe to be of divine origin, we cannot deny an equal freedom to those whose minds have not yet yielded to the evidence which has convinced us. If this freedom be abused, it is an offence against God, not against man: To God, therefore, not to man, must an account of it be rendered. As the Bill violates equality by subjecting some to peculiar burdens, so it violates the same principle, by granting to others peculiar exemptions. Are the Quakers and Menonists the only sects who think a compulsive support of their Religions unnecessary and unwarrantable? Can their piety alone be entrusted with the care of public worship? Ought their Religions to be endowed above all others with extraordinary privileges by which proselytes may be enticed from all others? We think too favorably of the justice and good sense of these denominations to believe that they either covet pre-eminences over their fel-

low citizens or that they will be seduced by them from the common opposition to the measure.

5. Because the Bill implies either that the Civil Magistrate is a competent Judge of Religious Truth; or that he may employ Religion as an engine of Civil policy. The first is an arrogant pretension falsified by the contradictory opinions of Rulers in all ages, and throughout the world: the second an unhallowed perversion of the means of salvation.

6. Because the establishment proposed by the Bill is not requisite for the support of the Christian Religion. To say that it is, is a contradiction to the Christian Religion itself, for every page of it disavows a dependence on the powers of this world: it is a contradiction to fact; for it is known that this Religion both existed and flourished, not only without the support of human laws, but in spite of every opposition from them, and not only during the period of miraculous aid, but long after it had been left to its own evidence and the ordinary care of Providence. Nay, it is a contradiction in terms; for a Religion not invented by human policy, must have preexisted and been supported, before it was established by human policy. It is moreover to weaken in those who profess this Religion a pious confidence in its innate excellence and the patronage of its Author; and to foster in those who still reject it, a suspicion that its friends are too conscious of its fallacies to trust it to its own merits.

7. Because experience witnesseth that ecclesiastical establishments, instead of maintaining the purity and efficacy of Religion, have had a contrary operation. During almost fifteen centuries has the legal establishment of Christianity been on trial. What have been its fruits? More or less in all places, pride and indolence in the Clergy, ignorance and servility in the laity, in both, superstition, bigotry and persecution. Enquire of the Teachers of Christianity for the ages in which it appeared in its greatest luster; those of every sect, point to the ages prior to its incorporation with Civil policy. Propose a restoration of this primitive State in which its Teachers depended on the voluntary rewards of their flocks, many of them predict its downfall. On which Side ought their testimony to have greatest weight, when for or when against their interest?

8. Because the establishment in question is not necessary for the support of Civil Government. If it be urged as necessary for the support of Civil Government only as it is a means of supporting Religion, and it be not necessary for the latter purpose, it cannot be necessary for the former. If Religion be not within the cognizance of Civil Government how can its legal establishment be necessary to Civil Government? What influence in fact have ecclesiastical establishments had on Civil Society? In some instances they have been seen to erect a spiritual tyranny on the ruins of the Civil authority; in many instances they have been seen upholding the thrones of political tyranny: in no instance have they been seen the guardians of the liberties of the peo-

ple. Rulers who wished to subvert the public liberty, may have found an established Clergy convenient auxiliaries. A just Government instituted to secure & perpetuate it needs them not. Such a Government will be best supported by protecting every Citizen in the enjoyment of his Religion with the same equal hand which protects his person and his property; by neither invading the equal rights of any Sect, nor suffering any Sect to invade those of another.

9. Because the proposed establishment is a departure from the generous policy, which, offering an Asylum to the persecuted and oppressed of every Nation and Religion, promised a luster to our country, and an accession to the number of its citizens. What a melancholy mark is the Bill of sudden degeneracy! Instead of holding forth an Asylum to the persecuted, it is itself a signal of persecution. It degrades from the equal rank of Citizens all those whose opinions in Religion do not bend to those of the Legislative authority. Distant as it may be in its present form from the Inquisition, it differs from it only in degree. The one is the first step, the other the last in the career of intolerance. The magnanimous sufferer under this cruel scourge in foreign Regions, must view the Bill as a Beacon on our Coast, warning him to seek some other haven, where liberty and philanthropy in their due extent, may offer a more certain repose from his Troubles.

10. Because it will have a like tendency to banish our Citizens. The allurements presented by other situations are every day thinning their number. To superadd a fresh motive to emigration by revoking the liberty which they now enjoy, would be the same species of folly which has dishonored and depopulated flourishing kingdoms.

11. Because it will destroy that moderation and harmony which the forbearance of our laws to intermeddle with Religion has produced among its several sects. Torrents of blood have been split in the old world, by vain attempts of the secular arm, to extinguish Religious discord, by proscribing all difference in Religious opinion. Time has at length revealed the true remedy. Every relaxation of narrow and rigorous policy, wherever it has been tried, has been found to assuage the disease. The American Theater has exhibited proofs that equal and complete liberty, if it does not wholly eradicate it, sufficiently destroys its malignant influence on the health and prosperity of the State. If with the salutary effects of this system under our own eyes, we begin to contract the bounds of Religious freedom, we know no name that will too severely reproach our folly. At least let warning be taken at the first fruits of the threatened innovation. The very appearance of the Bill has transformed "that Christian forbearance, love and charity," which of late mutually prevailed, into animosities and jealousies, which may not soon be appeased. What mischiefs may not be dreaded, should this enemy to the public quiet be armed with the force of a law?

12. Because the policy of the Bill is adverse to the diffusion of the light of Christianity. The first wish of those who enjoy this precious gift ought to be that it may be imparted to the whole race of mankind. Compare the number of those who have as yet received it with the number still remaining under the dominion of false

Religions; and how small is the former! Does the policy of the Bill tend to lessen the disproportion?

No; it at once discourages those who are strangers to the light of revelation from coming into the Region of it; and countenances by example the nations who continue in darkness, in shutting out those who might convey it to them. Instead of Leveling as far as possible, every obstacle to the victorious progress of Truth, the Bill with an ignoble and unchristian timidity would circumscribe it with a wall of defense against the encroachments of error.

13. Because attempts to enforce by legal sanctions, acts obnoxious to so great a proportion of Citizens, tend to enervate the laws in general, and to slacken the bands of Society. If it be difficult to execute any law which is not generally deemed necessary or salutary, what must be the case, where it is deemed invalid and dangerous? And what may be the effect of so striking an example of impotency in the Government, on its general authority?

14. Because a measure of such singular magnitude and delicacy ought not to be imposed, without the clearest evidence that it is called for by a majority of citizens, and no satisfactory method is yet proposed by which the voice of the majority in this case may be determined, or its influence secured. "The people of the respective counties are indeed requested to signify their opinion respecting the adoption of the Bill to the next Session of Assembly." But the representation must be made equal, before the voice either of the Representatives or of the Counties will be that of the people. Our hope is that neither of the former will, after due consideration, espouse the dangerous principle of the Bill. Should the event disappoint us, it will still leave us in full confidence, that a fair appeal to the latter will reverse the sentence against our liberties.

15. Because finally, "the equal right of every citizen to the free exercise of his Religion according to the dictates of conscience" is held by the same tenure with all our other rights. If we recur to its origin, it is equally the gift of nature; if we weigh its importance, it cannot be less dear to us; if we consult the "Declaration of those rights which pertain to the good people of Virginia, as the basis and foundation of Government," it is enumerated with equal solemnity, or rather studied emphasis. Either then, we must say, that the Will of the Legislature is the only measure of their authority; and that in the plenitude of this authority, they may sweep away all our fundamental rights; or, that they are bound to leave this particular right untouched and sacred: Either we must say, that they may controul the freedom of the press, may abolish the Trial by Jury, may swallow up the Executive and Judiciary Powers of the State; nay that they may despoil us of our very right of suffrage, and erect themselves into an independent and hereditary Assembly or, we must say, that they have no authority to enact into the law the Bill under consideration. We the Subscribers say, that the General Assembly of this Commonwealth have no such

authority: And that no effort may be omitted on our part against so dangerous an usurpation, we oppose to it, this remonstrance; earnestly praying, as we are in duty bound, that the Supreme Lawgiver of the Universe, by illuminating those to whom it is addressed, may on the one hand, turn their Councils from every act which would affront his holy prerogative, or violate the trust committed to them: and on the other, guide them into every measure which may be worthy of his blessing, may redound to their own praise, and may establish more firmly the liberties, the prosperity and the happiness of the Commonweath.

THOMAS JEFFERSON TO ABIGAIL ADAMS
June 21, 1785

Editor's note: This was written by Minister Jefferson, from Paris, to Abigail, with her husband, John, the Minister in London.

I have received duly the honor of your letter, and am now to return you thanks for your condescension in having taken the first step for settling a correspondence which I so much desired; for I now consider it as settled and proceed accordingly. I have always found it best to remove obstacles first. I will do so therefore in the present case by telling you that I consider your boasts of the splendour of your city and of it's superb hackney coaches as a flout, and declaring that I would not give the polite, self-denying, feeling, hospitable, goodhumoured people of this country and their amiability in every point of view, (tho' it must be confessed our streets are somewhat dirty, and our fiacres rather indifferent) for ten such races of rich, proud, hectoring, swearing, squibbing, carnivorous animals as those among whom you are; and that I do love this people with all my heart, and think that with a better religion and a better form of government and their present governors their condition and country would be most enviable.

JAMES MADISON TO JAMES MONROE
June 21, 1785

Editor's note: The words in brackets were deleted from the final version of this letter.

Finding from a letter of Mr. Mazzei that you have never been furnished with a copy of the Bill for establishing the Christian Religion in this State, I now inclose one, regretting that I had taken it for granted that you must have been supplied thro' some other channel. A very warm opposition will be made to this innovation by the people of the middle and back Counties, particularly the latter. They do not scruple to declare it an alarming usurpation on their fundamental rights and that tho' the Genl. Assembly should give it the form if they will not give it the validity of a law. If there be any limitation to the power of the Legislature, particularly if this limitation is to be sought in their Declaration of Rights or Form of Government, I own the Bill appears to me to [justify] warrant this [strong] language of the people.

JAMES MADISON TO EDMUND RANDOLPH
July 26, 1785

Your favour of the 17th. inst: inclosing a letter from Mr. Jones and a copy of the ecclesiastical Journal, came safe to hand. If I do not dislike the contents of the latter, it is because they furnish as I conceive fresh and forcible arguments against the Genl. Assessment. It may be of little consequence what tribunal is to judge of Clerical misdemesnors or how firmly the incumbent may be fastened on the parish, whilst the Vestry & people may hear & pay him or not as they like. But should a legal salary be annexed to the title, this phantom of power would be substantiated into a real monster of oppression. Indeed it appears to be so at present as far as the Glebes & donations extend. I had seen some prints of these proceedings before I recd. your letter, and had remarked the sprinklings of liberality to which you allude. My conjectures I believe did not err as the quarter from which they came.

THOMAS JEFFERSON TO JOHN ADAMS
July 28, 1785

What do you think of the inclosed Draught to be proposed to the courts of London and Versailles?...

3. The subjects or citizens of either party in the territories of the other shall be free in the exercise of their religion, shall not be required to conform in word or deed to any other, not suffer any molestation on account of religion, unless it be for a real insult on that of any other person.

JAMES MADISON TO THOMAS JEFFERSON
August 20, 1785

The opposition to the general assessment gains ground. At the instance of some of its adversaries, I drew up the remonstrance herewith inclosed. It has been sent thro' the medium of confidential persons in a member of the upper county[s] and I am told will be pretty extensively signed. The presbyterian clergy have at length espoused the side of the opposition, being moved either by a fear of their laity or a jealousy of the episcopalians. The mutual hatred of these sects has been much inflamed by the late act of incorporating the latter. I am far from being sorry for it as a coalition between them could alone endanger our religious rights and a tendency to such an event had been suspected.

JAMES MADISON TO JOHN BROWN
August 23, 1785

Editor's note: Brown had asked Madison for advice on a constitution for Kentucky, where a movement for separation from Virginia was growing.

If it were possible, it would be well to define the extent of the Legislative power; but the nature of it in many respects seems to be indefinite. It is very practicable, however, to enumerate the essential exceptions. The Constitution may expressly restrain them from meddling with religion; from abolishing Juries; from taking away the Habeas Corpus; from forcing a citizen to give evidence against himself; from controulling the press; from enacting retrospective laws, at least in criminal cases; from abridging the right of suffrage; from taking private property for public use without paying its full value; from licensing the importation of slaves; from infringing the confederation, &c., &c.

THOMAS JEFFERSON TO MARQUIS DE CHASTELLUX
September 2, 1785

Editor's note: De Chastellux had written Travels in North America *and Jefferson sent him a list of comments and corrections regarding Virginia.*

17. The clergy are excluded, because, if admitted into the legislature at all, the probability is that they would form it's majority. For they are dispersed through every county in the state, they have influence with the people, and great opportunities of persuading them to elect them into the legislature. This body, tho shattered, is still formidable, still forms a corps, and is still actuated by the esprit de corps. The nature of that spirit has been severely felt by mankind, and has filled the history of ten or twelve centuries with too many atrocities not to merit a proscription from meddling with government.

THOMAS JEFFERSON TO ABIGAIL ADAMS
September 4, 1785

You will have seen the affair of the Cardinal de Rohan so well detailed in the Leyden gazette that I need add nothing on that head. The Cardinal is still in the Bastille. It is certain that the Queen has been compromised without the smallest authority from her: and the probability is that the Cardinal has been duped into it by his mistress Madme. de la Motte. The results from this two consequences not to his honour, that he is a debauchee and a booby.

THOMAS JEFFERSON TO ABIGAIL ADAMS
September 25, 1785

Editor's note: This letter from Paris really belongs in my next book, Jefferson & Madison on dining well.

I fancy it must be the quantity of animal food eaten by the English which renders their character insusceptible of civilization. I suspect it is in their kitchens and not in their churches that their reformation must be worked, and that Missionaries of that description from hence would avail more than those who should endeavor to tame them by precepts of religion or philosophy.

THOMAS JEFFERSON TO CHARLES BELLINI
September 30, 1785

But you are perhaps curious to know how this new scene has struck a savage of the mountains of America. Not advantageously I assure you. I find the general fate of humanity here most deplorable. The truth of Voltaire's observation offers itself perpetually, that every man here must be either the hammer or the anvil. It is a true picture of that country to which they say we shall pass hereafter, and where we are to see god and his angels in splendor, and crouds of the damned trampled under their feet.

JAMES MADISON TO JAMES MONROE
December 17, 1785

The Bill proportioning crimes & punishments was the one at which we stuck after wading thro' the most difficult parts of it. A few subsequent bills however were excepted from the postponement. Among these was the Bill for establishing Religious freedom, which has got thro' the H. of Delegates without alteration, though not without warm opposition. Mr. Mercer & Mr. Corbin were the principal combatants against it.

JAMES MADISON TO JAMES MADISON SR.
December 24, 1785

The Bill for establishing Religious freedom passed the H. of Delegates as it stands in the Revised Code. The Senate have disagreed to the preamble and substituted the last article of the Declaration of Rights. Which house is to recede, is uncertain. Both are much attached to their respective ideas.

JAMES MADISON TO JAMES MONROE
December 24, 1785

The proceedings of the Assembly since my last dated this day week have related 1. to the Bill for establishing Religious freedom in the Revisal.... The first employed the H. of Delegates several days. The preamble being the principal subject of contention. It at length passed without alteration. The Senate I am told have exchanged after equal altercation. The preamble of the revisal for the last clause in the Declaration of Rights; an exchange wch. was proposed in the H. of D. and negatived by a Considerable Majority. I do not learn that they have made or will make any other alteration.

JAMES MADISON TO THOMAS JEFFERSON
January 22, 1786

Editor's note: Following the Memorial and Remonstrance, Madison succeeded in getting Jefferson's "Bill concerning Religious Freedom" through the House of Delegates.

Our Assembly last night closed a Session of 97 days, during the whole of which except the first seven, I have shared in the confinement.... The titles in the enclosed list will point out to you such of the bills as were adopted from the Revisal....

The only one of these which was pursued into an Act is the Bill concerning Religious freedom. The steps taken throughout the Country to defeat the Genl. Assessment, had produced all the effect that could have been wished. The table was loaded with petitions & remonstrances from all parts against the interposition of the Legislature in matters of Religion. A General convention of the Presbyterian church prayed expressly that the bill in the Revisal might be passed into a law, as the best safeguard short of a Constitutional one, for their religious rights. The bill was carried thro' the H. of Delegates, without alteration. The Senate objected to the preamble, and sent down a proposed substitution of the 16th. art: of the Declaration of Rights. The H. of D. disagreed. The Senate insisted, and asked a Conference. Their objections were frivolous indeed. In order to remove them as they were understood by the Managers of the H. of D. the preamble was sent up again from the H. of D. with one or two verbal alterations. As an amendment to these the Senate sent down a few others; which as they did not affect the substance though they somewhat defaced the composition, it was thought better to agree to than to run further risks, especially as it was getting late in the Session and the House growing thin. The enacting clauses past without a single alteration, and I flatter myself have in this Country extinguished forever the ambitious hope of making laws for the human mind.

THOMAS JEFFERSON TO JAMES MADISON
February 8, 1786

Houdon is returned. He called on me the other day to remonstrate against the inscription proposed for Genl. W.'s statue. He says it is too long to be put on the pedestal.... A propos of the Capitol. Do my dear friend exert yourself to get the plan begun on set aside, & that adopted which was drawn here. It was taken from a model which has been the admiration of 16. centuries, which has been the object of as many pilgrimages as the tomb of Mahomet: which will give unrivalled honour to our state, and furnish a model whereon to form the taste of our young men.

THOMAS JEFFERSON TO JOHN PAGE
May 4, 1786

The mechanical arts in London are carried to a wonderful perfection. But of these I need not speak, because of them my countrymen have unfortunately too many examples before their eyes. I consider the extravagance, which has seized them, as a more baneful evil than toryism was during the war. It is the more so, as the example is set by the best and most amiable characters among us. Would a missionary appear, who would make frugality the basis of his religious system, and go through the land, preaching it up as the only road to salvation, I would join his school, though not generally disposed to seek my religion out of the dictates of my own reason, and feelings of my own heart.

JAMES MADISON TO JAMES MONROE
June 21, 1786

Again can there be a more shortsighted or dishonorable policy than to concur with Spain in frustrating the benevolent views of nature to sell the affections of our ultramontane brethren ... and at the same time to court by the most precious sacrifices the alliance of a nation whose impotency is notorious, who has given no proof of regard for us and the genius of whose government religion & manners unfit them, of all the nations of Christendom for a coalition with this country.

THOMAS JEFFERSON TO JEAN NICHOLAS DÉ MEUNIER
June 22, 1786

Editor's note: Jean dé Meunier was writing an article on America for the Encyclopédie Methodique. The Society of the Cincinnati was set up by officers in the revolutionary army, and was to be hereditary through the first male child.

It should be further considered that, in America, no other distinction between man & man had ever been known, but that of persons in office exercising powers by authority of the laws, and private individuals.... But of distinctions by birth or badge they had no more idea than they had of the mode of existence in the moon or planets. They had heard only that there were such, & knew that they must be wrong. A due horror of the evils which flow from these distinctions could be excited in Europe only, where the dignity of man is lost in arbitrary distinctions, where the human species is classed into several stages of degradation, where the many are crushed under the weight of the few, & where the order established can present to the contemplation of a thinking being no other picture than that of God almighty & his angels trampling under foot the hosts of the damned. No wonder then that the institution of the Cincinnati should be innocently conceived by one order of American citizens, could raise in the other orders only a slow, temperate, & rational opposition, and could be viewed in Europe as a detestable parricide.

THOMAS JEFFERSON TO JEAN NICHOLAS DÉ MEUNIER
June 26, 1786

M. dé Meunier, where he mentions that the slave-law has been passed in Virginia, without the clause of emancipation, is pleased to mention that neither Mr. Wythe nor Mr. Jefferson were present to make the proposition they had meditated; from which people, who do not give themselves the trouble to reflect or enquire, might conclude hastily that their absence was the cause why the proposition was not made; & of course that there were not in the assembly persons of virtue & firmness enough to propose the clause for emancipation. This supposition would not be true. There were persons there who wanted neither the virtue to propose, nor talents to enforce the proposition had they seen that the disposition of the legislature was ripe for it. These worthy characters would feel themselves wounded, degraded, & discouraged by this idea. Mr. Jefferson would therefore be obliged to M. dé Meunier to mention it in some such manner as this....

"But they saw that the moment of doing it with success had not yet arrived, and that an unsuccessful effort, as too often happens, would only rivet still closer the chains of bondage, and retard the moment of delivery to this oppressed description of men. What a stupendous, what an incomprehensible machine is man! who can endure toil, famine, stripes, imprisonment, & death itself in vindication of his own liberty, and the next moment be deaf to all those motives whose power supported him thro' his trial and inflict on his fellow men a bondage, one hour of which is fraught with more misery than ages of that which he rose in rebellion to oppose. But we must await with patience the workings of an overruling providence, & hope that that is preparing the deliverance of these, our suffering brethren. When the measure of their tears shall be full, when their groans shall have involved heaven itself in darkness, a god of justice will awaken to their distress and by diffusing light and liberality among their oppressors, or, at length, by exterminating thunder, manifest his attention to the things of this world, and that they are not left to the guidance of a blind fatality."

THOMAS JEFFERSON TO WILLIAM SMITH
July 9, 1786

Cannot you invent some commissions for me here, by way of reprisal for the vexations I give you? Silk stockings, gillets, &c. for yourself, gewgaws and contrivances for Madame? À propos, all hail, Madame! May your nights and days be many and full of joy! May their fruits be such as to make you feel the sweet union of parent and lover, but not so many as that you may feel their weight! May they be handsome and good as their mother, wise and honest as their father, but more milky! — For your old age I will compose a prayer thirty years hence.

To return to business (for I am never tempted to pray but when a warm feeling for my friends comes athwart my heart) they tell me that they are altering Dr. Ramsay's book in London in order to accommodate it to the English palete and pride.

THOMAS JEFFERSON TO ABIGAIL ADAMS
August 9, 1786

Editor's note: The British king referred to was George III.

It is an age since I have had the honor of a letter from you, and an age and a half since I presumed to address one to you. I think my last was dated in the reign of king Amri, but under which of his successors you wrote, I cannot recollect. Ochosias, Joachar, Manahem or some such hard names....

We have a blind story here of somebody attempting to assassinate your king. No man upon earth has my prayers for his continuance in life more sincerely than him. He is truly the American Messias. The most precious life that ever god gave, and may god continue it. Twenty long years has he been labouring to drive us to our good, and he labours and will labour still for if he can be spared. We shall have need of him for twenty more. The Prince of Wales on the throne, Lansdowne and Fox in the ministry, and we are undone! We become chained by our habits to the tails of those who hate and despise us. I repeat it then that my anxieties are all alive for the health and long life of the king. He has not friend on earth who would lament his loss so much and so long as I should.

Here we have singing, dauncing, laugh, and merriment. No assassinations, no treasons, rebellions, nor other dark deeds. When our king goes out, they fall down and kiss the earth where he has trodden: and then they go to kissing one another. And this is the truest wisdom. They have so much happiness in one year as an Englishman in ten.... There are some little bickerings between the king and his parliament, but they end with a sic volo, sic jubeo [as I wish, so I rejoice]. The bottom of my page tells me it is time for me to end.

THOMAS JEFFERSON TO GEORGE WYTHE
August 13, 1786

Editor's note: Wythe had been Jefferson's law professor, and then a signatory of the Declaration of Independence.

The European papers have announced that the assembly of Virginia were occupied on the revisal of their code of laws. This, with some other similar intelligence, has contributed much to convince the people of Europe, that what the English papers are constantly publishing of our anarchy, is false; as they are sensible that such a work is that of a people only who are in perfect tranquillity. Our act for freedom of religion is extremely applauded. The ambassadors & ministers of the several nations of Europe resident at this court have asked of me copies of it to send to their sovereigns, and it is inserted at full length in several books now in the press; among others, in the new Encyclopédie. I think it will produce considerable good even in these countries where ignorance, superstition, poverty, & oppression of body & mind in every form, are so firmly settled on the mass of the people, that their redemption from them can never be hoped. If the Almighty had begotten a thousand sons, instead of one, they would not have sufficed for this task. If all the sovereigns of Europe were to set themselves to work to emancipate the minds of their subjects from their present ignorance & prejudices, & that as zealously as they now endeavor the contrary, a thousand years would not place them on that high ground on which our common people are now setting out. Ours could not have been so fairly put into the hands of their own common sense had they not been separated from their parent stock & kept from contamination, either from them, or the other people of the old world, by the intervention of so wide an ocean. To know the worth of this, one must see the want of it here. I think by far the most important bill in our whole code is that for the diffusion of knowlege among the people. No other sure foundation can be devised, for the preservation of freedom and happiness. If anybody thinks that kings, nobles, or priests are good conservators of the public happiness send them here. It is the best school in the universe to cure them of that folly. They will see here with their own eyes that these descriptions of men are an abandoned confederacy against the happiness of the mass of the people. The omnipotence of their effect cannot be better proved than in this country particularly, where notwithstanding the finest soil upon earth, the finest climate under heaven, and a people of the most benevolent, the most gay and amiable character of which the human form is susceptible, where such a people I say, surrounded by so many blessings from nature, are yet loaded with misery by kings, nobles and priests, and by them alone. Preach, my dear Sir, a crusade against ignorance; establish & improve the law for educating the common people. Let our countrymen know that the people alone can protect us against these evils, and that the tax which will be paid for this purpose is not more than the thousandth part of what will be paid to kings, priests & nobles who will rise up among us if we leave the people in ignorance.

THOMAS JEFFERSON TO MARIA COSWAY
October 12, 1786

Editor's note: Jefferson became infatuated with Mrs. Cosway but all historians doubt if they had an affair. He wrote this after she left Paris.

Seated by my fire side, solitary and sad, the following dialogue took place between my Head and my Heart,

Heart: But they are sensible people who think for themselves. They will ask impartial foreigners who been among us, whether they saw or heard on the spot any instances of anarchy. They will judge too that a people occupied as we are in opening rivers, digging navigable canals, making roads, building public schools, establishing academies, erecting busts and statues to our great men, protecting religious freedom, abolishing sanguinary punishments, reforming and improving our laws in general, they will judge I say for themselves whether these are not the occupations of a people at their ease, whether this is not better evidence of our true state than a London paper, hired to lie, and from which no truth can ever be extracted but by reversing everything it says....

Head: The most effectual means of being secure against pain is to retire within ourselves, and to suffice for our own happiness. Those, which depend on ourselves, are the only pleasures a wise man will count on: for nothing is ours which another may deprive us of. Hence the inestimable value of intellectual pleasures. Ever in our power, always leading us to something new, never cloying, we ride, serene and sublime, above the concerns of this mortal world, contemplating truth and nature, matter and motion, the laws which bind up their existence, and that eternal being who made and bound them up by these laws. Let this be our employ.

Heart: When Heaven has taken from us some object of our love, how sweet is it to have a bosom wherein to recline our heads, and into which we may pour the torrent of our tears!... Let the gloomy monk, sequestered from the world, seek unsocial pleasures in the bottom of his cell! Let the sublimated philosopher grasp visionary happiness while pursuing phantoms dressed in the garb of truth! Their supreme wisdom is supreme folly; & they mistake for happiness the mere absence of pain. Had they ever felt the solid pleasure of one generous spasm of the heart, they would exchange for it all the frigid speculations of their lives, which you have been vaunting in such elevated terms....

If our country, when pressed with wrongs at the point of the bayonet, had been governed by its heads instead of its hearts, where should be have been now? Hanging on a gallows as high as Haman's. You began to calculate, and to compare wealth and numbers: we threw up a few pulsations of our blood; we supplied enthusiasm against wealth and numbers; we put our existence to the hazard, when the hazard seemed against us, and we saved our country: justifying, at the same time, the ways of Providence, whose precept is, to do always what is right, and leave the issue to Him....

I thought this a favorable proposition whereon to rest the issue of the dialogue. So I put an end to it by calling for my nightcap. Methinks I hear you wish to heaven I had called a little sooner, and so spared you the ennui of such a tedious sermon. I did not interrupt them sooner because I was in a mood for hearing sermons.... But, on your part, no curtailing. If your letters are as long as the Bible, they will appear short to me. Only let them be brim full of affection.

THOMAS JEFFERSON TO JAMES MADISON
December 16, 1786

The Virginia act for religious freedom has been received with infinite approbation in Europe, and propagated with enthusiasm. I do not mean by governments, but by the individuals who compose them. It has been translated into French and Italian; has been sent to most of the courts of Europe, and has been the best evidence of the falsehood of those reports which stated us to be in anarchy. It is inserted in the new "Encyclopédie," and is appearing in most of the publications respecting America. In fact, it is comfortable to see the standard of reason at length erected, after so many ages, during which the human mind has been held in vassalage by kings, priests, and nobles; and it is honorable for us, to have produced the first legislature who had the courage to declare, that the reason of man may be trusted with the formation of his own opinions.

THOMAS JEFFERSON TO CHARLES THOMSON
December 17, 1786

I take the first moment I can however to acknowledge the receipt of your letters of Apr. 6. July 8. and 30. In one of these you say you have not been able to learn whether, in the new mills in London, steam is the immediate mover of the machinery, or raises water to move it?... You observe that Whitehurst supposes it to have been the agent which, bursting the earth, threw it up into mountains and vallies. You ask me what I think of his book? I find in it many interesting facts brought together and many ingenious commentaries on them. But there are great chasms in his facts, and consequently in his reasoning. These he fills up by suppositions which may be as reasonably denied as granted. A sceptical reader therefore, like myself, is left in the lurch. I acknolege however he makes more use of fact than any other writer of a theory of the earth. But I give one answer to all these theorists. That is as follows: they all suppose the earth a created existence. They must suppose a creator then: and that he possessed power and wisdom to a great degree. As he intended the earth for the habitation of animals and vegetables is it reasonable to suppose he made two jobs of his creation? That he first made a chaotic lump and set it into rotary motion, and then waiting the millions of ages necessary to form itself, that when it had done this he stepped in a second time to create the animals and plants which were to inhabit it? As the hand of a creator is to be called in, it may as well be called in at one stage of the process as another. We may as well suppose he created the earth at once nearly in the state in which we see it, fit for the preservation of the beings he placed on it. But it is said we have proof that he did not create it in it's present solid form, but in a state of fluidity, because its present shape as an oblate spheroid is precisely that which a fluid mass revolving on it's axis would assume. But I suppose that the same equilibrium between gravity and centrifugal force which would determine a fluid mass into a form of an oblate spheroid, would determine the wise creator of that mass, if he made it in a solid state, to give it the same spheroidical form. A revolving fluid will continue to change it's shape till it attains that in which it's principles of contrary motion are balanced: for if you suppose them not balanced, it will change it's form. Now the same balanced form is necessary for the preservation of a revolving solid. The creator therefore of a revolving solid would make it an oblate spheroid, that figure alone admitting a perfect equilibrium. He would make it in that form for another reason, that is, to prevent a shifting of the axis of rotation. Had he created the earth perfectly spherical, it's axis might have been perpetually shifting by the influence of other bodies in the system, and by placing the inhabitants of the earth successively under it's poles, it might have been depopulated: whereas being Spheroidical it has but one axis on which it can revolve in equilibrio. Suppose the axis of the earth to shift 45._ Then cut it into 180 slices, making every section in the plane of a circle of latitude, perpendicular to the axis. Every one of these slices, excepting the equatorial one would be unbalanced, as there would be more matter on one side of it's axis than on the other. There could be but one diameter drawn through such a slice which would divide it into two equal parts. On every other possible diameter the parts would hang unequal. This would produce an irregularity in the diurnal rotation. We may therefore conclude it impossible for the poles of the earth to shift, if it was made spheroidically, and that it would be made spheroidal, tho' solid, to obtain this end. I use this reasoning only on the supposition that the earth had a beginning. I am sure I shall read your conjectures on this subject with great pleasure, tho' I bespeak before hand a right to indulge my natural incredulity and scepticism.

THOMAS JEFFERSON TO JOHN JAY
January 9, 1787

You will have seen in the public papers that the King has called an Assemblée des Notables. This has not been done for one hundred and sixty years past. Of course it calls up all the attention of the people. The objects of this Assembly are not named. Several are conjectured. [The] tolerating the Protestant religion; removing all the internal custom houses to the frontier; equalizing the gabelles [tax] on salt through the kingdom; the sale of the King's domains to raise money; or, finally, the effecting this necessary end by some other means are talked of. But in truth, nothing is known about it. This government practices secrecy so systematically, that it never publishes its purposes or its proceedings sooner or more extensively than is necessary.

THOMAS JEFFERSON TO JOHN ADAMS
January 11, 1787

There is here an order of priests called the Mathurins, the object of whose institution is the begging of alms for the redemption of captives. About 18. months ago they redeemed 300, which cost them about 1500 livres a piece. They have agents residing in the Barbary states, who are constantly employed in searching and contracting for the captives of their nation, and they redeem at a lower price than any other people can. It occurred to me that their agency might be engaged for our prisoners at Algiers. I have had interviews with them, and the last night a long one with the General of the order. They offer their services with all the benignity and cordiality possible. The General told me he could not expect to redeem our prisoners as cheap as their own, but that he would use all the means in his power to do it on the best terms possible, which will be the better as there shall be the less suspicion that he acts for our public. I told him I would write to you on the subject, and speak to him again. What do you think of employing them, limiting them to a certain price, as 300 dollars for instance, or any other sum you think proper? He will write immediately to his instruments there, and in two or three months we can know the event. He will deliver them to Marseilles, Cadiz, or where we please, at our expence. The money remaining of the fund destined to the Barbary business may I suppose be drawn for this object. Write me your opinion if you please, on this subject, finally, fully, and immediately, that if you approve of the proposition, I may enter into arrangements with the General before my departure for the waters of Aix, which will be about the beginning of February.

THOMAS JEFFERSON TO JOHN ADAMS
January 25, 1787

The charitable, the humane, the Christian Mathurins deserve our kindest Thanks, and we should be highly obliged to them if they could discover at what Price, our

Countrymen may be redeemed: but I don't think we have the Authority to advance the Money without the further orders of Congress.

THOMAS JEFFERSON, NOTES OF A TOUR INTO THE SOUTHERN PARTS OF FRANCE, &c.
March 3, 1787

CHAMPAGNE. MARCH 3. SENS to VERMANTON.... Few chateaux. No farm houses, all the people being gathered in villages. Are they thus collected by that dogma of their religion which makes them believe that, to keep the Creator in good humor with his own works, they must mumble a mass every day? Certain it is that they are less happy and less virtuous in villages than they would be insulated with their families on the grounds they cultivate.

JAMES MADISON, VICES OF THE POLITICAL SYSTEM OF THE UNITED STATES
April 1787

11. If the multiplicity and mutability of laws prove a want of wisdom, their injustice betrays a defect still more alarming: more alarming not merely because it is a greater evil in itself, but because it brings more into question the fundamental principle of republican Government, that the majority who rule in such Governments, are the safest Guardians both of public Good and of private rights. To what causes is this evil to be ascribed?

These causes lie 1. in the Representative bodies.... 2. A still more fatal if not more frequent cause lies among the people themselves. All civilized societies are divided into different interests and factions, as they happen to be creditors or debtors — Rich or poor — husbandmen, merchants or manufacturers — members of different religious sects — followers of different political leaders — inhabitants of different districts — owners of different kinds of property &c &c. In republican Government the majority however composed, ultimately give the law. Whenever therefore an apparent interest or common passion unites a majority what is to restrain them from unjust violations of the rights and interests of the minority, or of individuals? Three motives only 1. a prudent regard to their own good as involved in the general and permanent good of the Community.... 2dly. respect for character.... 3dly. will Religion the only remaining motive be a sufficient restraint? It is not pretended to be such on men individually considered. Will its effect be greater on them considered in an aggregate view? Quite the reverse. The conduct of every popular assembly acting on oath, the strongest of religious Ties, proves that individuals join without remorse in acts, against which their consciences would revolt if proposed to them under the like sanction, separately in their closets. When indeed Religion is kindled into enthusiasm, its force like that of other passions, is increased by the sympathy of a multitude. But enthusiasm is only a temporary state of religion, and while it lasts will hardly be seen with pleasure at the helm of Government. Besides as religion in its coolest state, is not infallible, it may become a motive to oppression as well as a restraint from injustice.

JAMES MADISON, SPEECH IN THE FEDERAL CONSTITUTIONAL CONVENTION ON FACTIONS
June 6, 1787

Mr. MADISON considered an election of one branch at least of the Legislature by the people immediately, as a clear principle of free Govt. and that this mode under proper regulations had the additional advantage of securing better representatives, as well as of avoiding too great an agency of the State Governments in the General one. — He differed from the member from Connecticut [Mr. Sharman] in thinking the objects mentioned to be all the principal ones that required a National Govt. Those were certainly important and necessary objects; but he combined with them the necessity of providing more effectually for the security of private rights, and the steady dispensation of Justice. Interferences with these were evils which had more perhaps than any thing else, produced this convention. Was it to be supposed that republican liberty could long exist under the abuses of it practiced in some of the States. The gentleman [Mr. Sharman] had admitted that in a very small State, faction & oppression wd. prevail. It was to be inferred then that wherever these prevailed the State was too small. Had they not prevailed in the largest as well as the smallest tho' less than in the smallest; and were we not thence admonished to enlarge the sphere as far as the nature of the Govt. would admit. This was the only defence agst. the inconveniencies of democracy consistent with the democratic form of Govt. All civilized Societies would be divided into different Sects, Factions, & interests, as they happened to consist of rich & poor, debtors & creditors, the landed, the manufacturing, the commercial interests, the inhabitants of this district or that district, the followers of this political leader or that political leader, the disciples of this religious Sect or that religious Sect. In all cases where a majority are united by a common interest or passion, the rights of the minority are in danger. What motives are to restrain them? A prudent regard to the maxim that honesty is the best policy is found by experience to be as little regarded by bodies of men as by individuals. Respect for character is always diminished in proportion to the number among whom the blame or praise is to be divided. Conscience, the only remaining tie, is known to be inadequate in individuals: In large numbers, little is to be expected from it. Besides, Religion itself may become a motive to persecution & oppression. — These observations are verified by the Histories of every Country antient & modern.

THOMAS JEFFERSON TO PETER CARR
August 10, 1787

Editor's note: Carr was Jefferson's nephew.

I have received your two letters of Decemb. 30 and April 18. and am very happy to find by them, as well as by letters from Mr. Wythe, that you have been so fortunate as to attract his notice & good will.... I inclose you a sketch of the sciences to which I would wish you to apply in such order as Mr. Wythe shall advise; I mention also the books in them worth your reading....

3. Moral philosophy. I think it lost time to attend lectures in this branch. He who made us would have been a pitiful bungler if he had made the rules of our moral conduct a matter of science. For one man of science, there are thousands who are not. What would have become of them? Man was destined for society. His morality therefore was to be formed to this object. He was endowed with a sense of right & wrong merely relative to this. This sense is as much a part of his nature as the sense of hearing, seeing, feeling; it is the true foundation of morality, & not the το χαλον truth, &c. as fanciful writers have imagined. The moral sense, or conscience, is as much a part of man as his leg or arm. It is given to all human beings in a stronger or weaker degree, as force of members is given them in a greater or less degree. It may be strengthened by exercise, as may any particular limb of the body. This sense is submitted indeed in some degree to the guidance of reason; but it is a small stock which is required for this: even a less one than what we call common sense. State a moral case to a ploughman & a professor. The former will decide it as well, & often better than the latter, because he has not been led astray by artificial rules. In this branch therefore read good books because they will encourage as well as direct your feelings. The writings of Sterne particularly form the best course of morality that ever was written. Besides these read the books mentioned in the enclosed paper; and above all things lose no occasion of exercising your dispositions to be grateful, to be generous, to be charitable, to be humane, to be true, just, firm, orderly, courageous &c. Consider every act of this kind as an exercise which will strengthen your moral faculties, & increase your worth.

4. Religion. Your reason is now mature enough to examine this object. In the first place divest yourself of all bias in favour of novelty & singularity of opinion. Indulge them in any other subject rather than that of religion. It is too important, & the consequences of error may be too serious. On the other hand shake off all the fears & servile prejudices under which weak minds are servilely crouched. Fix reason firmly in her seat, and call to her tribunal every fact, every opinion. Question with boldness even the existence of a god; because, if there be one, he must more approve of the homage of reason, than that of blindfolded fear. You will naturally examine first the religion of your own country. Read the bible then, as you would read Livy or Tacitus. The facts which are within the ordinary course of nature you will believe on the authority of the writer, as you do those of the same kind in Livy & Tacitus. The testimony of the writer weighs in their favor in one scale, and their not being against the laws of nature does not weigh against them. But those facts in the bible which contradict the laws of nature, must be examined with more care, and under a variety of faces. Here you must recur to the pretensions of the writer to inspiration from god. Examine upon what evidence his pretensions are founded, and whether that evidence is so strong as that its falsehood would be more improbable than a change in the laws of nature in the case he relates. For example in the book of Joshua we are told the sun stood still several hours. Were we to read that fact in

Livy or Tacitus we should class it with their showers of blood, speaking of statues, beasts, &c. But it is said that the writer of that book was inspired. Examine therefore candidly what evidence there is of his having been inspired. The pretension is entitled to your inquiry, because millions believe it. On the other hand you are astronomer enough to know how contrary it is to the law of nature that a body revolving on its axis as the earth does, should have stopped, should not by that sudden stoppage have prostrated animals, trees, buildings, and should after a certain time have resumed its revolution, & that without a second general prostration. Is this arrest of the earth's motion, or the evidence which affirms it, most within the law of probabilities? You will next read the new testament. It is the history of a personage called Jesus. Keep in your eye the opposite pretensions

1. of those who say he was begotten by god, born of a virgin, suspended & reversed the laws of nature at will, & ascended bodily into heaven: and

2. of those who say he was a man of illegitimate birth, of a benevolent heart, enthusiastic mind, who set out without pretensions to divinity, ended in believing them, & was punished capitally for sedition by being gibbeted according to the Roman law which punished the first commission of that offence by whipping, & the second by exile or death in furcâ [on a two pronged instrument of punishment].

See this law in the Digest Lib. 48. tit. 19. 28. 3. & Lipsius Lib. 2. de cruce. cap. 2. These questions are examined in the books I have mentioned under the head of religion, & several others. They will assist you in your inquiries, but keep your reason firmly on the watch in reading them all. Do not be frightened from this inquiry by any fear of it's consequences. If it ends in a belief that there is no god, you will find incitements to virtue in the comfort & pleasantness you feel in it's exercise, and the love of others which it will procure you. If you find reason to believe there is a god, a consciousness that you are acting under his eye, & that he approves you, will be a vast additional incitement; if that there be a future state, the hope of a happy existence in that increases the appetite to deserve it; if that Jesus was also a god, you will be comforted by a belief of his aid and love. In fine, I repeat that you must lay aside all prejudice on both sides, & neither believe nor reject anything because any other persons, or description of persons have rejected or believed it. Your own reason is the only oracle given you by heaven, and you are answerable not for the rightness but uprightness of the decision. I forgot to observe when speaking of the new testament that you should read all the histories of Christ, as well of those whom a council of ecclesiastics have decided for us to be Pseudo-evangelists, as those they named Evangelists. Because these Pseudo-evangelists pretended to inspiration as much as the others, and you are to judge their pretensions by your own reason, & not by the reason of those ecclesiastics. Most of these are lost. There are some however still extant, collected by Fabricius which I will endeavor to get & send you.

THOMAS JEFFERSON TO JOHN ADAMS
August 30, 1787

Editor's note: The Monsieur Jefferson refers to was Louis XVI's brother, later Louis XVIII.

The Count d'Artois is detested, and Monsieur the general favorite. The Archbishop of Toulouse is made Ministre principale, a virtuous, patriotic and able character.

CONSTITUTION OF THE UNITED STATES OF AMERICA
September 17, 1787

Editor's note: Even in his day, Madison was commonly called "the father of the constitution" for his management of the constitutional convention.

Article l, Section 7:

If any bill shall not be returned by the President within ten days (Sundays excepted) after it shall have been presented to him, the same shall be a law....

Article ll, Section 1:

[Oath taken by the President. - 7] Before he enter on the execution of his office, he shall take the following oath or affirmation: - "I do solemnly swear (or affirm) that I will faithfully execute the office of President of the United States, and will to the best of my ability, preserve, protect, and defend the Constitution of the United States."

Article VI:

[Who shall take constitutional oath; no religious test as to official qualification. - 3] The Senators and Representatives before mentioned, and the members of the several State Legislatures, and all executive and judicial officers, both of the United States and the several States, shall be bound by oath or affirmation, to support this constitution; but no religious test shall ever be required as a qualification to any office or public trust under the United States....

Done in convention by the unanimous consent of the States present in the seventeenth day of September in the year of our Lord one thousand and eighty seven and of the independence of the United States of America the Twelfth. In witness whereof we have here-unto subscribed our names.

JAMES MADISON TO GEORGE WASHINGTON
October 18, 1787

I have been this day honoured with your favor of the 10th. instant, under the same cover with which is a copy of Col. Mason's objections to the Work of the Convention....

What can he mean by saying that the Common law is not secured by the new constitution, though it has been adopted by the State Constitutions. The common law is nothing more than the unwritten law, and is left by all the constitutions equally liable to legislative alterations. I am not sure that any notice is particularly taken of it in the Constitutions of the States.... What could the Convention have done? If they had in general terms declared the Common law to be in force, they would have broken in upon the legal Code of every State in the most material points: they wd. have done more, they would have brought over from G.B. a thousand heterogeneous & antirepublican doctrines, and even the ecclesiastical Hierarchy itself, for that is a part of the Common law. If they had undertaken a discrimination, they must have formed a digest of laws, instead of a Constitution. This objection surely was not brought forward in the Convention, or it wd. have been placed in such a light that a repetition of it out of doors would scarcely have been hazarded.

JAMES MADISON TO THOMAS JEFFERSON
October 24, 1787

You will herewith receive the result of the Convention, which continued its Session till the 17th. of September. I take the liberty of making some observations on the subject which will help to make up a letter, if they should answer no other purpose....

No distinction seems to be more obvious than that between spiritual and temporal matters. Yet wherever they have been made objects of Legislation, they have clashed and contended with each other, till one or the other has gained the supremacy....

We know however that no Society ever did or can consist of so homogeneous a mass of Citizens. In the savage State indeed, an approach is made towards it; but in that State little or no Government is necessary. In all civilized Societies, distinctions are various and unavoidable. A distinction of property results from that very protection which a free Government gives to unequal faculties of acquiring it. There will be rich and poor; creditors and debtors; a landed interest, a monied interest, a mercantile interest, a manufacturing interest. These classes may again be subdivided according to the different productions of different situations & soils, & according to different branches of commerce, and of manufactures.

In addition to these natural distinctions, artificial ones will be founded, on accidental differences in political, religious or other opinions, or an attachment to the persons of leading individuals. However erroneous or ridiculous these grounds of dissention and faction, may appear to the enlightened Statesman, or the benevolent philosopher, the bulk of mankind who are neither Statesmen nor Philosophers, will continue to view them in a different light. It remains then to be enquired whether a majority having any common interest, or feeling any common passion, will find sufficient motives to restrain them from oppressing the minority....

Three motives only can restrain in such cases.... 3. Religion. The inefficacy of this restraint on individuals is well known. The conduct of every popular Assembly, acting on oath, the strongest of religious ties, shews that individuals join without remorse in acts agst. which their consciences would revolt, if proposed to them separately in their closets. When Indeed Religion is kindled into enthusiasm, its force like that of other passions is increased by the sympathy of a multitude. But enthusiasm is only a temporary state of Religion, and whilst it lasts will hardly be seen with pleasure at the helm. Even in its coolest state, it has been much oftener a motive to oppression than a restraint from it....

The same security seems requisite for the civil as for the religious rights of individuals. If the same sect form a majority and have the power, other sects will be sure to be depressed. Divide et impera [divide and rule], the reprobated axiom of tyranny, is under certain qualifications, the only policy, by which a republic can be administered on just principles. It must be observed however that this doctrine can only hold within a sphere of a mean extent. As in too small a sphere oppressive combinations may be too easily formed agst. the weaker party; so in too extensive a one, a defensive concert may be rendered too difficult against the oppression of those entrusted with the administration. The great desideratum in Government is, so to modify the sovereignty as that it may be sufficiently neutral between different parts of the Society to controul one part from invading the rights of another, and at the same time sufficiently controuled itself, from setting up an interest adverse to that of the entire Society....

The final reception which will be given by the people at large to the proposed System can not yet be decided.... Penna. will be divided. The City of Philada., the Republican party, the Quakers, and most of the Germans espouse the Constitution.

JAMES MADISON TO EDMUND PENDLETON
October 28, 1787

I have recd. and acknowledge with great pleasure your favor of the 8th. instt. The remarks which you make on the Act of the Convention appear to me to be in general extremely well founded. Your criticism on the clause exempting vessels bound to or from a State from being obliged to enter &c in another is particularly so. This provision was dictated by the jealousy of some particular states, and was inserted pretty late in the Session. The object of it was what you conjecture. The expression is certainly not accurate. Is not a religious test as far as it is necessary, or would operate, involved in the oath itself? If the person swearing believes in the supreme Being who is invoked, and in the penal consequences of offending him, either in this or a future world or both, he will be under the same restraint from perjury as if he had previously subscribed a test requiring this belief. If the person in question be an unbeliever in these points and would notwithstanding take the oath, a previous test could have no effect. He would subscribe it as he would take the oath, without any principle that could be affected by either.

THOMAS JEFFERSON TO JOHN ADAMS
November 13, 1787

Editor's note: The Minister Principal and the Archbishop referred to are one and the same, Étienne Charles Loménie de Brienne, Archbishop of Toulouse.

Little is said lately of the progress of the negociations between the courts of Petersburg, Vienna, and Versailles.... Nor do I think that the Principal here will be easily induced to lend himself to any connection which shall threaten a war within a considerable number of years. His own reign will be that of peace only, in all probability; and were any accident to tumble him down, this country would immediately gird on it's sword and buckler, and trust to occurrences for supplies of money. The wound their honour has sustained festers in their hearts, and it may be said with truth that the Archbishop and a few priests, determined to support his measures because proud to see their order come again into power, are the only advocates for the line of conduct which has been pursued. It is said and believed thro' Paris literally that the Count de Montmorin *pleuroit comme un enfant* [cried like a baby] when obliged to sign the counter declaration. Considering the phrase as figurative, I believe it expresses the distress of his heart. Indeed he has made no secret of his individual opinion. In the mean time the Principal goes on with a firm and patriotic spirit, in reforming the cruel abuses of the government and preparing a new constitution which will give to this people as much liberty as they are capable of managing. This I think will be the glory of his administration, because, tho' a good theorist in finance, he is thought to execute badly.

JAMES MADISON, *THE FEDERALIST*, NO. 10
November 22, 1787

A zeal for different opinions concerning religion, concerning government, and many other points, as well of speculation as of practice; an attachment to different leaders ambitiously contending for pre-eminence and power; or to persons of other descriptions whose fortunes have been interesting to the human passions, have, in turn, divided mankind into parties, inflamed them with mutual animosity, and rendered them much more disposed to vex and oppress each other than to co-operate for their common good....

If the impulse and the opportunity be suffered to coincide, we well know that neither moral nor religious motives can be relied on as an adequate control....

A religious sect may degenerate into a political faction in a part of the Confederacy; but the variety of sects dispersed over the entire face of it must secure the national councils against any danger from that source.

JAMES MADISON, *THE FEDERALIST*, NO. 19
December 8, 1787

The examples of antient confederacies, cited in my last paper, have not exhausted the source of experimental instruction on this subject. There are existing institutions, founded on a similar principle, which merit particular consideration....

The connection among the Swiss cantons scarcely amounts to a confederacy; though it is sometimes cited as an instance of the stability of such institutions....

As far as the peculiarity of their case will admit of comparison with that of the United States; it serves to confirm the principle intended to be established. Whatever efficacy the union may have had in ordinary cases, it appears that the moment a cause of difference sprang up, capable of trying its strength, it failed. The controversies on the subject of religion, which in three instances have kindled violent and bloody contests, may be said in fact to have severed the league. The Protestant and Catholic cantons have since had their separate diets; where all the most important concerns are adjusted, and which have left the general diet little more business than to take care of the common bailages.

JAMES MADISON TO THOMAS JEFFERSON
December 9, 1787

The Constitution proposed by the late convention engrosses almost the whole political attention of America.... My information leads me to suppose there must be three parties in Virginia. The first for adopting without attempting amendments.... At the head of the 2d. party which urges amendments are the Govr. & Mr. Mason.... a third Class, at the head of which is Mr. Henry. This class concurs at present with the patrons of amendments, but will probably contend for such as strike at the essence of the system....

It is worthy of remark that whilst in Virga. and some of the other States in the middle & Southern Districts of the Union, the men of intelligence, patriotism, property, and independent circumstances, are thus divided: all of this description, with a few exceptions, in the Eastern States, and most of the middle States, are zealously attached to the proposed Constitution. In N. England, the men of letters, the principle officers of Government, the Judges and Lawyers, the Clergy, and men of property, furnish only here and there an adversary.

THOMAS JEFFERSON TO JAMES MADISON
December 20, 1787

I must thank you too for the information in Thos. Burke's case, tho' you will have found by a subsequent letter that I have asked of you a further investigation of that matter. It is to gratify the lady who is at the head of the Convent wherein my daughters are, and who, by her attachment and attention to them, lays me under great obligations....

I have little to fill a letter. I will therefore make up the deficiency by adding a few words on the Constitution proposed by our Convention.... I will now add what I do not like. First, the omission of a bill of rights providing clearly & without the aid of sophisms for freedom of religion, freedom of the press, protection against standing armies, restriction against monopolies, the eternal & unremitting force of the habeas corpus laws, and trials by jury in all matters of fact triable by the laws of the land & not by the law of nations. To say, as Mr. Wilson does that a bill of rights was not necessary because all is reserved in the case of the general government which is not given, while in the particular ones all is given which is not reserved, might do for the audience to whom it was addressed, but is surely a gratis dictum, opposed by strong inferences from the body of the instrument, as well as from the omission of the clause of our present confederation which had declared that in express terms.... Let me add that a bill of rights is what the people are entitled to against every government on earth, general or particular, & what no just government should refuse, or rest on inferences.

THOMAS JEFFERSON TO JOHN ADAMS
December 31, 1787

Editor's note: In September 1787, Jefferson rented rooms at the Carthusian monastery, whose monks took vows of silence.

Mr. Parker takes charge of the 10. aunes of double Florence for Mrs. Adams. The silk stockings are not yet ready. I had ordered them to be made by the Hermits of Mont Calvaire who are famous for the excellence and honesty of their work, and prices. They will come by the first opportunity.

JAMES MADISON, *THE FEDERALIST*, NO. 37
January 11, 1788

Would it be wonderful if, under the pressure of all these difficulties, the convention should have been forced into some deviations from that artificial structure and regular symmetry which an abstract view of the subject might lead an ingenious theorist to bestow on a Constitution planned in his closet or in his imagination? The real wonder is that so many difficulties should have been surmounted, and surmounted with a unanimity almost as unprecedented as it must have been unexpected. It is impossible for any man of candor to reflect on this circumstance without partaking of the astonishment. It is impossible for the man of pious reflection not to perceive in it a finger of that Almighty hand which has been so frequently and signally extended to our relief in the critical stages of the revolution.

THOMAS JEFFERSON TO ABIGAIL ADAMS
February 2, 1788

I doubt whether you may like the stockings on first appearance: but I will answer for their goodness, being woven expressly for me by the Hermits of Mont Calvaire with whom I go and stay sometimes, and am favoured by them.

THOMAS JEFFERSON TO WILLIAM STEPHENS SMITH
February 2, 1788

I am glad to learn by letters which come down to the 20th. of December that the new constitution will undoubtably be received by a sufficiency of the states to set it a going. Were I in America, I would advocate it warmly till nine should have adopted, and then as warmly take the other side to convince the remaining four that they ought not to come into it till the declaration of rights is annexed to it. By this means we should secure all the good of it, and procure so respectable an opposition as would induce the accepting states to offer a bill or rights.... But I own it astonishes me to find such a change wrought in the opinions of our countrymen since I left them, as that threefourths of them should be contented to live under a system which leaves to their governors the power of taking from them the trial by jury in civil cases, freedom of religion, freedom of the press, freedom of commerce, the habeus corpus laws, and of yoking with a standing army. This is a degeneracy in the principles of liberty to which I had given four centuries instead of four years. But I hope it will all come about. We are now vibrating between too much and too little government, and the pendulum will rest finally in the middle.

JAMES MADISON, *THE FEDERALIST*, NO. 51
February 6, 1788

But what is government itself, but the greatest of all reflections on human nature? If men were angels, no government would be necessary. If angels were to govern men, neither external nor internal controls on government would be necessary.... In a free government the security for civil rights must be the same as that for religious rights. It consists in the one case in the multiplicity of interests, and in the other in the multiplicity of sects. The degree of security in both cases will depend on the number of interests and sects; and this may be presumed to depend on the extent of country and number of people comprehended under the same government.

THOMAS JEFFERSON TO ALEXANDER DONALD
February 7, 1788

I wish with all my soul, that the nine first conventions may accept the new constitution, because this will secure to us the good it contains, which I think great and important. But I equally wish, that the four latest conventions, which ever they be, may refuse to accede to it, till a declaration of rights be annexed. This would probably command the offer of such a declaration, and thus give to the whole fabric, perhaps as much perfection as any one of that kind ever had. By a declaration of rights, I mean one which shall stipulate freedom of religion, freedom of the press, freedom of commerce against monopolies, trials by juries in all cases, no suspensions of the habeas corpus, no standing armies. These are fetters against doing evil, which no honest government should decline.

THOMAS JEFFERSON TO C. W. F. DUMAS
February 12, 1788

With respect to the new government, 9. or 10. states will probably have accepted it by the end of this month. The others may oppose it. Virginia I think will be of this number. Besides other objections of less moment, she will insist on annexing a bill of rights to the new constitution, i.e., a bill wherein the government shall declare that 1. Religion shall be free. 2. Printing presses free. 3. Trials by jury preserved in all cases. 4. No monopolies in commerce. 5. No standing army. Upon receiving this bill of rights, she will probably depart from her other objections; and this bill is so much of the interest of all the states that I presume they will offer it, and thus our constitution be amended and our union closed by the end of the present year. In this way there will have been opposition enough to do good, and not enough to do harm. I have such reliance on the good sense of the body of the people and the honesty of their leaders, that I am not afraid of their letting things go wrong to any length in any case.

JAMES MADISON, GENERAL DEFENSE OF THE CONSTITUTION, VIRGINIA RATIFICATION CONVENTION
June 6, 1788

Editor's note: Madison was responding to Patrick Henry. The celebrated orator was an opponent of the Constitution.

I confess to you, sir, were uniformity of religion to be introduced by this system, it would, in my opinion, be ineligible; but I have no reason to conclude that uniformity of government will produce that of religion. This subject is, for the honor of America, perfectly free and unshackled. The government has no jurisdiction over it: the least reflection will convince us there is no danger to be feared on this ground.

JAMES MADISON, GENERAL DEFENSE OF THE CONSTITUTION, VIRGINIA RATIFICATION CONVENTION
June 12, 1788

Editor's note: Again, this is in response to Patrick Henry.

The honorable member has introduced the subject of religion. Religion is not guarded; there is no bill of rights declaring that religion should be secure. Is a bill of rights a security for religion? Would the bill of rights, in this state, exempt the people from paying for the support of one particular sect, if such sect were exclusively established by law? If there were a majority of one sect, a bill of rights would be a poor protection for liberty. Happily for the states, they enjoy the utmost freedom of religion. This freedom arises from that multiplicity of sects which pervades America, and which is the best and only security for religious liberty in any society; for where there is such a variety of sects, there cannot be a majority of any one sect to oppress and persecute the rest. Fortunately for this commonwealth, a majority of the people are decidedly against any exclusive establishment. I believe it to be so in the other states. There is not a shadow of right in the general government to intermeddle with religion. Its least interference with it would be a most flagrant usurpation. I can appeal to my uniform conduct on this subject, that I have warmly supported religious freedom. It is better that this security should be depended upon from the general legislature, than from one particular state. A particular state might concur in one religious project. But the United States abound in such a variety of sects, that it is a strong security against religious persecution; and it is sufficient to authorize a conclusion, that no one sect will ever be able to outnumber or depress the rest.

THOMAS JEFFERSON TO J. P. P. DERIEUX
July 25, 1788

I am truly sensible, Sir, of the honour you do me in proposing to me that of becoming one of the Sponsors of your child, and return you my sincere thanks for it. At the same time I am not a little mortified that scruples, perhaps not well founded, forbid my undertaking this honourable office. The person who becomes sponsor for a child, according to the ritual of the church in which I was educated, makes a solemn profession, before god and the world, of faith in articles, which I had never sense enough to comprehend, and it has always appeared to me that comprehension must precede assent. The difficulty of reconciling the ideas of Unity and Trinity, have, from a very early part of my life, excluded me from the office of sponsorship, often proposed to me by my friends, who have trusted, for the faithful discharge of it, to morality alone instead of which the church requires faith. Accept therefore Sir this conscientious excuse which I make with regret, which must find it's apology in my heart, while perhaps it may do no great honour to my head, and after presenting me with respect and affection to Madame de Rieux, be assured of my constant dispositions to render you service, and of the sincerity of those sentiments of esteem with which I have the honor to be, Sir, your most obedient & most humble servant.

THOMAS JEFFERSON TO JAMES MADISON
July 31, 1788

My letter to Mr. Jay, containing all the public news that is well authenticated, I will not repeat it here, but add some details in the smaller way, which you may be glad to know....

The Archbishop's brother, and the new minister Villedeuil, and Lambert, have no will of their own. They cannot raise money for the peace establishment the next year, without the States General; much less if there be war; and their administration will probably end with the States General....

The new regulations present a preponderance of good over their evil. But they suppose that the king can model the constitution at will, or in other words that this government is a pure despotism: the question then arising is whether a pure despotism, in a single head, or one which is divided among a king, nobles, priesthood, and numerous magistracy is the least bad. I should be puzzled to decide: but I hope they will have neither, and that they are advancing to a limited, moderate government, in which the people will have a good share.

I sincerely rejoice at the acceptance of our new constitution by nine States. It is a good canvas, on which some strokes only want retouching. What these are, I think are sufficiently manifested by the general voice from north to south, which calls for a bill of rights. It seems generally understood, that this should go to juries, habeas corpus, standing armies, printing, religion and monopolies. I conceive there may be difficulty in finding general modifications of these, suited to the habits of all the States. But if such cannot be found, then it is better to establish trials by jury, the right of habeas corpus, freedom of the press and freedom of religion, in all cases, and to abolish standing armies in time of peace, and monopolies in all cases, than not to do it in any. The few cases wherein these things may do evil, cannot be weighed against the multitude wherein the want of them will do evil.... A declaration that the federal government will never restrain the presses from printing anything they please, will not take away the liability of the printers for false facts printed. The declaration, that religious faith shall be unpunished, does not give impunity to criminal acts, dictated by religious error.

THOMAS JEFFERSON TO ST. JOHN DE CREVECOEUR
August 9, 1788

The contest here is exactly what it was in Holland: a contest between the monarchical and aristocratical parts of the government, for a monopoly of despotism over the people.... The parliamentary part of the aristocracy is alone firmly united. The Noblesse and Clergy, but especially the former, are divided partly between the parliamentary and the despotic party, and partly united with the real patriots, who are endeavoring to gain for the nation what they can, both from the parliamentary and the single despotism.

THOMAS JEFFERSON TO JOHN BROWN CUTTING
August 23, 1788

The interesting question now is how the States general shall be composed. There are 3. opinions: 1. To place the three estates, Clergy, Noblesse, and Commons, in three different houses. The clergy would probably like this, and some of the nobility. But it has no partisans out of those orders. 2. To put the Clergy and Noblesse into one house, and the Commons into another. The Noblesse will be generally for this. 3. To put the three orders into one house, and make the Commons the majority of that house. This reunites the greatest number of partisans, and I suspect it is well patronized in the ministry, which I am persuaded are proceeding bonâ fide to improve the constitution of their country. As to the opposition which the English expect from the personal character of the king, it proves they do not know what his personal character is. He is the honestest man in his kingdom, and the most regular and economical. He has no foible which will enlist him against the good of his people; and whatever constitution will promote this, he will befriend.

THOMAS JEFFERSON TO JOHN JAY
September 3, 1788

In my letter of the 20th. I informed you of the act of public bankruptcy which has taken place here.... The Archbishop was hereupon removed ... and M. Necker called in as Director General of finance. To soften the Archbishop's dismission, a cardinal's hat is asked for him from Rome, and his nephew promised the succession to the archbishopric of Sens. The public joy, on this change of administration, was very great indeed. The people of Paris were amusing themselves with trying and burning the Archbishop in effigy, and rejoicing on the appointment of M. Necker. The commanding officer of the city guards undertook to forbid this, and not being obeyed, he charged the mob with fixed bayonets, killed two or three, and wounded many. This stopped their rejoicings for that day; but enraged at being thus obstructed in amusements wherein they had committed no disorder whatever, they collected in great numbers the next day, attacked the guards in various places, burned ten or twelve guard houses, killed two or three of the guards, and had about 6. or 8. of their own number killed. The city was, hereupon, put under martial law, and after a while, the tumult subsided, and peace was restored.

JAMES MADISON, OBSERVATIONS ON JEFFERSON'S DRAUGHT OF A CONSTITUTION FOR VIRGINIA
[ca. October 15, 1788]

Editor's note: Madison critiqued Jefferson's 1783 draft for John Brown who had asked Madison for advice on a constitution for Kentucky, where a movement for separation from Virginia was growing.

Exclusions. Does not the exclusion of Ministers of the Gospel as such violate a fundamental principle of liberty by punishing a religious profession with the privation of a civil right? Does it not violate another article of the plan itself which exempts religion from the cognizance of Civil power? Does it not violate justice by at once taking away a right and prohibiting a compensation for it. And does it not in fine violate impartiality by shutting the door agst the Ministers of one religion and leaving it open for those of every other.

JAMES MADISON TO THOMAS JEFFERSON
October 17, 1788

My own opinion has always been in favor of a bill of rights; provided it be so framed as not to imply powers not meant to be included in the enumeration. At the same time I have never thought the omission a material defect, nor been anxious to supply it even by subsequent amendment, for any other reason than that it is anxiously desired by others. I have favored it because I supposed it might be of use, and if properly executed could not be of disservice. I have not viewed it in an important light 1. because I conceive that in a certain degree, though not in the extent argued

---

by Mr. Wilson, the rights in question are reserved by the manner in which the federal powers are granted. 2. because there is great reason to fear that a positive declaration of some of the most essential rights could not be obtained in the requisite latitude. I am sure that the rights of Conscience in particular, if submitted to public definition would be narrowed much more than they are likely ever to be by an assumed power. One of the objections in New England was that the Constitution by prohibiting religious tests opened a door for Jews Turks & infidels. 3. because the limited powers of the federal Government and the jealousy of the subordinate Governments, afford a security which has not existed in the case of the State Governments, and exists in no other. 4. because experience proves the inefficacy of a bill of rights on those occasions when its controul is most needed. Repeated violations of these parchment barriers have been committed by overbearing majorities in every State. In Virginia I have seen the bill of rights violated in every instance where it has been opposed to a popular current. Notwithstanding the explicit provision contained in that instrument for the rights of Conscience it is well known that a religious establishment wd. have taken place in that State, if the legislative majority had found as they expected, a majority of the people in favor of the measure; and I am persuaded that if a majority of the people were now of one sect, the measure would still take place and on narrower ground than was then proposed, notwithstanding the additional obstacle which the law has since created.

JAMES MADISON TO EDMUND PENDLETON
October 20, 1788

It appears from late foreign intelligence that war is likely to spread its flames still farther among the unfortunate inhabitants of the Old world. France is certainly enough occupied already with her internal fermentations. At present the struggle is merely between the aristocracy and the monarchy. The only chance in favor of the people lies in the mutual attempts of the Competitors to make their side of the question the popular one. The late measures of the Court have that tendency. The nobility and Clergy who wish to accelerate the States General wish at the same time to have it formed on the anticent [sic] model established on the feudal idea which excluded the people almost altogether. The Court has at length agreed to convene this assembly in May, but is endeavoring to counteract the aristocratic policy, by admitting the people to a greater share of representation. In both the parties there are some real friends to liberty who will probably take advantage of circumstances to promote their object. Of this description on the anti-court side is our friend the Marquis.

THOMAS JEFFERSON TO GEORGE WASHINGTON
November 4, 1788

As soon as the convocation of the States General was announced, a tranquility took place thro' the whole kingdom.... The court, to clear itself of the dispute, convened the Notables who had acted with general approbation on the former occasion, and referred to them the forms of calling and organizing the States-general. These

Notables consist principally of nobility and clergy, the few of the Tiers etat among them being either parliament-men, or other privileged persons. The court wished that in the future States general the members of the Tiers etat should equal those of both the other orders, and that they should form but one house, all together, and vote by persons, not by orders. But the Notables, in the true spirit of priests and nobles, combining together against the people, have voted by 5 bureaux out of 6, that the people or tiers etat shall have no greater number of deputies than each of the other orders separately, and that they shall vote by orders: so that the two orders concurring in a vote, the third will be overruled; for it is not here as in England where each of the three branches has a negative on the other two. If this project of theirs succeeds, a combination between the two houses of clergy and nobles, will render the representation of the Tiers etat merely nugatory. The bureaux are to assemble together to consolidate their separate votes; but I see no reasonable hope of their changing this. Perhaps the king, knowing that he may count on the support of the nation and attach it more closely to him, may take on himself to disregard the opinions of the notables in this instance, and may call an equal representation of the people, in which precedents will support him. In every event, I think the present disquiet will end well. The nation has been awakened by our revolution, they feel their strength, they are enlightened, their lights are spreading, and they will not retrograde.

THOMAS JEFFERSON TO JOHN PARADISE
November 22, 1788

The Notables are in session. They have proven themselves a meer combination of priests and Nobles against the people. The court wishes to give to the tiers etat as many deputies as the other two orders should have jointly in the states general. One bureau decided in favor of it by a majority of one voice; the other five bureaux against it by almost an unanimity.

THOMAS JEFFERSON TO JOHN ADAMS
December 5, 1788

The internal tranquillity of this country, which had never been so far compromitted as to produce bloodshed, was entirely reestablished by the announcing of the parliament and substitution of Mr. Necker in the department of finance instead of the Archbishop of Sens. The parliament which had called for the States general only thro' fear that they could not obtain otherwise their own restoration, being once restored, began to fear those very States general and to prepare cavils at the forms of calling and organizing them. The court to debarrass itself of the dispute, referred these to the same Notables who had acted, on a former occasion, with approbation. These Notables, being composed of Clergy, Nobility, members of parliament and some privileged persons of the tiers etat, have shamelessly combined against the rights of the people. The court wished the tiers should equal the two other orders by the number of their deputies in the State general, and that they should form one house only. Five bureaux out of 6. of the Notables have voted that the people shall have only as many members as each of the other orders singly, and that they shall vote by orders: so that the votes of the two houses of clergy and nobles concurring, that of the tiers etat will be overruled. The votes of the bureaux are not yet consolidated, but I see no reason to suppose that the separate votes will be changed in the consolidation.

JAMES MADISON TO THOMAS JEFFERSON
December 8, 1788

The questions which divide the public at present relate 1. to the extent of the amendments that ought to be made to the Constitution. 2. to the mode in which they ought to be made. The friends of the Constitution, some from an approbation of particular amendments, others from a spirit of conciliation, are generally agreed that the System should be revised. But they wish the revisal to be carried no farther than to supply additional guards for liberty, without abridging the sum of power transferred from the States to the general Government or altering previous to trial, the particular structure of the latter and are fixed in opposition to the risk of another Convention, whilst the purpose can be as well answered, by the other mode provided for introducing amendments. Those who have opposed the Constitution, are on the other hand, zealous for a second Convention, and for a revisal which may either not be restrained at all, or extend at least as far as alterations have been proposed by any State. Some of this class, are, no doubt, friends to an effective Government, and even to the substance of the particular Government in question. It is equally certain that there are others, who urge a Second Convention with the insidious hope, of throwing all things into Confusion, and of subverting the fabric just established, if not the Union itself. If the first Congress embrace the policy which circumstances mark out, they will not fail to propose of themselves, every desireable safeguard for popular rights; and by thus separating the well meaning from the designing opponents, fix on the latter their true character, and give the Government its due popularity and stability.

THOMAS JEFFERSON TO THOMAS PAINE
December 23, 1788

As to the affairs of this country, they have hitherto gone on well. The Court being decided to call the States General, know that the form of calling and constituting them would admit of cavil. They asked the advice of the Notables. These advised that the form of the last States General of 1614 be observed. In that, the commons had but about one-third of the whole number of members, and they voted by orders. The Court wished now that they should have one-half of the whole number of members, and that they should form but one house, not three. The parliament have taken up the subject, and given the opinion which the Court would have wished. We are, therefore, in hopes that, availing themselves of these contrary opinions, they will follow that which they wished. The priests and nobles threaten schism; and we do not know yet what form will ultimately be adopted. If no schism of this kind prevents it, the States will meet about March or April, and will obtain, without opposition from the Court, 1. Their own periodical convocation; 2. A share in the legislation; 3. The exclusive right to tax and appropriate the public money. They will attempt also to obtain a habeas corpus law and free press; but it does not appear to me that the nation is ripe to accept of these, if offered.

THOMAS JEFFERSON TO WILLIAM CARMICHAEL
December 25, 1788

The internal affairs of this country will I hope go on well. Neither the time, place, nor form of the States general are yet announced. But they will certainly meet in March or April. The clergy and nobility, as clergy and nobility eternally will, are opposed to giving to the tiers etat so effectual a representation as may dismount them from their backs. The court wishes to give to the unprivileged order an equal number of votes with the privileged, and that they should sit in one house. But the court is timid. Some are of opinion that a majority of the nobles are also on the side of the people. I doubt it when so great a proportion of the Notables, indeed almost an unanimity were against them, and 5. princes of the blood out of 7.

THOMAS JEFFERSON TO PÈRE CHAUVIER
December 27, 1788

Editor's note: Chauvier was the Géneral et Grand Ministre of the Order of Mathurins.

I will now, according to your kind permission, take the liberty of troubling you with the details relative to the American captives now at Algiers.... My present prayer to you, Sir, is that you will find means to have these unfortunate men subsisted as comfortably as their condition will admit. You were so thoughtful as to suggest that it would not be prudent to supply them so liberally as to let it be suspected by the captors that our government interests itself for them. I leave this entirely to your discretion, and will replace at a moment's warning whatever you may be so good as to have furnished for their subsistence and cloathing. I cannot conclude my letter, Sir, without expressing with what sincere pleasure I have observed the truly fraternal spirit with which you have undertaken to aid us in the relief of these our unfortunate brethren. A conduct so conformable with the genuine character of that religion, whose basis is charity and benevolence, proves that it's concerns could not have been deposited in more worthy hands, and is a title the more to those sentiments of gratitude, veneration and esteem with which I have the honour to be, Sir, you most obedient and most humble servant.

JAMES MADISON TO GEORGE EVE
January 2, 1789

Editor's note: Eve was a leading Virginia Baptist preacher.

Being informed that reports prevail not only that I am opposed to any amendments whatever to the new federal Constitution; but that I have ceased to be a friend to the rights of Conscience; and inferring from a conversation with my brother William, that you are disposed to contradict such reports as far as your knowledge of my sentiments may justify, I am led to trouble you with this communication of them. As a private Citizen it could not be my wish that erroneous opinions should be entertained, with respect to either of those points, particularly, with respect to religious liberty. But having been induced to offer my services to this district as its representative in the federal Legislature, considerations of a public nature make it proper that, with respect to both, my principles and views should be rightly understood.

I freely own that I have never seen in the Constitution as it now stands those serious dangers which have alarmed many respectable Citizens. Accordingly whilst it remained unratified, and it was necessary to unite the States in some one plan, I opposed all previous alterations as calculated to throw the States into dangerous contentions, and to furnish the secret enemies of the Union with an opportunity of promoting its dissolution. Circumstances are now changed: The Constitution is established on the ratifications of eleven States and a very great majority of the people of America; and amendments, if pursued with a proper moderation and in a proper mode, will be not only safe, but may serve the double purpose of satisfying the minds of well meaning opponents, and of providing additional guards in favour of liberty. Under this change of circumstances, it is my sincere opinion that the Constitution ought to be revised, and that the first Congress meeting under it, ought to prepare and recommend to the States for ratification, the most satisfactory provisions for all essential rights, particularly the rights of Conscience in the fullest latitude, the freedom of the press, trials by jury, security against general warrants &c.

THOMAS JEFFERSON TO THOMAS PAINE
January 5, 1789

No conveiance for my letter having yet occurred, I have an opportunity of adding to it the great decision of the court that the tiers etat shall elect a moiety of the states general. Had the contrary been decided, I think danger would have ensued. The deputies of the tiers etat would have come up with express instructions to agree to no tax imposed by an assembly in which they would have been so unequally represented. But, the decision being against the privileged orders, will there be no danger from them? The clergy all move heaven and earth to defeat the effect of this [just ?] representation. They will endeavor now that the votes shall be by orders, and not by persons. The Princes of the blood (Monsieur and the D. d'Orleans excepted) have threatened scission and if the clergy can bring over the majority of the noblesse to the same sentiments, a scission may be effected. But the young part of the nobility are in favor of the tiers etat, and the more advanced are daily coming over to them. So that I am in hopes, by the meeting of the states, there will remain against them only those whom age has rendered averse to new reasons and reformations.

THOMAS JEFFERSON TO THOMAS SHIPPEN
January 5, 1789

The great news of this country is that the late decision of the court that the tiers etat shall elect one half the members for the states general. The clergy, the princes, and the old nobles cry out against this. The younger part of the noblesse approve of it, and it's justice is every day becoming more firmly established in the public opinion. So that by the meeting of the states general I hope they will be ripe to decide whether that body shall vote by orders or persons.

THOMAS JEFFERSON TO RICHARD PRICE
January 8, 1789

Editor's note: Price had written Jefferson that "There has been in almost all religions a melancholy separation of religion from morality."

I concur with you strictly in your opinion of the comparative merits of atheism and demonism, and really see nothing but the latter in the being worshipped by many who think themselves Christians. Your opinions and writings will have effect in bringing others to reason on this subject....

You say you are not sufficiently informed about the nature and circumstances of the present struggle here. Having been on the spot from its first origin, and watched its movements as an uninterested spectator, with no other bias than a love of mankind, I will give you my ideas of it. Though celebrated writers of this and other countries had already sketched good principles on the subject of government, yet the American war seems first to have awakened the thinking part of this nation in general from the sleep of despotism in which they were sunk....

Happily for the nation, it happened that, at the same moment, the dissipations of the court had exhausted the money and credit of the State, and M. de Calonnes found himself obliged to appeal to the nation.... The Notables concurred with the minister in the necessity of reformation, adroitly avoided the demand of money, got him displaced, and one of their leading men placed in his room. The archbishop of Toulouse, by the aid of the hopes formed of him, was able to borrow some money, and he reformed considerably the expenses of the court.

Notwithstanding the prejudices since formed against him, he appeared to me to pursue the reformation of the laws and constitution as steadily as a man could do who had to drag the court after him, and even to conceal from them the consequences of the measures he was leading them into. In his time the criminal laws were reformed, provincial assemblies and States established in most of the provinces, the States General promised, and a solemn acknowledgment made by the King that he could not impose a new tax without the consent of the nation. It is true he was continually goaded forward by the public clamors, excited by the writings and workings of the Patriots, who were able to keep up the public fermentation at the exact point which borders on resistance, without entering on it. They had taken into their alliance the Parliaments also, who were led, by very singular circumstances, to espouse, for the first time, the rights of the nation. They had from old causes had personal hostility against M. de Calonnes. They refused to register his laws or his taxes, and went so far as to acknowledge they had no power to do it. They persisted in this with his successor, who therefore exiled them. Seeing that the nation did not interest themselves much for their recall, they began to fear that the new judicatures proposed in their place would be established and that their own suppression would be perpetual. In short, they found their own strength insufficient to oppose that of the King. They therefore insisted that the States General should be called. Here they became united with and supported by the Patriots, and their joint influence was sufficient to produce the promise of that assembly. I always suspected that the archbishop had no objections to this force under which they laid him. But the Patriots and Parliament insisted it was their efforts which extorted the promise against his will....

The court was well disposed towards the people, not from principles of justice or love to them; but they want money. No more can be had from the people. They are squeezed to the last drop. The clergy and nobles, by their privileges and influence, have kept their property in a great measure untaxed hitherto. They then remain to be squeezed, and no agent is powerful enough for this but the people. The court therefore must ally itself with the people.

But the Notables, consisting mostly of privileged characters, had proposed a method of composing the States, which would have rendered the voice of the people, or Tiers États, in the States General, inefficient for the purpose of the court. It concurred then with the Patriots in intriguing with the Parliament to get them to pass a vote in favor of the rights of the people. This vote, balancing that of the Notables, has placed the court at liberty to follow its own views, and they have determined that the Tiers Etat shall have in the States General as many votes as the clergy and nobles put together. Still a great question remains to be decided, that is, shall the States General vote by orders, or by persons? Precedents are both ways. The clergy will move heaven and earth to obtain the suffrage by orders, because that parries the effect of all hitherto done for the people. The people will probably send their deputies expressly instructed to consent to no tax, to no adoption of the public debts, unless the unprivileged part of the nation has a voice equal to that of the privileged; that is to say, unless the voice of the Tiers Etat be equalled to that of the clergy and nobles. They will have the young noblesse in general on their side, and the King and court. Against them will be the antient nobles and the clergy. So that I hope, upon the whole, that by the time they meet, there will be a majority of the nobles themselves in favor of the Tiers Etat.

THOMAS JEFFERSON TO JOHN JAY
January 11, 1789

As the character of the Prince of Wales is becoming interesting, I have endeavoured to learn what it truly is.... He has not a single idea of justice, morality, religion, or the rights of men, nor any anxiety for the opinion of the world. He carries that indifference for fame so far, that he would probably not be hurt were he to lose his throne, provided he could be assured of having always meat, drink, horses and women....

This country advances with a steady pace towards the establishment of a constitution whereby the people will resume the great mass of powers so fatally lodged in the hands of the king....

The clergy and the nobles, by their privileges and their influence, have hitherto screened their property in a great degree, from public contribution. That half of the orange, then, remains yet to be squeezed, and for this operation there is no agent powerful enough but the people. They are, therefore, brought forward as the favorites of the Court, and will be supported by them. The moment of crisis will be the meeting of the States; because their first act will be, to decide whether they shall vote by persons or by orders. The Clergy will leave nothing unattempted to secure the latter; for they see that the spirit of reformation will not confine itself to the political, but will extend to the ecclesiastical establishment also.

JAMES MADISON TO THOMAS MANN RANDOLPH
January 13, 1789

Whilst the Constitution was unratified, those who viewed the difficulties of uniting the various interests, and prejudices of the States, and the various opinions, and speculations of their political leaders, in any one plan whatever, were naturally led to withstand all previous amendments, as a dangerous road to public confusion.... Whatever opinion may be entertained as to this point, however, it is evident, that the change of situation produced by the establishment of the Constitution, leaves me in common with other friends of the Constitution, free, and consistent in espousing such a revisal of it, as will either make it better in itself; or without making it worse, will make it appear better to those, who now dislike it. It is accordingly, my sincere opinion, and wish, that in order to effect these purposes, the Congress, which is to meet in March, should undertake the salutary work. It is particularly, my opinion, that the clearest, and strongest provision ought to be made, for all those essential rights, which have been thought in danger, such as the right of conscience, the freedom of the press, trials by jury, exemption from general warrants, &c.

THOMAS JEFFERSON TO EDWARD BANCROFT
January 16, 1789

I have deferred answering your letter on the subject of slaves, because you permitted me to do it till a moment of leisure.... I do not recollect the conversation at Vincennes to which you allude, but can repeat still on the same ground, on which I must have done then, that as far as I can judge from the experiments which have been made, to give liberty to, or rather, to abandon persons whose habits have been formed in slavery is like abandoning children. Many quakers in Virginia seated their slaves on their lands as tenants. They were distant from me, and therefore I cannot be particular in the details, because I never had very particular information. I cannot say whether they were to pay a rent in money, or a share of the produce: but I remember that the landlord was obliged to plan their crops for them, to direct all their operations during every season and according to the weather, but what is more afflicting, he was obliged to watch them daily and almost constantly to make them work, and even to whip them. A man's moral sense must be unusually strong, if slavery does not make him a thief.

THOMAS JEFFERSON TO WILLIAM SHORT
January 22, 1789

The affairs of this kingdom go on well. The determination of the council to give to the tiers etat a representation equal to that of the privileged classes is opposed bitterly by the clergy and antient nobles, secretly by the parliament; but has in it's favor the body of the nation, the younger part of the noblesse and the handsome young women.

JAMES MADISON TO A RESIDENT OF SPOTSYLVANIA COUNTY
January 27, 1789

That the change of circumstances produced by the secure establishment of the plan proposed, leaves me free to espouse such amendments as will, in the most satisfactory manner, guard essential rights, and will render certain vexatious abuses of power impossible. That it is my wish, particularly, to see specific provision made on the subject of the Rights of Conscience, the Freedom of the Press, Trial by Jury, Exemption from General Warrants &c, to see, effectual provision made also for the periodical increase of the representatives, until the number shall amount to the fullest security on that head, and for prohibiting appeals to the federal court in cases that might be vexatious or superfluous. That there are a variety of other alterations which ought to be inserted, as either eligible in themselves, or as to those who think them so.

THOMAS JEFFERSON TO FRANCIS HOPKINSON
March 13, 1789

You say that I have been dished up to you as an antifederalist, and ask me if it be just. My opinion was never worthy enough of notice to merit citing; but since you ask it I will tell it you. I am not a Federalist, because I never submitted the whole system of my opinions to the creed of any party of men whatever in religion, in philosophy, in politics, or in anything else where I was capable of thinking for myself. Such an addiction is the last degradation of a free and moral agent. If I could not go to heaven but with a party, I would not go there at all....

What I disapproved from the first moment also was the want of a bill of rights to guard liberty against the legislative as well as executive branches of the government, that is to say to secure freedom in religion, freedom of the press, freedom from monopolies, freedom from unlawful imprisonment, freedom from a permanent military, and a trial by jury in all cases determinable by the laws of the land....

These, my dear friend, are my sentiments, by which you will see I was right in saying I am neither federalist nor antifederalist; that I am of neither party, nor yet a trimmer between parties. These my opinions I wrote within a few hours after I had read the constitution, to one or two friends in America. I had not then read one single word printed on the subject. I never had an opinion in politics or religion which I was afraid to own. A costive reserve on these subjects might have procured me more esteem from some people, but less from myself.

THOMAS JEFFERSON TO JAMES MADISON
March 15, 1789

Your thoughts on the subject of the Declaration of rights in the letter of Oct 17. I have weighed with great satisfaction. Some of them had not occurred to me before, but were acknoleged just in the moment they were presented to my mind. In the arguments in favor of a declaration of rights, you omit one which has great weight with me, the legal check which it puts into the hands of the judiciary. This is a body, which if rendered independent & kept strictly to their own department merits great confidence for their learning & integrity. In fact what degree of confidence would be too much for a body composed of such men as Wythe, Blair & Pendleton? On characters like these the 'civium ardor prava jubentium' [Horace - The passion of citizens lusting after depravities] would make no impression. I am happy to find that on the whole you are a friend to this amendment. The Declaration of rights is like all other human blessings alloyed with some inconveniences, and not accomplishing fully it's object. But the good in this instance vastly overweighs the evil. I cannot refrain from making short answers to the objections which your letter states to have been raised.

1. That the rights in question are reserved by the manner in which the federal powers are granted. Answer. A constitutive act may certainly be so formed as to need no declaration of rights. The act itself has the force of a declaration as far as it goes; and if it goes to all material points nothing more is wanting. In the draught of a constitution which I had once a thought of proposing in Virginia, & printed afterwards, I endeavored to reach all the great objects of public liberty, and did not mean to add a declaration of rights. Probably the object was imperfectly executed; but the deficiencies would have been supplied by others, in the course of discussion. But in a constitutive act which leaves some precious articles unnoticed, and raises implications against others, a declaration of rights becomes necessary by way of supplement. This is the case of our new federal constitution. This instrument forms us into one state as to certain objects, and gives us a legislative & executive body for these objects. It should therefore guard us against their abuses of power within the field submitted to them.

2. A positive declaration of some essential rights could not be obtained in the requisite latitude. Answer. Half a loaf is better than no bread. If we cannot secure all our rights, let us secure what we can.

3. The limited powers of the federal government & jealousy of the subordinate governments afford a security which exists in no other instance. Answer. The first member of this seems resolvable into the first objection before stated. The jealousy of the subordinate governments is a precious reliance. But observe that those governments are only agents. They must have principles furnished them whereon to found their opposition. The declaration of rights will be the text whereby they will try all the acts of the federal government, In this view it is necessary to the federal government also; as by the same text they may try the opposition of the subordinate governments.

4. Experience proves the inefficacy of a bill of rights. True. But tho it is not absolutely efficacious under all circumstances, it is of great potency always, and rarely inefficacious. A brace the more will often keep up the building which would have fallen with that brace the less. There is a remarkable difference between the characters of the Inconveniences which attend a Declaration of rights, & those which attend the want of it. The inconveniences of the Declaration are that it may cramp government in it's useful exertions. But the evil of this is short-lived, trivial & reparable. The inconveniences of the want of a Declaration are permanent, afflicting & irreparable. They are in constant progression from bad to worse. The executive in our governments is not the sole, it is scarcely the principal object of my jealousy. The tyranny of the legislatures is the most formidable dread at present, and will be for long years. That of the executive will come in it's turn, but it will be at a remote period. I know there are some among us who would now establish a monarchy. But they are inconsiderable in number and weight of character. The rising race are all republicans. We were educated in royalism; no wonder if some of us retain that idolatry still. Our young people are educated in republicanism, an apostasy from that to royalism is unprecedented & impossible. I am much pleased with the prospect that a declaration of rights will be added; and hope it will be done in that way which will not endanger the whole frame of the government, or any essential part of it....

The English papers tell you the King is well: and even the English ministry say so. They will naturally set the best foot foremost: and they guard his person so well that it is difficult for the public to contradict them. The King is probably better, but not well by a great deal.... They have carried the king to church; but it was his private chapel. If he be well why do not they shew him publicly to the nation, & raise them from that consternation into which they have been thrown by the prospect of being delivered over to the profligate hands of the prince of Wales.

Thomas Jefferson to Thomas Paine
March 17, 1789

The question of voting by persons or orders is the most controverted: but even that seems to have gained already a majority among the Nobles.... The D. d'Orleans has given instructions to his proxies in the Baillages which would be deemed bold in England, and are reasonable beyond the reach of an Englishman, who slumbering under a kind of half reformation in politics and religion is not excited by any thing he sees or feels to question the remains of prejudice. The writers of this country now taking the field freely, and unrestrained or rather revolted by prejudice, will rouse us all from the errors in which we have been hitherto rocked.

THOMAS JEFFERSON TO COLONEL DAVID HUMPHREYS
March 18, 1789

The change in this country since you left it, is such as you can form no idea of. The frivolities of conversation have given way entirely to politics.... The King.... has not offered a participation in the legislature, but it will surely be insisted on. The public mind is so ripened on all these subjects, that there seems to be now but one opinion. The clergy, indeed, think separately, and the old men among the Nobles; but their voice is suppressed by the general one of the nation. The writings published on this occasion are some of them very valuable; because, unfettered by the prejudices under which the English labour, they give a full scope to reason, and strike out truths as yet unperceived and unacknoleged on the other side of the channel. An Englishman, dozing under a kind of half reformation, is not excited to think by such gross absurdities as stare a Frenchman in the face, wherever he looks, whether it be towards the throne or the alter.

THOMAS JEFFERSON TO JOHN PAUL JONES
March 23, 1789

In this country, things go on well. The States general are to meet the 27th.... The States will be composed of about 300 clergy, 300 Nobles, and 600 commoners, and their first question will be whether they shall vote by orders or persons. I think the latter will be decided. If this difficulty be got over, I see no other to a very happy settlement of their affairs.

JAMES MADISON, FIRST INAUGURAL ADDRESS OF GEORGE WASHINGTON
April 30, 1789

Editor's note: The University Press of Virginia edition of The Papers of James Madison, *declares that "Although no draft in his hand survives, there is good reason to believe that JM composed Washington's first inaugural address." Although no draft by Madison exists, a May 5th note by Washington to Madison asks him to write yet another speech: "as you have began (sic), so I would wish you to finish, the good work in a short reply to the Address of the House of Representatives."*

Fellow-Citizens of the Senate and of the House of Representatives....

Such being the impressions under which I have, in obedience to the public summons, repaired to the present station, it would be peculiarly improper to omit in this first official act my fervent supplications to that Almighty Being who rules over the universe, who presides in the councils of nations, and whose providential aids can supply every human defect, that His benediction may consecrate to the liberties and happiness of the people of the United States a Government instituted by themselves for these essential purposes, and may enable every instrument employed in its administration to execute with success the functions allotted to his charge. In tendering this homage to the Great Author of every public and private good, I assure myself that it expresses your sentiments not less than my own, nor those of my fellow-citizens at large less than either. No people can be bound to acknowledge and adore the Invisible Hand which conducts the affairs of men more than those of the United States. Every step by which they have advanced to the character of an independent nation seems to have been distinguished by some token of providential agency; and in the important revolution just accomplished in the system of their united government the tranquil deliberations and voluntary consent of so many distinct communities from which the event has resulted can not be compared with the means by which most governments have been established without some return of pious gratitude, along with an humble anticipation of the future blessings which the past seem to presage. These reflections, arising out of the present crisis, have forced themselves too strongly on my mind to be suppressed. You will join with me, I trust, in thinking that there are none under the influence of which the proceedings of a new and free government can more auspiciously commence....

Besides the ordinary objects submitted to your care, it will remain with your judgment to decide how far an exercise of the occasional power delegated by the fifth article of the Constitution is rendered expedient at the present juncture by the nature of objections which have been urged against the system, or by the degree of inquietude which has given birth to them. Instead of undertaking particular recommendations on this subject, in which I could be guided by no lights derived from official opportunities, I shall again give way to my entire confidence in your discernment and pursuit of the public good; for I assure myself that whilst you carefully avoid every alteration which might endanger the benefits of an united and effective government, or which ought to await the future lessons of experience, a reverence for the characteristic rights of freemen and a regard for the public harmony will sufficiently influence your deliberations on the question how far the former can be impregnably fortified or the latter be safely and advantageously promoted....

Having thus imparted to you my sentiments as they have been awakened by the occasion which brings us together, I shall take my present leave; but not without resorting once more to the benign Parent of the Human Race in humble supplication that, since He has been pleased to favor the American people with opportunities for deliberating in perfect tranquillity, and dispositions for deciding with unparalleled unanimity on a form of government for the security of their union and the advancement of their happiness, so His divine blessing may be equally conspicuous in the enlarged views, the temperate consultations, and the wise measures on which the success of this Government must depend.

JAMES MADISON, ADDRESS OF THE HOUSE OF REPRESENTATIVES
TO THE PRESIDENT
May 5, 1789

Editor's note: Madison wrote the address in his capacity as chair of a House committee.

In forming the pecuniary provision for the Executive department, we shall not lose sight of a wish resulting from motives which give it a peculiar claim to our regard. Your resolution, in a moment critical to the liberties of your Country, to renounce all personal emolument, was among the many presages of your patriotic services....

Such are the sentiments which we have thought fit to address to you. They flow from our own hearts; and we verily believe that among the millions we represent, there is not a virtuous citizen whose heart will disown them.

All that remains is that we join in your fervent supplication for the blessings of Heaven on our Country; and that we add our own for the choicest of these blessings on the MOST BELOVED OF HER CITIZENS.

THOMAS JEFFERSON TO MARQUIS DE LAFAYETTE
May 6, 1789

The Noblesse, and especially the Noblesse of Auvergne, will always prefer men who will do their dirty work for them. You are not made for that. They will, therefore, soon drop you, and the people, in that case, will perhaps not take you up. Suppose a scission should take place. The Priests and Nobles will secede, the nation will remain in place, and, with the King, will do its own business. If violence should be attempted, where will you be? You cannot then take side with the people in opposition to your own vote, that very vote which will have helped to produce the scission. Still less can you array yourself against the people. That is impossible. Your instructions are, indeed, a difficulty. But to state this at its worst it is only a single difficulty, which a single effort surmounts. Your instructions can never embarrass you a second time, whereas an acquiescence under them will reproduce greater difficulties every day, and without end. Besides, a thousand circumstances offer as many justifications of your departure from Your instructions. Will it be impossible to persuade all parties that (as for good legislation two Houses are necessary) the placing the privileged classes together in one House, and the unprivileged in another, would be better for both than a scission? I own, I think it would. People can never agree without some sacrifices; and it appears but a moderate sacrifice in each party, to meet on this middle ground. The attempt to bring this about might satisfy your instructions, and a failure in it would justify your siding with the people, even to those who think instructions are laws of conduct.

JAMES MADISON, GEORGE WASHINGTON'S REPLY OF THE PRESIDENT TO THE HOUSE OF REPRESENTATIVES
May 8, 1789

Editor's note: Nothing better demonstrates the centrality of Madison in the creation of the government of the United States than the fact that he ghostwrote the reply of the first President under the Constitution, of which he is called "the father," to an address of the first House, which he also wrote.

Your very affectionate Address produces emotions which I know not how to express. I feel my past endeavors in the service of my Country are far Overpaid by its goodness: and I fear much that my future ones may not fulfill you kind Anticipation. All that I can promise is, that they will be invariably directed by an honest and an ardent zeal. Of this resource my heart assures me. For all beyond, I rely on the wisdom and patriotism of those with whom I am to cooperate, and a continuance of the blessings of Heaven on our beloved Country.

THOMAS JEFFERSON TO WILLIAM CARMICHAEL
May 8, 1789

The States general were opened the day before yesterday. Viewing it as an Opera it was imposing; as a scene of business the king's speech was exactly what it should have been and very well delivered, not a word of the chancellor's was heard by any body, so that as yet I have never heard a single guess at what it was about. Mr. Necker's was as good as such a number of details would permit it to be. The picture of their resources was consoling and generally plausible. I could have wished him to have dwelt more on those great constitutional reformations which his 'Rapport au roy' had prepared us to expect. But they observe that these points were proper for the speech of the Chancellor. We are in hopes therefore they were in that speech, which, like the Revelations of St. John, were no revelations at all. The Noblesse on coming together shew that they are not as much reformed in the principles as we had hoped they would be. In fact there is real danger of their totally refusing to vote by persons. Some found hopes on the lower clergy which constitutes four fifths of the deputies of that order. If they do not turn the balance in favour of the tiers etat, there is real danger of a scission. But I shall not consider even that event as rendering things desperate. If the king will do business with the tiers etat which constitutes the nation, it may be well done without priests or nobles.

THOMAS JEFFERSON TO JOHN JAY
May 9, 1789

The progress of light and liberality in the order of the Noblesse, has equaled expectation in Paris only, and its vicinities. The great mass of deputies of that order, which come from the country, shew that the habits of tyranny over the people, are deeply rooted in them. They will consent, indeed, to equal taxation; but five-sixths of that chamber are thought to be, decidedly, for voting by orders; so that, had this great preliminary question rested on this body, which formed heretofore the sole hope, that hope would have been completely disappointed. Some aid, however, comes in from a quarter whence none was expected. It was imagined the ecclesiastical elections would have been generally in favor of the higher clergy; on the contrary, the lower clergy have obtained five-sixths of these deputations. These are the sons of peasants, who have done all the drudgery of the service, for ten, twenty and thirty guineas a year, and whose oppressions and penury, contrasted with the pride and luxury of the higher clergy, have rendered them perfectly disposed to humble the latter. They have done it, in many instances, with a boldness they were thought insusceptible of. Great hopes have been formed, that these would concur with the Tiers Etat, in voting by persons. In fact, about half of them seem as yet so disposed; but the bishops are intriguing, and drawing them over with the address which has ever marked ecclesiastical intrigue....

The Tiers Etat, as constituting the nation, may propose to do the business of the nation, either with or without the minorities in the Houses of Clergy and Nobles, which side with them. In that case, if the King should agree to it, the majorities in those two Houses would secede, and might resist the tax gatherers. This would bring on a civil war. On the other hand, the privileged orders, offering to submit to equal taxation, may propose to the King to continue the government in its former train, resuming to himself the power of taxation. Here, the tax gatherers might be resisted by the people. In fine, it is but too possible, that between parties so animated, the King may incline the balance as he pleases. Happy that he is an honest, unambitious man, who desires neither money nor power for himself; and that his most operative minister, though he has appeared to trim a little, is still, in the main, a friend to public liberty.

THOMAS JEFFERSON TO JAMES MADISON
May 11, 1789

The nobility of & about Paris have come over as was expected to the side of the people in the great question of voting by persons or orders.... The clergy seem at present much divided. Five sixths of that representation consists of the lower clergy, who, being the sons of the peasantry, are very well with the tiers etat. But the bishops are intrigueing & drawing them over daily. The tiers etat is so firm to vote by persons or to go home, that it is impossible to conjecture what will be the result.

JAMES MADISON, GEORGE WASHINGTON'S REPLY OF THE
PRESIDENT TO THE SENATE
May 18, 1789

Editor's note: Washington wrote Madison on the 17th: "Mr. Madison having been so obliging as to draw the answer to the Address of the House of Representatives - GW. would thank him for doing the same to that of the Senate."

I Thank you for your Address.... I now feel myself inexpressibly happy in a belief, that Heaven, which has done so much for our infant Nation will not withdraw its Providential influence before our political felicity shall have been completed; and in a conviction, that the Senate will at all times co-operate in every measure, which may tend to promote the welfare of this confederated Republic. Thus supported by a firm trust in a great Arbiter of the Universe, aided by the collected wisdom of the Union, and imploring the Divine benediction on our joint exertions in the service of our Country, I readily engage with you in the arduous, but pleasing, task of attempting to make a Nation happy.

THOMAS JEFFERSON TO THOMAS PAINE
May 19, 1789

You know that the States General have met, and probably have seen the speeches at the opening of them. The three orders sit in distinct chambers. The great question, whether they shall vote by orders or persons can never be surmounted amicably. It has not yet been proposed in form; but the votes which have been taken on the out-works of that question show that the Tiers Etat are unanimous, a good majority of the clergy (consisting of the Curés) disposed to side with the Tiers Etat, and in the chamber of the Noblesse, there are only fifty-four in that sentiment, against one hundred and ninety, who are for voting by orders. Committees to find means of conciliation are appointed by each chamber; but conciliation is impossible. Some think the Nobles could be induced to unite themselves with the higher Clergy into one House, the lower Clergy and Tiers Etat forming another. But the Tiers Etat are immovable. They are not only firm, but a little disdainful. The question is, what will ensue? One idea is to separate, in order to consult again their constituents, and to take new instructions. This would be doing nothing, for the same instructions would be repeated; and what, in the meantime, is to become of a government, absolutely without money, and which cannot be kept in motion with less than a million of livres a day? The more probable expectation is as follows. As soon as it shall become evident that no amicable determination of the manner of voting can take place, the Tiers Etat will send an invitation to the two other orders to come and take their places in the common chamber. A majority of the Clergy will go, and the minority of the Noblesse. The chamber thus composed will declare that the States General are constituted, will notify it to the King, and that they are ready to proceed to business. If the King refuses to do business with them, and adheres to the Nobles, the common chamber will declare all taxes at an end, will form a declaration of rights, and do such other acts as circumstances will permit, and go home. The tax-gatherers will then be resisted, and it may well be doubted whether the soldiery and their officers will not divide, as the Tiers Etat and Nobles. But it is more likely that the King will agree to do business with the States General.

JAMES MADISON, NOTES FOR SPEECH IN CONGRESS
[ca. June 8, 1789]

Reasons urging amendts.
1. to prove fedts. friends to liberty
2. remove remaining inquietudes
3. bring in N. C. and R. Island
4. to improve the Constitution

Reasons for moderating the plan
1. No stop if door opend to theoretic amendts.
2. as likely to make worse as better till trial
3. insure passage by 2/3 of Congs. & 3/4 of Sts.

Objectns. of 3 kinds vs the Constn:
1. vs. the theory of its structure
2. vs. substance of its powers - elections & direct taxes
3. vs. omission of guards in favr. of rights & libertys

The last most urged & easiest obviated.
Read the amendments

They relate 1st. to private rights

Bill of Rights - useful - not essential

fallacy on both sides - especy as to English Decln. of Rts
1. mere act of parlt.
2. no freedom of press - Conscience
     Gl. Warrants - Habs. corpus
     jury in Civil Causes - criml.
     attainders - arms to Protestts.

frequent parlts. cheif trust

freedom of press & Conscience unknown to Magna Cha. & Pet: Rts

Contents of Bills of Rhts
1. assertion of primitive equality &c.
2. do. of rights exerted in formg. Govts.
3. natural rights, retained - as Speech, Con:
4. positive rights resultg. - as trial by jury
5. Doctrinl. artics. as Depts. distinct - Electns free
6. moral precepts for the adminstrn. & natil. character - as justice - Oeconomy - &c

———

Object of Bill of Rhts

To limit & qualify powr. by exceptg. from grant cases in whc. it shall not be exercised or exd. in a particular manner.

to guard 1. vs. Executive & in Engd. &c
        2. Legislative as in Sts
        3. the majority of people

ought to point vs greatest danger which in Rep: is Prerogative of majority

Here proper, tho' less nessary., than in small Repubs

Objectns. vs. Bill of Rhts.

1. in Elective Govt. all power in people
    hence unnecessary & improper - this vs. Sts
2. In fedl. Govt. all not given retained
    Bill of powers - needs no bill of Rhts

Sweeping clause - Genl Warrants &c
3. St: Bills not repeald.

too uncertain

Some Sts have not bills - others defect: - others - injurious - as Protestts.
4. disparage other rights - or constructively enlarge

the first goes vs St: Bills

both guarded vs. by amendt.
5. Not effectl. vs Sts also - but some check

Courts will aid - also Ex: also.

Sts Legisls: watch

Time sanctify - incorporate public Sentiment

Bill of Rts ergo. proper

II increase of Reps. 2 for each H.

III pay of Congs.

IV Interdict to States as to Conscience - press - & Jury
this more necsy. to Sts. than Congs.

V Check on appeals & Common law

VI. partn. as to 3 Depts. & do. as to Genl. & St: Govts.

JAMES MADISON, PROPOSED AMENDMENTS TO THE CONSTITUTION, HOUSE OF REPRESENTATIVES
June 8, 1789

I will state my reasons why I think it proper to propose amendments; and state the amendments themselves, so far as I think they ought to be proposed....

That in article 1st, section 9, between clauses 3 and 4, be inserted these clauses, to wit: The civil rights of none shall be abridged on account of religious belief or worship, nor shall any national religion be established, nor shall the full and equal rights of conscience be in any manner, or on any pretext infringed.... The right of the people to keep and bear arms shall not be infringed; a well armed and well regulated militia being the best security of a free country: but no person religiously scrupulous of bearing arms shall be compelled to render military service in person....

That in article 1st, section 10, between clauses 1 and 2, be inserted this clause, to wit:

No State shall violate the equal rights of conscience, or the freedom of the press, or the trial by jury in criminal cases....

The first of these amendments relates to what may be called a bill of rights. I will own that I never considered this provision so essential to the federal constitution, as to make it improper to ratify it, until such an amendment was added; at the same time, I always conceived, that in a certain form and to a certain extent, such a provision was neither improper nor altogether useless. I am aware, that a great number of the most respectable friends to the government and champions for republican liberty, have thought such a provision, not only unnecessary, but even improper; nay, I believe some have gone so far as to think it even dangerous. Some policy has been made use of perhaps by gentlemen on both sides of the question: I acknowledge the ingenuity of those arguments which were drawn against the constitution, by a comparison with the policy of Great-Britain, in establishing a declaration of rights; but there is too great a difference in the case to warrant the comparison: therefore the arguments drawn from that source, were in a great measure inapplicable. In the declaration of rights which that country has established, the truth is, they have gone no farther, than to raise a barrier against the power of the crown; the power of the legislature is left altogether indefinite. Although I know whenever the great rights, the trial by jury, freedom of the press, or liberty of conscience, came in question in that body, the invasion of them is resisted by able advocates, yet their Magna Charta does not contain any one provision for the security of those rights, respecting which, the people of America are most alarmed. The freedom of the press and rights of conscience, those choicest privileges of the people, are unguarded in the British constitution.

But although the case may be widely different, and it may not be thought necessary to provide limits for the legislative power in that country, yet a different opinion prevails in the United States. The people of many states, have thought it necessary to raise barriers against power in all forms and departments of Government, and I am inclined to believe, if once bills of rights are established in all the states as well as the federal constitution, we shall find that although some of them are rather unimportant, yet, upon the whole, they will have a salutary tendency.

It may be said, in some instances, they do no more than state the perfect equality of mankind. This to be sure is an absolute truth, yet it is not absolutely necessary to be inserted at the head of a constitution....

It may be thought all paper barriers against the power of the community are too weak to be worthy of attention. I am sensible they are not so strong as to satisfy gentlemen of every description who have seen and examined thoroughly the texture of such a defence; yet, as they have a tendency to impress some degree of respect for them, to establish the public opinion in their favor, and rouse the attention of the whole community, it may be one means to control the majority from those acts to which they might be otherwise inclined....

I wish also, in revising the constitution, we may throw into that section, which interdicts the abuse of certain powers in the State Legislatures, some other provisions of equal if not greater importance than those already made. The words, "No state shall pass any bill of attainder, ex post facto law," etc. were wise and proper restrictions in the constitution. I think there is more danger of those powers being abused by the State Governments than by the Government of the United States. The same may be said of other powers which they possess, if not controlled by the general principle, that laws are unconstitutional which infringe the rights of the community. I should therefore wish to extend this interdiction, and add, as I have stated in the 5th resolution, that no State shall violate the equal right of conscience, freedom of the press, or trial by jury in criminal cases; because it is proper that every Government should be disarmed of powers which trench upon those particular rights. I know, in some of the state constitutions, the power of the Government is controlled by such a declaration, but others are not. I cannot see any reason against obtaining even a double security on those points; and nothing can give a more sincere proof of the attachment of those who opposed this constitution to these great and important rights, than to see them join in obtaining the security I have now proposed; because it must be admitted, on all hands, that the State Governments are as liable to attack these invaluable privileges as the general government is, and therefore ought to be as cautiously guarded against.

THOMAS JEFFERSON TO JAMES MADISON
June 18, 1789

Committees of conciliation having failed in their endeavors to bring together the three chambers of the States general, the king proposed a specific mode of verifying their powers: for that having been the first question which presented itself to them, was the one on which the question of voting by persons or orders was first brought on. The Clergy accepted unconditionally. The Noblesse accepted on conditions which reduced the acceptance to nothing at all....

We shall know, I think, within a day or two, whether the government will risk a bankruptcy & civil war, rather than see all distinction of orders done away, which is what the Commons will push for.... The Noblesse, on the contrary, are absolutely out of their senses. They are so furious, they can seldom debate at all. They have few men of moderate talents, & not one of great, in the majority. Their proceedings have been very injudicious. The Clergy are waiting to profit by every incident to secure themselves, & have no other object in view. Among the Commons there is an entire unanimity on the great question of voting by persons. Among the Noblesse there are about 60. for the Commons, and about three times that number against them. Among the Clergy, about 20 have already come over & joined the Commons, and in the course of a few days they will be joined by many more, not, indeed, making the majority of that House, but very near it. The bishops & archbishops have been very successful by bribes and intrigues, in detaching the Curés from the Commons, to whom they were at first attached to a man.... The Curés thro' the kingdom, form the mass of the Clergy; they are the only part favorably known to the people, because solely charged with the dues of baptism, burial, confession, visitation of the sick, instruction of the children, & aiding the poor; they are themselves of the people, & united with them. The carriages & equipage only of the higher Clergy, not their persons, are known to the people, & are in detestation with them. The souldiers will follow their officers, that is to say, their captains, lieutenants & ensigns.

THOMAS JEFFERSON TO JOHN JAY
June 24, 1789

The declaration prepared by Mr. Necker, while it censured in general the proceedings both of the Nobles and Commons, announced the King's views such as substantially to coincide with the Commons. It was agreed to in Council, as also that the séance royale should be held on the 22nd, and the meetings till then be suspended. While the Council was engaged in this deliberation at Marly, the Chamber of the Clergy was in debate, whether they should accept the invitation of the Tiers to unite with them in the common chamber. On the first question, to unite simply and unconditionally, it was decided in the negative by a very small majority. As it was known, however, that some members who had voted in the negative, would be for the affirmative with some modifications, the question was put with these modifications, and it was determined by a majority of eleven members, that their body should join the Tiers. These proceedings of the Clergy were unknown to the Council at Marly, and those of the Council were kept secret from everybody. The next morning (the 20th), the members repaired to the House as usual, found the doors shut and guarded, and a proclamation posted up for holding a séance royale on the 22nd, and a suspension of their meetings till then. They presumed, in the first moment, that their dissolution was decided, and repaired to another place, where they proceeded to business. They there bound themselves to each other by an oath, never to separate of their own accord, till they had settled a constitution for the nation on a solid basis, and if separated by force, that they would reassemble in some other place. It was intimated to them, however, that day, privately, that the proceedings of the séance royale would be favorable to them. The next day they met in a church, and were joined by a majority of the Clergy. The heads of the aristocracy saw that all was lost without some violent exertion.... They procured a committee to be held, consisting of the King and his ministers, to which Monsieur and the Count d'Artois should be admitted.... The nobility were in triumph, the people in consternation. When the King passed the next day through the lane ... there was a dead silence.... This must have been sensible to the King. He had ordered, in the close of his speech, that the members should follow him, and resume their deliberations the next day. The Noblesse followed him, and so did the Clergy, except about thirty, who, with the Tiers, remained in the room, and entered into deliberation. They protested against what the King had done, adhered to all their former proceedings, and resolved the inviolability of their own persons. An officer came twice to order them out of the room, in the King's name, but they refused to obey.... This is the state of things, as late as I am able to give them with certainty, at this moment. I shall go to Versailles tomorrow, and be able to add the transactions of this day and tomorrow.

June 25. Just returned from Versailles, I am enabled to continue my narration. On the 24th, nothing remarkable passed, except an attack by the mob of Versailles on the Archbishop of Paris, who had been one of the instigators of the court, to the proceedings of the séance royale. They threw mud and stones at his carriage, broke the windows of it, and he in a fright promised to join the Tiers.

This day (the 25th) forty-eight of the Nobles have joined the Tiers. Among them is the Duke d'Orleans. The Marquis de La Fayette could not be of the number, being restrained of his instructions or to accept his resignation. There are with the Tiers now, one hundred and sixty-four members of the Clergy, so that the common chamber consists of upwards of eight hundred members. The minority of the Clergy, however, call themselves the chamber of the Clergy, and pretend to go on with business....

During the continuance of this crisis and my own stay, I shall avail myself of every private conveyance to keep you informed of what passes.

THOMAS JEFFERSON TO JOHN JAY
June 29, 1789

My letter of the 25th gave you the transactions of the States General to the afternoon of that day. On the next, the Archbishop of Paris joined the Tiers, as did some others of the Clergy and Noblesse.... I have mentioned to you the ferment into which the proceedings at the séance royale of the 23rd, had thrown the people. The soldiery also were affected by it.... They began to quit their barracks.... The operation of this medicine, at Versailles, was as sudden as it was powerful. The alarm there was so complete, that in the afternoon of the 27th, the King wrote a letter to the President of the Clergy, the Cardinal de La Rochefoucault, in these words:

"My Cousin - Wholly engaged in promoting the general good of my kingdom, and desirous, above all things, that the Assembly of the States General should apply themselves to objects of general interest, after the voluntary acceptance by your order of my declaration of the 23d of the present month; I pass my word that my faithful Clergy will, without delay, unite themselves with the other two orders, to hasten the accomplishment of my paternal views. Those, whose powers are too limited, may decline voting until new powers are procured. This will be a new mark of attachment which my Clergy will give me. I pray God, my Cousin, to have you in his holy keeping. - Louis."

A like letter was written to the Duke de Luxemburgh, President of the Noblesse.... and they went in a body and took their seats with the Tiers, and thus rendered the union of the orders in one chamber complete....

Tomorrow they will recommence business, voting by persons on all questions; and whatever difficulties may be opposed in debate by the malcontents of the Clergy and Nobility, everything must be finally settled at the will of the Tiers.

THOMAS JEFFERSON TO THOMAS PAINE
July 11, 1789

The National Assembly then (for this is the name they take), have shown through every stage of these transactions a coolness, wisdom, and resolution to set fire to the four corners of the kingdom and to perish with it themselves, rather than relinquish an iota from their plan of a total change of government, are now in complete and undisputed possession of the sovereignty. The executive and aristocracy are at their feet; the mass of the nation, the mass of the clergy, and the army are with them; they have prostrated the old government, and are now beginning to build one from the foundation.... You see that these are the materials of a superb edifice, and the hands which have prepared them, are perfectly capable of putting them together, and filling up the work of which these are only the outlines.

THOMAS JEFFERSON TO RICHARD PRICE
July 12, 1789

Editor's note: The Socinian doctrine referred to below was enunciated by Lelio Sozzini (1525-1562) and Fausto Sozzini (1539-1604). They rejected the doctrines of the trinity and atonement but accepted Jesus as "a subaltern god to whom the supreme god gave over the command of the world."

I have already informed you that the proceedings of the states general were tied up by the difficulty which arose as to the manner of voting, whether it should be by persons or orders. The Tiers at length gave an ultimate invitation to the other two orders to come and join them, informing them at the same time that if they did not they would proceed without them. The majority of the clergy joined them. The king then interposed by the séance royale of which you have heard. The decision he undertook to pronounce was declared null by the assembly and they proceeded to business. Tumults in Paris and Versailles and still more the declared defection of the Souldiery to the popular cause produced from the king an invitation of the Nobles and the minority of the clergy to go and join the common assembly. They did so, and since that time the three orders are in one room, voting by persons, and without any sensible dissentions. Still the body of the nobles are rankling at the heart; but I see no reason to apprehend any great evil from it....

The Declaration of the rights of man, which constitutes the 1st. chapter of this work, was brought in the day before yesterday, and referred to the bureaus. You will observe that these are the outlines of a great work, and be assured that the body engaged in it are equal to a masterly execution of it. They may meet with some difficulties from within their body and some from without. There may be small and temporary checks. But I think they will persevere to it's accomplishment. The mass of the people is with them: the effective part of the clergy is with them: so I beleive is the souldiery and a respectable proportion of the officers. They have against them the high officers, the high clergy, the noblesse and the parliaments. This you see is an army of officers without souldiers. Should this revolution succeed, it is the beginning of the reformation of the governments of Europe....

Is there any good thing on the subject of the Socinian doctrine, levelled to a mind not habituated to abstract reasoning? I would thank you to recommend such a work to me. Or have you written any thing of that Kind? That is what I should like best, as none are so easy to be understood as those who understand themselves.

THOMAS JEFFERSON TO JOHN JAY
July 19, 1789

The demolition of the Bastille was now ordered, and begun. A body of the Swiss guards of the regiment of Ventimille, and the city horse guards, joined the people.... The aristocrats of the Nobles and Clergy in the States General, vied with each other in declaring how sincerely they were converted to the justice of voting by persons, and how determined to go with the nation all its lengths.... the Count d'Artois and Monsieur de Montisson (a deputy connected with him), Madame de Polignac, Madame de Guiche, and the Count de Vaudreuil, favorites of the Queen, the Abbé de Vermont, her confessor, the Prince of Condé and the Duke of Bourbon, all fled; we know not whither.... The churches are now occupied in singing "De profundis" and "Requiems" "for the repose of the souls of the brave and valiant citizens who have sealed with their blood the liberty of the nation."

THOMAS JEFFERSON TO JAMES MADISON
July 22, 1789

My last to you was of the 18th. of June. Within a day or two after, yours of May 9.

came to hand. In the rest of Europe nothing remarkeable has happened; but in France such events as will be for ever memorable in history. To begin where my last left them, the king took on himself to decide the great question of voting by persons or by orders, by a declaration made at a Séance royale on the 23d. of June. In the same declaration he inserted many other things, some good some bad. The Tiers undismayed resolved that the whole was a mere nullity, and proceeded as if nothing had happened. The majority of the clergy joined them, & a small part of the Nobles. The uneasiness produced by the king's declaration occasioned the people to collect about the palace in the evening of the same day. The king and queen were alarmed & sent for Mr. Necker. He was conducted <by the mob> to & from the palace amidst the acclamations of the people. The French guards were observed to be mixed in great numbers with the people & to participate of their passions. This made so decisive an impression that the king on the 27th. wrote to the Clergy & Nobles who had not yet joined the Tiers, recommending to them to go & join them. They did so, & it was imagined all was now settled. It was soon observed however that troops, and those the foreign troops, were marching towards Paris from different quarters. The States addressed the king to forbid their approach. He declared it was only to preserve the tranquility of Paris & Versailles; and I believe he thought so....

The insurrection became now universal. The next day (the 13th.) the people forced a prison & took some arms. On the 14th. a committee was named by the city, with powers corresponding to our committees of safety.

They resolved to raise a city militia of 48,000 men. The people attacked the Invalids & got a great store of arms. Then they attack & carry the Bastille, cut off the Governor's & Lieutenant governor's heads, and that also of the Prevost des marchands discovered in a treacherous correspondence. While these things were doing here, the council is said to have been agitating at Versailles a proposition to arrest a number of the members of the States, referring every thing to them, & ordered away the troops. The city committee named the Marquis de la Fayette commander in chief, they went on organising their militia, the tumults continued, & a noise spread about Versailles that they were coming there to massacre the court, the ministry &c. Every minister heeupon resigned & fled, the Count d' Artois, Prince of Condé, Duke de Bourbon, the family of Polignacs, the Ct. de Vaudreuil, Abbé Vermont, confessor of the queen and keystone of all the intrigues, all fled out of the kingdom. The king wrote to recall Mr. Necker....

All the streets thro which he passed were lined with Bourgeois armed with guns.... about 60,000. The States general on foot,... M. de la Fayette at their head on horse back.

JAMES MADISON, REMARKS IN CONGRESS ON PROPOSED CONSTITUTIONAL AMENDMENTS
August 15, 1789

Editor's note: The congressional committee was discussing the clause "No religion shall be established by Law, nor shall the equal rights of conscience be infringed."

MR. MADISON said he apprehended the meaning of the words to be, that congress should not establish a religion, and enforce the legal observation of it by law, nor compel men to worship God in any manner contrary to their conscience. Whether the words were necessary or not he did not mean to say, but they had been required by some of the state conventions, who seemed to entertain an opinion that under the clause of the constitution, which gave power to congress to make all laws necessary and proper to carry into execution the constitution, and the laws made under it, enabled them to make laws of such a nature as might infringe the rights of conscience, or establish a national religion. To prevent these effects he presumed the amendment was intended, and he thought it as well expressed as the nature of the language would admit....

MR. MADISON thought, if the word national was inserted before religion, it would satisfy the minds of honorable gentlemen. He believed that the people feared one sect might obtain a pre-eminence, or two combined together, and establish a religion to which they would compel others to conform. He thought if the word national was introduced, it would point the amendment directly to the object it was intended to prevent....

MR. MADISON withdrew his motion, but observed that the words "no national religion shall be established by law," did not imply that the Government was a national one; the question was then taken on Mr. Livermore's motion, and passed in the affirmative, thirty-one for, and twenty against it....

MR. MADISON was unwilling to take up any more of the time of the committee, but on the other hand, he was not willing to be silent after the charges that had been brought against the committee, and the gentleman who introduced the amendments, by the honorable members on each side of him, (Mr. Sumpter and Mr. Burke). Those gentlemen say that we are precipitating the business, and insinuate that we are not acting with candor; I appeal to the gentlemen who have heard the voice of their country, to those who have attended the debates of the State conventions, whether the amendments now proposed, are not those most strenuously required by the opponents to the constitution? It was wished that some security should be given for those great and essential rights which they had been taught to believe were in danger. I concurred, in the convention of Virginia, with those gentlemen, so far as to agree to a declaration of those rights which corresponded with my own judgment, and the other alterations which I had the honor to bring forward before the present Congress. I appeal to the gentlemen on this floor who are desirous of amending the constitution, whether these proposed are not compatible with what are required by our constituents? Have not the people been told that the rights of conscience, the freedom of speech, the liberty of the press, and trial by jury, were in jeopardy; that they ought not to adopt the constitution until those important rights were secured to them.

But while I approve of these amendments, I should oppose the consideration at this time, of such as are likely to change the principles of the Government, or that are of a doubtful nature; because I apprehend there is little prospect of obtaining the consent of two-thirds of both Houses of Congress, and three-fourths of the State Legislatures, to ratify propositions of this kind; therefore, as a friend to what is attainable, I would limit it to the plain, simple, and important security that has been required. If I was inclined to make no alteration in the constitution I would bring forward such amendments as were of a dubious cast, in order to have the whole rejected.

JAMES MADISON, REMARKS IN CONGRESS ON PROPOSED CONSTITUTIONAL AMENDMENTS
August 17, 1789

Editor's note: The congressional committee was discussing the clause "No State shall infringe the equal rights of conscience, nor the freedom of speech, or of the press, nor the right to trial by jury in criminal cases." The House accepted the clause but the Senate rejected it.

Mr. Madison Conceived this to be the most valuable amendment in the whole list; if there was any reason to restrain the Government of the United State from infringing upon these essential rights, it was equally necessary that they should be secured against the State Governments. He thought that if they provided against the one, it was as necessary to provide against the other, and was satisfied that it would be equally grateful to the people.

JAMES MADISON TO RICHARD PETERS
August 19, 1789

The papers inclosed will shew that the nauseous project of amendments has not yet been either dismissed or despatched. We are so deep in them now, that right or wrong some thing must be done. I say this not by way of apology, for to be sincere I think no apology requisite. 1. because a constitutional provision in favr. of essential rights is a thing not improper in itself and was always viewed in that light by myself. It may be less necessary in a republic, than a Monarchy, & in a fedl. Govt. than the former, but it is in some degree rational in every Govt., since in every Govt. power may oppress, and declarations on paper, tho' not an effectual restraint, are not without some influence. 2. In many States the Constn. was adopted under a tacit compact in favr. of some subsequent provisions on this head. In Virga. It would have been certainly rejected, had no assurances been given by its advocates that such provisions would be pursued. As an honest man I feel my self bound by this consideration. 3. If the Candidates in Virga. for the House of Reps. had not taken this conciliary ground at the election, that State would have [been] represented almost wholly by disaffected characters, instead of the federal reps. now in Congs. 4. If amendts. had not been proposed from the federal side of the House, the proposition would have come within three days, from the adverse side. It is certainly best that they should appear to be the free gift of the friends of the Constitution rather than to be extorted by the address & weight of its enemies. 5. It will kill the opposition every where, and by putting an end to the disaffection to the Govt. itself, enable the administration to venture on measures not otherwise safe. Those who hate the Govt. will always join the party disaffected to measures of the administration, and such a party will be created by every important measure. 6. If no amendts. be proposed the language of antifedl. leaders to the people, will be, we advised you not to adopt the Constn. witht. previous amendts—You listened to those who told you that subsequent securities for your rights would be most easily obtained—We urged you to insist on a Convention as the only effectual mode of obtaining these—You yielded to the assurances of those who told you that a Convention was unecessary, that Congs. wd. be the proper channel for getting what was wanted. &c &c. Here are fine texts for popular declaimers who wish to revive the antifedl. cause, and at the fall session of the Legislares. to blow the trumpet for a second Convention. In Virga. a majority of the Legislature last elected, is bitterly opposed to the Govt. and will be joined, if no amends. be proposed, by great nos. of the other side who will complain of being deceived. 7. Some amendts. are necssy for N. Carola. I am so informed by the best authorities in that State.

THOMAS JEFFERSON TO JAMES MADISON
August 28, 1789

It is impossible to desire better dispositions towards us than prevail in the National Assembly. Our proceedings have been viewed as a model for them on every occasion; and though in the heat of debate men are generally disposed to contradict every authority urged by their opponents, ours has been treated like that of the Bible, open to explanation but not to question. I am sorry that in the moment of such a disposition, anything should come from us to check it. The placing them on a mere footing with the English will have this effect.

THOMAS JEFFERSON TO JAMES MADISON
September 6, 1789

This principle, that the earth belongs to the living and not to the dead, is of very extensive application and consequences in every country, and most especially in France. It enters into the resolution of the questions, whether the nation may change the descent of land holden in tail; whether they may change the appropriation of lands given anciently to the church, to hospitals, colleges, orders of chivalry, and otherwise in perpetuity; whether they may abolish the charges and privileges attached on lands, including the whole catalogue, ecclesiastical and feudal; it goes to hereditary offices, authorities and jurisdictions, to hereditary orders, distinctions and applications, to perpetual monopolies in commerce, the arts and sciences, with a long train of et ceteras; renders the question of reimbursement, a question of generosity and not of right.

JAMES MADISON TO GEORGE WASHINGTON
November 20, 1789

I hear nothing certain from the Assembly. It is said that an attempt of Mr. H. to revive the project of cummutables has been defeated.... As far as I can gather, the great bulk of the late opponents are entirely at rest, and more likely to censure a further opposition to the Govt. as now Administered than the Government itself. One of the principle leaders of the Baptists lately sent me word that the amendments had entirely satisfied the disaffected of his Sect, and that it would appear in their subsequent conduct.

JAMES MADISON TO GEORGE WASHINGTON
January 4, 1790

Editor's note: Madison refers to Virginia's debate on ratification of the Bill of Rights. The Bill, numbered as we now know it, was ratified nationally on December 15, 1791.

You have probably seen by the papers that the contest in the Assembly on the subject of the amendments ended in the loss of them. The House of Delegates got over the objections to the 11 & 12, but the Senate revived them with the addition of the 3 & 8 articles, and by a vote of adherence prevented a ratification. On some accounts this event is no doubt to be regretted. But it will do no injury to the Genl. Government. On the contrary it will have the effect with many of turning their distrust towards their own Legislature. The miscarriage of the 3d. art. particularly, will have this effect.

Part 5

JEFFERSON, MADISON, AND GEORGE WASHINGTON

1790 – 1794

J efferson returned to the U.S. to become Washington's Secretary of State. The central foreign issue before the new republic was to be the relationship of the U.S. to Britain, which occupied forts in the Northwest Territories given to the U.S. in the treaty ending the revolution, and revolutionary France, its imperial rival. Jefferson was deeply committed to the anti-clerical Paris left, although he became increasingly critical of its evolution and decay into Jacobin state-terrorism and the drift towards authoritarianism.

Madison was in the House of Representatives, but his initial influence on Washington was enormous. He ghosted his first Inaugural Address.

Jefferson and Madison were now identified with anti-clericalism for their own efforts to disestablish religion in Virginia and with the French revolution that they supported. Many American clergy, particularly in Massachusetts and Connecticut, which still recognized religious establishments in their state constitutions, became identified with the increasingly pro-British "monarchists," as Jefferson called them, the pro-capitalists around Alexander Hamilton, Washington's Secretary of the Treasury and Vice President John Adams. The unity of the "Federalists," the supporters of the Constitution, ended in 1793 when Jefferson left the cabinet. In 1796, John Adams became the Federalist President, with the "Republican" Jefferson elected Vice President, meaning, under the then rules, that he got the second highest number of votes for President.

THOMAS JEFFERSON, RESPONSE TO THE CITIZENS OF ALBEMARLE
February 12, 1790

My feeble and obscure exertions in their service, and in the holy cause of freedom, have had no other merit than that they were my best. We have all the same. We have been fellow-labourers and fellow-sufferers, and heaven has rewarded us with a happy issue from our struggles. It rests now with ourselves alone to enjoy in peace and concord the blessings of self-government, so long denied to mankind: to shew by example the sufficiency of human reason for the care of human affairs and that the will of the majority, the Natural law of every society, is the only sure guardian of the rights of man.... That it may flow thro' all times, gathering strength as it goes, and spreading the happy influence of reason and liberty over the face of the earth, is my fervent prayer to heaven.

THOMAS JEFFERSON TO WILLIAM HUNTER
March 11, 1790

Convinced that the republican is the only form of government which is not eternally at open or secret war with the rights of mankind, my prayers and efforts shall be cordially distributed to the support of what we have so happily established. It is indeed an animating thought, that while we are securing the rights of ourselves and our posterity, we are pointing out the way to struggling nations, who wish like us to emerge from their tyrannies also. Heaven help their struggles, and lead them, as it has done us, triumphantly through them.

JAMES MADISON TO EDMUND RANDOLPH
March 21, 1790

Editor's note: The Quakers were the first religious denomination to oppose slavery. Some presented a petition to Congress in February, asking for action against the slave trade. Madison voted for a House declaration that Article l, section 9 of the Constitution guaranteed the right of states to import slaves until 1808, but Congress could "restrain" Americans from supplying slaves to foreigners, and could insist on "humane treatment" for slaves imported into the U.S.

The debates occasioned by the Quakers have not yet expired. The stile of them has been as shamefully indecent as the matter was evidently misjudged. The true policy of the Southn. members was to have let the affair proceed with as little noise as possible, and to have made use of the occasion to obtain along with an assertion of the powers of Congs. a recognition of the restraints imposed by the Constitution.

THOMAS JEFFERSON TO MADAME D'ENVILLE
April 2, 1790

The change in your government will approximate us more to one another. You have had some checks, some horrors since I left you. But the way to heaven, you know, has always been said to be strewed with thorns. Why your nation have had fewer than any other on earth, I do not know, unless it be that it is the best on earth.... Heaven send that the glorious example of your country may be but the beginning of the history of European liberty, and that you may live many years in health and happiness to see at length that heaven did not make man in it's wrath.

THOMAS JEFFERSON TO NOAH WEBSTER
December 4, 1790

It had become an universal and almost uncontroverted position in the several States that the purposes of society do not require a surrender of all our rights to our ordinary governors: that there are certain portions of right not necessary to enable them to carry on an effective government, and which experience has nevertheless proved they will be constantly encroaching on if submitted to them; that there are also certain fences which experience has proved peculiarly efficacious against wrong and rarely obstructive of right, which yet the governing powers have ever shown a disposition to weaken and remove. Of the first kind, for instance, is freedom of religion: of the second, trial by jury, Habeas corpus laws, free presses.

JAMES MADISON, SPEECH IN CONGRESS ON
RELIGIOUS EXEMPTIONS FROM MILITIA DUTY
December 22, 1790

Mr. Madison did not mean to object to the amendment under consideration, though he thought it too far, in making exceptions in favour of the members of Congress. But as the committee of the whole had decided that point against him by a respectable majority, he should not now renew the question. But there is a question of great magnitude, which I am desirous of having determined. I shall therefore take the liberty of moving it. That we add to the end of the amendment, the words, "and persons conscientiously scrupulous of bearing arms." I agree with the gentleman who was last up, that is the glory of this country, the boast of the revolution, and the pride of the present constitution, that here the rights of mankind are known and established on a basis more certain, and I trust, more durable, than any heretofore recorded in history, or existing in any other part of this globe, but above all, it is the particular glory of this country, to have secured the rights of conscience which in other nations are least understood or most strangely violated. In my opinion, were these things less clear, it would be a sufficient motive to indulge these men in the exercise of their religious sentiments — that they have evinced by an uniform conduct of moderation, their merit, and deserving of the high privilege, they knew its value, and generously extended it to all men, even when possessing the plenitude of legislative power, they are the only people in America who have not abused the rights of conscience, except the Roman Catholics, who anticipated them by an earlier settlement, in establishing a toleration of all religions in their governments in the United States. Their honorable example has procured them a merit with this country, which ought not to be disregarded — and could I reach to them this exemption, from the performance of what they conceive to be criminal, with justice to the other sects in the community, or if the other sects were willing to withdraw their plea for an equivalent, my own opinion would be, to grant them privilege on terms perfectly gratuitous.

It has been said, by a gentleman from Georgia, (Mr. Jackson) that if this privilege is extended to this class of citizens, all other denominations will be induced to secure it to themselves by counterfeiting their principles. I am persuaded, the gentleman indulged his imagination more than his judgment, when he predicted this effect. He cannot consult his own heart, nor the disposition of his fellow citizens, nor human nature itself, when he supposes either himself or the people of America, or of any nation, would apostatize from their God for reasons so inconsiderable. Would any man consent to put on the mask of hypocrisy in order to avoid a duty which is honorable? I cannot believe that one out of a thousand, nay not a single citizen will be found throughout the United States, who will usurp this privilege by hypocritical pretensions. But it will be in vain to attempt to force them into the field, by such an attempt we shall only expose the imbecility of the government: Compulsion being out of the question, we must, therefore, from necessity, exempt them; if we are actuated by no more generous motive. Let us make a virtue of this necessity, and grant the exemption. By penalties we may oppress them, but by no means hitherto discovered, can you make them undertake the defence of this nation. My view, at this time is, to bring the question fairly before the house. I am not, therefore, tenacious of the words or mode of the amendment, but beg attention only to the principle.

JAMES MADISON, SPEECH IN CONGRESS ON RELIGIOUS EXEMPTIONS FROM MILITIA DUTY
December 23, 1790

Editor's note: Madison withdrew his conscientious objection to militia service proposal for parliamentary reasons, and then raised the issue again. Some Representatives felt that exemptions should be handled by the states.

Mr. Madison then brought forward a clause, for exempting all persons conscientiously scrupulous of bearing arms, who should make a declaration thereof before a magistrate, or who should produce a certificate of their belonging to a religious society, who profess such tenets: that for this exemption, they should pay an equivalent in money, to be collected as hereafter provided, and appropriated to the purposes, to which the revenue, arising from the post-office, was appropriated. He again repeated, it was his opinion, that this exemption should be made gratuitous, if justice to other sects did not demand an equivalent. He hoped, gentlemen would not object to form, as his object was to decide the principle.

Mr. Madison had heard no reason, why the business of exemption should be left to the states, except that from local circumstances they would be better able to des-

ignate those, whom they thought entitled to such exemption. This is far from satisfactory, in a case, where uniformity is in a high degree necessary. If this object be
important, it is incumbent on us to make the regulation. It was objected, that the
equivalent should not be for the national use, but for that of the particular states.
This opinion does not seem well warranted by the reason of things. For whose benefit is the militia organized, armed and disciplined? For the benefit of the United
States. If the services are for the benefit of the United States, why shall a particular
state receive the money, which is taken as an equivalent? We will put a case: Suppose
one state in the union consists altogether of such persons, as are the object of this
clause: their fines are all to go into their state treasury. So then the United States not
only lose their proportion of personal service, but the equivalent likewise; for it is
taken for granted, that each state ought to contribute her proportion towards the
common defence. The more this argument is examined, the more gentlemen will
perceive, that this money ought to come into the treasury of the U. States.

It may be asked, why make a difference between the quantum of money laid as
an equivalent for an exemption from personal service, and what is laid as a fine for
non-attendance on muster-days — when the nation in each case sustains an equal
loss of public service? To this it may be replied, that there is an essential difference
between an omission of a duty from scruples of conscience, and a breach and open
infraction of the law, proceeding from want of respect, motives of disloyalty, selfish
indulgence or gratification.

He did not however wish the house to come to an immediate decision. As it was
possible, that his amendment was not clearly expressed, he would not oppose any
modification of it, that would give more general satisfaction, whilst it retained the
principle.

JAMES MADISON, SPEECH IN CONGRESS ON
RELIGIOUS EXEMPTIONS FROM MILITIA DUTY
December 24, 1790

*Editor's note: A Representative objected to Madison's militia exemption bill as vaguely
worded. Ultimately, Madison's move for exemption failed.*

Mr. Madison admitted that his proposition might not be designated with the most
desirable accuracy; but he conceived its imperfection might be overlooked, if it was
considered, that the whole bill was intended to be given to a select committee for
arrangement and correction. But if the test was not satisfactorily designated, he
thought it might have been expected of the candor and ability of the gentleman,
that he would have amended it, rather than have made it a reason for voting against
a proposition, the principle of which was approved. I do not know, continued he,
what better criterion can be suggested; some criterion must, however, be had. If we
do not take the declaration of the party, we must, perhaps, depend upon a certificate from the religious society of which he is a member, or other voucher, to satisfy the magistrate with respect to the scruples of conscience. Now, I will submit it to

the gentleman, whether we can confine our exemption to this or that particular sect; or whether, because a man happened to be dissevered from a meeting of the Quakers, he ought not to be equally excused if he had really the same scruple. If this would be improper, then our criterion must apply to individuals, and not to societies. If it should be found by experience, that the operation of the law was evaded by any person under such pretexts, as had been conjectured, the legislature will always be at hand to redress the evil, We do not presume to consider our regulations as perfect; if we get as near that desirable point as is practical, at present, we ought not to despair of approximating more and more, as experience shall point out.

With respect to the alliance which the gentleman from New Hampshire pleases himself in having formed with my colleague, I cannot but observe, that if he is right in his principles, his ally must be wrong. Yet his ally has incontestably shewn, that the power of designating the militia resides absolutely in the United States. Whether the probable object of the convention be considered, when they proposed to take away the power of regulating the militia from the state governments, and to place it in the hands of the federal government: or whether we can examine the nature and construction of the term itself, we cannot but be convinced, that the authority was intended to be given us for the establishment of an effective militia - a militia that hitherto was not so effectually established as to ensure a sufficient defence against foreign invaders: or efficient enough to destroy the necessity of a standing national force: or in case of such a force being raised, and turned against the liberties of our fellow citizens, adequate to repel the hostile attacks of mad ambition. Let us not, by a false construction, admit a doctrine subversive of the great end which the constitution aimed to secure, namely, perfection to the union, the means of insuring domestic tranquility, and providing for the common defence.

If then it belongs to the general government, to provide for the establishment of a militia, it should be done by us, in the best manner possible. Now, whether that may be by making the exemption in the manner proposed, by exempting and laying an equivalent or fine, is the question. Instead of denominating it a punishment, for a crime, let it be the effect of compassion, to an unfortunate, not a vicious class of the society. When this is done, and the mode of appropriation and collection both made convenient, there will be no apprehension of oppression, or cause of complaint.

THOMAS JEFFERSON, REPORT ON THE ALGERINE PRISONERS
December 28, 1790

The Secretary of State, having had under consideration the situation of the citizens of the United States in captivity at Algiers, makes the following report thereupon to the President of the United States:

When the House of Representatives, at their late session, were pleased to refer to the Secretary of State, the petition of our citizens in captivity at Algiers, there still existed some expectation that certain measures, which had been employed to effect their redemption, the success of which depended on their secrecy, might prove effectual. Information received during the recess of Congress has so far weakened those expectations, as to make it now a duty to lay before the President of the United States, a full statement of what has been attempted for the relief of these our suffering citizens, as well before, as since he came into office, that he may be enabled to decide what further is to be done....

Though the ransom of captives was not among the objects expressed in their commissions, because at their dates the case did not exist, yet they thought it their duty to undertake that ransom, fearing that the captives might be sold and dispersed through the interior and distant countries of Africa, if the previous orders of Congress should be waited for. They therefore added a supplementary instruction to the agent to negotiate their ransom. But, while acting thus without authority, they thought themselves bound to offer a price so moderate as not to be disapproved. They therefore restrained him to two hundred dollars a man; which was something less than had been just before paid for about three hundred French captives, by the Mathurins, a religious order of France, instituted in ancient times for the redemption of Christian captives from the infidel Powers....

In the beginning of the next year, 1787, the Minister Plenipotentiary of the United States at Paris procured an interview with the general of the religious order of Mathurins, before mentioned, to engage him to lend his agency, at the expense of the United States, for the redemption of their captive citizens. He proffered at once all the services he could render, with the liberality and the zeal which distinguish his character. He observed, that he had agents on the spot, constantly employed in seeking out and redeeming the captives of their own country; that these should act for us, as for themselves; that nothing could be accepted for their agency; and that he would only expect that the price of redemption should be ready on our part, so as to cover the engagement into which he should enter. He added, that, by the time all expenses were paid, their last redemption had amounted to near two thousand five hundred livres a man, and that he could by no means flatter us that they could redeem our captives as cheap as their own. The pirates would take advantage of its being out of their ordinary line. Still he was in hopes they would not be much higher.

The proposition was then submitted to Congress, that is to say, in February, 1787, and on the 19th of September, in the same year, their Minister Plenipotentiary at Paris received their orders to embrace the offers of the Mathurins. This he immediately notified to the general, observing, however, that he did not desire him to enter into any engagements till a sufficient sum to cover them should be actually deposited in Paris. The general wished that the whole might be kept rigorously secret, as, should the barbarians suspect him to be acting for the United States, they would demand such sums as he could never agree to give, even with our consent, because it would injure his future purchases from them....

Nothing further was known of his progress or prospects, when the House of Representatives were pleased, at their last session, to refer the petition of our captives at Algiers to the Secretary of State. The preceding narrative shows that no report could have then been made without risking the object, of which some hopes were still entertained. Later advices, however, from the Chargé des Affaires of the United States, at Paris, informs us, that these measures, though not yet desperate, are not to be counted on. Besides the exorbitance of price, before feared, the late transfer of the lands and revenues of the clergy in France to the public, by withdrawing the means, seems to have suspended the proceedings of the Mathurins in the purposes of their institution.

It is time, therefore, to look about for something more promising, without relinquishing, in the meanwhile, the chance of success through them....

Passing over the ransoms of the Mathurins, which are kept far below the common level by special circumstances:

In 1789, Mr. Logie, the English consul at Algiers, informed a person who wished to ransom one of our common sailors, that he would cost from £450 to £500 sterling, the mean of which is $2,137. In December of the same year, Captain O'Brien thinks our men will now cost $2,290 each, though a Jew merchant believes he could get them for $2,264....

But should it be thought better to repress force by force, another expedient for their liberation may perhaps offer. Captures made on the enemy may perhaps put us into possession of some of their mariners, and exchange be substituted for ransom. It is not indeed a fixed usage with them to exchange prisoners. It is rather their custom to refuse it. However, such exchanges are sometimes effected, by allowing them more or less of advantage. They have sometimes accepted of two Moors for a Christian, at others they have refused five or six for one.

Perhaps Turkish captives may be objects of greater partiality with them, as their government is entirely in the hands of Turks, who are treated in every instance as a superior order of beings. Exchange, too, will be more practicable in our case, as our captives have not been sold to private individuals, but are retained in the hands of the Government.

The liberation of our citizens has an intimate connection with the liberation of our commerce in the Mediterranean, now under the consideration of Congress. The distresses of both proceed from the same cause, and the measures which shall be adopted for the relief of the one, may, very probably, involve the relief of the other.

JAMES MADISON, SPEECH IN THE HOUSE OF REPRESENTATIVES OPPOSING THE NATIONAL BANK
February 2, 1791

Is the power of establishing an incorporated Bank among the powers vested by the Constitution in the Legislature of the United States?...

4. If Congress could incorporate a Bank merely because the act would leave the States free to establish Banks also, any other incorporations might be made by

Congress. They could incorporate companies of manufacturers, or companies for cutting canals, or even religious societies, leaving similar incorporations by the States, like State Banks to themselves: Congress might even establish religious teachers in every parish, and pay them out of the Treasury of the United States, leaving other teachers unmolested in their functions. These inadmissible consequences condemned the controversial principle....

The defence against the charge founded on the want of a bill of rights, presupposed, he said, that the powers not given were retained; and that those given were not to be extended by remote implications. On any other supposition, the power of Congress to abridge the freedom of the press, or the rights of conscience, &c. could not have been disproved.

THOMAS JEFFERSON TO JOHN ADAMS
July 17, 1791

Editor's note: A private letter by Jefferson had been attacked in an article written under the pseudonym Publicola and Adams had been accused of being Publicola.

That you and I differ in our ideas of the best form of government, is well known to us both; but we have differed as friends should do, respecting the purity of each other's motives, and confining our differences of opinion to private conversation. And I can declare with truth, in the presence of the Almighty, that nothing was further from my intention or expectation than to have either my own or your name brought before the public on this occasion.

THOMAS JEFFERSON TO JOHN ADAMS
August 30, 1791

Editor's note: Adams had complained of an article in a newspaper, which accused him of being a monarchist.

You speak of the execrable paragraph in the Connecticut paper. This it is true appeared before Publicola. But it had no more relation to Paine's pamphlet and my note, than to the Alcoran. I am satisfied the writer of it had never seen either.

FIRST AMENDMENT TO THE CONSTITUTION
Ratified December 15, 1791

Congress shall make no law respecting an establishment of religion, or prohibiting the free exercise thereof; or abridging the freedom of speech, or of the press; or the right of the people peacefully to assemble, and to petition the Government for a redress of grievances.

James Madison, "Property," National Gazette
March 27, 1792

This term in its particular application means "that dominion which one man claims and exercises over the external things of the world, in exclusion of every other individual."

In its larger and juster meaning, it embraces every thing to which a man may attach a value and have a right; and which leaves to every one else the like advantage.

In the former sense, a man's land, or merchandize, or money is called his property.

In the latter sense, a man has a property in his opinions and the free communication of them.

He has a property of peculiar value in his religious opinions, and in the profession and practice dictated by them....

Government is instituted to protect property of every sort.... According to this standard of merit, the praise of affording a just security to property, should be sparingly bestowed on a government which, however scrupulously guarding the possessions of individuals, does not protect them in the enjoyment and communication of their opinions, in which they have an equal, and in the estimation of some, a more valuable property.

More sparingly should this praise be allowed to a government, where a man's religious rights are violated by penalties, or fettered by tests, or taxed by a hierarchy. Conscience is the most sacred of all property; other property depending in part on positive law, the exercise of that, being a natural and unalienable right. To guard a man's house as his castle, to pay public and enforce private debts with the most exact faith, can give no title to invade a man's conscience which is more sacred than his castle, or to withhold from it that debt of protection, for which the public faith is pledged, by the very nature and original conditions of the social pact....

A just security to property is not afforded by that government, under which unequal taxes oppress one species of property and reward another species: where arbitrary taxes invade the domestic sanctuaries of the rich, and excessive taxes grind the faces of the poor; where the keenness and competitions of want are deemed an insufficient spur to labor, and taxes are again applied, by an unfeeling policy, as another spur; in violation of that sacred property, which Heaven, in decreeing man to earn his bread by the sweat of his brow, kindly reserves to him, in the small repose that could be spared from the supply of his necessities.

If there be a government then which prides itself in maintaining the inviolability of property; which provides that none shall be taken directly even for public use without indemnification to the owner, and yet directly violates the property which individuals have in their opinions, their religion, their persons, and their faculties; nay more, which indirectly violates their property, in their actual possessions, in the labor which ought to relieve their fatigues and soothe their cares, the influence will have been anticipated, that such a government is not a pattern for the United States.

If the United States means to obtain or deserve the full praise due to wise and just governments, they will equally respect the rights of property, and the property in rights: they will rival the government that most sacredly guards the former; and by repelling its example in violating the latter, will make themselves a pattern to that and all other governments.

THOMAS JEFFERSON TO THOMAS PAINE
June 19, 1792

I received with great pleasure the present of your pamphlets, as well for the thing itself as that it was a testimony of your recollection. Would you believe it possible that in this country there should be high & important characters who need your lessons in republicanism, & who do not heed them? It is but too true that we have a sect preaching up & pouting after an English constitution of king, lords, & commons, & whose heads are itching for crowns, coronets & mitres. But our people, my good friend, are firm and unanimous in their principles of republicanism & there is no better proof of it than that they love what you write and read it with delight. The printers season every newspaper with extracts from your last, as they did before from your first part of the Rights of Man. They have both served here to separate the wheat from the chaff, and to prove that tho' the latter appears on the surface, it is on the surface only. The bulk below is sound & pure. Go on then in doing with your pen what in other times was done with the sword: shew that reformation is more practicable by operating on the mind than on the body of man, and be assured that it has not a more sincere votary nor you a more ardent well-wisher than Yrs. &c.

THOMAS JEFFERSON TO GEORGE WASHINGTON
September 9, 1792

You will there see that my objection to the constitution was that it wanted a bill of rights securing freedom of religion, freedom of the press, freedom from standing armies, trial by jury, & a constant Habeus corpus act. Col. Hamilton's was that it wanted a king and a house of Lords. The sense of America has approved my objection & added the bill of rights, not the king and lords....

Freneau, as translating clerk, & the printer of a periodical paper likely to circulate thro' the states (uniting in one person the parts of Pintard & Fenno) revived my hopes that the thing could at length be effected. On the establishment of his paper therefore, I furnished him with the Leyden gazettes, with an expression of my wish that he could always translate & publish the material intelligence they contained; & have continued to furnish them from time to time, as regularly as I received them. But as to any other direction or indication of my wish how his press should be conducted, what sort of intelligence he should give, what essays encourage, I can protest in the presence of heaven, that I never did by myself or any other, directly or indirectly, say a syllable, nor attempt any kind of influence. I can further protest, in the same awful presence, that I never did by myself or any other, directly or indirectly, write, dictate or procure any one sentence or sentiment to be inserted in his, or any other gazette, to which my name was not affixed or that of my office....

No government ought to be without censors: & where the press is free, no one ever will. If virtuous, it need not fear the fair operation of attack & defence. Nature has given to man no other means of sifting out the truth either in religion, law, or politics.

JAMES MADISON, "WHO ARE THE BEST KEEPERS OF THE PEOPLE'S LIBERTIES?" *National Gazette*, December 22, 1792

Editor's note: The title question is answered in dialogue form. The followers of Jefferson and Madison were known as the Republicans. Decades later their party became the present Democratic Party. The anti-Republicans soon became the Federalists.

Republican - The people themselves. The sacred trust can be no where so safe as in the hands most interested in preserving it....

Anti-republican - You look at the surface only, where errors float, instead of fathoming the depths where truth lies hid. It is not the government that is disposed to fly off from the people; but the people that are ever ready to fly off from the government. Rather say then, enlighten the government, warn it to be vigilant, enrich it with influence, arm it with force, and to the people never pronounce but two words—Submission and Confidence.

Republican - The centrifugal tendency then is in the people, not in the government, and the secret art lies in restraining the tendency, by augmenting the attractive principle of the government with all the weight that can be added to it. What a perversion of the natural order of things! To make power the primary and central object of the social system, and Liberty but its satellite.

Anti-republican - The science of the stars can never instruct you in the mysteries of government. Wonderful as it may seem, the more you increase the attractive force of power, the more you enlarge the sphere of liberty; the more you make government independent and hostile towards the people, the better security you provide for their rights and interests....

Republican - Mysterious indeed! But mysteries belong to religion, not to government; to the ways of the Almighty, not to the works of man. And in religion itself there is nothing mysterious to its author; the mystery lies in the dimness of the human sight. So in the institutions of man let there be no mystery, unless for those inferior beings endowed with a ray perhaps of the twilight vouchsafed to the first order of terrestrial creation.

Anti-republican - You are destitute, I perceive, of every quality of a good citizen, or rather of a good subject. You have neither the light of faith nor the spirit of obedience. I denounce you to the government as an accomplice of atheism and anarchy.

Republican - And I forbear to denounce you to the people though a blasphemer of their rights and an idolater of tyranny: Liberty disdains to persecute.

THOMAS JEFFERSON, OPINION ON THE FRENCH TREATIES
April 28, 1793

Editor's note: Jefferson was Washington's Secretary of State.

I proceed, in compliance with the requisition of the President, to give an opinion in writing on the general question, Whether the U.S. have the right to renounce their treaties with France, or to hold them suspended till the government of that country shall be established?...

The Law of nations, by which this question is to be determined, is composed of three branches. 1. The Moral law of our nature. 2. The Usages of nations. 3. Their special Conventions. The first of these only, concerns this question, that is to say the Moral law to which Man has been subjected by his creator, & of which his feelings, or Conscience as it sometimes called, are the evidence with which his creator has furnished him. The Moral duties which exist between individual and individual in a state of nature, accompany them into a state of society & the aggregate of the duties of all individuals composing the society constitutes the duties of that society towards any other; so that between society & society the same moral duties exist as did between the individuals composing them while in an unassociated state, their maker not having released them from those duties on their forming themselves into a nation. Compacts then between nation & nation are obligatory on them by the same moral law which obliges individuals to observe their compacts. There are circumstances; however, which sometimes excuse the non-performance of contracts between man and man; so are there also between nation and nation. When performance, for instance, becomes impossible, non-performance is not immoral; so if performance becomes self-destructive to the party, the law of self-preservation overrules the laws of obligation in others. For the reality of these principles I appeal to the true fountains of evidence, the head and heart of every rational and honest man. It is there nature has written her moral laws, and where every man may read them for himself. He will never read there the permission to annul his obligations for a time, or forever, whenever they become dangerous, useless, or disagreeable; certainly not when merely useless or disagreeable, as seems to be said in an authority which has been quoted, (Vattel, p. 2, 197) and though he may, under certain degrees of danger, yet the danger must be imminent, and the degree great. Of these, it is true, that nations are to be judges for themselves; since no one nation has a right to sit in judgment over another, but the tribunal of our consciences remains, and that also of the opinion of the world. These will revise the sentence we pass in our own case, and as we respect these, we must see that in judging ourselves we have honestly done the part of impartial and rigorous judges.

THOMAS JEFFERSON TO MRS. CHURCH
November 27, 1793

Madame Cosway in a convent! I knew that to much goodness of heart she joined enthusiasm and religion; but I thought that very enthusiasm would have prevented her from shutting up her adoration of the God of the universe within the walls of a cloister; that she would rather have sought the mountain-top....

En attendant [In the mean time], God bless you.
Accept the homage of my sincere and constant affection.

THOMAS JEFFERSON TO TENCH COXE
May 1, 1794

Your letters give a comfortable view of French affairs, and later events seem to confirm it. Over the foreign powers I am convinced they will triumph completely, and I cannot but hope that that triumph, and the consequent disgrace of the invading tyrants, is destined, in order of events, to kindle the wrath of the people of Europe against those who have dared to embroil them in such wickedness, and to bring at length, kings, nobles and priests to the scaffolds which they have been so long deluging with human blood. I am still warm whenever I think of these scoundrels, though I do it as seldom as I can, preferring infinitely to contemplate the tranquil growth of my lucerne and potatoes.

Part 6

THE REPUBLICANS STRUGGLE
AGAINST FEDERALISM

1798 – 1800

T he central issue of Adams' administration became the 1798 "Alien and Sedition Acts." The Naturalization Act, Alien Act, Sedition Act, and Alien Enemies Act were passed midst quasi-war with France. The Sedition Act made it illegal to criticize the government or its officials publicly.

Jefferson and Madison lead the ideological struggle against the Acts. The Vice President drafted resolutions against the Acts and had them introduced into Kentucky's legislature. Madison drafted resolutions for Virginia. Both states passed their resolutions, declaring the Acts void. Their campaign is successful and in 1800 Jefferson was elected President.

THOMAS JEFFERSON TO JOHN TAYLOR
June 4, 1798

Seeing, therefore, that an association of men who will not quarrel with one another is a thing which never yet existed, from the greatest confederacy of nations down to a town meeting or a vestry; seeing that we must have somebody to quarrel with I had rather keep our New England associates for that purpose, than to see our bickerings transferred to others. They are circumscribed within such narrow limits, and their population so full, that their numbers will ever be the minority, and they are marked, like the Jews, with such a perversity of character, as to constitute, from that circumstance, the natural division of our parties. A little patience, and we shall see the reign of witches pass over, their spells dissolved, and the people recovering their true sight, restoring their government to its true principles.

THOMAS JEFFERSON, DRAFT OF THE KENTUCKY RESOLUTIONS
October 1798

Resolved.... that whensoever the General Government assumes undelegated powers, its acts are unauthoritative, void, and of no force.... that the government created by this compact was not made the exclusive or final judge of the extent of the powers delegated to itself; since that would have made its discretion, and not the Constitution, the measure of its powers; but that, as in all other cases of compact among powers having no common judge, each party has an equal right to judge for itself, as well of infractions as of the mode and measure of redress.... therefore the act of Congress, passed on the 14th day of July, 1798, and intituled "An Act in addition to the act intituled An Act for the punishment of certain crimes against the United States".... are altogether void....

Resolved.... that no power over the freedom of religion, freedom of speech, or freedom of the press being delegated to the United States by the Constitution, nor prohibited by it to the States, all lawful powers respecting the same did of right remain, and were reserved to the States or the people....

And thus also they guarded against all abridgment by the United States of the freedom of religious opinions and exercises, and retained to themselves the right of protecting the same, as this State, by a law passed on the general demand of its citizens, had already protected them from all human restraint or interference. And that in addition to this general principle and express declaration, another and more special provision has been made by one of the amendments to the Constitution, which expressly declares, that "Congress shall make no law respecting an establishment of religion, or prohibiting the free exercise thereof, or abridging the freedom of speech or of the press:" thereby guarding in the same sentence, and under the same words, the freedom of religion, of speech, and of the press: insomuch, that whatever violated either, throws down the sanctuary which covers the others, and that libels, falsehood, and defamation, equally with heresy and false religion, are withheld from the cognizance of federal tribunals. That, therefore, the act of Congress of the United States, passed on the 14th day of July, 1798, intituled "An Act in addition to the act intituled An Act for the punishment of certain crimes against the United States," which does abridge the freedom of the press, is not law, but is altogether void, and of no force.

JAMES MADISON, VIRGINIA RESOLUTIONS AGAINST
THE ALIEN AND SEDITION ACTS
December 21, 1798

That this State having by its convention which ratified the federal constitution, expressly declared, "that among other essential rights, the liberty of conscience and of the press cannot be cancelled, abridged, restrained or modified by any authority of the United States" and from its extreme anxiety to guard these rights from every possible attack of sophistry or ambition, having with other states recommended an amendment for that purpose, which amendment was in due time annexed to the Constitution, it would mark a reproachful inconsistency and criminal degeneracy, if an indifference were now shewn to the most palpable violation of one of these rights thus declared and secured, and to the establishment of a precedent which may be fatal to the other.

JAMES MADISON, ADDRESS TO THE PEOPLE,
VIRGINIA GENERAL ASSEMBLY
January 23, 1799

Editor's note: The Address was a follow up to Madison's 1798 Virginia Resolutions against the federal Alien and Sedition Acts, which he believed were destroying American civil liberties.

So insatiable is a love of power that it has resorted to a distinction between the freedom and licentiousness of the press for the purpose of converting the third amendment of the constitution which was dictated by the most lively anxiety to preserve that freedom, into an instrument for abridging it. Thus usurpation even justifies itself by a precaution against usurpation; and thus an amendment universally designed to quiet every fear is adduced as the source of an act which has produced general terror and alarm.

The distinction between liberty and licentiousness is still a repetition of the Protean doctrine of implication, which is ever ready to work its ends by varying its shape. By its help, the judge as to what is licentious may escape through any constitutional restriction. Under it men of a particular religious opinion might be excluded from office, because such exclusion would not amount to an establishment of religion, and because it might be said that their opinions are licentious. And under it Congress might denominate a religion to be heretical and licentious, and proceed to its suppression. Remember that precedents once established are so much positive power; and that the nation which reposes on the pillow of political confidence, will sooner or later end its political existence in a deadly lethargy. Remember, also that it is to the press mankind are indebted for having dispelled the clouds which long encompassed religion, for disclosing her genuine lustre, and disseminating her salutary doctrines....

Pledged as we are, fellow-citizens, to these sacred engagements, we yet humbly and fervently implore the Almighty Disposer of events to avert from our land war and usurpation, the scourges of mankind; to permit our fields to be cultivated in peace, to instill into nations the love of friendly intercourse; to suffer our youth to be educated in virtue, and to preserve our morality from the pollution invariably incident to habits of war; to prevent the laborer and husbandman from being harassed by taxes and imposts; to remove from ambition the means of disturbing the commonwealth; to annihilate all pretexts for power afforded by war; to maintain the Constitution; and to bless our nation with tranquillity, under whose benign influence we may reach the summit of happiness and glory, to which we are destined by nature and nature's God.

THOMAS JEFFERSON TO ELBRIDGE GERRY
January 26, 1799

I am for free commerce with all nations; political connection with none; & little or no diplomatic establishment. And I am not for linking ourselves by new treaties with the quarrels of Europe; entering that field of slaughter to preserve their balance, or joining in the confederacy of kings to war against the principles of liberty. I am for freedom of religion, & against all maneuvers to bring about a legal ascendancy of one sect over another: for freedom of the press, & against all violations of the constitution to silence by force & not by reason the complaints or criticisms, just or unjust, of our citizens against the conduct of their agents. And I am for encouraging the progress of science in all it's branches; and not for raising a hue and cry against the sacred name of philosophy; for awing the human mind by stories of rawhead & bloody bones to a distrust of its own vision, & to repose implicitly on that of others; to go backwards instead of forwards to look for improvement; to believe that government, religion, morality, & every other science were in the highest perfection in ages of the darkest ignorance, and that nothing can ever be devised more perfect than what was established by our forefathers....

In truth, we never differed but on one ground, the funding system; and as, from the moment of it's being adopted by the constituted authorities, I became religiously principled in the sacred discharge of it to the uttermost farthing, we are united now even on that single ground of difference.

THOMAS JEFFERSON TO THOMAS LOMAX
March 12, 1799

I join you therefore in branding as cowardly the idea that the human mind is incapable of further advances. This is precisely the doctrine which the present despots of the earth are inculcating, & their friends here re-echoing; & applying especially to religion & politics; 'that it is not probable that any thing better will be discovered than what was known to our fathers.' We are to look backwards then & not forwards for the improvement of science, & to find it amidst feudal barbarisms and the fires of Spital-fields. But thank heaven the American mind is already too much opened, to listen to these impostures; and while the art of printing is left to us, science can never be retrograde; what is once acquired of real knowlege can never be lost. To preserve the freedom of the human mind then & freedom of the press, every spirit should be ready to devote itself to martyrdom; for as long as we may think as we will, & speak as we think, the condition of man will proceed in improvement. The generation which is going off the stage has deserved well of mankind for the struggles it has made, & for having arrested that course of despotism which had overwhelmed the world for thousands & thousands of years.

JAMES MADISON, REPORT TO COMMITTEE OF VIRGINIA'S HOUSE OF DELEGATES ON THE ALIEN AND SEDITION ACTS
[Late 1799 - January 7, 1800]

Report of the committee to whom were referred the communications of various states relative to the resolutions of the General Assembly of this state, concerning the Alien and Sedition-Laws....

Nor can it ever be granted, that a power to act on a case when it actually occurs, includes a power over all the means that may tend to prevent the occurrence of the case. Such a latitude of construction would render unavailing, every practicable definition of particular and limited powers. Under the idea of preventing war in general, as well as invasion in particular, not only an indiscriminate removal of all aliens, might be enforced; but a thousand other things still more remote from the operations and precautions appurtenant to war, might take place. A bigoted or tyrannical nation might threaten us with war, unless certain religious or political regulations were adopted by us; yet it never could be inferred, if the regulations which would prevent war, were such as Congress had otherwise no power to make, that the power to make them would grow out of the purpose they were to answer. Congress have power to suppress insurrections, yet it would not be allowed to follow, that they might employ all the means tending to prevent them; of which a system of moral instruction for the ignorant, and of provident support for the poor, might be regarded as among the most efficacious....

ll. The next point which the resolution requires to be proved, is, that the power

---

over the press exercised by the sedition-act, is positively forbidden by one of the amendments to the Constitution.

The amendment stands in these words — "Congress shall make no law respecting an establishment of religion, or prohibiting the free exercise thereof, or abridging the freedom of speech or of the press; or the right of the people peaceably to assemble, and to petition the government for a redress of grievances"....

The nature of governments elective, limited and responsible, in all their branches, may well be supposed to require a greater freedom of animadversion, than might be tolerated by the genius of such a government as that of Great Britain.... Not withstanding the general doctrine of the common law, on the subject of the press, and the occasional punishment of those, who use it with a freedom offensive to the government, it is well known, that ... the freedom exercised by the press, and protected by public opinion, far exceeds the limits prescribed by the ordinary rules of law.... The practice in America must be entitled to much more respect.... To these observations one fact will be added, which demonstrates that the common law cannot be admitted as the universal expositor of American terms, which may be the same with those contained in that law. The freedom of conscience, and of religion, are found in the same instruments, which assert the freedom of the press. It will never be admitted, that the meaning of the former, in the common law of England, is to limit their meaning in the United States....

The resolution next in order is as follows:
That this state having by its Convention, which ratified the Federal Constitution expressly declared, that among other essential rights, "the liberty of conscience and of the press cannot be cancelled, abridged, restrained or modified by any authority of the United States," and from its extreme anxiety to guard these rights from every possible attack of sophistry and ambition, having with other states, recommended an amendment for that purpose, which amendment was, in due time, annexed to the constitution; it would mark a reproachful inconsistency, and criminal degeneracy, if an indifference were now shewn, to the most palpable violation of one of these rights, thus declared and secured; and the establishment of a precedent, which may be fatal to the other.

To place this resolution in its just light, it will be necessary to recur to the act of ratification by Virginia, which stands in the ensuing form:

We, the delegates of the people of Virginia, duly elected in pursuance of a recommendation from the General Assembly, and now met in convention, having fully and freely investigated and discussed the proceedings of the federal convention, and being prepared as well as the most mature deliberation hath enabled us to decide thereon; do, in the name and in behalf of the people of Virginia, declare and make known, that the powers granted under the Constitution, being derived from the people of the United States, may be resumed by them, whensoever the same shall be perverted to their injury or oppression; and that every power not granted thereby, remains with them, and at their will. That, therefore, no right of any denomination can be cancelled, abridged, restrained, or modified, by the Congress, by the Senate, or House of Representatives, acting in any capacity, by the President, or any department or officer of the United States, except in those instances in which power is given by the Constitution for those purposes; and that, among other essential rights, the liberty of conscience and of the press, cannot be cancelled, abridged, restrained, or modified, by any authority of the United States.

Here is an express and solemn declaration by the convention of the state, that they ratified the constitution in the sense that no right of any denomination can be cancelled, abridged, retrained or modified by the government of the United States or any part of it; except in those instances in which power is given by the constitution; and in the sense particularly, "that among other essential rights, the liberty of conscience and freedom of the press cannot be cancelled, abridged, restrained or modified, by any authority of the United States."

Words could not well express, in a fuller or more forcible manner, the understanding of the convention, that the liberty of conscience and the freedom of the press, were equally and completely exempted from all authority whatever of the United States.

Under an anxiety to guard more effectually these rights against every possible danger, the convention, after ratifying the Constitution, proceeded to prefix to certain amendments proposed by them, a declaration of rights, in which are two articles providing, the one for the liberty of conscience, the other for the freedom of speech and of the press.

Similar recommendations having proceeded from a number of other states, and Congress, as has been seen, having in consequence thereof, and with a view to extend the ground of public confidence, proposed, among other declaratory and restrictive clauses, a clause expressly securing the liberty of conscience and of the press; and Virginia having concurred in the ratifications which made them a part of the Constitution, it will remain with a candid public to decide, whether it would not mark an inconsistency and degeneracy, if an indifference were now shown to a palpable violation of one of those rights, the freedom of the press; and to a precedent therein, which may be fatal to the other, the free exercise of religion.

That the precedent established by the violation of the former of these rights, may, as is affirmed by the resolution, be fatal to the latter, appears to be demonstrable, by a comparison of the grounds on which they respectively rest; and from the scope of reasoning, by which the power over the former has been vindicated.

First. Both of these rights, the liberty of conscience and of the press, rest equally on the original ground of not being delegated by the Constitution, and consequently withheld from the government. Any construction, therefore, that would attack this original security for the one, must have the like effect on the other.

Secondly. They are both equally secured by the supplement to the Constitution; being both included in the same amendment, made at the same time, and by the same authority. Any construction or argument, then, which would turn the amendment into a grant or acknowledgment of power with respect to the press, might be equally applied to the freedom of religion.

Thirdly. If it be admitted that the extent of the freedom of the press, secured by the amendment, is to be measured by the common law on this subject, the same authority may be resorted to, for the standard which is to fix the extent of the "free exercise of religion." It cannot be necessary to say what this standard would be; whether the common law be taken solely as the unwritten, or as varied by the written law of England.

Fourthly. If the words and phrases in the amendment, are to be considered as chosen with a studied discrimination, which yields an argument for a power over the press, under the limitation that its freedom be not abridged, the same argument results from the same consideration, for a power over the exercise of religion, under the limitation that its freedom be not prohibited.

For, if Congress may regulate the freedom of the press, provided they do not abridge it, because it is said only "they shall not abridge it," and is not said, "they shall make no law respecting it," the analogy of reasoning is conclusive, that Congress may regulate and even abridge the free exercise of religion, provided they do not prohibit it, because it is said only "they shall not prohibit it," and is not said, "they shall make no law respecting, or no law abridging it."

The General Assembly were governed by the clearest reason, then, in considering the "sedition-act," which legislates on the freedom of the press, as establishing a precedent that may be fatal to the liberty of conscience; and it will be the duty of all, in proportion as they value the security of the latter, to take the alarm at every encroachment on the former.

THOMAS JEFFERSON TO DR. JOSEPH PRIESTLEY
January 27, 1800

Editor's note: Priestley was one of the great scientists of the day. He was the first to isolate oxygen, (without realizing its importance). Theologically, he was a father of Unitarianism. His support for the French revolution led to a British mob destroying his home and lab, whereupon he emigrated to the U.S.

I have a letter from M. Dupont, since his arrival at N. York, dated the 20th, in which he says he will be in Philadelphia within about a fortnight from that time; but only on a visit. How much would it delight me if a visit from you at the same time, were to shew us two such illustrious foreigners embracing each other in my country, as the asylum for whatever is great & good. Pardon, I pray you, the temporary deliri-

---

um which has been excited here, but which is fast passing away. The Gothic idea that we are to look backwards instead of forwards for the improvement of the human mind, and to recur to the annals of our ancestors for what is most perfect in government, in religion & in learning, is worthy of those bigots in religion & government, by whom it has been recommended, & whose purposes it would answer. But it is not an idea which this country will endure; and the moment of their showing it is fast ripening; and the signs of it will be their respect for you, & growing detestation of those who have dishonored our country by endeavors to disturb our tranquility in it. No one has felt this with more sensibility than, my dear Sir, your respectful & affectionate friend & servant.

THOMAS JEFFERSON TO BISHOP JAMES MADISON
January 31, 1800

I have lately by accident got a sight of a single volume (the 3d.) of the Abbe Barruel's 'Antisocial conspiracy,' which gives me the first idea I have ever had of what is meant by the Illuminatism against which 'illuminate Morse' as he is now called, & his ecclesiastical & monarchical associates have been making such a hue and cry. Barruel's own parts of the book are perfectly the ravings of a Bedlamite. But he quotes largely from Wishaupt whom he considers as the founder of what he calls the order. As you may not have had an opportunity of forming a judgment of this cry of 'mad dog' which has been raised against his doctrines, I will give you the idea I have formed from only an hour's reading of Barruel's quotations from him, which you may be sure are not the most favorable. Wishaupt seems to be an enthusiastic Philanthropist. He is among those (as you know the excellent Price and Priestley also are) who believe in the indefinite perfectibility of man. He thinks he may in time be rendered so perfect that he will be able to govern himself in every circumstance so as to injure none, to do all the good he can, to leave government no occasion to exercise their powers over him, & of course to render political government useless. This you know is Godwin's doctrine, and this is what Robinson, Barruel & Morse had called a conspiracy against all government. Wishaupt believes that to promote this perfection of the human character was the object of Jesus Christ. That his intention was simply to reinstate natural religion, & by diffusing the light of his morality, to teach us to govern ourselves. His precepts are the love of god & love of our neighbor. And by teaching innocence of conduct, he expected to place men in their natural state of liberty & equality. He says, no one ever laid a surer foundation for liberty than our grand master, Jesus of Nazareth. He believes the Free masons were originally possessed of the true principles & objects of Christianity, & have still preserved some of them by tradition, but much disfigured. The means he proposes to effect this improvement of human nature are 'to enlighten men, to correct their morals & inspire them with benevolence. Secure of our success, sais he, we abstain from violent commotions. To have foreseen the happiness of posterity & to have prepared it by irreproachable means, suffices for our felicity. The tranquility of our consciences is not troubled by the reproach of aiming at the ruin or overthrow of states or thrones.' As Wishaupt lived under the tyranny of a despot & priests, he knew that caution was necessary even in spreading information, & the principles of pure morality. He proposed therefore to lead the Free masons to adopt this object & to make the objects of their institution the diffusion of science & virtue. He proposed to initiate new members into his body by gradations proportioned to his fears of the thunderbolts of tyranny. This has given an air of mystery to his views, was the foundation of his banishment, the subversion of the masonic order, & is the colour for the ravings against him of Robinson, Barruel & Morse, whose real fears are that the craft would be endangered by the spreading of information, reason, & natural morality among men. This subject being new to me, I have imagined that if it be so to you also, you may receive the same satisfaction in seeing, which I have had in forming the analysis of it: & I believe you will think with me that if Wishaupt had written here, where no secrecy is necessary in our endeavors to render men wise & virtuous, he would not have thought of any secret machinery for that purpose. As Godwin, if he had written in Germany, might probably also have thought secrecy & mysticism prudent.

THOMAS JEFFERSON TO DR. BENJAMIN RUSH
September 23, 1800

Editor's note: The "XYZ plot" referred to by Jefferson took place in 1797-8, during the administration of John Adams, his predecessor as President, when three French agents tried to shake down the U.S. government, to end a period of semi-war between the two countries. The Federalists tried, unsuccessfully, to use the crisis against the Republicans, commonly identified with the anti-clericalism of the French revolution.

I have to acknolege the reciept of your favor of Aug. 22. and to congratulate you on the healthiness of your city. Still Baltimore, Norfolk and Providence admonish us that we are not clear of our new scourge. When great evils happen, I am in the habit of looking out for what good may arise from them as consolations to us: and Providence has in fact established the order of things as that most evils are the means of producing some good. The yellow fever will discourage the growth of great cities in our nation; and I view great cities as pestilential to the morals, the health and the liberties of man. True, they nourish some of the elegant arts; but the useful ones can thrive elsewhere, and less perfection in the others with more health virtue and freedom would be my choice....

    I promised you a letter on Christianity, which I have not forgotten. On the contrary, it is because I have reflected on it, that I find much more time necessary for it than I can at present dispose of. I have a view of the subject which ought to displease neither the rational Christian nor Deists, and would reconcile many to a character they have too hastily rejected. I do not know that it would reconcile the *genus irritabile vatum* [the irritable tribe of priests] who are all in arms against me. Their hostility is on too interested ground to be softened. The delusion into which the X.Y.Z.

plot shewed it possible to push the people; the successful experiment made under the prevalence of that delusion on the clause of the constitution, which, while it secured the freedom of the press, covered also the freedom of religion, had given to the clergy a very favorite hope of obtaining an establishment of a particular form of Christianity thro' the U.S.; and as every sect believes its own form the true one, every one perhaps hoped for his own, but especially the Episcopalians & Congregationalists. The returning good sense of our country threatens abortion to their hopes, & they believe that any portion of power confided to me, will be exerted in opposition to their schemes. And they believe rightly; for I have sworn upon the altar of god, eternal hostility against every form of tyranny over the mind of man. But this is all they have to fear from me: & enough too in their opinion, & this is the cause of their printing lying pamphlets against me, forging conversations for me with Mazzei, Bishop Madison, &c., which are absolute falsehoods without a circumstance of truth to rest on; falsehoods, too, of which I acquit Mazzei & Bishop Madison, for they are men of truth. - But enough of this. It is more than I have before committed to paper on the subject of all the lies which have been preached or printed against me.

THOMAS JEFFERSON TO JEREMIAH MOOR
August 14, 1800

You may remember perhaps that in the year 1783, after the close of the war there was a general idea that a convention would be called in this state to form a constitution. In that expectation I then prepared a scheme of constitution which I meant to have proposed.... I observe however in the same scheme of a constitution, an abridgement of the right of being elected, which after 17 years more of experience & reflection, I do not approve. It is the incapacitation of a clergyman from being elected. The clergy, by getting themselves established by law, & ingrafted into the machine of government, have been a very formidable engine against the civil and religious rights of man. They are still so in many countries & even in some of these United States. Even in 1783, we doubted the stability of our recent measures for reducing them to the footing of other useful callings. It now appears that our means were effectual. The clergy here seem to have relinquished all pretention to privilege and to stand on a footing with lawyers, physicians &c. They ought therefore to possess the same rights....

I have great confidence in the common sense of mankind in general: but it requires a great deal to get the better of notions which our tutors have instilled into our minds while incapable of questioning them, & to rise superior to antipathies strongly rooted.

THOMAS JEFFERSON, MEMORANDUM - SERVICES TO MY COUNTRY
[ca. 1800]

I have sometimes asked myself whether my country is the better for my having lived at all? I do not know that it is. I have been the instrument of doing the following things; but they would have been done by others; some of them, perhaps, a little better....

I proposed the demolition of the church establishment, and the freedom of religion. It could only be done by degrees; to wit, the Act of 1776, c. 2, exempted dissenters from contributions to the church, and left the church clergy to be supported by voluntary contributions of their own sect; was continued from year to year, and made perpetual 1779, c. 36. I prepared the act for religious freedom in 1777, as part of the revisal, which was not reported to the Assembly till 1779, and that particular law not passed till 1785, and then by the efforts of Mr. Madison.

Part 7

JEFFERSON BECOMES PRESIDENT. MADISON BECOMES SECRETARY OF STATE

1801 – 1805

Thomas Jefferson's administration was the triumph of American secularism. Unlike his predecessors, he would not issue thanksgiving proclamations. In 1804 the President of the United States took his razor to the Bible and constructed "The Philosophy of Jesus of Nazareth." He removed every trace of the divinity of Jesus from his edition of the four Gospels.

Madison was Jefferson's Secretary of State. Two shy scholars had to deal with Muslim Barbary pirates seizing American boats and holding crews for ransom. They sent the marines. The French revolution had decayed. Napoleon became consul. Then on December 12, 1804, as Jefferson waited for his second inaugural, in the last gasp of revolutionary anti-clericalism, he took the crown from the Pope's hands and placed it on his own head.

They were able to buy the Louisiana Territory from him in 1803. Their domestic accommodation to slavery meant that they did not try to keep slavery out of the new territory and they could not recognize the Haitian slave revolt against France and the regimes emerging from it.

THOMAS JEFFERSON, FIRST INAUGURAL ADDRESS
March 4, 1801

And let us reflect that, having banished from our land that religious intolerance under which mankind so long bled and suffered, we have yet gained little if we countenance a political intolerance as despotic, as wicked, and capable of as bitter and bloody persecutions....

Kindly separated by nature and a wide ocean from the exterminating havoc of one quarter of the globe; too high-minded to endure the degradations of the others; possessing a chosen country, with room enough for our descendants to the thousandth and thousandth generation; entertaining a due sense of our equal right to the use of our own faculties, to the acquisitions of our own industry, to honor and confidence from our fellow-citizens, resulting not from birth, but from our actions and their sense of them; enlightened by a benign religion, professed, indeed, and practiced in various forms, yet all of them inculcating honesty, truth, temperance, gratitude, and the love of man; acknowledging and adoring an overruling Providence, which by all its dispensations proves that it delights in the happiness of man here and his greater happiness hereafter — with all these blessings, what more is necessary to make us a happy and a prosperous people?...

About to enter, fellow-citizens, on the exercise of duties which comprehend everything dear and valuable to you, it is proper you should understand what I deem the essential principles of our Government, and consequently those which ought to shape its Administration. I will compress them within the narrowest compass they will bear, stating the general principle, but not all its limitations. Equal and exact justice to all men, of whatever state or persuasion, religious or political.... freedom of religion; freedom of the press, and freedom of person under the protection of the habeas corpus, and trial by juries impartially selected. These principles form the bright constellation which has gone before us and guided our steps through an age of revolution and reformation....

Relying, then, on the patronage of your good will, I advance with obedience to the work, ready to retire from it whenever you become sensible how much better choice it is in your power to make. And may that Infinite Power which rules the destinies of the universe lead our councils to what is best, and give them a favorable issue for your peace and prosperity.

THOMAS JEFFERSON TO JOHN DICKINSON
March 6, 1801

No pleasure can exceed that which I received from reading your letter of the 21st. ult. It was like the joy we expect in the mansions of the blessed, when received with the embraces of our fathers, we shall be welcomed with their blessing as having done our part not unworthy of them. The storm through which we have passed, has been tremendous indeed. The tough sides of our Argosie have been thoroughly tried. Her strength has stood the waves into which she was steered, with a view to sink her. We shall put her on her republican tack, & she will now show by the beauty of her motion the skill of her builders. Figure apart, our fellow citizens have been led hook-winked from their principles, by a most extraordinary combination of circumstances. But the band is removed, and they now see for themselves. I hope to see shortly a perfect consolidation, to effect which, nothing shall be spared on my part, short of the abandonment of the principles of our revolution. A just and solid republican government maintained here, will be a standing monument & example for the aim & imitation of the people of other countries; and I join with you in the hope and belief that they will see, from our example, that a free government is of all others the most energetic; that the inquiry which has been excited among the mass of mankind by our revolution & it's consequences, will ameliorate the condition of man over a great portion of the globe. What a satisfaction have we in the contemplation of the benevolent effects of our efforts, compared with those of the leaders on the other side, who have discountenanced all advances in science as dangerous innovations, have endeavored to render philosophy and republicanism terms of reproach, to persuade us that man cannot be governed but by the rod, &c. I shall have the happiness of living & dying in the contrary hope.

THOMAS JEFFERSON TO REV. JOHN HARGROVE
March 11, 1801

I beg leave to return you my thanks, and through you, to the Acting Committee of the New Jerusalem Church, in the city of Baltimore, for your friendly congratulations.

I deplore with you the present sanguinary and turbulent state of things in the Eastern world, and look forward to the restoration of peace, and progress of information, for the promotion of genuine charity, liberality, and brotherly kindness towards those who differ from us in opinion.

The Philanthropy which breathes through the several expressions of your letter is a pledge that you will endeavour to diffuse the sentiments of benevolence among our fellow-men, and to inculcate the important truth, that they promote their own happiness by nourishing kind and friendly dispositions towards others.

Commending your endeavours to the Being, in whose hands we are, I beg you to accept assurances of my perfect consideration and respect.

THOMAS JEFFERSON TO DR. JOSEPH PRIESTLEY
March 21, 1801

Yours is one of the few lives precious to mankind, & for the continuance of which every thinking man is solicitous. Bigots may be an exception. What an effort, my dear Sir, of bigotry in Politics & Religion have we gone through! The barbarians really flattered themselves they should be able to bring back the times of Vandalism, when ignorance put everything into the hands of power & priestcraft. All advances in science were proscribed as innovations. They pretended to praise and encourage education, but it was to be the education of our ancestors. We were to look backwards, not forwards, for improvement; the President himself declaring, in one of his answers to addresses, that we were never to expect to go beyond them in real science. This was the real ground of all the attacks on you. Those who live by mystery & charlatanerie, fearing you would render them useless by simplifying the Christian philosophy, — the most sublime & benevolent, but most perverted system that ever shone on man, — endeavored to crush your well-earnt & well-deserved fame. But it was the Lilliputians upon Gulliver. Our countrymen have recovered from the alarm into which art & industry had thrown them; science & honesty are replaced on their high ground; and you, my dear Sir, as their great apostle, are on it's pinnacle. It is with heartfelt satisfaction that, in the first moments of my public action, I can hail you with welcome to our land, tender to you the homage of it's respect & esteem, cover you under the protection of those laws which were made for the wise and good like you, and disdain the legitimacy of that libel on legislation, which under the form of a law, was for some time placed among them.

THOMAS JEFFERSON TO MOSES ROBINSON
March 23, 1801

I have to acknolege the reciept of your favor of the 3d inst. and to thank you for the friendly expressions it contains. I entertain real hope that the whole body of your fellow citizens (many of whom had been carried away by the XYZ. business) will shortly be consolidated in the same sentiments. When they examine the real principles of both parties, I think they will find little to differ about. I know, indeed, that there are some of their leaders who have so committed themselves, that pride, if no other passion, will prevent their coalescing. We must be easy with them. The eastern States will be the last to come over, on account of the dominion of the clergy, who had got a smell of union between Church and State, and began to indulge reveries which can never be realised in the present state of science. If, indeed, they could have prevailed on us to view all advances in science as dangerous innovations, and to look back to the opinions and practices of our forefathers, instead of looking forward, for improvement, a promising groundwork would have been laid. But I am in hopes their good sense will dictate to them, that since the mountain will not come to them, they had better go to the mountain: that they will find their interest in acquiescing in the liberty and science of their country, and that the Christian religion, when divested of the rags in which they have enveloped it, and brought to the original purity and simplicity of its benevolent institutor, is a religion of all others most friendly to liberty, science, and the freest expansion of the human mind.

THOMAS JEFFERSON TO ELBRIDGE GERRY
March 29, 1801

What with the natural current of opinion which has been setting over to us for 18. months, and the immense impetus which was given it from the 11th to the 17th of

Feb., we may now say that the U.S. from N.Y. southwardly, are as unanimous in the principles of '76, as they were in '76. The only difference is, that the leaders who remain behind are more numerous & bolder than the apostles of toryism in '76. The reason is, that we are now justly more tolerant than we could safely have been then, circumstanced as we were. Your part of the Union tho' as absolutely republican as ours, had drunk deeper of the delusion, & is therefore slower in recovering from it. The aegis of government, & the temples of religion & of justice, have all been prostituted there to toll us back to the times when we burnt witches. But your people will rise again. They will awake like Sampson from his sleep, & carry away the gates & posts of the city....

I was not deluded by the eulogiums of the public papers in the first moments of change. If they could have continued to get all the loaves & fishes, that is, if I would have gone over to them, they would continue to eulogise....

The right of opinion shall suffer no invasion from me. Those who have acted well have nothing to fear, however they may have differed from me in opinion: those who have done ill, however, have nothing to hope; nor shall I fail to do justice lest it should be ascribed to that difference of opinion. A coalition of sentiments is not for the interest of printers. They, like the clergy, live by the zeal they can kindle, and the schisms they can create. It is contest of opinion in politics as well as religion which makes us take great interest in them, and bestow our money liberally on those who furnish aliment to our appetite. The mild and simple principles of the Christian philosophy would produce too much calm, too much regularity of good, to extract from it's disciples a support for a numerous priesthood, were they not to sophisticate it, ramify it, split it into hairs, and twist it's texts till they cover the divine morality of it's author with mysteries, and require a priesthood to explain them. The Quakers seem to have discovered this. They have no priests, therefore no schisms. They judge of the text by the dictates of common sense & common morality. So the printers can never leave us in a state of perfect rest and union of opinion. They would be no longer useful, and would have to go to the plough.

THOMAS JEFFERSON TO PIERREPONT EDWARDS
July 1801

[If] the nature of ... government [were] a subordination of the civil to the ecclesiastical power, I [would] consider it as desperate for long years to come. Their steady habits [will] exclude the advances of information, and they [will] seem exactly where they [have always been]. And there [the] clergy will always keep them if they can. [They] will follow the bark of liberty only by the help of a tow-rope.

THOMAS JEFFERSON TO ATTORNEY GENERAL LEVI LINCOLN
August 26, 1801

I am glad to learn from you that the answer to New Haven had a good effect in Massachusetts on the Republicans, and no ill effects on the sincere federalists.... (Of the monarchical federalists, I have no expectations. They are incurables, to be taken care of in a mad-house if necessary, and on motives of charity.) I am much pleased, therefore, with your information that the republican federalists are still coming in to the desired union. The eastern newspapers had given me a different impression, because I suppose the printers knew the taste of their customers, and cooked their dishes to their palates. The Palladium is understood to be the clerical paper, and from the clergy I expect no mercy. They crucified their Savior who preached that their kingdom was not of this world, and all who practice on that precept must expect the extreme of their wrath. The laws of the present day withhold their hands from blood. But lies and slander still remain to them.

THOMAS JEFFERSON TO BISHOP CARROLL
September 3, 1801

I have recieved at this place the application signed by yourself and several respectable inhabitants of Washington on the purchase of a site for a Roman Catholic church from the Commissioners. As the regulation of price rests very much with them, I have refered the paper to them, recommending to them all the favor which the object of the purchase would [....], the advantages of every kind which it would promise, and their duties permit. I shall be happy on this and on every other occasion of showing my respect & concern for the religious society over which you preside in these states and in tendering to yourself assurances of my high esteem and consideration.

THOMAS JEFFERSON TO REV. ISAAC STORY
December 5, 1801

Your favor of Oct. 27. was recieved some time since, and read with pleasure. It is not for me to pronounce on the hypothesis you present of a transmigration of souls from one body to another in certain cases. The laws of nature have withheld from us the means of physical knowledge of the country of spirits and revelation has, for reasons unknown to us, chosen to leave us in the dark as we were. When I was young I was fond of speculations which seemed to promise some insight into that hidden country, but observing at length that they left me in the same ignorance in which they had found me, I have for very many years ceased to read or to think concerning them, and have reposed my head on that pillow of ignorance which a benevolent creator has made so soft for us knowing how much we should be forced to use it. I have thought it better by nourishing the good passions, and controuling the bad, to merit an inheritance in the state of being of which I can know so little, and to trust for the future to him who has been so good for the past. I percieve too that these speculations have been with you only the amusement of leisure hours; while your labours have been devoted to the education of your children, making them good members of society, to the instructing men in their duties, and performing the other offices of a large parish. I am happy in your approbation of the principles I avowed on entering on the government. Ingenious minds, availing themselves of the imperfection of language, have tortured the expressions out of their plain meaning in order to infer departures of them in practice. If revealed language has been able to guard itself against misinterpretations, I could not expect it.

THOMAS JEFFERSON, FIRST ANNUAL MESSAGE TO CONGRESS
December 8, 1801

It is a circumstance of sincere gratification to me that on meeting the great council of our nation, I am able to announce to them, on the grounds of reasonable certainty, that the wars and troubles which have for so many years afflicted our sister nations have at length come to an end, and that the communications of peace and commerce are once more opening among them. While we devoutly return thanks to the beneficent Being who has been pleased to breathe into them the spirit of conciliation and forgiveness, we are bound with peculiar gratitude to be thankful to him that our own peace has been preserved through so perilous a season, and ourselves permitted quietly to cultivate the earth and to practice and improve those arts which tend to increase our comforts.

THOMAS JEFFERSON TO THE DANBURY BAPTIST ASSOCIATION
January 1, 1802

Editor's note: The material in brackets was deleted in Jefferson's final draft, after discussion with his Attorney General. See the next letter.

The affectionate sentiments of esteem and approbation which you are so good as to express towards me, on behalf of the Danbury Baptist Association, give me the highest satisfaction. My duties dictate a faithful and zealous pursuit of the interests of my constituents, and in proportion as they are persuaded of my fidelity to those duties, the discharge of them becomes more and more pleasing.

Believing with you that religion is a matter which lies solely between man and his God, that he owes account to none other for his faith or his worship, that the legitimate powers of government reach actions only, and not opinions, I contemplate with sovereign reverence that act of the whole American people which declared that their legislature should "make no law respecting an establishment of religion, or prohibiting the free exercise thereof," thus building a wall of separation between Church and State. [Congress thus inhibited from acts respecting religion, and the Executive authorised only to execute their acts, I have refrained from prescribing even those occasional performances of devotion, practiced indeed by the Executive of another nation as the legal head of its church, but subject here, as religious exercises only to the voluntary regulations and discipline of each respective sect.] Adhering to this expression of the supreme will of the nation in behalf of the rights of conscience, I shall see with sincere satisfaction the progress of those sentiments which tend to restore to man all his natural rights, convinced he has no natural right in opposition to his social duties.

I reciprocate your kind prayers for the protection and blessing of the common Father and Creator of man, and tender you for yourselves and your religious association, assurances of my high respect and esteem.

THOMAS JEFFERSON TO ATTORNEY GENERAL LEVI LINCOLN
January 1, 1802

Editor's note: Historians presume that Lincoln told Jefferson to delete the passage in brackets in his reply to the Danbury Baptists, so as not to provoke an unnecessary political holy war.

Averse to recieve addresses, yet unable to prevent them, I have generally endeavored to turn them to some account, by making them the occasion, by way of answer, of sowing useful truths and principles among the people, which might germinate and become rooted among their political tenets. The Baptist address, now enclosed, admits of a condemnation of the alliance between Church and State, under the authority of the Constitution. It furnishes an occasion, too, which I have long wished to find, of saying why I do not proclaim fastings and thanksgivings, as my predecessors did. The address, to be sure, does not point at this, and its introduction is awkward. But I foresee no opportunity of doing it more pertinently. I know it will give great offense to the New England clergy; but the advocate of religious freedom is to expect neither peace nor forgiveness from them. Will you be so good as to examine the answer, and suggest any alterations which might prevent an ill effect, or promote a good one, among the people? You understand the temper of those in the North, and can weaken it, therefore, to their stomachs: it is at present seasoned to the Southern taste only. I would ask the favor of you to return it, with the address, in the course of the day or evening.

THOMAS JEFFERSON TO THE BROTHERS AND FRIENDS OF THE MIAMIS, POWTEWATAMIES AND WEEAUKS
January 7, 1802

I receive with great satisfaction the visit you have been so kind as to make us at this place, and I thank the Great Spirit who has conducted you to us in health and safety. It is well that friends should sometimes meet, open their minds mutually, and renew the chain of affection. Made by the same Great Spirit, and living in the same land with our brothers, the red men, we consider ourselves as of the same family; we wish to live with them as one people, and to cherish their interests as our own.

THOMAS JEFFERSON TO REVEREND DAVID AUSTIN
January 21, 1802

Editor's note: Presbyterian Austin convinced hundreds of New Jerseyites that Christ would arrive on "the fourth Sabbath of May, 1796." He then went bankrupt, building a New Haven pier for Jews to sail off to the Judeo-Christian holy land. He flooded Jefferson with applications for government jobs, from cabinet down and schemes to solve the world's problems. The < > hold Jefferson's deletions.

Having daily to read voluminous letters & documents for the dispatch of the public affairs, your letters have condemned a portion of my time which duty forbids me any longer to devote to them. Your talents as a divine I hold in due respect, but of their employment in a political line I must be allowed to judge for myself, bound as I am to select those which I suppose best suited to the public service. Of the special communications to you of his will by the supreme being, I can have no evidence, and therefore must ascribe <all of> them to the false perceptions of your mind. It is with real pain that I find myself at length obliged to say in <common> terms what I had hoped you would have inferred from silence. Accept my respects & best wishes.

THOMAS JEFFERSON TO THE BROTHERS OF THE DELAWARE AND SHAWANEE NATIONS
February 10, 1802

I thank the Great Spirit that he has conducted you hither in health and safety, and that we have an opportunity of renewing our amity, and of holding friendly conference together. It is a circumstance of great satisfaction to us that we are in peace and good understanding with all our red brethren, and that we discover in them the same disposition to continue so which we feel ourselves. It is our earnest desire to merit, and possess their affections, by rendering them strict justice, prohibiting injury from others, aiding their endeavors to learn the culture of the earth, and to raise useful animals, and befriending them as good neighbors, and in every other way in our power. By mutual endeavors to do good to each other, the happiness of both will be better promoted than by efforts of mutual destruction. We are all created by the same Great Spirit; children of the same family. Why should we not live then as brothers ought to do?

THOMAS JEFFERSON TO BROTHER HANDSOME LAKE
November 3, 1802

I have received the message in writing which you sent me through Captain Irvine, our confidential agent, placed near you for the purpose of communicating and transacting between us, whatever may be useful for both nations. I am happy to learn you have been so far favored by the Divine Spirit as to be made sensible of those things which are for your good and that of your people, and of those which are hurtful to you; and particularly that you and they see the ruinous effects which the abuse of spirituous liquors have produced upon them.

THOMAS JEFFERSON, SECOND ANNUAL MESSAGE TO CONGRESS
December 15, 1802

When we assemble together, fellow-citizens, to consider the state of our beloved country, our just attentions are first drawn to those pleasing circumstances which mark the goodness of that Being from whose favor they flow and the large measure of thankfulness we owe for His bounty. Another year has come around, and finds us still blessed with peace and friendship abroad; law, order, and religion at home; good affection and harmony with our Indian neighbors; our burthens lightened, yet our income sufficient for the public wants, and the produce of the year great beyond example. These, fellow-citizens, are the circumstances under which we meet, and we remark with special satisfaction those which under the smiles of Providence result from the skill, industry, and order of our citizens, managing their own affairs in their own way and for their own use, unembarrassed by too much regulation, unoppressed by fiscal exactions.

THOMAS JEFFERSON TO DR. JOSEPH PRIESTLEY
April 9, 1803

While on a short visit lately to Monticello, I recieved from you a copy of your comparative view of Socrates & Jesus, and I avail myself of the first moment of leisure after my return to acknolege the pleasure had in the perusal of it, and the desire it excited to see you take up the subject on a more extensive scale. In consequence of some conversation with Dr. Rush, in the year 1798-99, I had promised some day to write him a letter giving him my view of the Christian system. I have reflected often on it since, & even sketched the outlines in my own mind. I should first take a general view of the moral doctrines of the most remarkable of the antient philosophers, of whose ethics we have sufficient information to make an estimate, say of Pythagoras, Epicurus, Epictetus, Socrates, Cicero, Seneca, Antoninus. I should do justice to the branches of morality they have treated well; but point out the importance of those in which they are deficient. I should then take a view of the deism and ethics of the Jews, and show in what a degraded state they were, and the necessity they presented of a reformation. I should proceed to a view of the life, character, & doctrines of Jesus, who sensible of incorrectness of their ideas of the Deity, and of morality, endeavored to bring them to the principles of a pure deism, and juster notions of the attributes of God, to reform their moral doctrines to the standard of reason, justice & philanthropy, and to inculcate the belief of a future state. This view would purposely omit the question of his divinity, & even his inspiration. To do him justice, it would be necessary to remark the disadvantages his doctrines have to encounter, not having been committed to writing by himself, but by the most unlettered of men, by memory, long after they had heard them from him; when much was forgotten, much misunderstood, & presented in very paradoxical shapes. Yet such are the fragments remaining as to show a master workman, and that his system of morality was the most benevolent & sublime probably that has been ever taught, and consequently more perfect than those of any of the antient philosophers. His character & doctrines have received still greater injury from those who pretend to be his special disciples, and who have disfigured and sophisticated his actions & precepts, from views of personal interest, so as to induce the unthinking part of mankind to throw off the whole system in disgust, and to pass sentence as an impostor on the most innocent, the most benevolent, the most eloquent and sublime character that ever has been exhibited to man. This is the outline; but I have not the time, & still less the information which the subject needs. It will therefore rest with me in contemplation only. You are the person who of all others would do it best, and most promptly. You have all the materials at hand, and you put together with ease. I wish you could be induced to extend your late work to the whole subject.

THOMAS JEFFERSON TO EDWARD DOWSE
April 19, 1803

I now return the sermon you were so kind as to enclose me, having perused it with attention. The reprinting of it by me, as you have proposed, would very readily be ascribed to hypocritical affection, by those who, when they cannot blame our acts, have recourse to the expedient of imputing them to bad motives. This is a resource which can never fail them; because there is no act, however virtuous, for which ingenuity may not find some bad motive. I must also add that tho' I concur with the author in considering the moral precepts of Jesus as more pure, correct, and sublime than those of the ancient philosophers, yet I do not concur with him in the mode of proving it. He thinks it necessary to libel and decry the doctrines of the philosophers; but a man must be blinded, indeed, by prejudice, who can deny them a great degree of merit. I give them their just due, and yet maintain that the morality of Jesus, as taught by himself, and freed from the corruptions of latter times, is far superior. Their philosophy went chiefly to the government of our passions, so far as respected ourselves, and the procuring our own tranquillity. In our duties to others they were short and deficient. They extended their cares scarcely beyond our kindred and friends individually, and our country in the abstract. Jesus embraced with charity and philanthropy our neighbors, our countrymen, and the whole family of mankind. They confined themselves to actions; he pressed his sentiments into the region of our thoughts, and called for purity at the fountain head. In a pamphlet lately published in Philadelphia by Dr. Priestley, he has treated, with more justice and skill than Mr. Bennet, a small portion of this subject. His is a comparative view of Socrates only with Jesus. I have urged him to take up the subject on a broader scale.

Every word which goes forth from me, whether verbally or in writing, becomes the subject of so much malignant distortion, and perverted construction, that I am obliged to caution my friends against admitting the possibility of my letters getting into the public papers, or a copy of them to be taken under any degree of confidence. The present one is perhaps of a tenor to silence some calumniators. But I never will, by any word or act, bow to the shrine of intolerance, or admit the right of inquiry into the religious opinions of others. On the contrary, we are bound, you, I, and everyone, to make common cause, even with error itself, to maintain the common right of freedom of conscience. We ought with one heart and one hand hew down the daring and dangerous efforts of those who would seduce the public opinion to substitute itself into that tyranny over religious faith which the laws have so justly abdicated. For this reason, were my opinions up to the standard of those who arrogate the right of questioning them, I would not countenance that arrogance by descending to an explanation. Accept my friendly salutations & high esteem.

THOMAS JEFFERSON TO DR. BENJAMIN RUSH
April 21, 1803

In some of the delightful conversations with you, in the evenings of 1798–99, and which served as an Anodyne to the afflictions of the crisis through which our country was then laboring, the Christian religion was sometimes our topic: and I then promised you, that one day or other, would give you my views of it. They are the result of a life of inquiry & reflection, and very different from that Anti-Christian system imputed to me by those who know nothing of my opinions. To the corruptions of Christianity I am indeed opposed; but not to the genuine precepts of Jesus himself. I am a Christian, in the only sense he wished any one to be; sincerely attached to his doctrines, in preference to all others; ascribing to himself every human excellence; & believing he never claimed any other. At the short intervals since these conversations, when I could justifiably abstract my mind from public affairs, the subject has been under my contemplation. But the more I considered it, the more it expanded beyond the measure of either my time or information. In the moment of my late departure from Monticello, I received from Doctr. Priestley, his little treatise of 'Socrates & Jesus compared.' This being a section of the general view I had taken of the field, it became a subject of reflection while on the road, and unoccupied otherwise. The result was, to arrange in my mind a Syllabus, or Outline of such an estimate of the comparative merits of Christianity, as wished to see executed by some one of more leisure and information for the task, than myself. This I now send you, as the only discharge of my promise I can probably ever execute. And in confiding it to you, I know it will not be exposed to the malignant perversions of those who make every word from me a text for new misrepresentations & calumnies. I am moreover averse to the communication of my religious tenets to the public; because it would countenance the presumption of those who have endeavored to draw them before that tribunal, and to seduce public opinion to erect itself into that inquisition over the rights of conscience, which the laws have so justly proscribed. It behoves every man who values liberty of conscience for himself, to resist invasions of it in the case of others; or their case may, by change of circumstances, become his own. It behoves him, too, in his own case, to give no example of concession, betraying the common right of independent opinion, by answering questions of faith, which the laws have left between God & himself. Accept my affectionate salutations.

SYLLABUS OF AN ESTIMATE OF THE MERIT OF THE DOCTRINES OF JESUS, COMPARED WITH THOSE OF OTHERS
April 21, 1803

Editor's note: Jefferson's footnote follows the asterisk in brackets.
Translations are in parentheses.

In a comparative view of the Ethics of the enlightened nations of antiquity, of the Jews and of Jesus, no notice should be taken of the corruptions of reason among the antients, to wit, the idolatry & superstition of the vulgar, nor of the corruptions of Christianity by the learned among its professors.

Let a just view be taken of the moral principles inculcated by the most esteemed of the sects of ancient philosophy, or of their individuals; particularly Pythagoras, Socrates, Epicurus, Cicero, Epictetus, Seneca, Antoninus.

I. PHILOSOPHERS.
1. Their precepts related chiefly to ourselves, and the government of those passions which, unrestrained, would disturb our tranquillity of mind.* [To explain, I will exhibit the heads of Seneca's and Cicero's philosophical works, the most extensive of any we have recieved from the antients. Of 10. heads in Seneca, 7. relate to ourselves, to wit *de irá, Consolatio, de tranquilitate, de constantiá sapientis, de otio sapientis, de vitá beatá, de brevitate vitae.* (about anger, Consolation, constancy of the wise, leisure of the wise, the blessed life, briefness of life.) 2. relate to others, *de clementia, de beneficiis* (concerning clemency, concerning benefits), and 1. relates to the government of the world, *de providentiá* (concerning providence). Of 11. tracts of Cicero, 5 respect ourselves, viz. *de finibus* (namely of finality), *Tusculana, Academica, Paradoxa, de Senectute. 1. de officiis,* (Tusculan Disputations, Academics, Paradoxes, On Old Age, 1. Concerning Duties) partly to ourselves, partly to others. 1. *de amicitiá,* (Concerning Friendship) relates to others: and 4. are on different subjects, to wit, *de naturá deorum, de divinatione, de fato, Somnium Scipionis* (Concerning the nature of the Gods, divination, fate, Scipio's dream)].

In this branch of philosophy they were really great.

2. In developing our duties to others, they were short and defective. They embraced, indeed, the circles of kindred & friends, and inculcated patriotism, or the love of our country in the aggregate, as a primary obligation: toward our neighbors & countrymen they taught justice, but scarcely viewed them as within the circle of benevolence. Still less have they inculcated peace, charity & love to our fellow men, or embraced with benevolence the whole family of mankind.

II. JEWS.

1. Their system was Deism; that is, the belief of one only God. But their ideas of him & of his attributes were degrading & injurious.

2. Their Ethics were not only imperfect, but often irreconcilable with the sound dictates of reason & morality, as they respect intercourse with those around us; & repulsive & anti-social, as respecting other nations. They needed reformation, therefore, in an eminent degree.

III. JESUS.

In this state of things among the Jews, Jesus appeared. His parentage was obscure; his condition poor; his education null; his natural endowments great; his life correct and innocent: he was meek, benevolent, patient, firm, disinterested, & of the sublimest eloquence.

The disadvantages under which his doctrines appear are remarkable.

1. Like Socrates & Epictetus, he wrote nothing himself.

2. But he had not, like them, a Xenophon or an Arian to write for him. On the contrary, all the learned of his country, entrenched in its power and riches, were opposed to him, lest his labors should undermine their advantages; and the committing to writing his life & doctrines fell on the most unlettered & ignorant men; who wrote, too, from memory, & not till long after the transactions had passed.

3. According to the ordinary fate of those who attempt to enlighten and reform mankind, he fell an early victim to the jealousy & combination of the altar and the throne, at about 33. years of age, his reason having not yet attained the maximum of its energy, nor the course of his preaching, which was but of 3. years at most, presented occasions for developing a complete system of morals.

4. Hence the doctrines which he really delivered were defective as a whole, and fragments only of what he did deliver have come to us mutilated, misstated, & often unintelligible.

5. They have been still more disfigured by the corruptions of schismatising followers, who have found an interest in sophisticating & perverting the simple doctrines he taught by engrafting on them the mysticisms of a Grecian sophist, frittering them into subtleties, & obscuring them with jargon, until they have caused good men to reject the whole in disgust, & to view Jesus himself as an impostor.

Notwithstanding these disadvantages, a system of morals is presented to us, which, if filled up in the true style and spirit of the rich fragments he left us, would be the most perfect and sublime that has ever been taught by man.

The question of his being a member of the god-head, or in direct communication with it, claimed for him by some of his followers, and denied by others, is foreign to the present view, which is merely an estimate of the intrinsic merit of his doctrines.

1. He corrected the Deism of the Jews, confirming them in their belief of one only god, and giving them juster notions of his attributes and government.

2. His moral doctrines, relating to kindred & friends, were more pure & perfect than those of the most correct of the philosophers, and greatly more so than those of the Jews; and they went far beyond both in inculcating universal philanthropy, not only to kindred and friends, to neighbors and countrymen, but to all mankind, gathering all into one family, under the bonds of love, charity, peace, common wants and common aids. A development of this head will evince the peculiar superiority of the system of Jesus over all others.

3. The precepts of philosophy, & of the Hebrew code, laid hold of actions only. He pushed his scrutinies into the heart of man; erected his tribunal in the region of his thoughts, and purified the waters at the fountain head.

4. He taught, emphatically, the doctrines of a future state, which was either doubted, or disbelieved by the Jews; and wielded it with efficacy, as an important incentive, supplementary to the other motives to moral conduct.

THOMAS JEFFERSON TO HENRY DEARBORN, LEVI LINCOLN AND OTHERS
April 23, 1803

A promise to a friend sometime ago, executed but lately, has placed my religious creed on paper. I am desirous it should be perused by three or four particular friends, with whom tho' I never desired to make a mystery of it, yet no occasion has happened to occur of explaining it to them. It is communicated for their personal satisfaction, and to enable them to judge of the truth or falsehood of the libels published on that subject. When read, the return of the paper with this cover is asked.

THOMAS JEFFERSON TO DR. JOSEPH PRIESTLEY
April 24, 1803

In my letter of Apr. 9. I gave you the substance of a view I had taken of the morality taught by the antient philosophers and by Jesus. The subject being on my mind, I committed to writing a syllabus of it, as I would treat it had I time or information sufficient, and sent it to Dr. Rush in performance of the promise I had formerly made him. Tho' this differs no otherwise from my letter to you than in being more full and formal, yet I send you a copy of it. There is a point or two in which you and I probably differ. But the wonder would be that any two persons should see in the same point of view all the parts of an extensive subject. I did not know that any comparative view of these schemes of morality had been taken till I saw your tract on Socrates and Jesus, and learnt from that that a Mr. Toulmin had written a dissertation in the same way, but I am sure he has left enough of the field to employ your pen advantageously. Accept my sincere prayers for your health and life, and assurances of my affectionate esteem & respect.

THOMAS JEFFERSON TO LEVI LINCOLN
April 26, 1803

Editor's note: On several occasions Jefferson wrote of himself in the third person.

Mr. Lincoln is perfectly free to retain the copy of the syllabus, and to make any use of it his discretion would approve, confident as Th: J. is that his discretion would not permit him to let it be copied lest it should get into print. In the latter case Th: J. would become the butt of every set of disquisitions which every priest would undertake to write on every tenet it expresses. Their object is not truth, but matter whereon to write against Th: J. and this Synopsis would furnish matter for repeating in new forms all the volumes of divinity which are now mouldering on the shelves from which they should never more be taken. Th: J. would thank Mr. L. not to put his name on the paper in filing it away, lest in case of accident to Mr. L. it should get out.

THOMAS JEFFERSON, INSTRUCTIONS TO CAPTAIN MERIWETHER LEWIS
June 20, 1803

Editor's note: Jefferson here is asking Lewis to gather information on the Indians to be encountered on the famous expedition to the Pacific.

And, considering the interest which every nation has in extending & strengthening the authority of reason & justice among the people around them, it will be useful to acquire what knolege you can of the state of morality, religion, & information among them; as it may better enable those who may endeavor to civilize & instruct them, to adapt their measures to the existing notions & practices of those on whom they are to operate.

THOMAS JEFFERSON, THIRD ANNUAL MESSAGE TO CONGRESS
October 17, 1803

We have seen with sincere concern the flames of war lighted up again in Europe, and nations with which we have the most friendly and useful relations engaged in mutual destruction. While we regret the miseries in which we see others involved let us bow with gratitude to that kind Providence which, inspiring with wisdom and moderation our late legislative councils while placed under the urgency of the greatest wrongs, guarded us from hastily entering into the sanguinary contest, and left us only to look on and to pity its ravages.

THOMAS JEFFERSON TO THE BROTHERS OF THE CHOCTAW NATION
December 17, 1803

I am glad, brothers, you are willing to go and visit some other parts of our country. Carriages shall be ready to convey you, and you shall be taken care of on your journey; and when you shall have returned here and rested yourselves to your own mind, you shall be sent home by land. We had provided for your coming by land,

and were sorry for the mistake which carried you to Savannah instead of Augusta, and exposed you to the risks of a voyage by sea. Had any accident happened to you, though we could not help it, it would have been a cause of great mourning to us. But we thank the Great Spirit who took care of you on the ocean, and brought you safe and in good health to the seat of our great Council; and we hope His care will accompany and protect you, on your journey and return home; and that He will preserve and prosper your nation in all its just pursuits.

THOMAS JEFFERSON TO DR. JOSEPH PRIESTLEY
January 29, 1804

I rejoice that you have undertaken the task of comparing the moral doctrines of Jesus with those of the ancient Philosophers. You are so much in possession of the whole subject, that you will do it easier & better than any other person living. I think you cannot avoid giving, as preliminary to the comparison, a digest of his moral doctrines, extracted in his own words from the Evangelists, and leaving out everything relative to his personal history and character. It would be short and precious. With a view to do this for my own satisfaction, I had sent to Philadelphia to get two testaments Greek of the same edition, & two English, with a design to cut out the morsels of morality, and paste them on the leaves of a book, in the manner you describe as having been pursued in forming your Harmony. But I shall now get the thing done by better hands.

THOMAS JEFFERSON TO THE SOEUR THERESE DE ST. XAVIER FARJON, SUPERIOR, AND THE NUNS OF THE ORDER OF ST. URSULA AT NEW ORLEANS
May 15, 1804

I have received, holy sisters, the letter you have written me wherein you express anxiety for the property vested in your institution by the former governments of Louisiana. The principles of the constitution and government of the United States are a sure guarantee to you that it will be preserved to you sacred and inviolate, and that your institution will be permitted to govern itself according to it's own voluntary rules, without interference from the civil authority. Whatever diversity of shade may appear in the religious opinions of our fellow citizens, the charitable objects of your institution cannot be indifferent to any; and it's furtherance of the wholesome purposes of society by training up it's younger members in the way they should go, cannot fail to ensure it the patronage of the government it is under. Be assured it will meet all the protection which my office can give it.

I salute you, holy sisters, with friendship and respect.

THOMAS JEFFERSON TO THE OSAGE NATION
July 16, 1804

We are all now of one family, born in the same land, and bound to live as brothers; and the strangers from beyond the great water are gone from among us. The Great Spirit has given you strength, and has given us strength; not that we might hurt one another, but to do each other all the good in our power. Our dwellings, indeed, are very far apart, but not too far to carry on commerce and useful intercourse. You have furs and peltries which we want, and we have clothes and other useful things which you want. Let us employ ourselves, then, in mutually accommodating each other. To begin this on our part, it was necessary to know what nations inhabited the great country called Louisiana, which embraces all the waters of the Mississippi and Missouri, what number of peltries they could furnish, what quantities and kind of merchandise they would require, where would be the deposits most convenient for them, and to make an exact map of all those waters....

My children, these are my words, carry them to your nation, keep them in your memories, and our friendship in your hearts and may the Great Spirit look down upon us and cover us with the mantle of his love.

THOMAS JEFFERSON TO ABIGAIL ADAMS
July 22, 1804

Editor's note: Mrs. Adams had complained against Jefferson that he had freed someone, James Callender in reality, who had been imprisoned by Adams for nine months under the Sedition Law.

But another fact is that I 'liberated a wretch who was suffering for a libel against Mr. Adams.' I do not know who was the particular wretch alluded to: but I discharged every person under punishment or prosecution under the Sedition law, because I considered and now consider that law to be a nullity as absolute and as palpable as if Congress had ordered us to fall down and worship a golden image; and that it was as much my duty to arrest it's execution in every stage, as it would have been to have rescued from the fiery furnace those who should have been cast into it for refusing to worship their image.

THOMAS JEFFERSON TO BENJAMIN RUSH
August 8, 1804

I shall be happy to recieve your pamphlet, as I am whatever comes from you. I have also a little volume, a mere and faithful compilation which I shall some of these days ask you to read as containing the exemplification of what I advanced in a former letter as to the excellence of 'the Philosophy of Jesus of Nazareth.' Accept affectionate salutations & assurances of esteem and respect.

THOMAS JEFFERSON TO BENJAMIN BARTON
February 14, 1805

The correspondence between Dr. Priestley and myself was unfrequent and short. His fear of encroaching on my public duties deprived me of communications from him which would have been always welcome. I have examined all his letters to me since Mar. 1801. (those preceding being at Monticello) and find they do not contain a single fact interesting to your object. I hardly suppose the following one to be so. Having been long anxious to see a fair and candid comparison made between the doctrines of the Greek and Roman philosophers, and the genuine doctrines of Jesus, I pressed Dr. Priestley, early in 1803, to undertake that work. He at first declined it from the extent of the subject, his own age and infirmities: but he afterwards informed me that having viewed the subject more attentively and finding that his Common place book would refer him readily to the materials, he had undertaken it: and a little before his death he informed me he had finished it. I apprehend however that he meditated a 2nd. part which should have given a view of the genuine doctrines of Jesus divested of those engrafted into his by false followers. I suppose this because it is wanting to compleat the work, and because I observe he calls what is published Part 1st.

THOMAS JEFFERSON, NOTES FOR SECOND INAUGURAL ADDRESS
1805

The former one was an exposition of the principles on which I thought it my duty to administer the government.... The former was promise: this is performance. Yet the nature of the occasion requires that details should be avoided.... The heads are Foreign affairs, Domestic do., viz. Taxes, Debts, Louisiana, Religion, Indians. The Press. None of these heads need any commentary but that of the Indians. This is a proper topic not only to promote the work of humanizing our citizens towards these people, but to conciliate to us the good opinion of Europe on the subject of the Indians. This, however, might have been done in half the compass it here occupies. But every respecter of science, every friend of political reformation must have observed with indignation the hue & cry raised against philosophy & the rights of man; and it really seems as if they would be overbourne & barbarism, bigotry & despotism would recover the ground they have lost by the advance of public understanding. I have thought the occasion justified some discountenance of these antisocial doctrines, some testimony against them, but not to commit myself in direct warfare on them. I have thought it best to say what is directly applied to the Indians only, but admits by inference a more general extention.

JAMES MADISON, MEMORANDUMS FOR THOMAS JEFFERSON'S SECOND INAUGURAL ADDRESS
February 8-21, 1805

Editor's note: Two memos by Madison were with Jefferson's notes for the Address.

Feb. 8. 05

Substitute

"Religion. As religious exercises, could therefore be neither controuled nor prescribed by us. They have accordingly been left as the Constitution found them, under the direction & discipline acknowledged within the several states."

Feb. 21. 05

Instead of "acts of religious exercise suited to it (religion)" "exercises suited to it" or some equivalent variation is suggested.

Part 8

JEFFERSON'S SECOND ADMINISTRATION

1805 – 1809

B ritain and France at war harassed American shipping. In 1807 Jefferson and Madison got Congress to enact the Embargo Act, which banned all international trade with American ports. Eventually reality intruded and the law was repealed as Jefferson left office. But the ban on trade with British and French ports continued, sporadically, until the War of 1812. Concern for the threat from the British military in Canada made Jefferson take note of the rise of the Shawnee Prophet, Tenskwatawa, the brother of Tecumseh.

Religion was still a party question. The New England merchant class naturally opposed the embargo and their clergy denounced Jefferson's "atheism." But the future looked like it was with them regarding secularism. Unitarianism was beginning to grow roots in America and Jefferson thought it was going to be America's future. After the degeneration of the French revolution, Jefferson and Madison's America was the sole strong fort of republican secularism.

THOMAS JEFFERSON, SECOND INAUGURAL ADDRESS
March 4, 1805

In matters of religion, I have considered that its free exercise is placed by the constitution independent of the powers of the general government. I have therefore undertaken, on no occasion, to prescribe the religious exercises suited to it; but have left them, as the constitution found them, under the direction and discipline of state or church authorities acknowledged by the several religious societies.

The aboriginal inhabitants of these countries I have regarded with the commiseration their history inspires. Endowed with the faculties and the rights of men, breathing an ardent love of liberty and independence, and occupying a country which left them no desire but to be undisturbed, the stream of overflowing population from other regions directed itself on these shores; without power to divert, or habits to contend against, they have been overwhelmed by the current, or driven before it; now reduced within limits too narrow for the hunter's state, humanity enjoins us to teach them agriculture and the domestic arts; to encourage them to that industry which alone can enable them to maintain their place in existence, and to prepare them in time for that state of society, which to bodily comforts adds the improvement of the mind and morals. We have therefore liberally furnished them with the implements of husbandry and household use; we have placed among them instructors in the arts of first necessity; and they are covered with the aegis of the law against aggressors from among ourselves.

But the endeavors to enlighten them on the fate which awaits their present course of life, to induce them to exercise their reason, follow its dictates, and change their pursuits with the change of circumstances, have powerful obstacles to encounter; they are combated by the habits of their bodies, prejudice of their minds, ignorance, pride, and the influence of interested and crafty individuals among them, who feel themselves something in the present order of things, and fear to become nothing in any other. These persons inculcate a sanctimonious reverence for the customs of their ancestors; that whatsoever they did, must be done through all time; that reason is a false guide, and to advance under its counsel, in their physical, moral, or political condition, is perilous innovation; that their duty is to remain as their Creator made them, ignorance being safety, and knowledge full of danger; in short, my friends, among them is seen the action and counteraction of good sense and bigotry; they, too, have their anti-philosophers, who find an interest in keeping things in their present state, who dread reformation, and exert all their faculties to maintain the ascendancy of habit over the duty of improving our reason, and obeying its mandates....

Contemplating the union of sentiment now manifested so generally, as auguring harmony and happiness to our future course, I offer to our country sincere congratulations. With those, too, not yet rallied to the same point, the disposition to do so is gaining strength; facts are piercing through the veil drawn over them; and our doubting brethren will at length see, that the mass of their fellow citizens, with whom they cannot yet resolve to act, as to principles and measures, think as they think, and desire what they desire; that our wish, as well as theirs, is, that the public efforts may be directed honestly to the public good, that peace be cultivated, civil and religious liberty unassailed, law and order preserved; equality of rights maintained, and that state of property, equal or unequal, which results to every man from his own industry, or that of his fathers....

I shall now enter on the duties to which my fellow citizens have again called me, and shall proceed in the spirit of those principles which they have approved.... I shall need, too, the favor of that Being in whose hands we are, who led our forefathers, as Israel of old, from their native land, and planted them in a country flowing with all the necessaries and comforts of life; who has covered our infancy with his providence, and our riper years with his wisdom and power; and to whose goodness I ask you to join with me in supplications, that he will so enlighten the minds of your servants, guide their councils, and prosper their measures, that whatsoever they do, shall result in your good, and shall secure to you the peace, friendship, and approbation of all nations.

THOMAS JEFFERSON TO THE CHIEFS OF THE CHICKASAW NATION
March 7, 1805

I am happy to receive you at the seat of the government of the twenty-two nations, and to take you by the hand. Your friendship to the Americans has long been known to me. Our fathers have told us that your nation never spilled the blood of an American, and we have seen you fighting by our side and cementing our friendship by mixing our blood in battle against the same enemies. I rejoice, therefore, that the Great Spirit has covered you with His protection through so long a journey and so inclement a season, and brought you safe to the dwelling of a father who wishes well to all his red children, and to you especially.

THOMAS JEFFERSON TO THE CHIEFS OF THE CHEROKEE NATION
January 10, 1806

My children, I thank you for your visit and pray to the Great Spirit who made us all and planted us all in this land to live together like brothers that He will conduct you safely to your homes, and grant you to find your families and your friends in good health.

THOMAS JEFFERSON TO DOCTORS ROGERS AND SLAUGHTER
March 2, 1806

I deem it the duty of every man to devote a certain portion of his income for charitable purposes; and that it is his further duty to see it so applied as to do the most good of which it is capable. This I believe to be best insured, by keeping within the circle of his own inquiry and information the subjects of distress to whose relief his contributions shall be applied. If this rule be reasonable in private life, it becomes so necessary in my situation, that to relinquish it would leave me without rule or compass. The applications of this kind from different parts of our own, and from foreign countries, are far beyond any resources within my command. The mission of Serampore, in the East Indies, the object of the present application, is but one of many items. However disposed the mind may feel to unlimited good, our means having limits, we are necessarily circumscribed by them. They are too narrow to relieve even the distresses under my own eye; and to desert these for others which we neither see nor know, is to omit doing a certain good for one which is uncertain. I know, indeed, there have been splendid associations for effecting benevolent purposes in remote regions of the earth. But no experience of their effect has proved that more good would not have been done by the same means employed nearer home. In explaining, however, my own motives of action, I must not be understood as impeaching those of others. Their views are those of an expanded liberality. Mine may be too much restrained by the law of usefulness. But it is a law to me, and with minds like yours, will be felt as a justification. With this apology, I pray you to accept my salutations, and assurances of high esteem and respect.

THOMAS JEFFERSON TO THE CHIEFS OF THE OSAGE NATION
December 3, 1806

I welcome you sincerely to the seat of the government of the United States. The journey you have taken is long and fatiguing, and proved your desire to become acquainted with your new brothers of this country. I thank the Master of life, who has preserved you by the way and brought you safely here....

My children, these are my words, carry them to your nation, keep them in your memories and our friendship in your hearts, and may the Great Spirit look down upon us and cover us with the mantle of His love.

THOMAS JEFFERSON TO THE WOLF AND PEOPLE OF THE MANDAN NATION
December 30, 1806

The journey which you have taken to visit your fathers on this side of our island is a long one, and your having undertaken it is a proof that you desired to become acquainted with us. I thank the Great Spirit that he has protected you through the journey and brought you safely to the residence of your friends, and I hope He will have you constantly in His safe keeping, and restore you in good health to your nations and families.

THOMAS JEFFERSON TO THE MASSACHUSETTS LEGISLATURE
February 14, 1807

During the term which yet remains, of my continuance in the station assigned me, your confidence shall not be disappointed, so far as faithful endeavors for your service can merit it.

I feel with particular sensibility your kind expressions towards myself personally; and I pray that that Providence in whose hand are the nations of the earth, may continue towards ours His fostering care, and bestow on yourselves the blessings of His protection and favor.

THOMAS JEFFERSON TO MESSRS. THOMAS, ELLICOT AND OTHERS
November 13, 1807

I thank you for the address you have kindly presented me, on behalf of that portion of the Society of Friends of which you are the representatives, and I learn with satisfaction their approbation of the principles which have influenced the councils of the General Government in their decisions on several important subjects confided to them.

The desire to preserve our country from the calamities and ravages of war, by cultivating a disposition, and pursuing a conduct, conciliatory and friendly to all nations, has been sincerely entertained and faithfully followed. It was dictated by the principles of humanity, the precepts of the gospel, and the general wish of our country, and it was not to be doubted that the Society of Friends, with whom it is a religious principle, would sanction it by their support.

The same philanthropic motives have directed the public endeavors to ameliorate the condition of the Indian natives, by introducing among them a knowledge of agriculture and some of the mechanic arts, by encouraging them to resort to these as more certain, and less laborious resources for subsistence than the chase; and by withholding from them the pernicious supplies of ardent spirits. They are our brethren, our neighbors; they may be valuable friends, and troublesome enemies. Both duty and interest then enjoin, that we should extend to them the blessings of civilized life, and prepare their minds for becoming useful members of the American family. In this important work I owe to your society an acknowledgment that we have felt the benefits of their zealous co-operation, and approved its judicious direction towards producing among those people habits of industry, comfortable subsistence, and civilized usages, as preparatory to religious instruction and the cultivation of letters.

Whatever may have been the circumstances which influenced our forefathers to permit the introduction of personal bondage into any part of these States, and to participate in the wrongs committed on an unoffending quarter of the globe, we may rejoice that such circumstances, and such a sense of them, exist no longer. It is honorable to the nation at large that their legislature availed themselves of the first practicable moment for arresting the progress of this great moral and political error; and I sincerely pray with you, my friends, that all the members of the human family may, in the time prescribed by the Father of us all, find themselves securely established in the enjoyment of life, liberty, and happiness.

THOMAS JEFFERSON TO CAPTAIN JOHN THOMAS
November 18, 1807

I received on the 14th instant your favor of August 31, and I beg you to assure my fellow citizens of the Baptist church of Newhope meeting-house, that I learn with great satisfaction their approbation of the principles which have guided the present administration of the government. To cherish and maintain the rights and liberties of our citizens, and to ward from them the burdens, the miseries, and the crimes of war, by a just and friendly conduct towards all nations, were among the most obvious and important duties of those to whom the management of their public interests have been confided; and happy shall we be if a conduct guided by these views on our part, shall secure to us a reciprocation of peace and justice from other nations. Among the most inestimable of our blessings, also, is that you so justly particularize, of liberty to worship our Creator in the way we think most agreeable to His will; a liberty deemed in other countries incompatible with good government, and yet proved by our experience to be its best support.

THOMAS JEFFERSON, REPLY TO BAPTIST ADDRESS
1807

Among the most inestimable of our blessings is that ... of liberty to worship our Creator in the way we think most agreeable to His will; a liberty deemed in other countries incompatible with good government and yet proved by our experience to be its best support.

THOMAS JEFFERSON TO REV. SAMUEL MILLER
January 23, 1808

I have duly received your favor of the 18th and am thankful to you for having written it, because it is more agreeable to prevent than to refuse what I do not think myself authorized to comply with. I consider the government of the U.S. as interdicted by the Constitution from intermeddling with religious institutions, their doctrines, discipline, or exercises. This results not only from the provision that no law shall be made respecting the establishment, or free exercise, of religion, but from that also which reserves to the states the powers not delegated to the U.S. Certainly no power to prescribe any religious exercise, or to assume authority in religious discipline, has been delegated to the general government. It must then rest with the states, as far as it can be in any human authority. But it is only proposed that I should recommend, not prescribe a day of fasting & prayer. That is, that I should indirectly assume to the U.S. an authority over religious exercises which the Constitution has directly precluded them from. It must be meant too that this recommendation is to carry some authority, and to be sanctioned by some penalty on those who disregard it; not indeed of fine and imprisonment, but of some degree of proscription perhaps in public opinion. And does the change in the nature of the penalty make the recommendation the less a law of conduct for those to whom it is directed? I do not believe it is for the interest of religion to invite the civil magistrate to direct it's exercises, it's discipline, or it's doctrines; nor of the religious societies that the general government should be invested with the power of effecting any uniformity of time or matter among them. Fasting & prayer are religious exercises. The enjoining them an act of discipline. Every religious society has a right to determine for itself the times for these exercises, & the objects proper for them, according to their own particular tenets; and this right can never be safer than in their own hands, where the constitution has deposited it.

I am aware that the practice of my predecessors may be quoted. But I have ever believed that the example of state executives led to the assumption of that authority by the general government, without due examination, which would have discovered that what might be a right in a state government, was a violation of that right when assumed by another. Be this as it may, every one must act according to the dictates of his own reason, & mine tells me that civil powers alone have been given to the President of the U.S. and no authority to direct the religious exercises of his constituents.

I again express my satisfaction that you have been so good as to give me an opportunity of explaining myself in a private letter, in which I could give my reasons more in detail than might have been done in a public answer: and I pray you to accept the assurances of my high esteem & respect.

THOMAS JEFFERSON TO THE NEW YORK SOCIETY OF TAMMANY
February 29, 1808

I have received your address, fellow citizens, and, thankful for the expressions so personally gratifying to myself, I contemplate with high satisfaction the ardent spirit it breathes of love to our country, and of devotion to its liberty and independence. The crisis in which it is placed, cannot but be unwelcome to those who love peace, yet spurn at a tame submission to wrong. So fortunately remote from the theatre of European contests, and carefully avoiding to implicate ourselves in them, we had a right to hope for an exemption from the calamities which have afflicted the contending nations, and to be permitted unoffendingly to pursue paths of industry and peace.

I receive with sensibility your kind prayers for my future happiness, and I supplicate a protecting Providence to watch over your own and our country's freedom and welfare.

THOMAS JEFFERSON TO THE DELEGATES OF THE DEMOCRATIC REPUBLICANS OF PHILADELPHIA
May 25, 1808

Editor's note: Jefferson and Madison's supporters were known as the Republicans, but were gradually acquiring a reputation as "democrats," at the hands of the "monarchist" Federalists. By the time that Andrew Jackson became president, Republican fell out of usage and today's Democratic Party is the lineal descendant of their party.

It is to be lamented that any of our citizens, not thinking with the mass of the nation as to the principles of our government, or of its administration, and seeing all its proceedings with a prejudiced eye, should so misconceive and misrepresent our situation as to encourage aggressions from foreign nations. Our expectation is, that their distempered views will be understood by others as they are by ourselves; but should wars be the consequence of these delusions, and the errors of our dissatisfied citizens find atonement only in the blood of their sounder brethren, we must meet it as an evil necessarily flowing from that liberty of speaking and writing which guards our other liberties; and I have entire confidence in the assurances that your ardor will be animated, in the conflicts brought on, by considerations of the necessity, honor, and justice of our cause.

I sincerely thank you, fellow citizens, for the concern you so kindly express for my future happiness. It is a high and abundant reward for endeavors to be useful; and I supplicate the care of Providence over the well-being of yourselves and our beloved country.

Thomas Jefferson to the Members of the Baltimore Baptist Association
October 17, 1808

I receive with great pleasure the friendly address of the Baltimore Baptist Association, and am sensible how much I am indebted to the kind dispositions which dictated it.

In our early struggles for liberty, religious freedom could not fail to become a primary object. All men felt the right, and a just animation to obtain it was exhibited by all. I was one only among the many who befriended its establishment, and am entitled but in common with others to a portion of that approbation which follows the fulfillment of a duty.

Excited by wrongs to reject a foreign government which directed our concerns according to its own interests, and not to ours, the principles which justified us were obvious to all understandings, they were imprinted in the breast of every human being; and Providence ever pleases to direct the issue of our contest in favor of that side where justice was. Since this happy separation, our nation has wisely avoided entangling itself in the system of European interests, has taken no side between its rival powers, attached itself to none of its ever-changing confederacies. Their peace is desirable; and you do me justice in saying that to preserve and secure this, has been the constant aim of my administration. The difficulties which involve it, however, are now at their ultimate term, and what will be their issue, time alone will disclose. But be it what it may, a recollection of our former vassalage in religion and civil government, will unite the zeal of every heart, and the energy of every hand, to preserve that independence in both which, under the favor of heaven, a disinterested devotion to the public cause first achieved, and a disinterested sacrifice of private interests will now maintain.

I am happy in your approbation of my reasons for determining to retire from a station, in which the favor of my fellow citizens has so long continued and supported me: I return your kind prayers with supplications to the same almighty Being for your future welfare and that of our beloved country.

184

THOMAS JEFFERSON TO THE KETOCTON BAPTIST ASSOCIATION
October 18, 1808

I received with great pleasure the affectionate address of the Ketocton Baptist Association, and am sensible how much I am indebted to the kind dispositions which dictated it.

In our early struggles for liberty, religious freedom could not fail to become a primary object. All men felt the right, and a just animation to obtain it was excited in all. And although your favor selected me as the organ of your petition to abolish the religious denomination of a privileged church, yet I was but one of the many who befriended its object, and am entitled but in common with them to a portion of that approbation which follows the fulfillment of a duty.

The views you express of the conduct of the belligerent powers are as correct as they are afflicting to the lovers of justice and humanity. Those moral principles and conventional usages which have heretofore been the bond of civilized nations, which have so often preserved their peace by furnishing common rules for the measure of their rights, have now given way to force, the law of Barbarians, and the nineteenth century dawns with the Vandalism of the fifth. Nothing has been spared on our part to preserve the peace of our country, during this distempered state of the world. But the difficulties which involve it are now at their ultimate term, and what will be their issue, time alone will disclose. But be that what it may, a recollection of our former vassalage in religion and civil government will unite the zeal of every heart, and the energy of every hand, to preserve that independence in both, which, under the favor of Heaven, a disinterested devotion to the public cause first achieved, and a disinterested sacrifice of private interests will now maintain.

I am happy in your approbation of my reasons for determining to retire from a station in which the favor of my fellow citizens has so long continued and supported me; and I return your kind prayers by supplications to the same Almighty Being for your future welfare, and that of our beloved country.

THOMAS JEFFERSON, EIGHTH ANNUAL MESSAGE TO CONGRESS
November 8, 1808

Availing myself of this the last occasion which will occur of addressing the two houses of the legislature at their meeting, I cannot omit the expression of my sincere gratitude for the repeated proofs of confidence manifested to me by themselves and their predecessors since my call to the administration, and the many indulgences experienced at their hands.... Looking forward with anxiety to their future destinies, I trust that, in their steady character unshaken by difficulties, in their love of liberty, obedience to law, and support of the public authorities, I see a sure guaranty of the permanence of our republic; and retiring from the charge of their affairs, I carry with me the consolation of a firm persuasion that Heaven has in store for our beloved country long ages to come of prosperity and happiness.

THOMAS JEFFERSON TO THE SIX BAPTIST ASSOCIATIONS OF
CHESTERFIELD, VIRGINIA
November 21, 1808

Thank you, fellow citizens, for your affectionate address, and I receive with satisfaction your approbation of my motives for retirement. In reviewing the history of the times through which we have passed, no portion of it gives greater satisfaction, on reflection, than that which presents the efforts of the friends of religious freedom, and the success with which they were crowned. We have solved by fair experiment, the great and interesting question whether freedom of religion is compatible with order in government, and obedience to the laws. And we have experienced the quiet as well as the comfort which results from leaving every one to profess freely and openly those principles of religion which are the inductions of his own reason, and the serious convictions of his own inquiries....

I thank you sincerely for your kind wishes for my welfare, and with equal sincerity implore the favor of a protecting Providence for yourselves.

THOMAS JEFFERSON TO ALBERT GALLATIN
December 8, 1808

Editor's note: Jefferson is discussing applications for government jobs.

Mr. Harrison will continue in office till the 3rd of March. I send you tit for tat, one lady application for another. However our feelings are to be perpetually harrowed by these solicitations, our course is plain, and inflexible to right or left. But for God's sake get us relieved from this dreadful drudgery of refusal.

THOMAS JEFFERSON TO THE METHODIST EPISCOPAL CHURCH AT
PITTSBURG, PENNSYLVANIA
December 9, 1808

I am much indebted; fellow citizens, for your friendly address of November 20th, and gratified by its expressions of personal regard to myself. Having ever been an advocate for the freedom of religious opinion and exercise, from no person, certainly, was an abridgment of these sacred rights to be apprehended less than from myself.

In justice, too, to our excellent Constitution, it ought to be observed, that it has not placed our religious rights under the power of any public functionary. The power, therefore, was wanting, not less than the will, to injure these rights....

For that portion of your approbation which you are pleased to bestow on my conduct, I am truly thankful, and I offer my sincere prayers for your welfare, and a happy issue of our country from the difficulties impending over it.

THOMAS JEFFERSON TO THE CITIZENS OF PHILADELPHIA
February 3, 1809

I learn with great satisfaction your approbation of the several measures passed by the government and enumerated in your address. For the advantages flowing from them you are indebted principally to a wise and patriotic legislature, and to the able and inestimable coadjutors with whom it has been my good fortune to be associated in the direction of your affairs. That these measures may be productive of the ends intended, must be the wish of every friend of his country; and the belief that everything has been done to preserve our peace, secure the rights of our fellow citizens, and to promote their best interests, will be a consolation under every situation to which the great Disposer of events may destine us.

Your approbation of the motives for my retirement from the station so long confided to me, is a confirmation of their correctness. In no office can rotation be more expedient; and none less admits the indulgence of age. I am peculiarly sensible of your kind wishes for my happiness in the tranquillity of retirement. Nothing will contribute more to it than the hope of carrying with me the approbation of my fellow citizens, of the endeavors which I have faithfully exerted to be useful to them. To the all-protecting favor of Heaven I commit yourselves and our common country.

THOMAS JEFFERSON TO THE LEGISLATURE OF THE STATE OF GEORGIA
February 3, 1809

To no events which can concern the future welfare of my country, can I ever become an indifferent spectator; her prosperity will be my joy, her calamities my affliction.

Thankful for the indulgence with which my conduct has been viewed by the legislature of Georgia, and for the kind expressions of their good will, I supplicate the favor of Heaven towards them and our beloved country.

THOMAS JEFFERSON TO THE SOCIETY OF THE METHODIST EPISCOPAL CHURCH AT NEW LONDON, CONNECTICUT
February 4, 1809

The approbation you are so good as to express of the measures which have been recommended and pursued during the course of my administration of the national concerns, is highly acceptable. The approving voice of our fellow citizens, for endeavors to be useful, is the greatest of all earthly rewards.

No provision in our Constitution ought to be dearer to man than that which protects the rights of conscience against the enterprises of the civil authority. It has not left the religion of its citizens under the power of its public functionaries, were it possible that any of these should consider a conquest over the consciences of men either attainable or applicable to any desirable purpose. To me no information could be more welcome than that the minutes of the several religious societies should prove, of late, larger additions than have been usual, to their several associations, and I trust that the whole course of my life has proved me a sincere friend to religious as well as civil liberty.

I thank you for your affectionate good wishes for my future happiness.

Retirement has become essential to it; and one of its best consolations will be to witness the advancement of my country in all those pursuits and acquisitions which constitute the character of a wise and virtuous nation; and I offer sincere prayers to Heaven that its benediction may attend yourselves, our country and all its sons.

THOMAS JEFFERSON TO THE GENERAL ASSEMBLY OF VIRGINIA
February 16, 1809

To the sincere spirit of republicanism are naturally associated the love of country, devotion to its liberty, its rights, and its honor. Our preference to that form of government has been so far justified by its success, and the prosperity with which it has blessed us. In no portion of the earth were life, liberty and property ever so securely held; and it is with infinite satisfaction that withdrawing from the active scenes of life, I see the sacred design of these blessings committed to those who are sensible of their value and determined to defend them....

The assurances of your approbation, and that my conduct has given satisfaction to my fellow citizens generally, will be an important ingredient in my future happiness; and that the supreme Ruler of the universe may have our country under His special care, will be among the latest of my prayers.

THOMAS JEFFERSON TO THE CITIZENS OF WILMINGTON
February 16, 1809

I am thankful for the great indulgence with which you have viewed the measures of my administration. Of their wisdom, others must judge; but I may truly say they have been pursued with honest intentions, unbiased by any personal or interested views. It is a consolation to know that the motives for my retirement are approved; and although I withdraw from public functions, I shall continue an anxious spectator of passing events, and offer to Heaven my constant prayers for the preservation of our republic, and especially of those its best principles which secure to all its citizens a perfect equality of rights.

THOMAS JEFFERSON TO THE REPUBLICANS OF NIAGARA
February 24, 1809

The eventful crisis in our national affairs so truly portrayed in your very friendly address, has justly excited your serious attention. The nations of the earth prostrated at the foot of power, the ocean submitted to the despotism of a single nation, the laws of nature and the usages which have hitherto regulated the intercourse of nations and interposed some restraint between power and right, now totally disregarded. Such is the state of things when the United States are left single-handed to maintain the rights of neutrals, and the principles of public right against a warring world. Under these circumstances, it is a great consolation to receive the assurances of our faithful citizens that they will unite their destiny with their government, will rally under the banners of their country, and with their lives and fortunes, defend and support their civil and religious rights. This declaration, too, is the more honorable from those whose frontier residence will expose them particularly to the inroads of a foe....

I thank you for your kind wishes for my future happiness in retiring from public life to the bosom of my family. Nothing will contribute more to it than the assurance that my fellow citizens approve of my endeavors to serve them, and the hope that we shall be continued in the blessings we have enjoyed under the favor of Heaven.

THOMAS JEFFERSON TO THE REPUBLICAN YOUNG MEN OF NEW LONDON
February 24, 1809

You do justice to the government in believing that their utmost endeavors have been used to steer us clear of wars with other nations, and honor to yourselves in declaring that if these endeavors prove ineffectual, and your country is called upon to defend its rights and injured honor by an appeal to arms, you will be ready for the contest, and will meet our enemies at the threshold of our country. While prudence will endeavor to avoid this issue, bravery will prepare to meet it.

I thank you, fellow citizens, for your kind expressions of regard for myself, and prayers for my future happiness, and I join in supplications to that Almighty Being who has heretofore guarded our councils, still to continue His gracious benedictions towards our country, and that yourselves may be under the protection of His divine favor.

THOMAS JEFFERSON TO THE TAMMANY SOCIETY OF WASHINGTON
March 2, 1809

I learn with sincere pleasure that the measures I have pursued in directing the affairs of our nation have met with approbation. Their sole object has certainly been the good of my fellow citizens, which sometimes may have been mistaken, but never intentionally disregarded. This approbation is the more valued as being the spontaneous effusion of the feelings of those who have lived in the same city with myself, and having examined carefully and even jealously my conduct through every passing day, bear testimony to their belief in its fidelity. I am happy, in my retirement, to carry with me your esteem and your prayers for my health, peace, and happiness; and I sincerely supplicate Heaven that your own personal welfare may long make a part of the general prosperity of a great, a free, and a happy people.

Part 9

MADISON BECOMES PRESIDENT

1809 – 1812

J efferson returned to Virginia and never left it again. He remained in contact with the world through an immense correspondence.

The major preoccupation of the new President was the ever menacing foreign situation. But domestically the regime stayed on course. In 1811 Madison vetoed a bill incorporating a Washington Episcopal church. He immediately followed with another veto with regard to reserving land in the Mississippi territory for a Baptist church.

In 1811, the army defeated Tenskwatawa, Tecumseh's brother, at Tippecanoe, Indiana. Potential involvement of the Indian movement with Britain is his concern as the country headed to one last war with Britain, with Madison's declaration of war, June 18, 1812.

THOMAS JEFFERSON TO THE CITIZENS OF WASHINGTON
March 4, 1809

The station which we occupy among the nations of the earth is honorable, but awful. Trusted with the destinies of this solitary republic of the world, the only monument of human rights, and the sole depository of the sacred fire of freedom and self-government, from hence it is to be lighted up in other regions of the earth, if other regions of the earth shall ever become susceptible of its benign influence. All mankind ought then, with us, to rejoice in its prosperous, and sympathize in its adverse fortunes, as involving everything dear to man. And to what sacrifices of interest, or convenience, ought not these considerations to animate us? To what compromises of opinion and inclination, to maintain harmony and union among ourselves, and to preserve from all danger this hallowed ark of human hope and happiness. That differences of opinion should arise among men, on politics, on religion, and on every other topic of human inquiry, and that these should be freely expressed in a country where all our faculties are free, is to be expected. But these valuable privileges are much prevented when permitted to disturb the harmony of social intercourse, and to lessen the tolerance of opinion. To the honor of society here, it has been characterized by a just and generous liberality, and an indulgence of those affections which, without regard to political creeds, constitute the happiness of life.

JAMES MADISON, FIRST INAUGURAL ADDRESS
March 4, 1809

To cherish peace and friendly intercourse with all nations having correspondent dispositions; to maintain sincere neutrality toward belligerent nations; to prefer in all cases amicable discussion and reasonable accommodation of differences to a decision of them by an appeal to arms; to exclude foreign intrigues and foreign partialities, so degrading to all countries and so baneful to free ones; to foster a spirit of independence too just to invade the rights of others, too proud to surrender our own, too liberal to indulge unworthy prejudices ourselves and too elevated not to look down upon them in others; to hold the union of the States as the basis of their peace and happiness; to support the Constitution, which is the cement of the Union, as well in its limitations as in its authorities; to respect the rights and authorities reserved to the States and to the people as equally incorporated with and essential to the success of the general system; to avoid the slightest interference with the right of conscience or the functions of religion, so wisely exempted from civil jurisdiction; to preserve in their full energy the other salutary provisions in behalf of private and personal rights, and of the freedom of the press; to observe economy in public expenditures; to liberate the public resources by an honorable discharge of the public debts; to keep within the requisite limits a standing military force, always remembering that an armed and trained militia is the firmest bulwark of republics—that without standing armies their liberty can never be in danger, nor with large ones safe; to promote by authorized means improvements friendly to agriculture, to manufactures, and to external as well as internal commerce; to favor in like manner the advancement of science and the diffusion of information as the best aliment to true liberty; to carry on the benevolent plans which have been so meritoriously applied to the conversion of our aboriginal neighbors from the degradation and wretchedness of savage life to a participation of the improvements of which the human mind and manners are susceptible in a civilized state—as far as sentiments and intentions such as these can aid the fulfillment of my duty, they will be a resource which can not fail me....

But the source to which I look or the aids which alone can supply my deficiencies is in the well-tried intelligence and virtue of my fellow-citizens, and in the counsels of those representing them in the other departments associated in the care of the national interests. In these my confidence will under every difficulty be best placed, next to that which we have all been encouraged to feel in the guardianship and guidance of that Almighty Being whose power regulates the destiny of nations, whose blessings have been so conspicuously dispensed to this rising Republic, and to whom we are bound to address our devout gratitude for the past, as well as our fervent supplications and best hopes for the future.

THOMAS JEFFERSON TO STEPHEN CROSS
March 28, 1809

Sincerely and affectionately attached to our national Constitution, as the ark of our safety, and grand Palladium of our peace and happiness, I learn with pleasure that the number of those in the county of Essex, who read and think for themselves, is great, and constituted of men who will never surrender but with their lives, the invaluable liberties achieved by their fathers. Their elevated minds put all to the hazard for a threepenny duty on tea, by the same nation which now exacts a tribute equal to the value of half our exported produce.

I thank you, fellow citizens, for the kind interest you take in my future happiness, and I sincerely supplicate that overruling Providence which governs the destinies of men and nations; to dispense His choicest blessings on yourselves and our beloved country.

THOMAS JEFFERSON TO THE FRIENDS OF THE ADMINISTRATION OF THE UNITED STATES IN BRISTOL COUNTY, RHODE ISLAND
March 29, 1809

In retiring from the duties of my late station, I have the consolation of knowing that such is the character of those into whose hands they are transferred, and of a conviction that all will be done for us which wisdom and virtue can do. I thank you, fellow citizens, for the kind sentiments of your address, and am particularly gratified by your approbation of the course I have pursued; and I pray Heaven to keep you under its holy favor.

THOMAS JEFFERSON TO THE DEMOCRATIC REPUBLICAN DELEGATES FROM THE TOWNSHIPS OF WASHINGTON COUNTY, IN PENNSYLVANIA
March 31, 1809

Our lot has been cast, by the favor of Heaven, in a country and under circumstances, highly auspicious to our peace and prosperity, and where no pretence can arise for the degrading and oppressive establishments of Europe. It is our happiness that honorable distinctions flow only from public approbation; and that finds no object in titled dignitaries and pageants. Let us then, fellow citizens, endeavor carefully to guard this happy state of things, by keeping a watchful eye over the disaffection of wealth and ambition to the republican principles of our Constitution, and by sacrificing all our local and personal interests to the cultivation of the Union, and maintenance of the authority of the laws.

My warmest thanks are due to you, fellow citizens, for the affectionate sentiments expressed in your address, and my prayers will ever be offered for your welfare and happiness.

THOMAS JEFFERSON TO THE MEMBERS OF THE BAPTIST CHURCH OF BUCK MOUNTAIN IN ALBEMARLE
April 13, 1809

I thank you, my friends and neighbors, for your kind congratulations on my return to my native home, and on the opportunities it will give me of enjoying, amidst your affections, the comforts of retirement and rest. Your approbation of my conduct is the more valued as you have best known me, and is an ample reward for any services I may have rendered. We have acted together from the origin to the end of a memorable Revolution, and we have contributed, each in the line allotted us, our endeavors to render its issue a permanent blessing to our country. That our social intercourse may, to the evening of our days, be cheered and cemented by witnessing the freedom and happiness for which we have labored, will be my constant prayer. Accept the offering of my affectionate esteem and respect.

THOMAS JEFFERSON TO THE TAMMANY SOCIETY OF THE CITY OF BALTIMORE
May 25, 1809

The hope you express that my successor will continue in the same system of measures, is guaranteed, as far as future circumstances will permit, by his enlightened and zealous participation in them heretofore, and by the happy pacification he is now effecting for us. Your wishes for my future happiness are very thankfully felt, and returned by the sincerest desires that yourselves may experience the favors of the great Dispenser of all good.

THOMAS JEFFERSON TO JAMES FISHBACK
September 27, 1809

Editor's note: The letter is as received by Fishback except for the lengthy passage in brackets, from a copy of Jefferson's missing composition draft.

I thank you for the pamphlet you were so kind as to send me. At an earlier period of life I pursued enquiries of that kind with industry and care. Reading, reflection and time have convinced me [it is better to be quiet myself, and let others be quiet on these speculations. Every religion consists of moral precepts, and of dogmas. In the first they all agree. All forbid us to murder, steal, plunder, bear false witness & ca. and these are the articles necessary for the preservation of order, justice, and happiness in society. In their particular dogmas all differ; no two professing the same. These respect vestments, ceremonies, physical opinions, and metaphysical speculations, totally unconnected with morality, and unimportant to the legitimate objects of society. Yet these are the questions on which have hung the bitter schisms of Nazarenes, Socinians, Arians, Athanasians in former times, and now of Trinitarians, Unitarians, Catholics, Lutherans, Calvinists, Methodists, Baptists, Quakers & c. Among the Mahometans we are told that thousands fell victims to the dispute whether the first or second toe of Mahomet was longest; and what blood, how many human lives have the words 'this do in remembrance of me' cost the Christian world! We all agree in the obligation of the moral precepts of Jesus; but we schismatize and lose ourselves in subtleties about his nature, his conception maculate or immaculate, whether he was a god or not a god, whether his votaries are to be initiated by simple aspersion, by immersion, or without water; whether his priests must be robed in white, in black, or not robed at all; whether we are to use our own reason, or the reason of others, in the opinions we form, or as to the evidence we are to believe. It is on questions of this, and still less importance, that such oceans of human blood have been spilt, and whole regions of the earth have been desolated by wars and persecutions, in which human ingenuity has been exhausted in inventing new tortures for their brethren. It is time then to become sensible how insoluble these questions are by minds like ours, how unimportant, and how mischievous; and to consign them to the sleep of death, never to be awakened from it. The varieties in the structure and action of the human mind, as in those of the body, are the work of our creator, against which it cannot be a religious duty to erect the standard of uniformity. The practice of morality being necessary for the well being of society, he has taken care to impress it's precepts so indelibly on our hearts, that they shall not be effaced by the whimsies of our brain. Hence we see good men in all religions, and as many in one as another. It is then a matter of principle with me to avoid disturbing the tranquility of others by the expression of any opinion on the (unimportant points) innocent questions on which we schismatize, and think it enough to hold fast to those moral precepts which are of the essence of Christianity, and of all other religions. No where are these to be found in greater purity than in the discourses of the great reformer of religion whom

---

we follow. — I have been led into these reflections by your invitation to make observations on the subject of your pamphlet, as you have treated it. The only one I permit myself is on the candor, the moderation and the ingenuity with which you appear to have sought truth. that the interests of society require the observation of those moral precepts only in which all religions agree, (for all forbid us to murder, steal, plunder, or bear false witness,) and that we should not intermeddle with the particular dogmas in which all religions differ, and which are totally unconnected with morality. In all of them we see good men, and as many in one as another. The varieties in the structure and action of the human mind as in those of the body, are the work of our creator, against which it cannot be a religious duty to erect the standard of uniformity. The practice of morality being necessary for the well-being of society, he has taken care to impress its precepts so indelibly on our hearts that they shall not be effaced by the subtleties of our brain. We all agree in the obligation of the moral precepts of Jesus, and nowhere will they be found delivered in greater purity than in his discourses. It is, then, a matter of principle with me to avoid disturbing the tranquillity of others by the expression of any opinion on the innocent questions on which we schismatise.

On the subject of your pamphlet, and the mode of treating it, I permit myself only to observe the candor, moderation and ingenuity with which you appear to have sought truth. This is of good example, and worthy of commendation. If all the writers and preachers on religious questions had been of the same temper, the history of the world would have been of much more pleasing aspect.

THOMAS JEFFERSON TO WILLIAM BALDWIN
January 19, 1810

Editor's note: At a later period, Jefferson confused who he wrote this letter to, marking it to Samuel Kercheval, and it is found in some editions of his works as addressed to him.

Yours of the 7th. inst. has been duly recieved, with the pamphlet inclosed, for which I return you my thanks. Nothing can be more exactly and seriously true than what is there stated; that but a short time elapsed after the death of the great reformer of the Jewish religion, before his principles were departed from by those who professed to be his special servants, and perverted into an engine for enslaving mankind, and aggrandising their oppressors in church and state; that the purest system of morals ever before preached to man, has been adulterated and sophisticated by artificial constructions, into a mere contrivance to filch wealth and power to themselves; that rational men not being able to swallow their impious heresies, in order to force them down their throats, they raise the hue and cry of infidelity, while themselves are the greatest obstacles to the advancement of the real doctrines of Jesus, and do in fact constitute the real Anti-Christ.

You expect that your book will have some effect on the prejudices which the society of Friends entertain against the present and late administrations. In this I think you will be disappointed. The Friends are men, formed with the same passions, and swayed by the same natural principles and prejudices as others. In cases where the passions are neutral, men will display their respect for the religious professions of their sect. But where their passions are enlisted, these professions are no obstacle. You observe very truly that both the late and present administration conducted the government on principles professed by the Friends. Our efforts to preserve peace, our measures as to the Indians, as to slavery, as to religious freedom, were all in consonance with their professions. Yet I never expected we should get a vote from them, and in this I was neither decieved nor disappointed. There is no riddle in this, to those who do not suffer themselves to be duped by the professions of religious sectaries. The theory of American Quakerism is a very obvious one. The mother society is in England. Its members are English by birth and residence, devoted to their own country, as good citizens ought to be. The Quakers of these States are colonies or filiations from the mother society, to whom that society sends it's yearly lessons. On these the filiated societies model their opinions, their conduct, their passions and attachments. A Quaker is, essentially, an Englishman, in whatever part of the earth he is born or lives. The outrages of Great Britain on our navigation and commerce, have kept us in perpetual bickerings with her. The Quakers here have taken side against their own government; not on their profession of peace, for they saw that peace was our object also; but from devotion to the views of the mother-society. In 1797. and 8. when an administration sought war with France, the Quakers were the most clamorous for war. Their principle of peace, as a secondary one, yielded to the primary one of Adherence to the Friends in England, and what was patriotism in the Original became Treason in the Copy. On that occasion, they obliged their good old leader, Mr. Pemberton, to erase his name from a petition to Congress, against war, which had been delivered to a Representative of Pennsylvania, a member of the late and present administration. He accordingly permitted the old gentleman to erase his name. You must not, therefore, expect that your book will have any more effect on the society of Friends here, than on the English merchants settled among us. I apply this to the Friends in general, not universally. I know individuals among them as good patriots as we have. I thank you for the kind wishes and sentiments towards myself, expressed in your letter, & sincerely wish to yourself the blessings of health & happiness.

THOMAS JEFFERSON TO REV. SAMUEL KNOX
February 12, 1810

The times which brought us within mutual observation were awfully trying. But truth and reason are eternal. They have prevailed. And they will eternally prevail, however in times and places they may be overborne for a while by violence, military, civil, or ecclesiastical. The preservation of the holy fire is confided to us by the world, and the sparks which will emanate from it will ever serve to rekindle it in other quarters of the globe, numinibus secundis [with the help of the gods].

THOMAS JEFFERSON TO JOHN TYLER
May 26, 1810

I have long lamented with you the depreciation of law science. The opinion seems to be that Blackstone is to us what the Alcoran is to the Mahometans, that everything which is necessary is in him, and what is not in him is not necessary.

THOMAS JEFFERSON TO WILLIAM DUANE
August 12, 1810

Our laws, language, religion, politics and manners are so deeply laid in English foundations, that we shall never cease to consider their history as a part of ours, and to study ours in that as its origin.

JAMES MADISON, VETO MESSAGE TO THE HOUSE OF REPRESENTATIVES OF THE UNITED STATES
February 21, 1811

Editor's note: Readers should be aware that Madison slightly misquotes the First Amendment, which literally reads, "Congress shall make no law respecting an establishment of religion."

Having examined and considered the bill entitled "An Act incorporating the Protestant Episcopal Church in the town of Alexander, in the District of Columbia," I now return the bill to the House of Representatives, in which it originated, with the following objections:

Because the bill exceeds the rightful authority to which governments are limited by the essential distinction between civil and religious functions, and violates in particular the article of the Constitution of the United States which declares 'Congress shall make no law respecting a religious establishment.' The bill enacts into and establishes by law sundry rules and proceedings relative purely to the organization and policy of the church incorporated, and comprehending even the election and removal of the minister of the same, so that no change could be made therein by the particular society or by the general church of which it is a member, and whose authority it recognizes. This particular church, therefore, would so far be a religious establishment by law, a legal force and sanction being given to certain articles in its constitution and administration. Nor can it be considered that the articles thus established are to be taken as the descriptive criteria only of the corporate identity of the society, inasmuch as this identity must depend on other characteristics, as the regulations established are in general unessential and alterable according to the principles and canons by which churches of the denomination govern themselves, and as the injunctions and prohibitions contained in the regulations would be enforced by the penal consequences applicable to the violation of them according to the local law.

Because the bill vests in the said incorporated church an authority to provide for the support of the poor and the education of poor children of the same, an authority which, being altogether superfluous if the provision is to be the result of pious charity, would be a precedent for giving to religious societies as such a legal agency in carrying into effect a public and civil duty.

JAMES MADISON, VETO MESSAGE TO THE HOUSE OF REPRESENTATIVES OF THE UNITED STATES
February 28, 1811

Editor's note: Again, Madison slightly misquotes the First Amendment.

Having examined and considered the bill entitled "An Act for the relief of Richard Trevin, William Coleman, Edwin Lewis, Samuel Mims, Joseph Wilson, and the Baptist Church at Salem Meeting House, in the Mississippi Territory," I now return the same to the House of Representatives, in which it originated, with the following objection:

Because the bill in reserving a certain parcel of land of the United States for the use of said Baptist Church comprises a principle and precedent for the appropriation of funds of the United States for the use and support of religious societies, contrary to the article of the Constitution which declares the 'Congress shall make no law respecting a religious establishment.'

THOMAS JEFFERSON TO WILLIAM DUANE
March 28, 1811

If we move in mass, be it ever so circuitously, we shall attain our object; but if we break into squads, everyone pursuing the path he thinks most direct, we become an easy conquest to those who can now barely hold us in check. I repeat again, that we ought not to schismatize on either men or measures. Principles alone can justify that. If we find our government in all its branches rushing headlong, like our predecessors, into the arms of monarchy, if we find them violating our dearest rights, the trial by jury, the freedom of the press, the freedom of opinion, civil or religious, or opening on our peace of mind or personal safety the sluices of terrorism, if we see them raising standing armies, when the absence of all other danger points to these as the sole objects on which they are to be employed, then indeed let us withdraw and call the nation to its tents. But while our functionaries are wise, and honest, and vigilant, let us move compactly under their guidance, and we have nothing to fear....

God bless you and preserve you through a long and healthy old age.

THOMAS JEFFERSON TO GENERAL THADDEUS KOSCIUSKO
April 13, 1811

And behold! Another example of man rising in his might and bursting the chains of his oppressor, and in the same hemisphere. Spanish America is all in revolt. The insurgents are triumphant in many of the States, and will be so in all. But there the danger is that the cruel arts of their oppressors have enchained their minds, have kept them in the ignorance of children, and as incapable of self-government as children. If the obstacles of bigotry and priest-craft can be surmounted, we may hope that common sense will suffice to do everything else. God send them a safe deliverance.

THOMAS JEFFERSON TO ALEXANDER VON HUMBOLDT
April 14, 1811

The interruption of our intercourse with France for some time past, has prevented my writing to you. A conveyance now occurs.... It is the first safe opportunity offered of acknowledging ... the IIId part of your valuable work, 2d, 3d, 4th and 5th livraisons, and the IVth part, 2d, 3d, and 4th livraisons, with the Tableaux de la nature, and an interesting map of New Spain. For these magnificent and much esteemed favors, accept my sincere thanks. They give us a knowledge of that country more accurate than I believe we possess of Europe, the seat of the science of a thousand years. It comes out, too, at a moment when those countries are beginning to be interesting to the whole world. They are now becoming the scenes of political revolution, to take their stations as integral members of the great family of nations....

I imagine they will copy our outlines of confederation and elective government, abolish distinction of ranks, bow the neck to their priests, and persevere in intolerantism.

JAMES MADISON TO THE BAPTIST CHURCHES IN NEAL'S CREEK
AND ON THE BLACK CREEK, NORTH CAROLINA
June 3, 1811

I have received, fellow-citizens, your address, approving my objection to the Bill containing a grant of public land to the Baptist Church at Salem Meeting House: Mississippi Territory. Having always regarded the practical distinction between Religion and Civil Government as essential to the purity of both and as guaranteed by the Constitution of the United States, I could not have otherwise discharged my duty on the occasion which presented itself. Among the various religious societies in our Country, none has been more vigilant or constant in maintaining that distinction than the Society of which you make a part, and it is an honorable proof of your sincerity and integrity, that you are as ready to do so in a case favoring the interest of your brethren as in other cases. It is but just, at the same time, to the Baptist Church at Salem Meeting House, to remark that their application to the National legislature does not appear to have contemplated a grant of the land in question but on terms that might be equitable to the public as well as to themselves.

THOMAS JEFFERSON TO JOHN ADAMS
April 20, 1812

Editor's note: The Wabash prophet referred to below was Tenskwatawa, the brother of Tecumseh. Tenskwatawa lost the battle of Tippecanoe to General William Henry Harrison, November 7, 1811.

You wish to know something of the Richmond and Wabash prophets. Of Nimrod Hewes I never heard before. Christopher Macpherson I have known for 20. years. He is a man of color, brought up as a bookkeeper by a merchant, his master, and afterwards enfranchised. He had understanding enough to post up his ledger from his journal, but not enough to bear up against Hypochondriac affections and the gloomy forebodings they inspire. He became crazy, foggy, his head always in the clouds, and rhapsodizing what neither himself nor any one else could understand. I think he told me he had visited you personally while you were in the administration, and wrote you letters, which you have probably forgotten in the mass of correspondencies of that crazy class, of whose complaints, and terrors, and mysticisms, the several presidents have been the regular depositories. Macpherson was too honest to be molested by anybody, and too inoffensive to be a subject to the Mad-house; altho', I believe, we are told in the old book that 'every man that is mad, and maketh himself a prophet, thou shouldst put him in prison and in the stocks.'

The Wabash prophet is a very different character, more rogue than fool, if to be a rogue is not the greatest of all follies. He arose to notice while I was in the administration, and became of course a proper subject of enquiry for me. The enquiry was made with diligence. His declared object was the reformation of his red brethren, and their return to their pristine manner of living. He pretended to be in constant communication with the great spirit, and he was instructed by him to make known to the Indians that they were created by him distinct from the Whites, of different natures, for different purposes, and placed under different circumstances, adapted to their nature and destinies: that they must return from all the ways of the Whites to the habits and opinions of their forefathers. They must not eat the flesh of hogs, of bullocks, of sheep, etc., the deer and buffalo having been created for their food; they must not make bread of wheat, but of Indian corn. They must not wear linen nor woolen, but dress like their fathers in the skins and furs of wild animals. They must not drink ardent spirits; and I do not remember whether he extended his inhibitions to the gun and gunpowder, in favor of the bow and arrow. I concluded from all this that he was a visionary, enveloped in the clouds of their antiquities, and vainly endeavoring to lead back his brethren to the fancied beatitudes of their golden age. I thought there was little danger of his making many proselytes from the habits and comforts they had learned from the Whites to the hardships and privations of savages, and no great harm if he did. We let him go on therefore unmolested. But his followers increased till the English thought him worth corruption, and found him corruptible. I suppose his views were then changed; but his proceedings in consequence of them were after I left the administration, and are therefore unknown to me; nor have I ever been informed what were the particular acts on his part which produced an actual commencement of hostilities on ours. I have no doubt however that his subsequent proceedings are but a chapter apart, like that of Henry and Ld Liverpool in the Book of the Kings of England....

This letter, with what it encloses, has given you enough, I presume, of law and the prophets.

THOMAS JEFFERSON TO JOHN ADAMS
June 11, 1812

You ask if there is any book that pretends to give any account of the traditions of the Indians, or how one can acquire an idea of them? Some scanty accounts of their traditions, but fuller of their customs and characters are given us by most of the early travellers among them. These you know were chiefly French. Lafitau, among them, and Adair an Englishman, have written on this subject; the former two volumes, the latter one, all in 4to [quarto]. But unluckily Lafitau had in his head a preconcieved theory on the mythology, manners, institutions and government of the antient nations of Europe, Asia, and Africa, and seems to have entered on those of America only to fit them into the same frame, and to draw from them a confirmation of his general theory. He keeps up a perpetual parallel, in all those articles, between the Indians of America, and the antients of the other quarters of the globe. He selects therefore all the facts, and adopts all the falsehoods which favor his theory, and very gravely retails such absurdities as zeal for a theory could alone swallow. He was a man of much classical and scriptural reading, and has rendered his book not unentertaining. He resided five years among the Northern Indians, as a Missionary, but collects his matter much more from the writings of others, than from his own observation.

Adair too had his kink. He believed all the Indians of American to be descended from the Jews: the same laws, usages; rites and ceremonies, the same sacrifices, priests, prophets, fasts and festivals, almost the same religion, and that they all spoke Hebrew. For altho he writes particularly of the Southern Indians only, the Catawbas, Creeks, Cherokees, Chickasaws and Choctaws, with whom alone he was personally acquainted, yet he generalises whatever he found among them, and brings himself to believe that the hundred languages of America, differing fundamentally every one from every other, as much as Greek from Gothic, have yet all one common prototype. He was a trader, a man of learning, a self-taught Hebraist, a strong religionist, and of as sound a mind as Don Quixot in whatever did not touch his religious chivalry. His book contains a great deal of real instruction on it's subject, only requiring the reader to be constantly on his guard against the wonderful obliquities of his theory....

You ask further, if the Indians have any order of priesthood among them, like the Druids, Bards or Minstrels of the Celtic nations? Adair alone, determined to see what he wished to see in every object, metamorphoses their Conjurers into an order of priests, and describes their sorceries as if they were the great religious ceremonies of the nation. Lafitau calls them by their proper names, Jongleurs, Devins, Sortileges; De Bry praestigiatores [tricksters, fortune tellers, witches; disengaging sleight of hand artists], Adair himself sometimes Magi, Archimagi, cunning men, Seers, rain makers, and the modern Indian interpreters, call them Conjurers and Witches. They are persons pretending to have communications with the devil and other evil spirits, to foretell future events, bring down rain, find stolen goods, raise the dead, destroy some, and heal others by enchantment, lay spells, etc. And Adair, without departing from his parallel of the Jews and Indians, might have found their counterpart, much more aptly, among the Soothsayers, sorcerers and wizards of the Jews, their Jannes and Jambres, their Simon Magus, witch of Endor, and the young damsel whose sorceries disturbed Paul so much; instead of placing them in a line with their High-priest, their Chief priests, and their magnificent hierarchy generally. In the solemn ceremonies of the Indians, the persons who direct or officiate, are their chiefs, elders and warriors, in civil ceremonies or in those of war; it is the Head of the Cabin, in their private or particular feasts or ceremonies; and sometimes the Matrons, as in their Corn feasts. And, even here, Adair might have kept up his parallel, with ennobling his Conjurers. For the antient Patriarchs, the Noahs, the Abrahams, Isaacs and Jacobs, and, even after the consecration of Aaron, the Samuels and Elijahs, and we may say further every one for himself, offered sacrifices on the altars. The true line of distinction seems to be, that solemn ceremonies, whether public or private, addressed to the Great Spirit, are conducted by the worthies of the nation, Men, or Matrons, while Conjurers are resorted to only for the invocation of evil spirits. The present state of the several Indian tribes, without any public order of priests, is proof sufficient that they never had such an order. Their steady habits permit no innovations, not even those which the progress of science offers to increase the comforts, enlarge the understanding, and improve the morality of mankind. Indeed so little idea have they of a regular order of priests, that they mistake ours for their Conjurers, and call them by that name.

JAMES MADISON TO MY RED CHILDREN
August 1812

You have come through a long path to see your father, but it is a straight and a clean path, kept open for my red children who hate crooked walks. I thank the Great Spirit that he has brought you in health through the long journey, and that he gives us a clear sky and a bright sun for our meeting....

The red people who live on the same great Island with the White people of the 18 fires, are made by the Great Spirit out of the same earth, from parts of it differing in colour only. My regard for all my red children, has made me desirous that the bloody tomahawk should be buried between the Osages, the Cherokees, & the Choctaws.... The Great Spirit has given you, like your white brethren, good heads to contrive: strong arms, and active bodies. Use them like your white brethren; not all at once, which is difficult, but by little & little, which is easy. Especially live in peace with one another, like your white brethren of the 18 fires, and like them, your little sparks will grow into great fires. You will be well fed, well clothed, dwell in good houses, and enjoy the happiness for which you, like them, were created. The Great Spirit is the friend of man of all colours. He made them to be friends of one another. The more they are so, the more he will be their friend. These are the words of your father to his red children, The Great Spirit, who is the father of us all, approves them.

Part 10

MADISON'S SECOND ADMINISTRATION

1813 – 1817

M adison is the ultimate civilian fighting British imperialism. Under pressure from religious elements in Congress, the wartime President issues a thanksgiving proclamation on July 23, 1813.

On October 5th, Tecumseh died in battle as the U.S. defeated the British army in Ontario.

In August 1814, Madison had to flee from a British attack on Washington. The White House was burned. On November 16 he issued a Proclamation of a day of public humiliation and fasting and of prayer to Almighty God.

On December 24th, European negotiations ended the war but on January 8, 1815, the United States won a major victory at New Orleans, restoring Americans' military pride. Later a naval squadron defeated the Mediterranean Barbary pirates.

In 1817, after the inauguration of James Monroe, Madison retired to Montpelier.

Jefferson's prime political activity during his retirement was his involvement in establishing the University of Virginia on a secular basis. Then, in 1814, after the British burned down the federal library in Washington, he sold his library of nearly 6,700 volumes to the federal government. It became the foundation for the Library of Congress.

In 1816, he begins to discuss what will become "The Life and Morals of Jesus of Nazareth," clippings from the four Gospels of what he considers the moral teachings of Jesus.

JAMES MADISON, SECOND INAUGURAL ADDRESS
March 4, 1813

About to add the solemnity of an oath to the obligations imposed by a second call to the station in which my country heretofore placed me, I find in the presence of this respectable assembly an opportunity of publicly repeating my profound sense of so distinguished a confidence and of the responsibility united with it. The impressions on me are strengthened by such an evidence that my faithful endeavors to discharge my arduous duties have been favorably estimated, and by a consideration of the momentous period at which the trust has been renewed. From the weight and magnitude now belonging to it I should be compelled to shrink if I had less reliance on the support of an enlightened and generous people, and felt less deeply a conviction that the war with a powerful nation, which forms so prominent a feature in our situation, is stamped with that justice which invites the smiles of Heaven on the means of conducting it to a successful termination.

THOMAS JEFFERSON TO RICHARD RUSH
May 31, 1813

Editor's note: Richard was the son of Benjamin Rush, who he discusses below.

My acquaintance with him began in 1776. It soon became intimate, and from that time a warm friendship has been maintained by a correspondence of unreserved confidence. In the course of this, each had deposited in the bosom of the other communications which were never intended to go further. In the sacred fidelity of each to the other these were known to be safe: and above all things that they would be kept from the public eye. There may have been other letters of this character written by me to him: but two alone occur to me at present, about which I have any anxiety. These were of April 21, 1803 and January 16, 1811. The first of these was on the subject of religion, a subject on which I have ever been most scrupulously reserved. I have considered it as a matter between every man and his maker in which no other, and far less the public has a right to intermeddle. To your father alone I committed some views on this subject in the first of the letters above mentioned, led to it by previous conversations, and a promise on my part to digest and communicate them in writing.

THOMAS JEFFERSON TO JOHN ADAMS
June 15, 1813

Of Lindsay's Memoirs I had never before heard, and scarcely indeed of himself. It could not therefore but be unexpected that two letters of mine should have any thing to do with his life. The name of his editor was new to me, and certainly presents itself, for the first time, under unfavorable circumstances. Religion, I suppose, is the scope of his book: and that a writer on that subject should usher himself to the world in the very act of the grossest abuse of confidence, by publishing private letters which passed between two friends, with no views to their ever being made public, is an instance of inconsistency, as well as of infidelity of which I would rather be the victim than the author. By your kind quotation of the dates of my two letters I have been enabled to turn to them. They had compleatly evanished from my memory. The last is on the subject of religion, and by it's publication will gratify the priesthood with new occasion of repeating their Comminations against me. They wish it to be believed that he can have no religion who advocates it's freedom. This was not the doctrine of Priestley, and I honored him for the example of liberality he set to his order.

JAMES MADISON, A PROCLAMATION OF THANKSGIVING
July 23, 1813

Whereas the Congress of the United States, by a joint resolution of the two Houses, have signified a request that a day may be recommended, to be observed by the people of the United States with religious solemnity, as a day of Public Humiliation and Prayer and whereas in times of public calamity, such as that of the war, brought on the U. States by the injustice of a foreign government, it is especially becoming, that the hearts of all should be touched with the same, and the eyes of all be turned to that Almighty Power, in whose hand are the welfare and the destiny of nations: I do, therefore, issue this my Proclamation, recommending to all who shall be piously disposed to unite their teams and voices in addressing, at one and the same time their vows and adorations to the great Parent and Sovereign of the Universe, that they assemble on the second Thursday of September next, in their respective religious congregations, to render him thanks for the many blessings he has bestowed on the people of the United States; that he has blessed them with a land capable of yielding all the necessaries and requisites of human life, with ample means for convenient exchanges with foreign countries; that he has blessed the labors employed in its cultivation and improvement; that he is now blessing the exertions to extend and establish the arts and manufactures; which will secure within ourselves supplies too important to remain dependent on the precarious policy, or the peaceable dispositions of other nations, and particularly that he has blessed the United States with a political constitution founded on the will and authority of the whole people, and guaranteeing to each individual security, not only of his person and his property, but of those sacred rights of conscience, so essential to his present happiness, and so dear to his future hopes: - that with those expressions of devout thankfulness be joined supplications to the same Almighty Power, that he would look down with compassion on our infirmities, that he would pardon our manifold transgressions, and awaken and strengthen in all the wholesome purposes of repentance and amendment; that in this season of trial and calamity, he would preside, in a particular manner over our public councils, and inspire all citizens with a love of their country, and with those fraternal affections and that mutual confidence, which have so happy a tendency to make us safe at home and respected abroad; and that, as he was graciously pleased, heretofore, to smile on our struggles against the attempts of the government of the empire of which these states then made a part, to wrest from them the rights and privileges to which they were entitled in common with every other part, and to raise them to the station of an independent and sovereign people; so he would now be pleased, in like manner, to bestow his blessing on our arms in resisting the hostile and persevering efforts of the same power to degrade us on the ocean, the common inheritance of all, from rights and immunities, belonging and essential to the American people, as a co-equal member of the great community of independent nations; and that, inspiring our enemies with moderation, with justice and with that spirit of reasonable accommodation, which our country has continued to manifest, we may be enabled to beat our swords into plough-shares, and to enjoy in peace, every man; the fruits of his honest industry, and the rewards of his lawful enterprize.

If the public homage of a people can ever be worthy the favorable regard of the Holy and Omniscient Being to whom it is addressed, it must be that, in which those who join in it are guided only by their free choice, by the impulse of their hearts and the dictates of their consciences; and such a spectacle must be interesting to all Christian nations; as proving that religion, that gift of Heaven for the good of man, freed from all coercive edicts, from that unhallowed connexion with the powers of this world, which corrupts religion into an instrument or an usurper policy of the state, and making no appeal but to reason, to the heart and to the conscience, can spread its benign influence every where, and can attract to the Divine Altar those free will offerings of humble supplication, thanksgiving and praise, which alone can be acceptable to Him whom no hypocrisy can deceive, and no forced sacrifices propitiate.

Upon these principles, and with these views, the people of the United States are invited, in conformity with the resolution aforesaid, to dedicate the day above named to the religious solemnities therein recommended.

Given at Washington, this twenty-third day of July in the year or our Lord one thousand eight hundred and thirteen.

THOMAS JEFFERSON TO JOHN ADAMS
August 22, 1813

Your approbation of my outline to Dr. Priestley is a great gratification to me; and I very much suspect that if thinking men would have the courage to think for themselves, and to speak what they think, it would be found they do not differ in religious opinions, as much as is supposed. I remember to have heard Dr. Priestley say that if all England would candidly examine themselves, and confess, they would find that Unitarianism was really the religion of all: and I observe a bill is now depending in parliament for the relief of Anti-Trinitarians. It is too late in the day for men of sincerity to pretend they believe in the Platonic mysticism that three are one and one is three, and yet, that the one is not three, and the three not one: to divide mankind by a single letter into όμοουσians and όμοιουσians [homoousians: son of the same substance as the father, and homoiousians: son of like but not same substance]. But this constitutes the craft, the power, and profits of the priests. Sweep away their gossamer fabrics of fictitious religion, and they would catch no more flies. We should all then, like the quakers, live without an order of priests, moralise for ourselves, follow the oracle of conscience, and say nothing about what no man can understand, nor therefore believe; for I suppose belief to be the assent of the mind to an intelligible proposition.

It is with great pleasure I can inform you that Priestley finished the comparative view of the doctrines of the Philosophers of antiquity, and of Jesus, before his death; that I can have a copy of his work forwarded from Philadelphia, by a correspondent there, and presented for your acceptance, by the same mail which carries you this, or very soon after. The branch of the work which the title announces is executed with learning and candor, as was every thing Priestley wrote: but perhaps a little hastily, for he felt himself pressed by the hand of death. The Abbé Batteux had in fact laid the foundations of this part, in his Causes premieres; with which he has given us the originals of Ocellus and Timaeus, who first committed the doctrines of Pythagoras to writing; and Enfield, to whom the Doctor refers, had done it more copiously. But he has omitted the important branch, which in your letter of Aug. 9. you say you have never seen executed, a comparison of the morality of the old testament with that of the new. And yet no two things were ever more unlike. I ought not to have asked him to give it. He dared not. He would have been eaten alive by his intolerant brethren, the Cannibal priests. And yet this was really the most interesting branch of the work.

Very soon after my letter to Doctr. Priestley, the subject being still in my mind, I had leisure, during an abstraction from business, for a day or two while on the road, to think a little more on it, and to sketch more fully than I had done to him, a Syllabus of the matter which I thought should enter into the work. I wrote it to Dr. Rush; and there ended all my labor on the subject; himself and Dr. Priestley being the only depositories of my secret. The fate of my letter to Priestley, after his death, was a warning to me on that of Dr. Rush; and at my request his family was so kind as to quiet me by returning my original letter and Syllabus. By this you will be sensible how much interest I take in keeping myself clear of religious disputes before the public; and especially of seeing my Syllabus disembowelled by Aruspices [Roman priests, inspected entrails, made predictions] of the modern Paganism. Yet I enclose it to you with entire confidence, free to be perused by yourself and Mrs. Adams, but by no one else; and to be returned to me.

You are right in supposing, in one of yours, that I had not read much of Priestley's Predestination, his No-soul system, or his controversy with Horsley. But I have read his Corruptions of Christianity, and Early opinions of Jesus, over and over again; and I rest on them, and on Middleton's writings, especially his letters from Rome, and to Waterland, as the basis of my own faith. These writings have never been answered, nor can be answered, by quoting historical proofs, as they have done. For these facts therefore I cling to their learning, so much superior to my own.

THOMAS JEFFERSON TO WILLIAM CANBY
September 18, 1813

During a long life, as much devoted to study as a faithful transaction of the trusts committed to me would permit, no subject has occupied more of my consideration than our relations with all the beings around us, our duties to them, and our future prospects. After reading and hearing everything which probably can be suggested respecting them, I have formed the best judgment I could as to the course they prescribe, and in the due observance of that course, I have no recollections which give me uneasiness. An eloquent preacher of your religious society, Richard Motte, in a discourse of much emotion and pathos, is said to have exclaimed aloud to his congregation, that he did not believe there was a Quaker, Presbyterian, Methodist or Baptist in heaven, having paused to give his hearers time to stare and to wonder. He added, that in heaven, God knew no distinctions, but considered all good men as his children, and as brethren of the same family. I believe, with the Quaker preacher, that he who steadily observes those moral precepts in which all religions concur, will never be questioned at the gates of heaven, as to the dogmas in which they all differ. That on entering there, all these are left behind us, and the Aristides and Catos, the Penns and Tillotsons, Presbyterians and Baptists, will find themselves united in all principles which are in concert with the reason of the supreme mind. Of all the systems of morality, ancient or modern, which have come under my observation, none appear to me so pure as that of Jesus. He who follows this steadily need not, I think, be uneasy, although he cannot comprehend the subtleties and mysteries erected on his doctrines by those who, calling themselves his special followers and favorites, would make him come into the world to lay snares for all understandings but theirs. These metaphysical heads, usurping the judgment seat of God, denounce as his enemies all who cannot perceive the Geometrical logic of Euclid in the demonstrations of St. Athanasius, that three are one, and one is three; and yet that the one is not three nor the three one. In all essential points you and I are of the same religion; and I am too old to go into inquiries and changes as to the unessential.

THOMAS JEFFERSON TO JOHN ADAMS
October 12, 1813

I now send you, according to your request a copy of the Syllabus. To fill up this skeleton with arteries, with veins, with nerves, muscles and flesh, is really beyond my time and information. Whoever could undertake it would find great aid in Enfield's judicious abridgment of Brucker's history of Philosophy, in which he has reduced 5. or 6. quarto vols. of 1000. pages each of Latin closely printed, to two moderate 8 vos. of English, open, type.

To compare the morals of the old, with those of the new testament, would require an attentive study of the former, a search thro' all it's books for it's precepts, and through all it's history for it's practices, and the principles they prove. As commentaries too on these, the philosophy of the Hebrews must be enquired into, their Mishna, their Gemara, Cabbala, Jezirah, Sohar, Cosri, and their Talmud must be examined and understood, in order to do them full justice. Brucker, it should seem, has gone deeply into these Repositories of their ethics, and Enfield, his epitomiser, concludes in these words. 'Ethics were so little studied among the Jews, that, in their whole compilation called the Talmud, there is only one treatise on moral subjects. Their books of Morals chiefly consisted in a minute enumeration of duties. From the law of Moses were deduced 613. precepts, which were divided into two classes, affirmative and negative, 248 in the former, and 365 in the latter. It may serve to give the reader some idea of the low state of moral philosophy among the Jews in the Middle age, to add, that of the 248. affirmative precepts, only 3. were considered as obligatory upon women; and that, in order to obtain salvation, it was judged suffi- cient to fulfill any one single law in the hour of death; the observance of the rest being deemed necessary, only to increase the felicity of the future life. What a wretched depravity of sentiment and manners must have prevailed before such cor- rupt maxims could have obtained credit! It is impossible to collect from these writ- ings a consistent series of moral Doctrine.' Enfield, B. 4. chap. 3. It was the refor- mation of this 'wretched depravity' of morals which Jesus undertook. In extracting the pure principles which he taught, we should have to strip off the artificial vest- ments in which they have been muffled by priests, who have travestied them into various forms, as instruments of riches and power to them. We must dismiss the Platonists and Plotinists, the Stagyrites and Gamalielites, the Eclectics the Gnostics and Scholastics, their essences and emanations, their Logos and Demi-urgos, Aeons and Daemons male and female, with a long train of Etc. Etc. Etc. or, shall I say at once, of Nonsense. We must reduce our volume to the simple evangelists, select, even from them, the very words only of Jesus, paring off the Amphibologisms into which they have been led by forgetting often, or not understanding, what had fallen from him, by giving their own misconceptions as his dicta, and expressing unintelli- gibly for others what they had not understood themselves. There will be found remaining the most sublime and benevolent code of morals which has ever been offered to man. Have performed this operation for my own use, by cutting verse by verse out of the printed book, and arranging, the matter which is evidently his, and which is as easily distinguishable as diamonds in a dunghill. The result is an 8 vo. of 46. pages of pure and unsophisticated doctrines, such as were professed and acted on by the unlettered apostles, the Apostolic fathers, and the Christians of the 1st. century. Their Platonising successors indeed, in after times, in order to legitimate the corruptions which they had incorporated into the doctrines of Jesus, found it necessary to disavow the primitive Christians, who had taken their principles from the mouth of Jesus himself, of his Apostles, and the Fathers contemporary with them. They excommunicated their followers as heretics, branding them with the opprobrious name of Ebionites or Beggars.

For a comparison of the Graecian philosophy with that of Jesus, materials might be largely drawn from the same source. Enfield gives a history, and detailed account of the opinions and principles of the different sects. These relate to the gods, their natures, grades, places and powers; the demi-gods and daemons, and their agency with man; the Universe, it's structure, extent, production and duration; the origin of things from the elements of fire, water, air and earth; the human soul, it's essence and derivation; the summum bonum [supreme good] and finis bonorum [end of all good things]; with a thousand idle dreams and fancies on these and other subjects the knolege of which is withheld from man, leaving but a short chapter for his moral duties, and the principal section of that given to what he owes himself, to precepts for rendering him impassible, and unassailable by the evils of life, and for preserving his mind in a state of constant serenity.

Such a canvas is too broad for the age of seventy, and especially of one whose chief occupations have been in the practical business of life. We must leave therefore to others, younger and more learned than we are, to prepare this euthanasia for Platonic Christianity, and it's restoration to the primitive simplicity of it's founder. I think you give a just outline of the theism of the three religions when you say that the principle of the Hebrew was the fear, of the Gentile the honor, and of the Christian the love of God.

An expression in your letter of Sep. 14. that 'the human understanding is a revelation from it's maker' gives the best solution, that I believe can be given, of the question, What did Socrates mean by his Daemon? He was too wise to believe, and too honest to pretend that he had real and familiar converse with a superior and invisible being. He probably considered the suggestions of his conscience, or reason, as revelations, or inspirations from the Supreme mind, bestowed, on important occasions, by a special superintending providence.

I acknolege all the merit of the hymn of Cleanthes to Jupiter, which you ascribe to it. It is as highly sublime as a chaste and correct imagination can permit itself to go. Yet in the contemplation of a being so superlative, the hyperbolic flights of the Psalmist may often be followed with approbation, even with rapture; and I have no hesitation in giving him the palm over all the Hymnists of every language, and of every time. Turn to the 148th. psalm, in Brady and Tate's version. Have such conceptions been ever before expressed? Their version of the 15th. psalm is more to be esteemed for it's pithiness, than it's poetry. Even Sternhold, the leaden Sternhold, kindles, in a single instance, with the sublimity of his original, and expresses the majesty of God descending on the earth, in terms not unworthy of the subject.

'The Lord descended from
And bowed the heav'ns most
above high;
And underneath his feet he cast
The darkness of the sky.
On Cherubim and Seraphim
Full royally he rode;
And on the wings of mighty

Came flying all abroad.'
Psalm xviii. 9. 10.

The Latin versions of this passage by Buchanan and by Johnston, are but mediocres. But the Greek of Duport is worthy of quotation....

The best collection of these psalms is that of the Octagonian dissenters of Liverpool, in their printed Form of prayer; but they are not always the best versions. Indeed bad is the best of the English versions; not a ray of poetical genius having ever been employed on them. And how much depends on this may be seen by comparing Brady and Tate's XVth. psalm with Blacklock's Justum et tenacem propositi virum [a man just and steadfast of purpose] of Horace, quoted in Hume's history, Car. 2. ch. 65. A translation of David in this style, or in that of Pompei's Cleanthes, might give us some idea of the merit of the original. The character too of the poetry of these hymns is singular to us. Written in monostichs, each divided into strophe and antistrophe, the sentiment of the 1st. member responded with amplification or antithesis in the second.

THOMAS JEFFERSON TO JOHN ADAMS
October 28, 1813

The passage you quote from Theognis, I think has an Ethical, rather than a political object. The whole piece is a moral exhortation, παραινεσις, and this passage particularly seems to be a reproof to man, who, while with his domestic animals he is curious to improve the race by employing always the finest male, pays no attention to the improvement of his own race, but intermarries with the vicious, the ugly, or the old, for considerations of wealth or ambition. It is in conformity with the principle adopted afterwards by the Pythagoreans, and expressed by Ocellus in another form; Περι δε της εκ των αλληλων ανθρωπων γενεσεως etc., ουχ ήδονης ενεκαιήμιξις which, as literally as intelligibility will admit, may be thus translated. "Concerning the interprocreation of men, how, and of whom it shall be, in a perfect manner, and according to the laws of modesty and sanctity, conjointly, this is what I think right. First to lay it down that we do not commix for the sake of pleasure, but of the procreation of children. For the powers, the organs and desires for coition have not been given by god to man for the sake of pleasure, but for the procreation of the race. For as it were incongruous for a mortal born to partake of divine life, the immortality of the race being taken away, god fulfilled the purpose by making the generations uninterrupted and continuous. This therefore we are especially to lay down as a principle, that coition is not for the sake of pleasure." But Nature, not trusting to this moral and abstract motive, seems to have provided more securely for the perpetuation of the species by making it the effect of the oestrum [passion] implanted in the constitution of both sexes. And not only has the commerce of love been indulged on this unhallowed impulse, but made subservient also to wealth and ambition by marriages without regard to the beauty, the healthiness, the understanding, or virtue of the subject from which we are to breed. The selecting the best male for a Harem of well chosen females also, which Theognis seems to recommend from the example of our sheep and asses, would doubtless improve the human, as it does the brute animal, and produce a race of veritable αριστοι ["aristocrats"]. For experience proves that the moral and physical qualities of man, whether good or evil, are transmissible in a certain degree from father to son. But I suspect that the equal rights of men will rise up against this privileged Solomon, and oblige us to continue acquiescence under the Αμαυρωσις γενεος ἀστων ["the degeneration of the race of men"] which Theognis complains of, and to content ourselves with the accidental aristoi produced by the fortuitous concourse of breeders. For I agree with you that there is a natural aristocracy among men. The grounds of this are virtue and talents. Formerly bodily powers gave place among the aristoi. But since the invention of gunpowder has armed the weak as well as the strong with missile death, bodily strength, like beauty, good humor, politeness and other accomplishments, has become but an auxiliary ground of distinction....

It is probable that our difference of opinion may in some measure be produced by a difference of character in those among whom we live. From what I have seen of Massachusetts and Connecticut myself, and still more from what I have heard, and the character given of the former by yourself, [v I, page III - Adams, A Defence of the Constitutions of the Government of the United States of America - TJ] who know them so much better, there seems to be in those two states a traditionary reverence for certain families, which has rendered the offices of the government nearly hereditary in those families. I presume that from an early period of your history, members of these families happening to possess virtue and talents, have honestly exercised them for the good of the people, and by their services have endeared their names to them.

In coupling Connecticut with you, I mean it politically only, not morally. For having made the Bible the Common law of their land they seem to have modeled their morality on the story of Jacob and Laban. But altho' this hereditary succession to office with you may in some degree be founded in real family merit, yet in a much higher degree it has proceeded from your strict alliance of Church and State. These families are canonised in the eyes of the people on the common principle "you tickle me, and I will tickle you." In Virginia we have nothing of this. Our clergy, before the revolution, having been secured against rivalship by fixed salaries, did not give themselves the trouble of acquiring influence over the people. Of wealth, there were great accumulations in particular families, handed down from generation to generation under the English law of entails. But the only object of ambition for the wealthy was a seat in the king's council. All their court then was paid to the crown and it's creatures; and they Philipised in all collisions between the king and people. Hence they were unpopular; and that unpopularity continues attached to their names. A Randolph, a Carter, or a Burwell must have great personal superiority over a common competitor to be elected by the people, even at this day.

At the first session of our legislature after the Declaration of Independence, we passed a law abolishing entails. And this was followed by one abolishing the privilege of Primogeniture, and dividing the lands of intestates equally among all their children, or other representatives. These laws, drawn by myself, laid the axe to the root of Pseudoaristocracy. And had another which I prepared been adopted by the legislature, our work would have been compleat. It was a Bill for the more general diffusion of learning....

The law for religious freedom, which made a part of this system, having put down the aristocracy of the clergy, and restored to the citizen the freedom of the mind, and those of entails and descents nurturing an equality of condition among them, this on Education would have raised the mass of the people to the high ground of moral respectability necessary to their own safety, and to orderly government; and would have compleated the great object of qualifying them to select the veritable aristoi, for the trusts of government, to the exclusion of the Pseudalists: and the same Theognis who has furnished the epigraphs of your two letters assures us that 'ουδεμιαν πω, Κυρν· άγαθοι πολιν ώλεσαν άνδρες' ["Curnis, good men have never harmed any city"]'. Altho' this law has not yet been acted on but in a small and inefficient degree, it is still considered as before the legislature, with other bills of the revised code, not yet taken up, and I have great hope that some patriotic spirit will, at a favorable moment, call it up, and make it the key-stone of the arch of our government.

THOMAS JEFFERSON TO ALEXANDER VON HUMBOLDT
December 6, 1813

The livraison [revue] of your astronomical observations, and the 6th and 7th on the subject of New Spain, with the corresponding atlases, are duly received, as had been the preceding cahiers [letters]. For these treasures of a learning so interesting to us, accept my sincere thanks. I think it most fortunate that your travels in those countries were so timed as to make them known to the world in the moment they were about to become actors on its stage. That they will throw off their European dependence I have no doubt; but in what kind of government their revolution will end I am not so certain. History, I believe, furnishes no example of a priest-ridden people maintaining a free civil government. This marks the lowest grade of ignorance, of which their civil as well as religious leaders will always avail themselves for their own purposes. The vicinity of New Spain to the United States, and their consequent intercourse, may furnish schools for the higher, and example for the lower classes of their citizens. And Mexico, where we learn from you that men of science are not wanting, may revolutionize itself under better auspices than the Southern provinces. These last, I fear, must end in military despotisms. The different casts of their inhabitants, their mutual hatreds and jealousies, their profound ignorance and bigotry, will be played off by cunning leaders, and each be made the instrument of enslaving others. But of all this you can best judge, for in truth we have little knowledge of them to be depended on, but through you.

JAMES MADISON, REPORT ON THE STATE OF THE UNION
December 7, 1813

It would be improper to close this communication without expressing a thankfulness, in which all ought to unite, for the numerous blessings with which our beloved
Country continues to be favored, for the abundance which overspreads our land,
and the prevailing health of its inhabitants, for the preservation of our internal tranquility, and the stability of our free institutions, and above all for the light of divine
truth, and the protection of every man's conscience in the enjoyment of it. And
although among our blessings we cannot number an exemption from the evils of
war; yet these will never be regarded as the greatest of evils by the friends of liberty and the right of nations.

THOMAS JEFFERSON TO THOMAS LEIPER
January 1, 1814

Thus am I situated. I receive letters from all quarters, some from known friends,
some from those who write like friends, on various subjects. What am I to do? Am I
to button myself up in Jesuitical reserve, rudely declining any answer, or answering
in terms so unmeaning as only to prove my distrust? Must I withdraw myself from
all interchange of sentiment with the world? I cannot do this. It is at war with my
habits and temper. I cannot act as if all men were unfaithful because some are so; nor
believe that all will betray me, because some do. I had rather be the victim of occasional infidelities, than relinquish my general confidence in the honesty of man.

THOMAS JEFFERSON TO JOHN ADAMS
January 24, 1814

Editor's note: All material in brackets are the editor's clarifications.

You ask me if I have ever seen the work of J. W. Goethens Schristen? Never. Nor did
the question ever occur to me before Where get we the ten commandments? The
book indeed gives them to us verbatim. But where did it get them? For itself tells us
they were written by the finger of god on tables of stone, which were destroyed by
Moses: it specifies those on the 2d. set of tables in different form and substance, but
still without saying how the others were recovered. But the whole history of these
books is so defective and doubtful that it seems vain to attempt minute enquiry into
it: and such tricks have plaid with their text, and with the texts of other books relating to them, that we have a right, from that cause, to entertain much doubt what
parts of them are genuine. In the New testament there is internal evidence that
parts of it have proceeded from an extraordinary man; and that other parts are the
fabric of very inferior minds. It is easy to separate those parts, as to pick diamonds
from dunghills. The matter of the first was such as would be preserved in the memory of the hearers, and handed on by tradition for a long time; and the latter such
stuff as might be gathered up, for imbedding it, any where, and at any time.

I have nothing of Vives, or Budaeus, and little of Erasmus. If the familiar histories of the saints, the want of which they regret, would have given us the histories of those tricks, which these writers acknolege to have been practiced, and of the lies they agree have been invented for the sake of religion, I join them in their regrets. These would be the only parts of their histories worth reading. It is not only the sacred volumes they have thus interpolated, gutted, and falsified, but the works of others relating to them, and even the laws of the land. We have a curious instance of one of these pious frauds in the Laws of Alfred. He composed, you know, from the laws of the Heptarchy, a Digest for the government of the United kingdom, and in his preface to that work he tells us expressly the sources from which he drew it, to wit, the laws of Ina. of Offa and Aethelbert, (not naming the pentateuch). But his pious Interpolator, very awkwardly, premises to his work four chapters of Exodus (from the 20th. to the 23d.) as a part of the laws of the land; so that Alfred's preface is made to stand in the body of the work. Our judges too have lent a ready hand to further these frauds, and have been willing to lay the yoke of their own opinions on the necks of others; to extend the coercions of municipal law to the dogmas of their religion, by declaring that these make a part of the law of the land. In the Year Book 34. H. 6, fo. 38. in Quare impedit [wherefore hindered], where the question was how far the common law takes notice of the Ecclesiastical law, Prisot, Chief Justice, in the course of his argument says '*tiels leis que ils de Seint eglise on en ancien scripture, covient a nous a donner credence; car ces Common ley sur quels touts manners leis sont fondes: et auxy, Sir, nous sumus obliges de conustre lour ley de saint eglise* Etc.' [To such laws of the church as have warrant in ancient writing our law giveth credence; for it is the common law on which all laws are based; and also, Sir, we are obliged to recognize the law of the church, etc.] Finch begins the business of falsification by mistranslating and misstating the words of Prisot thus 'to such laws of the church as have warrant in holy scripture our law giveth credence,' citing the above case and the words of Prisot in the margin Finch's law. B. I. c. 3. Here then we find ancien scripture, antient writing, translated 'holy scripture.' This, Wingate in 1658. erects into a Maxim of law, in the very words of Finch, but citing Prisot, and not Finch. And Sheppard tit. Religion, in 1675 laying it down in the same words as Finch, quotes the Year Book, Finch and Wingate. Then comes Sr. Matthew Hale, in the case of the King vs. Taylor I Ventr. 293. e Keb. 607. and declares that 'Christianity is parcel of the laws of England.' Citing nobody, and resting it, with his judgment against the witches, on his own authority, which indeed was sound and good in all cases into which no superstition or bigotry could enter. Thus strengthened, the court in 1728 in the King v. Woolston, would not suffer it to be questioned whether to write against Christianity was punishable at Common law, saying it had been settled by Hale in Taylor's case. 2 Stra. 834. Wood therefore, 409. without scruple, lays down as a principle that all blasphemy and profaneness are offences at the Common law, and cites Strange. Blackstone, in 1763. repeats in the words of Sr. Matthew Hale that 'Christianity is part of the laws of England,' citing Ventris and Strange *ubi supra* [wherein above]. And Ld. Mansfield in the case of the Chamberlain of London v.

Evans, in 1767. qualifying somewhat the position, says that 'the essential principles of revealed religion are part of the Common law.' Thus we find this string of authorities all hanging by one another on a single hook, a mistranslation by Finch of the words of Prisot, or on nothing. For all quote Prisot, or one another, or nobody. Thus Finch misquotes Prisot; Wingate also, but using Finch's words; Sheppard quotes Prisot, Finch and Wingate; Hale cites nobody; the court in Woolston's case cite Hale; Wood cites Woolston's case; Blackstone that and Hale; and Ld. Mansfield volunteers in his own *ipse dixit* [he himself has spoken]. And who now can question but that the whole Bible and Testament are a part of the Common law? And that Connecticut, in her blue laws, laying it down as a principle that the laws of god should be the laws of their land, except where their own contradicted them, did anything more than express, with a salvo, what the English judges had less cautiously declared without any restriction? And I dare say our cunning Chief Justice [Marshall] would swear to, and find as many sophisms to twist it out of the general terms of our Declaration of rights, and even the stricter text of the Virginia 'act for the freedom of religion' as he did to twist Burr's neck out of the halter for treason. May we not say then with him who was all candor and benevolence, 'Woe unto you, ye lawyers, for ye lade men with burdens grievous to bear.'

I think with you that Priestley, in his comparison of the doctrines of Philosophy and of revelation, did not do justice to the undertaking, but he felt himself pressed by the hand of death. Enfield has given us a more distinct account of the ethics of the antient philosophers; but the great work, of which Enfield's is an abridgment, Bruckner's history of Philosophy, is the treasure which I would wish to possess, as a book of reference or of special research only, for who could read 6. vol. 4to. [quarto] of 1000 pages each, closely printed, of modern Latin? Your account of D'Argens' Ocellus makes me wish for him also. Ocellus furnishes a fruitful text for a sensible and learned commentator. The Abbé Batteaux, which I have, is a meagre thing.

You surprise me with the account you give of the strength of family distinction still existing in your state. With us it is so totally extinguished that not a spark of it is to be found but lurking in the hearts of some of our old tories. But all bigotries hand to one another; and this in the Eastern states hangs, as I suspect, to that of the priesthood. Here youth, beauty, mind and manners are more valued than a pedigree.

THOMAS JEFFERSON TO SAMUEL GREENHOW
January 31, 1814

Your letter on the subject of the Bible Society arrived here while I was on a journey to Bedford, which occasioned a long absence from home. Since my return, it has lain, with a mass of others accumulated during my absence, till I could answer them. I presume the views of the society are confined to our own country; for with the religion of other countries my own forbids intermeddling. I had not supposed there was a family in this State not possessing a Bible, and wishing without having the means to procure one. When, in earlier life, I was intimate with every class, I think I never was in a house where that was the case. However, circumstances may have changed, and the society, I presume, have evidence of the fact. I therefore enclose you cheerfully, an order on Messrs. Gibson & Jefferson for fifty dollars, for the purposes of the society, sincerely agreeing with you that there never was a more pure and sublime system of morality delivered to man than is to be found in the four evangelists. Accept the assurances of my esteem and respect.

THOMAS JEFFERSON TO DR. THOMAS COOPER
February 10, 1814

Editor's note: Translations in brackets are by the editor.

In my letter of January 16, I promised you a sample from my common-place book, of the pious disposition of the English judges, to connive at the frauds of the clergy, a disposition which has even rendered them faithful allies in practice. When I was a student of the law, now half a century ago, after getting through Coke Littleton, whose matter cannot be abridged, I was in the habit of abridging and common-placing what I read meriting it, and of sometimes mixing my own reflections on the subject. I now enclose you the extract from these entries which I promised. They were written at a time of life when I was bold in the pursuit of knowledge, never fearing to follow truth and reason to whatever results they led, and bearding every authority which stood in their way. This must be the apology, if you find the conclusions bolder than historical facts and principles will warrant. Accept with them the assurances of my great esteem and respect.

Common-place Book.
873. In Quare imp. in C. B. 34, H. 6, fo. 38, the def. Br. of Lincoln pleads that the church of the pl. became void by the death of the incumbent, that the pl. and J. S. each pretending a right, presented two several clerks; that the church being thus rendered litigious, he was not obliged, by the Ecclesiastical law to admit either, until an inquisition de jure patronatus [a questioning of the right of patronage], in the ecclesiastical court: that, by the same law, this inquisition was to be at the suit of either claimant, and was not ex-officio to be instituted by the bishop, and at his proper costs; that neither party had desired such an inquisition; that six months passed whereon it belonged to him of right to present as on a lapse, which he had done. The pl. demurred. A question was, How far the Ecclesiastical law was to be respected in this matter by the common law court? and Prisot C. 3, in the course of his argument uses this expression, *"A tiels leis que ils de seint eglise ont en ancien scripture, covient a nous a donner credence, car ces common ley sur quel touts manners leis sont fondes: et auxy, sin, nous sumus obliges de conustre nostre ley; et, sin, si poit apperer or a nous que lievesque ad fait comme un ordinary fera en tiel cas, adong nous devons ces adjuger bon autrement nemy,"* &c. ["to such laws as those of holy church have in antient writing, it is proper for us to give credence; for the law is common as regards all affairs for which laws were founded. And moreover, Sir, we are obliged to follow their laws

regards the holy church: and in like manner they are obliged to follow our law. And, Sir, should it seem to us that the bishop acted as a layman in such a case, we should do well to deem him a common man, as much as not."] It does not appear that judgment was given. Y. B. ubi supra [wherein above]. S. C. Fitzh. abr. Qu. imp. 89. Bro. abr. Qu. imp. 12. Finch mistakes this in the following manner: "To such laws of the church as have warrant in Holy Scripture, our law giveth credence," and cites the above case, and the words of Prisot on the margin. Finch's law. B. 1, ch. 3, published 1613. Here we find "ancien scripture" converted into "Holy Scripture," whereas it can only mean the ancient written laws of the church. It cannot mean the Scriptures, 1, because the "ancien scripture" must then be understood to mean the "Old Testament" or Bible, in opposition to the "New Testament," and to the exclusion of that, which would be absurd and contrary to the wish of those |P1323|p1 who cite this passage to prove that the Scriptures, or Christianity, is a part of the common law. 2. Because Prisot says, *"Ceo [est] common ley, sur quel touts manners leis sont fondes."* ["It is the common law upon which all manner of laws are founded."] Now, it is true that the ecclesiastical law, so far as admitted in England, derives its authority from the common law. But it would not be true that the Scriptures so derive their authority. 3. The whole case and arguments show that the question was how far the Ecclesiastical law in general should be respected in a common law court. And in Bro. abr. of this case, Littleton says Prisot says, *"Ceo [est] common ley, sur quel touts manners leis sont fondes."* ["It is the common law upon which all manner of laws are founded."]

4. Because the particular part of the Ecclesiastical law then in question, to wit, the right of the patron to present to his advowson, was not founded on the law of God, but subject to the modification of the lawgiver, and so could not introduce any such general position as Finch pretends. Yet Wingate [in 1658] thinks proper to erect this false quotation into a maxim of the common law, expressing it in the very words of Finch, but citing Prisot, wing. max. 3. Next comes Sheppard, [in 1675,] who states it in the same words of Finch, and quotes the Year-Book, Finch and Wingate. 3. Shepp. abr. tit. Religion. In the case of the King v. Taylor, Sir Matthew Hale lays it down in these words, "Christianity is parcel of the laws of England." 1 Ventr. 293, 3 Keb. 607. But he quotes no authority, resting it on his own, which was good in all cases in which his mind received no bias from his bigotry, his superstitions, his visions above sorceries, demons, &c. The power of these over him is exemplified in his hanging of the witches. So strong was this doctrine become in 1728, by additions and repetitions from one another, that in the case of the King v. Woolston, the court would not suffer it to be debated, whether to write against Christianity was punishable in the temporal courts at common law, saying it had been so settled in Taylor's case, ante 2, stra. 834; therefore, Wood, in his Institute, lays it down that all blasphemy and profaneness are offences by the common law, and cites Strange *ubi supra* [wherein above]. Wood 409. And Blackstone [about 1763] repeats, in the words of Sir Matthew Hale, that "Christianity is part of the laws of England," citing Ventris and

Strange *ubi supra* [wherein above]. 4. Blackst. 59. Lord Mansfield qualifies it a little by saying that "The essential |P1324|p1 principles of revealed religion are part of the common law." In the case of the Chamberlain of London v. Evans, 1767. But he cities no authority, and leaves us at our peril to find out what, in the opinion of the judge, and according to the measure of his foot or his faith, are those essential principles of revealed religion obligatory on us as a part of the common law.

Thus we find this string of authorities, when examined to the beginning, all hanging on the same hook, a perverted expression of Prisot's, or on one another, or nobody. Thus Finch quotes Prisot; Wingate also; Sheppard quotes Prisot, Finch and Wingate; Hale cites nobody; the court in Woolston's case cite Hale; Wood cites Woolston's case; Blackstone that and Hale; and Lord Mansfield, like Hale, ventures it on his own authority. In the earlier ages of the law, as in the year-books, for instance, we do not expect much recurrence to authorities by the judges, because in those days there were few or none such made public. But in latter times we take no judge's word for what the law is, further than he is warranted by the authorities he appeals to. His decision may bind the unfortunate individual who happens to be the particular subject of it; but it cannot alter the law. Though the common law may be termed "Lex non Scripta," yet the same Hale tells us "when I call those parts of our laws Leges non Scriptae, I do not mean as if those laws were only oral, or communicated from the former ages to the latter merely by word. For all those laws have their several monuments in writing, whereby they are transferred from one age to another, and without which they would soon lose all kind of certainty. They are for the most part extant in records of pleas, proceedings, and judgments, in books of reports and judicial decisions, in tractates of learned men's arguments and opinions, preserved from ancient times and still extant in writing." Hale's H. c. d. 22. Authorities for what is common law may therefore be as well cited, as for any part of the Lex Scripta, and there is no better instance of the necessity of holding the judges and writers to a declaration of their authorities than the present; where we detect them endeavoring to make law where they found none, and to submit us at one stroke to a whole system, no particle of which has its foundation in the common law. For we know that the common law is that system of law which was introduced by the Saxons on their settlement in England, and altered from time to time by proper legislative authority from that time to the date of Magna Charta, which terminates the period of the common law, or lex non scripta, and commences that of the statute law, or Lex Scripta. This settlement took place about the middle of the fifth century. But Christianity was not introduced till the seventh century; the conversion of the first christian king of the Heptarchy having taken place about the year 598, and that of the last about 686. Here, then, was a space of two hundred years, during which the common law was in existence, and Christianity no part of it. If it ever was adopted, therefore, into the common law, it must have been between the introduction of Christianity and the date of the Magna Charta. But of the laws of this period we have a tolerable collection by Lambard and Wilkins, probably not perfect, but neither very defective; and if any one chooses to build a doctrine on any law of that period, supposed to have been lost, it is incumbent on him to prove it to have existed, and what were its contents. These were so far alterations of the common law, and became themselves a part of it. But none of these adopt Christianity as a part of the common law. If, therefore, from the settlement of the Saxons to the introduction of Christianity among them, that system of religion could not be a part of the common law, because they were not yet Christians, and if, having their laws from that period to the close of the common law, we are all able to find among them no such act of adoption, we may safely affirm (though contradicted by all the judges and writers on earth) that Christianity neither is, nor ever was a part of the common law. Another cogent proof of this truth is drawn from the silence of certain writers on the common law. Bracton gives us a very complete and scientific treatise of the whole body of the common law. He wrote this about the close of the reign of Henry III., a very few years after the date of the Magna Charta. We consider this book as the more valuable, as it was written about fore gives us the former in its ultimate state. Bracton, too, was an ecclesiastic, and would certainly not have failed to inform us of the adoption of Christianity as a part of the common law, had any such adoption ever taken place. But no word of his, which intimates anything like it, has ever been cited. Fleta and Britton, who wrote in the succeeding reign (of Edward I.), are equally silent. So also is Glanvil, an earlier writer than any of them, (viz.: temp. H. 2,) but his subject perhaps might not have led him to mention it. Justice Fortescue Aland, who possessed more Saxon learning than all the judges and writers before mentioned put together, places this subject on more limited ground. Speaking of the laws of the Saxon kings, he says, "the ten commandments were made part of their laws, and consequently were once part of the law of England; so that to break any of the ten commandments was then esteemed a breach of the common law, of England; and why it is not so now, perhaps it may be difficult to give a good reason." Preface to Fortescue Aland's reports, xvii. Had he proposed to state with more minuteness how much of the scriptures had been made a part of the common law, he might have added that in the laws of Alfred, where he found the ten commandments, two or three other chapters of Exodus are copied almost verbatim. But the adoption of a part proves rather a rejection of the rest, as municipal law. We might as well say that the Newtonian system of philosophy is a part of the common law, as that the Christian religion is. The truth is that Christianity and Newtonianism being reason and verity itself, in the opinion of all but infidels and Cartesians, they are protected under the wings of the common law from the dominion of other sects, but not erected into dominion over them. An eminent Spanish physician affirmed that the lancet had slain more men than the sword. Doctor Sangrado, on the contrary, affirmed that with plentiful bleedings, and draughts of warm water, every disease was to be cured. The common law protects both opinions, but enacts neither into law. See post. 879.

879. Howard, in his Contumes Anglo-Normandes, 1.87, notices the falsification of

the laws of Alfred, by prefixing to them four chapters of the Jewish law, to wit: the 20th, 21st, 22d and 23d chapters of Exodus, to which he might have added the 15th chapter of the Acts of the Apostles, v. 23, and precepts from other parts of the scripture. These he calls a hors d'oeuvre [side dish] of some pious copyist. This awkward monkish fabrication makes the preface to Alfred's genuine laws stand in the body of the work, and the very words of Alfred himself prove the fraud; for he declares, in that preface, that he has collected these laws from those of Ina, of Offa, Aethelbert and his ancestors, saying nothing of any of them being taken from the Scriptures. It is still more certainly proved by the inconsistencies it occasions. For example, the Jewish legislator Exodus xxi. 12, 13, 14, (copied by the Pseudo Alfred [symbol omitted] 13,) makes murder, with the Jews, death. But Alfred himself, Le. xxvi., punishes it by a fine only, called a Weregild, proportioned to the condition of the person killed. It is remarkable that Hume (append. 1 to his History) examining this article of the laws of Alfred, without perceiving the fraud, puzzles himself with accounting for the inconsistency it had introduced. To strike a pregnant woman so that she dies is death by Exodus, xxi. 22, 23, and Pseud. Alfr. 18; but by the laws of Alfred ix., pays a Weregild for both woman and child. To smite out an eye, or a tooth, Exod. xxi. 24-27. Pseud. Alfr. 19, 20, if of a servant by his master, is freedom to the servant; in every other case retaliation. But by Alfr. Le. xl. a fixed indemnification is paid. Theft of an ox, or a sheep, by the Jewish law, Exod. xxii. 1, was repaid five-fold for the ox and four-fold for the sheep; by the Pseudograph 24, the ox double, the sheep four-fold; but by Alfred Le. xvi., he who stole a cow and a calf was to repay the worth of the cow and 40l for the calf. Goring by an ox was the death of the ox, and the flesh not to be eaten. Exod. xxi. 28. Pseud. Alfr. 21 by Alfred Le. xxiv., the wounded person had the ox. The Pseudograph makes municipal laws of the ten commandments, 1-10, regulates concubinage, 12, makes it death to strike or to curse father or mother, 14, 15, gives an eye for an eye, tooth for a tooth, hand for hand, foot for foot, burning for burning, wound for wound, strife for strife, 19; tells the thief to repay his theft, 24; obliges the fornicator to marry the woman he has lain with, 29; forbids interest on money, 35; makes the laws of bailment, 28, very different from what Lord Holt delivers in Coggs v. Bernard, ante 92, and what Sir William Jones tells us they were; and punishes witchcraft with death, 30, which Sir Matthew Hale, 1 H. P. C. B. 1, ch. 33, declares was not a felony before the Stat. 1, Jac. 12. It was under that statute, and not this forgery, that he hung Rose Cullendar and Amy Duny, 16 Car. 2, (1662,) on whose trial he declared "that there were such creatures as witches he made no doubt at all; for first the Scripture had affirmed so much, secondly the wisdom of all nations had provided laws against such persons, and such hath been the judgment of this kingdom, as appears by that act of Parliament which hath provided punishment proportionable to the quality of the offence." And we must certainly allow greater weight to this position that "it was no felony till James' Statute," laid down deliberately in his H. P. C., a work which he wrote to be printed, finished, and transcribed for the press in his life time, than to the hasty scripture that "at common law witchcraft was punished with death as heresy, by writ de

Heretico Comburendo" [the burning of heretics] in his Methodical Summary of the P. C. p. 6, a work "not intended for the press, not fitted for it, and which he declared himself he had never read over since it was written;" Pref. Unless we understand his meaning in that to be that witchcraft could not be punished at common law as witchcraft, but as heresy. In either sense, however, it is a denial of this pretended law of Alfred. Now, all men of reading know that these pretended laws of homicide, concubinage, theft, retaliation, compulsory marriage, usury, bailment, and others which might have been cited, from the Pseudograph, were never the laws of England, not even in Alfred's time; and of course that it is a forgery. Yet palpable as it must be to every lawyer, the English judges have piously avoided lifting the veil under which it was shrouded. In truth, the alliance between Church and State in England has ever made their judges accomplices in the frauds of the clergy; and even bolder than they are. For instead of being contented with these four surreptitious chapters of Exodus, they have taken the whole leap, and declared at once that the whole Bible and Testament in a lump, make a part of the common law; ante 873: the first judicial declaration of which was by this same Sir Matthew Hale. And thus they incorporate into the English code laws made for the Jews alone, and the precepts of the gospel, intended by their benevolent author as obligatory only in *foro concientiae* [in speaking of conscience]; and they arm the whole with the coercions of municipal law. In doing this, too, they have not even used the Connecticut caution of declaring, as is done in their blue laws, that the laws of God shall be the laws of their land, except where their own contradict them; but they swallow the yea and nay together. Finally, in answer to Fortescue Aland's question why the ten commandments should not now be a part of the common law of England? we may say they are not because they never were made so by legislative authority, the document which has imposed that doubt on him being a manifest forgery.

Thomas Jefferson to Horatio Gates Spafford
March 17, 1814

I join in your reprobation of our merchants, priests, and lawyers, for their adherence to England and monarchy, in preference to their own country and its Constitution. But merchants have no country. The mere spot they stand on does not constitute so strong an attachment as that from which they draw their gains. In every country and in every age, the priest has been hostile to liberty. He is always in alliance with the despot, abetting his abuses in return for protection to his own. It is easier to acquire wealth and power by this combination than by deserving them, and to effect this, they have perverted the purest religion ever preached to man into mystery and jargon, unintelligible to all mankind, and therefore the safer engine for their purposes.

THOMAS JEFFERSON TO N. G. DUFIEF
April 19, 1814

Your favor of the 6th instant is just received, and I shall with equal willingness and truth, state the degree of agency you had, respecting the copy of M. de Becourt's book, which came to my hands. That gentleman informed me, by letter, that he was about to publish a volume in French, *"Sur la Creation du Monde, un Systeme d'Organisation Primitive,"* which, its title promised to be, either a geological or astronomical work. I subscribed; and, when published, he sent me a copy; and as you were my correspondent in the book line in Philadelphia, I took the liberty of desiring him to call on you for the price, which, he afterwards informed me, you were so kind as to pay him for me, being, I believe, two dollars. But the sole copy which came to me was from himself directly, and, as far as I know, was never seen by you.

I am really mortified to be told that, in the United States of America, a fact like this can become a subject of inquiry, and of criminal inquiry too, as an offence against religion; that a question about the sale of a book can be carried before the civil magistrate. Is this then our freedom of religion? And are we to have a censor whose imprimatur shall say what books may be sold, and what we may buy? And who is thus to dogmatize religious opinions for our citizens? Whose foot is to be the measure to which ours are all to be cut or stretched? Is a priest to be our inquisitor, or shall a layman, simple as ourselves, set up his reason as the rule for what we are to read, and what we must believe? It is an insult to our citizens to question whether they are rational beings or not, and blasphemy against religion to suppose it cannot stand the test of truth and reason. If M. de Becourt's book be false in its facts, disprove them; if false in its reasoning, refute it. But, for God's sake, let us freely hear both sides, if we choose. I know little of its contents, having barely glanced over here and there a passage, and over the table of contents. From this, the Newtonian philosophy seemed the chief object of attack, the issue of which might be trusted to the strength of the two combatants; Newton certainly not needing the auxiliary arm of the government, and still less the holy author of our religion, as to what in it concerns him. I thought the work would be very innocent, and one which might be confided to the reason of any man; not likely to be much read if let alone, but, if persecuted, it will be generally read. Every man in the United States will think it a duty to buy a copy, in vindication of his right to buy, and to read what he pleases. I have been just reading the new constitution of Spain. One of its fundamental basis is expressed in these words: "The Roman Catholic religion, the only true one, is, and always shall be, that of the Spanish nation. The government protects it by wise and just laws, and prohibits the exercise of any other whatever." Now I wish this presented to those who question what you may sell, or we may buy, with a request to strike out the words, "Roman Catholic," and to insert the denomination of their own religion. This would ascertain the code of dogmas which each wishes should domineer over the opinions of all others, and be taken, like the Spanish religion, under the "protection of wise and just laws." It would shew to what they wish to reduce the liberty for which one generation has sacrificed life and happiness. It would present our boasted freedom of religion as a thing of theory only, and not of practice, as what would be a poor exchange for the theoretic thraldom, but practical freedom of Europe. But it is impossible that the laws of Pennsylvania, which set us the first example of the wholesome and happy effects of religious freedom, can permit the inquisitorial functions to be proposed to their courts. Under them you are surely safe.

THOMAS JEFFERSON TO CHEVALIER LUIS DE ONIS
April 28, 1814

I thank you, Sir, for the copy of the new constitution of Spain which you have been so kind as to send me; and I sincerely congratulate yourself and the Spanish nation on this great stride towards political happiness....

There are parts of this constitution, however, in which you should expect of course that we should not concur. One of these is the intolerance of all but the Catholic religion; and no security provided against the re-establishment of an Inquisition, the exclusive judge of Catholic opinions, and authorized to proscribe and punish those it shall deem anti-Catholic.

THOMAS JEFFERSON TO THOMAS LAW
June 13, 1814

The copy of your Second Thoughts on Instinctive Impulses, with the letter accompanying it, was recieved just as I was setting out on a journey to this place, two or three days distant from Monticello. I brought it with me and read it with great satisfaction, and with the more as it contained exactly my own creed on the foundation of morality in man. It is really curious that on a question so fundamental, such a variety of opinions should have prevailed among men, and those, too, of the most exemplary virtue and first order of understanding. It shows how necessary was the care of the Creator in making the moral principle so much a part of our constitution as that no errors of reasoning or of speculation might lead us astray from its observance in practice. Of all the theories on this question, the most whimsical seems to have been that of Woollaston, who considers truth as the foundation of morality. The thief who steals your guinea does wrong only inasmuch as he acts a lie in using your guinea as if it were his own. Truth is certainly a branch of morality, and a very important one to society. But presented as its foundation, it is as if a tree taken up by the roots, had its stem reversed in the air, and one of its branches planted in the ground. Some have made the love of God the foundation of morality. This, too, is but a branch of our moral duties, which are generally divided into duties to God and duties to man. If we did a good act merely from the love of God and a belief that it is pleasing to Him, whence arises the morality of the Atheist? It is idle to say, as some do, that no such being exists. We have the same evidence of the fact as of most of those we act on, to-wit: their own affirmations, and their reasonings in support of them. I have observed, indeed, generally, that while in protestant countries the defections from the Platonic Christianity of the priests is to Deism, in catholic countries they are to Atheism. Diderot, D'Alembert, D'Holbach, Condorcet, are known to have been among the most virtuous of men. Their virtue, then, must have had some other foundation than the love of God.

The Το καλον [the beautiful] of others is founded in a different faculty, that of taste, which is not even a branch of morality. We have indeed an innate sense of what we call beautiful, but that is exercised chiefly on subjects addressed to the fancy, whether through the eye in visible forms, as landscape, animal figure, dress, drapery, architecture, the composition of colors, &c. or to the imagination directly, as imagery, style, or measure in prose or poetry, or whatever else constitutes the domain of criticism or taste, a faculty entirely distinct from the moral one. Self-interest, or rather self-love, or egoism, has been more plausibly substituted as the basis of morality. But I consider our relations with others as constituting the boundaries of morality. With ourselves we stand on the ground of identity, not of relation, which last, requiring two subjects, excludes self-love confined to a single one. To ourselves, in strict language, we can owe no duties, obligation requiring also two parties. Self-love, therefore, is no part of morality. Indeed it is exactly its counterpart. It is the sole antagonist of virtue, leading us constantly by our propensities to self-gratification in violation of our moral duties to others. Accordingly, it is against this enemy that are erected the batteries of moralists and religionists, as the only obstacle to the practice of morality. Take from man his selfish propensities, and he can have nothing to seduce him from the practice of virtue. Or subdue those propensities by education, instruction or restraint, and virtue remains without a competitor. Egoism, in a broader sense, has been thus presented as the source of moral action. It has been said that we feed the hungry, clothe the naked, bind up the wounds of the man beaten by thieves, pour oil and wine into them, set him on our own beast and bring him to the inn, because we receive ourselves pleasure from these acts. So Helvetius, one of the best men on earth, and the most ingenious advocate of this principle, after defining "interest" to mean not merely that which is pecuniary, but whatever may procure us pleasure or withdraw us from pain, [de l'Esprit 2. 1.] says, [ib. 2. 2.] "the humane man is he to whom the sight of misfortune is insupportable, and who to rescue himself from this spectacle, is forced to succor the unfortunate object." This indeed is true. But it is one step short of the ultimate question. These good acts give us pleasure, but how happens it that they give us pleasure? Because nature hath implanted in our breasts a love of others, a sense of duty to them, a moral instinct, in short, which prompts us irresistibly to feel and to succor their distresses, and protests against the language of Helvetius [ib. 2. 5.] "what other motive than self-interest could determine a man to generous actions? It is as impossible for him to love what is good for the sake of good, as to love evil for the sake of evil."

The Creator would indeed have been a bungling artist, had he intended man for a social animal, without planting in him social dispositions. It is true they are not planted in every man, because there is no rule without exceptions; but it is false reasoning which converts exceptions into the general rule. Some men are born without the organs of sight, or of hearing, or without hands. Yet it would be wrong to say that man is born without these faculties, and sight, hearing, and hands may with truth enter into the general definition of man. The want or imperfection of the moral sense in some men, like the want or imperfection of the senses of sight and hearing in others, is no proof that it is a general characteristic of the species. When it is wanting, we endeavor to supply the defect by education, by appeals to reason and calculation, by presenting to the being so unhappily conformed, other motives to do good and to eschew evil, such as the love, or the hatred, or rejection of those among whom he lives, and whose society is necessary to his happiness and even existence; demonstrations by sound calculation that honesty promotes interest in the long run; the rewards and penalties established by the laws; and ultimately the prospects of a future state of retribution for the evil as well as the good done while here. These are the correctives which are supplied by education, and which exercise the functions of the moralist, the preacher, and legislator; and they lead into a course of correct action all those whose disparity is not too profound to be eradicated.

Some have argued against the existence of a moral sense, by saying that if nature had given us such a sense, impelling us to virtuous actions, and warning us against those which are vicious, then nature would also have designated, by some particular ear-marks, the two sets of actions which are, in themselves, the one virtuous and the other vicious. Whereas, we find, in fact, that the same actions are deemed virtuous in one country and vicious in another. The answer is that nature has constituted utility to man the standard and best of virtue. Men living in different countries, under different circumstances, different habits and regimens, may have different utilities; the same act, therefore, may be useful, and consequently virtuous in one country which is injurious and vicious in another differently circumstanced. I sincerely, then, believe with you in the general existence of a moral instinct. I think it the brightest gem with which the human character is studded, and the want of it as more degrading than the most hideous of the bodily deformities. I am happy in reviewing the roll of associates in this principle which you present in your second letter, some of which I had not before met with. To these might be added Ld. Kaims, one of the ablest of our advocates, who goes so far as to say, in his Principles of Natural Religion, that a man owes no duty to which he is not urged by some impulsive feeling. This is correct, if referred to the standard of general feeling in the given case, and not to the feeling of a single individual. Perhaps I may misquote him, it being fifty years since I read his book.

The leisure and solitude of my situation here has led me to the indiscretion of taxing you with a long letter on a subject whereon nothing new can be offered you. I will indulge myself no further than to repeat the assurances of my continued esteem & respect.

THOMAS JEFFERSON TO JOHN ADAMS
July 5, 1814

I am just returned from one of my long absences, having been at my other home for five weeks past. Having more leisure there than here for reading, I amused myself with reading seriously Plato's republic. I am wrong however in calling it amusement, for it was the heaviest task-work I ever went through. I had occasionally before taken up some of his other works, but scarcely ever had patience to go through a whole dialogue. While wading thro' the whimsies, the puerilities, and unintelligible jargon of this work, I laid it down often to ask myself how it could have been that the world should have so long consented to give reputation to such nonsense as this? How the *soi-disant* [self-styled] Christian world indeed should have done it, is a piece of historical curiosity. But how could the Roman good sense do it? And particularly how could Cicero bestow such eulogies on Plato? Altho' Cicero did not wield the dense logic of Demosthenes, yet he was able, learned, laborious, practiced in the business of the world, and honest. He could not be the dupe of mere style, of which he was himself the first master in the world. With the Moderns, I think, it is rather a matter of fashion and authority. Education is chiefly in the hands of persons who, from their profession, have an interest in the reputation and the dreams of Plato. They give the tone while at school, and few, in their after-years, have occasion to revise their college opinions. But fashion and authority apart, and bringing Plato to the test of reason, take from him his sophisms, futilities, and incomprehensibilities, and what remains? In truth, he is one of the race of genuine Sophists, who has escaped the oblivion of his brethren, first by the elegance of his diction, but chiefly by the adoption and incorporation of his whimsies into the body of artificial Christianity. His foggy mind, is forever presenting the semblances of objects which, half seen thro' a mist, can be defined neither in form or dimension. Yet this which should have consigned him to early oblivion really procured him immortality of fame and reverence. The Christian priesthood, finding the doctrines of Christ leveled to every understanding, and too plain to need explanation, saw, in the mysticisms of Plato, materials with which they might build up an artificial system which might, from it's indistinctness, admit everlasting controversy, give employment for their order, and introduce it to profit, power and pre-eminence. The doctrines which flowed from the lips of Jesus himself are within the comprehension of a child; but thousands of volumes have not yet explained the Platonisms engrafted on them: and for this obvious reason that nonsense can never be explained. Their purposes however are answered. Plato is canonized; and it is now deemed as impious to question his merits as those of an Apostle of Jesus. He is peculiarly appealed to as an advocate of the immortality of the soul; and yet I will venture to say that were there no better arguments than his in proof of it, not a man in the world would believe it. It is fortunate for us that Platonic republicanism has not obtained the same favor as Platonic Christianity; or we should now have been all living, men, women and children, pell mell together, like beasts of the field or forest.

Yet 'Plato is a great Philosopher,' said La Fontaine. But says Fontenelle 'do you find his ideas very clear'? 'Oh no! He is of an obscurity impenetrable.' 'Do you not find him full of contradictions?' 'Certainly,' replied La Fontaine, 'he is but a Sophist.' Yet immediately after, he exclaims again, 'Oh Plato was a great Philosopher.' Socrates had reason indeed to complain of the misrepresentations of Plato; for in truth his dialogues are libels on Socrates.

THOMAS JEFFERSON TO EDWARD COLES
August 25, 1814

Your favour of July 31, was duly received, and was read with peculiar pleasure. The sentiments breathed through the whole do honor to both the head and heart of the writer. Mine on the subject of slavery of negroes have long since been in possession of the public, and time has only served to give them stronger root. The love of justice and the love of country plead equally the cause of these people, and it is a moral reproach to us that they should have pleaded it so long in vain, and should have produced not a single effort, nay I fear not much serious willingness to relieve them & ourselves from our present condition of moral & political reprobation....

Your solitary but welcome voice is the first which has brought this sound to my ear; and I have considered the general silence which prevails on this subject as indicating an apathy unfavorable to every hope. Yet the hour of emancipation is advancing, in the march of time. It will come; and whether brought on by the generous energy of our own minds; or by the bloody process of St. Domingo, excited and conducted by the power of our present enemy, if once stationed permanently within our Country, and offering asylum & arms to the oppressed, is a leaf of our history not yet turned over....

For men probably of any color, but of this color we know, brought from their infancy without necessity for thought or forecast, are by their habits rendered as incapable as children of taking care of themselves, and are extinguished promptly wherever industry is necessary for raising young. In the mean time they are pests in society by their idleness, and the depredations to which this leads them. Their amalgamation with the other color produces a degradation to which no lover of his country, no lover of excellence in the human character can innocently consent....

The laws do not permit us to turn them loose, if that were for their good: and to commute them for other property is to commit them to those whose usage of them we cannot control. I hope then, my dear sir, you will reconcile yourself to your country and its unfortunate condition; that you will not lessen its stock of sound disposition by withdrawing your portion from the mass. That, on the contrary you will come forward in the public councils, become the missionary of this doctrine truly christian; insinuate & inculcate it softly but steadily, through the medium of writing and conversation; associate others in your labors, and when the phalanx is formed, bring on and press the proposition perseveringly until its accomplishment. It is an encouraging observation that no good measure was ever proposed, which, if duly pursued, failed to prevail in the end. We have proof of this in the history of the endeavors in the English parliament to suppress that very trade which brought this evil on us. And you will be supported by the religious precept, "be not weary in well-doing."

That your success may be as speedy & complete, as it will be of honorable & immortal consolation to yourself, I shall as fervently and sincerely pray as I assure you of my great friendship and respect.

THOMAS JEFFERSON TO MILES KING
September 26, 1814

I duly recieved your letter of Aug. 20. and I thank you for it, because I believe it was written with kind intentions, and a personal concern for my future happiness. Whether the particular revelation, which you suppose to have been made to your-self were real or imaginary, your reason alone is the competent judge. For, dispute as long as we will on religious tenets, our reason at last must ultimately decide, as it is the only oracle which god has given us to determine between what really comes from him, and the phantasms of a disordered or deluded imagination. When he means to make a personal revelation he carries conviction of it's authenticity to the reason he has bestowed as the umpire of truth. You believe you have been favored with such a special communication. Your reason, not mine, is to judge of this: and if it shall be his pleasure to favor me with a like admonition, I shall obey it with the same fidelity which I would obey his known will in all cases. Hitherto I have been under the guidance of that portion of reason which he has thought proper to deal out to me. I have followed it faithfully in all important cases, to such a degree at least as leaves me without uneasiness; and if on minor occasions I have erred from it's dic-tates, I have trust in him who made us what we are, and knows it was not his plan to make us always unerring. He has formed us moral agents. Not that, in the per-fection of the state, he can feel pain or pleasure from anything we may do: he is far above our power: but that we may promote the happiness of those with whom he has placed us in society, by acting honestly towards all, benevolently to those who fall within our way respecting sacredly their rights bodily and mental, and cherish-ing especially their freedom of conscience, as we value our own. I must ever believe that religion substantially good which produces an honest life, and we have been authorized by one whom you and I equally respect, to judge of the tree by its fruit. Our particular principles of religion are a subject of accountability to our god alone. I inquire after no man's, and trouble none with mine; nor is it given to us in this life to know whether your's or mine, our friend's or our foe's, are exactly the right. Nay, we have heard it said that there is not a quaker or a baptist, a presbyterian or an epis-copalian, a catholic or a protestant in heaven: that, on entering that gate, we leave those badges of schism behind, and find ourselves united in those principles only in which god has united us all. Let us not be uneasy then about the different roads we may pursue, as believing them the shortest, to that our last abode: but, following the guidance of a good conscience, let us be happy in the hope that, by these different paths, we shall all meet in the end — and that you and I may there meet and embrace is my earnest prayer: and with assurance I salute you with brotherly esteem and respect.

THOMAS JEFFERSON TO THOMAS COOPER
October 7, 1814

I agree with yours of the 22d, that a professorship of Theology should have no place in our institution. But we cannot always do what is absolutely best. Those with whom we act, entertaining different views, have the power and the right of carrying them into practice. Truth advances, and error recedes step by step only; and to do to our fellow men the most good in our power, we must lead where we can, follow where we cannot, and still go with them, watching always the favorable moment for helping them to another step.

JAMES MADISON, PROCLAMATION OF A DAY OF PUBLIC HUMILIATION AND FASTING AND OF PRAYER TO ALMIGHTY GOD
November 16, 1814

The two Houses of the National Legislature having by a joint resolution expressed their desire that in the present time of public calamity and war a day may be recommended to be observed by the people of the United States as a day of public humiliation and fasting and of prayer to Almighty God for the safety and welfare of these States, His blessing on their arms, and a speedy restoration of peace, I have deemed it proper by this proclamation to recommend that Thursday, the 12th of January next, be set apart as a day on which all may have an opportunity of voluntarily offering at the same time in their respective religious assemblies their humble adoration to the Great Sovereign of the Universe, of confessing their sins and transgressions, and of strengthening their vows of repentance and amendment. They will be invited by the same solemn occasion to call to mind the distinguished favors conferred on the American people in the general health which has been enjoyed, in the abundant fruits of the season, in the progress of the arts instrumental to their comfort, their prosperity, and their security, and in the victories which have so powerfully contributed to the defense and protection of our country, a devout thankfulness for all which ought to be mingled with their supplications to the Beneficent Parent of the Human Race that He would be graciously pleased to pardon all their offenses against Him; to support and animate them in the discharge of their respective duties; to continue to them the precious advantages flowing from political institutions so auspicious to their safety against dangers from abroad, to their tranquillity at home, and to their liberties, civil and religious; and that He would in a special manner preside over the nation in its public councils and constituted authorities, giving wisdom to its measures and success to its arms in maintaining its rights and in overcoming all hostile designs and attempts against it; and, finally, that by inspiring the enemy with dispositions favorable to a just and reasonable peace its blessings may be speedily and happily restored.

THOMAS JEFFERSON TO WILSON CARY NICHOLAS
November 26, 1814

You are not mistaken in viewing the conduct of the Eastern States as the source of our greatest difficulties in carrying on the war, as it certainly is the greatest, if not the sole, inducement with the enemy to persevere in it. The greater part of the people in that quarter have been brought by their leaders, aided by their priests, under a delusion scarcely exceeded by that recorded in the period of witchcraft; and the leaders are becoming daily more desperate in the use they make of it. Their object is power. If they could obtain it by menaces, their efforts would stop there. These failing, they are ready to go every length for which they can train their followers. Without foreign co-operation, revolts & separation will be hardly risked; and what the effect of so profligate an experiment may be, first on deluded partizans, and next on those remaining faithful to the nation who are respectable for their consistency, and even for their numbers, is for conjecture only. The best may be hoped, but the worst ought to be kept in view.

THOMAS JEFFERSON TO CHARLES CLAY
January 29, 1815

Your letter of Dec. 20. was 4. weeks on it's way to me. I thank you for it: for altho' founded on a misconception, it is evidence of the friendly concern for my peace and welfare which I have ever believed you to feel. Of publishing a book on religion, my dear Sir, I never had an idea. I should as soon think of writing for the reformation of Bedlam, as of the world of religious sects. Of these there must be at least ten thousand, every individual of every one of which believes all are wrong but his own. To undertake to bring them all right, would be like undertaking, single handed, to fell the forests of America. Probably you have heard me say I had taken the four evangelists, had cut out from them every text they had recorded of the moral precepts of Jesus, and arranged them in a certain order, and altho' they appeared but as fragments, yet fragments of the most sublime edifice of morality which had ever been exhibited to man. This I have probably mentioned to you, because it is true, and the idea of it's publication may have suggested itself as an inference of your own mind. I not only write nothing on religion, but rarely permit myself to speak on it, and never but in a reasonable society. I have probably said more to you than to any other person, because we have had more hours of conversation in duetto in our meetings at the Forest. I abuse the priests indeed, who have so much abused the pure and holy doctrines of their master, and who have laid me under no obligations of reticence as to the tricks of their trade. The genuine system of Jesus, and the artificial structures they have erected, to make them the instruments of wealth, power, and preeminence to themselves, are as distinct things in my view as light and darkness: and while I have classed them with soothsayers and necromancers, I place him among the greatest of the reformers of morals, and scourges of priest-craft that have ever existed. They felt him as such, and never rested until they had silenced him by death. But his heresies against Judaism prevailing in the long run, the priests have tacked about, and rebuilt upon them the temple which he destroyed, as splendid, as profitable, and as imposing as that.

Government, as well as religion, has furnished it's schisms, it's persecutions, and it's devices for fattening idleness on the earnings of the people. It has it's hierarchy of emperors, kings, princes, and nobles, as that has of popes, cardinals, archbishops, bishops, and priests. In short, Cannibals are not to be found in the wilds of America only, but are reveling on the blood of every living people. Turning then from this loathsome combination of church and state, and weeping over the follies of our fellow-men, who yield themselves the will dupes and drudges of these Mountebanks, I consider reformation and redress as desperate, and abandon them to Quixotism of more enthusiastic minds.

THOMAS JEFFERSON TO MARQUIS DE LAFAYETTE
February 14, 1815

I learn, with real sorrow, the deaths of Monsieur and Madame de Tessé. They made an interesting part in the idle reveries in which I have sometimes indulged myself, of seeing all my friends of Paris once more, for a month or two; a thing impossible, which, however, I never permitted myself to despair of. The regrets, however, of seventy-three at the loss of friends, may be the less, as the time is shorter within which we are to meet again, according to the creed of our education.

THOMAS JEFFERSON TO P. H. WENDOVER
March 13, 1815

Your favor of January 30 was received after long delay on the road, and I have to thank you for the volume of discourses which you have been so kind as to send me. I have gone over them with great satisfaction, and concur with the able preacher in his estimate of the character of the belligerents in our late war, and lawfulness of defensive war....

All this Mr. McLeod has well proved, and from these sources of argument particularly which belong to his profession. On one question only I differ from him, and it is that which constitutes the subject of his first discourse, the right of discussing public affairs in the pulpit. I add the last words, because I admit the right in general conversation and in writing; in which last form it has been exercised in the valuable book you have now favored me with.

The mass of human concerns, moral and physical, is so vast, the field of knowledge requisite for man to conduct them to the best advantage is so extensive, that no human being can acquire the whole himself, and much less in that degree necessary for the instruction of others. It has of necessity, then, been distributed into different departments, each of which, singly, may give occupation enough to the whole time and attention of a single individual. Thus we have teachers of languages, teachers of mathematics, of natural philosophy, of chemistry, of medicine, of law, of history, of government, etc. Religion, too, is a separate department, and happens to be the only one deemed requisite for all men, however high or low.

Collections of men associate together, under the name of congregations, and employ a religious teacher of the particular sect of opinions of which they happen to be, and contribute to make up a stipend as a compensation for the trouble of delivering them, at such periods as they agree on, lessons in the religion they profess. If they want instruction in other sciences or arts, they apply to other instructors; and this is generally the business of early life. But I suppose there is not an instance of a single congregation which has employed their preacher for the mixed purposes of lecturing them from the pulpit in chemistry, in medicine, in law, in the science and principles of government, or in anything but religion exclusively. Whenever, therefore, preachers, instead of a lesson in religion, put them off with a discourse on the Copernican system, on chemical affinities, on the construction of government, or the characters or conduct of those administering it, it is a breach of contract, depriving their audience of the kind of service for which they are salaried, and giving them, instead of it, what they did not want, or, if wanted, would rather seek from better sources in that particular art or science. In choosing our pastor we look to his religious qualifications, without inquiring into his physical or political dogmas, with which we mean to have nothing to do. I am aware that arguments may be found which may twist a thread of politics into the cord of religious duties. So may they for every other branch of human art or science.

Thus, for example, it is a religious duty to obey the laws of our country; the teacher of religion, therefore, must instruct us in those laws, that we may know how to obey them. It is a religious duty to assist our sick neighbors; the preacher must, therefore, teach us medicine, that we may do it understandingly. It is a religious duty to preserve our own health; our religious teacher, then, must tell us what dishes are wholesome, and give us recipes in cookery, that we may learn how to prepare them. And so, ingenuity, by generalizing more and more, may amalgamate all the branches of science into any one of them, and the physician who is paid to visit the sick may give a sermon instead of medicine, and the merchant to whom money is sent for a hat may send a handkerchief instead of it.

But notwithstanding this possible confusion of all sciences into one, common sense draws lines between them sufficiently distinct for the general purposes of life, and no one is at a loss to understand that a recipe in medicine or cookery, or a demonstration in geometry is not a lesson in religion. I do not deny that a congregation may, if they please, agree with their preacher that he shall instruct them in medicine also, or law, or politics. Then, lectures in these, from the pulpit, become not only a matter of right, but of duty also. But this must be with the consent of every individual; because the association being voluntary, the mere majority has no right to apply the contributions of the minority to purposes unspecified in the agreement of the congregation.

I agree, too, that on all other occasions, the preacher has the right, equally with every other citizen, to express his sentiments, in speaking or writing, on the subjects of medicine, law, politics, etc., his leisure time being his own, and his congregation not obliged to listen to his conversation or to read his writings; and no one would have regretted more than myself, had any scruple as to this right withheld from us the valuable discourses which have led to the expression of an opinion as to the true limits of the right. I feel my portion of indebtedness to the reverend author for the distinguished learning, the logic, and the eloquence with which he has proved that religion, as well as reason, confirms the soundness of those principles on which our government has been founded and its rights asserted.

These are my views on this question. They are in opposition to those of the highly respected and able preacher, and are, therefore, the more doubtingly offered. Difference of opinion leads to inquiry, and inquiry to truth; and that, I am sure, is the ultimate and sincere object of us both. We both value too much the freedom of opinion sanctioned by our Constitution not to cherish its exercise even where in opposition to ourselves.

Unaccustomed to reserve or mystery in the expression of my opinions, I have opened myself frankly on a question suggested by your letter and present. And although I have not the honor of your acquaintance, this mark of attention, and still more the sentiments of esteem so kindly expressed in your letter, are entitled to a confidence that observations not intended for the public will not be ushered to their notice, as has happened to me sometimes. Tranquillity, at my age, is the balm of life. While I know I am safe in the honor and charity of a McLeod, I do not wish to be cast forth to the Marats, the Dantons, and the Robespierres of the priesthood; I mean the Parishes, the Ogdens, and the Gardiners of Massachusetts.

I pray you to accept the assurances of my esteem and respect.

THOMAS JEFFERSON TO JOHN ADAMS
June 10, 1815

In the first place, Peace, God bless it! has returned to put us all again into a course of lawful and laudable pursuits: a new trial of the Bourbons has proved to the world their incompetence to the functions of the station they have occupied: and the recall of the Usurper has clothed him with the semblance of a legitimate Autocrat.

THOMAS JEFFERSON TO JOHN ADAMS
August 10-11, 1815

You ask information on the subject of Camus.... Of his report to the National Institute on the subject of the Bollandists your letter gives me the first information. I had supposed them to be defunct with the society of Jesuits, of which they were:

and that their works, altho' above ground, were, from their bulk and insignificance, as effectually entombed on their shelves, as if in the graves of their authors. Fifty-two volumes in folio of the Acta Sanctorum, in dog-Latin, would be a formidable enterprize to the most laborious German. I expect, with you, they are the most enormous mass of lies, frauds, hypocrisy and imposture that ever was heaped together on this globe. By what chemical process M. Camus supposed that an Extract of truth could be obtained from such a farrago of falsehood, I must leave to the Chemists and Moralists of the age to divine....

At length Bonaparte has got on the right side of a question. From the time of his entering the legislative hall to his retreat to Elba, no man has execrated him more than myself. I will not except even the members of the Essex junto; altho' for very different reasons: I, because he was warring against the liberty of his own country, and independance of others; they because he was the enemy of England, the Pope, and the Inquisition. But, at length, and as far as we can judge, he seems to have become the choice of his nation. At least he is defending the cause of his nation, and that of all mankind, the rights of every people to independance and self-government....

Aug. 11. P.S. I had finished my letter yesterday, and this morning recieved the news of Bonaparte's second abdication. Very well. For him personally, I have no feeling but of reprobation.

THOMAS JEFFERSON TO DR. BENJAMIN WATERHOUSE
October 13, 1815

I was highly gratified with the receipt of your letter of Sep. 1.... and by the evidence it furnished me of your bearing up with firmness and perseverance against the persecutions of your enemies, religious, political and professional. These last I suppose have not yet forgiven you the introduction of vaccination and annihilation of the great variolous field of profit to them; and none of them pardon the proof you have established that the condition of man may be meliorated, if not infinitely, as enthusiasm alone pretends, yet indefinitely, as bigots alone can doubt. In lieu of these enmities you have the blessings of all the friends of human happiness, for this great peril from which they are rescued.

I have read with pleasure the orations of Mr. Holmes & Mr. Austin.... Both have set the valuable example of quitting the beaten ground of the revolutionary war, and making the present state of things the subject of annual animadversion and instruction. A copious one it will be and highly useful if properly improved. Cobbet's address would of itself have mortified and humbled the Cossac priests; but brother Jonathan has pointed his arrow to the hearts of the worst of them. These reverend leaders of the Hartford nation it seems then are now falling together about religion, of which they have not one real principle in their hearts. Like bawds, religion becomes to them a refuge from the despair of their loathsome vices. They seek in it only an oblivion of the disgrace with which they have loaded themselves, in their political ravings, and of their mortification at the ridiculous issue of their Hartford convention. No event, more than this, has shewn the placid character of our constitution. Under any other their treasons would have been punished by the halter. We let them live as laughing stocks for the world, and punish them by the torment of eternal contempt. The emigrations you mention from the Eastern states are what I have long counted on. The religious & political tyranny of those in power with you, cannot fail to drive the oppressed to milder associations of men, where freedom of mind is allowed in fact as well as in pretence. The subject of their present clawings and caterwaulings is not without it's interest to rational men. The priests have so disfigured the simple religion of Jesus that no one who reads the sophistications they have engrafted on it, from the jargon of Plato, of Aristotle & other mystics, would conceive these could have been fathered on the sublime preacher of the sermon on the mount. Yet, knowing the importance of names, they have assumed that of Christians, while they are mere Platonists, or anything rather than disciples of Jesus. One of these parties beginning now to strip off these meretricious trappings their followers may take courage to make thorough work, and restore to us the figure in it's original simplicity and beauty. The effects of this squabble therefore, whether religious or political, cannot fail to be good in some way.

The visit to Monticello, of which you hold up an idea, would be a favor indeed of the first order. I know however the obstacles of age & distance and should therefore set due value on it's vicarious execution, should business or curiousity lead a son of yours to visit this Sodom and Gomorrah of parsons Osgood, Parish & Gardiner.

THOMAS JEFFERSON TO HORATIO GATES SPAFFORD
1816

I am not afraid of the priests. They have tried upon me all their various batteries, of pious whining, hypocritical canting, lying and slandering, without being able to give me one moment of pain. I have contemplated their order from the Magi of the East to the Saints of the West, and I have found no difference of character, but of more or less caution, in proportion to their information or ignorance of those on whom their interested duperies were to be plaid off. Their sway in New England is indeed formidable. No mind beyond mediocrity dares there to develop itself.

THOMAS JEFFERSON TO ARCHIBALD CAREY
1816

On the dogmas of religion, as distinguished from moral principles, all mankind, from the beginning of the world to this day, have been quarreling, fighting, burning and torturing one another, for abstractions unintelligible to themselves and to all others, and absolutely beyond the comprehension of the human mind. Were I to enter on that arena, I should only add an unit to the number of Bedlamites.

THOMAS JEFFERSON TO CHARLES YANCEY
January 6, 1816

Like a dropsical man calling out for water, water, our deluded citizens are clamoring for more banks, more banks. The American mind is now in that state of fever which the world has so often seen in the history of other nations. We are under the bank bubble, as England was under the South Sea bubble, France under the Mississippi bubble, and as every nation is liable to be, under whatever bubble, design, or delusion may puff up in moments when off their guard. We are now taught to believe that legerdemain tricks upon paper can produce as solid wealth as hard labor in the earth. It is vain for common sense to urge that nothing can produce but nothing; that it is an idle dream to believe in a philosopher's stone which is to turn everything into gold, and to redeem man from the original sentence of his Maker, "in the sweat of his brow shall he eat his bread."

Not Quixote enough, however, to attempt to reason Bedlam to rights, my anxieties are turned to the most practicable means of withdrawing us from the ruin into which we have run. Two hundred millions of paper in the hands of the people, (and less can not be from the employment of a banking capital known to exceed one hundred millions,) is a fearful tax to fall at haphazard on their heads. The debt which purchased our independence was but of eighty millions, of which twenty years of taxation had in 1809 paid but the one half. And what have we purchased with this tax of two hundred millions which we are to pay by wholesale but usury, swindling, and new forms of demoralization.

THOMAS JEFFERSON TO CHARLES THOMSON
January 9, 1816

An acquaintance of 52 years, for I think ours dates from 1764, calls for an interchange of notice now and then, that we remain in existence, the monuments of another age, and examples of a friendship unaffected by the jarring elements by which we have been surrounded, of revolutions, of government, of party and of opinion. I am reminded of this duty by the receipt, thro' our friend Dr. Patterson, of your Synopsis of the four Evangelists. I had procured it as soon as I saw it advertized, and had become familiar with it's use, but this copy is the more valued as it comes from your hand. This work bears the stamp of that accuracy which marks everything from you, and will be useful to those who, not taking things on trust, recur for themselves to the fountain of pure morals. I, too, have made a wee little book from the same materials, which I call the Philosophy of Jesus. It is a paradigma of his doctrines, made by cutting the texts out of the book, and arranging them on the pages of a blank book, in a certain order of time or subject. A more beautiful or precious morsel of ethics I have never seen. It is a document in proof that I am a real Christian, that is to say, a disciple of the doctrines of Jesus, very different from the Platonists, who call me infidel and themselves Christians and preachers of the Gospel, while they draw all their characteristic dogmas from what it's author never said nor saw. They have compounded from the heathen mysteries a system beyond the comprehension of man, of which the great reformer of the vicious ethics and deism of the Jews, were he to return on earth, would not recognize one feature. If I had time I would add to my little book the Greek, Latin and French texts, in columns side by side. And I wish I could subjoin a translation of Gassendi's Syntagma of the doctrines of Epicurus, which, notwithstanding the calumnies of the Stoics and caricatures of Cicero, is the most rational system remaining of the philosophy of the ancients, as frugal of vicious indulgence, and fruitful of virtue as the hyperbolical extravagances of his rival sects.

THOMAS JEFFERSON TO BENJAMIN AUSTIN
January 9, 1816

Editor's note: Although Jefferson writes below of "Algerine slavery," and American sailors were indeed captured by pirates from Tripoli, given the context discussed, the domination of the seas by Britain and France, what he actually was referring to was the seizure of American sailors by Britain, alleging them to be British. This was the prime cause of the war of 1812.

Who could have imagined that the two most distinguished in the rank of nations, for science and civilization, would have suddenly descended from that honorable eminence, and setting at defiance all those moral laws established by the Author of nature between nation and nation, as between man and man, would cover earth and sea with robberies and piracies, merely because strong enough to do it with temporal impunity; and that under this disbandment of nations from social order, we should have been despoiled of a thousand ships, and have thousands of our citizens reduced to Algerine slavery. Yet all this has taken place. One of these nations interdicted to our vessels all harbors of the globe without having first proceeded to some one of hers, there paid a tribute proportionate to the cargo, and obtained her license to proceed to the port of destination. The other declared them to be lawful prize if they had touched at the port, or been visited by a ship of the enemy nation.

THOMAS JEFFERSON TO HORATIO GATES SPAFFORD
January 10, 1816

Editor's note: The bracketed material was written into a reply to Spafford, who sent him a tract, and then deleted. However a transcript was sent to Richmond Enquirer editor Thomas Ritchie.

[You judge truly that I am not afraid of the priests. They have tried upon me all their various batteries, of pious whining, hypocritical canting, lying and slandering, without being able to give me one moment of pain. I have contemplated their order from the Magi of the East to the Saints of the West, and I have found no difference of character, but of more or less caution, in proportion to their information or ignorance of those on whom their interested duperies were to be plaid off. Their sway in New England is indeed formidable. No mind beyond mediocrity dares there to develop itself. If it does, they excite against it the public opinion which they command, & by little, but incessant and teasing persecutions, drive it from among them. Their present emigrations to the Western country are real flights from persecution, religious & political, but the abandonment of the country by those who wish to enjoy freedom of opinion leaves the despotism over the residue more intense, more oppressive.

They are now looking to the flesh pots of the South and aiming at foothold there by their missionary teachers. They have lately come forward boldly with their plan to establish "a qualified religious instructor over every thousand souls in the US." And they seem to consider none as qualified but their own sect. Thus, in Virginia, they say there are but 60, qualified, and that 914 are still wanting of the full quota. All besides the 60, are "mere nominal ministers, unacquainted with theology." Now the 60, they allude to are exactly in the string of counties at the Western foot of the Blue ridge, settled originally by Irish presbyterians, and composing precisely the tory district of the state. There indeed is found in full vigor the hypocrisy, the despotism, and anti-civism of the New England qualified religious instructors.

The country below the mountains, inhabited by Episcopalians, Methodists & Baptists (under mere nominal ministers, unacquainted with theology) are pronounced "destitute of the means of grace, and as sitting in darkness and under the shadow of death." They are quite in despair too at the insufficient means of New England to fill this fearful void. "with Evangelical light, with catechetical instructions, weekly lectures, & family visiting." That Yale cannot furnish above 80 graduates annually, and Harvard perhaps not more. That there must therefore be an immediate, universal, vigorous & systematic effort made to evangelize the nation. To see that there is a bible for every family, a school for every district, and a qualified (i.e. Presbyterian) "pastor for every thousand souls; that newspapers, tracts, magazines must be employed; the press be made to groan, & every pulpit in the land to sound it's trumpet long and loud. A more homogeneous (I.E. New England) "character must be produced thro' the nation." That section then of our union having lost it's political influence by disloyalty to it's country is now to recover it under the mask of religion. It is to send among us their Gardiners, their Osgoods, their Parishes & Pearsons, as apostles to teach us their orthodoxy. This is the outline of the plan as published by Messrs. Beecher, Pearson & Co.

It has uttered however one truth. "That the nation must be awakened to save itself by it's own exertions, or we are undone." And I trust that this publication will do not a little to awaken it; and that in aid of it newspapers, tracts and magazines must sound the trumpet. Yours I hope will make itself heard, and the louder as yours is the nearest house in the course of conflagration.]

THOMAS JEFFERSON TO JOHN ADAMS
January 11, 1816

Of the last five months I have past four at my other domicile, for such it is in a considerable degree. No letters are forwarded to me there, because the cross post to that place is circuitous and uncertain. During my absence therefore they are accumulating here, and awaiting acknolegments. This has been the fate of your favor of Nov. 13.

I agree with you in all it's eulogies on the 18th. century. It certainly witnessed the sciences and arts, manners and morals, advanced to a higher degree than the world had ever before seen....

How then has it happened that these nations, France especially and England, so great, so dignified, so distinguished by science and the arts, plunged at once into all the depths of human enormity, threw off suddenly and openly all the restraints of morality, all sensation to character, and unblushingly avowed and acted on the principle that power was right? Can this sudden apostacy from national rectitude be accounted for? The treaty of Pilnitz seems to have begun it, suggested perhaps by the baneful precedent of Poland. Was it from the terror of monarchs, alarmed at the light returning on them from the West, and kindling a Volcano under their thrones? Was it a combination to extinguish that light, and to bring back, as their best auxiliaries, those enumerated by you, the Sorbonne, the Inquisition, the Index expurgatorius, and the knights of Loyola? Whatever it was, the close of the century saw the moral world thrown back again to the age of the Borgias, to the point from which it had departed 300. years before....

Your prophecies to Dr. Price proved truer than mine; and yet fell short of the fact, for instead of a million, the destruction of 8. or 10. millions of human beings has probably been the effect of these convulsions. I did not, in 89. believe they would have lasted so long, nor have cost so much blood. But altho' your prophecy has proved true so far, I hope it does not preclude a better final result. That same light from our West seems to have spread and illuminated the very engines employed to extinguish it. It has given them a glimmering of their rights and their power. The idea of representative government has taken root and growth among them....

Even France will yet attain representative government. You observe it makes the basis of every constitution which has been demanded or offered: of that demanded by their Senate; of that offered by Bonaparte; and of that granted by Louis XVIII. The idea then is rooted, and will be established, altho' rivers of blood may yet flow between them and their object. The allied armies now couching upon them are first to be destroyed, and destroyed they will surely be. A nation united can never be conquered. We have seen what the ignorant bigotted and unarmed Spaniards could do against the disciplined veterans of their invaders. What then may we not expect from the power and character of the French nation? The oppressors may cut off heads after heads, but like those of the Hydra, they multiply at every stroke.

THOMAS JEFFERSON TO PETER WILSON
January 20, 1816

I think, therefore, the pious missionaries who shall go to the several tribes to instruct them in the Christian religion will have to learn a language for every tribe they go to; nay, more, that they will have to create a new language for every one, that is to say, to add to theirs new words for the new ideas they will have to communicate. Law, medicine, chemistry, mathematics, every science has a language of its own, and divinity not less than others. Their barren vocabularies cannot be vehicles for ideas of the fall of man, his redemption, the triune composition of the Godhead, and other mystical doctrines considered by most Christians of the present date as essential elements of faith. The enterprise is therefore arduous, but the more inviting perhaps to missionary zeal, in proportion as the merit of surmounting it will be greater.

THOMAS JEFFERSON TO THOMAS RITCHIE
January 21, 1816

In answering the letter of a Northern correspondent lately, I indulged in a tirade against a pamphlet recently published in this quarter. On revising my letter, however, I thought it unsafe to commit myself so far to a stranger. I struck out the passage, therefore, yet I think the pamphlet of such a character as not to be unknown, or unnoticed by the people of the United States. It is the most bold and impudent stride New England has ever made in arrogating an ascendancy over the rest of the Union. The first form of the pamphlet was an address from the Reverend Lyman Beecher, chairman of the Connecticut Society for the education of pious young men for the ministry. Its matter was then adopted and published in a sermon by Reverend Mr. Pearson of Andover in Massachusetts, where they have a theological college; and where the address "with circumstantial variations to adapt it to more general use" is reprinted on a sheet and a half of paper, in so cheap a form as to be distributed, I imagine, gratis, for it has a final note indicating six thousand copies of the first edition printed. So far as it respects Virginia, the extract of my letter gives the outline. I therefore send it to you to publish or burn, abridge or alter, as you think best. You understand the public palate better than I do. Only give it such a title as may lead to no suspicion from whom you received it. I am the more induced to offer it to you because it is possible mine may be the only copy in the State, and because, too, it may be à propos for the petition for the establishment of a theological society now before the legislature, and to which they have shown the unusual respect of hearing an advocate for it at their bar. From what quarter this theological society comes forward I know not; perhaps from our own tramontaine clergy, of New England religion and politics; perhaps it is an entering wedge from its theological sister in Andover, for the body of "qualified religious instructors" proposed by their pious brethren of the East "to evangelize and catechize," to edify our daughters by weekly lectures, and our wives by "family visits" from these pious young monks from

Harvard and Yale. However, do with this what you please, and be assured of my friendship and respect.

THOMAS JEFFERSON TO REVEREND NOAH WORCESTER
January 29, 1816

Your letter bearing date October 18, 1815, came only to hand the day before yester-day.... I have to thank you for the pamphlets accompanying it, to wit, the Solemn Review, the Friend of Peace or Special Interview, and the Friend of Peace, No. 2.... I have not read the last two steadily through, because where one assents to proposi-tions as soon as announced it is loss of time to read the arguments in support of them. These numbers discuss the first branch of the causes of war, that is to say, wars undertaken for the point of honor, which you aptly analogize with the act of duelling between individuals, and reason with justice from the one to the other. Undoubtably this class of wars is, in the general, what you state them to be, "need-less, unjust and inhuman, as well as anti-Christian." The second branch of this sub-ject, to wit, wars undertaken on account of wrong done, and which may be likened to the act of robbery in private life, I presume will be treated of in your future num-bers. I observe this class mentioned in the Solemn Review, p. 10, and the question asked, "Is it common for a nation to obtain a redress of wrongs by war? The answer to this question you will of course draw from history. In the meantime, reason will answer it on grounds of probability, that where the wrong has been done by a weak-er nation, the stronger one has generally been able to enforce redress; but where by a stronger nation, redress by war has been neither obtained nor expected by the weaker. On the contrary, the loss has been increased by the expenses of the war in blood and treasure. Yet it may have obtained another object equally securing itself from future wrong.

THOMAS JEFFERSON TO JOSEPH CABELL
February 2, 1816

No, my friend, the way to have good and safe government, is not to trust it all to one, but to divide it among the many, distributing to every one exactly the functions he is competent to....

And I do believe that if the Almighty has not decreed that man shall never be free, (and it is a blasphemy to believe it,) that the secret will be found to be in the making himself the depository of the powers respecting himself, so far as he is com-petent to them, and delegating only what is beyond his competence by a synthetical process, to higher and higher orders of functionaries, so as to trust fewer and fewer powers in proportion as the trustees become more and more oligarchical....

God bless you, and all our rulers, and give them the wisdom, as I am sure they have the will, to fortify us against the degeneracy of one government, and the con-centration of all its powers in the hands of the one, the few, the well-born or the many.

THOMAS JEFFERSON TO JOHN ADAMS
April 8, 1816

Did I know Baron Grimm while at Paris? Yes, most intimately.... Altho' I never heard Grimm express the opinion, directly, yet I always supposed him to be of the school of Diderot, D'Alembert, D'Holbach, the first of whom committed their system of atheism to writing in *"Le bon sens,"* and the last in his *"Systeme de la Nature."* It was a numerous school in the Catholic countries, while the infidelity of the Protestant took generally the form of theism. The former always insisted that it was a mere question of definition between them, the hypostasis of which on both sides was "Nature" or "the Universe;" that both agreed in the order of the existing system, but the one supposed it from eternity, the other as having begun in time. And when the atheist descanted on the unceasing motion and circulation of matter through the animal, vegetable and mineral kingdoms, never resting, never annihilated, always changing form, and under all forms gifted with the power of reproduction; the theist pointing "to the heavens above, and to the earth beneath, and to the waters under the earth," asked if these did not proclaim a first cause, possessing intelligence and power; power in the production, and intelligence in the design and constant preservation of the system; urged the palpable existence of final causes, that the eye was made to see, and the ear to hear, and not that we see because we have eyes, and hear because we have ears; an answer obvious to the senses, as that of walking across the room was to the philosopher demonstrating the non-existence of motion. It was in D'Holbach's conventicles that Rousseau imagined all the machinations against him were contrived; and he left, in his Confessions the most biting anecdotes of Grimm. These appeared after I left France; but I have heard that poor Grimm was so much afflicted by them, that he kept his bed several weeks. I have never seen these Memoirs of Grimm. Their volume has kept them out of our market.

I have been lately amusing myself with Levi's book in answer to Dr. Priestley. It is a curious and tough work. His style is inelegant and incorrect, harsh and petulent to his adversary, and his reasoning flimsy enough. Some of his doctrines were new to me, particularly that of his two resurrections: the first a particular one of all the dead, in body as well as soul, who are to live over again, the Jews in a state of perfect obedience to god, the other nations in a state of corporeal punishment for the sufferings they have inflicted on the Jews. And he explains this resurrection of bodies to be only of the original stamen of Leibnitz, or the *homunculus in semine masculino* [male penis in begetting], considering that as a mathematical point, insusceptible of separation, or division. The second resurrection a general one of souls and bodies, eternally to enjoy divine glory in the presence of the supreme being. He alledges that the Jews alone preserve the doctrine of the unity of god. Yet their god would be deemed a very indifferent man with us: and it was to correct their Anamorphosis of the deity that Jesus preached, as well as to establish the doctrine of a future state. However Levi insists that that was taught in the old testament, and even by Moses himself and the prophets. He agrees that an anointed prince was prophecied and promised: but denies that the character and history of Jesus has any analogy with that of the person promised. He must be fearfully embarrassing to the Hierophants of fabricated Christianity; because it is their own armour in which he clothes himself for the attack. For example, he takes passages of Scripture from their context (which would give them a very different meaning) strings them together, and makes them point towards what object he pleases; he interprets them figuratively, typically, analogically, hyperbolically; he calls in the aid of emendation, transposition, ellipsis, metonymy, and every other figure of rhetoric; the name of one man is taken for another, one place for another, days and weeks for months and years; and finally avails himself of all his advantage over his adversaries by his superior knolege of the Hebrew, speaking in the very language of the divine communication, while they can only fumble on with conflicting and disputed translations. Such is this war of giants. And how can such pigmies as you and I decide between them? For myself I confess that my head is not formed tantas componere lites [of a size for such sacrifices].

And as you began your Mar. 2. with a declaration that you were about to write me the most frivolous letter I had ever read, so I will close mine by saying I have written you a full match for it, and by adding my affectionate respects to Mrs. Adams, and the assurance of my constant attachment and consideration for yourself.

THOMAS JEFFERSON TO PIERRE DUPONT DE NEMOURS
April 24, 1816

Enlighten the people generally, and tyranny and oppressions of body and mind will vanish like evil spirits at the dawn of day. Although I do not, with some enthusiasts, believe that the human condition will ever advance to such a state of perfection as that there shall no longer be pain or vice in the world, yet I believe it susceptible of much improvement, and most of all, in matters of government and religion; and that the diffusion of knowledge among the people is to be the instrument by which it is to be effected. The constitution of the Cortes had defects enough; but when I saw in it this amendatory provision, I was satisfied all would come right in time, under its salutary operation. No people have more need of a similar provision than those for whom you have felt so much interest. No mortal wishes them more success than I do. But if what I have heard of the ignorance and bigotry of the mass be true, I doubt their capacity to understand and to support a free government; and fear that their emancipation from the foreign tyranny of Spain, will result in a military despotism at home.

THOMAS JEFFERSON TO FRANCIS VAN DER KEMP
April 25, 1816

The Syllabus, which is the subject of your letter, was addressed to a friend to whom I had promised a more detailed view. But finding that I should never have time for that, I sent him what I thought should be the Outlines of such a work. The same subject entering sometimes into the correspondence between Mr. Adams and myself, I sent him a copy of it. The friend to whom it had been first addressed dying soon after, I asked from his family the return of the original, as a confidential communication, which they kindly sent me. So that no copy of it, but that in possession of Mr. Adams, now exists out of my own hands. I have used this caution, lest it should get out in connection with my name; and I was unwilling to draw on myself a swarm of insects, whose buz is more disquieting than their bite - As an abstract thing, and without any intimation from what quarter derived, I can have no objection to it's being committed to the consideration of the world. I believe it may even do good by producing discussion, and finally a true view of the merits of this great reformer. Pursuing the same ideas after writing the Syllabus, I made, for my own satisfaction, an Extract from the Evangelists of the texts of his morals, selecting those only whose style and spirit proved them genuine, and his own: and they are as distinguishable from the matter in which they are imbedded as diamonds in dunghills. A more precious morsel of ethics was never seen. It was too hastily done however, being the work of one or two evenings only, while I lived at Washington, overwhelmed with other business: and it is my intention to go over it again at more leisure. This shall be the work of the ensuing winter. I gave it the title of 'The Philosophy of Jesus extracted from the texts of the Evangelists.' - To this Syllabus and Extract, if a history of his life can be added, written with the same view of the subject, the world will see, after the fogs shall be dispelled, for 14. centuries he has been inveloped by Jugglers to make money of him, when the genuine character shall be exhibited, which they have dressed up in the rags of an Impostor, the world, I say, will at length see the immortal merit of this first of human Sages. I rejoice that you think of undertaking this work. It is one I have long wished to see written on the scale of a Laertius or a Nepos. Nor can it be a work of labor, or of volume. For his journeyings from Judaea to Samaria, and Samaria to Galilee, do not cover much country; and the incidents of his life require little research. They are all at hand, and need only to be put into human dress; noticing such only as within the physical laws of nature, and offending none by a denial, or even a mention, of what is not. If the Syllabus and Extract (which is short) either in substance, or at large, are worth a place under the same cover with your biography, they are at your service. I ask one only condition, that no possibility shall be admitted of my name being even intimated with the publication. If done in England, as you seem to contemplate, there will be the less likelihood of my being thought of. I shall be much gratified to learn that you pursue your intention of writing the life of Jesus, and pray to accept the assurances of my great respect and esteem.

THOMAS JEFFERSON TO JOHN TAYLOR
May 28, 1816

On my return from a long journey and a considerable absence from home, I found here a copy of your "Enquiry into the Principles of our Government," which you have been so kind as to send me; and for which I pray you accept my thanks.... Funding I consider as limited, rightfully, to a redemption of the debt within the lives of a majority of the generation contracting it; every generation coming equally, by the laws of the Creator of the world to the free possession of the earth He made for their subsistence, unincumbered by their predecessors, who, like them, were but tenants for life.... Indeed, it must be acknoleged, that the term republic is of very vague application in every language. Witness the self-styled republics of Holland, Switzerland, Genoa, Venice, Poland. Were I to assign to this term a precise and definite idea, I would say, purely and simply, it means a government by its citizens in mass, acting directly and personally, according to rules established by the majority; and that every other government is more or less republican, in proportion as it has in its composition more or less of this ingredient of the direct action of the citizens.... And we have examples of it in some of our State Constitutions, which, if not poisoned by priest-craft, would prove its excellence over all mixtures with other elements; and with only equal doses of poison, would still be the best.

THOMAS JEFFERSON TO FRANCIS VAN DER KEMP
July 30, 1816

Your favor of July 14. is recieved, and I am entirely satisfied with the disposition you have made of the Syllabus, keeping my name unconnected with it, as I am sure you have done. I should really be gratified to see a full and fair examination of the ground it takes. I believe it to be the only ground on which reason and truth can take their stand, and that only against which we are told that the gates of hell shall not finally prevail. Yet I have little expectation that the affirmative can be freely maintained in England. We know it could not here. For altho' we have freedom of religious opinion by law, we are yet under the inquisition of public opinion: and in England it would have both law and public opinion to encounter. The love of peace, and a want of either time or taste for these disquisitions, induce silence on my part as to the contents of this paper, and all explanations and discussions which might arise out of it; and this must be my apology for observing the same silence on the questions of your letter. I leave the thing to the evidence of the books on which it claims to be founded, and with I am persuaded you are more familiar then myself.

Altho' I rarely waste time in reading on theological subjects, as mangled by our Pseudo-Christians, yet I can readily suppose Basanistos may be amusing. Ridicule is the only weapon which can be used against unintelligible propositions. Ideas must be distinct before reason can act upon them; and no man ever had a distinct idea of the trinity. It is mere Abracadabra of the mountebanks calling themselves the priests of Jesus. If it could be understood it would not answer their purpose. Their security is in their faculty of shedding darkness, like the scuttle fish, thro' the element in which they move, and making it impenetrable to the eye of a pursuing enemy. And there they will skulk, until some rational creed can occupy the void which the obliteration of their duperies would leave in the minds of our honest and unsuspecting brethren. Whenever this shall take place, I believe that Christianism may be universal and eternal. I salute you with great esteem and respect.

THOMAS JEFFERSON TO JOHN ADAMS
August 1, 1816

I know nothing of the history of the Jesuits you mention in 4. vols. Is it a good one? I dislike, with you, their restoration: because it marks a retrograde step from light towards darkness. We shall have our follies without doubt. Some one or more of them will always be afloat. But ours will be the follies of enthusiasm, not of bigotry, not of Jesuitism. Bigotry is the disease of ignorance, of morbid minds; enthusiasm of the free and buoyant. Education and free discussion are antidotes of both. We are destined to be a barrier against the returns of ignorance and barbarism. Old Europe will have to lean on our shoulders, and to hobble along by our side, under the monkish trammels of priests and kings, as she can. What a colossus shall we be when the southern continent comes up to our mark! What a stand will it secure as a ralliance for the reason and freedom of the globe! I like the dreams of the future better than the history of the past. So good night! I will dream on, always fancying that Mrs. Adams and yourself are by my side marking the progress and obliquities of ages and countries.

THOMAS JEFFERSON TO MARGARET BAYARD SMITH
August 6, 1816

I have recieved, dear Madam, your very friendly letter of July 21st. and Assure you that I feel with deep sensibility it's kind expressions towards myself, and the more as from a person than whom no other's could be more in sympathy with my own affections. I often call to mind the occasions of knowing your worth, which the societies of Washington furnished; and none more than those derived from your much valued visit to Monticello. I recognize the same motives of goodness in the solicitude you express on the rumor supposed to proceed from a letter of mine to Charles Thomson, on the subject of the Christian religion. It is true that, in writing to the translator of the Bible and Testament, that subject was mentioned; but equally so that no adherence to any particular mode of Christianity was there expressed, nor any change of opinions suggested. A change from what? The priests indeed have heretofore thought proper to ascribe to me religious, or rather antireligious sentiments, of their own fabric, but such as soothed their resentments against the Act of Virginia for establishing religious freedom. They wished him to be thought Atheist, Deist, or Devil, who could advocate freedom from their religious dictations. But I have ever thought religion a concern purely between our god and our consciences, for which we were accountable to him, and not to the priests. I never told my own religion, nor scrutinized that of another. I never attempted to make a convert, nor wished to change another's creed. I have ever judged of the religion of others by their lives, and by this test, my dear Madam, I have been satisfied yours must be an excellent one, to have produced a life of such exemplary virtue and correctness. For it is in our lives, and not from our words, that our religion must be read. By the same test the world must judge me. But this does not satisfy the priesthood. They must have a positive, a declared assent to all their interested absurdities. My opinion is that there would never have been an infidel, if there had never been a priest. The artificial structures they have built on the purest of all moral systems, for the purpose of deriving from it pence and power, revolts those who think for themselves, and who read in that system only what is really there. These, therefore, they brand with such nicknames as their enmity chuses gratuitously to impute. I have left the world, in silence, to judge of causes from their effects; and I am consoled in this course, my dear friend, when I perceive the candor with which I am judged by your justice and discernment; and that, notwithstanding the slanders of the Saints, my fellow-citizens have thought me worthy of trusts. The imputations of irreligion having spent their force, they think an imputation of change might now be turned to account as a boulster for their duperies. I shall leave them, as heretofore, to grope on in the dark.

THOMAS JEFFERSON TO JOHN ADAMS
October 14, 1816

Your undertaking the 12. volumes of Dupuis is a degree of heroism to which I could not have aspired even in my younger days. I have been contented with the humble atchievment of reading the Analysis of his work by Destutt-Tracy.... and his Conclusion, are worth more in my eye than the body of the work. For the object of that seems to be to smother all history under mantle of allegory. If histories so unlike as those of Hercules and Jesus, can, by a fertile imagination, and Allegorical interpretations, be brought to the same tally, no line of distinction remains between fact and fancy....

I gather from his other works that he adopts the principle of Hobbes, that justice is founded in contract solely, and does not result from the construction of man. I believe, on the contrary, that it is instinct, and innate, that the moral sense is as much a part of our constitution as that of feeling, seeing, or hearing; as a wise creator must have seen to be necessary in an animal destined to live in society: that every human mind feels pleasure in doing good to another; that the non-existence of justice is not to be inferred from the fact that the same act is deemed virtuous and right in one society, which is held vicious and wrong in another; because as the circumstances and opinions of different societies vary, so the acts which may do them right or wrong must vary also: for virtue does not consist in the act we do, but in the end it is to effect....

Your history of the Jesuits, by what name of the author, or other description is it to be enquired for?

THOMAS JEFFERSON TO GEORGE LOGAN
November 12, 1816

I recieved your favor of Oct. 16. at this place, where I pass much of my time, very distant from Monticello. I am quite astonished at the idea which seems to have gotten abroad; that I propose publishing something on the subject of religion. And this is said to have arisen from a letter of mine to my friend Charles Thomson, in which certainly there is no trace of such an idea. When we see religion split into so many thousands of sects, and I may say Christianity itself divided into it's thousands also, who are disputing, anathemizing and where the laws permit, burning and torturing one another for abstractions which no one of them understand, and which are indeed beyond the comprehension of the human mind, into which of the chambers of this Bedlam would a man wish to thrust himself. The sum of all religion as expressed by it's best preacher, 'fear God and love thy neighbor,' contains no mystery, needs no explanation — but this wont do. It gives no scope to make dupes; priests could not live by it. Your ideas of the moral obligations of governments are perfectly correct. The man who is dishonest as a statesman would be a dishonest man in any station. It is strangely absurd to suppose that a million of human beings collected together are not under the same moral laws which bind each of them separately. It is a great consolation to me that our government, as it cherishes most it's duties to it's own citizens, so is the most exact in it's moral conduct towards other nations.

THOMAS JEFFERSON TO FRANCIS VAN DER KEMP
November 24, 1816

I recieved your favor of Nov. 1. at this place at which I make occasionally a temporary residence; and I have perused with great satisfaction the magnificent skeleton you inclose me of what would indeed be a compleat Encyclopedia of Christian philosophy. It's execution would require a Newton in physics, a Locke in metaphysics, and one who to a possession of all history, adds a judgment and candor to estimate it's evidence and credibility in proportion to the character of the facts it presents and he should have a long life before him. I fear we shall not see this canvas filled in our day, and that we must be contented to have all this light blaze upon us when the curtain shall be removed which limits our mortal sight. I had however persuaded myself to hope that we should have from your own pen, one branch of this great work, the mortal biography of Jesus. This candidly and rationally written, without any regard to sectarian dogmas, would reconcile to his character a weighty multitude who do not properly estimate it; and would lay the foundation of a genuine christianity.

THOMAS JEFFERSON TO JOHN ADAMS
November 25, 1816

My books are all arrived, some at New York, some at Boston; and I am glad to hear that those for Harvard are safe also; and the Uranologia you mention, without telling me what it is. It is something good, I am sure, from the name connected with it, and if you would add your Fable of the bees, we should recieve valuable instruction as to the Uranologia both of the father and son; more valuable than the Chinese will from our bible-societies. These Incendiaries, finding that the days of fire and faggot are over in the Atlantic hemisphere, are now preparing to put the torch to the Asiatic regions. What would they say were the Pope to send annually to this country colonies of Jesuit priests with cargoes of their Missal and translations of their Vulgate, to be put gratis into the hands of every one who would accept them? And to act thus nationally on us as a nation?

I proceed to the letter you were so good as to inclose to me. It is an able letter, speaks volumes in few words, presents a profound view of awful truths, and lets us see truths more awful, which are still to follow. George the IIId. then, and his minister Pitt, and successors, have spent the fee-simple of the kingdom, under pretence of governing it. Their sinecures, salaries, pensions, priests, prelates, princes and eternal wars have mortgaged to it's full value the last foot of their soil. They are reduced to the dilemma of a bankrupt spendthrift who, having run thro' his whole fortune, now asks himself what he is to do?... But it is not in the character of man to come to any peaceful compromise of such a state of things. The princes and priests will hold to the flesh-pots, the empty bellies will seize on them, and these being the multitude, the issue is obvious, civil war, massacre, exile as in France, until the stage is cleared of everything but the multitude, and the lands get into their hands by such processes as the revolution will engender. They will then want peace and a government, and what will it be? Certainly not a renewal of that which has already ruined them. Their habits of law and order, their ideas almost innate of the vital elements of free government, of trial by jury, habeus corpus, freedom of the press, freedom of opinion, and representative government, make them, I think, capable of bearing a considerable portion of liberty.

JAMES MADISON, LAST ANNUAL MESSAGE
December 3, 1816

And may I not be allowed to add to this gratifying spectacle, that I shall read in the character of the American people, in their devotion to true liberty, and to the constitution which is its palladium, sure presages, that the destined career of my country will exhibit a Government, pursuing the public good as it's sole object, and regulating its means by the great principles, to which they are so well allied: a Government, which watches over the purity of elections, the freedom of speech and of the press, the trial by Jury, and the equal interdict against encroachments and compacts, between religion and the State; which maintains inviolably the maxims of public faith, the security of persons and property, and encourages, in every authorized mode, that general diffusion of knowledge which guarantees to public liberty its permanency, and to those who possess the blessing, the true enjoyment of it....

These contemplations, sweetening the remnant of my days, will animate my prayers for the happiness of my beloved Country, and a perpetuity of the Institutions, under which it is enjoyed.

THOMAS JEFFERSON, SCHOOL ACT
1817

Editor's note: Jefferson was discussing Visitors, i.e., supervisors of Virginia's County elementary schools, and teachers. A note to the bill declared that

Ministers of the Gospel are excluded to avoid jealousy from the other sects, were the public education committed to the ministers of a particular one; and with more reason than in the case of their exclusion from the legislative and executive functions.

THOMAS JEFFERSON TO JOHN ADAMS
January 11, 1817

The result of your 50. or 60. years of religious reading in the four words 'be just and good' is that in which all our enquiries must end; as the riddles of the priesthoods end in four more '*ubi panis, ibi deus* [where there is bread, there is God].' What all agree upon is probably right; what no two agree in most probably is wrong. One of our fan-coloured biographers, who paints small men as very great, enquired of me lately, with real affection too, whether he might consider as authentic, the change in my religion much spoken of in some circles. Now this supposed that they knew what had been my religion before, taking for it the word of their priests, whom I certainly never made the confidants of my creed. My answer was 'say nothing of my religion. It is known to my god and myself alone. It's evidence before the world is to be sought in my life. If that has been honest and dutiful to society, the religion which has regulated it cannot be a bad one.'

THOMAS JEFFERSON TO ABIGAIL ADAMS
January 11, 1817

But those 20. years, alas! where are they? With those beyond the flood. Our next meeting must then be in the country to which they have flown, a country, for us, not now very distant. For this journey we shall need neither gold nor silver in our purse, nor scrip, nor coats, nor staves. Nor is the provision for it more easy than the preparation has been kind. Nothing proves more than this that the being who presides over the world is essentially benevolent, stealing from us, one by one, the faculties of enjoyment, searing our sensibilities, leading us, like the horse in his mill, round and round the same beaten circle.

To see what we have seen,
To taste the tasted, and at each return,
Less tasteful; o'er our palates to decant
Another vintage.

Until satiated and fatigued with the leaden iteration, we ask our own *Congé* [leave]. I heard once a very old friend, who had troubled himself with neither poets nor philosophers, say the same thing in plain prose, that he was tired of pulling off his shoes and stockings at night, and putting them on again in the morning. The wish to stay here is thus gradually extinguished: but not so easily that of returning once in a while to see how things have gone on. Perhaps however one of the elements of future felicity is to be a constant and unimpassioned view of what is passing here. If so, this may well supply the wish of occasional visits. Mercier has given us a vision of the year 2440, but prophecy is one thing, history another. On the whole however, perhaps it is wise and well to be contented with the good things which the master of the feast places before us, and to be thankful for what we have, rather than thoughtful about what we have not.

Thomas Jefferson to William Lee
January 16, 1817

I received, three days ago, a letter from M. Martin, 2d Vice President, and M. Parmantier, Secretary of "the French Agricultural and Manufacturing Society," dated at Philadelphia the 5th instant. It covered resolutions proposing to apply to Congress for a grant of two hundred and fifty thousand acres of land on the Tombigbee, and stating some of the general principles on which the society was to be founded; and their letter requested me to trace for them the basis of a social pact for the local regulations of their society, and to address the answer to yourself, their 1st Vice President at Washington....

I feel all the presumption it would manifest, should I undertake to do what this respectable society is alone qualified to do suitably for itself. There are some preliminary questions, too, which are particularly for their own consideration. It is proposed that this shall be a separate State? Or a county of a State? Or a mere voluntary association, as those of the Quakers, Dunkers, Menonists? A separate State it cannot be, because from the tract it asks it would not be more than twenty miles square; and in establishing new States regard is had to a certain degree of equality in size. If it is to be a county of a State, it cannot be governed by its own laws, but must be subject to those of the State of which it is a part.

If merely a voluntary association, the submission of its members will be merely voluntary also; as no act of coercion would be permitted by the general law. These considerations must control the society, and themselves alone can modify their own intentions and wishes to them. With this apology for declining a task to which I am so unequal, I pray them to be assured of my sincere wishes for their success and happiness, and yourself particularly of my high consideration and esteem.

Thomas Jefferson to Charles Thomson
January 29, 1817

I should regret you had thought the incident with Mr. Delaplaine worth an explanation. He wrote to me on the subject of my letter to you of Jan. 9. 1816. and asked me questions which I answer only to one being. To himself therefore I replied 'say nothing of my religion; it is known to my god and myself alone. It's evidence before the world is to be sought in my life. If that has been honest and dutiful to society, the religion which has regulated it cannot be a bad one.' It is a singular anxiety which some people have that we should all think alike. Would the world be more beautiful were all our faces alike? Were our tempers, our talents, our tastes, our forms, our wishes, aversions and pursuits cast exactly in the same mould? If no varieties existed in the animal, vegetable, or mineral creation, but all were strictly uniform, catholic and orthodox, what a world of physical and moral monotony would it be! These are the absurdities into which those run who usurp the throne of god, and dictate to him what he should have done. May they, with all their metaphysical riddles, appear before that tribunal with as clean hands and hearts as you and I shall. There, suspended in the scales of eternal justice, faith and works will shew their worth by their weight. God bless you and preserve you long in life & health.

Part 11

THE REVOLUTIONARIES IN
RETIREMENT

1817 – 1819

The University was still Jefferson's political preoccupation as 1817 saw the Virginia Assembly defeat a bill presenting his general education plan. But October 6 saw the cornerstone laid for the University. In 1818 he chaired the commission to plan the University and wrote its report. By 1819 the Assembly charters the University. His campaign required him to clarify the relationship between religion and the secular university.

As he tried to withdraw from involvement with contemporary politics, and the slavery question, which came to the fore when a Northern Representative proposed an amendment prohibiting slavery in Missouri, Jefferson began *The Life & Morals of Jesus of Nazareth,* a mature redo of his Presidential effort in 1804.

On retiring to Montpelier, Madison helped found the American Colonization Society as a solution to slavery. But 1819 saw him oppose a federal ban on slavery in Missouri. As with Jefferson, he could still think progressively about issues where they had achieved success, while he was unable to think realistically about the consequences of their compromise with slavery.

Between leaving the White House in 1817 and his death, he wrote the Detatched Memoranda. Among other things, it contains his fullest thoughts on separation of religion and state. As the mature thoughts of the presenter of the Bill of Rights, it is as important as that document and it is our duty and pleasure to bring it to the attention of the public.

THOMAS JEFFERSON TO MARQUIS DE LAFAYETTE
May 4, 1817

Here all is quiet. The British war has left us in debt; but that is a cheap price for the good it has done us.... But its best effect has been the complete suppression of party. The federalists who were truly American, and their great mass was so, have separated from their brethren who were mere Anglomen, and are received with cordiality into the republican ranks. Even Connecticut, as a State, and the last one expected to yield its steady habits (which were essentially bigoted in politics as well as religion), has chosen a republican governor, and republican legislature. Massachusetts indeed still lags; because most deeply involved in the parricide crimes and treasons of the war. But her gangrene is contracting, the sound flesh advancing on it, and all there will be well. I mentioned Connecticut as the most hopeless of our States. Little Delaware had escaped my attention. That is essentially a Quaker State, the fragment of a religious sect which, there, in the other States, in England, are a homogeneous mass, acting with one mind, and that directed by the mother society in England. Dispersed, as the Jews, they still form, as those do, one nation, foreign to the land they live in. They are Protestant Jesuits, implicitly devoted to the will of their superior, and forgetting all duties to their country in the execution of the policy of their order. When war is proposed with England, they have religious scruples; but when with France, these are laid by, and they become clamorous for it. They are, however, silent, passive, and give no other trouble than of whipping them along....

I wish I could give better hopes of our southern brethren. The achievement of their independence of Spain is no longer a question. But it is a very serious one, what will then become of them? Ignorance and bigotry, like other insanities, are incapable of self-government. They will fall under military despotism, and become the murderous tools of the ambition of their respective Bonapartes; and whether this will be for their greater happiness, the rule of one only has taught you to judge. No one, I hope, can doubt my wish to see them and all mankind exercising self-government, and capable of exercising it. But the question is not what we wish, but what is practicable? As their sincere friend and brother then, I do believe the best thing for them, would be for themselves to come to an accord with Spain, under the guarantee of France, Russia, Holland, and the United States, allowing to Spain a nominal supremacy, with authority only to keep the peace among them, leaving them otherwise all the powers of self-government, until their experience in them, their emancipation from their priests, and advancement in information, shall prepare them for complete independence.

THOMAS JEFFERSON TO JOHN ADAMS
May 5, 1817

Editor's note: Jefferson's comments on Massachusetts and Connecticut are in reference to the fact that Adam's state continued to maintain congregationalism as the established religion until 1833, while Connecticut did away with it in 1817.

Your recommendations are always welcome, for indeed the subjects of them always merit welcome, and some of them in an extraordinary degree. They make us acquainted with what there is of excellent in our ancient sister state of Massachusetts, once venerated and beloved, and still hanging on our hopes, for what need we despair after the resurrection of Connecticut to light and liberality. I had believed that, the last retreat of Monkish darkness, bigotry, and abhorrence of those advances of the mind which had carried the other states a century ahead of them. They seemed still to be exactly where their forefathers were when they schismatised from the Covenant of works, and to consider, as dangerous heresies, all innovations good or bad. I join you therefore in sincere congratulations that this den of the priesthood is at length broken up, and that a protestant popedom is no longer to disgrace the American history and character. If by religion we are to understand sectarian dogmas, in which no two of them agree, then your exclamation on that hypothesis is just, "that this would be the best of all possible worlds, if there were no religion in it." But if the moral precepts, innate in man, and made a part of his physical constitution, as necessary for a social being, if the sublime doctrines of philanthropism and deism taught us by Jesus of Nazareth, in which all agree, constitute true religion, then, without it, this would be, as you again say, "something not fit to be named even, indeed, a hell."

THOMAS JEFFERSON TO ALEXANDER VON HUMBOLDT
June 13, 1817

The physical information you have given us of a country hitherto so shamefully unknown, has come exactly in time to guide our understandings in the great political revolution now bringing it into prominence on the stage of the world. The issue of its struggles, as they respect Spain, is no longer matter of doubt. As it respects their own liberty, peace and happiness, we cannot be quite so certain. Whether the blinds of bigotry, the shackles of the priesthood, and the fascinating glare of rank and wealth, give fair play to the common sense of the mass of their people, so far as to qualify them for self-government, is what we do not know. Perhaps our wishes may be stronger than our hopes.

THOMAS JEFFERSON TO ALBERT GALLATIN
June 16, 1817

Three of our papers have presented us the copy of an act of the legislature of New York, which, if it has really passed, will carry us back to the times of the darkest bigotry and barbarism, to find a parallel. Its purport is, that all those who shall hereafter join in communion with the religious sect of Shaking Quakers, shall be deemed civilly dead, their marriages dissolved, and all their children and property taken out of their hands. This act being published nakedly in the papers, without the usual signatures, or any history of the circumstances of its passage, I am not without a hope it may have been a mere abortive attempt. It contrasts singularly with a contemporary vote of the Pennsylvania legislature, who, on a proposition to make the belief in God a necessary qualification for office, rejected it by a great majority, although assuredly there was not a single atheist in their body. And you remember to have heard, that when the act for religious freedom was before the Virginia Assembly, a motion to insert the name of Jesus Christ before the phrase, "the author of our holy religion," which stood in the bill, was rejected, although that was the creed of a great majority of them.

THOMAS JEFFERSON TO GEORGE TICKNOR
November 25, 1817

I had before heard of the military ingredients which Bonaparte had infused into all the schools of France, but have never so well understood them as from your letter. The penance he is now doing for all his atrocities must be soothing to every virtuous heart. It proves that we have a god in heaven. That he is just, and not careless of what passes in this world. And we cannot but wish to this inhuman wretch, a long, long life, that time as well as intensity may fill up his sufferings to the measure of his enormities.

JAMES MADISON, DETATCHED MEMORANDA
[1817-1832]

Editor's note: In 1856, Congress authorized William Rives, Madison's historian friend, to prepare his papers for publication. The Detatched (sic) Memoranda was among these. Rives worked on them in his home, publishing several volumes of papers. However, although he quoted it in a biography of Madison, he did not include it in these volumes. Eventually it was misplaced, ending up in a pile of Rives' personal papers.

The document was recovered in 1946 by Elizabeth Fleet, working on a biography of Rives, and published in the October 1946 issue of The William and Mary Quarterly, *a leading journal devoted to the founding fathers. There is no doubt of its authenticity and it has been cited by the Supreme Court. As the notepaper has no watermark, Rives dated it as "subsequent to" Madison's "retirement from the presidency in 1817," and Gaillard Hunt, another major Madison scholar, considered it as "before 1832."*

It is given here in 1817 because it deals at length with aspects of separation of religion and state that Madison takes up in passages in later letters, and illuminates those remarks. The text is Fleet's. Thus some parentheses are not closed, etc. I add translations from Latin. The memorandum ends incompletely, but it is suggested that readers reexamine his July 23, 1813 Proclamation of Thanksgiving, and his Proclamation of a day of public humiliation and fasting and of prayer to Almighty God, November 16, 1814, both above.

I did not become acquainted with Dr. Franklin till after his return from France and election to the Chief Magistracy of Pennsylvania.... I never passed half an hour in his company without hearing some observation or anicdote worth remembering.... In a conversation with him one day whilst he was confined to his bed, the subject of religion with its various dotrines & modes happening to turn up, the Dr. remarked that he should be glad to see an experiment made of a religion that admitted of no pardon for transgressions; the hope of impunity being the great encouragement to them. In illustration of this tendency, he said that when he was a young man he was much subject to fits of indigestion brought on by indulgence at the table. On complaining of it to a friend, he recommended as a remedy a few drops of oil of wormwood, whenever that happened; and that he should carry a little viol of it about him. On trial he said he found the remedy to answer, and then said he, having my absolution in my pocket, I went on sinning more freely than ever....

The Docr was more apprehensive of encroachment by the States, and in support of his opinion related what had occurred when the Union of 1706 between England & Scotland was on foot. The Scotch orators & patriots opposed the measure as pregnant with ruin to their country. In a Sermon one of their Preachers vehemently declaimed agst it. Not only would the dignity the independence & commerce of Scotland be lost. Her religion as well as Civil interests would be sacrificed in favor of England. In a word the whale would swallow Jonas. But how said the Docr has it turned out, Why that Jonas had in fact swallowed the whale (Bute & other Scotsmen having then the sway in the Br. Cabinet) case of the story concerning Abraham and the angels against persecution - Dialogue with   — see F's (Franklin's) Gazette See the sundry accts of it in   & his improvemt by adding to the alleged original in the appeal to Abraham—the words "who art thyself a sinner"....

The danger of silent accumulations & encroachments by Ecclesiastical Bodies have not sufficiently engaged attention in the U.S. They have the noble merit of first unshackling the conscience from persecuting laws, and of establishing among religious Sects a legal equality. If some of the States have not embraced this just and this truly Xn principle in its proper latitude, all of them present examples by which the most enlightened States of the old world may be instructed; and there is one State at least, Virginia, where religious liberty is placed on its true foundation and is defined in its full latitude. The general principle is contained in her declaration of rights, prefixed to her Constitution: but it is unfolded and defined, in its precise extent, in the act of the Legislature, usually named the Religious Bill, which passed into a law in the year 1786. Here the separation between the authority of human laws, and the natural rights of Man excepted from the grant on which all political authority is founded, is traced as distinctly as words can admit, and the limits to this authority established with as much solemnity as the forms of legislation can express. The law has the further advantage of having been the result of a formal appeal to the sense of the Community and a deliberate sanction of a vast majority, comprizing every sect of Christians in the State. This act is a true standard of Religious liberty: its principle the great barrier agst usurpations on the rights of conscience. As long as it is respected & no longer, these will be safe. Every provision for them short of this principle, will be found to leave crevices at least thro' which bigotry may introduce persecution; a monster, that feeding & thriving on its own venom, gradually swells to a size and strength overwhelming all laws divine & human.

Ye States of America, which retain in your Constitutions or Codes, any aberration from the sacred principle of religious liberty, by giving to Caesar what belongs to God, or joining together what God has put asunder, hasten to revise & purify your systems, and make the example of your Country as pure & compleat, in what relates to the freedom of the mind and its allegiance to its maker, as in what belongs to the legitimate objects of political & civil institutions.

Strongly guarded as is the separation between Religion & Govt in the Constitution of the United States the danger of encroachment by Ecclesiastical Bodies, may be illustrated by precedents already furnished in their short history. (See the cases in which negatives were put by J. M. on two bills passd by Congs and his signature withheld from another. See also attempt in Kentucky for example, where it was proposed to exempt Houses of Worship from taxes.

The most notable attempt was that in Virga to establish a Genl assessment for the support of all Xn sects. This was proposed in the year   by P. H. and supported by all his eloquence, aided by the remaining prejudices of the Sect which before the Revolution had been established by law. The progress of the measure was arrested by urging that the respect due to the people required in so extraordinary a case an appeal to their deliberate will. The bill was accordingly printed & published with that view. At the instance of Col: George Nicholas, Col: George Mason & others, the memorial & remonstrance agst it was drawn up, (which see) and printed Copies of it circulated thro' the State, to be signed by the people at large. It met with the approbation of the Baptists, the Presbyterians, the Quakers, and the few Roman Catholics, universally; of the Methodists in part; and even of not a few of the Sect formerly established by law. When the Legislature assembled, the number of Copies & signatures prescribed displayed such an overwhelming opposition of the people, that the proposed plan of a genl assessmt was crushed under it; and advantage taken of the crisis to carry thro' the Legisl: the Bill above referred to, establishing religious liberty. In the course of the opposition to the bill in the House of Delegates, which was warm & strenuous from some of the minority, an experiment was made on the reverence entertained for the name & sanctity of the Saviour, by proposing to insert the words "Jesus Christ" after the words "our lord" in the preamble, the object of which would have been, to imply a restriction of the liberty defined in the Bill, to those professing his religion only. The amendment was discussed, and rejected by a vote of   agst (See letter of J. M. to Mr. Jefferson dated   ) The opponents of the amendment having turned the feeling as well as judgment of the House agst it, by successfully contending that the better proof of reverence for that holy name wd be not to profane it by making it a topic of legisl. discussion, & particularly by making his religion the means of abridging the natural and equal rights of all men, in defiance of his own declaration that his Kingdom was not of this world. This view of the subject was much enforced by the circumstance that it was espoused by some members who were particularly distinguished by their reputed piety and Christian zeal.

But besides the danger of a direct mixture of Religion & civil Government, there is an evil which ought to be guarded agst in the indefinite accumulation of property

---

from the capacity of holding it in perpetuity by ecclesiastical corporations. The power of all corporations, ought to be limited in this respect. The growing wealth acquired by them never fails to be a source of abuses. A warning on this subject is emphatically given in the example of the various Charitable establishments in G. B. the management of which has been lately scrutinized. The excessive wealth of ecclesiastical Corporations and the misuse of it in many Countries of Europe has Long been a topic of complaint. In some of them the Church has amassed half perhaps the property of the nation. When the reformation took place, an event promoted if not caused, by that disordered state of things, how enormous were the treasures of religious societies, and how gross the corruptions engendered by them; so enormous & so gross as to produce in the Cabinets & Councils of the Protestant states a disregard, of all the pleas of the interested party drawn from the sanctions of the law, and the sacredness of property held in religious trust. The history of England during the period of the reformation offers a sufficient illustration for the present purpose.

Are the U. S. duly awake to the tendency of the precedents they are establishing, in the multiplied incorporations of Religious Congregations with the faculty of acquiring & holding property real as well as personal? Do not many of these acts give this faculty, without limit either as to time or as to amount? And must not bodies, perpetual in their existence, and which may be always gaining without ever losing, speedily gain more than is useful, and in time more than is safe? Are there not already examples in the U. S. of ecclesiastical wealth equally beyond its object and the foresight of those who laid the foundation of it? In the U. S. there is a double motive for fixing limits in this case, because wealth may increase not only from additional gifts, but from exorbitant advances in the value of the primitive one. In grants of vacant lands, and of lands in the vicinity of growing towns & Cities the increase of value is often such as if foreseen, would essentially controul the liberality confirming them. The people of the U. S. owe their Independence &. their liberty, to the wisdom of descrying in the minute tax of 3 pence on tea, the magnitude of the evil comprized in the precedent. Let them exert the same wisdom, in watching agst every evil lurking under plausible disguises, and growing up from small beginnings. *Obsta principiis* [resist beginnings].

see the Treatise of Father Paul on benificiary matters.

Is the appointment of Chaplains to the two Houses of Congress consistent with the Constitution, and with the pure principle of religious freedom?

In strictness the answer on both points must be in the negative. The Constitution of the U. S. forbids everything like an establishment of a national religion. The law appointing Chaplains establishes a religious worship for the national representatives, to be performed by Ministers of religion, elected by a majority of them; and these are to be paid out of the national taxes. Does not this involve the principle of a national establishment, applicable to a provision for a religious worship for the Constituent as well as of the representative Body, approved by the majority, and conducted by Ministers of religion paid by the entire nation.

The establishment of the chaplainship to Congs is a palpable violation of equal rights, as well as of Constitutional principles: The tenets of the chaplains elected [by the majority] shut the door of worship agst the members whose creeds & consciences forbid a participation in that of the majority. To say nothing of other sects, this is the case with that of Roman Catholics & Quakers who have always had members in one or both of the Legislative branches. Could a Catholic clergyman ever hope to be appointed a Chaplain? To say that his religious principles are obnoxious or that his sect is small, is to lift the evil at once and exhibit in its naked deformity the doctrine that religious truth is to be tested by numbers or that the major sects have a right to govern the minor.

If Religion consist in voluntary acts of individuals, singly, or voluntarily associated, and it be proper that public functionaries, as well as their Constituents shd discharge their religious duties, let them like their Constituents, do so at their own expence. How small a contribution from each member of Cong wd suffice for the purpose? How just wd it be in its principle? How noble in its exemplary sacrifice to the genius of the Constitution; and the divine right of conscience? Why should the expence of a religious worship be allowed for the Legislature, be paid by the public, more than that for the Ex. or Judiciary branch of the Govt.

Were the establishment to be tried by its fruits, are not the daily devotions conducted by these legal Ecclesiastics, already degenerating into a scanty attendance, and a tiresome formality?

Rather than let this step beyond the landmarks of power have the effect of a legitimate precedent, it will be better to apply to it the legal aphorism *de minimis non curat lex* [the law doesn't care about minute things]: or to class it cum *"maculis quas aut incuria fudit, aut humana parum cavit natura."* [with "the stains which either negligence has poured out or which human nature could hardly anticipate."]

Better also to disarm in the same way, the precedent of Chaplainships for the army and navy, than erect them into a political authority in matters of religion. The object of this establishment is seducing; the motive to it is laudable. But is it not safer to adhere to a right principle, and trust to its consequences, than confide in the reasoning however specious in favor of a wrong one. Look thro' the armies & navies of the world, and say whether in the appointment of their ministers of religion, the spiritual interest of the flocks or the temporal interest of the Shepherds, be most in view: whether here, as elsewhere the political care of religion is not a nominal more than a real aid. If the spirit of armies be devout, the spirit out of the armies will never be less so; and a failure of religious instruction &, exhortation from a voluntary source within or without, will rarely happen: if such be not the spirit of armies, the official services of their Teachers are not likely to produce it. It is more likely to flow from the labours of a spontaneous zeal. The armies of the Puritans had their appointed Chaplains; but without these there would have been no lack of public devotion in that devout age.

The case of navies with insulated crews may be less within the scope of these reflections. But it is not entirely so. The chance of a devout officer, might be of as much worth to religion, as the service of an ordinary chaplain. [were it admitted that religion has a real interest in the latter.] But we are always to keep in mind that it is safer to trust the consequences of a right principle, than reasonings in support of a bad one.

Religious proclamations by the Executive recommending thanksgivings & fasts are shoots from the same root with the legislative acts reviewed.

Altho' recommendations only, they imply a religious agency, making no part of the trust delegated to political rulers.

The objections to them are 1. that Govts ought not to interpose in relation to those subject to their authority but in cases where they can do it with effect. An advisory Govt is a contradiction in terms. 2. The members of a Govt as such can in no sense, be regarded as possessing an advisory trust from their Constituents in their religious capacities. They cannot form an ecclesiastical Assembly, Convocation, Council, or Synod, and as such issue decrees or injunctions addressed to the faith or the Consciences of the people. In their individual capacities, as distinct from their official station, they might unite in recommendations of any sort whatever, in the same manner as any other individuals might do. But then their recommendations ought to express the true character from which they emanate. 3. They seem to imply and certainly nourish the erronious idea of a national religion. The idea just as it related to the Jewish nation under a theocracy, having been improperly adopted by so many nations which have embraced Xnity, is too apt to lurk in the bosoms even of Americans, who in general are aware of the distinction between religious & political societies. The idea also of a union of all to form one nation under one Govt in acts of devotion to the God of all is an imposing idea. But reason and the principles of the Xn religion require that all the individuals composing a nation even of the same precise creed & wished to unite in a universal act of religion at the same time, the union ought to be effected thro' the intervention of their religious not of their political representatives. In a nation composed of various sects, some alienated widely from others, and where no agreement could take place thro' the former, the interposition of the latter is doubly wrong: 4. The tendency of the practice, to narrow the recommendation to the standard of the predominant sect. The Ist proclamation of Genl Washington dated Jany 1. 1795 (see if this was the 1st) recommending a day of thanksgiving, embraced all who believed in a supreme ruler of the Universe. That of Mr. Adams called for a Xn worship. Many private letters reproached the Proclamations issued by J. M. for using general terms, used in that of Presidt W—n; and some of them for not inserting particulars according with the faith of certain Xn sects. The practice if not strictly guarded naturally terminates in a conformity to the creed of the majority and a single sect, if amounting to a majority. 5. The last & not the least objection is the liability of the practice to a subserviency to political views; to the scandal of religion, as well as the increase of party animosities. Candid or incautious politicians will not always disown such views. In truth it is difficult to frame such a religious Proclamation generally suggested by a political State of things, without referring to them in terms having some bearing on party questions. The Proclamation of Pres: W. which was issued just after the suppression of the Insurrection in Penna and at a time when the public mind was divided on several topics, was so construed by many. Of this the Secretary of State himself, E. Randolph seems to have had an anticipation.

The original draught of that Instrument filed in the Dept. of State (see copies of these papers on the files of J. M.) in the hand writing of Mr Hamilton the Secretary of the Treasury. It appears that several slight alterations only had been made at the suggestion of the Secretary of State; and in a marginal note in his hand, it is remarked that "In short this proclamation ought to savour as much as possible of religion, & not too much of having a political object." In a subjoined note in the hand of Mr. Hamilton, this remark is answered by the counter-remark that "A proclamation of a Government which is a national act, naturally embraces objects which are political" so naturally, is the idea of policy associated with religion, whatever be the mode or the occasion, when a function of the latter is assumed by those in power.

During the administration of Mr Jefferson no religious proclamation was issued. It being understood that his successor was disinclined to such interpositions of the Executive and by some supposed moreover that they might originate with more propriety with the Legislative Body, a resolution was passed requesting him to issue a proclamation. (see the resolution in the Journals of Congress.

It was thought not proper to refuse a compliance altogether; but a form & language were employed, which were meant to deaden as much as possible any claim of political right to enjoin religious observances by resting these expressly on the voluntary compliance of individuals, and even by limiting the recommendation to such as wished simultaneous as well as voluntary performance of a religious act on the occasion. The following is a copy of the proclamation: (see it in

THOMAS JEFFERSON, ANAS
February 4, 1818

Editor's note: On February 4, 1818, Jefferson wrote an introduction to a collection of letters, confidential notes and reports, written while he was Secretary of State. Later, material from his Vice-Presidential and Presidential period was added. Thomas Jefferson Randolph, his grandson, called them "Anas," as with the Greek plural of the suffix employed to form the term "Jeffersoniana." The passages below refer to February 1, 1800, when Vice President Jefferson was waiting to take office as President, in March.

February the 1st. Doctor Rush tells me that he had it from Asa Green, that when the clergy addressed General Washington on his departure from the Government, it was observed in their consultation, that he had never, on any occasion, said a word to the public which showed a belief in the Christian religion, and they thought they should so pen their address, as to force him at length to declare publicly whether he was a Christian or not. They did so.

However, he observed, the old fox was too cunning for them. He answered every article of their address particularly except that, which he passed over without notice. Rush observes, he never did say a word on the subject in any of his public papers, except in his valedictory letter to the Governors of the States, when he resigned his commission in the army, wherein he speaks of "the benign influence of the Christian religion." I know that Gouverneur Morris, who pretended to be in his secrets and believed himself to be so, has often told me that General Washington believed no more of that system than he himself did.

THOMAS JEFFERSON TO COUNT ANTONIO DUGNANI
February 14, 1818

Editor's note: Dugnani was the Papal Nuncio to France in 1789.

During the terrible revolutions of Europe I felt great anxiety for you, and have never yet learnt with certainty how far they affected you. Your letter to the Archbishop being from Rome and so late in September makes me hope that all is well, and thanks be to God the tiger who revelled so long in the blood and spoils of Europe is at length, like another Prometheus, chained to his rock, where the vulture of remorse for his crimes will be preying on his vitals and in like manner without consuming them.

THOMAS JEFFERSON TO BENJAMIN WATERHOUSE
March 3, 1818

When I contemplate the immense advances in science and discoveries in the arts which have been made within the period of my life, I look forward with confidence to equal advances by the present generation, and have no doubt they will consequently be as much wiser than we have been as we than our fathers were, and they than the burners of witches. Even the metaphysical contest, which you so pleasantly described to me in a former letter, will probably end in improvement, by clearing the mind of Platonic mysticism and unintelligible jargon.

THOMAS JEFFERSON TO SAMUEL WELLS AND GABRIEL LILLY
April 1, 1818

I make you my acknolegement for the sermon on the Unity of God, and am glad to see our countrymen looking that question in the face. It must end in a return to primitive christianity, and the disbandment of the unintelligible Athanasian jargon of 3. being 1. and 1. being 3. This sermon is one of the strongest pieces against it. I observe you are about printing a work of Belsham's on the same subject, for which I wish to be a subscriber, and inclose you a 5 D. bill, there being none of fractional denominations. The surplus therefore may stand as I shall be calling for other things.

THOMAS JEFFERSON TO JOHN ADAMS
May 17, 1818

I was so unfortunate as not to receive from Mr. Holly's own hand your favor of January the 28th, being then at my other home. He dined only with my family, and left them with an impression which has filled me with regret that I did not partake of the pleasure his visit gave them. I am glad he is gone to Kentucky. Rational Christianity will thrive more rapidly there than here. They are freer from prejudices than we are, and bolder in grasping at truth. The time is not distant, though neither you nor I shall see it, when we shall be but a secondary people to them. Our greediness for wealth, and fantastical expense, have degraded, and will degrade, the minds of our maritime citizens. These are the peculiar vices of commerce....

I enter into all your doubts as to the event of the revolution of South America. They will succeed against Spain. But the dangerous enemy is within their own breasts. Ignorance and superstition will chain their minds and bodies under religious and military despotism. I do believe it would be better for them to obtain freedom by degrees only; because that would qualify them to take charge of themselves understandingly; with more certainty, if in the meantime, under so much control as may keep them at peace with one another. Surely, it is our duty to wish them independence and self-government, because they wish it themselves, and they have the right, and we none, to choose for themselves; and I wish, moreover, that our ideas may be erroneous, and theirs prove well founded. But these are speculations, my friend, which we may as well deliver over to those who are to see their development. We shall only be lookers on, from the clouds above, as now we look down on the labors, the hurry and bustle of the ants and bees. Perhaps in that supermundane region, we may be amused with seeing the fallacy of our own guesses, and even the nothingness of those labors which have filled and agitated our own time here.

JAMES MADISON TO PRESIDENT JAMES MONROE
May 21, 1818

Editor's note: Madison refers here to Tsar Alexander of Russia.

The character and views of Alexander appear to be more and more wrapped in mystery. It would seem that he aspired to be the conservator of the peace of the world, in contrast with the conquering genius of Napoleon, and that he mingles with his ambition a spice of fanaticism, which, whether, as often happens, it ends in hypocrisy, or, on the contrary, grows into stronger delusions of supernatural guidance, may transform the Saint into the Despot.

JAMES MADISON TO MORDECAI NOAH
May 15, 1818

Editor's note: Madison appointed Noah consul at Tunis in 1813. Two years later he was recalled, under accusation of misappropriating funds. Eventually the charge was dropped.

I have recd. your letter of the 6th, with the eloquent discourse delivered at the Consecration of the Jewish Synagogue. Having ever regarded the freedom of religious opinions and worship as equally belonging to every sect, and the secure enjoyment of it as the best human provision for bringing all either into the same way of thinking, or into that mutual charity which is the only substitute, I observe with pleasure the view you give of the spirit in which your Sect partake of the blessings offered by our Govt and Laws.

As your foreign Mission took place whilst I was in the Administration, it cannot but be agreeable to me to learn that your accts. have been closed in a manner so favorable to you. And I know too well the justice & candor of the present Executive to doubt, that an official [illegible] will be readily allowed to explanations necessary to protect your character against the effect of any impressions whatever ascertained to be erroneous. It is certain that your religious profession was well known at the time you recd. your Commission; and that in itself could not be a motive for your recall.

THOMAS JEFFERSON TO MORDECAI NOAH
May 28, 1818

I thank you for the Discourse on the consecration of the Synagogue in your city, with which you have been pleased to favor me. I have read it with pleasure and instruction, having learnt from it some valuable facts in Jewish history which I did not know before. Your sect by its sufferings has furnished a remarkable proof of the universal spirit of religious intolerance inherent in every sect, disclaimed by all while feeble, and practiced by all when in power. Our laws have applied the only antidote to this vice, protecting our religious, as they do our civil rights, by putting all on an equal footing. But more remains to be done, for although we are free by the law, we are not so in practice. Public opinion erects itself into an inquisition, and exercises its office with as much fanaticism as fans the flames of an *Auto-da-fé*. The prejudice still scowling on your section of our religion altho' the elder one, cannot be unfelt by ourselves. It is to be hoped that individual dispositions will at length mould themselves to the model of the law, and consider the moral basis, on which all our religions rest, as the rallying point which unites them in a common interest; while the peculiar dogmas branching from it are the exclusive concern of the respective sects embracing them, and no rightful subject of notice to any other. Public opinion needs reformation on that point, which would have the further happy effect of doing away the hypocritical maxim of "intus et lubet, foris ut moris" ["within as pleases, without how maintained"]. Nothing, I think, would be so likely to effect this, as to your sect particularly, as the more careful attention to education, which you recommend, and which, placing its members on the equal and commanding benches of science, will exhibit them as equal objects of respect and favor. I should not do full justice to the merits of your Discourse, were I not, in addition to that of its matter, to express my consideration of it as a fine specimen of style and composition. I salute you with great respect and esteem.

THOMAS JEFFERSON TO SALMA HALE
July 26, 1818

I thank you for the pamphlets you have been so kind as to send me, which I now return. They give a lively view of the state of religious dissension now prevailing in the North, and making it's way to the South. Most controversies begin with a discussion of principles; but soon degenerate into episodical, verbal, or personal cavils. Too much of this is seen in these pamphlets, and, as usual, those whose dogmas are the most unintelligible are the most angry. The truth is that Calvinism has introduced into the Christian religion more new absurdities than it's leader had purged it of old ones. Our saviour did not come into the world to save metaphysicians only. His doctrines are levelled to the simplest understandings and it is only by banishing Hierophantic mysteries and Scholastic subtleties, which they have nick-named Christianity, and getting back to the plain and unsophisticated precepts of Christ, that we become real Christians. The half reformation of Luther and Calvin did something towards a restoration of his genuine doctrines; the present contest will, I hope, compleat what they begun, and place us where the evangelists left us. I salute you with esteem and respect.

THOMAS JEFFERSON, REPORT OF THE COMMISSIONERS
FOR THE UNIVERSITY OF VIRGINIA
August 4, 1818

What, but education, has advanced us beyond the condition of our indigenous neighbors? And what chains them to their present state of barbarism and wretchedness, but a bigoted veneration for the supposed superlative wisdom of their fathers, and the preposterous idea that they are to look backward for better things and not forward, longing as it should seem to return to the days of eating acorns and roots, rather than indulge in the degeneracies of civilization. And how much more encouraging to the achievements of science and improvement is this, than the desponding view that the condition of man cannot be ameliorated, that what has been must ever be, and that to secure ourselves where we are, we must tread with awful reverence in the footsteps of our fathers. This doctrine is the genuine fruit of the alliance between Church and State; the tenants of which, finding themselves but too well in their present condition, oppose all advances which might unmask their usurpations, and monopolies of honors, wealth, and power, and fear every change, as endangering the comforts they now hold....

In conformity with the principles of our Constitution, which places all sects of religion on an equal footing, with the jealousies of the different sects in guarding that equality from encroachment and surprise, and with the sentiments of the Legislature in favor of freedom of religion, manifested on former occasions, we have proposed no professor of divinity; and the rather as the proofs of the being of a God, the creator, preserver, and supreme ruler of the universe, the author of all the relations of morality, and of the laws and obligations these infer, will be within the province of the professor of ethics to which adding the developments of these moral obligations, of those in which all sects agree, with a knowledge of the languages, Hebrew, Greek, and Latin, a basis will be formed common to all sects. Proceeding thus far without offence to the Constitution, we have thought it proper at this point to leave every sect to provide, as they think fittest, the means of further instruction in their own peculiar tenets.

JAMES MADISON TO ROBERT WALSH
March 2, 1819

I recd. some days ago your letter of Feby 15, in which you intimate your intention to vindicate our Country against misrepresentations propagated abroad, and your desire of information on the subject of Negro slavery, of moral character, of religion, and of education in Virginia, as affected by the Revolution, and our public Institutions....

With respect to the moral features of Virga. it may be observed, that pictures which have been given of them are, to say the least, outrageous caricatures even when taken from the state of Society previous to the Revolution; and that so far as there was any ground or colour for them, then, the same cannot be found for them now.

Omitting more minute or less obvious causes tainting the habits and manners of the people under the Colonial Govt., the following offer themselves, 1. the negro slavery chargeable in so great a degree on the very quarter which has furnished most of the libellers. It is well known that during the Colonial dependence of Virga. repeated attempts were made to stop the importation of slaves each of which attempts was successively defeated by the foreign negative on the laws, and that one of the first offsprings of independent & Republican legislation was an Act of perpetual prohibition. 2. the too unequal distribution of property favored by laws derived from the British code, which generated examples in the opulent class inauspicious to the habits of the other classes. 3. the indolence of most & the irregular lives of many of the established Clergy, consisting, in a very large proportion, of foreigners, and these in no inconsiderable proportion, of men willing to leave their homes in the parent Country where their demerit was an obstacle to a provision for them, and whose degeneracy here was promoted by their distance from the controuling eyes of their kindred & friends, by the want of Ecclesiastical superiors in the Colony, or efficient ones in G. B. who might maintain a salutary discipline among them, and finally by their independence both of their congregations and of the Civil authority for their stipends....

That there has been an increase of religious instruction since the revolution can admit of no question. The English church was originally the established religion, the character of the clergy that above described. Of other sects there were but few adherents, except the Presbyterians who predominated on the W. side of the Blue

Mountains. A little time previous to the Revolutionary struggle the Baptists sprang up, and made a very rapid progress. Among the early acts of the Republican Legislature, were those abolishing the Religious establishment, and putting all Sects at full liberty and on a perfect level. At present the population is divided, with small exceptions, among the Protestant Episcopalians, the Presbyterians, the Baptists & the Methodists. Of their comparative numbers I can command no sources of information. I conjecture the Presbyterians & Baptists to form each abt a third, & the two other sects together of which the Methodists are much the smallest, to make up the remaining third. The Old churches, built under the establisht at the public expence, have in many instances gone to ruin, or are in a very dilapidated state, owing chiefly to a transition desertion of the flocks to other worships. A few new ones have latterly been built particularly in the towns. Among the other sects, Meeting Houses, have multiplied & continue to multiply, tho' in general they are of the plainest and cheapest sort. But neither the number nor the style of the Religious edifices is a true measure of the state of religion. Religious instruction is now diffused throughout the Community by preachers of every sect with almost equal zeal, tho' with very unequal acquirements, and at private houses & open stations and occasionally in such as are appropriated to Civil use, as well as buildings appropriated to that use. The qualifications of the Preachers, too among the new sects where there was the greatest deficiency, are understood to be improving. On a general comparison of the present & former times, the balance is certainly & vastly on the side of the present, as to the number of religious teachers the zeal which actuates them, the purity of their lives, and the attendance of the people on their instructions. It was the Universal opinion of the Century preceding the last, that Civil Govt could not stand without the prop of a Religious establishment, & that the Xn religion itself, would perish if not supported by a legal provision for its Clergy. The experience of Virginia conspicuously corroborates the disproof of both opinions. The Civil Govt, tho' bereft of everything like an associated hierarchy, possesses the requisite stability and performs its functions with complete success, Whilst the number, the industry, and the morality of the Priesthood, & the devotion of the people have been manifestly increased by the total separation of the Church from the State.

THOMAS JEFFERSON TO THOMAS PARKER
May 15, 1819

I thank you, Sir, for the pamphlet you have been so kind as to send me on the reveries, not to say insanities of Calvin and Hopkins; yet the latter, I believe, is the proper term. Mr. Locke defines a madman to be someone who has a kink in his head on some particular subject, which neither reason nor fact can untangle. Grant him that postulate, and he reasons as correctly as other men. This was the real condition of Calvin and Hopkins, on whom reasoning was wasted. The strait jacket alone was their proper remedy. You ask my opinion on this subject, but when we see so many Hopkinsonian religions in the world, all different, yet every one confident it is the only true one, a man must be very clear-sighted who can see the impression of the finger of God on any particular one of them. Were I to be the founder of a new sect, I would call them Apriarians, and, after the example of the bee, advise them to extract the honey of every sect. My fundamental principle would be the reverse of Calvin's, that we are to be saved by our good works which are within our power, and not by our faith which is not within our power. I salute you with respect and good-will.

JAMES MADISON TO ROBERT J. EVANS
June 15, 1819

I have recd. your letter of the 3d instant, requesting such hints as may have occurred to me on the subject of an eventual extinguishment of slavery in the U. S....

The colonizing plan on foot, has as far as it extends, a due regard to these requisites; with the additional object of bestowing new blessings civil & religious on the quarter of the Globe most in need of them. The Society proposes to transport to the African Coast all free & freed blacks who may be willing to remove thither; to provide by fair means, &, it is understood with a prospect of success, a suitable territory for their reception; and to initiate them into such an establishment as may gradually and indefinitely expand itself.

The experiment, under this view of it, merits encouragement from all who regard slavery as an evil, who wish to see it diminished and abolished by peaceable & just means; and who have themselves no better mode to propose. Those who have most doubted the success of the experiment must at least have wished to find themselves in an error.

THOMAS JEFFERSON TO EZRA STILES ELY
June 25, 1819

Your favor Sir, of the 14th. has been duly recieved, and with it the book you were so kind as to forward to me....

On looking over the summary of the contents of your book, it does not seem likely to bring into collision any of the sectarian differences which you suppose may exist between us. In that branch of religion which regards the moralities of life, and the duties of a social being, which teaches us to love our neighbors as ourselves, and to do good to all men, I am sure that you and I do not differ. We probably differ on that which relates to the dogmas of theology, the foundation of all sectarianism, and on which no two sects dream alike; for if they did they would then be of the same. You say you are a Calvinist. I am not. I am of a sect by myself, as far as I know. I am not a Jew, and therefore do not adopt their theology, which supposes the god of infinite justice to punish the sins of the fathers upon their children, unto the 3d. and 4th. generation: and the benevolent and sublime reformer of that religion has told us only that god is good and perfect, but has not defined him. I am therefore of his theology, believing that we have neither words nor ideas adequate to that definition. And if we could all, after his example, leave the subject as undefinable, we should all be of one sect, doers of good and eschewers of evil. No doctrines of his lead to schism. It is the speculations of crazy theologists which have made a Babel of a religion the most moral and sublime ever preached to man, and calculated to heal, and not to create differences. These religious animosities I impute to those who call themselves his ministers, and who engraft their casuistries on the stock of his simple precepts. I am sometimes more angry with them than is authorized by the blessed charities which he preached. To yourself I pray the acceptance of my great respect.

THOMAS JEFFERSON TO JOHN BRAZIER
August 24, 1819

The acknowledgment of your favor of July 15th, and thanks for the Review which it covered of Mr. Pickering's Memoir on the Modern Greek, have been delayed by a visit to an occasional but distant residence from Monticello, and to an attack here of rheumatism which is just now moderating. I had been much pleased with the memoir, and was much also with your review of it. I have little hope indeed of the recovery of the ancient pronunciation of that finest of human languages, but still I rejoice at the attention the subject seems to excite with you, because it is an evidence that our country begins to have a taste for something more than merely as much Greek as will pass a candidate for clerical ordination....

But to whom are these things useful?... To the moralist they are valuable, because they furnish ethical writings highly and justly esteemed: although in my own opinion, the moderns are far advanced beyond them in this line of science, the divine finds in the Greek language a translation of his primary code, of more importance to him than the original because better understood; and, in the same language, the newer code, with the doctrines of the earliest fathers, who lived and wrote before the simple precepts of the founder of this most benign and pure of all systems of morality became frittered into subtleties and mysteries, and hidden under jargons incomprehensible to the human mind. To these original sources he must now, therefore, return, to recover the virgin purity of his religion.

THOMAS JEFFERSON TO WILLIAM SHORT
October 31, 1819

Editor's note: After sending the letter, Jefferson added a comment in his polygraphic copy. It included an asterisk, referring to a footnote which he placed at the bottom of his page containing the comment. For clarity, all of Jefferson's addition is placed in brackets after the sentence to which it refers. The footnoted material is in a parenthesis following the asterisk, within the brackets. Jefferson's closing line in Latin is translated by the editor.

As you say of yourself, I too am an Epicurean. I consider the genuine (not the imputed) doctrines of Epicurus as containing everything rational in moral philosophy which Greece and Rome have left us. Epictetus, indeed, has given us what was good of the Stoics; all beyond, of their dogmas, being hypocrisy and grimace. Their great crime was in their calumnies of Epicurus and misrepresentations of his doctrines; in which we lament to see the candid character of Cicero engaging as an accomplice. Diffuse, vapid, rhetorical, but enchanting. His prototype Plato, eloquent as himself, dealing out mysticisms incomprehensible to the human mind, has been deified by certain sects usurping the name of Christians; because, in his foggy conceptions, they found a basis of impenetrable darkness whereon to rear fabrications as delirious, of their own invention. These they fathered blasphemously on him whom they claimed as their founder, but who would disclaim them with the indignation which their caricatures of his religion so justly excite. Of Socrates we have nothing genuine but in the Memorabilia of Xenophon. For Plato makes him one of his Collocutors merely to cover his own whimsies under the mantle of his name; a liberty of which we are told Socrates himself complained. Seneca is indeed a fine moralist, disfiguring his work at times with some stoicisms, and affecting too much of antithesis and point, yet giving us on the whole a great deal of sound and practical morality. But the greatest of all the reformers of the depraved religion of his own country, was Jesus of Nazareth. Abstracting what is really his from the rubbish in which it is buried, easily distinguished by it's lustre from the dross of his biographers, and as separable from that as the diamond from the dung hill, we have the outlines of a system of the most sublime morality which has ever fallen from the lips of man: outlines which it is lamentable he did not live to fill up. Epictetus and Epicurus give us laws for governing ourselves, Jesus a supplement of the duties and charities we owe to others. The establishment of the innocent and genuine character of this benevolent Moralist, and the rescuing it from the imputation of imposture, which has resulted from misconstructions of his words by his pretended votaries, is a most desirable object, and one to which Priestley has successfully devoted his labors and learning. [which has resulted from artificial systems,* (e.g. the immaculate conception of Jesus, his deification, the creation of the world by him, his miraculous powers, his resurrection and visible ascension, his corporal presence in the Eucharist, the Trinity, original sin, atonement, regeneration, election, orders of Hierarchy, & c.) invented by ultra-Christian sects, unauthorized by a single word ever uttered by him.] It would in time, it is to be hoped, effect a quiet euthanasia of the heresies of bigotry and fanaticism which have so long triumphed over human reason, and so generally and deeply afflicted mankind. But this work is to be begun by winnowing the grain from the chaff of the historians of his life. I have sometimes thought of translating Epictetus (for he has never been tolerably translated into English) by adding the genuine doctrines of Epicurus from the Syntagma of Gassendi, and an abstract from the Evangelists of whatever has the stamp of the eloquence and fine imagination of Jesus. The last I attempted too hastily some 12. or 15. years ago. It was the work of 2. or 3. nights only, at Washington, after getting thro' the evening task of reading the letters and papers of the day. But with one foot in the grave, these are now idle projects for me. My business is to beguile the wearisomeness of declining life, as I endeavor to do, by the delights of classical reading and of Mathematical truths, and by the consolations of a sound philosophy, equally indifferent to hope and fear....

I will place under this a Syllabus of the doctrines of Epicurus, somewhat in the lapidary style, which I wrote some 20. years ago. A like one of the philosophy of Jesus, of nearly the same age, is too long to be copied. *Vale, et tibi persuade carissimum te esse mihi.* [Farewell, and know in your heart that you are most dear to me.]

THOMAS JEFFERSON, A SYLLABUS OF THE DOCTRINES OF EPICURUS
October 31, 1819

Editor's note: The translation from the Latin is the editor's.

Physical. The Universe eternal.
    It's parts, great and small, interchangeable.
  Matter and Void alone.
    Motion inherent in matter which is weighty and declining.
    Eternal circulation of the elements of bodies.
  Gods, an order of beings next superior to man,
    enjoying in their sphere, their own felicities;
    but not meddling with the concerns of the scale of
    beings below them.
Moral. Happiness the aim of life.
    Virtue the foundation of happiness.
    Utility the test of virtue.
  Pleasure active and In-do-lent.
    In-do-lence is the absence of pain, the true felicity.
    Active, consists in agreeable motion
      It is not happiness, but the means to produce it.
      Thus the absence of hunger is an article of felicity;
      eating the means to obtain it.
The *summum bonum* [highest good] is to be not pained in body, nor troubled in mind.
      i. e. In-do-lence of body, tranquillity of mind.
    To procure tranquillity of mind we must avoid desire and fear
    the two principal diseases of the mind.
Man is a free agent.
Virtue consists in
1. Prudence. 2. Temperance. 3. Fortitude. 4. Justice.
To which are opposed
1. Folly. 2. Desire. 3. Fear. 4. Deceit.

Part 12

JEFFERSON TAKES HIS RAZOR
TO THE BIBLE

1819

The scholars are divided as to when Jefferson completed *The Life and Morals*, with some saying late 1819, others believing it was finished in early 1820. In any case, we know that he had come to feel that his missing 1804 work, *The Philosophy of Jesus*, had been too hastily done, while he was busy with Presidential affairs. Certainly the work of his retirement was a major effort. He laid out selected verses, and parts of verses, which he cut out of Bibles with a razor, in parallel columns in English, French, Latin and Greek, being careful to remove all traces of supernatural miracles.

Only the four Gospels were used, interweaving selections from them into what readers will immediately see is a coherent narrative. Indeed it is so coherent that readers are urged to read it with a King James Bible handy, as the only way to see just how much of the traditional stories he scorned.

THOMAS JEFFERSON, THE LIFE AND MORALS OF JESUS OF NAZARETH
1819-20

L. 2:1 AND it came to pass in those days, that there went out a decree from Caesar Augustus, that all the world should be taxed.

2:2 (And this taxing was first made when Cyrenius was governor of Syria.)

2:3 And all went to be taxed, every one into his own city.

2:4 And Joseph also went up from Galilee, out of the city of Nazareth, into Judaea, unto the city of David, which is called Bethlehem; (because he was of the house and lineage of David,)

2:5 To be taxed with Mary his espoused wife, being great with child.

2:6 And so it was, that, while they were there, the days were accomplished that she should be delivered.

2:7 And she brought forth her firstborn son, and wrapped him in swaddling clothes, and laid him in a manger; because there was no room for them in the inn.

2:21 And when eight days were accomplished for the circumcising of the child, his name was called JESUS,

2:39 And when they had performed all things according to the law of the Lord, they returned into Galilee, to their own city Nazareth.

2:40 And the child grew, and waxed strong in spirit, filled with wisdom:

2:42 And when he was twelve years old, they went up to Jerusalem, after the custom of the feast.

2:43 And when they had fulfilled the days, as they returned, the child Jesus tarried behind in Jerusalem; and Joseph and his mother knew not of it.

2:44 But they, supposing him to have been in the company, went a day's journey; and they sought him among their kinsfolk and acquaintances.

2:45 And when they found him not, they turned back again to Jerusalem, seeking him.

2:46 And it came to pass, that after three days they found him in the temple, sitting in the midst of the doctors, both hearing them, and asking them questions.

2:47 And all that heard him were astonished at his understanding and answers.

2:48 And when they saw him, they were amazed: and his mother said unto him, Son, why hast thou thus dealt with us? Behold, thy father and I have sought thee sorrowing.

2:51 And he went down with them, and came to Nazareth, and was subject unto them.

2:52 And Jesus increased in wisdom and stature.

3:1 Now in the fifteenth year of the reign of Tiberius Caesar, Pontius Pilate being governor of Judaea, and Herod being tetrarch of Galilee, and his brother Philip tetrarch of Ituraea and of the region of Trachonitis, and

Lysanias the tetrarch of Abilene,

3:2   Annas and Caiaphas being the high priests,

MK. 1:4   John did baptize in the wilderness.

MT. 3:4   And the same John had his raiment of camel's hair, and a leathern girdle about his loins; and his meat was locusts and wild honey.

3:5   Then went out to him Jerusalem, and all Judaea, and all the region round about Jordan,

3:6   And were baptized of him in Jordan,

3:13   Then cometh Jesus from Galilee to Jordan unto John, to be baptized of him.

L. 3:23   And Jesus himself began to be about thirty years of age,

J. 2:12   After this he went down to Capernaum, he, and his mother, and his brethren, and his disciples: and they continued there not many days.

2:13   And the Jews' passover was at hand, and Jesus went up to Jerusalem.

2:14   And found in the temple those that sold oxen and sheep and doves, and the changers of money sitting:

2:15   And when he had made a scourge of small cords, he drove them all out of the temple, and the sheep, and the oxen; and poured out the changers' money, and overthrew the tables;

2:16   And said unto them that sold doves, Take these things hence; make not my Father's house an house of merchandise.

J. 3:22   After these things came Jesus and his disciples into the land of Judaea; and there he tarried with them, and baptized.

4:12   Now when Jesus had heard that John was cast into prison, he departed into Galilee;

MK. 6:17   For Herod himself had sent forth and laid hold upon John, and bound him in prison for Herodias' sake, his brother Philip's wife: for he had married her.

6:18   For John had said unto Herod, It is not lawful for thee to have thy brother's wife.

6:19   Therefore Herodias had a quarrel against him, and would have killed him; but she could not:

6:20   For Herod feared John, knowing that he was a just man and an holy, and observed him; and when he heard him, he did many things, and heard him gladly.

6:21   And when a convenient day was come, that Herod on his birthday made a supper to his lords, high captains, and chief estates of Galilee;

6:22   And when the daughter of the said Herodias came in, and danced, and pleased Herod and them that sat with him, the king said unto the damsel, Ask of me whatsoever thou wilt, and I will give it thee.

6:23 And he sware unto her, Whatsoever thou shalt ask of me, I will give it thee, unto the half of my kingdom.

6:24 And she went forth, and said unto her mother, What shall I ask? And she said, The head of John the Baptist.

6:25 And she came in straightway with haste unto the king, and asked, saying, I will that thou give me, by and by in a charger, the head of John the Baptist.

6:26 And the king was exceeding sorry; yet for his oath's sake, and for their sakes which sat with him, he would not reject her.

6:27 And immediately the king sent an executioner, and commanded his head to be brought: and he went and beheaded him in the prison;

6:28 And brought his head in a charger, and gave it to the damsel: and the damsel gave it to her mother.

MK. 1:21 And they went into Capernaum; and straightway on the sabbath day he entered into the synagogue, and taught.

MK. 1:22 And they were astonished at his doctrine: for he taught them as one that had authority, and not as the scribes.

MT. 12:1 At that time Jesus went on the sabbath day through the corn; and his disciples were an hungered, and began to pluck the ears of corn and to eat.

12:2 But when the Pharisees saw it, they said unto him, Behold, thy disciples do that which is not lawful to do upon the sabbath day.

12:3 But he said unto them, Have ye not read what David did, when he was an hungered, and they that were with him;

12:4 How he entered into the house of God, and did eat the shewbread, which was not lawful for him to eat, neither for them which were with him, but only for the priests?

12:5 Or have ye not read in the law, how that on the sabbath days the priests in the temple profane the sabbath, and are blameless?

12:9 And when he was departed thence, he went into their synagogue:

12:10 And, behold, there was a man which had his hand withered. And they asked him, saying, Is it lawful to heal on the sabbath days? that they might accuse him.

12:11 And he said unto them, What man shall there be among you, that shall have one sheep, and if it fall into a pit on the sabbath day, will he not lay hold on it, and lift it out?

12:12 How much then is a man better than a sheep? Wherefore it is lawful to do well on the sabbath days.

MK. 2:27 And he said unto them, The sabbath was made for man, and not man for the sabbath:

MT. 12:14 Then the Pharisees went out, and held a council against him, how they might destroy him.

12:15 But when Jesus knew it, he withdrew himself from thence: and great multitudes followed him.

L. 6:12 And it came to pass in those days, that he went out into a mountain to pray, and continued all night in prayer to God.

6:13 And when it was day, he called unto him his disciples: and of them he chose twelve, whom also he named apostles;

6:14 Simon (whom he also named Peter), and Andrew his brother, James and John, Philip and Bartholomew,

6:15 Matthew and Thomas, James the son of Alphaeus, and Simon called Zelotes,

6:16 And Judas the brother of James, and Judas Iscariot, which also was the traitor.

6:17 And he came down with them, and stood in the plain, and the company of his disciples, and a great multitude of people out of all Judaea and Jerusalem, and from the sea coast of Tyre and Sidon, which came to hear him.

MT. 5:1 And seeing the multitudes, he went up into a mountain: and when he was set, his disciples came unto him:

5:2 And he opened his mouth, and taught them, saying,

5:3 Blessed are the poor in spirit: for theirs is the kingdom of heaven.

5:4 Blessed are they that mourn: for they shall be comforted.

5:5 Blessed are the meek: for they shall inherit the earth.

5:6 Blessed are they which do hunger and thirst after righteousness: for they shall be filled.

5:7 Blessed are the merciful: for they shall obtain mercy.

5:8 Blessed are the pure in heart: for they shall see God.

5:9 Blessed are the peacemakers: for they shall be called the children of God.

5:10 Blessed are they which are persecuted for righteousness' sake: for theirs is the kingdom of heaven.

5:11 Blessed are ye, when men shall revile you, and persecute you, and shall say all manner of evil against you falsely, for my sake.

5:12 Rejoice, and be exceeding glad: for great is your reward in heaven: for so persecuted they the prophets which were before you.

L. 6:24 But woe unto you that are rich! for ye have received your consolation.

6:25 Woe unto you that are full! for ye shall hunger. Woe unto you that laugh now! for ye shall mourn and weep.

6:26 Woe unto you, when all men shall speak well of you! for so did their fathers to the false prophets.

MT. 5:13 Ye are the salt of the earth: but if the salt have lost his savour, wherewith shall it be salted? it is thenceforth good for nothing, but to be cast out, and to be trodden under foot of men.

5:14 Ye are the light of the world. A city that is set on an hill cannot be hid.

5:15 Neither do men light a candle, and put it under a bushel, but on a candlestick; and it giveth light unto all that are in the house.

5:16 Let your light so shine before men, that they may see your good works, and glorify your Father which is in heaven.

5:17 Think not that I am come to destroy the law, or the prophets: I am not come to destroy, but to fulfil.

5:18 For verily I say unto you, Till heaven and earth pass, one jot or one tittle shall in no wise pass from the law, till all be fulfilled.

5:19 Whosoever therefore shall break one of these least commandments, and shall teach men so, he shall be called the least in the kingdom of heaven: but whosoever shall do and teach them, the same shall be called great in the kingdom of heaven.

5:20 For I say unto you, That except your righteousness shall exceed the righteousness of the scribes and Pharisees, ye shall in no case enter into the kingdom of heaven.

5:21 Ye have heard that it was said by them of old time, Thou shalt not kill; and whosoever shall kill shall be in danger of the judgment:

5:22 But I say unto you, That whosoever is angry with his brother without a cause shall be in danger of the judgment: and whosoever shall say to his brother, Raca, shall be in danger of the council: but whosoever shall say, Thou fool, shall be in danger of hell fire.

5:23 Therefore if thou bring thy gift to the altar, and there rememberest that thy brother hath ought against thee;

5:24 Leave there thy gift before the altar, and go thy way; first be reconciled to thy brother, and then come and offer thy gift.

5:25 Agree with thine adversary quickly, whilst thou art in the way with him; lest at any time the adversary deliver thee to the judge, and the judge deliver thee to the officer, and thou be cast into prison.

5:26 Verily I say unto thee, Thou shalt by no means come out thence, till thou hast paid the uttermost farthing.

5:27 Ye have heard that it was said by them of old time, Thou shalt not commit adultery:

5:28 But I say unto you, That whosoever looketh on a woman to lust after her hath committed adultery with her already in his heart.

5:29 And if thy right eye offend thee, pluck it out, and cast it from thee: for it is profitable for thee that one of thy members should perish, and not that thy whole body should be cast into hell.

5:30 And if thy right hand offend thee, cut it off, and cast it from thee: for it is profitable for thee that one of thy members should perish, and not that thy whole body should be cast into hell.

5:31 It hath been said, Whosoever shall put away his wife, let him give her a writing of divorcement:

5:32 But I say unto you, That whosoever shall put away his wife, saving for the cause of fornication, causeth her to commit adultery: and whosoever shall marry her that is divorced committeth adultery.

5:33 Again, ye have heard that it hath been said by them of old time, Thou shalt not forswear thyself, but shalt perform unto the Lord thine oaths:

5:34 But I say unto you, Swear not at all; neither by heaven; for it is God's throne:

5:35 Nor by the earth; for it is his footstool: neither by Jerusalem; for it is the city of the great King.

5:36 Neither shalt thou swear by thy head, because thou canst not make one hair white or black.

5:37 But let your communication be, Yea, yea; Nay, nay: for whatsoever is more than these cometh of evil.

5:38 Ye have heard that it hath been said, An eye for an eye, and a tooth for a tooth:

5:39 But I say unto you, That ye resist not evil: but whosoever shall smite thee on thy right cheek, turn to him the other also.

5:40 And if any man will sue thee at the law, and take away thy coat, let him have thy cloak also.

5:41 And whosoever shall compel thee to go a mile, go with him twain.

5:42 Give to him that asketh thee, and from him that would borrow of thee turn not thou away.

5:43 Ye have heard that it hath been said, Thou shalt love thy neighbour, and hate thine enemy.

5:44 But I say unto you, Love your enemies, bless them that curse you, do good to them that hate you, and pray for them that despitefully use you, and persecute you;

5:45 That ye may be the children of your Father which is in heaven: for he maketh his sun to rise on the evil and on the good, and sendeth rain on the just and on the unjust.

5:46 For if ye love them which love you, what reward have ye? do not even the publicans the same?

5:47 And if ye salute your brethren only, what do ye more than others? do not even the publicans so?

L. 6:34 And if ye lend to them of whom ye hope to receive, what thank have ye? for sinners also lend to sinners, to receive as much again.

6:35 But love ye your enemies, and do good, and lend, hoping for nothing again; and your reward shall be great, and ye shall be the children of the Highest: for he is kind unto the unthankful and to the evil.

6:36 Be ye therefore merciful, as your Father also is merciful.

MT. 6:1 Take heed that ye do not your alms before men, to be seen of them: otherwise ye have no reward of your Father which is in heaven.

6:2 Therefore when thou doest thine alms, do not sound a trumpet before thee, as the hypocrites do in the synagogues and in the streets, that they may have glory of men. Verily I say unto you, They have their reward.

6:3 But when thou doest alms, let not thy left hand know what thy right hand doeth:

6:4 That thine alms may be in secret: and thy Father which seeth in secret himself shall reward thee openly.

6:5 And when thou prayest, thou shalt not be as the hypocrites are: for they love to pray standing in the synagogues and in the corners of the streets, that they may be seen of men. Verily I say unto you, They have their reward.

6:6 But thou, when thou prayest, enter into thy closet, and when thou hast shut thy door, pray to thy Father which is in secret; and thy Father which seeth in secret shall reward thee openly.

6:7 But when ye pray, use not vain repetitions, as the heathen do: for they think that they shall be heard for their much speaking.

6:8 Be not ye therefore like unto them: for your Father knoweth what things ye have need of, before ye ask him.

6:9 After this manner therefore pray ye: Our Father which art in heaven, Hallowed be thy name.

6:10 Thy kingdom come, Thy will be done in earth, as it is in heaven.

6:11 Give us this day our daily bread.

6:12 And forgive us our debts, as we forgive our debtors.

6:13 And lead us not into temptation, but deliver us from evil: For thine is the kingdom, and the power, and the glory, for ever. Amen.

6:14 For if ye forgive men their trespasses, your heavenly Father will also forgive you:

6:15 But if ye forgive not men their trespasses, neither will your Father forgive your trespasses.

6:16 Moreover when ye fast, be not, as the hypocrites, of a sad countenance: for they disfigure their faces, that they may appear unto men to fast. Verily I say unto you, They have their reward.

6:17 But thou, when thou fastest, anoint thine head, and wash thy face;

6:18 That thou appear not unto men to fast, but unto thy Father which is in secret: and thy Father, which seeth in secret, shall reward thee openly.

6:19 Lay not up for yourselves treasures upon earth, where moth and rust doth corrupt, and where thieves break through and steal:

6:20 But lay up for yourselves treasures in heaven, where neither moth nor rust doth corrupt, and where thieves do not break through nor steal:

6:21   For where your treasure is, there will your heart be also.

6:22   The light of the body is the eye: if therefore thine eye be single, thy whole body shall be full of light.

6:23   But if thine eye be evil, thy whole body shall be full of darkness. If therefore the light that is in thee be darkness, how great is that darkness!

6:24   No man can serve two masters: for either he will hate the one, and love the other; or else he will hold to the one, and despise the other. Ye cannot serve God and mammon.

6:25   Therefore I say unto you, Take no thought for your life, what ye shall eat, or what ye shall drink; nor yet for your body, what ye shall put on. Is not the life more than meat, and the body than raiment?

6:26   Behold the fowls of the air: for they sow not, neither do they reap, nor gather into barns; yet your heavenly Father feedeth them. Are ye not much better than they?

6:27   Which of you by taking thought can add one cubit to his stature?

6:28   And why take ye thought for raiment? Consider the lilies of the field, how they grow; they toil not, neither do they spin:

6:29   And yet I say unto you, That even Solomon in all his glory was not arrayed like one of these.

6:30   Wherefore, if God so clothe the grass of the field, which to day is, and to morrow is cast into the oven, shall he not much more clothe you, O ye of little faith?

6:31   Therefore take no thought, saying, What shall we eat? or, What shall we drink? or, Wherewithal shall we be clothed?

6:32   (For after all these things do the Gentiles seek:) for your heavenly Father knoweth that ye have need of all these things.

6:33   But seek ye first the kingdom of God, and his righteousness; and all these things shall be added unto you.

6:34   Take therefore no thought for the morrow: for the morrow shall take thought for the things of itself. Sufficient unto the day is the evil thereof.

MT. 7:1   Judge not, that ye be not judged.

     7:2   For with what judgment ye judge, ye shall be judged: and with what measure ye mete, it shall be measured to you again.

L.   6:38   Give, and it shall be given unto you; good measure, pressed down, and shaken together, and running over, shall men give into your bosom.

MT. 7:3   And why beholdest thou the mote that is in thy brother's eye, but considerest not the beam that is in thine own eye?

     7:4   Or how wilt thou say to thy brother, Let me pull out the mote out of thine eye; and, behold, a beam is in thine own eye?

     7:5   Thou hypocrite, first cast out the beam out of thine own eye; and then shalt thou see clearly to cast out the mote out of thy brother's eye.

7:6   Give not that which is holy unto the dogs, neither cast ye your pearls before swine, lest they trample them under their feet, and turn again and rend you.

7:7   Ask, and it shall be given you; seek, and ye shall find; knock, and it shall be opened unto you:

7:8   For every one that asketh receiveth; and he that seeketh findeth; and to him that knocketh it shall be opened.

7:9   Or what man is there of you, whom if his son ask bread, will he give him a stone?

7:10   Or if he ask a fish, will he give him a serpent?

7:11   If ye then, being evil, know how to give good gifts unto your children, how much more shall your Father which is in heaven give good things to them that ask him?

7:12   Therefore all things whatsoever ye would that men should do to you, do ye even so to them: for this is the law and the prophets.

7:13   Enter ye in at the strait gate: for wide is the gate, and broad is the way, that leadeth to destruction, and many there be which go in thereat:

7:14   Because strait is the gate, and narrow is the way, which leadeth unto life, and few there be that find it.

7:15   Beware of false prophets, which come to you in sheep's clothing, but inwardly they are ravening wolves.

7:16   Ye shall know them by their fruits. Do men gather grapes of thorns, or figs of thistles?

7:17   Even so every good tree bringeth forth good fruit; but a corrupt tree bringeth forth evil fruit.

7:18   A good tree cannot bring forth evil fruit, neither can a corrupt tree bring forth good fruit.

7:19   Every tree that bringeth not forth good fruit is hewn down, and cast into the fire.

7:20   Wherefore by their fruits ye shall know them.

MT. 12:35 A good man out of the good treasure of the heart bringeth forth good things: and an evil man out of the evil treasure bringeth forth evil things.

12:36 But I say unto you, That every idle word that men shall speak, they shall give account thereof in the day of judgment.

12:37 For by thy words thou shalt be justified, and by thy words thou shalt be condemned.

MT. 7:24 Therefore whosoever heareth these sayings of mine, and doeth them, I will liken him unto a wise man, which built his house upon a rock:

7:25   And the rain descended, and the floods came, and the winds blew, and beat upon that house; and it fell not: for it was founded upon a rock.

7:26   And every one that heareth these sayings of mine, and doeth them not, shall be likened unto a foolish man, which built his house upon the sand:

7:27 And the rain descended, and the floods came, and the winds blew, and beat upon that house; and it fell: and great was the fall of it.

7:28 And it came to pass, when Jesus had ended these sayings, the people were astonished at his doctrine:

7:29 For he taught them as one having authority, and not as the scribes.

MT. 8:1 When he was come down from the mountain, great multitudes followed him.

MK. 6:6 And he went round about the villages, teaching.

MT. 11:28 Come unto me, all ye that labour and are heavy laden, and I will give you rest.

11:29 Take my yoke upon you, and learn of me; for I am meek and lowly in heart: and ye shall find rest unto your souls.

11:30 For my yoke is easy, and my burden is light.

L. 7:36 And one of the Pharisees desired him that he would eat with him. And he went into the Pharisee's house, and sat down to meat.

7:37 And, behold, a woman in the city, which was a sinner, when she knew that Jesus sat at meat in the Pharisee's house, brought an alabaster box of ointment,

7:38 And stood at his feet behind him weeping, and began to wash his feet with tears, and did wipe them with the hairs of her head, and kissed his feet, and anointed them with the ointment.

7:39 Now when the Pharisee which had bidden him saw it, he spake within himself, saying, This man, if he were a prophet, would have known who and what manner of woman this is that toucheth him: for she is a sinner.

7:40 And Jesus answering said unto him, Simon, I have somewhat to say unto thee. And he saith, Master, say on.

7:41 There was a certain creditor which had two debtors: the one owed five hundred pence, and the other fifty.

7:42 And when they had nothing to pay, he frankly forgave them both. Tell me therefore, which of them will love him most?

7:43 Simon answered and said, I suppose that he, to whom he forgave most. And he said unto him, Thou hast rightly judged.

7:44 And he turned to the woman, and said unto Simon, Seest thou this woman? I entered into thine house, thou gavest me no water for my feet: but she hath washed my feet with tears, and wiped them with the hairs of her head.

7:45 Thou gavest me no kiss: but this woman since the time I came in hath not ceased to kiss my feet.

7:46 My head with oil thou didst not anoint: but this woman hath anointed my feet with ointment.

MK. 3:31 There came then his brethren and his mother, and, standing without, sent unto him, calling him.

3:32 And the multitude sat about him, and they said unto him, Behold, thy mother and thy brethren without seek for thee.

3:33 And he answered them, saying, Who is my mother, or my brethren?

3:34 And he looked round about on them which sat about him, and said, Behold my mother and my brethren!

3:35 For whosoever shall do the will of God, the same is my brother, and my sister, and mother.

L. 12:1 In the mean time, when there were gathered together an innumerable multitude of people, insomuch that they trode one upon another, he began to say unto his disciples first of all, Beware ye of the leaven of the Pharisees, which is hypocrisy.

12:2 For there is nothing covered, that shall not be revealed; neither hid, that shall not be known.

12:3 Therefore whatsoever ye have spoken in darkness shall be heard in the light; and that which ye have spoken in the ear in closets shall be proclaimed upon the housetops.

12:4 And I say unto you my friends, Be not afraid of them that kill the body, and after that have no more that they can do.

12:5 But I will forewarn you whom ye shall fear: Fear him, which after he hath killed hath power to cast into hell; yea, I say unto you, Fear him.

12:6 Are not five sparrows sold for two farthings? And not one of them is forgotten before God?

12:7 But even the very hairs of your head are all numbered. Fear not therefore: ye are of more value than many sparrows.

12:13 And one of the company said unto him, Master, speak to my brother, that he divide the inheritance with me.

12:14 And he said unto him, Man, who made me a judge or a divider over you?

12:15 And he said unto them, Take heed, and beware of all manner of covetousness: for a man's life consisteth not in the abundance of the things which he possesseth.

12:16 And he spake a parable unto them, saying, The ground of a certain rich man brought forth plentifully:

12:17 And he thought within himself, saying, What shall I do, because I have no room where to bestow my fruits?

12:18 And he said, This will I do: I will pull down my barns, and build greater; and there will I bestow all my fruits and my goods.

12:19 And I will say to my soul, Soul, thou hast much goods laid up for many years; take thine ease, eat, drink, and be merry.

12:20 But God said unto him, Thou fool, this night thy soul shall be required of thee: then whose shall those things be, which thou hast provided?

12:21 So is he that layeth up treasure for himself, and is not rich toward God.

12:22 And he said unto his disciples, Therefore I say unto you, Take no thought for your life, what ye shall eat; neither for the body, what ye shall put on.

12:23 The life is more than meat, and the body is more than raiment.

12:24 Consider the ravens: for they neither sow nor reap; which neither have storehouse nor barn; and God feedeth them: how much more are ye better than the fowls?

12:25 And which of you with taking thought can add to his stature one cubit?

12:26 If ye then be not able to do that thing which is least, why take ye thought for the rest?

12:27 Consider the lilies how they grow: they toil not, they spin not; and yet I say unto you, that even Solomon in all his glory was not arrayed like one of these.

12:28 If then God so clothe the grass, which is to day in the field, and to morrow is cast into the oven; how much more will he clothe you, O ye of little faith?

12:29 And seek not ye what ye shall eat, or what ye shall drink, neither be ye of doubtful mind.

12:30 For all these things do the nations of the world seek after: and your Father knoweth that ye have need of these things.

12:31 But rather seek ye the kingdom of God; and all these things shall be added unto you.

12:32 Fear not, little flock; for it is your Father's good pleasure to give you the kingdom.

12:33 Sell that ye have, and give alms; provide yourselves bags which wax not old, a treasure in the heavens that faileth not, where no thief approacheth, neither moth corrupteth.

12:34 For where your treasure is, there will your heart be also.

12:35 Let your loins be girded about, and your lights burning;

12:36 And ye yourselves like unto men that wait for their lord, when he will return from the wedding feast; that when he cometh and knocketh, they may open unto him immediately.

12:37 Blessed are those servants, whom the lord when he cometh shall find watching: verily I say unto you, that he shall gird himself, and make them to sit down to meat, and will come forth and serve them.

12:38 And if he shall come in the second watch, or come in the third watch, and find them so, blessed are those servants.

12:39 And this know, that if the good-man of the house had known what hour the thief would come, he would have watched, and not have suffered his house to be broken through.

12:40 Be ye therefore ready also: for the Son of man cometh at an hour when ye think not.

12:41 Then Peter said unto him, Lord, speakest thou this parable unto us, or even to all?

12:42 And the Lord said, Who then is that faithful and wise steward, whom his lord shall make ruler over his household, to give them their portion of meat in due season?

12:43 Blessed is that servant, whom his lord when he cometh shall find so doing.

12:44 Of a truth I say unto you, that he will make him ruler over all that he hath.

12:45 But and if that servant say in his heart, My lord delayeth his coming; and shall begin to beat the menservants and maidens, and to eat and drink, and to be drunken;

12:46 The lord of that servant will come in a day when he looketh not for him, and at an hour when he is not aware, and will cut him in sunder.

12:47 And that servant, which knew his lord's will, and prepared not himself, neither did according to his will, shall be beaten with many stripes.

12:48 But he that knew not, and did commit things worthy of stripes, shall be beaten with few stripes. For unto whomsoever much is given, of him shall be much required: and to whom men have committed much, of him they will ask the more.

12:54 And he said also to the people, When ye see a cloud rise out of the west, straightway ye say, There cometh a shower; and so it is.

12:55 And when ye see the south wind blow, ye say, There will be heat; and it cometh to pass.

12:56 Ye hypocrites, ye can discern the face of the sky and of the earth; but how is it that ye do not discern this time?

12:57 Yea, and why even of yourselves judge ye not what is right?

12:58 When thou goest with thine adversary to the magistrate, as thou art in the way, give diligence that thou mayest be delivered from him; lest he hale thee to the judge, and the judge deliver thee to the officer, and the officer cast thee into prison.

12:59 I tell thee, thou shalt not depart thence, till thou hast paid the very last mite.

L.   13:1 There were present at that season some that told him of the Galileans, whose blood Pilate had mingled with their sacrifices.

13:2 And Jesus answering said unto them, Suppose ye that these Galileans were sinners above all the Galileans, because they suffered such things?

13:3 I tell you, Nay: but, except ye repent, ye shall all likewise perish.

13:4 Or those eighteen, upon whom the tower in Siloam fell, and slew them, think ye that they were sinners above all men that dwelt in Jerusalem?

13:5 I tell you, Nay: but, except ye repent, ye shall all likewise perish.

13:6 He spake also this parable; A certain man had a fig tree planted in his vineyard; and he came and sought fruit thereon, and found none.

13:7 Then said he unto the dresser of his vineyard, Behold, these three years I come seeking fruit on this fig tree, and find none: cut it down; why cumbereth it the ground?

13:8 And he answering said unto him, Lord, let it alone this year also, till I shall dig about it, and dung it:

13:9 And if it bear fruit, well: and if not, then after that thou shalt cut it down.

L.   11:37 And as he spake, a certain Pharisee besought him to dine with him: and he went in, and sat down to meat.

11:38 And when the Pharisee saw it, he marvelled that he had not first washed before dinner.

11:39 And the Lord said unto him, Now do ye Pharisees make clean the outside of the cup and the platter; but your inward part is full of ravening and wickedness.

11:40 Ye fools, did not he that made that which is without make that which is within also?

11:41 But rather give alms of such things as ye have; and, behold, all things are clean unto you.

11:42 But woe unto you, Pharisees! for ye tithe mint and rue and all manner of herbs, and pass over judgment and the love of God: these ought ye to have done, and not to leave the other undone.

11:43 Woe unto you, Pharisees! for ye love the uppermost seats in the synagogues, and greetings in the markets.

11:44 Woe unto you, scribes and Pharisees, hypocrites! for ye are as graves which appear not, and the men that walk over them are not aware of them.

11:45 Then answered one of the lawyers, and said unto him, Master, thus saying thou reproachest us also.

11:46 And he said, Woe unto you also, ye lawyers! for ye lade men with burdens grievous to be borne, and ye yourselves touch not the burdens with one of your fingers.

11:52 Woe unto you, lawyers! for ye have taken away the key of knowledge: ye entered not in yourselves, and them that were entering in ye hindered.

11:53 And as he said these things unto them, the scribes and the Pharisees began to urge him vehemently, and to provoke him to speak of many things:

11:54 Laying wait for him, and seeking to catch something out of his mouth, that they might accuse him.

MT.   13:1 The same day went Jesus out of the house, and sat by the sea side.

13:2 And great multitudes were gathered together unto him, so that he went into a ship, and sat; and the whole multitude stood on the shore.

13:3 And he spake many things unto them in parables, saying, Behold, a sower went forth to sow;

13:4 And when he sowed, some seeds fell by the way side, and the fowls came and devoured them up:

13:5 Some fell upon stony places, where they had not much earth: and forthwith they sprung up, because they had no deepness of earth:

13:6 And when the sun was up, they were scorched; and because they had no root, they withered away.

13:7 And some fell among thorns; and the thorns sprung up, and choked them:

13:8 But other fell into good ground, and brought forth fruit, some an hundredfold, some sixtyfold, some thirtyfold.

13:9 Who hath ears to hear, let him hear.

MK. 4:10 And when he was alone, they that were about him with the twelve asked of him the parable.

MT. 13:18 Hear ye therefore the parable of the sower.

13:19 When any one heareth the word of the kingdom, and understandeth it not, then cometh the wicked one, and catcheth away that which was sown in his heart. This is he which received seed by the way side.

13:20 But he that received the seed into stony places, the same is he that heareth the word, and anon with joy receiveth it;

13:21 Yet hath he not root in himself, but dureth for a while: for when tribulation or persecution ariseth because of the word, by and by he is offended.

13:22 He also that received seed among the thorns is he that heareth the word; and the care of this world, and the deceitfulness of riches, choke the word, and he becometh unfruitful.

13:23 But he that received seed into the good ground is he that heareth the word, and understandeth it; which also beareth fruit, and bringeth forth, some an hundredfold, some sixty, some thirty.

MK. 4:21 And he said unto them, Is a candle brought to be put under a bushel, or under a bed? and not to be set on a candlestick?

4:22 For there is nothing hid, which shall not be manifested; neither was any thing kept secret, but that it should come abroad.

4:23 If any man have ears to hear, let him hear.

MT. 13:24 Another parable put he forth unto them, saying, The kingdom of heaven is likened unto a man which sowed good seed in his field:

13:25 But while men slept, his enemy came and sowed tares among the wheat, and went his way.

13:26 But when the blade was sprung up, and brought forth fruit, then appeared the tares also.

13:27 So the servants of the householder came and said unto him, Sir, didst not thou sow good seed in thy field? from whence then hath it tares?

13:28 He said unto them, An enemy hath done this. The servants said unto him, Wilt thou then that we go and gather them up?

13:29 But he said, Nay; lest while ye gather up the tares, ye root up also the wheat with them.

13:30 Let both grow together until the harvest: and in the time of harvest I will say to the reapers, Gather ye together first the tares, and bind them in bundles to burn them: but gather the wheat into my barn.

13:36 Then Jesus sent the multitude away, and went into the house: and his disciples came unto him, saying, Declare unto us the parable of the tares of the field.

13:37 He answered and said unto them, He that soweth the good seed is the Son of man;

13:38 The field is the world; the good seed are the children of the kingdom; but the tares are the children of the wicked one;

13:39 The enemy that sowed them is the devil; the harvest is the end of the world; and the reapers are the angels.

13:40 As therefore the tares are gathered and burned in the fire; so shall it be in the end of this world.

13:41 The Son of man shall send forth his angels, and they shall gather out of his kingdom all things that offend, and all them which do iniquity;

13:42 And shall cast them into a furnace of fire: there shall be wailing and gnashing of teeth.

13:43 Then shall the righteous shine forth as the sun in the kingdom of their Father. Who hath ears to hear, let him hear.

13:44 Again, the kingdom of heaven is like unto treasure hid in a field; the which when a man hath found, he hideth, and for joy thereof goeth and selleth all that he hath, and buyeth that field.

13:45 Again, the kingdom of heaven is like unto a merchant man, seeking goodly pearls:

13:46 Who, when he had found one pearl of great price, went and sold all that he had, and bought it.

13:47 Again, the kingdom of heaven is like unto a net, that was cast into the sea, and gathered of every kind:

13:48 Which, when it was full, they drew it to shore, and sat down, and gathered the good into vessels, but cast the bad away.

13:49 So shall it be at the end of the world: the angels shall come forth, and sever the wicked from among the just,

13:50 And shall cast them into the furnace of fire: there shall be wailing and gnashing of teeth.

13:51 Jesus saith unto them, Have ye understood all these things? They say unto him, Yea, Lord.

13:52 Then said he unto them, Therefore every scribe which is instructed unto the kingdom of heaven is like unto a man that is an householder, which bringeth forth out of his treasure things new and old.

MK. 4:26 And he said, So is the kingdom of God, as if a man should cast seed into the ground;

4:27 And should sleep, and rise night and day, and the seed should spring and grow up, he knoweth not how.

4:28 For the earth bringeth forth fruit of herself; first the blade, then the ear, after that the full corn in the ear.

4:29 But when the fruit is brought forth, immediately he putteth in the sickle, because the harvest is come.

4:30 And he said, Whereunto shall we liken the kingdom of God? or with what comparison shall we compare it?

4:31 It is like a grain of mustard seed, which, when it is sown in the earth, is less than all the seeds that be in the earth:

4:32 But when it is sown, it groweth up, and becometh greater than all herbs, and shooteth out great branches; so that the fowls of the air may lodge under the shadow of it.

4:33 And with many such parables spake he the word unto them, as they were able to hear it.

4:34 But without a parable spake he not unto them: and when they were alone, he expounded all things to his disciples.

L. 9:57 And it came to pass that, as they went in the way, a certain man said unto him, Lord, I will follow thee whithersoever thou goest.

9:58 And Jesus said unto him, Foxes have holes, and birds of the air have nests; but the Son of man hath not where to lay his head.

9:59 And he said unto another, Follow me. But he said, Lord, suffer me first to go and bury my father.

9:60 Jesus said unto him, Let the dead bury their dead: but go thou and preach the kingdom of God.

9:61 And another also said, Lord, I will follow thee; but let me first go bid them farewell, which are at home at my house.

9:62 And Jesus said unto him, No man, having put his hand to the plough, and looking back, is fit for the kingdom of God.

L. 5:27 And after these things he went forth, and saw a publican, named Levi, sitting at the receipt of custom: and he said unto him, Follow me.

5:28 And he left all, rose up, and followed him.

5:29 And Levi made him a great feast in his own house: and there was a great company of publicans and

MK. 2:15 Many publicans and sinners sat also together with Jesus and his disciples: for there were many, and they followed him.

2:16 And when the scribes and Pharisees saw him eat with publicans and sinners, they said unto his disciples, How is it that he eateth and drinketh with publicans and sinners?

2:17 When Jesus heard it, he saith unto them, They that are whole have no need of the physician, but they that are sick: I came not to call the righteous, but sinners to repentance.

L.   5:36 And he spake also a parable unto them; No man putteth a piece of a new garment upon an old; if otherwise, then both the new maketh a rent, and the piece that was taken out of the new agreeth not with the old.

5:37 And no man putteth new wine into old bottles; else the new wine will burst the bottles, and be spilled, and the bottles shall perish.

5:38 But new wine must be put into new bottles; and both are preserved.

MT. 13:53 And it came to pass, that when Jesus had finished these parables, he departed thence.

13:54 And when he was come into his own country, he taught them in their synagogue, insomuch that they were astonished, and said, Whence hath this man this wisdom, and these mighty works?

13:55 Is not this the carpenter's son? is not his mother called Mary? and his brethren, James, and Joses, and Simon, and Judas?

13:56 And his sisters, are they not all with us? Whence then hath this man all these things?

13:57 And they were offended in him. But Jesus said unto them, A prophet is not without honour, save in his own country, and in his own house.

MT. 9:36 But when he saw the multitudes, he was moved with compassion on them, because they fainted, and were scattered abroad, as sheep having no shepherd.

MK. 6:7 And he called unto him the twelve, and began to send them forth by two and two;

MT. 10:5 And commanded them, saying, Go not into the way of the Gentiles, and into any city of the Samaritans enter ye not:

10:6 But go rather to the lost sheep of the house of Israel.

10:9 Provide neither gold, nor silver, nor brass in your purses,

10:10 Nor scrip for your journey, neither two coats, neither shoes, nor yet staves: for the workman is worthy of his meat.

10:11 And into whatsoever city or town ye shall enter, enquire who in it is worthy; and there abide till ye go thence.

10:12 And when ye come into an house, salute it.

10:13 And if the house be worthy, let your peace come upon it: but if it be not worthy, let your peace return to you.

10:14 And whosoever shall not receive you, nor hear your words, when ye depart out of that house or city, shake off the dust of your feet.

10:15 Verily I say unto you, It shall be more tolerable for the land of Sodom and Gomorrha in the day of judgment, than for that city.

10:16 Behold, I send you forth as sheep in the midst of wolves: be ye therefore wise as serpents, and harmless as doves.

10:17 But beware of men: for they will deliver you up to the councils, and they will scourge you in their synagogues;

10:18 And ye shall be brought before governors and kings for my sake, for a testimony against them and the Gentiles.

10:23 But when they persecute you in this city, flee ye into another:

10:26 Fear them not therefore: for there is nothing covered, that shall not be revealed; and hid, that shall not be known.

10:27 What I tell you in darkness, that speak ye in light: and what ye hear in the ear, that preach ye upon the housetops.

10:28 And fear not them which kill the body, but are not able to kill the soul: but rather fear him which is able to destroy both soul and body in hell.

10:29 Are not two sparrows sold for a farthing? and one of them shall not fall on the ground without your Father.

10:30 But the very hairs of your head are all numbered.

10:31 Fear ye not therefore, ye are of more value than many sparrows.

MK. 6:12 And they went out, and preached that men should repent.

6:30 And the apostles gathered themselves together unto Jesus, and told him all things, both what they had done, and what they had taught.

J. 7:1 After these things Jesus walked in Galilee: for he would not walk in Jewry, because the Jews sought to kill him.

MK. 7:1 Then came together unto him the Pharisees, and certain of the scribes, which came from Jerusalem.

7:2 And when they saw some of his disciples eat bread with defiled, that is to say, with unwashen, hands, they found fault.

7:3 For the Pharisees, and all the Jews, except they wash their hands oft, eat not, holding the tradition of the elders.

7:4 And when they come from the market, except they wash, they eat not. And many other things there be, which they have received to hold, as the washing of cups, and pots, brasen vessels, and of tables.

7:5 Then the Pharisees and scribes asked him, Why walk not thy disciples according to the tradition of the elders, but eat bread with unwashen hands?

7:14 And when he had called all the people unto him, he said unto them, Hearken unto me every one of you, and understand:

7:15 There is nothing from without a man, that entering into him can defile him: but the things which come out of him, those are they that defile the man.

7:16 If any man have ears to hear, let him hear.

7:17 And when he was entered into the house from the people, his disciples asked him concerning the parable.

7:18 And he saith unto them, Are ye so without understanding also? Do ye not perceive, that whatsoever thing from without entereth into the man, it cannot defile him;

7:19 Because it entereth not into his heart, but into the belly, and goeth out into the draught, purging all meats?

7:20 And he said, That which cometh out of the man, that defileth the man.

7:21 For from within, out of the heart of men, proceed evil thoughts, adulteries, fornications, murders,

7:22 Thefts, covetousness, wickedness, deceit, lasciviousness, an evil eye, blasphemy, pride, foolishness:

7:23 All these evil things come from within, and defile the man.

7:24 And from thence he arose, and went into the borders of Tyre and Sidon, and entered into an house, and would have no man know it: but he could not be hid.

MT. 18:1 At the same time came the disciples unto Jesus, saying, Who is the greatest in the kingdom of heaven?

18:2 And Jesus called a little child unto him, and set him in the midst of them,

18:3 And said, Verily I say unto you, Except ye be converted, and become as little children, ye shall not enter into the kingdom of heaven.

18:4 Whosoever therefore shall humble himself as this little child, the same is greatest in the kingdom of heaven.

18:7 Woe unto the world because of offences! for it must needs be that offences come; but woe to that man by whom the offence cometh!

18:8 Wherefore if thy hand or thy foot offend thee, cut them off, and cast them from thee: it is better for thee to enter into life halt or maimed, rather than having two hands or two feet to be cast into everlasting fire.

18:9 And if thine eye causeth offend thee, pluck it out, and cast it from thee: it is better for thee to enter into life with one eye, rather than having two eyes to be cast into hell fire.

18:12 How think ye? if a man have an hundred sheep, and one of them be gone astray, doth he not leave the ninety and nine and goeth into the mountains, and seeketh that which is gone astray?

18:13 And if so be that he find it, verily I say unto you, he rejoiceth more of that sheep, than of the ninety and nine which went not astray.

18:14 Even so it is not the will of your Father which is in heaven, that one of these little ones should perish.

18:15 Moreover if thy brother shall trespass against thee, go and tell him his fault between thee and him alone: if he shall hear thee, thou hast gained thy brother.

18:16 But if he will not hear thee, then take with thee one or two more, that in the mouth of two or three witnesses every word may be established.

18:17 And if he shall neglect to hear them, tell it unto the church: but if he neglect even to hear the church, let him be unto thee as a Gentile man and an heathen.

18:21 Then came Peter to him, and said, Lord, how oft shall my brother sin against me, and I forgive him? till seven times?

18:22 Jesus saith unto him, I say not unto thee, Until seven times: but, Until seventy times seven.

18:23 Therefore is the kingdom of heaven likened unto a certain king, which would take account of his servants.

18:24 And when he had begun to reckon, one was brought unto him, which owed him ten thousand talents.

18:25 But forasmuch as he had not wherewith to pay, his lord commanded him to be sold, and his wife, and children, and all that he had, and payment to be made.

18:26 The servant therefore fell down, and worshipped him, saying, Lord, have patience with me, and I will pay thee all.

18:27 Then the lord of that servant was moved with compassion, and loosed him, and forgave him the debt.

18:28 But the same servant went out, and found one of his fellowservants, which owed him an hundred pence: and he laid hands on him, and took him by the throat, saying, Pay me that thou owest.

18:29 And his fellowservant fell down at his feet, and besought him, saying, Have patience with me, and I will pay thee all.

18:30 And he would not: but went and cast him into prison, till he should pay the debt.

18:31 So when his fellowservants saw what was done, they were very sorry, and came and told unto their lord all that was done.

18:32 Then his lord, after that he had called him, said unto him, O thou wicked servant! I forgave thee all that debt, because thou desiredst me:

18:33 Shouldest not thou also have had compassion on thy fellowservant, even as I had pity on thee?

18:34 And his lord was wroth, and delivered him to the tormentors, till he should pay all that was due unto him.

18:35 So likewise shall my heavenly Father do also unto you, if ye from your hearts forgive not every one his brother their trespasses.

L. 10:1 After these things the Lord appointed other seventy also, and sent them two and two before his face into every city and place, whither he himself would come.

10:2 Therefore said he unto them, The harvest truly is great, but the labourers are few: pray ye therefore the Lord of the harvest, that he would send forth labourers into his harvest.

10:3 Go your ways: behold, I send you forth as lambs among wolves.

10:4 Carry neither purse, nor scrip, nor shoes: and salute no man by the way.

10:5 And into whatsoever house ye enter, first say, Peace be to this house.

10:6 And if the son of peace be there, your peace shall rest upon it: if not, it shall turn to you again.

10:7 And in the same house remain, eating and drinking such things as they give: for the labourer is worthy of his hire. Go not from house to house.

10:8 And into whatsoever city ye enter, and they receive you, eat such things as are set before you:

10:10 But into whatsoever city ye enter, and they receive you not, go your ways out into the streets of the same, and say,

10:11 Even the very dust of your city, which cleaveth on us, we do wipe off against you: notwithstanding be ye sure of this, that the kingdom of God is come nigh unto you.

10:12 But I say unto you, that it shall be more tolerable in that day for Sodom, than for that city.

J. 7:2 Now the Jews' feast of tabernacles was at hand.

7:3 His brethren therefore said unto him, Depart hence, and go into Judea, that thy disciples also may see the works that thou doest.

7:4 For there is no man that doeth any thing in secret, and he himself seeketh to be known openly. If thou do these things, shew thyself to the world.

7:5 For neither did his brethren believe in him.

7:6 Then Jesus said unto them, My time is not yet come: but your time is always ready.

7:7 The world cannot hate you; but me it hateth, because I testify of it, that the works thereof are evil.

7:8 Go ye up unto this feast: I go not up yet unto this feast: for my time is not yet full come.

7:9 When he had said these words unto them, he abode still in Galilee.

7:10 But when his brethren were gone up, then went he also up unto the feast, not openly, but as it were in secret.

7:11 Then the Jews sought him at the feast, and said, Where is he?

7:12 And there was much murmuring among the people concerning him: for some said, He is a good man: others said, Nay; but he deceiveth the people.

7:13 Howbeit no man spake openly of him for fear of the Jews.

7:14 Now about the midst of the feast Jesus went up into the temple, and taught.

7:15 And the Jews marvelled, saying, How knoweth this man letters, having never learned?

7:16 Jesus answered them, and said,

7:19 Did not Moses give you the law, and yet none of you keepeth the law? Why go ye about to kill me?

7:20 The people answered and said, Thou hast a devil: who goeth about to kill thee?

7:21 Jesus answered and said unto them, I have done one work, and ye all marvel.

7:22 Moses therefore gave unto you circumcision; (not because it is of Moses, but of the fathers;) and ye on the sabbath day circumcise a man.

7:23 If a man on the sabbath day receive circumcision, that the law of Moses should not be broken; are ye angry at me, because I have made a man every whit whole on the sabbath day?

7:24 Judge not according to the appearance, but judge righteous judgment.

7:25 Then said some of them of Jerusalem, Is not this he, whom they seek to kill?

7:26 But, lo, he speaketh boldly, and they say nothing unto him. Do the rulers know indeed that this is the very Christ?

7:32 The Pharisees heard that the people murmured such things concerning him; and the Pharisees and the chief priests sent officers to take him.

7:43 So there was a division among the people because of him.

7:44 And some of them would have taken him; but no man laid hands on him.

7:45 Then came the officers to the chief priests and Pharisees; and they said unto them, Why have ye not brought him?

7:46 The officers answered, Never man spake like this man.

7:47 Then answered them the Pharisees, Are ye also deceived?

7:48 Have any of the rulers or of the Pharisees believed on him?

7:49 But this people who knoweth not the law are cursed.

7:50 Nicodemus saith unto them, (he that came to Jesus by night, being one of them,)

7:51 Doth our law judge any man, before it hear him, and know what he doeth?

7:52 They answered and said unto him, Art thou also of Galilee? Search, and look: for out of Galilee ariseth no prophet.

7:53 And every man went unto his own house.

J. 8:1 Jesus went unto the mount of Olives.

8:2 And early in the morning he came again into the temple, and all the people came unto him; and he sat down, and taught them.

8:3 And the scribes and Pharisees brought unto him a woman taken in adultery; and when they had set her in the midst,

8:4 They say unto him, Master, this woman was taken in adultery, in the very act.

8:5 Now Moses in the law commanded us, that such should be stoned: but what sayest thou?

8:6 This they said, tempting him, that they might have cause to accuse him. But Jesus stooped down, and with his finger wrote on the ground, as though he heard them not.

8:7   So when they continued asking him, he lifted up himself, and said unto them, He that is without sin among you, let him first cast a stone at her.

8:8   And again he stooped down, and wrote on the ground.

8:9   And they which heard it, being convicted by their own conscience, went out one by one, beginning at the eldest, even unto the last: and Jesus was left alone, and the woman standing in the midst.

8:10   When Jesus had lifted up himself, and saw none but the woman, he said unto her, Woman, where are those thine accusers? hath no man condemned thee?

8:11   She said, No man, Lord. And Jesus said unto her, Neither do I condemn thee: go, and sin no more.

J.   9:1   And as Jesus passed by, he saw a man which was blind from his birth.

9:2   And his disciples asked him, saying, Master, who did sin, this man, or his parents, that he was born blind?

9:3   Jesus answered, Neither hath this man sinned, nor his parents: but that the works of God should be made manifest in him.

J.   10:1   Verily, verily, I say unto you, He that entereth not by the door into the sheepfold, but climbeth up some other way, the same is a thief and a robber.

10:2   But he that entereth in by the door is the shepherd of the sheep.

10:3   To him the porter openeth; and the sheep hear his voice: and he calleth his own sheep by name, and leadeth them out.

10:4   And when he putteth forth his own sheep, he goeth before them, and the sheep follow him: for they know his voice.

10:5   And a stranger will they not follow, but will flee from him: for they know not the voice of strangers.

10:11 I am the good shepherd: the good shepherd giveth his life for the sheep.

10:12 But he that is an hireling, and not the shepherd, whose own the sheep are not, seeth the wolf coming, and leaveth the sheep, and fleeth: and the wolf catcheth them, and scattereth the sheep.

10:13 The hireling fleeth, because he is an hireling, and careth not for the sheep.

10:14 I am the good shepherd, and know my sheep, and am known of mine.

10:16 And other sheep I have, which are not of this fold: them also I must bring, and they shall hear my voice; and there shall be one fold, and one shepherd.

L.   10:25 And, behold, a certain lawyer stood up, and put tempted him, saying, Master, what shall I do to inherit eternal life?

10:26 He said unto him, What is written in the law? how readest thou?

10:27 And he answering said, Thou shalt love the Lord thy God with all thy heart, and with all thy soul, and with all thy strength, and with all thy mind; and thy neighbour as thyself.

10:28 And he said unto him, Thou hast answered right: this do, and thou shalt live.

10:29 But he, willing to justify himself, said unto Jesus, And who is my neighbour?

10:30 And Jesus answering said, A certain man went down from Jerusalem to Jericho, and fell among thieves, which stripped him of his raiment, and wounded him, and departed, leaving him half dead.

10:31 And by chance there came down a certain priest that way: and when he saw him, he passed by on the other side.

10:32 And likewise a Levite, when he was at the place, came and looked on him, and passed by on the other side.

10:33 But a certain Samaritan, as he journeyed, came where he was: and when he saw him, he had compassion on him,

10:34 And went to him, and bound up his wounds, pouring in oil and wine, and set him on his own beast, and brought him to an inn, and took care of him.

10:35 And on the morrow when he departed, he took out two pence, and gave them to the host, and said unto him, Take care of him; and whatsoever thou spendest more, when I come again, I will repay thee.

10:36 Which now of these three, thinkest thou, was neighbour unto him that fell among the thieves?

10:37 And he said, He that shewed mercy on him. Then said Jesus unto him, Go, and do thou likewise.

L.   11:1 And it came to pass, that, as he was praying in a certain place, when he ceased, one of his disciples said unto him, Lord, teach us to pray, as John also taught his disciples.

11:2 And he said unto them, When ye pray, say, Our Father which art in heaven, Hallowed be thy name. Thy kingdom come. Thy will be done, as in heaven, so in earth.

11:3 Give us day by day our daily bread.

11:4 And forgive us our sins; for we also forgive every one that is indebted to us. And lead us not into temptation; but deliver us from evil.

11:5 And he said unto them, Which of you shall have a friend, and shall go unto him at midnight, and say unto him, Friend, lend me three loaves;

11:6 For a friend of mine in his journey is come to me, and I have nothing to set before him?

11:7 And he from within shall answer and say, Trouble me not: the door is now shut, and my children are with me in bed; I cannot rise and give thee.

11:8 I say unto you, Though he will not rise and give him, because he is his friend, yet because of his importunity he will rise and give him as many as he needeth.

11:9 And I say unto you, Ask, and it shall be given you; seek, and ye shall find; knock, and it shall be opened unto you.

11:10 For every one that asketh receiveth; and he that seeketh findeth; and to him that knocketh it shall be opened.

11:11 If a son shall ask bread of any of you that is a father, will he give him a stone? or if he ask a fish, will he for a fish give him a serpent?

11:12 Or if he shall ask an egg, will he offer him a scorpion?

11:13 If ye then, being evil, know how to give good gifts unto your children: how much more shall your heavenly Father give the Holy Spirit to them that ask him?

L.   14:1 And it came to pass, as he went into the house of one of the chief Pharisees to eat bread on the sabbath day, that they watched him.

14:2 And, behold, there was a certain man before him which had the dropsy.

14:3 And Jesus answering spake unto the lawyers and Pharisees, saying, Is it lawful to heal on the sabbath day?

14:4 And they held their peace.

14:5 And he saith unto them, Which of you shall have an ass or an ox fallen into a pit, and will not straightway pull him out on the sabbath day?

14:6 And they could not answer him again to these things.

14:7 And he put forth a parable to those which were bidden, when he marked how they chose out the chief rooms; saying unto them.

14:8 When thou art bidden of any man to a wedding, sit not down in the highest room; lest a more honourable man than thou be bidden of him;

14:9 And he that bade thee and him shall come and say to thee, Give this man place; and thou begin with shame to take the lowest room.

14:10 But when thou art bidden, go and sit down in the lowest room; that when he that bade thee cometh, he may say unto thee, Friend, go up higher: then shalt thou have worship in the presence of them that sit at meat with thee.

14:11 For whosoever exalteth himself shall be abased; and he that humbleth himself shall be exalted.

14:12 Then said he also to him that bade him, When thou makest a dinner or a supper, call not thy friends, nor thy brethren, neither thy kinsmen, nor thy rich neighbours; lest they also bid thee again, and a recompence be made thee.

14:13 But when thou makest a feast, call the poor, the maimed, the lame, the blind:

14:14 And thou shalt be blessed; for they cannot recompense thee: for thou shalt be recompensed at the resurrection of the just.

14:16 Then said he unto him, A certain man made a great supper, and bade many:

14:17 And sent his servant at supper time to say to them that were bidden, Come; for all things are now ready.

14:18 And they all with one consent began to make excuse. The first said unto him, I have bought a piece of ground, and I must needs go and see it: I pray thee have me excused.

14:19 And another said, I have bought five yoke of oxen, and I go to prove them: I pray thee have me excused.

14:20 And another said, I have married a wife, and therefore I cannot come.

14:21 So that servant came, and shewed his lord these things. Then the master of the house being angry said to his servant, Go out quickly into the streets and lanes of the city, and bring in hither the poor, and the maimed, and the halt, and the blind.

14:22 And the servant said, Lord, it is done as thou hast commanded, and yet there is room.

14:23 And the lord said unto the servant, Go out into the highways and hedges, and compel them to come in, that my house may be filled.

14:24 For I say unto you, That none of those men which were bidden shall taste of my supper.

14:28 For which of you, intending to build a tower, sitteth not down first, and counteth the cost, whether he have sufficient to finish it?

14:29 Lest haply, after he hath laid the foundation, and is not able to finish it, all that behold it begin to mock him,

14:30 Saying, This man began to build, and was not able to finish.

14:31 Or what king, going to make war against another king, sitteth not down first, and consulteth whether he be able with ten thousand to meet him that cometh against him with twenty thousand?

14:32 Or else, while the other is yet a great way off, he sendeth an ambassage, and desireth conditions of peace.

L. 15:1 Then drew near unto him all the publicans and sinners for to hear him.

15:2 And the Pharisees and scribes murmured, saying, This man receiveth sinners, and eateth with them.

15:3 And he spake this parable unto them, saying,

15:4 What man of you, having an hundred sheep, if he lose one of them, doth not leave the ninety and nine in the wilderness, and go after that which is lost, until he find it?

15:5 And when he hath found it, he layeth it on his shoulders, rejoicing.

15:6 And when he cometh home, he calleth together his friends and neighbours, saying unto them, Rejoice with me; for I have found my sheep which was lost.

15:7 I say unto you, that likewise joy shall be in heaven over one sinner that repenteth, more than over ninety and nine just persons, which need no repentance.

15:8 Either what woman having ten pieces of silver, if she lose one piece, doth not light a candle, and sweep the house, and seek diligently till she find it?

15:9 And when she hath found it, she calleth her friends and her neighbours together, saying, Rejoice with me; for I have found the piece which I had lost.

15:10 Likewise, I say unto you, there is joy in the presence of the angels of God over one sinner that repenteth.

15:11 And he said, A certain man had two sons:

15:12 And the younger of them said to his father, Father, give me the portion of goods that falleth to me. And he divided unto them his living.

15:13 And not many days after the younger son gathered all together, and took his journey into a far country, and there wasted his substance with riotous living.

15:14 And when he had spent all, there arose a mighty famine in that land; and he began to be in want.

15:15 And he went and joined himself to a citizen of that country; and he sent him into his fields to feed swine.

15:16 And he would fain have filled his belly with the husks that the swine did eat: and no man gave unto him.

15:17 And when he came to himself, he said, How many hired servants of my father's have bread enough and to spare, and I perish with hunger!

15:18 I will arise and go to my father, and will say unto him, Father, I have sinned against heaven, and before thee,

15:19 And am no more worthy to be called thy son: make me as one of thy hired servants.

15:20 And he arose, and came to his father. But when he was yet a great way off, his father saw him, and had compassion, and ran, and fell on his neck, and kissed him.

15:21 And the son said unto him, Father, I have sinned against heaven, and in thy sight, and am no more worthy to be called thy son.

15:22 But the father said to his servants, Bring forth the best robe, and put it on him; and put a ring on his hand, and shoes on his feet:

15:23 And bring hither the fatted calf, and kill it; and let us eat, and be merry:

15:24 For this my son was dead, and is alive again; he was lost, and is found. And they began to be merry.

15:25 Now his elder son was in the field: and as he came and drew nigh to the house, he heard musick and dancing.

15:26 And he called one of the servants, and asked what these things meant.

15:27 And he said unto him, Thy brother is come; and thy father hath killed the fatted calf, because he hath received him safe and sound.

15:28 And he was angry, and would not go in: therefore came his father out, and intreated him.

15:29 And he answering said to his father, Lo, these many years do I serve thee, neither transgressed I at any time thy commandment: and yet thou never gavest me a kid, that I might make merry with my friends:

15:30 But as soon as this thy son was come, which hath devoured thy living with harlots, thou hast killed for him the fatted calf.

15:31 And he said unto him, Son, thou art ever with me, and all that I have is thine.

15:32 It was meet that we should make merry, and be glad: for this thy brother was dead, and is alive again; and was lost, and is found.

L. 16:1 And he said also unto his disciples, There was a certain rich man, which had a steward; and the same was accused unto him that he had wasted his goods.

16:2 And he called him, and said unto him, How is it that I hear this of thee? give an account of thy stewardship; for thou mayest be no longer steward.

16:3 Then the steward said within himself, What shall I do? for my lord taketh away from me the stewardship: I cannot dig; to beg I am ashamed.

16:4 I am resolved what to do, that, when I am put out of the stewardship, they may receive me into their houses.

16:5 So he called every one of his lord's debtors unto him, and said unto the first, How much owest thou unto my lord?

16:6 And he said, An hundred measures of oil. And he said unto him, Take thy bill, and sit down quickly, and write fifty.

16:7 Then said he to another, And how much owest thou? And he said, An hundred measures of wheat. And he said unto him, Take thy bill, and write fourscore.

16:8 And the lord commended the unjust steward, because he had done wisely: for the children of this world are in their generation wiser than the children of light.

16:9 And I say unto you, Make to yourselves friends of the mammon of unrighteousness; that, when ye fail, they may receive you into everlasting habitations.

16:10 He that is faithful in that which is least is faithful also in much: and he that is unjust in the least is unjust also in much.

16:11 If therefore ye have not been faithful in the unrighteous mammon, who will commit to your trust the true riches?

16:12 And if ye have not been faithful in that which is another man's, who shall give you that which is your own?

16:13 No servant can serve two masters: for either he will hate the one, and love the other; or else he will hold to the one, and despise the other. Ye cannot serve God and mammon.

16:14 And the Pharisees also, who were covetous, heard all these things: and they derided him.

16:15 And he said unto them, Ye are they which justify yourselves before men; but God knoweth your hearts: for that which is highly esteemed among men is abomination in the sight of God.

16:18 Whosoever putteth away his wife, and marrieth another, committeth

---

adultery: and whosoever marrieth her that is put away from her husband committeth adultery.

16:19 There was a certain rich man, which was clothed in purple and fine linen, and fared sumptuously every day:

16:20 And there was a certain beggar named Lazarus, which was laid at his gate, full of sores,

16:21 And desiring to be fed with the crumbs which fell from the rich man's table: moreover the dogs came and licked his sores.

16:22 And it came to pass, that the beggar died, and was carried by the angels into Abraham's bosom: the rich man also died, and was buried;

16:23 And in hell he lift up his eyes, being in torments, and seeth Abraham afar off, and Lazarus in his bosom.

16:24 And he cried and said, Father Abraham, have mercy on me, and send Lazarus, that he may dip the tip of his finger in water, and cool my tongue; for I am tormented in this flame.

16:25 But Abraham said, Son, remember that thou in thy lifetime receivedst thy good things, and likewise Lazarus evil things: but now he is comforted, and thou art tormented.

16:26 And beside all this, between us and you there is a great gulf fixed: so that they which would pass from hence to you cannot; neither can they pass to us, that would come from thence.

16:27 Then he said, I pray thee therefore, father, that thou wouldest send him to my father's house:

16:28 For I have five brethren; that he may testify unto them, lest they also come into this place of torment.

16:29 Abraham saith unto him, They have Moses and the prophets; let them hear them.

16:30 And he said, Nay, father Abraham: but if one went unto them from the dead, they will repent.

16:31 And he said unto him, If they hear not Moses and the prophets, neither will they be persuaded, though one rose from the dead.

L. 17:1 Then said he unto the disciples, It is impossible but that offences will come: but woe unto him, through whom they come!

17:2 It were better for him that a millstone were hanged about his neck, and he cast into the sea, than that he should offend one of these little ones.

17:3 Take heed to yourselves: If thy brother trespass against thee, rebuke him; and if he repent, forgive him.

17:4 And if he trespass against thee seven times in a day, and seven times in a day turn again to thee, saying, I repent; thou shalt forgive him.

17:7 But which of you, having a servant plowing or feeding cattle, will say unto him by and by, when he is come from the field, Go and sit down to meat?

17:8 And will not rather say unto him, Make ready wherewith I may sup, and gird thyself, and serve me, till I have eaten and drunken; and afterward thou shalt eat and drink?

17:9 Doth he thank that servant because he did the things that were commanded him? I trow not.

17:10 So likewise ye, when ye shall have done all those things which are commanded you, say, We are unprofitable servants: we have done that which was our duty to do.

17:20 And when he was demanded of the Pharisees, when the kingdom of God should come, he answered them and said, The kingdom of God cometh not with observation:

17:26 And as it was in the days of Noe, so shall it be also in the days of the Son of man.

17:27 They did eat, they drank, they married wives, they were given in marriage, until the day that Noe entered into the ark, and the flood came, and destroyed them all.

17:28 Likewise also as it was in the days of Lot; they did eat, they drank, they bought, they sold, they planted, they builded;

17:29 But the same day that Lot went out of Sodom it rained fire and brimstone from heaven, and destroyed them all.

17:30 Even thus shall it be in the day when the Son of man is revealed.

17:31 In that day, he which shall be upon the housetop, and his stuff in the house, let him not come down to take it away: and he that is in the field, let him likewise not return back.

17:32 Remember Lot's wife.

17:33 Whosoever shall seek to save his life shall lose it; and whosoever shall lose his life shall preserve it.

17:34 I tell you, in that night there shall be two men in one bed; the one shall be taken, and the other shall be left.

17:35 Two women shall be grinding together; the one shall be taken, and the other left.

17:36 Two men shall be in the field; the one shall be taken, and the other left.

L. 18:1 And he spake a parable unto them to this end, that men ought always to pray, and not to faint;

18:2 Saying, There was in a city a judge, which feared not God, neither regarded man:

18:3 And there was a widow in that city; and she came unto him, saying, Render justice for me against mine adversary.

18:4 And he would not for a while: but afterward he said within himself, Though I fear not God, nor regard man;

18:5 Yet because this widow troubleth me, I will render her justice, lest by her continual coming she weary me.

18:6 And the Lord said, Hear what the unjust judge saith.

18:7 And shall not God render justice for his own elect, which cry day and night unto him, though he bear long with them?

18:8 I tell you that he will avenge them speedily. Nevertheless when the Son of man cometh, shall he find faith on the earth?

18:9 And he spake this parable unto certain which trusted in themselves that they were righteous, and despised others:

18:10 Two men went up into the temple to pray; the one a Pharisee, and the other a publican.

18:11 The Pharisee stood and prayed thus with himself, God, I thank thee, that I am not as other men are, extortioners, unjust, adulterers, or even as this publican.

18:12 I fast twice in the week, I give tithes of all that I possess.

18:13 And the publican, standing afar off, would not lift up so much as his eyes unto heaven, but smote upon his breast, saying, God be merciful to me a sinner.

18:14 I tell you, this man went down to his house justified rather than the other: for every one that exalteth himself shall be abased; and he that humbleth himself shall be exalted.

L. 10:38 Now it came to pass, as they went, that he entered into a certain village: and a certain woman named Martha received him into her house.

10:39 And she had a sister called Mary, which also sat at Jesus' feet, and heard his word.

10:40 But Martha was cumbered about much serving, and came to him, and said, Lord, dost thou not care that my sister hath left me to serve alone? bid her therefore that she help me.

10:41 And Jesus answered and said unto her, Martha, Martha, thou art careful and troubled about many things:

10:42 But one thing is needful: and Mary hath chosen that good part, which shall not be taken away from her.

MT. 19:1 And it came to pass, that when Jesus had finished these sayings, he departed from Galilee, and came into the coasts of Judaea beyond Jordan;

19:2 And great multitudes followed him.

19:3 The Pharisees also came unto him, tempting him, and saying unto him, Is it lawful for a man to put away his wife for every cause?

19:4 And he answered and said unto them, Have ye not read, that he which made them at the beginning made them male and female,

19:5 And said, For this cause shall a man leave father and mother, and shall cleave to his wife: and they twain shall be one flesh?

19:6 Wherefore they are no more twain, but one flesh. What therefore God hath joined together, let not man put asunder.

19:7 They say unto him, Why did Moses then command to give a writing of divorcement, and to put her away?

19:8 He saith unto them, Moses because of the hardness of your hearts suffered you to put away your wives: but from the beginning it was not so.

19:9 And I say unto you, Whosoever shall put away his wife, except it be for fornication, and shall marry another, committeth adultery: and whoso marrieth her which is put away doth commit adultery.

19:10 His disciples say unto him, If the case of the man be so with his wife, it is not good to marry.

19:11 But he said unto them, All men cannot receive this saying, save they to whom it is given.

19:12 For there are some eunuchs, which were so born from their mother's womb: and there are some eunuchs, which were made eunuchs of men: and there be eunuchs, which have made themselves eunuchs for the kingdom of heaven's sake. He that is able to receive it, let him receive it.

19:13 Then were there brought unto him little children, that he should put his hands on them, and pray: and the disciples rebuked them.

19:14 But Jesus said, Suffer little children, and forbid them not, to come unto me: for of such is the kingdom of heaven.

19:15 And he laid his hands on them, and departed thence.

19:16 And, behold, one came and said unto him, Good Master, what good thing shall I do, that I may have eternal life?

19:17 And he said unto him, Why callest thou me good? there is none good but one, that is God: but if thou wilt enter into life, keep the commandments.

19:18 He saith unto him, Which? Jesus said, Thou shalt do no murder, Thou shalt not commit adultery, Thou shalt not steal, Thou shalt not bear false witness,

19:19 Honour thy father and thy mother: and, Thou shalt love thy neighbour as thyself.

19:20 The young man saith unto him, All these things have I kept from my youth up: what lack I yet?

19:21 Jesus said unto him, If thou wilt be perfect, go and sell that thou hast, and give to the poor, and thou shalt have treasure in heaven: and come and follow me.

19:22 But when the young man heard that saying, he went away sorrowful: for he had great possessions.

19:23 Then said Jesus unto his disciples, Verily I say unto you, That a rich man shall hardly enter into the kingdom of heaven.

19:24 And again I say unto you, It is easier for a camel to go through the eye of a needle, than for a rich man to enter into the kingdom of God.

19:25 When his disciples heard it, they were exceedingly amazed, saying, Who then can be saved?

19:26 But Jesus beheld them, and said unto them, With men this is impossible; but with God all things are possible.

MT. 20:1 For the kingdom of heaven is like unto a man that is an householder, which went out early in the morning to hire labourers into his vineyard.

20:2 And when he had agreed with the labourers for a penny a day, he sent them into his vineyard.

20:3 And he went out about the third hour, and saw others standing idle in the marketplace,

20:4 And said unto them; Go ye also into the vineyard, and whatsoever is right I will give you. And they went their way.

20:5 Again he went out about the sixth and ninth hour, and did likewise.

20:6 And about the eleventh hour he went out, and found others standing idle, and saith unto them, Why stand ye here all the day idle?

20:7 They say unto him, Because no man hath hired us. He saith unto them, Go ye also into the vineyard: and whatsoever is right, that shall ye receive.

20:8 So when even was come, the lord of the vineyard saith unto his steward, Call the labourers, and give them their hire, beginning from the last unto the first.

20:9 And when they came that were hired about the eleventh hour, they received every man a penny.

20:10 And when the first came, they supposed that they should receive more; but they likewise received every man a denarius.

20:11 And when they had received it, they murmured against the goodman of the house,

20:12 Saying, These last have wrought but one hour, and thou hast made them equal unto us, which have borne the burden and heat of the day.

20:13 But he answered one of them, and said, Friend, I do thee no wrong: didst not thou agree with me for a penny?

20:14 Take that thine is, and go thy way: I will give unto this last, even as unto thee.

20:15 Is it not lawful for me to do what I will with mine own? Is thine eye evil, because I am good?

20:16 So the last shall be first, and the first last: for many be called, but few chosen.

L. 19:1 And Jesus entered and passed through Jericho.

19:2 And, behold, there was a man named Zacchaeus, which was the chief among the publicans, and he was rich.

19:3 And he sought to see Jesus who he was; and could not for the press, because he was little of stature.

19:4 And he ran before, and climbed up into a sycomore tree to see him: for he was to pass that way.

19:5 And when Jesus came to the place, he looked up, and saw him, and said unto him, Zacchaeus, make haste, and come down; for to day I must abide at thy house.

19:6 And he made haste, and came down, and received him joyfully.

19:7 And when they saw it, they all murmured, saying, That he was gone to be guest with a man that is a sinner.

19:8 And Zacchaeus stood, and said unto the Lord: Behold, Lord, the half of my goods I give to the poor; and if I have taken any thing from any man by false accusation, I restore him fourfold.

19:9 And Jesus said unto him, This day is salvation come to this house, forsomuch as he also is a son of Abraham.

19:10 For the Son of man is come to seek and to save that which was lost.

19:11 And as they heard these things, he added and spake a parable, because he was nigh to Jerusalem, and because they thought that the kingdom of God should immediately appear.

19:12 He said therefore, A certain nobleman went into a far country to receive for himself a kingdom, and to return.

19:13 And he called his ten servants, and delivered them ten pounds, and said unto them, Occupy till I come.

19:14 But his citizens hated him, and sent a message after him, saying, We will not have this man to reign over us.

19:15 And it came to pass, that when he was returned, having received the kingdom, then he commanded these servants to be called unto him, to whom he had given the money, that he might know how much every man had gained by trading.

19:16 Then came the first, saying, Lord, thy pound hath gained ten pounds.

19:17 And he said unto him, Well, thou good servant: because thou hast been faithful in a very little, have thou authority over ten cities.

19:18 And the second came, saying, Lord, thy pound hath gained five pounds.

19:19 And he said likewise to him, Be thou also over five cities.

19:20 And another came, saying, Lord, behold, here is thy pound, which I have kept laid up in a napkin:

19:21 For I feared thee, because thou art an austere man: thou takest up that thou layedst not down, and reapest that thou didst not sow.

19:22 And he saith unto him, Out of thine own mouth will I judge thee, thou wicked servant. Thou knewest that I was an austere man, taking up that I laid not down, and reaping that I did not sow:

19:23 Wherefore then gavest not thou my money into the bank, that at my coming I might have required mine own with usury?

19:24 And he said unto them that stood by, Take from him the pound, and give it to him that hath ten pounds.

19:25 (And they said unto him, Lord, he hath ten pounds.)

19:26 For I say unto you, That unto every one which hath shall be given; and from him that hath not, even that he hath shall be taken away from him.

19:27 But those mine enemies, which would not that I should reign over them, bring hither, and slay them before me.

19:28 And when he had thus spoken, he went before, ascending up to Jerusalem.

MT. 21:1 And when they drew nigh unto Jerusalem, and were come to Bethphage, unto the mount of Olives, then sent Jesus two disciples,

21:2 Saying unto them, Go into the village over against you, and straightway ye shall find an ass tied, and a colt with her: loose them, and bring them unto me.

21:3 And if any man say ought unto you, ye shall say, The Lord hath need of them; and straightway he will send them.

21:6 And the disciples went, and did as Jesus commanded them,

21:7 And brought the ass, and the colt, and put on them their clothes, and they set him thereon.

21:8 And a very great multitude spread their garments in the way; others cut down branches from the trees, and strawed them in the way.

21:10 And when he was come into Jerusalem, all the city was moved, saying, Who is this?

J. 12:19 The Pharisees therefore said among themselves, Perceive ye how ye prevail nothing? behold, the world is gone after him.

12:20 And there were certain Greeks among them that came up to worship at the feast:

12:21 The same came therefore to Philip, which was of Bethsaida of Galilee, and desired him, saying, Sir, we would see Jesus.

12:22 Philip cometh and telleth Andrew: and again Andrew and Philip tell Jesus.

12:23 And Jesus answered them, saying, The hour is come, that the Son of man should be glorified.

12:24 Verily, verily, I say unto you, Except a corn of wheat fall into the ground and die, it abideth alone: but if it die, it bringeth forth much fruit.

MT. 21:17 And he left them, and went out of the city into Bethany; and he lodged there.

MK. 11:12 And on the morrow, when they were come from Bethany,

11:15 Jesus went into the temple, and began to cast out them that sold and bought in the temple, and overthrew the tables of the moneychangers, and the seats of them that sold doves;

11:16 And would not suffer that any man should carry any vessel through the temple.

11:17 And he taught, saying unto them, Is it not written, My house shall be called of all nations the house of prayer? but ye have made it a den of thieves.

11:18 And the scribes and chief priests heard it, and sought how they might destroy him: for they feared him, because all the people was astonished at his doctrine.

11:19 And when even was come, he went out of the city.

11:27 And they come again to Jerusalem: and as he was walking in the temple, there come to him the chief priests, and the scribes, and the elders,

MT. 21:28 And he said unto them, But what think ye? A certain man had two sons; and he came to the first, and said, Son, go work today in my vineyard.

21:29 He answered and said, I will not: but afterward he repented, and went.

21:30 And he came to the second, and said likewise. And he answered and said, I go, sir: and went not.

21:31 Whether of them twain did the will of his father? They say unto him, The first. Jesus saith unto them, Verily I say unto you, That the publicans and the harlots go into the kingdom of God before you.

21:33 Hear another parable:

MK. 12:1 A certain man planted a vineyard, and set an hedge about it, and digged a place for the winevat, and built a tower, and let it out to husbandmen, and went into a far country.

12:2 And at the season he sent to the husbandmen a servant, that he might receive from the husbandmen of the fruit of the vineyard.

12:3 And they caught him, and beat him, and sent him away empty.

12:4 And again he sent unto them another servant; and at him they cast stones, and wounded him in the head, and sent him away shamefully handled.

12:5 And again he sent another; and him they killed, and many others: beating some, and killing some.

12:6 Having yet therefore one son, his wellbeloved, he sent him also last unto them, saying, They will reverence my son.

12:7 But those husbandmen said among themselves, This is the heir; come, let us kill him, and the inheritance shall be ours.

12:8 And they took him, and killed him, and cast him out of the vineyard.

12:9 What shall therefore the lord of the vineyard do? he will come and destroy the husbandmen, and will give the vineyard unto others.

MT. 21:45 And when the chief priests and Pharisees had heard his parables, they perceived that he spake of them.

21:46 But when they sought to lay hands on him, they feared the multitude, because they took him for a prophet.

MT. 22:1 And Jesus answered and spake unto them again by parables, and said,

22:2 The kingdom of heaven is like unto a certain king, which made a marriage for his son,

22:3 And sent forth his servants to call them that were bidden to the wedding: and they would not come.

22:4 Again, he sent forth other servants, saying, Tell them which are bidden,

Behold, I have prepared my dinner: my oxen and my fatlings are killed, and all things are ready: come unto the marriage.

22:5 But they made light of it, and went their ways, one to his farm, another to his merchandise:

22:6 And the remnant took his servants, and entreated them spitefully and slew them.

22:7 But when the king heard thereof, he was wroth: and he sent forth his armies, and destroyed those murderers, and burned up their city.

22:8 Then saith he to his servants, The wedding is ready, but they which were bidden were not worthy.

22:9 Go ye therefore into the highways, and as many as ye shall find, bid to the marriage.

22:10 So those servants went out into the highways, and gathered together all as many as they found, both bad and good: and the wedding was furnished with guests.

22:11 And when the king came in to see the guests, he saw there a man which had not on a wedding garment:

22:12 And he saith unto him, Friend, how camest thou in hither not having a wedding garment? And he was speechless.

22:13 Then saith the king to the servants, Bind him hand and foot, and take him away, and cast him into outer darkness; there shall be weeping and gnashing of teeth.

22:14 For many are called, but few are chosen.

22:15 Then went the Pharisees, and took counsel how they might entangle him in his talk.

22:16 And they sent out unto him their disciples with the Herodians, saying, Master, we know that thou art true, and teachest the way of God in truth, neither carest thou for any man: for thou regardest not the person of men.

22:17 Tell us therefore, What thinkest thou? Is it lawful to give tribute unto Caesar, or not?

22:18 But Jesus perceived their wickedness, and said, Why tempt yea me, ye hypocrites?

22:19 Shew me the tribute money. And they brought unto him a penny.

22:20 And he saith unto them, Whose is this image and superscription?

22:21 They say unto him, Caesar's. Then saith he unto them, Render therefore unto Caesar the things which are Caesar's; and unto God the things that are God's.

22:22 When they had heard these words, they marvelled, and left him, and went their way.

22:23 The same day came to him the Sadducees, which say that there is no resurrection, and asked him,

22:24 Saying, Master, Moses said, If a man die, having no children, his brother shall marry his wife, and raise up seed unto his brother.

22:25 Now there were with us seven brethren: and the first, when he had married a wife, deceased, and, having no issue, left his wife unto his brother:

22:26 Likewise the second also, and the third, unto the seventh.

22:27 And last of all the woman died also.

22:28 Therefore in the resurrection whose wife shall she be of the seven? for they all had her.

22:29 Jesus answered and said unto them, Ye do err, not knowing the scriptures, nor the power of God.

22:30 For in the resurrection they neither marry, nor are given in marriage, but are as the angels of God in heaven.

22:31 But as touching the resurrection of the dead, have ye not read that which was spoken unto you by God, saying,

22:32 I am the God of Abraham, and the God of Isaac, and the God of Jacob? God is not the God of the dead, but of the living.

22:33 And when the multitude heard this, they were astonished at his doctrine.

MK. 12:28 And one of the scribes came, and having heard them reasoning together, and perceiving that he had answered them well, asked him, Which is the first commandment of all?

12:29 And Jesus answered him, The first of all the commandments is, Hear, O Israel; The Lord our God is one Lord:

12:30 And thou shalt love the Lord thy God with all thy heart, and with all thy soul, and with all thy mind, and with all thy strength: this is the first commandment.

12:31 And the second is like, namely this: Thou shalt love thy neighbour as thyself. There is none other commandment greater than these.

MT. 22:40 On these two commandments hang all the law and the prophets.

MK. 12:32 And the scribe said unto him, Well, Master, thou hast said the truth: for there is one God; and there is none other but he:

12:33 And to love him with all the heart, and with all the understanding, and with all the soul, and with all the strength, and to love his neighbour as himself, is more than all whole burnt-offerings and sacrifices.

MT. 23:1 Then spake Jesus to the multitude, and to his disciples,

23:2 Saying, The scribes and the Pharisees sit in Moses' seat:

23:3 All therefore whatsoever they bid you observe, that observe and do; but do not ye after their works: for they say, and do not accordingly.

23:4 For they bind heavy burdens and grievous to be borne, and lay them on men's shoulders; but they themselves will not move them with one of their fingers.

23:5 But all their works they do for to be seen of men: they make broad their phylacteries, and enlarge the borders of their garments,

23:6 And love the uppermost rooms at feasts, and the chief seats in the synagogues,

23:7 And greetings in the markets, and to be called of men, Rabbi, Rabbi.

23:8 But be not ye called Rabbi: for one is your Master, even Christ, and all ye are brethren.

23:9 And call no man your father upon the earth: for one is your Father, which is in heaven.

23:10 Neither be ye called masters: for one is your Master, even Christ.

23:11 But he that is greatest among you shall be your servant.

23:12 And whosoever shall exalt himself shall be abased; and he that shall humble himself shall be exalted.

23:13 But woe unto you, scribes and Pharisees, hypocrites! for ye shut up the kingdom of heaven against men: for ye neither go in yourselves, neither suffer ye them that are entering to go in.

23:14 Woe unto you, scribes and Pharisees, hypocrites! for ye devour widows' houses, and for a pretence make long prayer: therefore ye shall receive the greater damnation.

23:15 Woe unto you, scribes and Pharisees, hypocrites! for ye compass sea and land to make one proselyte, and when he is made, ye make him twofold more the child of hell than yourselves.

23:16 Woe unto you, ye blind guides, which say, Whosoever shall swear by the temple, it is nothing; but whosoever shall swear by the gold of the temple, he is a debtor!

23:17 Ye fools and blind: for whether is greater, the gold, or the temple that sanctifieth the gold?

23:18 And, Whosoever shall swear by the altar, it is nothing; but whosoever sweareth by the gift that is upon it, he is guilty.

23:19 Ye fools and blind: for whether is greater, the gift, or the altar that sanctifieth the gift?

23:20 Whoso therefore shall swear by the altar, sweareth by it, and by all things thereon.

23:21 And whoso shall swear by the temple, sweareth by it, and by him that dwelleth therein.

23:22 And he that shall swear by heaven, sweareth by the throne of God, and by him that sitteth thereon.

23:23 Woe unto you, scribes and Pharisees, hypocrites! for ye pay tithe of mint and anise and cummin, and have omitted the weightier matters of the law, judgment, mercy, and faith: these ought ye to have done, and not to leave the other undone.

23:24 Ye blind guides! which strain at a gnat, and swallow a camel.

23:25 Woe unto you, scribes and Pharisees, hypocrites! for ye make clean the outside of the cup and of the platter, but within they are full of extortion and excess.

23:26 Thou blind Pharisee, cleanse first that which is within the cup and platter, that the outside of them may be clean also.

23:27 Woe unto you, scribes and Pharisees, hypocrites! for ye are like unto whited sepulchres, which indeed appear beautiful outward, but are within full of dead men's bones, and of all uncleanness.

23:28 Even so ye also outwardly appear righteous unto men, but within ye are full of hypocrisy and iniquity.

23:29 Woe unto you, scribes and Pharisees, hypocrites! because ye build the tombs of the prophets, and garnish the sepulchres of the righteous,

23:30 And say, If we had been in the days of our fathers, we would not have been partakers with them in the blood of the prophets.

23:31 Wherefore ye be witnesses unto yourselves, that ye are the children of them which killed the prophets.

23:32 Fill ye up then the measure of your fathers.

23:33 Ye serpents, ye generation of vipers, how can ye escape the damnation of hell?

MK. 12:41 And Jesus sat over against the treasury, and beheld how the people cast money into the treasury: and many that were rich cast in much.

12:42 And there came a certain poor widow, and she threw in two mites, which make a farthing.

12:43 And he called unto him his disciples, and saith unto them, Verily I say unto you, That this poor widow hath cast more in, than all they which have cast into the treasury:

12:44 For all they did cast in of their abundance; but she of her want did cast in all that she had, even all her living.

MT. 24:1 And Jesus went out, and departed from the temple: and his disciples came to him for to shew him the buildings of the temple.

24:2 And Jesus said unto them, See ye not all these things? verily I say unto you, There shall not be left here one stone upon another, that shall not be thrown down.

24:16 Then let them which be in Judaea flee into the mountains:

24:17 Let him which is on the housetop not come down to take any thing out of his house:

24:18 Neither let him which is in the field return back to take his clothes.

24:19 And woe unto them that are with child, and to them that give suck in those days!

24:20 But pray ye that your flight be not in the winter, neither on the sabbath day:

24:21 For then shall be great tribulation, such as was not since the beginning of the world to this time, no, nor ever shall be.

24:29 Immediately after the tribulation of those days shall the sun be darkened, and the moon shall not give her light, and the stars shall fall from heaven, and the powers of the heavens shall be shaken:

24:32 Now learn a parable of the fig tree; When his branch is yet tender, and putteth forth leaves, ye know that summer is nigh:

24:33 So likewise ye, when ye shall see all these things, know that it is near, even at the doors.

24:36 But of that day and hour knoweth no man, no, not the angels of heaven, but my Father only.

24:37 But as the days of Noe were, so shall also the coming of the Son of man be.

24:38 For as in the days that were before the flood they were eating and drinking, marrying and giving in marriage, until the day that Noe entered into the ark,

24:39 And knew not until the flood came, and took them all away; so shall also the coming of the Son of man be.

24:40 Then shall two be in the field; the one shall be taken, and the other left.

24:41 Two women shall be grinding at the mill; the one shall be taken, and the other left.

24:42 Watch therefore: for ye know not what hour your Lord doth come.

24:43 But know this, that if the goodman of the house had known in what watch the thief would come, he would have watched, and would not have suffered his house to be broken up.

24:44 Therefore be ye also ready.

24:45 Who then is a faithful and wise servant, whom his lord hath made ruler over his household, to give them meat in due season?

24:46 Blessed is that servant, whom his lord when he cometh shall find so doing.

24:47 Verily I say unto you, That he shall make him ruler over all his goods.

24:48 But and if that evil servant shall say in his heart, My lord delayeth his coming;

24:49 And shall begin to smite his fellowservants, and to eat and drink with the drunken;

24:50 The lord of that servant shall come in a day when he looketh not for him, and in an hour that he is not aware of,

24:51 And shall cut him asunder, and appoint him his portion with the hypocrites: there shall be weeping and gnashing of teeth.

MT. 25:1 Then shall the kingdom of heaven be likened unto ten virgins, which took their lamps, and went forth to meet the bridegroom.

25:2 And five of them were wise, and five were foolish.

25:3 They that were foolish took their lamps, and took no oil with them:

25:4 But the wise took oil in their vessels with their lamps.

25:5 While the bridegroom tarried, they all slumbered and slept.

25:6 And at midnight there was a cry made, Behold, the bridegroom cometh; go ye out to meet him.

25:7 Then all those virgins arose, and trimmed their lamps.

25:8 And the foolish said unto the wise, Give us of your oil; for our lamps are gone out.

25:9 But the wise answered, saying, Not so; lest there be not enough for us and you: but go ye rather to them that sell, and buy for yourselves.

25:10 And while they went to buy, the bridegroom came; and they that were ready went in with him to the marriage; and the door was shut.

25:11 Afterward came also the other virgins, saying, Lord, Lord, open to us.

25:12 But he answered and said, Verily I say unto you, I know you not.

25:13 Watch therefore.

25:14 For the kingdom of heaven is as a man travelling into a far country, who called his own servants, and delivered unto them his goods.

25:15 And unto one he gave five talents, to another two, and to another one; to every man according to his several ability; and straightway took his journey.

25:16 Then he that had received the five talents went and traded with the same, and made them other five talents.

25:17 And likewise he that had received two, he also gained other two.

25:18 But he that had received one went and digged in the earth, and hid his lord's money.

25:19 After a long time the lord of those servants cometh, and reckoneth with them.

25:20 And so he that had received five talents came and brought other five talents, saying, Lord, thou deliveredst unto me five talents: behold, I have gained beside them five talents more.

25:21 His lord said unto him, Well done, thou good and faithful servant: thou hast been faithful over a few things, I will make thee ruler over many things: enter thou into the joy of thy lord.

25:22 He also that had received two talents came and said, Lord, thou deliveredst unto me two talents: behold, I have gained two other talents beside them.

25:23 His lord said unto him, Well done, good and faithful servant; thou hast been faithful over a few things, I will make thee ruler over many things: enter thou into the joy of thy lord.

25:24 Then he which had received the one talent came and said, Lord, I knew thee that thou art an hard man, reaping where thou hast not sown, and gathering where thou hast not strawed:

25:25 And I was afraid, and went and hid thy talent in the earth: lo, there thou hast that is thine.

25:26 His lord answered and said unto him, Thou wicked and slothful servant, thou knewest that I reap where I sowed not, and gather where I have not strawed:

25:27 Thou oughtest therefore to have put my money to the exchangers, and then at my coming I should have received mine own with usury.

25:28 Take therefore the talent from him, and give it unto him which hath ten talents.

25:29 For unto every one that hath shall be given, and he shall have abundance: but from him that hath not shall be taken away even that which he hath.

25:30 And cast ye the unprofitable servant into outer darkness: there shall be weeping and gnashing of teeth.

L.   21:34 And take heed to yourselves, lest at any time your hearts be overcharged with surfeiting, and drunkenness, and cares of this life, and so that day come upon you unawares.

25:35 For as a snare shall it come on all them that dwell on the face of the whole earth.

25:36 Watch ye therefore, and pray always, that ye may be accounted worthy to escape all these things that shall come to pass, and to stand before the Son of Man.

MT. 25:31 When the Son of Man shall come in his glory, and all the holy angels with him, then shall he sit upon the throne of his glory:

25:32 And before him shall be gathered all nations: and he shall separate them one from another, as a shepherd divideth his sheep from the goats:

25:33 And he shall set the sheep on his right hand, but the goats on the left.

25:34 Then shall the King say unto them on his right hand, Come, ye blessed of my Father, inherit the kingdom prepared for you from the foundation of the world:

25:35 For I was an hungered, and ye gave me meat: I was thirsty, and ye gave me drink: I was a stranger, and ye took me in:

25:36 Naked, and ye clothed me: I was sick, and ye visited me: I was in prison, and ye came unto me.

25:37 Then shall the righteous answer him, saying, Lord, when saw we thee an hungred, and fed thee? or thirsty, and gave thee drink?

25:38 When saw we thee a stranger, and took thee in? or naked, and clothed thee?

25:39 Or when saw we thee sick, or in prison, and came unto thee?

25:40 And the King shall answer and say unto them, Verily I say unto you, Inasmuch as ye have done it unto one of the least of these my brethren, ye have done it unto me.

25:41 Then shall he say also unto them on the left hand, Depart from me, ye cursed, into everlasting fire, prepared for the devil and his angels:

25:42 For I was an hungered, and ye gave me no meat: I was thirsty, and ye gave me no drink:

25:43 I was a stranger, and ye took me not in: naked, and ye clothed me not:

sick, and in prison, and ye visited me not.

25:44 Then shall they also answer him, saying, Lord, when saw we thee an hungered, or athirst, or a stranger, or naked, or sick, or in prison, and did not minister unto thee?

25:45 Then shall he answer them, saying, Verily I say unto you, Inasmuch as ye did it not to one of the least of these, ye did it not to me.

25:46 And these shall go away into everlasting punishment: but the righteous into life eternal.

MK. 14:1 After two days was the feast of the passover, and of unleavened bread: and the chief priests and the scribes sought how they might take him by craft, and put him to death.

14:2 But they said, Not on the feast day, lest there be an uproar of the people.

14:3 And being in Bethany in the house of Simon the leper, as he sat at meat, there came a woman having an alabaster box of ointment of spikenard very precious; and she brake the box, and poured it on his head.

14:4 And there were some that had indignation within themselves, and said, Why was this waste of the ointment made?

14:5 For it might have been sold for more than three hundred pence, and have been given to the poor. And they murmured against her.

14:6 And Jesus said, Let her alone; why trouble ye her? she hath wrought a good work on me.

14:7 For ye have the poor with you always, and whensoever ye will ye may do them good: but me ye have not always.

14:8 She hath done what she could: she is come aforehand to anoint my body to the burying.

MT. 26:14 Then one of the twelve, called Judas Iscariot, went unto the chief priests,

26:15 And said unto them, What will ye give me, and I will deliver him unto you? And they covenanted with him for thirty pieces of silver.

26:16 And from that time he sought opportunity to betray him.

26:17 Now the first day of the feast of unleavened bread the disciples came to Jesus, saying unto him, Where wilt thou that we prepare for thee to eat the passover?

26:18 And he said, Go into the city to such a man, and say unto him, The Master saith, My time is at hand; I will keep the passover at thy house with my disciples.

26:19 And the disciples did as Jesus had appointed them; and they made ready the passover.

26:20 Now when the even was come, he sat down with the twelve.

L. 22:24 And there was also a strife among them, which of them should be accounted the greatest.

22:25 And he said unto them, The kings of the Gentiles exercise lordship over them; and they that exercise authority upon them are called benefactors.

22:26 But ye shall not be so: but he that is greatest among you, let him be as the younger; and he that is chief, as he that doth serve.

22:27 For whether is greater, he that sitteth at meat, or he that serveth? is not he that sitteth at meat? but I am among you as he that serveth.

J.   13:2   And supper being ended,

13:4   He riseth from supper, and laid aside his garments; and took a towel, and girded himself.

13:5   After that he poureth water into a bason, and began to wash the disciples feet, and to wipe them with the towel wherewith he was girded.

13:6   Then cometh he to Simon Peter: and Peter saith unto him, Lord, dost thou wash my feet?

13:7   Jesus answered and said unto him, What I do thou knowest not now; but thou shalt know hereafter.

13:8   Peter saith unto him, Thou shalt never wash my feet. Jesus answered him, If I wash thee not, thou hast no part with me.

13:9   Simon Peter saith unto him, Lord, not my feet only, but also my hands and my head.

13:10 Jesus saith to him, He that is washed needeth not save to wash his feet, but is clean every whit: and ye are clean, but not all.

13:11 For he knew who should betray him; therefore said he, Ye are not all clean.

13:12 So after he had washed their feet, and had taken his garments, and was set down again, he said unto them, Know ye what I have done to you?

13:13 Ye call me Master and Lord: and ye say well; for so I am.

13:14 If I then, your Lord and Master, have washed your feet; ye also ought to wash one another's feet.

13:15 For I have given you an example, that ye should do as I have done to you.

13:16 Verily, verily, I say unto you, The servant is not greater than his lord; neither he that is sent greater than he that sent him.

13:17 If ye know these things, happy are ye if ye do them.

13:21 When Jesus had thus said, he was troubled in spirit, and testified, and said, Verily, verily, I say unto you, that one of you shall betray me.

13:22 Then the disciples looked one on another, doubting of whom he spake.

13:23 Now there was leaning on Jesus' bosom one of his disciples, whom Jesus loved.

13:24 Simon Peter therefore beckoned to him, that he should ask who it should be of whom he spake.

13:25 He then lying on Jesus' breast saith unto him, Lord, who is it?

13:26 Jesus answered, He it is, to whom I shall give a sop, when I have dipped it. And when he had dipped the sop, he gave it to Judas Iscariot, the son of Simon.

13:31 Therefore, when he was gone out, Jesus said:

13:34 A new commandment I give unto you, That ye love one another; as I have loved you, that ye also love one another.

13:35 By this shall all men know that ye are my disciples, if ye have love one to another.

MT. 26:31 Then saith Jesus unto them, All ye shall be offended because of me this night:

26:33 Peter answered and said unto him, Though all men shall be offended because of thee, yet will I never be offended.

L. 22:33 I am ready to go with thee, both into prison, and to death.

22:34 And he said, I tell thee, Peter, the cock shall not crow this day, before that thou shalt thrice deny that thou knowest me.

MT. 26:35 Peter said unto him, Though I should die with thee, yet will I not deny thee. Likewise also said all the disciples.

26:36 Then cometh Jesus with them unto a place called Gethsemane, and saith unto the disciples, Sit ye here, while I go and pray yonder.

26:37 And he took with him Peter and the two sons of Zebedee, and began to be sorrowful and very heavy.

26:38 Then saith he unto them, My soul is exceeding sorrowful, even unto death: tarry ye here, and watch with me.

26:39 And he went a little farther, and fell on his face, and prayed, saying, O my Father, if it be possible, let this cup pass from me: nevertheless not as I will, but as thou wilt.

26:40 And he cometh unto the disciples, and findeth them asleep, and saith unto Peter, What, could ye not watch with me one hour?

26:41 Watch and pray, that ye enter not into temptation: the spirit indeed is willing, but the flesh is weak.

26:42 He went away again the second time, and prayed, saying, O my Father, if this cup may not pass away from me, except I drink it, thy will be done.

26:43 And he came and found them asleep again: for their eyes were heavy.

26:44 And he left them, and went away again, and prayed the third time, saying the same words.

26:45 Then cometh he to his disciples, and saith unto them, Sleep on now, and take your rest.

J. 18:1 When Jesus had spoken these words, he went forth with his disciples over the brook Cedron, where was a garden, into the which he entered, and his disciples.

18:2 And Judas also, which betrayed him, knew the place: for Jesus ofttimes resorted thither with his disciples.

18:3 Judas then, having received a band of men and officers from the chief priests and Pharisees, cometh thither with lanterns and torches and weapons.

MT. 26:48 Now he that betrayed him gave them a sign, saying, Whomsoever I shall kiss, that same is he: hold him fast.

26:49 And forthwith he came to Jesus, and said, Hail, master; and kissed him.

26:50 And Jesus said unto him, Friend, wherefore are thou come?

J. 18:4 Jesus therefore, knowing all things that should come upon him, went forth, and said unto them, Whom seek ye?

18:5 They answered him, Jesus of Nazareth. Jesus saith unto them, I am he. And Judas also, which betrayed him, stood with them.

18:6 As soon then as he had said unto them, I am he, they went backward, and fell to the ground.

18:7 Then asked he them again, Whom seek ye? And they said, Jesus of Nazareth.

18:8 Jesus answered, I have told you that I am he: if therefore ye seek me, let these go their way:

MT. 26:50 Then came they, and laid hands on Jesus and took him.

26:51 And, behold, one of them which were with Jesus stretched out his hand, and drew his sword, and struck a servant of the high priest's, and smote off his ear.

26:52 Then said Jesus unto him, Put up again thy sword into his place: for all they that take the sword shall perish with the sword.

26:55 In that same hour said Jesus to the multitudes, Are ye come out as against a thief with swords and staves for to take me? I sat daily with you teaching in the temple, and ye laid no hold on me.

26:56 Then all the disciples forsook him, and fled.

MK. 14:51 And there followed him a certain young man, having a linen cloth cast about his naked body; and the young men laid hold on him:

14:52 And he left the linen cloth, and fled from them naked.

MT. 26:57 And they that had laid hold on Jesus led him away to Caiaphas the high priest, where the scribes and the elders were assembled.

J. 18:15 And Simon Peter followed Jesus, and so did another disciple: that disciple was known unto the high priest, and went in with Jesus into the palace of the high priest.

18:16 But Peter stood at the door without. Then went out that other disciple, which was known unto the high priest, and spake unto her that kept the door, and brought in Peter.

18:18 And the servants and officers stood there, who had made a fire of coals; for it was cold: and they warmed themselves: and Peter stood with them, and warmed himself.

18:17 Then saith the damsel that kept the door unto Peter, Art not thou also one of this man's disciples? He saith, I am not.

18:25 And Simon Peter stood and warmed himself. They said therefore unto him, Art not thou also one of his disciples? He denied it, and said, I am not.

18:26 One of the servants of the high priest, being his kinsman whose ear Peter cut off, saith, Did not I see thee in the garden with him?

18:27 Peter then denied again: and immediately the cock crew.

MT. 26:75 And Peter remembered the word of Jesus, which said unto him, Before the cock crow, thou shalt deny me thrice. And he went out, and wept bitterly.

J. 18:19 The high priest then asked Jesus of his disciples, and of his doctrine.

18:20 Jesus answered him, I spake openly to the world; I ever taught in the synagogue, and in the temple, whither the Jews always resort; and in secret have I said nothing.

18:21 Why askest thou me? ask them which heard me, what I have said unto them: behold, they know what I said.

18:22 And when he had thus spoken, one of the officers which stood by struck Jesus with the palm of his hand, saying, Answerest thou the high priest so?

18:23 Jesus answered him, If I have spoken evil, bear witness of the evil: but if well, why smitest thou me?

MK. 14:53 And they led Jesus away to the high priest: and with him were assembled all the chief priests and the elders and the scribes.

14:55 And the chief priests and all the council sought for witness against Jesus to put him to death; and found none.

14:56 For many bare false witness against him, but their witness agreed not together.

14:57 And there arose certain, and bare false witness against him, saying,

14:58 We heard him say, I will destroy this temple that is made with hands, and within three days I will build another made without hands.

14:59 But neither so did their witness agree together.

14:60 And the high priest stood up in the midst, and asked Jesus, saying, Answerest thou nothing? what is it which these witness against thee?

14:61 But he held his peace, and answered nothing. Again the high priest asked him, and said unto him, Art thou the Christ, the Son of the Blessed?

L. 22:67 And he said unto them, If I tell you, ye will not believe:

22:68 And if I also ask you, ye will not answer me, nor let me go.

22:70 Then said they all, Art thou then the Son of God? And he said unto them, Ye say that I am.

MK. 14:63 Then the high priest rent his clothes, and saith, What need we any further witnesses?

14:64 Ye have heard the blasphemy: what think ye? And they all condemned him to be guilty of death.

14:65 And some began to spit on him, and to cover his face, and to buffet him, and to say unto him, Prophesy: and the servants did strike him with the palms of their hands.

J. 18:28 Then led they Jesus from Caiaphas unto the hall of judgment: and it was early; and they themselves went not into the judgment hall, lest they should be defiled; but that they might eat the passover.

18:29 Pilate then went out unto them, and said, What accusation bring ye against this man?

18:30 They answered and said unto him, If he were not a malefactor, we would not have delivered him up unto thee.

18:31 Then said Pilate unto them, Take ye him, and judge him according to your law. The Jews therefore said unto him, It is not lawful for us to put any man to death:

18:33 Then Pilate entered into the judgment hall again, and called Jesus, and said unto him, Art thou the King of the Jews?

18:34 Jesus answered him, Sayest thou this thing of thyself, or did others tell it thee of me?

18:35 Pilate answered, Am I a Jew? Thine own nation and the chief priests have delivered thee unto me: what hast thou done?

18:36 Jesus answered, My kingdom is not of this world: if my kingdom were of this world, then would my servants fight, that I should not be delivered to the Jews: but now is my kingdom not from hence.

18:37 Pilate therefore said unto him, Art thou a king then? Jesus answered, Thou sayest that I am a king. To this end was I born, and for this cause came I into the world, that I should bear witness unto the truth. Every one that is of the truth heareth my voice.

18:38 Pilate saith unto him, What is truth? And when he had said this, he went out again unto the Jews, and saith unto them, I find in him no fault at all.

L. 23:5 And they were the more fierce, saying, He stirreth up the people, teaching throughout all Jewry, beginning from Galilee to this place.

MT. 27:13 Then said Pilate unto him, Hearest thou not how many things they witness against thee?

L. 23:6 When Pilate heard of Galilee, he asked whether the man were a Galilean.

23:7 And as soon as he knew that he belonged unto Herod's jurisdiction, he sent him to Herod, who himself also was at Jerusalem at that time.

L. 23:8 And when Herod saw Jesus, he was exceeding glad: for he was desirous to see him of a long season, because he had heard many things of him; and he hoped to have seen some miracle done by him.

23:9 Then he questioned with him in many words; but he answered him nothing.

23:10 And the chief priests and scribes stood and vehemently accused him.

23:11 And Herod, with his men of war, set him at nought, and mocked him, and arrayed him in a gorgeous robe, and sent him again to Pilate.

23:12 And the same day Pilate and Herod were made friends together: for before they were at enmity between themselves.

23:13 And Pilate, when he had called together the chief priests and the rulers and the people,

23:14 Said unto them, Ye have brought this man unto me, as one that perverteth the people: and, behold, I, having examined him before you, have found no fault in this man touching those things whereof ye accuse him:

23:15 No, nor yet Herod: for I sent you to him; and, lo, nothing worthy of death is done unto him.

23:16 I will therefore chastise him, and release him.

MT. 27:15 Now at that feast the governor was wont to release unto the people a prisoner, whom they would.

27:16 And they had then a notable prisoner, called Barabbas.

27:17 Therefore when they were gathered together, Pilate said unto them, Whom will ye that I release unto you? Barabbas, or Jesus which is called Christ?

27:18 For he knew that for envy they had delivered him.

27:19 When he was set down on the judgment seat, his wife sent unto him, saying, Have thou nothing to do with that just man: for I have suffered many things this day in a dream because of him.

27:20 But the chief priests and elders persuaded the multitude that they should ask Barabbas, and destroy Jesus.

27:21 The governor answered and said unto them, Whether of the twain will ye that I release unto you? They said, Barabbas.

27:22 Pilate saith unto them, What shall I do then with Jesus which is called Christ? They all say unto him, Let him be crucified.

27:23 And the governor said, Why, what evil hath he done? But they cried out the more, saying, Let him be crucified.

27:26 Then released he Barabbas unto them: and when he had scourged Jesus, he delivered him to be crucified.

27:27 Then the soldiers of the governor took Jesus into the common hall, and gathered unto him the whole band of soldiers.

27:29 And when they had platted a crown of thorns, they put it upon his head, and a reed in his right hand: and they bowed the knee before him, and mocked him, saying, Hail, King of the Jews!

27:30 And they spit upon him, and took the reed, and smote him on the head.

27:31 And after that they had mocked him, they took the robe off from him, and put his own raiment on him, and led him away to crucify him.

27:3 Then Judas, which had betrayed him, when he saw that he was condemned, repented himself, and brought again the thirty pieces of silver to the chief priests and elders,

27:4 Saying, I have sinned in that I have betrayed the innocent blood. And they said, What is that to us? see thou to that.

27:5 And he cast down the pieces of silver in the temple, and departed, and went and hanged himself.

27:6 And the chief priests took the silver pieces, and said, It is not lawful for to put them into the treasury, because it is the price of blood.

27:7 And they took counsel, and bought with them the potter's field, to bury strangers in.

27:8 Wherefore that field was called, The Field of Blood, unto this day.

L. 23:26 And as they led him away, they laid hold upon one Simon, a Cyrenian, coming out of the country, and on him they laid the cross, that he might bear it after Jesus.

23:27 And there followed him a great company of people, and of women, which also bewailed and lamented him.

23:28 But Jesus turning unto them said, Daughters of Jerusalem, weep not for me, but weep for yourselves, and for your children.

23:29 For, behold, the days are coming, in the which they shall say, Blessed are the barren, and the wombs that never bare, and the paps which never gave suck.

23:30 Then shall they begin to say to the mountains, Fall on us; and to the hills, Cover us.

23:31 For if they do these things in a green tree, what shall be done in the dry?

23:32 And there were also two other, malefactors, led with him to be put to death.

J. 19:17 And he bearing his cross went forth into a place called the place of a skull, which is called in the Hebrew, Golgotha:

19:18 Where they crucified him, and two other with him, on either side one, and Jesus in the midst.

19:19 And Pilate wrote a title, and put it on the cross. And the writing was JESUS OF NAZARETH THE KING OF THE JEWS.

19:20 This title then read many of the Jews: for the place where Jesus was crucified was nigh to the city: and it was written in Hebrew, and Greek, and Latin.

19:21 Then said the chief priests of the Jews to Pilate, Write not, The King of the Jews; but that he said, I am King of the Jews.

19:22 Pilate answered, What I have written I have written.

19:23 Then the soldiers, when they had crucified Jesus, took his garments, and made four parts, to every soldier a part; and also his coat: now the coat was without seam, woven from the top throughout.

19:24 They said therefore among themselves, Let us not rend it, but cast lots for it, whose it shall be.

MT. 27:39 And they that passed by reviled him, wagging their heads,

27:40 And saying, Thou that destroyest the temple, and buildest it in three days, save thyself. If thou be the Son of God, come down from the cross.

27:41 Likewise also the chief priests mocking him, with the scribes and elders, said,

27:42 He saved others; himself he cannot save. If he be the King of Israel, let him now come down from the cross, and we will believe him.

27:43 He trusted in God; let him deliver him now, if he will have him: for he said, I am the Son of God.

L. 23:39 And one of the malefactors which were hanged railed on him, saying, If thou be the Christ, save thyself and us.

23:40 But the other answering rebuked him, saying, Dost not thou fear God, seeing thou art in the same condemnation?

23:41 And we indeed justly; for we receive the due reward of our deeds: but this man hath done nothing amiss.

23:34 Then said Jesus, Father, forgive them; for they know not what they do.

J. 19:25 Now there stood by the cross of Jesus his mother, and his mother's sister, Mary the wife of Cleophas, and Mary Magdalene.

19:26 When Jesus therefore saw his mother, and the disciple standing by, whom he loved, he saith unto his mother, Woman, behold thy son!

19:27 Then saith he to the disciple, Behold thy mother! And from that hour that disciple took her unto his own home.

MT. 27:46 And about the ninth hour Jesus cried with a loud voice, saying, *Eli, Eli, lama sabachthani?* that is to say, My God, my God, why hast thou forsaken me?

27:47 Some of them that stood there, when they heard that, said, This man calleth for Elias.

27:48 And straightway one of them ran, and took a spunge, and filled it with vinegar, and put it on a reed, and gave him to drink.

27:49 The rest said, Let be, let us see whether Elias will come to save him.

27:50 Jesus, when he had cried again with a loud voice, yielded up the ghost.

27:55 And many women were there beholding afar off, which followed Jesus from Galilee, ministering unto him:

27:56 Among which was Mary Magdalene, and Mary the mother of James and Joses, and the mother of Zebedee's children.

J. 19:31 The Jews therefore, because it was the preparation, that the bodies should not remain upon the cross on the sabbath day, (for that sabbath day was an high day,) besought Pilate that their legs might be broken, and that they might be taken away.

19:32 Then came the soldiers, and brake the legs of the first, and of the other which was crucified with him.

19:33 But when they came to Jesus, and saw that he was dead already, they brake not his legs:

19:34 But one of the soldiers with a spear pierced his side, and forthwith came there out blood and water.

19:38 And after this Joseph of Arimathaea, being a disciple of Jesus, but secretly for fear of the Jews, besought Pilate that he might take away the body of Jesus: and Pilate gave him leave. He came therefore, and took the body of Jesus.

19:39 And there came also Nicodemus, which at the first came to Jesus by night, and brought a mixture of myrrh and aloes, about an hundred pound weight.

19:40 Then took they the body of Jesus, and wound it in linen clothes with the spices, as the manner of the Jews is to bury.

19:41 Now in the place where he was crucified there was a garden; and in the garden a new sepulchre, wherein was never man yet laid.

19:42 There laid they Jesus,

MT. 27:60 And rolled a great stone to the door of the sepulchre, and departed.

Part 13

JEFFERSON'S LAST YEARS

1820 – 1826

I n 1820, Jefferson criticized the Missouri Compromise, maintaining the balance of free and slave states by admitting Maine with Missouri. He saw the attacks on slavery as no better than attempts at a Federalist come back.

From January 6 to July 29, 1821, he worked on his *Autobiography*, which fills in details with regard to many of his writings herein excerpted.

In 1823, a letter to the President helped formulate the Monroe Doctrine against European expansion in the Western Hemisphere. He continued to be involved with the University and education, preparing instructions for recruiting faculty in Europe.

Lafayette, on a triumphal tour of America, visited Monticello, November 3-15, 1824. The crowd of hundreds who accompanied him to the plantation burst into tears of joy at the meeting of the two old revolutionaries.

On March 7, 1825, he saw the University opened to students.

On June 24, 1826, Jefferson penned his last written words, in response to an invitation to visit Washington on the fiftieth Anniversary of the Declaration. He died on July 4th, shortly after 12 noon. Only five slaves were emancipated in his will. They were relatives of Sally Hemings, quietly freed by herself a short time later.

Like Jefferson, Madison opposed a federal ban on slavery in Missouri and was much concerned for the future of his republic. Lafayette visited Madison on his 1824-25 tour of the U.S. and Madison last visited Jefferson in 1825. "Take care of me when dead" was Jefferson's last request of his old friend. Indeed, after his death, Madison replaced Jefferson as Rector of the University of Virginia.

THOMAS JEFFERSON TO DR. THOMAS COOPER
March 13, 1820

I must explain to you the state of religious parties with us. About 1/3 of our state is Baptist, 1/3 Methodist, and of the remaining third two parts may be Presbyterian and one part Anglican. The Baptists are sound republicans and zealous supporters of their government. The Methodists are republican mostly, satisfied with the governmt. Medling with nothing but the concerns of their own calling and opposing nothing. These two sects are entirely friendly to our university. The Anglicans are the same. The Presbyterian clergy alone (not their followers) remain bitterly federal and malcontent with their government. They are violent, ambitious of power, and intolerant in politics as in religion and want nothing but license from the laws to kindle again the fires of their leader John Knox, and to give us a 2d blast from his trumpet. Having a little more monkish learning than the clergy of the other sects, they are jealous of the general diffusion of science, and therefore hostile to our Seminary lest it should qualify their antagonists of the other sects to meet them in equal combat. Not daring to attack the institution with the avowel of their real motives, they peck at you, at me, and every feather they can spy out. But in this they have no weight, even with their own followers. Excepting a few old men among them who may still be federal & Anglomen, their mainbody are good citizens, friends to their government, anxious for reputation, and therefore friendly to the University.

THOMAS JEFFERSON TO JOHN ADAMS
March 14, 1820

Mr. Locke, you know, and other materialists have charged with blasphemy the Spiritualists who have denied to the Creator the power of endowing certain forms of matter with the faculty of thought. These however are speculations and subtleties in which, for my own part, I have little indulged myself. When I meet with a proposition beyond finite comprehension, I abandon it as I do a weight which human strength cannot lift: and I think ignorance, in these cases, is truly the softest pillow on which I can lay my head. Were it necessary however to form an opinion, I confess I should, with Mr. Locke, prefer swallowing one incomprehensibility rather than two. It requires one effort only to admit the single incomprehensibility of matter endowed with thought: and two to believe, 1st. that of an existence called Spirit, of which we have neither evidence nor idea, and then 2ndly. how that spirit which has neither extention nor solidity, can put material organs into motion. These are things which you and I may perhaps know ere long. We have so lived as to fear neither horn of the dilemma. We have, willingly, done injury to no man; and have done for our country the good which has fallen in our way, so far as commensurate with the faculties given us. That we have not done more than we could cannot be imputed to us as a crime before any tribunal. I look therefore to that crisis, as I am sure you also do, as one *'qui summum nec metuit diem nec optat.'* [Who neither fears the final day nor hopes for it.] In the mean time be our last as cordial as were our first affections.

THOMAS JEFFERSON TO JOSÉ FRANCESCO CORRÈA DA SERRA
April 11, 1820

Editor's note: The translation from the Latin is the editor's.

It would particularly grieve me were you leave us without having seen our University in it's present advanced state. This is such as to give an idea of what it will be. We are enabled now to accomplish the buildings of the whole establishment (the Library excepted) by the close of the next year; and this being secured, it is impossible that the legislature, or it's constituents, can see with indifference such a suite of buildings standing compleat, and unoccupied. There exists indeed an opposition to it by the friends of William and Mary, which is not strong. The most restive is that of the priests of the different religious sects, who dread the advance of science as witches do the approach of day-light; and scowl on it the fatal harbinger announcing the subversion of the duperies on which they live. In this the Presbyterian clergy take the lead. The tocsin is sounded in all their pulpits, and the first alarm denounced is against the particular creed of Doctr. Cooper; and as impudently denounced as if they really knew what it is. But, of this we will talk when you see us at Monticello. in the mean time cura ut valeas, *et me ut amaris ama* [be as strong as my feeling for you].

THOMAS JEFFERSON TO WILLIAM SHORT
April 13, 1820

Your favor of Mar. 27. is recieved, and my granddaughter Ellen has undertaken to copy the Syllabus, which will therefore be inclosed. It was originally written to Dr. Rush. On his death, fearing that the inquisition of the public might get hold of it. I asked the return of it from the family, which they kindly replied with. At the request of another friend, I had given him a copy. He lent it to his friend to read, who copied it, and in a few months it appeared in the theological magazine of London. Happily that repository is scarcely known in this country, and the Syllabus, therefore, is still a secret, and in your hands I am sure it will continue so.

But while this syllabus is meant to place the character of Jesus in its true and high light, as no imposter himself, but a great reformer of the Hebrew code of religion, it is not to be understood that I am with him in all His doctrines. I am a Materialist; he takes the side of spiritualism: he preaches the efficacy of repentance towards forgiveness of sin; I require a counterpoise of good works to redeem it &c. &c. It is the innocence of his character, the purity and sublimity of his moral precepts, the eloquences of his inculcations, the beauty of the apologues in which he conveys them, that I so much admire; sometimes, indeed, needing indulgence to Eastern hyperbolism. My eulogies, too, may be founded on a postulate which all may not be ready to grant. Among the sayings and discourses imputed to him by his biographers, I find many passages of fine imagination, correct morality, and of the most lovely benevolence; and others, again, of so much ignorance, so much absurdity, so much untruth, charlatanism and imposture, as to pronounce it impossible that such contradictions should have proceeded from the same being. I separate, therefore, the gold from the dross; restore to him the former, and leave the latter to the stupidity of some, and roguery of others of his disciples. Of this band of dupes and impostors, Paul was the great Coryphaeus, and first corruptor of the doctrines of Jesus. These palpable interpolations and falsifications of His doctrines, led me to try to sift them apart. I found the work obvious and easy, and that His past composed the most beautiful morsel of morality which has been given to us by man. The syllabus is therefore of His doctrines, not all of mine. I read them as I do those of other ancient and modern moralists, with a mixture of approbation and dissent....

The history of our University you know.... An opposition in the mean time has been got up. That of our alma mater William and Mary, is not of much weight. She must descend into the second rank of academies of preparation for the University. The serious enemies are the priests of the different religious sects, to whose spells on the human mind it's improvement is ominous. Their pulpits are now resounding with denunciations against the appointment of Dr. Cooper whom they charge as a Monotheist in opposition to their tritheism. Hostile as these sects are in every other point, to one another, they unite in maintaining their mystical theogony against those who believe there is one god only. The Presbyterian clergy are loudest, the most intolerant of all sects, the most tyrannical and ambitious; ready at the word of the lawgiver, if such a word could be now obtained, to put the torch to the pile, and to rekindle in this virgin hemisphere, the flames in which their oracle Calvin consumed the poor Servetus, because he could not find in his Euclid the proposition which has demonstrated that three are one and one is three, nor subscribe to that of Calvin that magistrates have a right to exterminate all heretics to Calvinistic Creed. They pant to re-establish, by law that holy inquisition, which they can now only infuse into public opinion. We have most unwisely committed to the hierophants of our particular superstition, the direction of public opinion, that lord of the Universe. We have given them stated and privileged days to collect and catechise us, opportunities of delivering their oracles to the people in mass, and of molding their minds as wax in the hollow of their hands. But in despite of their fulminations against endeavors to enlighten the general mind, to improve the reason of the people, and to encourage them in the use of it, the liberality of this State will support this institution, and give fair play to the cultivation of reason.

THOMAS JEFFERSON TO JOSEPH MARX
July 8, 1820

Editor's note: Marx sent Jefferson the proceedings of the Sanhedrin, a French national Jewish assembly organized by Napoleon. Jefferson frequently wrote letters in the third person.

Th: Jefferson presents to Mr. Marx his complements & thanks for the Transactions of the Paris Sanhedrin, which he shall read with great interest, and with the regret he has ever felt at seeing a sect, the parent and basis of all those of Christendom, singled out by all of them for a persecution and oppression which proved they have profited nothing from the benevolent doctrines of him whom they profess to make the model of their principle and practice.

I have thought it a cruel addition to the wrongs which that injured sect have suffered, that their youth should be excluded from the instructions in science afforded to all others in our public seminaries, by imposing upon them a course of Theological Reading which their consciences do not permit them to pursue; and in the University lately established here, we have set the example of ceasing to violate the rights of conscience by any injunction on the different sects respecting their religion.

JAMES MADISON TO DR. JACOB DE LA MOTTA
August 1820

I have received your letter of the 7th inst. with the Discourse delivered at the Consecration of the Hebrew Synagogue at Savannah, for which you will please to accept my thanks.

The history of the Jews must forever be interesting. The modern part of it is, at the same time, so little generally known, that every ray of light on the subject has its value.

Among the features peculiar to the political system of the U. States, is the perfect equality of rights which it secures to every religious Sect. And it is particularly pleasing to observe in the good citizenship of such as have been most distrusted and oppressed elsewhere, a happy illustration of the safety & success of this experiment of a just & benignant policy. Equal laws, protecting equal rights, are found, as they ought to be presumed, the best guarantee of loyalty & love of country; as well as best calculated to cherish that mutual respect & good will among citizens of every religious denomination which are necessary to social harmony, and most favorable to the advancement of truth. The account you give of the Jews of your Congregation brings them fully within the scope of these observations.

THOMAS JEFFERSON TO WILLIAM SHORT
August 4, 1820

I owe you a letter for your favor of June 29, which was recieved in due time; and there being no subject of the day of particular interest, I will make this a supplement to mine of Apr. 13. My aim in that was to justify the character of Jesus against the fictions of his pseudo-followers, which have exposed him to the inference of being an impostor. For if we could believe that he really countenanced the follies, the falsehoods and the charlatanisms which his biographers father on him, and admit the misconstructions, interpolations and theorisations of the fathers of the early, and fanatics of the latter ages, the conclusion would be irresistible by every sound mind, that he was an impostor. I give no credit to their falsifications of his actions and doctrines; and to rescue his character, the postulate in my letter asked only what is granted in reading every other historian. When Livy and Siculus, for example, tell us things which coincide with our experience of the order of nature, we credit them on their word, and place their narrations among the records of credible history. But when they tell us of calves speaking, of statues sweating blood, and other things against the course of nature, we reject these as fables, not belonging to history. In like manner, when an historian, speaking of a character well known and established on satisfactory testimony, imputes to it things incompatible with that character, we reject them without hesitation, and assent to that only of which we have better evidence. Had Plutarch informed us that Caesar and Cicero passed their whole lives in religious exercises, and abstinence from the affairs of the world, we should reject what was so inconsistent with their established characters, still crediting what he relates in conformity with our ideas of them. So again, the superlative wisdom of Socrates is testified by all antiquity, and placed on ground not to be questioned. When therefore Plato puts into his mouth such fancies, such paralogisms and sophisms as a school boy would be ashamed of, we conclude they were the whimsies of Plato's own foggy brain, and acquit Socrates of puerilities so unlike his character. (Speaking of Plato, I will add, that no writer, antient or modern, has bewildered the world with more *ignes fatui* [delusions], than this renowned philosopher, in Ethics, in Politics and Physics. In the latter, to specify a single example, compare his views of the animal economy, in his Timaeus, with those of Mrs. Bryan in her Conversations on Chemistry, and weigh the science of the canonised philosopher against the good sense of the unassuming lady. But Plato's visions have furnished a basis for endless systems of mystical theology, and he is therefore all but adopted as a Christian saint. — It is surely time for men to think for themselves, and to throw off the authority of names so artificially magnified. But to return from this parenthesis, I say that) this free exercise of reason is all I ask for the vindication of the character of Jesus. We find in the writings of his biographers matter of two distinct descriptions. First a groundwork of vulgar ignorance, of things impossible, of superstitions, fanaticisms and fabrications. Intermixed with these again are sublime ideas of the supreme being, aphorisms and precepts of the purest morality and benevolence, sanctioned by a life of humility, innocence and simplicity of manners, neglect of riches, absence of worldly ambition and honors, with an eloquence and persuasiveness which have not been surpassed. These could not be inventions of the groveling authors who relate them. They are far beyond the powers of their feeble minds. They shew that there was a character, the subject of their history, whose splendid conceptions were above all suspicion of being interpolations from their hands. Can we be at a loss in separating such materials, and ascribing each to its genuine author? The difference is obvious to the eye and to the understanding, and we may read as we run, to each his part; and I will venture to affirm that he who, as I have done, will undertake to winnow this grain from it's chaff, will find it not to require a moment's consideration. The parts fall asunder of themselves as would those of an image of metal and clay.

There are, I acknolege, passages not free from objection, which we may with probability ascribe to Jesus himself; but claiming indulgence from the circumstances under which he acted. His object was the reformation of some articles in the religion of the Jews, as taught by Moses. That Seer had presented, for the object of their worship, a being of terrific character, cruel, vindictive, capricious and unjust. Jesus, taking for his type the best qualities of the human head and heart, wisdom, justice, goodness, and adding to them power, ascribed all of these but in infinite perfection, to the supreme being, and formed him really worthy of their adoration. Moses had either not believed in a future state of existence, or had not thought it essential to be explicitly taught to his people. Jesus inculcated that doctrine with emphasis and precision. Moses had bound the Jews to many idle ceremonies, mummeries and observances, of no effect towards producing the social utilities which constitute the essence of virtue. Jesus exposed their futility and insignificance. The one instilled into his people the most anti-social spirit towards other nations; the other preached philanthropy and universal charity and benevolence. — The office of reformer of the superstitions of a nation is ever dangerous. Jesus had to walk on the perilous confines of reason and religion: and a step to right or left might place him within the gripe of the priests of the superstition, a bloodthirsty race, as cruel and remorseless as the being whom they represented as the family god of Abraham, of Isaac and of Jacob, and the local god of Israel. They were constantly laying snares too to entangle him in the web of the law. He was justifiable therefore in avoiding these by evasions, by sophisms, by misconstructions and misapplications of scraps of the prophets, and in defending himself with these their own weapons, as sufficient, *ad homines*, at least. That Jesus did not mean to impose himself on mankind as the son of god physically speaking I have been convinced by the writings of men more learned than myself in that lore. But that he might conscientiously believe himself inspired from above, is very possible. The whole religion of the Jews, inculcated on him from his infancy, was founded in the belief of divine inspiration. The fumes of the most disordered imaginations were recorded in their religious code, as special communications of the deity; and as it could not but happen that, in the course of ages, events would now and then turn up to which some of these vague rhapsodies might be accommodated by the aid of allegories, figures, types, and other tricks upon words, they have not only preserved their credit with the Jews of all subsequent times, but are the foundation of much of the religions of those who have schismatised from them. Elevated by the enthusiasm of a warm and pure heart, conscious of the high strains of an eloquence which had not been taught him, he might readily mistake the coruscations of his own fine genius for inspirations of an higher order. This belief carried therefore no more personal imputation, than the belief of Socrates, that himself was under the care and admonitions of a guardian daemon. And how many of our wisest men still believe in the reality of these inspirations, while perfectly sane on all other subjects. Excusing therefore, on these considerations, those passages in the gospels which seem to bear marks of weakness in Jesus, ascribing to him what alone is consistent with the great and pure character of which the same writings furnish proofs, and to their proper authors their own trivialities and imbecilities, I think myself authorised to conclude the purity and distinction of his character in opposition to the impostures which those authors would fix upon him: and that the postulate of my former letter is no more than is granted in all other historical works.

THOMAS JEFFERSON TO JOHN ADAMS
August 15, 1820

Editor's note: Jefferson's additions to his copy are in brackets, as are translations from Greek and Latin. De haeretico comburendo, the burning of heretics, cited by Jefferson was an English writ utilized when heretics were convicted, abjured their sin, then relapsed.

But enough of criticism: let me turn to your puzzling letter of May 12. on matter, spirit, motion, &c. It's croud of scepticisms kept me from sleep. I read it, and laid it down: read it, and laid it down, again and again: and to give rest to my mind, I was obliged to recur ultimately to my habitual anodyne, 'I feel: therefore I exist.' I feel bodies which are not myself: there are other existences then. I call them matter. I feel them changing place. This gives me motion. Where there is an absence of matter, I call it void, or nothing, or immaterial space. On the basis of sensation, of matter and motion, we may erect the fabric of all the certainties we can have or need. I can conceive thought to be an action of a particular organisation of matter, formed for that purpose by its creator, as well as that attraction is an action of matter, or magnetism of loadstone. When he who denies to the Creator the power of endowing matter with the mode of action called thinking shall show how he could endow the Sun with the mode of action called attraction, which reins the planets in the tract of their orbits, or how an absence of matter can have a will, and, by that will, put matter into motion, then the materialist may be lawfully required to explain the process by which matter exercises the faculty of thinking. When once we quit the basis of sensation, all is in the wind. To talk of immaterial existences is to talk of nothings. To say that the human soul, angels, god, are immaterial, is to say, they are nothings, or that there is no god, no angels, no soul. I cannot reason otherwise: but I believe I am supported in my creed of materialism by Locke, Tracy, and Stewart. [by the Lockes, the Tracys, and the Stewarts.] At what age [that of Athanasius and the Council of Nicaea anno 324.] of the Christian church this heresy of immaterialism, this masked atheism, crept in, I do not know. [I do not exactly know.] But a heresy it certainly is. Jesus taught nothing of it. He told us indeed that 'God is a spirit,' but he has not defined what a spirit is, nor said that it is not matter. And the antient fathers generally, if not universally, [of the three first centuries.] held it to be matter: light and thin indeed, an etherial gas; but still matter. Origen says *'Deus reapse corporalis est; sed graviorum tantum corporum ratione, incorporeus.'* [God is in very fact corporeal, but, by reason of so much heavier bodies, incorporeal.] *Tertullian 'quid enim deus nisi corpus?'* [for what is God except body?] and again *'quis negabit deum esse corpus? Etsi deus spiritus, spiritus etiam corpus est, sui generis, in sua effigie.'* [Who will deny that God is body? Although God is spirit, yet spirit is body, of his own nature, in his own image,]

St. Justin Martyr says 'το θειον φαμεν ειναι ασωματον ουκ ότι ασωματον·— επειδη δε το μηκρατεισθαι ύπο τινος, του κρατεισθαι τιμιωτερον εστι, δια τουτο καλουμεν αυτον ασωματον' ['We say that the divinity is incorporeal, not that it is bodyless, but since the state of not being bounded by anything is a more honorable one than that of being bounded, for this reason we call him incorporeal.'] And St. Macarius, speaking of angels says *'quamvis enim subtilia sint, tamen in substantiâ, formâ et figurâ, secundum tenuitatem naturae eorum, corpora sunt tenuia.'* [For although their bodies are of light texture, nevertheless in substance, form, and figure, their bodies are rare, according to the rarity of their nature.] And St. Austin, St. Basil, Lactantius, Tatian, Athenagoras and others, with whose writings I pretend not a familiarity, are said by those who are, to deliver the same doctrine. Turn to your Ocellus d'Argens 97. 105. and to his Timaeus 17. for these quotations. In England these Immaterialists might have been burnt until the 29. Car. 2. when the writ de haeretico comburendo was abolished: and here until the revolution, that statute not having extended to us. All heresies being now done away with us, these schismatists are merely atheists, differing from the material Atheist only in their belief that 'nothing made something,' and from the material deist who believes that matter alone can operate on matter.

Rejecting all organs of information, therefore, but my senses, I rid myself of the Pyrrhonisms with which an indulgence in speculations hyperphysical and antiphysical, so uselessly occupy and disquiet the mind. A single sense may indeed be sometimes deceived, but rarely; and never all our senses together, with their faculty of reasoning. They evidence realities, and there are enough of these for all the purposes of life, without plunging into the fathomless abyss of dreams and phantasms. I am satisfied, and sufficiently occupied with the things which are, without tormenting or troubling myself about those which may indeed be, but of which I have no evidence. I am sure that I really know many, many things, and none more surely than that I love you with all my heart, and pray for the continuence of your life until you shall be tired of it yourself.

THOMAS JEFFERSON TO JACOB DE LA MOTTA
September 1, 1820

Th. Jefferson returns his thanks to Dr. De La Motta for the eloquent discourse on the Consecration of the Synagogue of Savannah, which he has been so kind as to send him. It excites in him the gratifying reflection that his country has been the first to prove to the world two truths, the most salutary to human society, that man can govern himself, and that religious freedom is the most effectual anodyne against religious dissension: the maxim of civil government being reversed in that of religion, where its true form is "divided we stand, united, we fall." He is happy in the restoration of the Jews, particularly, to their social rights, and hopes they will be seen taking their seats on the benches of science as preparatory to their doing the same at the board of government. He salutes Dr. De La Motta with sentiments of great respect.

THOMAS JEFFERSON TO REVEREND JARED SPARKS
November 4, 1820

Your favor of Sep. 18 is just recieved, with the book accompanying it. It's delay was owing to that of the box of books from Mr. Guegan, in which it was packed. Being just setting out on a journey I have time only to look over the summary of contents. In this I see nothing in which I am likely to differ materially from you. I hold the precepts of Jesus, as delivered by himself, to be the most pure, benevolent, and sublime which have ever been preached to man. I adhere to the principles of the first age; and consider all subsequent innovations as corruptions of his religion, having no foundation in what came from him. The metaphysical insanities of Athanasius, of Loyola, and of Calvin, are, to my understanding, mere relapses into polytheism, differing from paganism only by being more unintelligible. The religion of Jesus is founded in the Unity of God, and this principle chiefly, gave it triumph over the rabble of heathen gods then acknoleged. Thinking men of all nations rallied readily to the doctrine of one only god, and embraced it with the pure morals which Jesus inculcated. If the freedom of religion, guaranteed to us by law in theory, can ever rise in practice under the overbearing inquisition of public opinion, truth will prevail over fanaticism, and the genuine doctrines of Jesus, so long perverted by His pseudo priests, will again be restored to their original purity. This reformation will advance with the other improvements of the human mind but too late for me to witness it. Accept my thanks for your book, in which I shall read with pleasure your developments of the subject, and with them the assurance of my high respect.

THOMAS JEFFERSON, *AUTOBIOGRAPHY*
January 6 - July 29, 1821

My father's education had been quite neglected; but being of a strong mind, sound judgment and eager after information, he read much and improved himself.... He placed me at the English school at 5. years of age and at the Latin at 9. where I continued until his death. My teacher Mr. Douglas a clergyman from Scotland was but a superficial Latinist, less instructed in Greek, but with the rudiments of these languages he taught me French, and on the death of my father I went to the revd Mr. Maury a correct classical scholar, with whom I continued two years, and then went to Wm. and Mary college....

In 1769, I became a member of the legislature by the choice of the county in which I live, & continued in that until it was closed by the revolution. I made one effort in that body for the permission of the emancipation of slaves, which was rejected: and indeed, during the regal government, nothing liberal could expect success. Our minds were circumscribed within narrow limits by an habitual belief that it was our duty to be subordinate to the mother country in all matters of government, to direct all our labors in subservience to her interests, and even to observe a bigoted intolerance for all religions but hers....

The next event which excited our sympathies for Massachusetts was the Boston port bill, by which that port was to be shut up on the 1st of June, 1774.... We were under conviction of the necessity of arousing our people from the lethargy into which they had fallen as to passing events; and thought that the appointment of a day of general fasting & prayer would be most likely to call up & alarm their attention. No example of such a solemnity had existed since the days of our distresses in the war of 55. since which a new generation had grown up. With the help therefore of Rushworth, whom we rummaged over for the revolutionary precedents & forms of the Puritans of that day, preserved by him, we cooked up a resolution, somewhat modernizing their phrases, for appointing the 1st day of June, on which the Port bill was to commence, for a day of fasting, humiliation & prayer, to implore heaven to avert from us the evils of civil war, to inspire us with firmness in support of our rights, and to turn the hearts of the King & parliament to moderation & justice. To give greater emphasis to our proposition, we agreed to wait the next morning on Mr. Nicholas, whose grave & religious character was more in unison with the tone of our resolution and to solicit him to move it. We accordingly went to him in the morning. He moved it the same day; the 1st of June was proposed and it passed without opposition....

The first settlers of this colony were Englishmen, loyal subjects to their king and church, and the grant to Sr. Walter Raleigh contained an express Proviso that their laws "should not be against the true Christian faith, now professed in the church of England." As soon as the state of the colony admitted, it was divided into parishes, in each of which was established a minister of the Anglican church, endowed with a fixed salary, in tobacco, a glebe house and land with the other necessary appendages. To meet these expenses all the inhabitants of the parishes were assessed, whether they were or not, members of the established church. Towards Quakers who came here they were most cruelly intolerant, driving them from the colony by the severest penalties. In process of time however, other sectarisms were introduced, chiefly of the Presbyterian family; and the established clergy, secure for life in their glebes and salaries, adding to these generally the emoluments of a classical school, found employment enough, in their farms and schoolrooms for the rest of the week, and devoted Sunday only to the edification of their flock, by service, and a sermon at their parish church. Their other pastoral functions were little attended to. Against this inactivity the zeal and industry of sectarian preachers had an open and undisputed field; and by the time of the revolution, a majority of the inhabitants had become dissenters from the established church, but were still obliged to pay contributions to support the Pastors of the minority. This unrighteous compulsion to maintain teachers of what they deemed religious errors was grievously felt during the regal government, and without a hope of relief. But the first republican legislature which met in 76. was crowded with petitions to abolish this spiritual tyranny. These brought on the severest contests in which I have ever been engaged. Our great opponents were Mr. Pendleton & Robert Carter Nicholas, honest men, but zealous churchmen. The petitions were referred to the commee of the whole house on the state of the country; and after desperate contests in that committee, almost daily from the 11th of Octob. to the 5th of December, we prevailed so far only as to repeal the laws which rendered criminal the maintenance of any religious opinions, the forbearance of repairing to church, or the exercise of any mode of worship: and further, to exempt dissenters from contributions to the support of the established church; and to suspend, only until the next session levies on the members of that church for the salaries of their own incumbents. For although the majority of our citizens were dissenters, as has been observed, a majority of the legislature were churchmen. Among these however were some reasonable and liberal men, who enabled us, on some points, to obtain feeble majorities. But our opponents carried in the general resolutions of the commee of Nov. 19. a declaration that religious assemblies ought to be regulated, and that provision ought to be made for continuing the succession of the clergy, and superintending their conduct. And in the bill now passed was inserted an express reservation of the question, Whether a general assessment should not be established by law, on every one, to the support of the pastor of his choice; or whether all should be left to voluntary contributions; and on this question, debated at every session from 76 to 79 (some of our dissenting allies, having now secured their particular object, going over to the advocates of a general assessment) we could only obtain a suspension from session to session until 79. when the question against a general assessment was finally carried, and the establishment of the Anglican church entirely put down. In justice to the two honest but zealous opponents, who have been named I must add that altho', from their natural temperaments, they were more disposed generally to acquiesce in things as they are, than to risk innovations, yet whenever the public will had once decided, none were more faithful or exact in their obedience to it....

So far we were proceeding in the details of reformation only; selecting points of legislation prominent in character & principle, urgent, and indicative of the strength of the general pulse of reformation. When I left Congress, in 76. it was in the persuasion that our whole code must be reviewed, adapted to our republican form of government, and, now that we had no negatives of Councils, Governors & Kings to restrain us from doing right, that it should be corrected, in all it's parts, with a single eye to reason, & the good of those for whose government it was framed....

I proposed to abolish the law of primogeniture, and to make real estate descendible in parcenary to the next of kin, as personal property is by the statute of distribution. Mr. Pendleton wished to preserve the right of primogeniture, but seeing at once that that could not prevail, he proposed we should adopt the Hebrew principle, and give a double portion to the elder son. I observed that if the eldest son could eat twice as much, or do double work, it might be a natural evidence of his right to a double portion; but being on a par in his powers & wants, with his brothers and sisters, he should be on a par also in the partition of the patrimony, and such was the decision of the other members....

On the subject of the Criminal law, all were agreed that the punishment of death should be abolished, except for treason and murder; and that, for other felonies should be substituted hard labor in the public works, and in some cases, the *Lex talionis*. How this last revolting principle came to obtain our approbation, I do not remember. There remained indeed in our laws a vestige of it in a single case of a slave. It was the English law in the time of the Anglo-Saxons, copied probably from the Hebrew law of "an eye for an eye, a tooth for a tooth," and it was the law of several antient people. But the modern mind had left it far in the rear of it's advances....

The bill for establishing religious freedom, the principles of which had, to a certain degree, been enacted before, I had drawn in all the latitude of reason & right. It still met with opposition; but, with some mutilations in the preamble, it was finally passed; and a singular proposition proved that it's protection of opinion was meant to be universal. Where the preamble declares that coercion is a departure from the plan of the holy author of our religion, an amendment was proposed, by inserting the word "Jesus Christ," so that it should read "a departure from the plan of Jesus Christ, the holy author of our religion." The insertion was rejected by a great majority, in proof that they meant to comprehend, within the mantle of it's protection, the Jew and the Gentile, the Christian and Mahometan, the Hindoo, and infidel of every denomination....

The second bill proposed to amend the constitution of Wm. & Mary College, to enlarge it's sphere of science, and to make it in fact an University.... The College of Wm. & Mary was an establishment purely of the Church of England, the Visitors were required to be all of that Church; the Professors to subscribe it's 39 Articles, it's Students to learn it's Catechism, and one of its fundamental objects was declared to be to raise up Ministers for that church. The religious jealousies therefore of all the dissenters took alarm lest this might give an ascendancy to the Anglican sect and refused acting on that bill....

The bill on the subject of slaves was a mere digest of the existing laws respecting them, without any intimation of a plan for a future & general emancipation. It was thought better that this should be kept back, and attempted only by way of amendment whenever the bill should be brought on. The principles of the amendment however were agreed on, that is to say, the freedom of all born after a certain day, and deportation at a proper age. But it was found that the public mind would not yet bear the proposition, nor will it bear it even at this day. Yet the day is not distant when it must bear and adopt it, or worse will follow. Nothing is more certainly written in the book of fate than that these people are to be free. Nor is it less certain that the two races, equally free, cannot live in the same government. Nature, habit, opinion has drawn indelible lines of distinction between them. It is still in our power to direct the process of emancipation and deportation peaceably and in such slow degree as that the evil will wear off insensibly, and their place be *pari passu* [at an equal pace] filled up by free white laborers. If on the contrary it is left to force itself on, human nature must shudder at the prospect held up. We should in vain look for an example in the Spanish deportation or deletion of the Moors. This precedent would fall far short of our case.

The restoration of the rights of conscience relieved the people from taxation for the support of a religion not theirs; for the establishment was truly of the religion of the rich, the dissenting sects being entirely composed of the less wealthy people; and these, by the bill for a general education, would be qualified to understand their rights, to maintain them, and to exercise with intelligence their parts in self-government: and all this would be effected without the violation of a single natural right of any one individual citizen....

On the 1st of June 1779. I was appointed Governor of the Commonwealth and retired from the legislature. Being elected also one of the Visitors of Wm. & Mary college, a self-electing body, I effected, during my residence in Williamsburg that year, a change in the organization of that institution by abolishing the Grammar school, and the two professorships of Divinity & Oriental languages, and substituting a professorship of Law & Police, one of Anatomy Medicine and Chemistry, and one of Modern languages; and the charter confining us to six professorships, we added the law of Nature & Nations, & the Fine Arts to the duties of the Moral professor, and Natural history to those of the professor of Mathematics and Natural philosophy....

On the 7th. of May [1784] Congress resolved that a Minister Plenipotentiary should be appointed in addition to Mr. Adams & Dr. Franklin for negotiating treaties of commerce with foreign nations, and I was elected to that duty....

During the war of Independance, while the pressure of an external enemy hooped us together, and their enterprises kept us necessarily on the alert, the spirit of the people, excited by danger, was a supplement to the Confederation, and urged them to zealous exertions, whether claimed by that instrument, or not.... Yet this state of things afforded a happy augury of the future march of our confederacy, when it was seen that the good sense and good dispositions of the people, as soon as they perceived the incompetence of their first compact, instead of leaving it's correction to insurrection and civil war, agreed with one voice to elect deputies to a general convention, who should peaceably meet and agree on such a constitution as "would ensure peace, justice, liberty, the common defence & general welfare."

This Convention met at Philadelphia on the 25th. of May '87. It sat with closed doors and kept all it's proceedings secret, until it's dissolution on the 17th. of September, when the results of their labors were published all together. I received a copy early in November, and read and contemplated it's provisions with great satisfaction. As not a member of the Convention however, nor probably a single citizen of the Union, had approved it in all it's parts, so I too found articles which I thought objectionable. The absence of express declarations ensuring freedom of religion, freedom of the press, freedom of the person under the uninterrupted protection of the Habeas corpus, & trial by jury in civil as well as in criminal cases excited my jealousy; and the re-eligibility of the President for life, I quite disapproved. I expressed freely in letters to my friends, and most particularly to Mr. Madison & General Washington, my approbations and objections. How the good should be secured, and the ill brought to rights was the difficulty. To refer it back to a new Convention might endanger the loss of the whole. My first idea was that the 9. states first acting should accept it unconditionally, and thus secure what in it was good, and that the 4. last should accept on the previous condition that certain amendments should be agreed to, but a better course was devised of accepting the whole and trusting that the good sense & honest intentions of our citizens would make the alterations which should be deemed necessary. Accordingly all accepted, 6. without objection, and 7. with recommendations of specified amendments. Those respecting the press, religion, & juries, with several others, of great value, were accordingly made; but the Habeas corpus was left to the discretion of Congress, and the amendment against the reeligibility of the President was not proposed by that body....

Mr. Adams ... was now elected Vice President of the U. S. was soon to return to America, and.... our bankers in Amsterdam had notified me that the interest on our general debt would be expected in June; that if we failed to pay it, it would be deemed an act of bankruptcy and would effectually destroy the credit of the U S.... On my return from Holland, I had found Paris still in high fermentation as I had left it. Had the Archbishop, on the close of the assembly of Notables, immediately carried into operation the measures contemplated, it was believed they would all have been registered by the parliament, but he was slow, presented his edicts, one after another, & at considerable intervals of time, which gave time for the feelings excited by the proceedings of the Notables to cool off, new claims to be advanced, and a pressure to arise for a fixed constitution, not subject to changes at the will of the King. Nor should we wonder at this pressure when we consider the monstrous abuses of power under which this people were ground to powder, when we pass in review the weight of their taxes, and inequality of their distribution; the oppressions of the tythes, of the tailles, the corvees, the gabelles, the farms & barriers; the shackles on Commerce by monopolies; on Industry by gilds & corporations; on the freedom of conscience, of thought, and of speech; on the Press by the Censure; and of person by lettres de Cachet; the cruelty of the criminal code generally, the atrocities of the Rack, the venality of judges, and their partialities to the rich; the Monopoly of Military honors by the Noblesse; the enormous expenses of the Queen, the princes & the Court; the prodigalities of pensions; & the riches, luxury, indolence & immorality of the clergy. Surely under such a mass of misrule and oppression, a people might justly press for a thoro' reformation, and might even dismount their rough-shod riders, & leave them to walk on their own legs....

The parliament immediately protested that the votes for the enregistry had not been legally taken, and that they gave no sanction to the loans proposed. This was enough to discredit and defeat them.... and the Archbishop finding the times beyond his faculties, accepted the promise of a Cardinal's hat, was removed [Sep. 88] from the ministry, and Mr. Necker was called to the department of finance....

The effect of this change of ministers, and the promise of the States General at an early day, tranquillized the nation. But two great questions now occurred. 1. What proportion shall the number of deputies of the tiers etat bear to those of the Nobles and Clergy? And 2. shall they sit in the same, or in distinct apartments? Mr. Necker, desirous of avoiding himself these knotty questions, proposed a second call of the same Notables, and that their advice should be asked on the subject. They met Nov. 9. 88. and, by five bureaux against one, they recommended the forms of the States General of 1614. wherein the houses were separate, and voted by orders, not by persons. But the whole nation declaring at once against this, and that the tiers etat should be, in numbers, equal to both the other orders, and the Parliament deciding for the same proportion, it was determined so to be, by a declaration of Dec. 27. 88.... concessions came from the very heart of the King. He had not a wish but for the good of the nation, and for that object no personal sacrifice would ever have cost him a moment's regret. But his mind was weakness itself, his constitution timid, his judgment null, and without sufficient firmness even to stand by the faith of his word. His Queen too, haughty and bearing no contradiction, had an absolute ascendency over him; and around her were rallied the King's brother d'Artois, the court generally, and the aristocratic part of his ministers.... Against this host the good counsels of Necker, Montmorin, St. Priest, altho' in unison with the wishes of the King himself, were of little avail. The resolutions of the morning formed under their advice, would be reversed in the evening by the influence of the Queen & court. But the hand of heaven weighed heavily indeed on the machinations of this junto; producing collateral incidents, not arising out of the case, yet powerfully co-exciting the nation to force a regeneration of it's government, and overwhelming with accumulated difficulties this liberticide resistance. For, while laboring under the want of money for even ordinary purposes, in a government which required a million of livres a day, and driven to the last ditch by the universal call for liberty, there came on a winter of such severe cold, as was without example in the memory of man, or in the written records of history....

So great indeed was the scarcity of bread that from the highest to the lowest citizen, the bakers were permitted to deal but a scanty allowance per head, even to those who paid for it; and in cards of invitation to dine in the richest houses, the guest was notified to bring his own bread. To eke out the existence of the people, every person who had the means, was called on for a weekly subscription, which the Cures collected and employed in providing messes for the nourishment of the poor, and vied with each other in devising such economical compositions of food as would subsist the greatest number with the smallest means....

The States General were opened on the 5th. of May 89.... The composition of the assembly, altho' equivalent on the whole to what had been expected, was something different in it's elements. It has been supposed that a superior education would carry into the scale of the Commons a respectable portion of the Noblesse. It did so as to those of Paris, of it's vicinity and of the other considerable cities, whose greater intercourse with enlightened society had liberalized their minds, and prepared them to advance up to the measure of the times. But the Noblesse of the country, which constituted two thirds of that body, were far in their rear.... They were willing to submit to equality of taxation, but not to descend from their rank and prerogatives to be incorporated in session with the tiers etat. Among the clergy, on the other hand, it had been apprehended that the higher orders of the hierarchy, by their wealth and connections, would have carried the elections generally. But it proved that in most cases the lower clergy had obtained the popular majorities. These consisted of the Cures, sons of the peasantry who had been employed to do all the drudgery of parochial services for 10. 20. or 30 Louis a year; while their superiors were consuming their princely revenues in palaces of luxury & indolence....

The objects for which this body was convened being of the first order of importance, I felt it very interesting to understand the views of the parties of which it was composed, and especially the ideas prevalent as to the organization contemplated for their government. I went therefore daily from Paris to Versailles.... As preliminary to all other business, the awful questions came on, Shall the States sit in one, or in distinct apartments? And shall they vote by heads or houses? The opposition was soon found to consist of the Episcopal order among the clergy, and two thirds of the Noblesse; while the tiers etat were, to a man, united and determined. After various propositions of compromise had failed, the Commons undertook to cut the Gordian knot. The Abbe Sieyes, the most logical head of the nation, (author of the pamphlet *Qu'est ce que le tiers etat?* [What is the 3rd Estate?] which had electrified that country, as Paine's Common sense did us, after an impressive speech on the 10th of June, moved that a last invitation should be sent to the Nobles and Clergy, to attend in the Hall of the States, collectively or individually for the verification of powers, to which the commons would proceed immediately, either in their presence or absence. This verification being finished, a motion was made, on the 15th. that they should constitute themselves a National assembly; which was decided on the 17th. by a majority of four fifths. During the debates on this question, about twenty of the Cures had joined them, and a proposition was made in the chamber of the clergy that their whole body should join them. This was rejected at first by a small majority only; but, being afterwards somewhat modified, it was decided affirmatively, by a majority of eleven. While this was under debate and unknown to the court, to wit, on the 19th. a council was held in the afternoon at Marly, wherein it was proposed that the King should interpose by a declaration of his sentiments, in a séance royale. A form of declaration was proposed by Necker, which, while it censured in general the proceedings both of the Nobles and Commons, announced the King's views, such as substantially to coincide with the Commons. It was agreed to in council, the séance was fixed for the 22d. the meetings of the States were till then to be suspended, and everything, in the meantime, kept secret. The members the next morning (20th.) repairing to their house as usual, found the doors shut and guarded, a proclamation posted up for a seance royale on the 22d. and a suspension of their meetings in the meantime. Concluding that their dissolution was now to take place, they repaired to a building called the *"Jeu de paume"* (or Tennis court) and there bound themselves by oath to each other, never to separate of their own accord, till they had settled a constitution for the nation, on a solid basis, and if separated by force, that they would reassemble in some other place. The next day they met in the church of St. Louis, and were joined by a majority of the clergy....

The court party were now all rage and desperate. They procured a committee to be held consisting of the King and his ministers, to which Monsieur & the Count d'Artois should be admitted.... The Noblesse were in triumph; the people in consternation. I was quite alarmed at this state of things. The soldiery had not yet indicated which side they should take, and that which they should support would be sure to prevail. I considered a successful reformation of government in France, as ensuring a general reformation thro' Europe, and the resurrection, to a new life, of their people, now ground to dust by the abuses of the governing powers. I was much acquainted with the leading patriots of the assembly. Being from a country which had successfully passed thro' a similar reformation, they were disposed to my acquaintance, and had some confidence in me. I urged most strenuously an immediate compromise; to secure what the government was now ready to yield, and trust to future occasions for what might still be wanting. It was well understood that the King would grant at this time 1. Freedom of the person by Habeas corpus. 2. Freedom of conscience. 3. Freedom of the press. 4. Trial by jury. 5. A representative legislature. 6. Annual meetings. 7. The origination of laws. 8. The exclusive right of taxation and appropriation. And 9. The responsibility of ministers; and with the exercise of these powers they would obtain in future whatever might be further necessary to improve and preserve their constitution. They thought otherwise however, and events have proved their lamentable error. For after 30. years of war, foreign and domestic, the loss of millions of lives, the prostration of private happiness, and foreign subjugation of their own country for a time, they have obtained no more, nor even that securely....

When the King passed, the next day, thro' the lane formed from the Chateau to the Hotel des etats, there was a dead silence. He was about an hour in the House delivering his speech & declaration. On his coming out a feeble cry of "Vive le Roy" was raised by some children, but the people remained silent & sullen. In the close of his speech he had ordered that the members should follow him, & resume their deliberations the next day. The Noblesse followed him, and so did the clergy, except about thirty, who, with the tiers, remained in the room, and entered into deliberation....

The King went out to ride.... As Mr. Necker followed him universal acclamations were raised of "vive Monsr. Necker, vive le sauveur de la France opprimee." He was conducted back to his house with the same demonstrations of affection and anxiety. About 200. deputies of the Tiers, catching the enthusiasm of the moment, went to his house, and extorted from him a promise that he would not resign. On the 25th. 48. of the Nobles joined the tiers, & among them the D. of Orleans. There were then with them 164 members of the Clergy, altho' the minority of that body still sat apart & called themselves the chamber of the clergy. On the 26th. the Archbp. of Paris joined the tiers, as did some others of the clergy and of the Noblesse.

These proceedings had thrown the people into violent ferment. It gained the souldiery.... They began to quit their barracks, to assemble in squads, to declare they would defend the life of the King, but would not be the murderers of their fellow-citizens.... The operation of this medicine at Versailles was as sudden as it was powerful. The alarm there was so compleat that in the afternoon of the 27th. the King wrote with his own hand letters to the Presidents of the clergy and Nobles, engaging them immediately to join the Tiers. These two bodies were debating & hesitating when notes from the Ct. d'Artois decided their compliance. They went in a body and took their seats with the tiers, and thus rendered the union of the orders in one chamber compleat....

The Assembly now entered on the business of their mission, and first proceeded to arrange the order in which they would take up the heads of their constitution.... But the quiet of their march was soon disturbed by information that troops, and particularly the foreign troops, were advancing on Paris from various quarters.... This drew people to the spot, who thus accidentally found themselves in front of the troops, merely at first as spectators; but as their numbers increased, their indignation rose. They retired a few steps, and posted themselves on and behind large piles of stones, large and small, collected in that Place for a bridge which was to be built adjacent to it. In this position, happening to be in my carriage on a visit, I passed thro' the lane they had formed, without interruption. But the moment after I had passed, the people attacked the cavalry with stones....

The people, now openly joined by the French guards, force the prison of St. Lazare, release all the prisoners, and take a great store of corn, which they carry to the Corn-market. Here they get some arms, and the French guards begin to form & train them. The City-committee determined to raise 48.000. Bourgeoise, or rather to restrain their numbers to 48.000. On the 14th. they send one of their members (Mons. de Corny) to the Hotel des Invalides, to ask arms for their Garde-Bourgeoise....

M. de Corny and five others were then sent to ask arms of M. de Launay, governor of the Bastille. They found a great collection of people already before the place, and they immediately planted a flag of truce, which was answered by a like flag hoisted on the Parapet. The deputation prevailed on the people to fall back a little, advanced themselves to make their demand of the Governor, and in that instant a discharge from the Bastille killed four persons, of those nearest to the deputies. The deputies retired. I happened to be at the house of M. de Corny when he returned to it, and received from him a narrative of these transactions. On the retirement of the deputies, the people rushed forward & almost in an instant were in possession of a fortification defended by 100. men, of infinite strength, which in other times had stood several regular sieges, and had never been taken. How they forced their entrance has never been explained....

The demolition of the Bastille was now ordered and begun.... Every minister resigned.... and the next morning the Count D'Artois and M. de Montesson a deputy connected with him, Madame de Polignac, Madame de Guiche, and the Count de Vaudreuil, favorites of the queen, the Abbe de Vermont her confessor, the Prince of Conde and Duke of Bourbon fled....

The King landed at the Hotel de Ville. There M. Bailly presented and put into his hat the popular cockade, and addressed him. The King being unprepared, and unable to answer, Bailly went to him, gathered from him some scraps of sentences, and made out an answer, which he delivered to the audience as from the king. On their return the popular cries were *"vive le roy et la nation"*....

And here again was lost another precious occasion of sparing to France the crimes and cruelties thro' which she has since passed, and to Europe, & finally America the evils which flowed on them also from this mortal source. The king was now become a passive machine in the hands of the National assembly, and had he been left to himself, he would have willingly acquiesced in whatever they should devise as best for the nation. A wise constitution would have been formed, hereditary in his line, himself placed at it's head, with powers so large as to enable him to do all the good of his station, and so limited as to restrain him from it's abuse. This he would have faithfully administered, and more than this I do not believe he ever wished. But he had a Queen of absolute sway over his weak mind, and timid virtue; and of a character the reverse of his in all points.... I have ever believed that had there been no queen, there would have been no revolution....

The deed which closed the mortal course of these sovereigns, I shall neither approve nor condemn. I am not prepared to say that the first magistrate of a nation cannot commit treason against his country, or is unamenable to it's punishment.... Of those who judged the king, many thought him wilfully criminal, many that his existence would keep the nation in perpetual conflict with the horde of kings, who would war against a regeneration which might come home to themselves, and that it were better that one should die than all. I should not have voted with this portion of the legislature. I should have shut up the Queen in a Convent, putting harm out of her power, and placed the king in his station, investing him with limited powers, which I verily believe he would have honestly exercised, according to the measure of his understanding....

M. Necker had reached Basle before he was overtaken by the letter of the king, inviting him back.... and... a new administration was named, to wit St. Priest & Montmorin were restored; the Archbishop of Bordeaux was appointed Garde des sceaux [Keeper of the Seal]....

In the evening of Aug. 4.... the assembly abolished all titles of rank, all the abusive privileges of feudalism, the tythes and casuals of the clergy, all provincial privileges, and, in fine, the Feudal regimen generally. To the suppression of tythes the Abbe Sieyes was vehemently opposed; but his learned and logical arguments were unheeded, and his estimation lessened by a contrast of his egoism (for he was beneficed on them) with the generous abandonment of rights by the other members of the assembly....

They then appointed a Committee for the "reduction of a projet" of a Constitution, at the head of which was the Archbishop of Bordeaux. I received from him, as Chairman of the Committee a letter of July 20. requesting me to attend and assist at their deliberations; but I excused myself on the obvious considerations that my mission was to the king as Chief Magistrate of the nation, that my duties were limited to the concerns of my own country, and forbade me to intermeddle with the internal transactions of that in which I had been received under a specific character only....

These questions found strong differences of opinion, and produced repulsive combinations among the Patriots. The Aristocracy was cemented by a common principle of preserving the ancient regime, or whatever should be nearest to it.... In this uneasy state of things, I received one day a note from the Marquis de La Fayette, informing me that he should bring a party of six or eight friends to ask a dinner of me the next day.... These were leading patriots, of honest but differing opinions sensible of the necessity of effecting a coalition by mutual sacrifices, knowing each other, and not afraid therefore to unbosom themselves mutually. This last was a material principle in the selection. With this view the Marquis had invited the conference and had fixed the time & place inadvertently as to the embarrassment under which it might place me.

The discussions began at the hour of four, and were continued till ten o'clock in the evening; during which time I was a silent witness to a coolness and candor of argument unusual in the conflicts of political opinion; to a logical reasoning, and chaste eloquence, disfigured by no gaudy tinsel of rhetoric or declamation, and truly worthy of being placed in parallel with the finest dialogues of antiquity....

The Patriots all rallied to the principles thus settled, carried every question agreeably to them, and reduced the Aristocracy to insignificance and impotence. But duties of exculpation were now incumbent on me. I waited on Count Montmorin the next morning, and explained to him with truth and candor how it had happened that my house had been made the scene of conferences of such a character. He told me he already knew everything which had passed, that, so far from taking umbrage at the use made of my house on that occasion, he earnestly wished I would habitually assist at such conferences, being sure I should be useful in moderating the warmer spirits, and promoting a wholesome and practicable reformation only. I told him I knew too well the duties I owed to the king, to the nation, and to my own country to take any part in councils concerning their internal government, and that I should persevere with care in the character of a neutral and passive spectator, with wishes only and very sincere ones, that those measures might prevail which would be for the greatest good of the nation.....

Here I discontinue my relation of the French revolution. The minuteness with which I have so far given it's details is disproportioned to the general scale of my narrative. But I have thought it justified by the interest which the whole world must take in this revolution. As yet we are but in the first chapter of it's history. The appeal to the rights of man, which had been made in the U. S. was taken up by France, first of the European nations. From her the spirit has spread over those of the South. The tyrants of the North have allied indeed against it, but it is irresistible. Their opposition will only multiply it's millions of human victims; their own satellites will catch it, and the condition of man thro' the civilized world will be finally and greatly ameliorated. This is a wonderful instance of great events from small causes. So inscrutable is the arrangement of causes & consequences in this world that a two-penny duty on tea, unjustly imposed in a sequestered part of it, changes the condition of all it's inhabitants.

THOMAS JEFFERSON TO FRANCIS EPPES
January 19, 1821

Editor's note: Viscount Henry Bolingbroke's writings were a major influence on Jefferson's collegiate thinking on religion. He copied out or paraphrased many of his statements on Christianity and general philosophy.

You ask my opinion of Lord Bolingbroke and Thomas Paine. They were alike in making bitter enemies of the priests and pharisees of their day. Both were honest men; both advocates for human liberty. Paine wrote for a country which permitted him to push his reasoning to whatever length it would go. Lord Bolingbroke in one restrained by a constitution, and by public opinion. He was called indeed a tory; but his writings prove him a stronger advocate for liberty than any of his countrymen, the whigs of the present day. Irritated by his exile, he committed one act unworthy of him, in connecting himself momentarily with a prince rejected by his country. But he redeemed that single act by his establishment of the principles which proved it to be wrong. These two persons differed remarkably in the style of their writing, each leaving a model of what is most perfect in both extremes of the simple and the sublime. No writer has exceeded Paine in ease and familiarity of style, in perspicuity of expression, happiness of elucidation, and in simple and unassuming language. In this he may be compared with Dr. Franklin; and indeed his *Common Sense* was, for awhile, believed to have been written by Dr. Franklin, and published under the borrowed name of Paine, who had come over with him from England. Lord Bolingbroke's, on the other hand, is a style of the highest order. The lofty, rhythmical, full-flowing eloquence of Cicero. Periods of just measure, their members proportioned, their close full and round. His conceptions, too, are bold and strong, his diction copious, polished and commanding as his subject. His writings are certainly the finest samples in the English language, of the eloquence proper for the Senate. His political tracts are safe reading for the most timid religionist, his philosophical, for those who are not afraid to trust their reason with discussions of right and wrong.

You have asked my opinion of these persons, and, to you, I have given it freely. But, remember, that I am old, that I wish not to make new enemies, nor to give offence to those who would consider a difference of opinion as sufficient ground for unfriendly dispositions.

God bless you, and make you what I wish you to be.

THOMAS JEFFERSON TO JOHN ADAMS
January 22, 1821

Editor's note: Adams had proposed that Massachusetts abolish state constitutional recognition of religious groups.

I was quite rejoiced, dear Sir, to see that you had the health and spirits enough to take part in the late convention of your state for revising its constitution, and to bear your share in its debates and labors. The amendments of which we have as yet heard prove the advance of liberalism in the intervening period; and encourage a hope that the human mind will some day get back the freedom it enjoyed 2000 years ago. This country, which has given to the world the example of physical liberty, owes to it that of moral emancipation also. For, as yet, it is but nominal with us. The inquisition of public opinion overwhelms in practice the freedom asserted by the laws in theory....

But let us turn from our own uneasiness to the miseries of our Southern friends. Bolivar and Morillo it seems, have come to a parlay with dispositions at length to stop the useless effusions of human blood in that quarter. I feared from the beginning that these people were not yet sufficiently enlightened for self-government.... For freedom of religion they are not yet prepared. The scales of bigotry are not sufficiently fallen from their eyes to accept it for themselves individually, much less to trust others with it. But that will come in time, as well as a general ripeness to break entirely from the parent stem.

You see, my dear Sir, how easily we prescribe for others a cure for their difficulties, while we cannot cure our own. We must leave both, I believe, to heaven, and wrap ourselves up in the mantle of resignation, and of friendship of which I tender you the most sincere assurances.

THOMAS JEFFERSON TO TIMOTHY PICKERING
February 27, 1821

I thank you for Mr. Channing's discourse, which you have been so kind as to forward me. It is not yet at hand, but is doubtless on it's way. I had recieved it thro' another channel, and read it with high satisfaction. No one sees with greater pleasure than myself the progress of reason in it's advances toward rational Christianity. When we shall have done away the incomprehensible jargon of the Trinitarian arithmetic, that three are one, and one is three; when we shall have knocked down the artificial scaffolding, reared to mask from view the simple structure of Jesus, when, in short, we shall have unlearned every thing which has been taught since his day, and got back to the pure and simple doctrines he inculcated, we shall then be truly and worthily his disciples: and my opinion is that if nothing had ever been added to what flowed purely from his lips, the whole world would at this day have been Christian. I know that the case that you cite, of Dr. Drake, has been a common one. The religion-builders have so distorted and deformed the doctrines of Jesus, so muffled them in mysticisms, fancies and falsehoods, have caricatured them into forms so monstrous and inconcievable, as to shock reasonable thinkers, to revolt them against the whole, and drive them rashly to pronounce it's founder an impostor. Had there never been a Commentator, there never would have been an infidel. In the present advance of truth, which we both approve, I do not know that you and I may think alike on all points. As the Creator has made no two faces alike, so no two minds, and probably no two creeds. We well know that among Unitarians themselves there are strong shades of difference, as between Doctors Price and Priestley for example. So there may be peculiarities in your creed and in mine. They are honestly formed without doubt. I do not wish to trouble the world with mine, nor be troubled by them. These accounts are to be settled only with him who made us; and to him we leave it, with charity for all others, of whom also he is the only rightful and competent judge. I have little doubt that the whole of our country will soon be rallied to the Unity of the Creator, and, I hope, to the pure doctrines of Jesus also.

In saying to you so much, and without reserve, on a subject on which I never permit myself to go before the public, I know that I am safe against the infidelities which have so often betrayed my letters to the strictures of those for whom they were not written, and to whom I never meant to commit my peace. To yourself I wish every happiness, and will conclude, as you have done, in the same simple style of antiquity, *da operam ut Valeas. Hoc mihi gratius facere nihil potes* [you are able to do nothing more gracious for me than to farewell yourself].

JAMES MADISON TO RICHARD RUSH
November 20, 1821

I have been for some time a debtor for your favor of June 21, which was accompanied by the "Apocryphal New Testament." Accept my thanks for both....

We have seen, not without some little disappointment, the latter development of character in the Emperor Alexander. He is no longer the patron of the liberal ideas of the age, of the independence of nations, and of their relief from the burdens imposed by warlike establishments.... What, too, must be thought of his having no scruples at stepping into the domestic quarrels of Naples against the people contending for their rights, and his scrupling to intermeddle in the domestic affairs of Turkey against the most atrocious of despotisms, wreaking its worst cruelties on a people having peculiar claims to the sympathy of the Christian, as well as the civilized, world?

JAMES MADISON TO F. L. SCHAEFFER
December 3, 1821

I have received, with your letter of November 19th, the copy of your address at the ceremonial of laying the corner-stone of St. Matthew's Church in New York.

It is a pleasing and persuasive example of pious zeal, united with pure benevolence and of a cordial attachment to a particular creed, untinctured with sectarian illiberality. It illustrates the excellence of a system which, by a due distinction, to which the genius and courage of Luther led the way, between what is due and Caesar and what is due God, best promotes the discharge of both obligations. The experience of the United States is a happy disproof of the error so long rooted in the unenlightened minds of well-meaning Christians, as well as in the corrupt hearts of persecuting usurpers, that without a legal incorporation of religious and civil polity, neither could be supported. A mutual independence is found most friendly to practical Religion, to social harmony, and to political prosperity.

THOMAS JEFFERSON TO JEDIDIAH MORSE
March 6, 1822

Editor's note: Jefferson's footnote is bracketed after the sentence to which it refers.

I have duly received your letter of February the 16th, and have now to express my sense of the honorable station proposed to my ex-brethren and myself, in the constitution of the society for the civilization and improvement of the Indian tribes. The object too expressed, as that of the association, is one which I have ever had much at heart, and never omitted an occasion of promoting, while I have been in situations to do it with effect, and nothing, even now, in the calm of age and retirement, would excite in me a more lively interest than an approvable plan of raising that respectable and unfortunate people from the state of physical and moral abjection, to which they have been reduced by circumstances foreign to them. That the plan now proposed is entitled to unmixed approbation, I am not prepared to say, after mature consideration, and with all the partialities which its professed object would rightfully claim from me.

I shall not undertake to draw the line of demarcation between private associations of laudable views and unimposing numbers, and those whose magnitude may rivalise and jeopardise the march of regular government. Yet such a line does exist. I have seen the days, they were those which preceded the Revolution, when even this last and perilous engine became necessary; but they were days which no man would wish to see a second time. That was the case where the regular authorities of the government had combined against the rights of the people, and no means of correction remained to them, but to organise a collateral power, which, with their support, might rescue and secure their violated rights. But such is not the case with our government. We need hazard no collateral power, which, by a change of its original views, and assumption of others we know not how virtuous or how mischievous, would be ready organised and in force sufficient to shake the established foundations of society, and endanger its peace and the principles on which it is based. Is not the machine now proposed of this gigantic stature? It is to consist of the ex-Presidents of the United States, the Vice President, the Heads of all the executive departments, the members of the supreme judiciary, the Governors of the several States and territories, all the members of both Houses of Congress, all the general officers of the army, the commissioners of the navy, all Presidents and Professors of colleges and theological seminaries, all the clergy of the United States, the Presidents and Secretaries of all associations having relation to Indians, all commanding officers within or near Indian territories, all Indian superintendants and agents; all these ex-officio; and as many private individuals as will pay a certain price for membership. Observe too, that the clergy will constitute (1) nineteen twentieths of this association, and, by the law of the majority, may command the twentieth part, which, composed of all the high authorities of the United States, civil and military, may be outvoted and wielded by the nineteen parts with uncontrollable power, both as to purpose and process. [The clergy of the United States may probably be estimated at eight thousand. The residue of this society at four hundred; but if the former number be halved, the reasoning will be the same.] Can this formidable array be reviewed without dismay? It will be said, that in this association will be all the confidential officers of the government; the choice of the people themselves. No man on earth has more implicit confidence than myself in the integrity and discretion of this chosen band of servants. But is confidence or discretion, or is strict limit, the principle of our constitution? It will comprehend, indeed, all the functionaries of the government; but seceded from their constitutional stations as guardians of the nation, and acting not by the laws of their station, but by those of a voluntary society, having no limit to their purposes but the same will which constitutes their existence. It will be the authorities of the people and all influential characters from among them, arrayed on one side, and on the other, the people themselves deserted by their leaders. It is a fearful array. It will be said, that these are imaginary fears. I know they are so at present. I know it is as impossible for these agents of our choice and unbounded confidence, to harbor machinations against the adored principles of our constitution, as for gravity to change its direction, and gravid bodies to mount upwards. The fears are indeed imaginary: but the example is real. Under its authority, as a precedent, future associations will arise with objects at which we should shudder at this time. The society of Jacobins, in another country, was instituted on principles and views as virtuous as ever kindled the hearts of patriots. It was the pure patriotism of their purposes which extended their association to the limits of the nation, and rendered their power within it boundless; and it was this power which degenerated their principles and practices to such enormities, as never before could have been imagined. Yet these were men; and we and our descendants will be no more. The present is a case where, if ever, we are to guard against ourselves; not against ourselves as we are, but as we may be; for who can now imagine what we may become under circumstances not now imaginable? The object too of this institution, seems to require so hazardous an example as little as any which could be proposed. The government is, at this time, going on with the process of civilising the Indians, on a plan probably as promising as any one of us is able to devise, and with resources more competent than we could expect to command by voluntary taxation. Is it that the new characters called into association with those of the government, are wiser than these? Is it that a plan originated by a meeting of private individuals, is better than that prepared by the concentrated wisdom of the nation, of men not self-chosen, but clothed with the full confidence of the people? Is it that there is no danger that a new authority, marching, independently, along side of the government, in the same line and to the same object, may not produce collision, may not thwart and obstruct the operations of the government, or wrest the object entirely from their hands? Might we not as well appoint a committee for each department of the government, to counsel and direct its head separately, as volunteer ourselves to counsel and direct the whole, in mass? And might we not do it as well for their foreign, their fiscal, and their military, as for their Indian affairs? And how many societies, auxiliary to the government, may we expect to see spring up, in imitation of this, offering to associate themselves in this and that of its functions? In a word, why not take the government out of its constitutional hands, associate them indeed with us, to preserve a semblance that the acts are theirs, but insuring them to be our own by allowing them a minor vote only?

These considerations have impressed my mind with a force so irresistible, that (in duty bound to answer your polite letter, without which I should not have obtruded an opinion) I have not been able to withhold the expression of them. Not knowing the individuals who have proposed this plan, I cannot be conceived as entertaining personal disrespect for them. On the contrary, I see in the printed list persons for whom I cherish sentiments of sincere friendship, and others, for whose opinions and purity of purpose I have the highest respect. Yet thinking as I do, that this association is unnecessary; that the government is proceeding to the same object under control of the law; that they are competent to it in wisdom, in means, and inclination.; that this association, this wheel within a wheel, is more likely to produce collision than aid; and that it is, in its magnitude, of dangerous example; I am bound to say, that, as a dutiful citizen, I cannot in conscience become a member of this society, possessing as it does my entire confidence in the integrity of its views. I feel with awe the weight of opinion to which I may be opposed, and that, for myself, I have need to ask the indulgence of a belief that the opinion I have given is the best result I can deduce from my own reason and experience, and that it is sincerely conscientious. Repeating, therefore, my just acknowledgments for the honor proposed to me, I beg leave to add the assurances to the society and yourself of my highest confidence and consideration.

THOMAS JEFFERSON TO THOMAS WHITTEMORE
June 5, 1822

I thank you, Sir, for the pamphlets you have been so kind as to send me, and am happy to learn that the doctrine of Jesus, there is but one God, is advancing prosperously among our fellow-citizens. Had his doctrines, pure as they came from himself, been never sophisticated for unworthy purposes, the whole civilized world would at this day have formed but a single sect. You ask my opinion on the items of doctrine in your catechism. I have never permitted myself to meditate a specific creed. These formulas have been the bane and ruin of the Christian church, it's own fatal invention, which, through so many ages, made of Christendom a slaughterhouse, and at this day divides it into Casts of inextinguishable hatred to one another. Witness the present internecine rage of all other sects against the Unitarian. The religions of antiquity had no particular formulas of creed, those of the modern world none; except those of the religionists calling themselves Christians, and even among these, the Quakers have none. And hence alone the harmony, the quiet, the brotherly affections, the exemplary and unschismatising society of the Friends. And I hope the Unitarians will follow their happy example. — With these sentiments of the mischiefs of creeds and Confessions of faith, I am sure you will excuse my not giving opinions on the items of any particular one; and that you will accept at the same time the assurance of the high respect and consideration which I bear to it's author.

THOMAS JEFFERSON TO DR. BENJAMIN WATERHOUSE
June 26, 1822

Editor's note: Jefferson refers here to Aceldama, the field Judas bought with the money he got by betraying Jesus, hence a field of bloodshed and betrayal.

I have recieved and read with thankfulness and pleasure your denunciation of the abuses of tobacco and wine. Yet, however sound in it's principles, I expect it will be but a sermon to the wind. You will find it as difficult to inculcate these sanative precepts on the sensualists of the present day, as to convince an Athanasian that there is but one God. I wish success to both attempts, and am happy to learn from you that the latter, at least, is making progress, and the more rapidly in proportion as our Platonising Christians make more stir and noise about it.

The doctrines of Jesus are simple, and tend all to the happiness of man.

1. That there is one only God, and he all-perfect.
2. That there is a future state of rewards and punishments.
3. That to love God with all thy heart and thy neighbor as thyself, is the sum of religion.

These are the great points on which he endeavored to reform the religion of the Jews. But compare with these the demoralizing dogmas of Calvin.

1. That there are three Gods.
2. That good works, or the love of our neighbor are nothing.
3. That Faith is every thing; and the more incomprehensible the proposition, the more merit in it's faith.
4. That reason in religion is of unlawful use.
5. That God, from the beginning, elected certain individuals to be saved, and certain others to be damned; and that no crimes of the former can damn them; no virtues of the latter save.

Now, which of these is the true and charitable Christian? He who believes and acts on the simple doctrines of Jesus? Or the impious dogmatists, as Athanasius and Calvin? Verily I say these are the false shepherds foretold as to enter, not by the door into the sheep-fold, but to climb up some other way. They are mere usurpers of the Christian name, teaching a Counter-religion made up of the deliria of crazy imaginations, as foreign from Christianity as is that of Mahomet. Their blasphemies have driven thinking men into infidelity, who have too hastily rejected the supposed Author himself, with the horrors so falsely imputed to him. Had the doctrines of Jesus been preached always as pure as they came from his lips, the whole civilized world would now have been Christian. I rejoice that in this blessed country of free inquiry and belief, which has surrendered it's creed and conscience to neither kings nor priests, the genuine doctrine of one only God is reviving, and I trust that there is not a young man now living in the United States who will not die an Unitarian.

But much I fear, that when this great truth shall be re-established, its Votaries will fall into the fatal error of fabricating formulas of creed and Confessions of faith, the engines which so soon destroyed the religion of Jesus, and made of Christendom a mere Aceldama; that they will give up morals for mysteries, and Jesus for Plato. How much wiser are the Quakers, who, agreeing in the fundamental doctrines of the gospel, schismatize about no mysteries, and, keeping within the pale of Common sense, suffer no speculative differences of opinion, any more than of feature, to impair the love of their brethren. Be this the wisdom of Unitarians; this the holy mantle which shall cover within it's charitable circumference all who believe in one God, and who love their neighbor. — I conclude my sermon with sincere assurances of my friendly esteem and respect.

JAMES MADISON TO EDWARD LIVINGSTON
July 10, 1822

I observe with particular pleasure the view you have taken of the immunity of Religion from civil jurisdiction, in every case where it does not trespass on private rights or the public peace. This has always been a favorite principle with me; and it was not with my approbation, that the deviation from it took place in Congs. when they appointed Chaplains, to be paid from the Natl. Treasury. It would have been a much better proof to their constituents of their pious feeling if the members had contributed for the purpose, a pittance from their own pockets. As the precedent is not likely to be rescinded, the best that can now be done, may be to apply the Constn. the maxim of the law, *de minimis non curat* [the law doesn't care about minute things].

There has been another deviation from the strict principle in the Executive Proclamations of fasts & festivals, so far, at least, as they have spoken the languages of injunction, or have lost sight of the equality of all religious sects in the eye of the Constitution. Whilst I was honored with the Executive Trust I found it necessary on more than one occasion to follow the example of predecessors. But I was always careful to make the Proclamations absolutely indiscriminate, and merely recommendatory; or rather mere designations of a day, on which all who thought proper might unite in consecrating it to religious purposes, according to their own faith & forms. In this sense, I presume you reserve to the Govt. a right to appoint particular days for religious worship throughout the State, without any penal sanction enforcing the worship. I know not what may be the way of thinking on this subject in Louisiana. I should suppose the Catholic portion of the people, at least, as a small & even unpopular sect in the U. States, would rally, as they did in Virga. when religious liberty was a Legislative topic, to its broadest principle. Notwithstanding the general progress made within the two last centuries in favour of this branch of liberty, & the full establishment of it, in some parts of our Country, there remains in others a strong bias towards the old error, that without some sort of alliance or coalition between Govt. & Religion neither can be duly supported. Such indeed is the tendency to such a coalition, and such its corrupting influence on both the parties, that the danger cannot be too carefully guarded agst. And in a Govt. of opinion, like ours, the only effectual guard must be found in the soundness and stability of the general opinion on the subject. Every new & successful example therefore of a perfect separation between ecclesiastical and civil matters, is of importance. And I have no doubt that every new example, will succeed, as every past one has done, in shewing that religion & Govt. will both exist in greater purity, the less they are mixed together. It was the belief of all sects at one time that the establishment of Religion by law, was right & necessary; that the true religion ought to be established in exclusion of every other; And that the only question to be decided was which was the true religion. The example of Holland proved that a toleration of sects, dissenting from the established sect, was safe & even useful. The example of the Colonies, now States, which rejected religious establishments altogether, proved that all Sects might be safely & advantageously put on a footing of equal & entire freedom; and a continuance of their example since the declaration of Independence, has shewn that its success in Colonies was not to be ascribed to their connection with the parent Country. If a further confirmation of the truth could be wanted, it is to be found in the examples furnished by the States, which have abolished their religious establishments. I cannot speak particularly of any of the cases excepting that of Virga. where it is impossible to deny that Religion prevails with more zeal, and a more exemplary priesthood than it ever did when established and patronised by Public authority. We are teaching the world the great truth that Govts. do better without

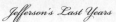

Kings & Nobles than with them. The merit will be doubled by the other lesson that Religion flourishes in greater purity, without than with the aid of Govt.

THOMAS JEFFERSON TO BENJAMIN WATERHOUSE
July 19, 1822

An antiently dislocated, and now stiffening wrist makes writing an operation so slow and painful to me that I should not so soon have troubled you with an acknolegement of your favor of the 8th. but for the request it contained of my consent to the publication of my letter of June 26. No, my dear Sir, not for the world. Into what a nest of hornets would it thrust my head! The *genus irretabile vatum* [the awful race of soothsayers], on whom argument is lost, and reason is, by themselves, disclaimed in matters of religion. Don Quixot undertook to redress the bodily wrongs of the world, but the redressment of mental vagaries would be an enterprise more than Quixotic. I should as soon undertake to bring the crazy skulls of Bedlam to sound understanding, as to inculate reason into that of an Athanasian. I am old, and tranquility is now my *summum bonum* [greatest good]. Keep me therefore from the fires and faggots of Calvin and his victim Servetus. Happy in the prospect of a restoration of primitive Christianity, I must leave to younger Athletes to encounter and lop off the false branches which have been engrafted into it by the mythologies of the middle and modern ages.

I am not aware of the peculiar resistance to Unitarianism which you ascribe to Pennsylvania. When I lived in Philadelphia there was a respectable congregation of that sect, with a meeting house and regular service which I attended, and in which Dr. Priestley officiated to numerous audiences. Baltimore has one or two churches, and their pastor, author of an inestimable book on this subject, was elected Chaplin to the late Congress. That doctrine has not yet been preached to us: but the breeze begins to be felt which precedes the storm; and fanaticism is all in a bustle, shutting it's doors and windows to keep it out. But it will come, and will drive before it the foggy mists of Platonism which have so long obscured our Atmosphere. I am in hopes that some of the disciples of your institution will become missionaries to us, of these doctrines truly evangelical, an open our eyes to what has been so long hidden from them. A bold and eloquent preacher would be no where listened to with more freedom than in this state, nor with more firmness of mind. They might need a preparatory discourse on the text of 'prove all things, hold fast that which is good' in order to unlearn the lesson that reason is an unlawful guide in religion. They might startle on being first awakened from the dreams of the night, but they would rub their eyes at once and look the spectres boldly in the face. The preacher might be excluded by our hierophants from their churches and meeting houses, but would be attended in the fields by whole acres of hearers and thinkers. Missionaries from Cambridge would soon be greeted with more welcome, than from the tritheistical school or Andover. Such are my wishes, such would be my welcomes, warm and cordial as the assurances of my esteem and respect for you.

Thomas Jefferson, Report to the President and Directors of the Literary Fund
October 7, 1822

In the same report of the commissioners of 1818 it was stated by them that "in conformity with the principles of our constitution, which places all sects of religion on an equal footing, with the jealousies of the different sects in guarding that equality from encroachment or surprise, and with the sentiments of the legislature in freedom of religion, manifested on former occasions, they had not proposed that any professorship of divinity should be established in the University; that provision, however, was made for giving instruction in the Hebrew, Greek and Latin languages, the depositories of the originals, and of the earliest and most respected authorities of the faith of every sect, and for courses of ethical lectures, developing those moral obligations in which all sects agree. That, proceeding thus far, without offence to the constitution, they had left, at this point, to every sect to take into their own hands the office of further instruction in the peculiar tenet of each."

It was not, however, to be understood that instruction in religious opinion and duties was meant to be precluded by the public authorities, as indifferent to the interests of society. On the contrary, the relations which exist between man and his Maker, and the duties resulting from those relations, are the most interesting and important to every human being, and the most incumbent on his study and investigation. The want of instruction in the various creeds of religious faith existing among our citizens presents, therefore, a chasm in a general institution of the useful sciences. But it was thought that this want, and the entrustment to each society of instruction in its own doctrine, were evils of less danger than a permission to the public authorities to dictate modes or principles of religious instruction, or than opportunities furnished them by giving countenance or ascendancy to any one sect over another. A remedy, however, has been suggested of promising aspect, which, while it excludes the public authorities from the domain of religious freedom, will give to the sectarian schools of divinity the full benefit the public provisions made for instruction in the other branches of science. There branches are equally necessary to the divine as to the other professional or civil characters, to enable them to fulfill the duties of their calling with understanding and usefulness. It has, therefore, been in contemplation, and suggested by some pious individuals, who perceive the advantages of associating other studies with those of religion, to establish their religious schools on the confines of the University, so as to give to their students ready and convenient access and attendance on the scientific lectures of the University; and to maintain, by that means, those destined for the religious professions on as high a standing of science, and of personal weight and respectability, as may be obtained by others from the benefits of the University. Such establishments would offer the further and greater advantage of enabling the students of the University to attend religious exercises with the professor of their particular sect, either in the rooms of the building still to be erected, and destined to that purpose under impartial regulations, as proposed in the same report of the commissioners, or in the lecturing room of such professor. To such propositions the Visitors are disposed to lend a willing ear, and would think it their duty to give every encouragement, by assuring to those who might choose such a location for their schools, that the regulations of the University should be so modified and accommodated as to give every facility of access and attendance to their students, with such regulated use also as may be permitted to the other students, of the library which may hereafter be acquired, either by public or private munificence. But always understanding that these schools shall be independent of the University and of each other. Such an arrangement would complete the circle of the useful sciences embraced by this institution, and would fill the chasm now existing, on principles which would leave inviolate the constitutional freedom of religion, the most inalienable and sacred of all human rights, over which the people and authorities of this state, individually and publicly, have ever manifested the most watchful jealousy: and could this jealousy be now alarmed, in the opinion of the legislature, by what is here suggested, the idea will be relinquished on any surmise of disapprobation which they might think proper to express.

THOMAS JEFFERSON TO DR. THOMAS COOPER
November 2, 1822

The atmosphere of our country is unquestionably charged with a threatening cloud of fanaticism, lighter in some parts, denser in others, but too heavy in all. I had no idea, however, that in Pennsylvania, the cradle of toleration and freedom of religion, it could have arisen to the height you describe. This must be owing to the growth of Presbyterianism. The blasphemy and absurdity of the five points of Calvin, and the impossibility of defending them, render their advocates impatient of reasoning, irritable, and prone to denunciation. In Boston, however, and its neighborhood, Unitarianism has advanced to so great strength, as now to humble this haughtiest of all religious sects; insomuch that they condescend to interchange with them and the other sects, the civilities of preaching freely and frequently in each others' meeting-houses. In Rhode Island, on the other hand, no sectarian preacher will permit an Unitarian to pollute his desk. In our Richmond there is much fanaticism, but chiefly among the women. They have their night meetings and praying parties, where, attended by their priests, and sometimes by a hen-pecked husband, they pour forth the effusions of their love to Jesus, in terms as amatory and carnal, as their modesty would permit them to use to a mere earthly lover. In our village of Charlottesville, there is a good degree of religion, with a small spice only of fanaticism. We have four sects, but without either church or meeting-house. The courthouse is the common temple, one Sunday in the month to each. Here, Episcopalian and Presbyterian, Methodist and Baptist, meet together, join in hymning their Maker, listen with attention and devotion to each others' preachers, and all mix in society with perfect harmony. It is not so in the districts where Presbyterianism prevails undividedly. Their ambition and tyranny would tolerate no rival if they had power. Systematical in grasping at an ascendency over all other sects, they aim, like the Jesuits, at engrossing the education of the country, are hostile to every institution which they do not direct, and jealous at seeing others begin to attend at all to that object. The diffusion of instruction, to which there is now so growing an attention, will be the remote remedy to this fever of fanaticism; while the more proximate one will be the progress of Unitarianism. That this will, ere long, be the religion of the majority from north to south, I have no doubt.

In our university you know there is no Professorship of Divinity. A handle has been made of this, to disseminate an idea that this is an institution, not merely of no religion, but against all religion. Occasion was taken at the last meeting of the Visitors, to bring forward an idea that might silence this calumny, which weighed on the minds of some honest friends to the institution. In our annual report to the legislature, after stating the constitutional reasons against a public establishment of any religious instruction, we suggest the expediency of encouraging the different religious sects to establish, each for itself, a professorship of their own tenets, on the confines of the university, so near as that their students may attend the lectures there, and have the free use of our library, and every other accommodation we can give them; preserving, however, their independence of us and of each other. This fills the chasm objected to ours, as a defect in an institution professing to give instruction in all useful sciences. I think the invitation will be accepted, by some sects from candid intentions, and by others from jealousy and rivalship. And by bringing the sects together, and mixing them with the mass of other students, we shall soften their asperities, liberalize and neutralize their prejudices, and make the general religion a religion of peace, reason, and morality.

THOMAS JEFFERSON TO JAMES SMITH
December 8, 1822

I have to thank you for your pamphlets on the subject of Unitarianism, and to express my gratification with your efforts for the revival of primitive Christianity in your quarter. No historical fact is better established, than that the doctrine of one god, pure and uncompounded, was that of the early ages of Christianity; and was among the efficacious doctrines which gave it triumph over the polytheism of the antients, sickened with the absurdities of their own theology. Nor was the unity of the supreme being ousted from the Christian creed by the force of reason, but by the sword of civil government, wielded at the will of the fanatic Athanasius. The hocus-pocus phantasm of a god like another Cerberus, with one body and three heads, had it's birth and growth in the blood of thousands and thousands of martyrs. And a strong proof of the solidity of the primitive faith, is it's restoration, as soon as a nation arises which vindicates to itself the freedom of religious opinion, and it's eternal divorce from the civil authority. The pure and simple unity of the creator of the universe, is now all but ascendant in the Eastern States; it is dawning in the West, and advancing towards the South; and I confidently expect that the present generation will see Unitarianism become the general religion of the United States. The Eastern presses are giving us many excellent pieces on the subject, and Priestley's learned writings on it are, or should be, in every hand. In fact, the Athanasian paradox that one is three, and three but one, is so incomprehensible to the human mind that no candid man can say he has any idea of it, and how can he believe what presents no idea? He who thinks he does, only decieves himself. He proves also that man, once surrendering his reason, has no remaining guard against absurdities the most monstrous, and like a ship without rudder, is the sport of every wind. With such persons gullibility which they call faith takes the helm from the hand of reason and the mind becomes a wreck.

I write with freedom, because, while I claim a right to believe in one god, if so my reason tells me, I yield as freely to others that of believing in three. Both religions I find make honest men, and that is the only point society has any right to look to. — Altho' this mutual freedom should produce mutual indulgence, yet I wish not to be brought in question before the public on this or any other subject, and I pray you to consider me as writing under that trust. I take no part in controversies, religious or political. At the age of 80. tranquility is the greatest good of life, and the strongest of our desires that of dying in the good will of all mankind. And with the assurance of all my good will to Unitarian & Trinitarian, to whig and tory, accept for yourself that of my entire respect.

JAMES MADISON TO EDWARD EVERETT
March 19, 1823

Our University has lately recd. a further loan from the Legislature which will prepare the Buildings for ten professors and about 200 Students.... the Visitors, with an annuity of $15,000 settled on the Institution, will turn their thoughts towards opening it, and to the preliminary engagement of Professors.

I am not surprised at the dilemma produced at your University by making theological professorships an integral part of the System. The anticipation of such an one led to the omission in ours; the Visitors being merely authorized to open a public Hall for religious occasions, under impartial regulations; with the opportunity to the different sects to establish Theological schools so near that the Students of the University may respectively attend the religious exercises in them. The village of Charlottesville also, where different religious worships will be held, is also so near, that resort may conveniently be had to them.

A University with sectarian professorships, becomes, of course, a Sectarian Monopoly: with professorships of rival sects, it would be an Arena of Theological Gladiators. Without any such professorships, it may incur for a time at least, the imputation of irreligious tendencies, if not designs. The last difficulty was thought more manageable than either of the others.

On this view of the subject, there seems to be no alternative but between a public University without a theological professorship, and sectarian Seminaries without a University.

I recollect to have seen, many years ago, a project of a prayer, by Govr. Livingston father of the present Judge, intended to comprehend & conciliate College Students of every Xn denomination, by a Form composed wholly of texts & phrases of scripture. If a trial of the expedient was ever made, it must have failed, notwithstanding its winning aspect from the single cause that many sects reject all set forms of Worship.

The difficulty of reconciling the Xn mind to the absence of a religious tuition from a University established by law and at the common expence, is probably less with us than with you. The settled opinion here is that religion is essentially distinct from Civil Govt and exempt from its cognizance; that a connexion between them is injurious to both; that there are causes in the human breast, which ensure the perpetuity of religion without the aid of the law; that rival sects, with equal rights, exercise mutual censorships in favor of good morals; that if new sects arise with absurd opinions or overheated maginations, the proper remedies lie in time, forbearance and example; that a legal establishment of religion without a toleration could not be thought of, and with a toleration, is no security for public quiet & harmony, but rather a source itself of discord & animosity; and finally that these opinions are supported by experience, which has shewn that every relaxation of the alliance between Law & religion, from the partial example of Holland, to its consummation in Pennsylvania Delaware N. J., &c., has been found as safe in practice as it is sound in theory. Prior to the Revolution, the Episcopal Church was established by law in this State. On the Declaration of independence it was left with all other sects, to a self-support. And no doubt exists that there is much more of religion among us now than there ever was before the change; and particularly in the Sect which enjoyed the legal patronage. This proves rather more than, that the law is not necessary to the support of religion.

With such a public opinion, it may be expected that a University with the feature peculiar to ours will succeed here if anywhere. Some of the Clergy did not fail to arraign the peculiarity; but it is not improbable that they had an eye to the chance of introducing their own creed into the professor's chair. A late resolution for establishing an Episcopal school within the College of William & Mary, tho' in a very guarded manner, drew immediate animadversions from the press, which if they have not put an end to the project, are a proof of what would follow such an experiment in the University of the State, endowed and supported as this will be, altogether by the Public authority and at the common expense.

THOMAS JEFFERSON TO JOHN ADAMS
April 11, 1823

The wishes expressed, in your last favor, that I may continue in life and health until I become a Calvinist, at least in his exclamation of *'mon Dieu! jusque à quand'!* ['my God! Till when'!] would make me immortal. I can never join Calvin in addressing his god. He was indeed an Atheist, which I can never be; or rather his religion was Daemonism. If ever man worshipped a false god, he did. The being described in his 5. points is not the God whom you and I acknolege and adore, the Creator and benevolent governor of the world; but a daemon of malignant spirit. It would be more pardonable to believe in no god at all, than to blaspheme him by the atrocious attributes of Calvin. Indeed, I think that every Christian sect gives a great handle to Atheism by their general dogma that, without a revelation, there would not be sufficient proof of the being of a god. Now one sixth of mankind only are supposed to be Christians; the other five sixths then, who do not believe in the Jewish and Christian revelation, are without a knolege of the existence of a god! This gives compleatly a gain de cause to the disciples of Ocellus, Timaeus, Spinosa, Diderot and D'Holbach. The argument which they rest on as triumphant and unanswerable is that, in every hypothesis of Cosmogony you must admit an eternal pre-existence of something; and according to the rule of sound philosophy, you are never to employ two principles to solve a difficulty when one will suffice. They say then that it is more simple to believe at once in the eternal pre-existence of the world, as it is now going on, and may for ever go on by the principle of reproduction which we see and witness, than to believe in the eternal pre-existence of an ulterior cause, or Creator of the world, a being whom we see not and know not, of whose form, substance and mode or place of existence, or of action no sense informs us, no power of the mind enables us to delineate or comprehend. On the contrary I hold (without appeal to revelation) that when we take a view of the Universe, in it's parts general or particular, it is impossible for the human mind not to percieve and feel a conviction of design, consummate skill, and indefinite power in every atom of it's composition. The movements of the heavenly bodies, so exactly held in their course by the balance of centrifugal and centripetal forces, the structure of our earth itself, with its distribution of lands, waters and atmosphere; animal and vegetable bodies, examined in all their minutest particles, insects mere atoms of life, yet as perfectly organised as man or mammoth, the mineral substances, their generation and uses, it is impossible, I say, for the human mind not to believe that there is, in all this, design, cause and effect, up to an ultimate cause, a fabricator of all things from matter and motion, their preserver and regulator while permitted to exist in their present forms, and their regenerator into new and other forms. We see, too, evident proofs of the necessity of a superintending power, to maintain the Universe in it's course and order. Stars, well known, have disappeared, new ones have come into view, comets, in their incalculable courses, may run foul of suns and planets and require renovation under other laws; certain races of animals are become extinct; and, were there no restoring power, all existences might extinguish successively, one by one, until all should be reduced to a shapeless chaos. So irresistible are these evidences of an intelligent and powerful Agent that, of the infinite numbers of men who have existed thro' all time, they have believed, in the proportion of a million at least to Unit, in the hypothesis of an eternal pre-existence of a creator, rather than in that of a self-existent Universe. Surely this unanimous sentiment renders this more probable, than that of the few in the other hypothesis. Some early Christians indeed have believed in the coeternal pre-existence of both the Creator and the world, without changing their relation of cause and effect. That this was the opinion of St. Thomas, we are informed by Cardinal Toleto, in these words '*Deus ab aeterno fuit jam omnipotens, sicut cum produxit mundum. Ab aeterno potuit producere mundum. — Si sol ab aeterno esset, lumen ab aeterno esset; et si pes, similiter vestigium. At lumen et vestigium effectus sunt efficientis solis et pedis; potuit ergo cum causa aeterna effectus coaeterna esse. Cujus sententiae est S. Thomas Theologorum primus.*' - [God was omnipotent forever, just as when he formed the world. He was able to make the world forever. If the sun were in existence from eternity, then light would have existed forever; and if a foot then likewise a footprint. But light and footprints are the effects of a sun and foot; therefore, with reason, the effect has the power to be co-eternal with the cause. St. Thomas was the first theologian of this opinion.] - Cardinal Toleto.

Of the nature of this being we know nothing. Jesus tells us that 'God is a spirit.' 4. John 24. but without defining what a spirit is 'πνευμα ὁ θεος.' Down to the 3d. century we know that it was still deemed material; but of a lighter subtler matter than our gross bodies. So says Origen. '*Deus igitur, cui anima similis est, juxta Originem, reapte corporalis est; sed graviorum tantum ratione corporum incorporeus.*' [God, therefore, to whom the soul is similar, in consequence of its origin, is in reality corporeal; but He is incorporeal in comparison with so much heavier bodies.]

These are the words of Huet in his commentary on Origen. Origen himself says '*appelatio* ἀσωματον *apud nostros scriptores est inusitata et incognita.*' [The word (incorporeal), among our writers, is not used or known.] So also Tertullian '*quis autem negabit Deum esse corpus, etsi deus spiritus? Spiritus etiam corporis sui generis, in sua effigie.*' [Yet who will deny that God is body, although God is spirit? Indeed He is spirit of His own type of body, in his own image.] Tertullian. These two fathers were of the 3d. century. Calvin's character of this supreme being seems chiefly copied from that of the Jews. But the reformation of these blasphemous attributes, and substitution of those more worthy, pure and sublime, seems to have been the chief object of Jesus in his discources to the Jews: and his doctrine of the Cosmogony of the world is very clearly laid down in the 3 first verses of the 1st. chapter of John, in these words, 'εν αρχη ην ὁ λογος, και ὁ λογος ην προς τον θεον και θεος ην ὁ λογος. 'Ꝃτος ην εν αρχη προς τον θεον. Παντα δε αυτꝃ εγενετο, και χωρις αυτꝃ εγενετο 8δε ἐν, ὁ γεγονεν. Which truly translated means 'in the beginning God existed, and reason (or mind) was with God, and that mind was God. This was in the beginning with God. All things were created by it, and without it was made not one thing which was made.' Yet this text, so plainly declaring the doctrine of Jesus that the world was created by the supreme, intelligent being, has been perverted by modern Christians to build up a second person of their tritheism by a mistranslation of the word λογος. One of it's legitimate meanings indeed is 'a word.' But, in that sense, it makes an unmeaning jargon: while the other meaning 'reason', equally legitimate, explains rationally the eternal preexistence of God, and his creation of the world. Knowing how incomprehensible it was that 'a word,' the mere action or articulation of the voice and organs of speech could create a world, they undertake to make of this articulation a second preexisting being, and ascribe to him, and not to God, the creation of the universe. The Atheist here plumes himself on the uselessness of such a God, and the simpler hypothesis of a self-existent universe. The truth is that the greatest enemies to the doctrines of Jesus are those calling themselves the expositors of them, who have perverted them for the structure of a system of fancy absolutely incomprehensible, and without any foundation in his genuine words. And the day will come when the mystical generation of Jesus, by the supreme being as his father in the womb of a virgin will be classed with the fable of the generation of Minerva in the brain of Jupiter. But we may hope that the dawn of reason and freedom of thought in these United States will do away [with] all this artificial scaffolding, and restore to us the primitive and genuine doctrines of this the most venerated reformer of human errors.

So much for your quotation of Calvin's 'mon dieu! jusqu' a quand' in which, when addressed to the God of Jesus, and our God, I join you cordially, and await his time and will with more readiness than reluctance. May we meet there again, in Congress, with our antient Colleagues, and recieve with them the seal of approbation 'Well done, good and faithful servants.'

THOMAS JEFFERSON TO MICHAEL MEGEAR
May 29, 1823

I thank you, Sir, for the copy of the letters of Paul and Amicus, which you have been so kind as to send me, and shall learn from them with satisfaction the peculiar tenets of the Friends, and particularly their opinions on the incomprehensibilities (otherwise called the mysteries) of the Trinity. I think with them on many points, and especially on missionary and Bible societies. While we have so many around us, within the same social pale, who need instruction and assistance, why carry to a distance, and to strangers what our own neighbors need? It is a duty certainly to give our sparings to those who want; but to see also that they are faithfully distributed, and duly apportioned to the respective wants of those receivers. And why give through agents whom we know not, to persons whom we know not, and in countries from which we get no account, when we can do it at short hand, to objects under our eye, through agents we know, and to supply wants we see? I do not know that it is a duty to disturb by missionaries the religion and peace of other countries, who may think themselves bound to extinguish by fire and fagot the heresies to which we give the name of conversions, and quote our own example for it. Were the Pope, or his holy allies, to send in mission to us some thousands of Jesuit priests to convert us to their orthodoxy, I suspect that we should deem and treat it as a national aggression on our peace and faith.

JAMES MADISON TO THOMAS JEFFERSON
June 27, 1823

I wish the rather that the Judge may be put on his guard, because, with all his good qualities, he has been betrayed into errors which shew that his discretion is not always awake.... And what is worse than all, I perceive from one of Cooper's publications, casually falling within my notice, that, among the effects of Judge Johnson's excitement, he has stooped to invoke the religous prejudices circulated against Cooper.

THOMAS JEFFERSON TO JOHN ADAMS
September 4, 1823

Your letter of Aug. 15. was recieved in due time, and with the welcome of every thing which comes from you. With it's opinions on the difficulties of revolutions, from despotism to freedom, I very much concur. The generation which commences a revolution can rarely compleat it. Habituated from their infancy to passive submission of body and mind to their kings and priests, they are not qualified, when called on, to think and provide for themselves and their inexperience, their ignorance and bigotry make them instruments often, in the hands of the Bonapartes and Iturbides to defeat their own rights and purposes. This is the present situation of Europe and Spanish America. But it is not desperate.

The light which has been shed on mankind by the art of printing has eminently changed the condition of the world. As yet that light has dawned on the midling classes only of the men of Europe. The kings and the rabble of equal ignorance, have not yet recieved it's rays; but it continues to spread. And, while printing is preserved, it can no more recede than the sun return on his course. A first attempt to recover the right of self-government may fail; so may a 2d. a 3d. etc., but as a younger, and more instructed race comes on, the sentiment becomes more and more intuitive, and a 4th. a 5th. or some subsequent one of the ever renewed attempts will ultimately succeed. In France the 1st. effort was defeated by Robespierre, the 2d. by Bonaparte, the 3d. by Louis XVIII. and his holy allies; another is yet to come, and all Europe, Russia excepted, has caught the spirit, and all will attain representative government, more or less perfect. This is now well understood to be a necessary check on kings, whom they will probably think it more prudent to chain and tame, than to exterminate. To attain all this however rivers of blood must yet flow, and years of desolation pass over. Yet the object is worth rivers of blood, and years of desolation for what inheritance so valuable can man leave to his posterity? The spirit of the Spaniard and his deadly and eternal hatred to a Frenchman, gives me much confidence that he will never submit, but finally defeat this atrocious violation of the laws of god and man under which he is suffering; and the wisdom and firmness of the Cortes afford reasonable hope that that nation will settle down in a temperate representative government, with an Executive properly subordinated to that. Portugal, Italy, Prussia, Germany, Greece will follow suit. You and I shall look down from another world on these glorious atchievements to man, which will add to the joys even of heaven.

JAMES MADISON TO THOMAS JEFFERSON
September 6, 1823

I am afraid the people of Spain as well as of Portugal need still further light, and heat, too, from the American example, before they will be a match for the crimes, the intrigues, and the bribes of their enemies, the treachery of their leaders, and, what is most of all to be dreaded, their Priests and their prejudices. Still, their cause is so just, that whilst there is life in it hope ought not to be abandoned.

THOMAS JEFFERSON TO A. CORAY
October 31, 1823

The government of Athens, for example, was that of the people of one city making laws for the whole country subjected to them. That of Lacedaemon was the rule of military monks over the laboring class of the people, reduced to abject slavery.

THOMAS JEFFERSON TO JOHN DAVIS
January 18, 1824

I thank you, Sir, for the copy you were so kind as to send me of the revd. Mr. Bancroft's Unitarian sermons. I have read them with great satisfaction, and always rejoice in efforts to restore us to primitive Christianity, in all the simplicity in which it came from the lips of Jesus. Had it never been sophisticated by the subtleties of Commentators, nor paraphrased into meanings totally foreign to it's character, it would at this day have been the religion of the whole civilized world. But the metaphysical abstractions of Athanasius, and the maniac ravings of Calvin, tinctured plentifully with the foggy dreams of Plato, have so loaded it with absurdities and incomprehensibilities, as to drive into infidelity men who had not the time, patience, or opportunity to strip it of it's meretricious trappings, and to see it in all it's native simplicity and purity. I trust however that the same free exercise of private judgment which gave us our political reformation will extend it's effects to that of religion, which the present volume is well calculated to encourage and promote.

Not wishing to give offence to those who differ from me in opinion, nor to be implicated in a theological controversy, I have to pray that this letter may not get into print, and to assure you of my great respect and good will.

THOMAS JEFFERSON TO GEORGE THACHER
January 26, 1824

I have read with much satisfaction the Sermon of Mr. Pierpont which you have been so kind as to send me, and am much pleased with the spirit of brotherly forbearance in matters of religion which it breathes, and the sound distinction it inculcates between the things which belong to us to judge, and those which do not. If all Christian sects would rally the Sermon in the mount, make that the central point of Union in religion, and the stamp of genuine Christianity, (since it gives us all the precepts of our duties to one another) why should we further ask, with the text of our sermon, 'What think ye of Christ'? And if one should answer 'he is a member of the Godhead,' another 'he is a being of eternal pre-existence,' a third 'he was a man divinely inspired,' a fourth 'he was the Herald of truths reformatory of the religions of mankind in general, but more immediately of that of his own countrymen, impressing them with more sublime and more worthy ideas of the Supreme being, teaching them the doctrine of a future state of rewards and punishments, and inculcating the love of mankind, instead of the anti-social spirit with which the Jews viewed all other nations,' What right, or what interest has either of these respondents, to claim pre-eminence for his dogma, and, usurping the judgment-seat of God, to condemn all the others to his wrath? In this case, I say with the wiser heathen *'deorum injuriae, diis curae.'* [The injuries of the gods are their concern.]

You press me to consent to the publication of my sentiments and suppose they might have effect even on Sectarian bigotry. But have they not the Gospel? If they hear not that, and the charities it teacheth, neither will they be persuaded though one rose from the dead. Such is the malignity of religious antipathies that, altho' the laws will no longer permit them, with Calvin, to burn those who not exactly of their Creed, they raise the Hue and cry of Heresy against them, place them under the ban of public opinion, and shut them out from all the kind affections of society. I must pray permission therefore to continue in quiet during the short time remaining to me: and, at a time of life when the afflictions of the body weigh heavily enough, not to superadd those which corrode the spirit also, and might weaken it's resignation to continuance in a joyless state of being which providence may yet destine. With these sentiments accept those of good will and respect to yourself.

THOMAS JEFFERSON TO ISAAC ENGELBRECHT
February 25, 1824

The kindness of the motive which led to the request of your letter of the 14th instant, and which would give some value to an article from me, renders compliance a duty of gratitude; knowing nothing more moral, more sublime, more worthy of your preservation than David's description of the good man, in his 15th Psalm, I will here transcribe it from Brady and Tate's version:

Lord, who's the happy man that may to Thy blest courts repair, Not stranger-like to visit them, but to inhabit there?

'Tis he whose every thought and deed by rules of virtue moves, Whose generous tongue disdains to speak the thing his heart disproves.

Who never did a slander forge, his neighbor's fame to wound,
Nor hearken to a false report, by malice whispered round.

Who vice, in all its pomp and power, can treat with just neglect;
And piety, though clothed in rags, religiously respect.
Who to his plighted vows and trust has ever firmly stood,
And though he promise to his loss, he makes his promise good.
Whose soul in usury disdains his treasure to employ,
Whom no rewards can ever bribe the guiltless to destroy.
The man who, by this steady course, has happiness ensur'd,
When earth's foundations shake, shall stand, by Providence secur'd.

Accept this as a testimony of my respect for your request, an acknowledgment of a due sense of the favor of your opinion, and an assurance of my good will and best wishes.

THOMAS JEFFERSON TO AUGUSTUS WOODWARD
March 24, 1824

I have to thank you, dear Sir, for the copy I have received of your System of Universal Science, for which, I presume, I am indebted to yourself. It will be a monument of the learning of the author and of the analyzing powers of his mind. Whether it may be adopted in general use is yet to be seen. These analytical views indeed must always be ramified according to their object. Yours is on the great scale of a methodical encyclopedia of all human sciences, taking for the basis of their distribution, matter, mind, and the union of both. Lord Bacon founded his first great division on the faculties of the mind which have cognizance of these sciences. It does not seem to have been observed by any one that the origination of this division was not with him. It had been proposed by Charron more than twenty years before, in his book *de la Sagesse*, B. 1, c. 14, and an imperfect ascription of the sciences to these respective faculties was there attempted. This excellent moral work was published in 1600. Lord Bacon is said not to have entered on his great work until his retirement from public office in 1621. Where sciences are to be arranged in accommodation to the schools of an university, they will be grouped to coincide with the kindred qualifications of Professors in ordinary. For a library, which was my object, their divisions and subdivisions will be made such as to throw convenient masses of books under each separate head. Thus, in the library of a physician, the books of that science, of which he has many, will be subdivided under many heads; and those of law, of which he has few, will be placed under a single one. The lawyer, again, will distribute his law books under many subdivisions, his medical under a single one. Your idea of making the subject matter of the sciences the basis of their distribution, is certainly more reasonable than that of the faculties to which they are addressed. The materialists will perhaps criticise a basis, one-half of which they will say is a non-existence; adhering to the axiom of Aristotle, *"nihil est in intellectu quod prius non fuerit in sensu,"* and affirming that we can have no evidence of any existence which impresses no sense. Of this opinion were most of the ancient philosophers, and several of the early and orthodox fathers of the Christian Church. Indeed, Jesus Himself, the Founder of our religion, was unquestionably a Materialist as to man. In all His doctrines of the resurrection, He teaches expressly that the body is to rise in substance. In the Apostles' Creed, we all declare that we believe in the "resurrection of the body." Jesus said that God is Spirit without defining it. Tertullian supplies the definition, *"quis negabit Deum esse corpus, etsi Deus Spiritus? spiritus etiam corporis sui generis in sua effigie."* [Who denies god to be material even if god is spirit? Spirit is material's unique reproduction.] And Origen, *"accipi, docet, pro eo quod non est simile huic nostro crassiori et visibli corpori, sed quod est naturaliter subtile et velut aura tenue."* [We receive and learn before accepting a fact. Spirit is material not as our dense and visible substance, but in fact spirit is natural as thin air]. The modern philosophers mostly consider thought as a function of our material organization; and Locke particularly among them, charges with blasphemy those who deny that Omnipotence could give the faculty of thinking to certain combinations of matter. Were I to recompose my tabular view of the sciences, I should certainly transpose a particular branch. The naturalists, you know, distribute the history of nature into three kingdoms or departments: zoology, botany, mineralogy. Ideology or mind, however, occupies so much space in the field of science, that we might perhaps erect it into a fourth kingdom or department. But, inasmuch as it makes a part of the animal construction only, it would be more proper to subdivide zoology into physical and moral. The latter including ideology, ethics, and mental science generally, in my catalogue, considering ethics, as well as religion, as supplements to law in the government of man, I had placed them in that sequence. But certainly the faculty of thought belongs to animal history, is an important portion of it, and should there find its place. But these are speculations in which I do not now permit myself to labor. My mind unwillingly engages in severe investigations. Its energies, indeed, are no longer equal to them. Being to thank you for your book, its subject has run away with me into a labyrinth of ideas no longer familiar, and writing also has become a slow and irksome operation with me. I have been obliged to avail myself of the pen of a granddaughter for this communication. I will here, therefore, close my task of thinking, hers of writing, and yours of reading, with assurances of my constant and high respect and esteem.

THOMAS JEFFERSON TO MAJOR JOHN CARTWRIGHT
June 5, 1824

Editor's note: The last line of the translation of an extensive medieval quote from Prisot below is conjectural. The language is provincial demotic, beyond the then bounds of official Latin turning into French.

I am much indebted for your kind letter of February the 29th, and for your valuable volume on the English Constitution. I have read this with pleasure and much approbation, and think it has deduced the Constitution of the English nation from its rightful root, the Anglo-Saxon. It is really wonderful, that so many able and learned men should have failed in their attempts to define it with correctness. No wonder then, that Paine, who thought more than he read, should have credited the great authorities who have declared, that the will of parliament is the Constitution of England. So Marbois, before the French revolution, observed to me, that the Almanac Royal was the Constitution of France. Your derivation of it from the Anglo-Saxons, seems to be made on legitimate principles. Having driven out the former inhabitants of that part of the island called England, they became aborigines as to you, and your lineal ancestors. They doubtless had a constitution; and although they have not left it in a written formula, to the precise text of which you may always appeal, yet they have left fragments of their history and laws, from which it may be inferred with considerable certainty....

Our Revolution commenced on more favorable ground. It presented us an album on which we were free to write what we pleased. We had no occasion to search into musty records, to hunt up royal parchments, or to investigate the laws and institutions of a semi-barbarous ancestry. We appealed to those of nature, and found them engraved on our hearts. Yet we did not avail ourselves of all the advantages of our position. We had never been permitted to exercise self-government. When forced to assume it, we were novices in its science. Its principles and forms had entered little into our former education. We established however some, although not all its important principles. The constitutions of most of our States assert, that all power is inherent in the people; that they may exercise it by themselves, in all cases to which they think themselves competent, (as in electing their functionaries executive and legislative, and deciding by a jury of themselves, in all judiciary cases in which any fact is involved,) or they may act by representatives, freely and equally chosen; that it is their right and duty to be at all times armed; that they are entitled to freedom of person, freedom of religion, freedom of property, and freedom of the press. In the structure of our legislatures, we think experience has proved the benefit of subjecting questions to two separate bodies of deliberants; but in constituting these, natural right has been mistaken, some making one of these bodies, and some both, the representatives of property instead of persons; whereas the double deliberation might be as well obtained without any violation of true principle, either by requiring a greater age in one of the bodies, or by electing a proper number of representatives of persons, dividing them by lots into two chambers, and renewing the division at frequent intervals, in order to break up all cabals. Virginia, of which I am myself a native and resident, was not only the first of the States, but, I believe I may say, the first of the nations of the earth, which assembled its wise men peaceably together to form a fundamental constitution, to commit it to writing, and place it among their archives, where every one should be free to appeal to its text....

With respect to our State and federal governments, I do not think their relations correctly understood by foreigners. They generally suppose the former subordinate to the latter. But this is not the case. They are co-ordinate departments of one simple and integral whole. To the State governments are reserved all legislation and administration, in affairs which concern their own citizens only, and to the federal government is given whatever concerns foreigners, or the citizens of other States; these functions alone being made federal. The one is the domestic, the other the foreign branch of the same government; neither having control over the other, but within its own department. There are one or two exceptions only to this partition of power. But, you may ask, if the two departments should claim each the same subject of power, where is the common umpire to decide ultimately between them? In cases of little importance or urgency, the prudence of both parties will keep them aloof from the questionable ground: but if it can neither be avoided nor compromised, a convention of the States must be called, to ascribe the doubtful power to that department which they may think best. You will perceive by these details, that we have not yet so far perfected our constitutions as to venture to make them unchangeable. But still, in their present state, we consider them not otherwise changeable than by the authority of the people, on a special election of representatives for that purpose expressly: they are until then the *lex legum* [the law of laws].

But can they be made unchangeable? Can one generation bind another, and all others, in succession forever? I think not. The Creator has made the earth for the living, not the dead. Rights and powers can only belong to persons, not to things, not to mere matter, unendowed with will. The dead are not even things. The particles of matter which composed their bodies, make part now of the bodies of other animals, vegetables, or minerals, of a thousand forms. To what then are attached the rights and powers they held while in the form of men? A generation may bind itself as long as its majority continues in life; when that has disappeared, another majority is in place, holds all the rights and powers their predecessors once held, and may change their laws and institutions to suit themselves. Nothing then is unchangeable but the inherent and unalienable rights of man.

I was glad to find in your book a formal contradiction, at length, of the judiciary usurpation of legislative powers; for such the judges have usurped in their repeated decisions, that Christianity is a part of the common law. The proof of the contrary, which you have adduced, is incontrovertible; to wit, that the common law existed while the Anglo-Saxons were yet Pagans, at a time when they had never yet heard the name of Christ pronounced, or knew that such a character had ever existed. But it may amuse you, to shew when, and by what means, they stole this law in upon us. In a case of *quare impedit* ['wherefore it obstructs'] in the Year-book 34. H. 6. folio 38. (anno 1458,) a question was made, how far the ecclesiastical law was to be respected in a common law court? And Prisot, Chief Justice, gives his opinion in these words,

"A tiel leis qu' ils de seint eglise ont en ancien scripture, covient à nous à donner credence; car

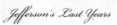

ceo common ley sur quels touts manners leis sont fondés. Et auxy, Sir, nous sumus oblègés de conustre lour ley de saint eglise; et semblablement ils sont obligés de conustre nostre ley. Et, Sir, si poit apperer or à nous que l'evesque ad fait come un ordinary fera en tiel cas, adong nous devons ceo adjuger bon, ou auterment nemy,"

["to such laws as those of holy church have in antient writing, it is proper for us to give credence; for the law is common as regards all affairs for which laws were founded. And moreover, Sir, we are obliged to follow their laws regards the holy church: and in like manner they are obliged to follow our law. And, Sir, should it seem to us that the bishop acted as a layman in such a case, we should do well to deem him a common man, as much as not."] &c. See S. C. Fitzh. Abr. Qu. imp. 89. Bro. Abr. Qu. imp. 12. Finch in his first book, c. 3. is the first afterwards who quotes this case, and mistakes it thus. 'To such laws of the church as have warrant in holy scripture, our law giveth credence.' And cites Prisot; mistranslating 'ancien scripture,' into 'holy scripture.' Whereas Prisot palpably says, 'to such laws as those of holy church have in antient writing, it is proper for us to give credence;' to wit, to their antient written laws. This was in 1613, a century and a half after the dictum of Prisot. Wingate, in 1658, erects this false translation into a maxim of the common law, copying the words of Finch, but citing Prisot. Wing. Max. 3. And Sheppard, title, 'Religion,' in 1675, copies the same mistranslation, quoting the Y. B. Finch and Wingate. Hale expresses it in these words; 'Christianity is parcel of the laws of England.' 1 Ventr. 293. 3 Keb. 607. But he quotes no authority. By these echoings and re-echoings from one to another, it had become so established in 1728, that in the case of the King vs. Woolston, 2 Stra. 834, the court would not suffer it to be debated, whether to write against Christianity was punishable in the temporal court at common law? Wood, therefore, 409, ventures still to vary the phrase, and say, that all blasphemy and profaneness are offences by the common law; and cites 2 Stra. Then Blackstone, in 1763, IV. 59, repeats the words of Hale, that 'Christianity is part of the laws of England,' citing Ventris and Strange. And finally, Lord Mansfield, with a little qualification, in Evans' case, in 1767, says, that 'the essential principles of revealed religion are part of the common law.' Thus ingulphing Bible, Testament and all into the common law, without citing any authority. And thus we find this chain of authorities hanging link by link, one upon another, and all ultimately on one and the same hook, and that a mistranslation of the words 'ancien scripture,' [ancient scripture] used by Prisot. Finch quotes Prisot; Wingate does the same. Sheppard quotes Prisot, Finch and Wingate. Hale cites nobody. The court in Woolston's case, cites Hale. Wood cites Woolston's case. Blackstone quotes Woolston's case and Hale. And Lord Mansfield, like Hale, ventures it on his own authority. Here I might defy the best read lawyer to produce another scrip of authority for this judiciary forgery; and I might go on further to shew, how some of the Anglo-Saxon priests interpolated into the text of Alfred's laws, the 20th, 21st, 22nd and 23rd chapters of Exodus, and the 15th of the Acts of the Apostles, from the 23rd to the 29th verses. But this would lead my pen and your patience too far. What a conspiracy this, between Church and State! Sing Tantarara, rogues all, rogues all, Sing Tantarara, rogues all!...

Your age of eighty-four and mine of eighty-one years, insure us a speedy meeting. We may then commune at leisure, and more fully, on the good and evil, which, in the course of our long lives, we have both witnessed; and in the mean time, I pray you to accept assurances of my high veneration and esteem for your person and character.

THOMAS JEFFERSON TO MARTIN VAN BUREN
June 29, 1824

I have to thank you for Mr. Pickering's elaborate philippic against Mr. Adams, Gerry, Smith, and myself; and I have delayed the acknowledgment until I could read it and make some observations on it. I could not have believed, that for so many years, and to such a period of advanced age, he could have nourished passions so vehement and viperous....

Mr. Pickering quotes, too, (page 34) the expression in the letter, of "the men who were Samsons in the field, and Solomons in the council, but who had had their heads shorn by the harlot England;" or, as expressed in their re-translation, "the men who were Solomons in council, and Samsons in combat, but whose hair had been cut off by the whore England." Now this expression also was perfectly understood by General Washington. He knew that I meant it for the Cincinnati generally, and that from what had passed between us at the commencement of that institution, I could not mean to include him. When the first meeting was called for its establishment, I was a member of the Congress then sitting at Annapolis. General Washington wrote to me, asking my opinion on that proposition, and the course, if any, which I thought Congress would observe respecting it. I wrote him frankly my own disapprobation of it....

Disapproving thus of the institution as much as I did, and conscious that I knew him to do so, he could never suppose that I meant to include him among the Samsons in the field, whose object was to draw over us the form, as they made the letter say, of the British government, and especially its aristocratic member, an hereditary House of Lords.... General Washington was himself sincerely a friend to the republican principles of our Constitution. His faith, perhaps, in its duration, might not have been as confident as mine; but he repeatedly declared to me, that he was determined it should have a fair chance for success, and that he would lose the last drop of his blood in its support, against any attempt which might be made to change it from its republican form.

THOMAS JEFFERSON TO PETER DUPONCEAU
August 1824

If the Common Law has been called our birthright, it has been done with little regard to any precise meaning. It could have been no more our birthright than the

Statute law of England, or than the English Constitution itself. If the one was brought by our ancestors with them, so must the others; and the whole consequently as it stood during the Dynasty of the Stuarts, the period of their emigration, with no other exceptions than such as necessarily resulted from inapplicability to the colonial state of things. As men our birthright was from a much higher source than the common or any other human law and of much greater extent than is imparted or admitted by the common law. And as far as it might belong to us as British subjects it must with its correlative obligations have expired when we ceased to be such. It would seem more correct therefore & preferable in every respect that the common law, even during the Colonial State, was in force not by virtue of its adhesion to the emigrants & their descendants in their individual capacity but by virtue of its adoption in their social & political capacity.

JAMES MADISON TO THOMAS JEFFERSON
September 20, 1824

On the receipt of yours of Aug. 8, I turned my thoughts to its request on the subject of a theological catalogue for the library of the University; and not being aware that so early an answer was wished, as I now find was the case, I had proceeded very leisurely in noting such authors as seemed proper for the collection. Supposing, also, that although theology was not to be taught in the University, its Library ought to contain pretty full information for such as might voluntarily seek it in that branch of learning. I had contemplated as much of a comprehensive and systematic selection as my scanty materials admitted, and had gone through the five first centuries of Christianity when yours of the 3d instant came to hand, which was the evening before last. This conveyed to me more distinctly the limited object your letter had in view, and relieved me from a task which I found extremely tedious; especially considering the intermixture of the doctrinal and controversial part of Divinity with the moral and metaphysical part, and the immense extent of the whole. I send you the list I had made out, with an addition on the same paper of such books as a hasty glance of a few catalogues and my recollection suggested. Perhaps some of them may not have occured to you, and may suit the blank you have not filled.

THOMAS JEFFERSON TO EDWARD EVERETT
October 15, 1824

Your letter of September the 10th gave me the first information that mine to Major Cartwright had got into the newspapers; and the first notice, indeed, that he had received it. I was a stranger to his person, but not to his respectable and patriotic character. I received from him a long and interesting letter, and answered it with frankness, going without reserve into several subjects, to which his letter had led, but on which I did not suppose I was writing for the newspapers. The publication of a letter in such a case, without the consent of the writer, is not a fair practice.

The part which you quote, may draw on me the host of judges and divines.

They may cavil, but cannot refute it. Those who read Prisot's opinion with a candid view to understand, and not to chicane it, cannot mistake its meaning. The reports in the Year-books were taken very short. The opinions of the judges were written down sententiously, as notes or memoranda, and not with all the development which they probably used in delivering them.

Prisot's opinion, to be fully expressed, should be thus paraphrased: "To such laws as those of holy church have recorded, and preserved in their ancient books and writings, it is proper for us to give credence; for so is, or so says the common law, or law of the land, on which all manner of other laws rest for their authority, or are founded; that is to say, the common law, or the law of the land common to us all, and established by the authority of us all, is that from which is derived the authority of all other special and subordinate branches of law, such as the canon law, law merchant, law maritime, law of Gavelkind, Borough English, corporation laws, local customs and usages, to all of which the common law requires its judges to permit authority in the special or local cases belonging to them. The evidence of these laws is preserved in their ancient treatises, books and writings, in like manner as our own common law itself is known, the text of its original enactments having been long lost, and its substance only preserved in ancient and traditionary writings. And if it appears, from their ancient books, writings, and records, that the bishop, in this case, according to the rules prescribed by these authorities, has done what an ordinary would have done in such case, then we should adjudge it good, otherwise not." To decide this question, they would have to turn to the ancient writings and records of the canon law, in which they would find evidence of the laws of advowsons, *quare impedit* [wherefore hindered], the duties VOL. XVI-6 of bishops and ordinaries, for which terms Prisot could never have meant to refer them to the Old or New Testament, *les saincts scriptures* [the holy scriptures], where surely they would not be found. A license which should permit "ancien scripture" to be translated "holy scripture," annihilates at once all the evidence of language. With such a license, we might reverse the sixth commandment into "thou shalt not omit murder." It would be the more extraordinary in this case, where the mistranslation was to effect the adoption of the whole code of the Jewish and Christian laws into the text of our statutes, to convert religious offences into temporal crimes, to make the breach of every religious precept a subject of indictment, submit the question of idolatry, for example, to the trial of a jury, and to a court, its punishment, to the third and fourth generation of the offender. Do we allow to our judges this lumping legislation?

The term "common law," although it has more than one meaning, is perfectly definite, *secundum subjectam materiem* [after looking at the matter]. Its most probable origin was on the conquest of the Heptarchy by Alfred, and the amalgamation of their several codes of law into one, which became common to them all. The authentic text of these enactments has not been preserved; but their substance has been committed to many ancient books and writings, so faithfully as to have been deemed genuine from generation to generation, and obeyed as such by all. We have some fragments of them collected by Lambard, Wilkins and others, but abounding with proofs of their spurious authenticity. Magna Charta is the earliest statute, the text of which has come down to us in an authentic form, and thence downward we have them entire. We do not know exactly when the common law and statute law, the *lex scripta et non scripta,* began to be contra-distinguished, so as to give a second acceptation to the former term; whether before, or after Prisot's day, at which time we know that nearly two centuries and a half of statutes were in preservation. In later times, on the introduction of the chancery branch of law, the term common law began to be used in a third sense, as the correlative of chancery law. This, however, having been long after Prisot's time, could not have been the sense in which he used the term. He must have meant the ancient lex non scripta, because, had he used it as inclusive of the *lex scripta,* he would have put his finger on the statute which had enjoined on the judges a deference to the laws of holy church. But no such statute existing, he must have referred to the common law in the sense of a *lex non scripta.* Whenever, then, the term common law is used in either of these senses, and it is never employed in any other, it is readily known in which of them, by the context and subject matter under consideration; which, in the present case, leave no room for doubt. I do not remember the occasion which led me to take up this subject, while a practitioner of the law.

But I know I went into it with all the research which a very copious law library enabled me to indulge; and I fear not for the accuracy of any of my quotations. The doctrine might be disproved by many other and different topics of reasoning; but having satisfied myself of the origin of the forgery, and found how, like a rolling snowball, it had gathered volume, I leave its further pursuit to those who need further proof, and perhaps I have already gone further than the feeble doubt you expressed might require.

I salute you with great esteem and respect.

JAMES MADISON TO FREDERICK BEASLEY
December 22, 1824

I have just received your letter of the 13th.... I can only observe that the system of polity for the University of Virginia being not yet finally digested and adopted, I cannot venture to say what it will be in its precise form and details....

The peculiarity in the Institution which excites at first most attention, and some animadversion, is the omission of a theological professorship. The public opinion seems now to have sufficiently yielded to its incompatibility with a State Institution, which necessarily excludes sectarian preferences. The best provision which occurred was that of authorizing the Visitors to open the public rooms for Religious uses, under impartial regulations, (a task that may occasionally involve some difficulties), and admitting the establishment of Theological Seminaries by the respective sects contiguous to the precincts of the University, and within the reach of a familiar intercourse distinct from the obligatory pursuits of the students. The growing village of Charlottesville, also, is not distant more than a mile, and contains already congregations and clergymen of the sects to which the students will mostly belong.

JAMES MADISON TO THOMAS JEFFERSON
December 31, 1824

I approve entirely the course you recommend to the friends of the University at Richmond, on the proposed removal of the College at Williamsburg. It would be fortunate if the occasion could be improved for the purpose of filling up the general plan of education, by the introduction of the grade of Seminaries between the primary schools and the University. I have little hope, however, that the College will accede to any arrangement which is to take from it a part of its funds, and subject it to the Legislative authority. And in resisting this latter innovation it will probably be supported by all the sectarian Seminaries, though to be adopted as legal establishments of the intermediate grade. It is questionable, also, whether the sectarian Seminaries would not take side with William and Mary in combating the right of the public to interfere in any manner with the property it holds. The perpetual inviolability of charters, and of donations, both public and private, for pious and charitable uses, seems to have been too deeply imprinted on the public mind to be readily given up. But the time surely cannot be distant when it must be seen by all that what is granted by the public authority for the public good, not for that of individuals, may be withdrawn and otherwise applied when the public good so requires; with an equitable saving or indemnity only in behalf of the individuals actually enjoying vested emoluments. Nor can it long be believed that, although the owner of property cannot secure its descent but for a short period, even to those who inherit his blood, he may entail it irrevocably and forever on those succeeding to his creed, however absurd or contrary to that of a more enlightened age. According to such doctrines, the Great Reformation of Ecclesiastical abuses in the 16th century was itself the greatest of abuses; and entails or other fetters attached to the descent of property by legal acts of its owners, must be as lasting as the society suffering from them.

THOMAS JEFFERSON TO JOHN ADAMS
January 8, 1825

Cabanis has proved by the anatomical structure of certain portions of the human frame, that they might be capable of receiving from the hand of the Creator the faculty of thinking; Flourens proves that they have received it; that the cerebrum is the thinking organ; and that life and health may continue, and the animal be entirely without thought, if deprived of that organ. I wish to see what the spiritualists will say to this. Whether, in this state, the soul remains in the body, deprived of its essence of thought? Or whether it leaves it, as in death, and where it goes? His memoirs and experiments have been reported on with approbation by a committee of the Institute, composed of Cuvier, Bertholet, Dumaril, Portal and Pinel. But all this, you and I shall know better when we meet again, in another place, and at no distant period.

THOMAS JEFFERSON TO DR. BENJAMIN WATERHOUSE
January 8, 1825

I am anxious to see the doctrine of one god commenced in our state. But the population of my neighborhood is too slender, and is too much divided into other sects to maintain any one preacher well. I must therefore be contented to be an Unitarian by myself, although I know there are many around me who would become so, if once they could hear the questions fairly stated.

THOMAS JEFFERSON TO ALEXANDER SMYTH
January 17, 1825

I have duly recieved 4 proof sheets of your explanation of the Apocalypse, with your letters of Dec. 29. and Jan. 8. in the last of which you request that, so soon as I shall be of opinion that the explanation you have given is correct, I would express it in a letter to you. From this you must be so good as to excuse me, because I make it an invariable rule to decline ever giving opinions on new publications in any case whatever. No man on earth has less taste or talent for criticism than myself, and least and last of all should I undertake to criticise works on the Apocalypse. It is between 50. and 60. years since I read it, and I then considered it as merely the ravings of a Maniac, no more worthy, nor capable of explanation than the incoherences of our own nightly dreams. I was therefore well pleased to see, in your first proof-sheet, that it was said to be not the production of St. John, but of Cerinthus, a century after the death of that Apostle. Yet the change of the Author's name does not lessen the extravagances of the composition, and come they from whomsoever they may, I cannot so far respect them as to consider them as an allegorical narrative of events, past or subsequent. The is not enough coherence enough in them to countenance any suite of rational ideas. You will judge therefore from this how impossible I think it that either your explanation, or that of any man in the heavens above, or on the earth beneath, can be a correct one. What has no meaning admits no explanation. And pardon me if I say, with the candor of friendship, that I think your time too valuable, and your understanding of too high an order, to be wasted on these paralogisms. You will percieve, I hope, also that I do not consider them as revelations of the supreme being, whom I would so far blaspheme as to impute to him a pretension of revelation, couched at the same time in terms which, he would know, were never to be understood by those to whom they were addressed. In the candor of these observations, I hope you will see the confidence, esteem and respect which I truly entertain for you.

JAMES MADISON TO THOMAS JEFFERSON
February 8, 1825

In framing a political creed, a like difficulty occurs as in the case of religion tho' the public right be very different in the two cases. If the Articles be in very general terms, they do not answer the purpose; if in very particular terms, they divide & exclude where meant to unite & fortify. The best that can be done in our case seems to be, to avoid the two extremes, by referring to selected Standards without requiring an unqualified conformity to them, which indeed might not in every instance be possible.

THOMAS JEFFERSON TO THOMAS JEFFERSON SMITH
February 21, 1825

This letter will, to you, be as one from the dead. The writer will be in the grave before you can weigh its counsels. Your affectionate and excellent father has requested that I would address to you something which might possibly have a favorable influence on the course of life you have to run, and I too, as a namesake, feel an interest in that course. Few words will be necessary, with good dispositions on your part. Adore God. Reverence and cherish your parents. Love your neighbor as yourself, and your country more than yourself. Be just. Be true. Murmur not at the ways of Providence. So shall the life into which you have entered, be the portal to one of eternal and ineffable bliss. And if to the dead it is permitted to care for the things of this world, every action of your life will be under my regard. Farewell.

The portrait of a good man by the most sublime of poets, for your imitation

Lord, who's the happy man that may to thy blest courts repair,
Not stranger-like to visit them, but to inhabit there?
'Tis he whose every thought and deed by rules of virtue moves,
Whose generous tongue disdains to speak the thing his heart disproves.
Who never did a slander forge, his neighbor's fame to wound,
Nor hearken to a false report, by malice whispered round.
Who vice, in all its pomp and power, can treat with just neglect;
And piety, though clothed in rages, religiously respect.
Who to his plighted vows and trust has ever firmly stood,
And though he promise to his loss, he makes his promise good.
Whose soul in usury disdains his treasure to employ,
Whom no rewards can ever bribe the guiltless to destroy.
The man, who, by his steady course, has happiness insur'd.
When earth's foundations shake, shall stand, by Providence secur'd.

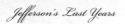

THOMAS JEFFERSON TO ELLEN COOLIDGE
August 27, 1825

I am glad you took the delightful tour which you describe in your letter. It is almost exactly that which Mr. Madison and myself pursued in May and June, 1791.... But from Saratoga till we got back to Northampton was then mostly desert. Now it is what thirty-four years of free and good government have made it. It shows how soon the labor of men would make a paradise of the whole earth, were it not for misgovernment, and a diversion of all his energies from the proper object — the happiness of man — to the selfish interests of kings, nobles, and priests.

JAMES MADISON TO MISS FRANCES WRIGHT
September 1, 1825

In cases where portions of time have been allotted to slaves, as among the Spaniards, with a view to their working out their freedom, it is believed that but few have availed themselves of the opportunity by a voluntary industry; and such a result could be less relied on in a case where each individual would feel that the fruit of his exertions would be shared by others, whether equally or unequally making them, and that the exertions of others would equally avail him, notwithstanding a deficiency in his own. Skillful arrangements might palliate this tendency, but it would be difficult to counteract it effectually.

The examples of the Moravians, the Harmonites, and the Shakers, in which the united labours of many for a common object have been successful, have, no doubt, an imposing character. But it must be recollected that in all these establishments there is a religious impulse in the members, and a religious authority in the head, for which there will be no substitutes of equivalent efficacy in the emancipating establishment.

JAMES MADISON TO FREDERICK BEASLEY
November 20, 1825

I have duly recd the copy of your little tract on the proofs of the Being & Attributes of God. To do full justice to it, would require not only a more critical attention than I have been able to bestow on it, but a resort to the celebrated work of Dr. Clarke, which I read fifty years ago only, and to that of Dr. Waterland also which I never read.

The reasoning that could satisfy such a mind as that of Clarke, ought certainly not to be slighted in the discussion. And the belief in a God, All Powerful wise & good, is so essential to the moral order of the World & to the happiness of man, that arguments which enforce it cannot be drawn from too many sources nor adapted with too much solicitude to the different characters & capacities to be impressed with it.

But whatever effect may be produced on some minds by the more abstract train of ideas which you so strongly support, it will probably always be found that the course of reasoning from the effect to the cause, "from Nature to Nature's God," Will be the more universal & more persuasive application.

The finiteness of the human understanding betrays itself on all subjects, but more especially when it contemplates such as involve infinity. What may safely be said seems to be, that the infinity of time & space forces itself on our conception, a limitation of either being inconceivable; that the mind prefers at once the idea of a self-existing cause to that of an infinite series of cause & effect, which augments, instead of avoiding the difficulty; and that it finds more facility in assenting to the self-existence of an invisible cause, possessing infinite power, wisdom & goodness, than to the self-existence of the universe, visibly destitute of those attributes, and which may be the effect of them. In this comparative facility of conception & belief, all philosophical Reasoning on the subject must perhaps terminate. But that I may not get farther beyond my depth, and without the resources which bear you up in fathoming efforts, I hasten to thank you for the favour which has made me your debtor, and to assure you of my esteem & my respectful regards.

JAMES MADISON TO DOCTOR C. CALDWELL
November 1825

I am sorry that the claims on my decreasing remnant of time do not permit me to enlarge on the profound subjects embraced in the memoir. I must not omit saying, however, that they are profoundly treated, and that I concur with you at once in rejecting the idea maintained by some divines, or more zeal than discretion, that there is no road from nature up to nature's God, and that all the knowledge of his existence and attributes which preceded the written revelation of them was derived from oral tradition. The doctrine is more extraordinary, as it so directly contradicts the declarations you have cited from the written authority itself. To my thanks for the memoir, I must add those due to your kind references to the best sources of information on the subject of phrenology. At an earlier stage of life, I might be tempted to avail myself of them. In that which it has reached, I must narrow, instead of widening, the scope of my researches.

THOMAS JEFFERSON TO ISAAC HARBY
January 6, 1826

Editor's note: Harby, of Charleston, SC, was one of the founders of American Reformed Judaism.

I have to thank you for the copy you have been so kind as to send me of your "Discourse before the reformed society of Israelites." I am little acquainted with the liturgy of the Jews or their mode of worship but the reformation proposed and explained in the Discourse appears entirely reasonable. Nothing is wiser than that all our institutions should keep pace with the advance of time and be improved with the improvement of the human mind. I have thought it a cruel addition to the wrongs which that injured sect have suffered that their youths should be excluded from the instructions in science afforded to all others in our public seminaries by imposing a course of theological reading which their consciences do not permit them to pursue, and in the University lately established here we have set the example of ceasing to violate the rights of conscience by any injunction on the different sects respecting their religion.

THOMAS JEFFERSON TO JAMES MADISON
February 17, 1826

The friendship which has subsisted between us, now half a century, and the harmony of our political principles and pursuits, have been sources of constant happiness to me through that long period. And if I remove beyond the reach of attentions to the University, or beyond the bourne of life itself, as I soon must, it is a comfort to leave that institution under your care, and an assurance that it will not be wanting. It has also been a great solace to me, to believe that you are engaged in vindicating to posterity the course we have pursued for preserving to them, in all their purity, the blessings of self-government, which we had assisted too in acquiring for them. If ever the earth has beheld a system of administration conducted with a single and steadfast eye to the general interest and happiness of those committed to it, one which, protected by truth, can never know reproach, it is that to which our lives have been devoted. To myself you have been a pillar of support through life. Take care of me when dead, and be assured that I shall leave with you my last affections.

THOMAS JEFFERSON TO ROGER WEIGHTMAN
June 24, 1826

Editor's note: This letter, declining to attend the fiftieth anniversary of the Declaration of Independence in the District of Columbia, was the last by Jefferson, who died ten days later, on July 4, 1826.

Respected Sir,

The kind invitation I receive from you, on the part of the citizens of the city of Washington, to be present with them at their celebration of the fiftieth anniversary of American Independence, as one of the surviving signers of an instrument pregnant with our own, and the fate of the world, is most flattering to myself, and heightened by the honorable accompaniment proposed for the comfort of such a journey. It adds sensibly to the sufferings of sickness, to be deprived by it of a personal participation in the rejoicings of that day. But acquiescence is a duty, under circumstances not placed among those we are permitted to control. I should, indeed, with peculiar delight, have met and exchanged there congratulations personally with the small band, the remnant of that host of worthies, who joined with us on that day, in the bold and doubtful election we were to make for our country, between submission or the sword; and to have enjoyed with them the consolatory fact, that our fellow citizens, after half a century of experience and prosperity, continue to approve the choice we made. May it be to the world, what I believe it will be, (to some parts sooner, to others later, but finally to all,) the signal of arousing men to burst the chains under which monkish ignorance and superstition had persuaded them to bind themselves, and to assume the blessings and security of self-government. That form which we have substituted, restores the free right to the unbounded exercise of reason and freedom of opinion. All eyes are opened, or opening, to the rights of man.

The general spread of the light of science has already laid open to every view the palpable truth, that the mass of mankind has not been born with saddles on their backs, nor a favored few booted and spurred, ready to ride them legitimately, by the grace of God. These are grounds of hope for others. For ourselves, let the annual return of this day forever refresh our recollections of these rights, and an undiminished devotion to them.

THOMAS JEFFERSON, EPITAPH
1826

On the faces of the Obelisk the following inscription, and not a word more

"Here was buried
Thomas Jefferson

Author of the Declaration of American Independance
of the Statute of Virginia for religious freedom
and Father of the University of Virginia."

Because by these, as testimonials that I have lived, I wish most to
be remembered.

Part 14

MADISON AFTER THE DEATH OF THOMAS JEFFERSON

1826 – 1834

Madison lived on for ten years after Jefferson, the last of the first four presidents to die. As such he received requests for his opinion on slavery, and his memories of events that he was involved with. The relation between religion and government was also a considerable concern to many of his correspondents.

Slavery gave him anxiety and he feared for the union. He particularly was concerned that his and Jefferson's arguments against the federal government during the strife over the Alien and Sedition Acts were being used by Southern politicians to threaten state nullification of federal laws and even disunion in the event of a threat to the southern institution.

On the other hand, he had made freedom of religion his lifetime cause. He had, despite compromises and failings along the way, kept the federal government apart from sectarianism. He was rightly proud of his accomplishment and could still vigorously present many definitive arguments in favor of separation of religion and state.

JAMES MADISON TO GEORGE MASON
July 14, 1826

Editor's note: Madison is discussing his Memorial and Remonstrance Against Religious Assessments.

During the session of the General Assembly, 1784-5, a bill was introduced into the House of Delegates providing for the legal support of Teachers of the Christian Religion, and being patronized by the most popular talents in the House, seemed likely to obtain a majority of votes. In order to arrest its progress, it was insisted with success, that the bill should be postponed till the ensuing session, and in the meantime be printed for public consideration, that the sense of the people might be the better called forth. Your highly distinguished ancestor, Col. Geo. Mason, Col. Geo. Nicholas also possessing much public weight, and some others, thought it advisable that a remonstrance against the bill should be prepared for general circulation and signature, and imposed on me the task of drawing up such a paper. This draught having received their sanction, a large number of printed copies were distributed, and so extensively signed by the people of every religious denomination, that at the ensuing session the projected measure was entirely frustrated; and under the influence of the public sentiment thus manifested the celebrated bill "Establishing Religious Freedom" enacted into a permanent barrier against Future attempts on the rights of conscience as declared in the Great Charter prefixed to the Constitution of the State.

JAMES MADISON TO MARQUIS DE LA FAYETTE
November 24, 1826

The Anglican hierarchy existing in Virginia prior to the Revolution was abolished by an early act of the Independent Legislature. In the year 1785, a bill was introduced under the auspices of Mr. Henry, imposing a general tax for the support of "Teachers of the Christian Religion." It made a progress, threatening a majority in its favor. As an expedient to defeat it, we proposed that it should be postponed to another session, and printed in the meantime for public consideration. Such an appeal in a case so important and so unforeseen could not be resisted. With a view to arouse the people, it was thought proper that a memorial should be drawn up, the task being assigned to me, to be printed and circulated throughout the State for a general signature. The experiment succeeded. The memorial was so extensively signed by the various religious sects, including a considerable portion of the old hierarchy, that the projected innovation was crushed, and under the influence of the popular sentiment thus called forth, the well-known Bill prepared by Mr. Jefferson, for "Establishing Religious freedom," passed into a law, as it now stands in our code of statutes.

JAMES MADISON TO J. K. PAULDING
March 10, 1827

Monopolies and perpetuities are objects of just abhorrence. The former are unjust to the existing, the latter, usurpations on the right of future generations. Is it not strange that the law, which will not permit an individual to bequeath his property to the descendants of his own loins for more than a short and strictly-defined term, should authorize an associated few to entail perpetual and indefeasible appropriations, and that not only to objects visible and tangible, but to particular opinions, consisting, sometimes, of the most metaphysical niceties, as is the case with ecclesiastical corporations?

JAMES MADISON TO GEORGE MASON
December 29, 1827

I am much obliged by your polite attention in sending me the copies of the Remonstrance in favour of Religious liberty, which, with your letter of the 10th, came duly to hand.... I wished a few copies on account of applications now and then made to me, and I preferred the edition of which you had sent me a sample, as being in the simplest of forms; and for the further reason that the pamphlet edition had inserted in the caption the term "toleration," not in the article declaring the right. The term being of familiar use in the English Code, had been admitted into the original draught of the Declaration of Rights; but, on a suggestion from myself, was readily exchanged for the phraseology excluding it.

JAMES MADISON, AUTOBIOGRAPHICAL NOTES
1832

Editor's note: Madison wrote this in third person.

Being young & in the midst of distinguished and experienced members of the convention he did not enter into its debates; tho' he occasionally suggested amendments; the most material of which was a change of the terms in which the freedom of Conscience was expressed in the proposed Declaration of Rights. This important and meritorious instrument was drawn by Geo. Mason, who had inadvertently adopted the word "toleration" in the article on that subject. The change suggested and accepted, substituted a phraseology which declared the freedom of conscience to be a natural and absolute right.

JAMES MADISON TO REVEREND JASPER ADAMS
Spring 1833

Editor's note: Adams challenged the notion "that Christianity had no connection with our civil government." Rather, he insisted, "the people of the United States have retained the Christian religion as the foundation of their civil, legal, and political institutions."

I recd in due time, the printed copy of your Convention sermon on the relation of Xnity to Civil Govt with a manuscript request of my opinion on the subject.

There appears to be in the nature of man what insures his belief in an invisible cause of his present existence, and anticipation of his future existence. Hence the propensities & susceptibilities in that case of religion which with a few doubtful or individual exceptions have prevailed throughout the world.

Waiving the rights of Conscience, not included in the surrender implied by the social State, and more or less invaded by all religious Establishments, the simple question to be decided is whether a support of the best & purest religion, the Xn religion itself ought, not so far at least as pecuniary means are involved, to be provided for by the Govt rather than be left to the voluntary provisions of those who profess it. And on this question experience will be an admitted Umpire, the more adequate as the connection between Govts & Religion have existed in such various degrees & forms, and now can be compared with examples where connection has been entirely dissolved.

In the Papal System, Government and Religion are in a manner consolidated, & that is found to be the worst of Govts.

In most of the Govts of the old world, the legal establishment of a particular religion and without or with very little toleration of others makes a part of the Political and Civil organization and there are few of the most enlightened judges who will maintain that the system has been favorable either to Religion or to Govt.

Until Holland ventured on the experiment of combining toleration with the establishment of a particular creed, it was taken for granted, that an exclusive & intolerant establishment was essential, and notwithstanding the light thrown on the subject by that experiment, the prevailing opinion in Europe, England not excepted, has been that Religion could not be preserved without the support of Govt nor Govt be supported with an established religion that there must be a least an alliance of some sort between them.

It remained for North America to bring the great & interesting subject to a fair, and finally to a decisive test.

In the Colonial State of the Country, there were four examples, R. I, N. J., Penna, and Delaware, & the greater part of N. Y. where there were no religious Establishments; the support of Religion being left to the voluntary associations & contributions of individuals; and certainly the religious condition of those Colonies, will well bear a comparison with that where establishments existed.

As it may be suggested that experiments made in Colonies more or less under the Controul of a foreign Government, had not the full scope necessary to display their tendency, it is fortunate that the appeal can now be made to their effects under a complete exemption from any such Controul.

It is true that the New England States have not discontinued establishments of Religion formed under very peculiar circumstances; but they have by successive relaxations advanced towards the prevailing example; and without any evidence of disadvantage either to Religion or good Government.

And if we turn to the Southern States where there was, previous to the Declaration of independence, a legal provision for the support of Religion; and since that event a surrender of it to a spontaneous support by the people, it may be said that the difference amounts nearly to a contrast in the greater purity & industry of the Pastors and in the greater devotion of their flocks, in the latter period than in the former. In Virginia the contrast is particularly striking, to those whose memories can make the comparison. It will not be denied that causes other than the abolition of the legal establishment of Religion are to be taken into view in accountg for the change in the Religious character of the community. But the existing character, distinguished as it is by its religious features, and the lapse of time now more than 50 years since the legal support of Religion was withdrawn sufficiently prove that it does not need the support of Govt and it will scarcely be contended that Government has suffered by the exemption of Religion from its cognizance, or its pecuniary aid.

The apprehension of some seems to be that Religion left entirely to itself may run into extravagances injurious both to Religion and to social order; but besides the question whether the interference of Govt in any form wd not be more likely to increase than Controul the tendency, it is a safe calculation that in this as in other cases of excessive excitement, Reason will gradually regain its ascendancy. Great excitements are less apt to be permanent than to vibrate to the opposite extreme.

Under another aspect of the subject there may be less danger that Religion, if left to itself, will suffer from a failure of the pecuniary support applicable to it than that an omission of the public authorities to limit the duration of their Charters to Religious Corporations, and the amount of property acquirable by them, may lead to an injurious accumulation of wealth from the lavish donations and bequests prompted by a pious zeal or by an atoning remorse. Some monitory examples have already appeared.

Whilst I thus frankly express my view of the subject presented in your sermon, I must do you the justice to observe that you very ably maintained yours. I must admit moreover that it may not be easy, in every possible case, to trace the line of separation between the rights of religion and the Civil authority with such distinctness as to avoid collisions & doubts on unessential points. The tendency to a usurpation on one side or the other, or to a corrupting coalition or alliance between them, will be best guarded agst by an entire abstinence of the Govt from interference in any way whatever, beyond the necessity of preserving public order, & protecting each sect agst trespasses on its legal rights by others.

I owe you Sir an apology for the delay in complying with the request of my opinion on the subject discussed in your sermon; if not also for the brevity & it may be thought crudeness of the opinion itself. I must rest the apology on my great age now in its 83rd year, with more than the ordinary infirmities, and especially on the effect of a chronic Rheumatism, combined with both, which makes my hand & fingers as averse to the pen as they are awkward in the use of it.

JAMES MADISON TO THOMAS GRIMKE
January 6, 1834

You wish to be informed of the errors in your pamphlet alluded to in my last. The first related to the proposition of Doctor Franklin in favor of a religious service in the Federal Convention. The proposition was received and treated with the respect due to it; but the lapse of time which had preceded, with considerations growing out of it, had the effect of limiting what was done, to a reference of the proposition to a highly respectable Committee. The issue of it may be traced in the printed Journal. The Quaker usage, never discontinued in the State and the place where the Convention held its sittings, might not have been without an influence as might also, the discord of religious opinions within the Convention, as well as among the clergy of the spot. The error into which you had fallen may have been confirmed by a communication in the National Intelligencer some years ago, said to have been received through a respectable channel from a member of the Convention. That the communication was erroneous is certain; whether from misapprehension or mis-recollection, uncertain.

SCHOLAR'S AFTERWORD

Historians don't invent history. They reinvent it. Traditionally, Jefferson was seen as America's font of political wisdom. Yet, in recent decades, the most discussed aspect of American revolutionary history was his sexual relation with his slave, Sally Hemings. Indeed the founding fathers were slaveholders. And they never gave women the vote.

Nevertheless, the revolution produced a government with two features that begin the modern age. It was a republic. It had no state religion. Those features are permanent positive additions to human consciousness. Our first task is to understand why the contributions of Jefferson and Madison are such a mix of major success and failure—by their standards and ours.

The answers are simple enough. They created modern politics. As youths they were opposed to slavery. However they soon realized that the forces—black or white—weren't there for full abolition. They were successful in stopping its spread north of the Ohio River. They also stopped the import of slaves. But then they made decisions that produced an America of unworkable compromises on slavery.

Now we read their aged pessimism regarding slavery with pity for them—for their inability, as pioneers without a map, to understand the consequences of their bow to the god of political necessity. They could not foresee the price their society was going to pay for it, in the form of the Civil War.

Yet, thru this, their religious thinking remained, if not perfect, vigorous. In their prime, they succeeded in separating church and state in Virginia. In their maturity they thought they did a good job of separating them at the federal level. They made compromises along the way, but triumphed on most principled issues. There were no religious tests for government posts. No one was persecuted for religion.

Real success meant they could acknowledge what still needed to be done. Massachusetts didn't fully disestablish religion until 1833. Indeed the First Amendment wasn't judicially declared binding on states until 1925. But a president refusing to proclaim Thanksgivings is several million miles more principled than anyone in Jefferson's party today, regarding maintaining or extending his "wall of separation" between all religions and our government.

That wall is now integral to the serious worldwide intellectual agenda. Indeed, some of our authors' later work now assumes supreme contemporary significance. Madison presented the Bill of Rights to the First Congress, hence he is the best authority on it. Now, given the importance of religion in United States policies at home and abroad, Madison's Detatched Memoranda must be ranked in historical importance with the Bible and Koran. "Jefferson's Bible" is as significant for American culture as the King James Bible. Yet the Memoranda and Jefferson's razor are as yet unknown to most Americans.

Jefferson thought that Unitarianism would conquer America. It didn't. Freedom of religion triumphed, but the sects and priestcraft he despised spread among white American Protestants, rich and poor. The land that produced the world's most politically successful anti-clerics became famous for its often fanatic popular religion.

Jefferson & Madison were advance thinkers among America's minuscule educated class of their day. Moreover, Jefferson never thought it his duty to convert anyone to non-denominational skepticism. His "Bible" only became public in 1902. Madison's Memoranda wasn't revealed until 1946. But now, with the 2004 election, when every other word out of the mouths of the Republican and Democratic presidential candidates is "faith," it is our duty and pleasure to bring their religious thinking to the widest American public. Their writings are classics, the best possible standard by which to measure the bawling of today's demagogues.

RELIGION IN AMERICAN POLITICS, FROM THE CIVIL WAR TO THE COLD WAR

Lincoln, devoted to Jefferson, never joined a church. He was the last President of Jeffersonian mentality. From then until now, an examination of politics and American religion takes us through less than inspiring aspects of U.S. history.

Pro-slavery Protestant sects were the mass base of post-civil war southern racism. But their issue was color. Religion per se became a national issue with the surging 19th century Catholic immigrant wave. The upshot, so-called Blaine Amendments to thirty-six state constitutions, designed to keep tax money out of thrusting "papist" hands, reinforced Protestantism as the unofficial cultural religion, rather than generated secularism. But Catholics weren't persecuted.

The Democratic Party, the descendent of Jefferson & Madison's Republicans, assumed its present name in the late 1820s. Our GOP Republicans took that vacant name to show that they were restoring Jefferson's politics. But the imposition of the 1924 immigration quotas was fueled by nativist Democratic and Republican worry about the dilution of their country's Protestant character by Catholic and Jewish immigrants. The giant KKK marches of the 1920s were Protestant events. Democrat William Jennings Bryan represented millions of such Protestants when he fought evolution in Tennessee schools in 1925. Democrat Al Smith lost the 1928 election to Protestant opposition to a Catholic President.

In the '30s, the Nazi German-American Bund played on nativist Protestant racism. Gerald L. K. Smith, a Huey Long lieutenant, became a well-known isolationist anti-Semite. With the Spanish civil war, Father Charles Coughlin, a pro-fascist radio-priest, developed a wide following among Catholics. During this time many Jews had to defend themselves against physical attacks. But it is important to remember that despite growing anti-semitism at the social level, thanks to Madison and Jefferson, no sane person believed they could pass anti-Jewish laws here.

U.S. anti-Semitism was discredited by the holocaust. In its wake, Zionism became a mass Jewish movement in reaction to the slaughter in Europe. Ninety percent of American Jewry, from Orthodox to Stalinist, supported Washington, backing crucial to the creation of Israel in 1948. For them, the issue was refuge for Jews fleeing European anti-Semitism. For the politicians, Margaret Truman, President Harry's daughter, later described how the National Chairman "almost made a speech, pointing out how many Jews were major contributors to the Democratic Party's campaign fund and were expecting the United States to support the Zionists' positions on Palestine."

In short, religion was all over American politics in different ways. But it wasn't a front and center political concern until after WW II, with its international consequences.

CHRIST, CAPITALISM, AND CLASS STRUGGLE

The major postwar factor pushing religion into the front lines of American political consciousness was the rise of atheist Stalinism as Wall Street's prime enemy. There were millions of Catholics from Eastern European countries taken over by Stalin, plus Italians, who might be mobilized against Communism in their ancestral homes. In 1954, in this environment, there was no serious opposition to the addition of "under God" to the Pledge of Allegiance, at the request of the Knights of Columbus and Catholic War Veterans.

Politician after politician got up on any occasion to defend "the Judeo-Christian way of life" against Communism. In life, Republican President Dwight Eisenhower, who organized Allied success in western Europe in WW II, was born into a fanatic pacifist sect. He saw religion as confining and himself as escaping from it. But, pressured by propaganda advisers, he became the first President baptized in office.

Jack Kennedy's 1960 election meant the effective end of "no Pope here" populism. His assassination went further into making him a national icon. But Americans didn't know that, behind the scenes, Kennedy committed the greatest governmental violation of freedom of religion in U.S. history. The President and his Attorney General, brother Bobby, signed papers authorizing bugging and wiretapping of Martin Luther King.

The story came out during the release of a flood of post-Watergate FBI files. They were looking for Communists in his entourage. All post WW II Democratic and Republican Presidents violated our free speech rights in the interest of anti-Communism and no one saw the church as implicated in it. When the facts were uncovered, lefts and liberals denounced it as an example of racism and/or government spying, with no thought given to its implications on church/state separation.

THE '60S COME AND RELIGION BEGINS TO GO

America is culturally Protestant and legally secularist, but the Roman Catholic Church is our biggest sect at twenty-five percent. However, while the election of Kennedy meant full acceptance for Catholics into the American family, the Church soon began to disintegrate. "Vatican II," the 1962-65 church council, tried to bring the church up to date. Latin was abandoned. The calendar was purged of bogus saints. Nuns abandoned medieval robes. The church admitted that its teachings contributed to modern anti-Semitism. The reforms deflated the Church's authority in the eyes of many faithful. The number becoming priests began its steep decline. More laymen, forgive the pun, began to use contraception.

Since then, recent immigrants from Latin America have poured out of the church. On February 18, 1999, the *New York Times* ran a survey of the city's Catholics, asking what kind of new Archbishop they preferred. So many surveyed declared themselves ex-Catholics that, for the first time, the paper set up a separate statistical column for this now-significant phenomena.

Engulfed by pedophile scandals, a morbid quality hovers over what is left of the Church. The reigning Pope has made a career of apologizing to Muslims for the crusades; to the Czechs for the burning of Jan Huss, their national Protestant hero; to Jews for fomenting anti-Semitism; and to Africans for slavery.

For all this, identification with the church doesn't hurt politicians with Catholics or others, if they enforce abortion, divorce and other democratically decided laws in conflict with dogma. However, as it continues to lose the respect of the faithful and the larger public, such identification will come to be taken as certified proof of either demagogic pandering to the older flock, as with New Jersey's Jim McGreevey, or worse, an utter lack of intellect.

Blacks are the most religious U.S. stratum. Forty-seven percent of Yanks believe that god created the world about 10,000 years ago. Fifty-seven percent of blacks believe that. Condoleezza Rice is the daughter of a minister. Black clerical rightists have gotten more publicity since Bush became President, and some black preachers demonstrate against gay marriage. But the vast majority of Black Christians don't support him. They aren't calling for an official Christian America. On the other hand, Bush's Christian persona, support for vouchers, and attempts to put churches on the government payroll via "faith-based" drug clinics, etc., doesn't hurt him among black Christians.

American black clerical political activity was most significant in the '50s and '60s, when the issue was simple: Mobilizing the masses for equality before the law. Since that was obtained, clergy are tested, like everyone else, by what they do about contemporary America. Typically, involvement with the Democratic Party, riddled with corruption and openly seeking money from the rich, limits their capacity to gain important benefits for poor blacks. Their influence wanes among educated young blacks, religiously, culturally and politically.

Southern white Protestantism had to undergo a dramatic ideological facelift after the collapse of legal segregation. The Southern Baptist Convention, America's largest Protestant sect, apologized for its racism. But it doesn't understand that supporting slavery against Lincoln, then segregation against King, disqualifies any organization to speak, forever after, on religion or politics.

The Southern Baptist Convention continues on its merry way to political hell. President Jimmy Carter left them. He ran the U.S. Eventually he came to believe women are as good as men. He believes in women ministers. They hold to male-only ministers. They stood by Bush as he invaded Iraq, even as his own Methodist leadership spoke for peace. But here again decline has set in. The convention was told that new baptisms have declined for four straight years.

THE RISE OF POPULAR SECULARISM

Jefferson's comment—American freethinkers tended to stay Protestant, unlike co-thinkers in Catholic countries, who were atheists—was true until 19th century German immigrants, including Marxists and other radicals, formed the first sociologically significant layer of American atheists. After Darwin, they were joined by some scientists from a larger minority of Freethinkers and Rationalists—most famously Mark Twain and Jack London. Jefferson's heritage reserved a place for the atheist's elbow at the American bar.

The Communist Party of the '20s was active in the larger atheist movement. But its efforts stopped in the '30s. Moscow sought an alliance with Britain, France, and America against Hitler. Archbishops were sought for their coalitions and atheist propaganda got in the way.

The '60s new left was focused on racism, opposition to the Vietnam War, and then feminism. Church-state separation wasn't an issue. Religion even became respectable in left circles with the rise of Martin Luther King and Malcolm X.

In 1952, when I entered into the world of ideological organizations, there was next to nothing in the way of organized atheism. But social evolution was generating growing percentages of educated atheists and freethinkers. In 1940, only 4.6 percent of adult Americans had bachelor degrees. The 2000 census came up with 24.4 percent.

Science is at the center of modern universities, with astronomy, biology, and physics as atheist strongholds, with approximately half such scientists calling themselves atheist. Their ethos—send an article into *Scientific American* about how physics proves that god exists and it gets flung into the round file—dominates state universities.

Few atheist scientists see themselves as recruiters to their ideology. Nevertheless, it spreads with mass higher education. Fourteen percent of Americans, one out of seven, say they have no religion. Twenty-seven percent of Jews, the most educated U.S. stratum, are atheists. Major upper class Protestant denominations, Episcopalians, Presbyterians, also lose their young elite to atheism. Whatever their politics, atheists are seen as the most consistent partisans of science. Indeed, it isn't a sociological accident that Ron Reagan, an open atheist, is the best-known proponent of stem cell research.

The late Egon Mayer of City University of New York, distinguished among pollsters and demographers, told me that his American Religious Identification Survey 2001 showed that the notion that the religious right was the wave of the future was wrong. They were empty barrels making the most noise.

The direction is away from religious orthodoxies, towards liberalization of old religions or outright abandonment of them. Increasingly the remnant Catholic laity believe in married priests. The Reform and Conservative Jewish sects have women rabbis. Fights over gay rights, up to ordinations as clergy, goes on in one sect after another.

According to the National Opinion Research Center, Protestants will become less than 50 percent of our population in late 2004 or 2005. The young, particularly the educated, are falling away. Among the still faithful, conversions from one sect to another are common. Zen and Tibetan Buddhism have followings here among native-born Americans. A majority of young Jews intermarry, and Protestant-Catholic marriages are skyrocketing.

According to Mayer, the religious right's shrillness is their reaction to a culture that is overwhelming them. At the same time, the growing atheist stratum, religious liberals, evolutionists, gay rights advocates, movers from one religion to another, Baptists and other Christians who know the history of their denomination's past persecution and draw separationist conclusions; these diverse elements now collectively constitute a mass social base for a movement that can ultimately come to power and produce the educated freethinking America that Jefferson, father of the University of Virginia, wished for.

NEW TIMES, OLD ISSUES

The civil rights and antiwar movements united progressive religious activist with atheist leftists. Church-state questions didn't come up. But their example generated a massive wave of other ethical and cultural challenges that confronted all religious forces head on.

In 1969, tens of thousands of women and their supporters marched in New York for female equality. Feminism rapidly triumphed. Serious sexual education in public schools became a national concern as unwed mothers became more common in all social stratums. Abortion became legal.

A nationwide mass gay movement sprang up after the 1969 riot at the Stonewall Inn in Greenwich Village. Since then it has won many legal victories, often against public opinion. Now, friend and foe alike see George Bush trying to mobilize backward Christian elements opposing gay marriage for his federal constitutional amendment. Everyone acknowledges that he is playing for votes. Thanks to Bush's open religious pandering, concern for church/state separation is at a high. But what many liberals don't want to fully acknowledge is that the Democrats are also into theological demagoguery.

Party strategists know they have the Black, Hispanic, and Jewish votes. They hope their minorities in the white Protestant and Catholic communities will be as big as possible. If that happens, they beat George W. Bush. In 2000, they got 39 percent of the voters who attended religious services at least once a week. They will do whatever they think they can get away with to maximize their minority of pious whites, without losing their liberal and gay supporters.

The party specialty is called "voting my district." Dennis Kucinich sat in the House of Representatives from Cleveland. With lots of Polish Catholics there, Kucinich was against abortion. When he took it into his head to become president, he suddenly sounded like he believed that abortion is a blessing.

In 2003, during the legal process involving Alabama's Chief Justice Roy Moore's Ten Commandments monument in the state court house, the 11th Federal Circuit Court of Appeals demanded removal of "Roy's Rock," On July 23, the U.S. House of Representatives voted 307 to 119 to amend an appropriations bill. It prohibited use of federal money to enforce the Court's decision demanding the rock's removal. Fifty out of 197 Democrats voted to ban U.S. money for enforcement of the order against Moore. Cynics understood that this was demagoguery. They knew the bill wouldn't get past the Senate. But it made fifty Representatives look good in the eyes of white Protestant voters.

In 2002, an atheist got the 9th U.S. Circuit Court of Appeals to rule that "under God" in the Pledge of Allegiance for school kids violates the First Amendment. It was to be banned in the Circuit's nine western states. On two occasions the Senate voted, 99 to 0 and 94 to 0, to denounce the 9th's ruling in non-binding statements. Among those denouncing the court was John Kerry.

The House voted 307 to 119 for an amendment to an appropriations bill. It prohibited use of federal money to enforce the 9th's ruling. Ninety-one of 199 Democrats voted to ban funding the "under God" decision.

CRUSADERS, ZIONISTS, AND JIHADIS

Internationally, Washington's manipulation of religion against atheist Stalinism developed to war-crimes proportions, with horrific consequences carrying through to this day.

In 1979, Jimmy Carter supported the Shah of Iran, infamous for torture, against the Shia Islamic revolutionary movement. The Shah lost and Jimmy brought him here. The U.S. became Shatan Bozarog—Great Satan. Ayatollah Khomeini's victory inspired many Muslims, Shia and Sunni. He proved it was possible to beat Great Satan.

The U.S. vs. Iran's regime was constantly in the media during the Carter administration, and carried over to Ronald Reagan's administration beginning in 1981. What the public didn't know was that in 1979, Jimmy, emeshed in a struggle against Shia fundamentalism, covertly involved the U.S. in Afghanistan, on the side of Sunni fundamentalism against a Soviet puppet regime.

Afghanistan bordered on the Soviet Union. At 9 percent, it was one of the least literate countries in the world. The Soviets were popular with the city dwellers among the 9 percent, as they represented modernity. In 1973, the last king was overthrown by Lt. General Muhammad Daoud Khan. The local pro-Russian Communist Party, on its own, killed him and took power in 1978. Their dominant element was analogous to Cambodia's Pol Pot. They fanatically imposed social change on a traditional rural Islamic society. They began to jail an internal rival faction.

The strength of the resistance convinced the Soviets that they would be faced with a triumphant Islamic state on their border unless they intervened to replace the local Stalinist tyrant with a less menacing face to the traditional society, while preserving the secular gains, particularly for women, under the republican regime. In 1979, the Soviets invaded, killed then President Hafizulla Amin and replaced him with the leader of the suppressed Stalinist faction.

Carter misunderstood the events. He saw the Soviet invasion as expansionist, when it was defensive in purpose. He started covertly arming fundamentalists against the Soviets. He was defeated for reelection, Ronald Reagan took over and in time the expense of fighting U.S.-armed Islamists forced Moscow out. At this writing, Gulbuddin Hekmatyar, the favorite U.S. anti-Soviet fanatic, is still in the field, against the U.S., in tandem with the Taliban and Bin Laden.

No mincing words: Bipartisan Washington committed war crimes in patronizing fundamentalism against the Soviets. Worst of all, what they put into Afghanistan's kettle, came back afterwards into America's spoon. Al Qaeda and 9/11 was the "blowback"—CIA slang for disastrous consequences of their missions.

Between 1929 and 1933, in the depths of the Depression, Germany's capitalists supported Hitler against the threat to their wealth represented by the working class—the Social Democratic and Communist Parties. Killing Jews, invading Russia—none of that was on their minds. They needed a Commie basher. Hitler was handy. He won with their crucial support. He took on the world and Germany lost five million dead, its eastern provinces, etc. These events are all consequences of helping right-wing fanatics against the left.

Likewise, Washington didn't want the consequences of patronage to fundamentalists. It had no interest in taking away women's rights under the Soviet sponsored regime. But that's what happened because they backed resident Commie-bashing fanatics.

Without U.S. patronage, fundamentalism couldn't win. But the fanatics interpreted it differently. They won because they were on Allah's side, craftily using "Crusader" money and military training in a good cause, beating atheist Soviets.

Saddam Hussein's attack on Kuwait brought U.S. troops into Saudi Arabia to protect the regime and its oil. Bin Laden realized that the dynasty there were Christian clients. Now it was time to take on the Crusaders. Wall Street trained terrorists, they learned their lessons well, and 9/11 was the result.

The circumstances and actors were different, but U.S. involvement with Afghan fundamentalism will come to be seen to be as a replay of German capitalism's patronage of Nazism.

JEFFERSON & MADISON TO THE RESCUE!!!

At this very moment, we certainly have a surreal situation. The U.S. is constitutionally Madison's creation. He vetoed a bill because it vested in a church "an authority to provide for the support of the poor and the education of poor children of the same, an authority which, being altogether superfluous if the provision is to be the result of pious charity, would be a precedent for giving to religious societies as such a legal agency in carrying into effect a public and civil duty."

If that isn't clear, nothing is. Yet we have Bush's Executive Order on Faith-Based Initiatives and Kerry's answer, a "Presidential Advisory Group on Expanding Faith-Based Initiatives." At the same time, the U.S. simultaneously trains Islamic fundamentalist Saudi Arabia's National Guard and helps fund and arm Orthodox Jewish Israel.

If we could scroll him up to our times, is it possible to imagine that Madison would tolerate this. You, dear reader, have read him. You know the answer: No.

We, 168 years after Madison's death, have much experience with religious manipulation by politicians. The South is dotted with Confederate cemeteries, full of Christian and Jewish slave holders, inspired by their constitution:

"We, the people of the Confederate States, each State acting in its sovereign and independent character, in order to form a permanent federal government, establish justice, insure domestic tranquillity, and secure the blessings of liberty to ourselves and our posterity invoking the favor and guidance of Almighty God do ordain and establish this Constitution for the Confederate States of America."

King was indeed spied upon by Madison's party. The Democratic and Republican parties share criminal responsibility for the triumph of Islamic fundamentalism in Afghanistan. The cemeteries of America are now full of innocent dead, because of unforeseen consequences of their joint crime. The cemeteries of Palestine/Israel are likewise full of Arabs and Israelis, as a consequence of U.S. patronage of Orthodox Israel.

It took 9/11 to give us to a new commandment: Thou shalt not pander to religious fanatics. Do that abroad, and it has direct consequences on Americans' lives and rights. What Americans must realize is that such outrages abroad have their origin in hustling them here. "Blow jobs in the White House" became part of polite reportage, even as Bill Clinton's military trained Saudia's Islamic fundamentalist military. All the while, Jesus passed thru his lips on every convenient occasion as he sought to keep his white Protestant supporters.

Being neither a prophet nor a prophet's son, I don't predict election winners. But, given the history of the current candidates, Bush and Kerry, you don't have to be a prophet to understand that whoever wins the 2004 election will be a "faith-based" trashmouth. Domestically this means money wasted via vouchers going to sectarian schools, instead of towards shaping up public schools. Internationally this means our tax money funding Israeli religious apartheid, our military training the Saudi dynasty's shock troops. Bluntly put, we will still be in the fast lane to death and disaster if politicians do not begin to heed the lessons of Jefferson and Madison.

There can only be one answer to this orgy of demagoguery: An informed mass movement for separation of religion and state, against all politicians who would combine them. In this inevitable battle we have some powerful advantages, if we utilize them.

Currently, the Iraq war is increasingly unpopular, with demonstrations becoming common events. All the monkey chatter about the war on terrorism serves to bring the political conversation around to the ugly fact that bipartisan Washington funded and trained Afghanistan's Islamic fundamentalist fanatics.

Above all, the mass social forces are present for the final triumph of separatism. America's young educated will increase. The politicians, so skilled in playing to the uneducated, have nothing to offer them intellectually, but we have Jefferson's razor to present to them.

The hacks claim to represent patriotism. Every year July 4th rolls around and they pay lipservice to Jefferson's ideals. They can still get away with it because the broad public has no awareness of what he and Madison really stood for. So, let us take Jefferson's Bible and Madison's Memoranda to the people. With time, they will take that critical blade to their own religious values, to the ranting of the politicians, and finally to the failings of our political and social systems.

Lenni Brenner
September 2004

Thomas Jefferson's

CHRONOLOGY

1743

April 13 (April 2, Old Style). Born at Shadwell plantation in Goochland (later Albemarle) County, Virginia, to Peter Jefferson, a planter and surveyor, and Jane Randolph.

1752

Attends a local school run by a Scot, Rev. William Douglas.

1757

Peter Jefferson dies.

1758-60

Attends Rev. James Maury's school in Fredericksville Parish, 12 miles from Shadwell. Begins a literary commonplace book, entering extracts from Greek, Latin, and English literature.

1760-62

Attends William and Mary College in Williamsburg. Studies mathematics, philosophy, French and the violin. Attends dinners with Virginia governor. Graduated in 1762.

1762

Begins law studies with George Wythe, his former teacher at college.

1764

Comes of age, inherits 2,750 acres and slaves.

1765

Passes bar examination. Returns to Shadwell.

1766
Spring-Summer. Tours Annapolis, Philadelphia, and New York.

1767
Begins practicing law.

1768
Begins building Monticello, on a 867-foot mountain near Shadwell.

1769
May. Takes seat as representative from Albemarle County in Virginia's House of Burgesses. Serves in House until 1776.

1770
November. Takes up residence at Monticello.

1772
January 1. Marries Martha Wayles Skelton, widow, age twenty-three. They have six children. Only two live to adulthood.

1773
Takes possession of father-in-law's 11,000 acres and slaves. Sells more than half the land. Purchasers later pay in depreciated revolutionary money. Jefferson spends life trying to repay father-in-law's creditors.

1774
January 14. Through division of estate of Jefferson's wife's father, acquires additional slaves, including Elizabeth (Betty) Hemings (c.1735-1807).

July. Drafts instructions for Virginia delegates to first Continental Congress. Friends have his instructions published in August as *A Summary View of the Rights of British America*.

1775
March 27. Jefferson is a delegate to the second Continental Congress. He attends the House of Burgesses until mid-June departure for Philadelphia.

June 20. Jefferson arrives in Philadelphia.
June-July. Drafts address, "A Declaration of the Causes & Necessity for Taking Up Arms."

August 9. Returns to Virginia. Attends Convention, an interim state government in early revolution.

October 1. Returns to Philadelphia.

December. Returns to Monticello.

1776

January. Writes an "alternative" history of the colonies elaborating on what he wrote in 1774 in *A Summary View of the Rights of British America*.

May 14 – September. In Philadelphia at second Continental Congress.

May 15. Virginia Convention appoints a committee to draft a constitution.

May-June. Although not on the committee, Jefferson writes drafts of constitution. Reforms include gradual abolition of slavery, extension of suffrage, independent judiciary and easy immigrant naturalization.

June 7. Richard Henry Lee, on Virginia instructions, calls for declaration of independence. Congress appoints a committee: Jefferson, John Adams, Benjamin Franklin, Robert Livingston, and Roger Sherman. Jefferson drafts document. Other members make 47 changes.

June 28. The committee submits draft to Congress.

July 1-4. Congress debates draft. Jefferson objects to many of thirty-nine further changes. Most significant are deletion of arguments holding George III responsible for slave trade in the colonies, and his ending, replaced by Lee's resolution.

July 4. Congress prints Declaration.

July 8. First public reading takes place in Philadelphia.

October 11. Jefferson returns to Virginia House of Delegates. James Madison, also serving, becomes a political colleague until Jefferson's death. They exchange approximately 1,200 letters.

October 11 – November 19, 1776. Writes Rough Draft of Resolutions for Disestablishing the Church of England and for Repealing Laws Interfering with Freedom of Worship.

November 30. Draft of Bill Exempting Dissenters from Contributing to the Support of the Church.

1777

Member of committee to revise Virginia's laws.
Drafts Virginia Statute for Religious Freedom.

1778

Daughter Mary (Polly) born August 1.

1779

June 1. Elected governor with one-year term.

June 18. Jefferson submits Report of the Committee of Revisors to House. Worked on since 1776, it includes Statute for Religious Freedom; Bill for Proportioning Crimes and Punishments; Bill for the More General Diffusion of Knowledge; and measures expanding suffrage, abolishing feudal land inheritance laws. Only measures for abolition of primogeniture and entail as forms of land inheritance, pass. The House passed Statute for Religious Freedom.

1780
June 2. Reelected governor.

December 20. Jefferson answers a French questionnaire regarding information about the states. After sending answers, Jefferson makes further changes.

December 29. British army, commanded by Benedict Arnold, invades Virginia.

1781
June 2. Second term expires, but before a new governor can be elected, the British attack Monticello on June 4. Jefferson, with family and friends, flees.

June 12. Virginia House calls inquiry into adequacy of preparations against British invasion, and his flight.

December 15. House accepts committee report absolving Jefferson.
Writes *Notes On The State Of Virginia, 1781-82.*

1782
September 6. Wife, Martha Wayles Skelton, dies after illness following May 8 birth of their sixth child.

1783
June 6. Delegate to Congress from Virginia.

November-December. Attends Congress at Princeton and Annapolis.

1784
March 1. Submits to Congress his Report of a Plan of Government for the Western Territory. He proposes that slavery be abolished in new states by 1800. Congress rejects this part and passes revised Ordinance April 23. Jefferson blames Southern representatives for rejection of his plan, high point of his opposition to slavery.

May 7. Congress appoints Jefferson Minister plenipotentiary to join John Adams and Benjamin Franklin in negotiating treaties in Europe.
June-July. Jefferson travels throughout eastern states, collecting information on history, geography, agriculture and commerce for role as minister.

July 5. Sails to Europe with Patsy.

August 3. Arrives in France.

1785

March. Succeeds Franklin as Minister to France.

April-May. Adams and Jefferson negotiate loan from Dutch bankers to consolidate U.S. debts, pay French veterans of the American Revolution, and ransom captives held by Algerian and Moroccan pirate rulers.

Notes on the State of Virginia privately printed in France, author's name omitted, 200 copies.

1786

January 16. Virginia House passes the Statute for Religious Freedom.

March-April. Jefferson visits John Adams, Minister in London. He is presented to and snubbed by George III.

1787

March-June. Jefferson travels through southern France and northern Italy.

May-September. Constitutional Convention meets in Philadelphia. Madison keeps Jefferson informed. In November, he receives draft of the Constitution and generally approves, but urges adding Bill of Rights.

July. Daughter, 9 year old Polly arrives in Paris with 14 year old slave, Sally Hemings.

1788

March-April. Travels through Holland and the Rhineland.

1789

May 5. Attends opening of Estates-General at Versailles. Jefferson drafts charter of rights with Marquis de Lafayette in June. It is the basis for the Declaration of Rights that Lafayette presents to the National Assembly in July.

July 14. Bastille is stormed.
August. Lafayette and other patriots discuss constitution at Jefferson's home.

September 26. The Senate confirms Jefferson's appointment as Washington's Secretary of State.

September 28. Jefferson departs for home. He learns of his appointment on arriving in Virginia on November 23.

1790

March 21. Assumes office of Secretary of State.

1791

May 8. Jefferson explains to Washington his involvement in the publication of Thomas Paine's *The Rights of Man*. He wrote endorsement published in the preface, describing "heresies" against republicanism, and readers assume the remarks aim at Vice President Adams.

May-June. Jefferson and Madison go on nature tour of northern states.

1793
January 3. Jefferson wrote the U.S. chargé d'affaires in Paris, criticizing his dismay at French revolutionary violence. Sacrifices of "innocent blood" is a small price to pay for the liberty he believes will follow excesses.

April 28. Secretary of State Jefferson writes opinion for Washington arguing that acceptance of the new French minister is acceptance of the revolutionary Paris government, led by the Girondins.

Mid-August. Washington criticizes the Democratic-Republican clubs that have sprung up in support of France. Jacobins gain control of France. Many Girondists are imprisoned.

Jefferson resigns as Secretary of State, effective December 31.

1795
October. Madison visits Monticello to discuss the Jay Treaty with Great Britain. They oppose ratification. It addresses issues left unresolved since the 1783 peace treaty. It provides compensation to British creditors from American debtors, and arranges evacuation of British troops occupying northwestern U.S. posts. But it fails to address American trading rights and impressment of American seamen by the British navy.

1796
April 24. Jefferson writes letter. An "Anglican monarchical and aristocratical party has sprung up" aiming to return the country to "forms" of British government. He refers to revolutionary heroes, "Samsons in the field and Solomons in the council," who have "gone over to these heresies." Washington assumes Jefferson included him among the "Samsons" and ends correspondence with him.

December 7. John Adams is elected President. Jefferson is elected Vice President, receiving second largest number of electoral votes.

1797
March 4. Inaugurated as Vice President.

1798
Jefferson helps pay for publication of James Callender's pamphlet *The Prospect Before Us*. It claims to expose Adams as a monarchist.

June-July. Congress passes the "Alien and Sedition Acts." The Naturalization Act, Alien Act, Sedition Act, and Alien Enemies Act are passed midst quasi-war with France. The Sedition Act makes it illegal to criticize the government or its officials publicly.

September-October. Jefferson and Madison consult on blocking Alien and Sedition Acts. The Vice President drafts resolutions against the Acts and has them introduced into Kentucky's legislature. Madison drafts resolutions for Virginia. In November, Kentucky passes Jefferson's resolutions declaring the Acts void, and in December Virginia passes Madison's.

1799

March 1. Jefferson leaves Philadelphia for Monticello.

1800

December 3. Electors meet in their states and vote for next president. Tie between Jefferson and Aaron Burr does not become known until the end of the month. This throws the election into the House of Representatives.

1801

February 11. The electors' votes are counted in Congress. The House of Representatives meets separately. On February 17, on the 36th ballot, Jefferson is elected President.

March 2. President John Adams appoints sixteen federal judges in a series of "midnight appointments." Republicans see a Federalist plot to control courts. Jefferson and Adams cease correspondence and do not resume until 1812.

March 4. Jefferson is the first President inaugurated in Washington. Walks to inauguration as act of republican simplicity.

March 8. Judiciary Act repealed.

May. The Pasha of Tripoli declares war on the U.S. because it has been paying Tripoli less in tribute than it pays Algiers. On May 20, Jefferson sends a naval squadron.

1802

January 1. Jefferson replies to Connecticut's Danbury Baptist Association. He writes of "building a wall of separation between Church and State."

September. When Jefferson failed to reward James Callender with the office of postmaster, Callender makes accusation that Jefferson "for many years past kept, as his concubine, one of his own slaves," Sally Hemings.

1803

April 30. The U.S. purchases the Louisiana territory from France for $15 million dollars.

1804

February. Compiles "The Philosophy of Jesus." It is lost after his death.

April 17. Jefferson's daughter dies. Abigail Adams writes a letter of condolence.

June 13. Jefferson responds. Correspondence follows. It ceases over arguments regarding Jefferson's support of Callender's pamphlet and Adams's appointment of "midnight judges."

November. Reelected president.

1805
March 4. Inaugurated for a second term.

1808
James Madison is elected president.

1809
March 4. Madison is inaugurated president. Jefferson returns to Virginia and never leaves it again.

1814
February 20. Jefferson's bill for the establishment of free public education in Virginia is defeated in the state legislature.

September 21. Jefferson sells his library of nearly 6,700 volumes to the federal government after its library was destroyed in August when the British burned the Capitol.

1815
Jefferson's library becomes the foundation for the Library of Congress.

1816
January 9. Jefferson writes letter telling of what will become "The Life and Morals of Jesus of Nazareth," clippings from the four Gospels of what he considers the moral teachings of Jesus.

1817
Virginia Assembly defeats bill presenting Jefferson's general education plan.
October 6. Cornerstone is laid for the University of Virginia.

1818
February 4. Jefferson writes introduction for letters, notes, and reports written while Secretary of State. His grandson inherits his papers, names them the "Anas," Greek plural of the suffix employed to form "Jeffersoniana."

August 1-4. Jefferson chairs commission to plan the University. He writes its report.

1819
January 25. The Assembly charters the University.

Jefferson begins "The Life & Morals of Jesus of Nazareth," (first published in 1902).

A Northern Representative proposed an amendment prohibiting slavery in Missouri.

1820

April 22. Jefferson criticizes the Missouri Compromise, maintaining the balance of free and slave states by admitting Maine with Missouri. Sees attacks on slavery as no better than attempts at a Federalist come back.

1821

January 6-July 29. Jefferson works on *Autobiography*.

1823

Letter to President helps formulate Monroe Doctrine against European expansion in the Western Hemisphere.

1824

April. Jefferson prepares instructions for recruiting faculty in Europe for the University of Virginia.

November 3-15. Lafayette, on triumphal tour of America, visits Monticello. Crowd of hundreds burst into tears of joy at the meeting of the two old revolutionaries.

1825

March 7. University of Virginia opened to students.

1826

July 4. Jefferson dies shortly after 12 noon, on the fiftieth anniversary of the Declaration of Independence. Only five slaves are emancipated in his will. They are relatives of Sally Hemings, who is quietly freed a short time later.

James Madison's

CHRONOLOGY

1751
March 16 (March 5, Old Style). Born in King George County, Virginia, to James Madison Sr., and Nelly Conway.

1762
Attends local boarding school. Learns Latin, Greek, and French.

1767
Studies at home with Rev. Thomas Martin, rector of his family's Anglican church.

1769
Studies at College of New Jersey, today Princeton University. Studies Hebrew.

1771
Receives baccalaureate, continues study.

1772
Returns to Virginia. Develops nervous disorder, fears early death.

1773
Studies law.

1774
Visits New York and Pennsylvania. Elected to Orange County Committee of Safety. It embargoes British goods.

1775
Becomes militia Colonel but never sees combat due to poor health.

1776
Delegate to Virginia convention and then General Assembly.

May 29-June 12, 1776. Madison drafts Amendments to the Virginia Declaration of Rights.

October 11. Jefferson returns to serve in Virginia House of Delegates. Madison, also serving, becomes friend until Jefferson's death. They exchange approximately 1,200 letters.

1777
Defeated for Assembly.

1778
Serves in Council of State, Governor's cabinet, under Patrick Henry.

1779
Serves in Council of State under Thomas Jefferson.

1780
March 20. Delegate to Continental Congress.

1781
June 14. Reelected to Congress.

1782
June 15. Reelected to Congress.

1783
Unpaid Pennsylvania soldiers surrounded the State House where Congress met, on June 21. When the state declined to use militia to keep the peace, Madison took refuge with Congress in Princeton, where it reconvened on June 26.

November 7. Leaves Congress, as delegates cannot serve more than three years out of six.

1784
Fights for religious freedom in Virginia Assembly. Accompanies Marquis de Lafayette to New York for negotiations with Iroquois.

1785
June 20. Writes Memorial and Remonstrance Against Religious Assessments.

1786
Secures enactment of Virginia Statute for Religious Freedom proposed by Jefferson in 1777.

Elected to Constitutional Convention in Philadelphia.

1787
Writes Vices of the Political System of the United States.

September 17. Constitution of the United States of America finalized. Madison is the major figure at the Constitutional Convention. Contributes to Federalist Papers.

1788
June 6-12. Leads fight for ratification of Constitution in Virginia Convention.

Ca. October 15. Observations on the Draught of a Constitution for Virginia.

Defeated in Assembly vote for seat in new federal Senate. Elected by people to House of Representatives.

1789
Advises Washington on inaugural address and writes the House reply.

June 8. Presents Bill of Rights.

1790
Reelected to House.

December 22. Speech in Congress on Religious Exemptions from Militia Duty.

1791
May-June. Nature tours North with Jefferson.

December 15. Bill of Rights ratified.

1792
Leads Republican opposition in House.

1793
Reelected to House.

1794
Marries Dolley Payne Todd.

1795
Reelected to House.

1796
December 9. Announces retirement from House.

1797
Retires to home in Montpelier.

1798
September-October. Madison consults Jefferson on how to block the Alien and Sedition Acts. Madison drafts resolutions against the Acts for Virginia legislature. In December Virginia passes Madison's Resolution. Makes Address to the People.

1799
Elected to state legislature.

1800

Virginia approves Madison's Report on Alien and Sedition Acts.

1801

Becomes Secretary of State under Jefferson. Withholds diplomatic recognition of Toussaint L'Ouverture's black revolutionary Haitian regime.

1802

Begins negotiations to buy Louisiana from Napoleon.

1803

United States buys Louisiana.

1804

Protests British impressment of sailors on American ships.

1805

Protests Royal navy seizures of American ships.

1806

Law passed restricting British imports. Operation suspended until 1807 to allow for negotiations.

1807

British frigate fires on American frigate Chesapeake, killing three and removing four "British" seamen from boat. U.S. embargoes all U.S. overseas trade on December 22.

1808

December 7. Madison is elected President.

1809

March 4. Inaugurated as President.

1810

Madison annexes Western Florida to the U.S.

1811

February 21. Veto Message to the House of Representatives of the United States regarding a bill incorporating a Washington Episcopal church.

February 28. Veto Message to the House of Representatives of the United States regarding reserving land in Mississippi territory for Baptist church.

U.S. frigate fires on British corvette, killing nine.

Army defeats Tenskwatawa, Tecumseh's brother, at Tippecanoe, Indiana.

1812

Sends declaration of war to Congress.

1813
March 4. Second Inauguration.

July 23. Madison issues Thanksgiving proclamation.

October 5th. Tecumseh dies in battle as U.S. defeats British army in Ontario.

1814
August. Madison flees from British attack on Washington. The White House is burned.

November 16. Proclamation of a day of public humiliation and fasting and of prayer to Almighty God.

December 24. Negotiations end war.

1815
January 8. Major British defeat at New Orleans, after peace treaty is signed.

Naval squadron defeats Mediterranean Barbary pirates.

1816
Charters new national bank.

1817
Retires to Montpelier. Helps found American Colonization Society as solution to slavery.

1817-32
After leaving the White House, Madison writes "Detached Memoranda."

1818
Gives major address on agriculture in Virginia.

1819
Opposes federal ban on slavery in Missouri.

1824
Lafayette visits Madison and Jefferson on triumphant tour of U.S.

1825
Last visit with Jefferson.

1826
After Jefferson's death, replaces him as Rector of the University of Virginia.

1828
Madison opposes South Carolina slaveholders' doctrine of state nullification of federal laws.

1829

Attends Virginia constitutional convention. Proposes adoption of federal three-fifths rule for counting slaves in state reapportionment. The measure, reducing power of major slave counties, is defeated.

1830

Madison again opposes nullification.

1833

Accepts honorary presidency of American Colonization Society.

1834

Resigns as University Rector.

1835

Will does not provide for emancipation of his slaves.

1836

June 28. Dies at Montpelier.

DOCUMENTS AND LETTERS LISTS

January 19, 1764, 4
January 23, 1764, 5
July 30, 1776, 26
May 4, 1786, 77
Paine, Thomas,
December 23, 1788, 102
January 5, 1789, 104
March 17, 1789, 110
May 19, 1789, 116
July 11, 1789, 123
June 19, 1792, 141
Paradise, John,
November 22, 1788, 101
Parker, Thomas,
May 15, 1819, 272
Philadelphia Citizens,
February 3, 1809, 186
Pickering, Timothy,
February 27, 1821, 355
Price, Richard,
January 8, 1789, 105
July 12, 1789, 123
Priestley, Dr. Joseph,
January 27, 1800, 152
March 21, 1801, 159
April 9, 1803, 166
April 24, 1803, 171
January 29, 1804, 173
Randolph, John,
November 29, 1775, 21
Randolph, Peyton,
July 23, 1770, 6
Richie, Thomas,
January 21, 1816, 240
Rittenhouse, David,
July 19, 1778, 48
Robinson, Moses,
March 23, 1801, 160
Rogers, Dr., and Slaughter Dr.,
March 2, 1806, 179
Rush, Dr. Benjamin,
September 23, 1800, 154
April 23, 1803, 168
August 8, 1804, 174
Rush, Richard,
May 31, 1813, 206
Shippen, Thomas,
January 5, 1789, 105
Short, William,
January 22, 1789, 108
October 31, 1819, 274
April 13, 1820, 335
August 4, 1820, 337
Six Baptist Associations of Chesterfield,
Virginia,
November 21, 1808, 186

Skipworth, Robert,
August 3, 1771, 8
Smith, James,
December 8, 1822, 366
Smith, Margaret Bayard,
August 6, 1816, 249
Smith, Thomas Jefferson,
February 21, 1825, 386
Smith, William,
July 9, 1786, 79
Smith, William Stephens,
February 2, 1788, 95
Smyth, Alexander,
January 17, 1825, 385
Spafford, Horatio Gates,
March 17, 1814, 224
1816, 238
January 10, 1816, 240
Sparks, Rev. Jared,
November 4, 1820, 342
Story, Rev. Isaac,
December 5, 1801, 162
Tammany Society of Baltimore,
May 25, 1809, 194
Tammany Society of New York,
February 29, 1808, 183
Tammany Society of Washington,
March 2, 1809, 189
Taylor, John,
June 4, 1798, 146
May 28, 1816, 247
Thatcher, George,
January 26, 1824, 373
Thomas, Captain John,
November 18, 1807, 181
Thomas, Ellicot, Messrs., and Others,
November 13, 1807, 181
Thompson, Charles,
December 17, 1786, 82
January 9, 1816, 239
January 29, 1817, 254
Ticknor, George,
November 25, 1817, 260
Trist, Eliza,
December 11, 1783, 60
Tyler, John,
May 26, 1820, 198
Van Buren, Martin,
June 29, 1824, 380
Van Der Kemp, Francis,
April 25, 1816, 246
July 30, 1816, 248
November 24, 1816, 251
Von Humboldt, Alexander,
April 14, 1811, 200

INDEX

203, 230, 271, 273, 333, 345, 391, 399-401, 403, 407, 408, 410, 414, 415, 420, 421
Blackstone, William, 198, 217, 218, 220, 221, 379
Blaine, James, 398
Blair, John, 109
Bolingbroke, Vicount Henry, 9, 354
Bolivar, Simón, 355
Bollandists, 236. *See* Jesuits
Bonaparte, Napoleon, 157, 236, 237, 242, 258, 267, 268, 372, 420
Borgias, 242
Bourbon, Duke, 124, 125, 352
Bourdaloue, 6
Boyle, Mrs., 53
Brackton, 222
Bradford, William, 9-12, 17, 18, 20
Brady, 212, 213, 374
Brafferton, 53
Brazier, John, 274
Brienne, Etienne, 89, 92, 97, 99
Britton, 222
Broughton, 37
Brown, John, 74, 99
Brucker, Johann, 210, 211
Bryan, Mrs., 338
Bryan, William Jennings, 398
Buchanan, 213
Budaeus, 217
Buddhism, 402
Burke, Mr., 126
Burke, Thomas, 93
Burr, Aaron, 218, 413
Burwell, Lewis, 214
Burwell, Miss Rebecca, 3,
Bush, George, W., 400, 401-03, 405
Bute, John, 261

Cabanis, Pierre, 384
Cabell, Joseph, 244
Caesar, Augustus, 278, 315, 357
Caesar, Julius, 338
Caiaphas, 279
Caldwell, Doctor C., 388
Callender, James, 174, 412, 413, 414
Calvin, John, 270, 272, 273, 336, 342, 360, 361, 363, 365, 368, 369, 370, 371, 373, 374
Calvinists, 28, 37, 195, 270, 273, 368
Cambden, 39
Canby, William, 210
Carey, Archibald, 238
Carmichael, William, 103, 114
Carr, Peter, 86
Carroll, Bishop John, 162
Carter, 214

Carter, Jimmy, 401, 403, 404
Carter, Mrs., 9
Cartesn, 43
Carthusians, 94
Cartwright, Major John, 376, 381
Catholic War Veterans, 399
Catholics, 20, 26, 31, 35, 37, 42-44, 57, 84, 85, 89, 92-94, 97, 99, 101, 103, 121, 124, 133, 137, 162, 173, 195, 200, 210, 215, 225-227, 231, 236, 237, 242, 245, 246, 249, 250, 252, 258, 259, 262, 264, 267, 268, 340-42, 347-354 passim, 360, 361, 366, 370, 394, 398-403
Cato, 210
Cauvier, Pére, 103
Cerinthus, 385
Channing, Mr., 355
Charles, King of England, 18
Charles, King of Spain, 57
Charron, 375
Chastellux, Marquis de, 75
Christ. *See* Jesus
Church, Mrs., 144
Church of England. *See* Episcopalians
Cicero, 6, 9, 166, 169, 229, 240, 275, 338, 354
Clarke, Dr., 387
Clay, Charles, 233
Cleanthes, 212, 213
Clinton, Bill, 405
Cobbet, William, 237
Coke, 2
Coleman, William, 199
Coles, Edward, 230
Collins, 9
Communists, 401. *See also* Stalinism
Conde, Prince, 124, 125, 352
Condorcet, Marie Jean, 6, 227
Congregationalists, 155
Constantine, 36
Conway, Nelly, 417
Coolidge, Ellen, 387
Cooper, Dr. Thomas, 219, 232, 334-6, 365, 372
Copernicus, 235
Coray, A., 373
Corbin, Mr., 76
Cosway, Maria, 81, 144
Coughlin, Father Charles, 399
Coxe, Tench, 144
Crevecoeur, St. John de, 98
Cromwell, Oliver, 51
Cross, Stephen, 193
Cullendar, Rose, 223
Curnis, 215
Cutting, John Brown, 98
Cuvier, Georges, 385
Cyprian, 39